World Development Report 1988

Published for The World Bank
Oxford University Press

Oxford University Press

NEW YORK OXFORD LONDON GLASGOW
TORONTO MELBOURNE WELLINGTON HONG KONG
TOKYO KUALA LUMPUR SINGAPORE JAKARTA
DELHI BOMBAY CALCUTTA MADRAS KARACHI
NAIROBI DAR ES SALAAM CAPE TOWN

ISBN 0-19-520649-5 clothbound
ISBN 0-19-520650-9 paperback
ISSN 0163-5085

The Library of Congress has cataloged this serial publication as follows:
World development report. 1978–
[New York] Oxford University Press.
v. 27 cm. annual.
Published for The World Bank.
1. Underdeveloped areas—Periodicals.   2. Economic development—
Periodicals.   I. International Bank for Reconstruction and Development.

HC59.7.W659   330.9′172′4   78-67086

This book is printed on paper that adheres to
the American National Standard for Permanence of Paper
for Printed Library Materials, Z39.48-1984.

Foreword

This Report is the eleventh in the annual series assessing major development issues. Part I reviews recent trends in the world economy and their implications for the future prospects of developing countries. Part II examines the role of public finance in development. Like its predecessors the Report includes the World Development Indicators, which provide selected social and economic indicators for more than 100 countries.

World economic growth has continued through 1987 and into 1988, but two problems have characterized the recent trends: unsustainable economic imbalances within and among industrial countries, and highly uneven economic growth among developing countries. Part I of the Report concludes that three interdependent policy challenges need to be addressed.

First, industrial countries need to reduce their external payments imbalances. Without such action the world economy as a whole, and especially the developing countries, could face a serious risk of recession and financial upheaval. Second, developing countries need to persevere in restructuring their domestic economic policies in order to gain creditworthiness and growth. The divergences among developing countries in their adjustment to the external shocks of the 1980s demonstrate the importance of sound economic management. Third, net resource transfers from the developing countries must be trimmed so that investment and growth can resume. Further adjustment by industrial and developing countries will help. But debtors and creditors will also have to continue the search, case by case, for ways to

reduce the debt overhang. For the poorest countries, especially those in Sub-Saharan Africa, concessional debt relief and increased aid are necessary to facilitate resumed growth.

The rapid expansion of the public sector in recent decades and the emergence of fiscal crises in most developing countries during the 1980s have made public finance the focus of the development and adjustment challenge. Part II of this Report explores how public finance policies are best designed and implemented.

Most of the developing countries that were able to avoid economic crises in the 1980s maintained moderate and stable fiscal deficits. Those that ran into trouble generally had unsustainably high fiscal deficits. Once crises occur, fiscal retrenchment is essential for effective stabilization, but by itself is not sufficient to generate growth. The manner in which deficits are reduced—how additional revenues are raised and how expenditures are cut—is crucial.

The costs of revenue mobilization can and must be reduced in the interest of more efficient resource allocation and growth. Tax reform in certain developing countries shows that governments can simplify overly complex and costly tax systems, broaden tax bases, lower tax rates, and improve tax administration, while maintaining or even increasing revenues. Greater reliance on user charges will also lead to a more efficient and equitable allocation of resources.

Where fiscal deficits are excessive, public spending generally has to be cut. Setting careful priorities when public spending is cut is as important as when it is increased. Good fiscal planning, budgeting, and project evaluation are important tools to ensure that public spending conforms with sound sectoral strategies and complements rather than competes with private initiatives.

The efficiency of public services and the scope for raising revenue can often be strengthened by decentralizing decisionmaking to local governments and to state-owned enterprises, and by improving accountability and transparency in financial relations among public agencies. The capacity of local governments to raise revenue needs to be enlarged and their administrative capabilities strengthened. Reform of state-owned enterprises will often require an expansion of the role of the market and of private sector involvement.

Poverty remains the ultimate challenge of development policy. Stable fiscal policy is essential to sustain economic growth and thus to relieve poverty in the long term. Public spending, if properly designed, provides the poor with access to basic services, helps to protect them from the social costs of adjustment, and buttresses the development of human resources.

Like all previous *World Development Reports*, this is a study by the staff of the World Bank and the judgments in it do not necessarily reflect the views of the Board of Directors or the governments they represent.

Barber B. Conable
President
The World Bank

June 1, 1988

This Report has been prepared by a team led by Johannes F. Linn and comprising William R. Easterly, Cheryl Williamson Gray, Emmanuel Y. Jimenez, Govindan G. Nair, Anthony J. Pellechio, Zmarak M. Shalizi, and Eugene L. Versluysen. The team was assisted by David Dunn, Anastasios Filippides, M. Shahbaz Khan, Fayez S. Omar, Clifford W. Papik, Subramanian S. Sriram, Lynn E. Steckelberg, and Deborah L. Wetzel.

Many others in and outside the Bank provided helpful comments and contributions (see the Bibliographical note). The International Economics Department prepared the data and projections presented in Part I and the Statistical appendix. It is also responsible for the World Development Indicators. The production staff of the Report included Connie Eysenck, Virginia deHaven Hitchcock, Pensri Kimpitak, Joyce C. Petruzzelli, Kathy S. Rosen, Walton Rosenquist, and Brian J. Svikhart. Library assistance was provided by Iris Anderson. The support staff was headed by Rhoda Blade-Charest and included Trinidad Angeles, Carlina Jones, María Guadalupe M. Mattheisen, and Patricia Smith. The work was carried out under the general direction of W. David Hopper and Stanley Fischer, with Clive Crook as the principal editor.

Contents

Text figures

Text tables

Statistical appendix tables

Acronyms and initials

ADP Automated data processing
AETR Average effective tax rate
BIS Bank for International Settlements
CAP Common Agricultural Policy of the EC
CPI Consumer price index
EC The European Community, comprising Belgium, Denmark, France, Federal Republic of Germany, Greece, Ireland, Italy, Luxembourg, Netherlands, Portugal, Spain, and the United Kingdom
EMS European Monetary System
ERP Effective rate of protection
FDI Foreign direct investment
FY Fiscal year
G-7 The Group of Seven, comprising Canada, France, Federal Republic of Germany, Italy, Japan, United Kingdom, and United States
GATT General Agreement on Tariffs and Trade
GDP Gross domestic product
GFS *Government Finance Statistics Yearbook*, published annually by the IMF
GNP Gross national product
IBRD International Bank for Reconstruction and Development (The World Bank)
IDA International Development Association
IFS *International Financial Statistics*, published monthly by the IMF
IMF International Monetary Fund

LIBOR London interbank offered rate
MDF Municipal development fund
METR Marginal effective tax rate
MFA Multifibre Arrangement
MIGA Multilateral Investment Guarantee Agency
MTR Marginal tax rate
NIE Newly industrialized economy
NTB Nontariff barrier
O&M Operation and maintenance
ODA Official development assistance
OECD Organisation for Economic Co-operation and Development, comprising Australia, Austria, Belgium, Canada, Denmark, Finland, France, Federal Republic of Germany, Greece, Iceland, Ireland, Italy, Japan, Luxembourg, Netherlands, New Zealand, Norway, Portugal, Spain, Sweden, Switzerland, Turkey, United Kingdom, and United States
PAYE Pay as you earn
PSBR Public sector borrowing requirement
SOE State-owned enterprise
Unesco United Nations Educational, Scientific and Cultural Organization
VAT Value added tax
VER Voluntary export restraint

Definitions and data notes

The principal country groups used in the text of this Report and in the World Development Indicators are defined below. The overall classification uses GNP per capita as the main criterion.

- *Developing countries* are divided into *low-income economies*, with 1986 GNP per person of $425 or less, and *middle-income economies*, with 1986 GNP per person of $426 or more.
- *High-income oil exporters* comprise Bahrain, Brunei, Kuwait, Libya, Qatar, Saudi Arabia, and the United Arab Emirates.
- *Industrial market economies* are the members of the Organisation for Economic Co-operation and Development, apart from Greece, Portugal, and Turkey, which are included among the middle-income developing countries. This group is commonly referred to in the text as *industrial economies* or *industrial countries*.
- *Nonreporting nonmember economies* are Albania, Angola, Bulgaria, Cuba, Czechoslovakia, German Democratic Republic, Democratic People's Republic of Korea, Mongolia, and the Union of Soviet Socialist Republics.

For analytical purposes several other overlapping classifications based predominantly on exports or external debt are used in addition to geographic country groupings:

- *Oil exporters* are middle-income developing countries with exports of petroleum and gas, including reexports, accounting for 30 percent of merchandise exports: Algeria, Cameroon, People's Republic of the Congo, Ecuador, Arab Republic of Egypt, Gabon, Indonesia, Islamic Republic of Iran, Iraq, Mexico, Nigeria, Oman, Syrian Arab Republic, Trinidad and Tobago, and Venezuela.
- *Exporters of manufactures* are developing economies with exports of manufactures (defined for this purpose as SITC 5, 6, 7, and 8, less 68, 651, 652, 654, 655, 667) accounting for more than 30 percent of exports of goods and services: Brazil, China, Hong Kong, Hungary, India, Israel, Republic of Korea, Poland, Portugal, Romania, Singapore, and Yugoslavia.
- *Highly indebted countries* are seventeen countries deemed to have encountered severe debt servicing difficulties: Argentina, Bolivia, Brazil, Chile, Colombia, Costa Rica, Côte d'Ivoire, Ecuador, Jamaica, Mexico, Morocco, Nigeria, Peru, Philippines, Uruguay, Venezuela, and Yugoslavia.
- *Sub-Saharan Africa* comprises all of the countries south of the Sahara excluding South Africa.
- *Middle East and North Africa* comprises Afghanistan, Algeria, Arab Republic of Egypt, Islamic Republic of Iran, Iraq, Israel, Jordan, Kuwait, Lebanon, Libya, Morocco, Oman, Saudi Arabia, Syrian Arab Republic, Tunisia, Turkey, United Arab Emirates, People's Democratic Republic of Yemen, and Yemen Arab Republic.
- *East Asia* comprises all low- and middle-income economies of East and Southeast Asia and the Pacific, east of and including China, Mongolia, and Thailand.
- *South Asia* comprises Bangladesh, Bhutan, Burma, India, Nepal, Pakistan, and Sri Lanka.
- *Latin America and the Caribbean* comprise all American and Caribbean countries south of the United States.

Economic and demographic terms are defined in the technical notes to the World Development Indicators. The Indicators use the country groupings given above but include only countries with a population of 1 million or more.

Billion is 1,000 million.

Trillion is 1,000 billion.

Tons are metric tons, equal to 1,000 kilograms, or 2,204.6 pounds.

Growth rates are calculated as least squares exponential rates of growth and are in real terms unless otherwise stated. Growth rates for spans of years in tables cover the period from the beginning of the base year to the end of the last year given.

Dollars are current U.S. dollars unless otherwise specified.

All tables and figures are based on World Bank data unless otherwise specified.

The symbol .. in tables means "not available."

The symbol — in tables means "not applicable."

Data from secondary sources are not always available from 1986 onward. The numbers in this *World Development Report* shown for historical data may differ from those shown in previous Reports because of continuous updating as better data become available and because of recompilation of certain data for a ninety-country sample.

Public finance in development: an overview

Public finance shapes the course of development. It affects aggregate resource use and financing patterns and, together with monetary and exchange rate policies, influences the balance of payments, the accumulation of foreign debt, and the rates of inflation, interest, and exchange. Public spending, taxes, user charges, and borrowing also affect the behavior of producers and consumers and influence the distribution of wealth and income in an economy. Balance of payments crises and foreign debt problems are at least aggravated, and are often caused, by imprudent fiscal policy. Their solution almost invariably involves some combination of cutting public spending and raising additional revenue, thus freeing resources for exports and debt service. Careless fiscal austerity can lead to prolonged recession, however, and can place a disproportionately heavy burden on the poor. For this reason the structural aspects of public finance policy—how spending is allocated and revenue raised—matter as much as the overall macroeconomic balance.

World Development Report 1988 examines public finance in developing countries against the backdrop of today's uncertain economic outlook. The Report's main concern is how appropriate public finance policies can improve the quality of government. The discussion is timely for two reasons. First, budget deficits and external debts pose a dilemma for many governments: how can they achieve short-term stabilization without retarding long-term development? Second, the perception of government has shifted during the past decade; where government was once commonly seen as

a catalyst of development, many now think it an obstacle.

The Report is in two parts. Part I explores recent developments in the world economy, including the emergence of severe macroeconomic imbalances among industrial countries and the effect of these imbalances on the developing world. It concludes that a significant reduction in the budget deficit of the United States, together with stronger domestic demand in the Federal Republic of Germany, Japan, and the newly industrialized economies (NIEs), is necessary to reduce today's sizable current account imbalances and avoid the risk of a slowdown in the world economy. Developing countries must continue to reform domestic policies, while the net resource transfers from the developing countries must be reduced if these countries are to resume sustained economic growth.

Part II concentrates on public finance in developing countries. Five broad conclusions emerge.

- Prudent and stable macroeconomic fiscal management is far preferable to successive phases of extreme fiscal expansion and contraction. Modest and sustainable fiscal deficits promote growth, while shielding the poor from the heavy burdens of fiscal austerity.

- Greater reliance on user charges and simplified, restructured general tax systems can increase public revenue and reduce economic distortions.

- Clear priorities and concentration on quality are necessary for efficient and effective public spending. Priorities tend to emerge more forcefully if decisionmakers are aware of their specific

Table 1 Growth of real per capita GDP, 1965 to 1995
(annual percentage change)

| | Actual | | | Projected, 1987–95 | |
Country group	1965–73	1973–80	1980–87	Base	High
Industrial countries	3.6	2.1	1.9	1.8	2.6
Developing countries	3.9	3.2	1.8	2.2	3.6
Exporters of manufactures	4.8	4.0	4.6	3.4	4.9
Highly indebted countries	4.2	2.9	−1.3	1.0	2.5
Sub-Saharan Africa	3.8	0.5	−2.9	0.0	0.7

Note: All growth rates for developing countries are based on a sample of ninety countries.

resource constraints and expect to abide by them in planning and budgeting.

• Autonomous and accountable decentralized public entitites, including subnational levels of government and state-owned enterprises, can improve the efficiency of both spending and revenue gathering. But administrative constraints limit the scope for speedy decentralization; increased private sector involvement in the provision of public services should therefore be explored wherever feasible.

• Well-designed public finance policies can be powerful tools for relieving poverty.

Figure 1 Ratios of investment to GDP in developing countries, 1970 to 1986

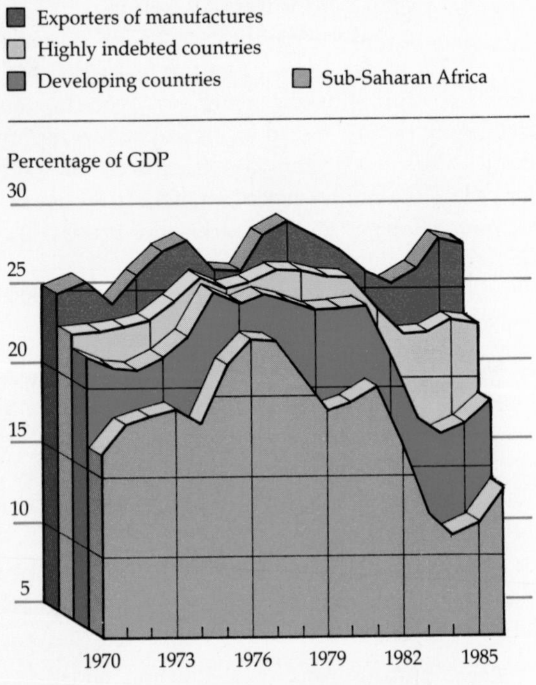

■ Exporters of manufactures
□ Highly indebted countries
■ Developing countries   ■ Sub-Saharan Africa

Percentage of GDP

Note: Data are based on a sample of ninety developing countries.

Although the focus of Part II is on developing countries, many of the issues addressed are also problems for the industrial countries. Solving these problems is a difficult task for any government. Reform must span the full range of macroeconomic and microeconomic concerns as well as deal comprehensively with all parts of the public sector: central, state, and local governments and state-owned enterprises. The relations between fiscal and other policies are pervasive and complex. The lack of accurate fiscal data in developing countries further complicates the task of policy design. In addition public finance reform usually involves politically sensitive tradeoffs that most governments, whether in developing or industrial countries, would rather avoid. Yet the many examples of fiscal policy cited in this Report indicate that reform is both possible and highly beneficial.

Policy options for global adjustment

As the 1980s draw to a close, economic turbulence and uncertainty persist. Since 1983 governments in industrial countries have managed to reduce inflation and maintain a positive rate of growth. But significant problems remain: high real interest rates, declining investment rates, volatile exchange rates, growing current account imbalances, rising protectionism, and—in Europe—high unemployment. These problems are mainly the legacy of past inflationary policies and structural rigidities. But they are also a consequence of the mismatch of macroeconomic policies during much of the 1980s—expansionary in the United States and contractionary in Europe and Japan—and of the combination of loose fiscal policy and tight monetary policy, particularly in the United States. This has led to slowed growth of both production and trade. As a result, the world economy faces continuing risks.

Growth has also slowed substantially in the developing countries. Some African and highly indebted, middle-income countries have suffered significant declines in per capita income (see Table 1). Their investments have fallen to levels at which even minimal replacement may no longer occur in important sectors of their economies (see Figure 1). Their debts are growing, but they still face negative net resource transfers because debt service obligations exceed the limited amounts of new financing. In some developing countries the severity of this prolonged economic slump already surpasses that of the Great Depression in the industrial countries (see Figure 2), and in many countries poverty is on the rise (see Box 1).

To improve the economic outlook for industrial and developing countries alike, policymakers must achieve progress toward three related goals:

• Reducing economic imbalances among industrial countries
• Restructuring economic policies in developing countries
• Reducing the net transfer of financial resources from developing countries.

Reducing economic imbalances among industrial countries

While the immediate outlook in mid-1988 is for continued modest world economic expansion, three main steps are needed to enhance growth prospects and reduce the risks of further instability in the financial market and, possibly, a sharp slowdown in activity beyond the near term. The first is credible action to reduce the U.S. federal budget deficit. This is essential to bring about a lasting reduction in the country's current account deficit and to lower real interest rates. Second, Japan should maintain, and Germany accelerate, the growth of domestic demand through appropriate macroeconomic and structural policies. Third, those NIEs of East Asia that are running sizable current account surpluses could do even more to accelerate the growth of domestic demand, appreciate their currencies against the dollar, and reduce the degree of protection of their domestic producers.

In the present climate of economic uncertainty, judging the appropriate stance of macroeconomic policy will be unavoidably difficult. However, concerted and credible change along the lines suggested here would help reduce the sizable current account imbalances among industrial countries (and the East Asian NIEs) and lessen the risks of a recession. It would also stabilize exchange rates. Economic growth, moreover, could be faster, as indicated in the "high-case" scenario of Table 1.

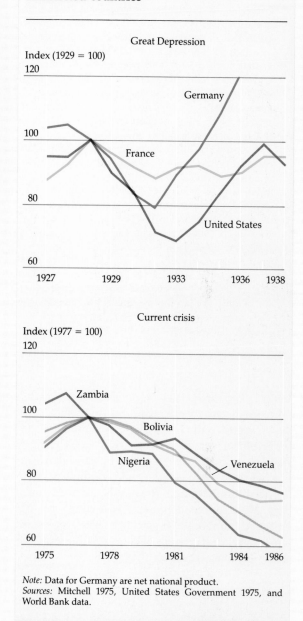

Figure 2 Per capita GDP during the Great Depression and the current crisis in selected countries

Note: Data for Germany are net national product.
Sources: Mitchell 1975, United States Government 1975, and World Bank data.

These policies should also be accompanied by a reduction of protection. The current Uruguay Round of the General Agreement on Tariffs and Trade (GATT) negotiations provides a timely forum to promote multilateral reductions in the barriers to trade.

Without concerted policy action by the industrial countries, the global economic outlook is more likely to conform to the "base-case" scenario of

Box 1   The continuing need to alleviate poverty

Poverty in the developing countries is on the rise. Between 1970 and 1980 the number of people with inadequate diets in developing countries (excluding China) increased from 650 million to 730 million. Since 1980 matters have turned from bad to worse: economic growth rates have slowed, real wages have dropped, and growth in employment has faltered in most developing countries. Precipitous declines in commodity prices have cut rural incomes, and governments have reduced their real spending on social services.

Comprehensive data on poverty are lacking, especially for the most recent years, but scattered information from individual countries confirms the general impression of deteriorating social conditions in many developing countries. A recent study found that the number of people below the poverty line increased at least up to 1983–84 in Brazil, Chile, Ghana, Jamaica, Peru, and the Philippines. It also found that there has been a sharp and widespread reversal in the trend toward improved standards of child health, nutrition, and education. Other sources show that in twenty-one out of thirty-five low-income developing countries, the daily calorie supply per capita was lower in 1985 than in 1965. Between 1979 and 1983 life expectancy declined in nine Sub-Saharan African countries. In Zambia deaths from malnutrition among infants and children doubled during 1980–84, and in Sri Lanka the calorie consumption of the poorest tenth of the population fell 9 percent between 1979 and 1982. In Costa Rica falling real wages during 1979–82 increased the incidence of poverty by more than two-thirds. Real per capita public spending on health and education in low-income developing countries stagnated between 1975 and 1984. For six low-income countries the number of physicians per capita decreased between 1965 and 1981, and enrollment ratios for primary education declined in twelve low-income Sub-Saharan African countries.

In the aftermath of the second oil price shock, the subsequent worldwide recession, and the debt crisis, it is not surprising that governments have focused their attention on stabilization and adjustment and that fiscal austerity has reduced spending on the relief of poverty. However, increases in the incidence of poverty make it essential for the issue to move again into the forefront of policy design—and especially the design of public spending programs.

Table 1. Per capita incomes in many parts of the developing world would continue to stagnate or, at best, reverse only very slowly the dramatic declines of the past few years. Trade would remain sluggish and commodity prices depressed. Negative net resource transfers would continue to drain financial resources from the highly indebted countries. More serious downside risks would persist. Further disruptions in financial markets, higher interest rates, and a more severe slowdown of the world economy would all be possible.

Restructuring economic policies in developing countries

The responsibility for the second task of policy adjustment lies with the developing countries. Their pace of development depends greatly on the effectiveness of the domestic economic policies that each government pursues. Those policies can be effective even in a generally unfavorable international environment. Examples go beyond the East Asian NIEs, whose achievements are so often cited: they include Botswana, China, Colombia, India, Indonesia, Thailand, and Turkey. In each of these countries strong economic performance in recent years can be traced to sound policies—not just to special factors such as external aid or natural resource endowments.

Reducing the net resource transfers from developing countries

Finally, the net resource transfers from developing countries to the rest of the world need to be reduced to improve the debtor countries' economic performance. Improved policies in industrial countries could lower real interest rates and improve trading prospects for the highly indebted developing countries. This, in conjunction with sound policies in the developing world, would enhance the creditworthiness of the highly indebted countries and help them to attract new capital. Combining better policies and inflows of new capital with various available methods of stretching out or reducing debt repayments would reduce the resource drain and allow increased investment to support growth. Finally, there is the challenge for most highly indebted, middle-income countries to find new financial options, including ways to pass on current market discounts on debt to the debtor countries under case by case, market-based approaches. For the debt-distressed, low-income countries of Sub-Saharan Africa, proposals to ease their debt burdens by official support need careful consideration.

Concerted action in all three areas—industrial country policies, developing country policies, and resource transfers—provides the best chance to avoid a worldwide economic downturn and to return developing countries to a level of growth comparable with that of the 1950s and 1960s. However, inaction on any front should not become an excuse for inaction elsewhere. Developing countries can still do much to influence their own economic prospects, regardless of the international economic environment. This is true especially in the area of public finance.

The role of public finance in development

Many of today's public finance issues have troubled policymakers for centuries—how to raise and allocate public funds effectively while limiting budget deficits and how to delegate authority while maintaining accurate accounts and financial discipline, for example (see Box 2). But these issues are of even greater importance now because of the expansion of the public sector during the past 100 years—beginning in the industrial countries around 1880 and in the developing countries after 1940. From a share of 5 to 10 percent of gross national product (GNP), central government spending has grown to an average of about 25 percent of GNP in developing countries and 30 percent in industrial countries. In some countries the share exceeds 50 percent of GNP. The public sector affects the economy not only through its taxation and spending, but also through interventions such as price controls and licensing. Although country experiences vary widely and rigorous assessment is difficult, the public sector now appears to be as important in developing countries as in the industrial countries.

The expanded role of the public sector carries with it risks and opportunities, however. The risks

---

Box 2   Insights from the history of public finance

From the earliest days of recorded history one of the principal challenges to government has been the management of public finance. In their book, *A History of Taxation and Expenditure in the Western World,* Carolyn Webber and Aaron Wildavsky explore taxation and expenditure policies from ancient times to the present. In the final chapter they concluded:

No matter what a society's patterns of taxing and spending are, supporting government has always been problematic. In this respect, at least, past and present merge.

Virtually every aspect of modern budgetary behavior that we regard as especially distinctive has its analogue in ancient practices. Governments, from the Mauryan kings of ancient India to early Roman emperors to the feudal monarchies of medieval Europe and the new nation-states of the early-modern era, have tried to maintain accounts of tax receipts, and sometimes (but never successfully) to keep records of spending for different purposes. Though the technology differs, the results are often the same: as with the off-budget trust funds in modern governments, detailed line-item accounts of spending did not help much if receipts in a given fund were insufficient to cover mandated spending.

. . . .

Ancient, medieval, and early-modern governments certainly lacked effective technical and administrative instruments, but they did use expedients to help stay afloat. They taxed the land and necessities; they debased currency and confiscated as much as possible; they sold offices, crown lands, and sometimes the king's jewels; they conquered and pillaged. When officials could not get inside houses, they taxed columns, windows, and doors. They levied hundreds of taxes on the production and sale of commodities and services. In doing this, governments alienated their subjects, debased public morality, and wrought havoc with trade. But, for the most part, they got by. And when, after centuries of reform, such venal and inefficient practices were abolished, governments still faced financial crises. The big difference today is that crises take place at much higher levels of expenditure and revenue.

What stands out in the ebb and flow of financial tides is problem succession: old solutions give rise to new problems that are in their turn superseded. No policy instrument is good for all seasons.

. . . .

Whether or not governments stay solvent, at the very least our lengthy chronicle of the difficulties continuously associated with efforts by governments at diverse times and places to raise and spend revenue should convey the message that taxing and expenditure are never a straightforward matter.

arise from the ineffective use of public resources and from the overextension of government into areas that are better left to private markets. The opportunities arise from the government's power, in principle, to allocate resources efficiently when markets fail to do so and from its ability to provide relief to those in poverty. It is the task of public finance to balance the opportunities and the risks, and thus improve the quality of government. The most important aspects of public finance within which pragmatic policies should be pursued are the management of public deficits, revenue mobilization, allocation of public spending, and decentralization of public functions.

Fiscal policy for stabilization and adjustment

Large fiscal deficits are often at the root of both external and internal macroeconomic imbalances. External imbalances express themselves as current account deficits, capital flight, and rapidly expanding external debts. Internal imbalances take the form of high real interest rates, falling private investment, and rising inflation. Prudent fiscal policy—that is, fiscal deficits consistent with low and stable inflation, a sustainable level of foreign debt, and a favorable climate for private investment—is indispensable to stabilization and adjustment. Furthermore, reforms in many other areas—financial liberalization, currency devaluation, price deregulation, trade reform, and so on—can work only if the fiscal implications are taken into account.

With a few exceptions, the fiscal deficits of today's "problem debtors" increased significantly in the late 1970s and early 1980s. Current account deficits widened in step with fiscal expansion, and the ratio of public debt to gross domestic product (GDP) increased correspondingly. Capital flight worsened the debt problem as domestic savers responded to unsustainable fiscal deficits by sheltering their assets abroad. Unlike the problem debtors, other countries (such as Indonesia, the Republic of Korea, and Thailand) had more sustainable fiscal policies during the 1970s. They accumulated smaller stocks of public debt in relation to their capacity to service it. They also adjusted their fiscal policies quickly in the early 1980s and took steps to prevent their real exchange rates from rising excessively. As a result these countries—which might easily have joined the problem debtors—steered clear of debt troubles.

Countries with commodity booms are a special example of the importance of prudent fiscal policy. In many countries public revenues accelerated rapidly as the export prices of commodities soared in the 1970s. The windfall encouraged governments to increase spending—sometimes by more than the windfall, as higher domestic revenues were leveraged through foreign borrowing. However, much of this spending went to higher consumer subsidies or investment projects of dubious economic merit. After the boom, spending kept rising while revenue contracted sharply. The resulting fiscal deficits led to fiscal and external debt crises that finally forced spending cuts. Some commodity exporters—Botswana, Cameroon, and Indonesia, for example—managed to avoid destructive boom and bust cycles by cautious fiscal management of the boom revenues. They moderated spending increases during the boom and used the rise in public savings to accumulate external assets or repay external debt. They also adjusted rapidly to the end of the boom by cutting spending and maintaining low inflation, stable exchange rates, and solid performance in other exports. These contrasting country experiences demonstrate that erring on the side of caution is less costly than falsely assuming a temporary boom to be permanent.

Low-income Africa faces even greater difficulties than the middle-income debtors. It depends heavily on erratic flows of concessional and nonconcessional lending; the public revenue base is narrow and volatile. After borrowing heavily to finance fiscal expansion in the 1970s, African countries have been forced to adjust as lending has been cut back. Adjustment has been complicated by dual exchange rate systems, which are especially common in low-income Africa and which, in effect, tax exports. Removing this tax through exchange rate unification and devaluation helps the export sector, but the temporary loss of revenue can lead to bigger fiscal deficits and higher inflation. These countries therefore need to synchronize exchange rate reform with fiscal reform.

Prudent fiscal policy guards against the risks of excessive foreign debt and overvalued currencies. But sound macroeconomic policy is not enough. Many developing countries need to make structural changes if they are to resume satisfactory long-term growth. Public finance offers many opportunities for reform of this kind. The ways in which governments raise revenue can substantially affect economic efficiency. Similarly, the quality and composition of public spending strongly influence development. This Report considers each side of the budget balance in turn.

Reforming tax systems

When public deficits need to be reduced, the economic cost of raising more revenue must be weighed against the cost of cutting public spending. More revenue and less spending will both be needed as a rule. The temptation in the short term is to rely on ad hoc increases in revenue because they are administratively and politically convenient. But in many countries this approach has led to complex and highly distortionary revenue systems that not only fail to collect sufficient revenue but also damage long-term growth. Most of today's systems could be restructured to increase yield, reduce distortions, and minimize the burden on the poor.

The two main types of public revenue are general taxes (compulsory charges unrelated to particular expenditure items) and user charges (payments from beneficiaries in exchange for goods provided by public agencies). General taxes make up the bulk of central government revenue, whereas user charges are the main source of revenue for state-owned enterprises. State and local governments commonly collect both.

Tax revenue as a share of GNP has increased during the past decade in many developing countries in response to the need for fiscal adjustment. Taxes on international trade are still the largest source of central government revenue in low-income countries, particularly in Sub-Saharan Africa. But the revenue share of trade taxes has been declining, since most developing countries are shifting gradually to domestic taxes. Among the domestic taxes, commodity taxes such as sales, excise, and value added taxes are more important than income taxes. In industrial countries, however, income taxes are often the more important source of revenue.

In general, the economic cost of taxation increases with the tax rate and is higher when the base is narrow, as is the case in most developing countries. Recent reforms in developing countries such as Colombia, Indonesia, Jamaica, and Malawi have rightly concentrated on expanding the base, thus avoiding higher tax rates and adverse effects on incentives. To make the tax structure more transparent and to ease administration and enforcement, the reforms have also favored fewer rates and fewer exemptions. They have tried to promote equity by improving the collection of taxes from the wealthy through limited exemptions and improved tax administration and by avoiding taxes on the poor. Progressive income taxes are hard to collect in developing countries.

Successful tax reforms have also demonstrated that variants of the value added tax (VAT) can generate substantial revenue with fewer distortions than import, turnover, or excise taxes. Joint reform of trade and commodity taxes is particularly effective in meeting the dual goals of raising revenue and reducing inefficiency.

Many developing countries have a limited capacity for administration, so tax reform must be confined to what is administratively feasible. In most developing countries, especially the poorer ones, simplicity is essential. However, modern techniques, such as the use of computers and tax identification codes, can make it easier to collect most taxes.

Improving the allocation of public spending

Central government spending grew substantially until 1982 in many developing countries but then tended to decline as a percentage of GDP until 1985 as resources grew tighter. Although the breakdown of spending by category varies tremendously among countries, some generalizations are possible. For example, industrial countries spend much more (as a share of both total spending and GDP) on subsidies and transfers, primarily for health and social security, while developing countries tend to allocate more of their spending to investment.

Governments can promote both economic growth and equity by supplying the physical infrastructure needed for productive private investment and by providing social services to meet the basic needs and improve the productivity of the population. But the high cost of raising revenue means that it is vital to set priorities and attain quality in public spending. Priorities can be set by considering what governments do best and what markets do best. Governments must provide "public goods" that benefit all citizens, such as law and order and national defense. They should also be involved in providing goods and services with large external benefits to society, such as primary education, basic health care, and immunization programs. Direct investment or regulation is needed to control monopolies caused by a single source of supply or large returns to scale relative to the size of the market—water supply, sanitation, and power, for instance. Finally, government subsidies on goods and services consumed by the poor are sometimes justified, but, to contain the cost, they should be accurately targeted.

These criteria help to explain the widespread public provision of infrastructure for transport, communications, power, water supply, and irrigation—areas critical for growth in the early stages of development. They also support public spending on basic education and health, which has been instrumental in producing higher literacy rates and skill levels, reducing mortality and morbidity, and lowering fertility rates. In contrast, these criteria generally do not support direct public production or marketing of industrial or agricultural products, or direct public provision of bus transport or housing.

Setting priorities is only the first step. All dimensions of investment projects—economic, technical, administrative, and financial—must be appropriately designed and implemented in a policy environment that provides incentives for good performance. Priorities and quality must also be considered in allocating recurrent public spending: adequate spending on operation and maintenance will often be more important than new investment, hiring fewer civil servants and paying them competitive wages will generally be preferable to using the government as the employer of last resort, and subsidies will be more efficient when targeted to the poor rather than dispersed across the entire populace.

Improving the efficiency and effectiveness of public spending requires reform of fiscal planning, budgeting, implementation, and monitoring. Fiscal planning ideally involves formulating a phased investment program, projecting current spending needs, and assessing revenue availability and borrowing requirements for three to five years, all set in the context of a consistent macroeconomic framework. The annual budget would then be a comprehensive one-year slice of the medium-term plan. For plans and budgets to promote effective decisionmaking by individual public agents, the tradeoffs among agencies, programs, and projects must be explicit, and the budget constraint for each agency, once set, must be firm so that an agency may not exceed a budget on its own initiative.

Although the capacity to carry out medium-term fiscal planning and comprehensive annual budgeting is limited in most developing countries, some have coped well. Botswana, for example, has developed procedures to ensure that careful attention is paid to the recurrent cost implications of its investment spending. Chile has used economic analysis—primarily cost-benefit analysis—to screen potential investments thoroughly. Others

are trimming government payrolls through hiring freezes, civil service censuses, and voluntary retirement schemes; a few countries are trying to rationalize the civil service wage structure. Mexico is moving toward targeted food subsidies. These and other examples show that it is possible to improve the efficiency and effectiveness of public spending.

Spending priorities and revenue options in selected sectors

Sectoral perspectives on public finance highlight the need to consider revenue and spending jointly. Similar problems—insufficient spending on cost-effective activities, inefficient public programs, and limited access by the poor—beset current public involvement in education, health, urban services, and rural infrastructure in many countries. Solving these problems calls for three sorts of public finance reform: redirecting spending toward activities in which government participation is most critical, increasing the reliance on user and other benefit-related charges to finance such spending, and decentralizing some public responsibilities to those in closer touch with local needs and conditions.

Spending should be more sharply focused within each of the sectors mentioned above. In education, a pressing need exists to expand and improve primary schooling, particularly in the poorest countries. In health, more public resources should be allocated to basic health measures such as immunization and prenatal care. Public spending on these basic services is not only socially more profitable than spending on higher education, nonessential drugs, and expensive curative hospital care, but it is also more equitable, because the more expensive services are used primarily by the relatively wealthy. In urban services, public provision of roads, water, electricity, and sanitation is critical, whereas bus services and housing infrastructure can often be more efficiently provided by the private sector. In rural infrastructure, roads, potable water, irrigation, and electricity are areas in which the public sector has been, and should continue to be, involved; but in each case spending can often be shifted toward more cost-effective techniques. Such reforms can expand the access of the poor to basic services, while increasing the contribution of the public sector to economic growth and development.

User charges provide the link between spending and revenue decisions for many sectors. Unlike taxes, user charges can raise revenue to finance the expansion of priority services, while increasing rather than decreasing efficiency. Publicly provided goods and services will be used efficiently if they are priced to reflect the cost of production as well as externalities and other market imperfections. In contrast, subsidized (that is, underpriced) services result in excessive consumption and demands for additional spending, and the taxes needed to pay for such subsidies create distortions elsewhere in the economy. User charges thus lead to a double efficiency gain: they allocate the supply of public goods and services efficiently, and their use avoids the need for distortionary taxes.

The case for user charges is well established for public utilities such as gas, water, power, and telephones. But selective user charges can be increased even in health and education. Although sound economic and social reasons exist for continuing to subsidize primary education and basic health programs, whose benefits spill over to society at large, the generous subsidies so common for other education and health services in developing countries can be reduced. Charging users of public facilities that have large private benefits—including curative outpatient hospital care and university education—will increase efficiency in production and consumption. It will also mobilize resources to finance the expansion of priority services, many of which are used primarily by the poor. This is an important goal during times of severe budgetary restraint. Some subsidies will likely have to remain, but these need to be carefully targeted primarily to the poor. Selective scholarships, for example, are one way to give poor students access to higher education, for which others would have to pay at least part of the cost.

For some public services, such as the distribution of irrigated water and the maintenance of local feeder roads, shifting some responsibilities to local providers will free central authorities to focus on priority tasks. With appropriate training, regulation, and monitoring from the center, many local initiatives can identify needs and mobilize resources more easily. Where services are already provided locally, the decentralized agencies need to be strengthened, as discussed below.

Financing local government

Many developing countries would benefit from an increase in the responsibility of state and local governments for certain public functions. Decentralization is advisable for goods and services that are regional or local, rather than national, in character, such as water supply and sanitation, transport, and even some health and education services. In such cases it can increase public accountability and responsiveness to local preferences. The scope for decentralizing is greatest in urban areas, but broadening the involvement of rural communities in water supply, irrigation, and rural roads can also improve the quality of public services.

Despite these benefits, state and local governments frequently face restrictions in raising resources to finance present or potential spending. Central authorities often regulate the few local sources of revenue by controlling tax rates, prohibiting increases in user charges, and limiting the means for revenue collection and enforcement. As a rule these restrictions can be safely eased, which increases the revenue-raising capability of subnational governments and reduces their dependence on central transfers.

User charges are especially helpful at the local level because local governments generally concentrate on services whose direct cost can be recovered. Although central government restrictions, lack of local technical expertise, and political opposition may limit the extent of charging, local governments in some developing countries have managed to develop successful cost recovery programs, usually in conjunction with improved service.

Among local taxes the property tax has many desirable features but is often administratively and politically difficult to collect. Even so, property tax reform should be considered as part of any broader local finance reform. Other local taxes, which are often complex and excessive in number and thus costly to collect and poorly enforced, can generally be streamlined to reduce administrative costs.

Central or state government grants are also common sources of local finance. If properly designed and administered, such grants can adjust for income differences, ensure national benefits from certain local public functions such as education, and provide incentives for greater local fiscal effort.

Credit can provide an alternative way to finance local capital investment. Municipal development funds have been successful in some developing countries in channeling credit, training, and technical assistance to local governments. Raising more revenue locally remains desirable in order to increase the debt service capacity of local government and to complement or replace grants from higher tiers of government.

Weak administrative capacity limits the ability of local governments to raise and spend revenue effectively. Efforts to increase this capacity—including training, technical assistance, and even central government staff deployed at the local level—is an essential task for the central authorities.

Strengthening public finance through reform of state-owned enterprises

State-owned enterprises (SOEs) were usually established either to decentralize some key public sector activities or to move others from the private sector to the public domain. In some developing countries certain SOEs have succeeded as commercial ventures, contributing to public revenues and playing important roles in nation-building. In most countries, however, the achievements of SOEs have fallen short of what was hoped for. Their success has been hampered by a multiplicity of conflicting objectives and a lack of fiscal discipline.

Many SOEs are expected to finance themselves through internally generated funds or nongovernmental borrowing. In practice, however, the need to finance persistent gaps between SOE saving and investment has added greatly to the public deficits and public indebtedness in developing countries. Direct budgetary subsidies to SOEs have substantially increased central government deficits. Furthermore, direct foreign borrowing by SOEs typically has grown faster than that of the private sector. Governments frequently guaranteed these borrowings without overall borrowing strategies or controls, and poor SOE performance forced many governments to assume debts that SOEs could not service.

Many governments now see the critical importance of reforming SOE finance as part of the broader task of fiscal reform. The first step is to reduce SOE claims on the government budget by improving operational efficiency and ensuring that charges cover costs. Transparency in financial relations between the government and SOEs is also critical. If all subsidies to SOEs are explicitly budgeted, their cost can be subject to annual review, rather than hidden or simply forgotten. Increasing the availability of reliable information on SOEs' financial and operational performance, eliminating arrears between public agencies, and controlling government guarantees of SOE borrowings will also help to restore fiscal discipline. Finally, private sector involvement can often improve the efficiency of SOE operations and reduce their drain on fiscal resources. Because the barriers to full and rapid privatization are often daunting, intermediate solutions—such as subcontracting, leasing, or allowing private competition—are often more feasible.

Directions for reform

Prudent budget policies, reduced costs of raising revenue, efficient and effective public spending, strengthened decentralization in government, and public finance policies consistent with poverty alleviation—these are the five broad directions which public finance policies should strive to pursue. Progress simultaneously on all fronts will be difficult to attain in most countries. Nonetheless, neglect of any one area can easily lead to problems in the others. A comprehensive approach to public finance reform is therefore essential to produce consistent policy advice and to implement sustainable reform.

Opportunities and Risks in Managing the World Economy

1

Policy options for global adjustment

The global economy remains fragile despite reasonable short-term growth prospects. Although average GDP growth in the industrial countries was marginally higher in 1987 than in 1986, it was well below the high levels of the 1950s and 1960s. Moreover large international payment imbalances persist, and there is a risk of further volatility in stock markets, exchange rates, and interest rates. This fragility is a direct consequence of lasting divergences in the macroeconomic policies of the leading industrial countries. Without significant changes in these policies the present economic uncertainty may soon be followed by a worldwide recession. For developing countries—despite considerable stabilization and adjustment efforts—the outlook remains worrying, especially for those with acute debt problems. These countries face the risk of prolonged stagnation in real per capita income, greater poverty, and social unrest.

Three issues need to be addressed if the growth prospects of industrial and developing countries are to improve.

• The leading industrial countries must persevere in adjusting their macroeconomic and structural policies so as gradually to reduce external imbalances to a sustainable level. This would improve the longer term outlook for growth in the industrial countries—a precondition for faster growth in developing countries.
• Developing countries must pursue policy reforms designed to advance their development prospects, even if the international environment is unfavorable.

• Net resource transfers from developing countries to the rest of the world must be reduced.

Resolving these issues poses an enormous challenge for governments in industrial and developing countries and for the international financial community. These issues are closely linked. Progress on all three would lessen the risks in the outlook and make it possible to resume healthy economic growth.

The legacy of the 1970s

The 1970s were a period of turmoil and transition for the world economy. Following the long postwar expansion, GDP growth in the industrial countries became generally more erratic. For the decade as a whole it declined to 3.1 percent a year, compared with 5.0 percent during the 1960s. The first oil price shock, mounting fiscal deficits, rising inflation, and greater rigidity in the functioning of domestic markets were the main reasons for this slowdown. The volatility of exchange rates following the collapse of the Bretton Woods exchange rate system in 1971 added to the financial tensions.

In the developing countries, economic growth during the 1970s remained largely unaffected by the slowdown in industrial countries. It averaged 5.4 percent, or broadly the same as in the previous decade. As documented in earlier *World Development Reports*, however, this relatively strong performance was achieved by a rapid accumulation of external debt and—in many countries—at the expense of growing domestic imbalances. These in-

13

Figure 1.1 Actual and projected growth of GDP, 1960 to 1990

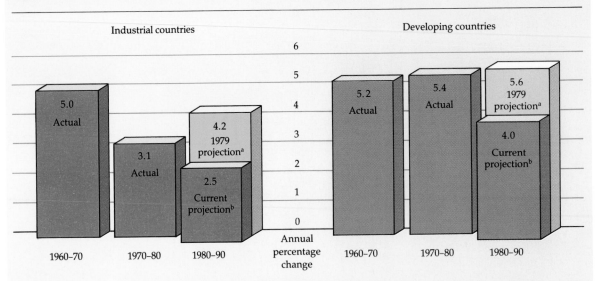

a. From the central case scenario of *World Development Report 1979*. This projection did not include China, which was expected to have higher than average growth.
b. Based on actual growth for 1980–87 and projected growth for 1987–90 under the base case.
Sources: World Bank, *World Development Report 1979,* and World Bank data.

cluded large fiscal deficits, inflation, overvalued currencies, and distorted incentives for industry and agriculture. As a result many developing countries were left vulnerable to new external shocks.

Despite the increased economic uncertainty of the 1970s the global outlook toward the end of the decade generally permitted cautious optimism. The oil price shock of 1973 appeared to have been weathered successfully and without lasting damage to world trade and capital markets. A modest resurgence of growth in industrial countries, closer to the averages of the 1950s and 1960s, together with steady growth in the developing countries, seemed a likely outcome for the 1980s. Like other forecasts prepared at the time, projections for the world economy presented in *World Development Report 1979* envisaged average real GDP growth of 4.2 percent in industrial countries and 5.6 percent in developing countries for 1980–90 (see Figure 1.1).

Combining the outcome for 1980–87 and projections for the remainder of the 1980s, the average rate of growth for the decade as a whole is likely to be little more than half that projected in 1979 for the industrial countries and roughly two-thirds that projected for the developing countries. This is

a large discrepancy. It underlines the reversal in world economic fortunes in three main areas.

• Sharp fluctuations in the price of oil—starting with the second price shock in late 1979—caused serious disruptions for oil-importing and oil-exporting developing countries alike. Those that had accumulated large external debts were the worst hit.

• Faced by high and rising inflation, most industrial countries redirected their macroeconomic policies to reduce inflationary pressures.

• The unexpected deterioration in the international environment—slower growth in world trade, falling commodity prices, reduced access to foreign financing, and steep increases in real interest rates—compounded the structural weaknesses and past economic policy failures of many developing countries.

The next section reviews macroeconomic policy in industrial countries during the 1980s and its effect on the world economy. It also considers current policy options for these countries. The chapter goes on to analyze the effect of changes in the external environment facing developing countries, and explores options to deal with their trade and debt problems. It concludes with an assessment of the outlook for the world economy until 1995.

Macroeconomic policies and imbalances in industrial countries

In most industrial countries the policy response to the high inflation and widening fiscal deficits inherited from the late 1970s was rapid and vigorous. Starting in late 1979, these countries turned to strict anti-inflationary monetary policy. For the seven largest countries (the G-7) the rate of growth of narrow money (M1) declined from 10 percent in 1979 to 6 percent in 1980. Together with the second oil shock this helped to trigger a severe recession in 1981–82. Most industrial countries also shifted the emphasis of their fiscal policies, aiming for lower structural budget deficits. Although recession-related automatic stabilizers caused offsetting increases in budget deficits—in most industrial countries central and general government deficits remained high until the middle of the decade (see Table 1.1)—the new direction of fiscal policy had a procyclical effect that deepened the recession. In 1982 average GDP growth tumbled to −0.4 percent in industrial countries and to 2.0 percent in developing countries.

The United States was the main exception to the new orientation of fiscal policy; its combination of lower tax rates and higher spending caused budget deficits to rise after 1981. In the United States and the United Kingdom, among others, efforts were also initiated to curb the role of the public sector in the economy and to loosen the regulation of private enterprise. This involved far-reaching liberalization of financial markets and other sectors of the economy. The privatization of some state-owned enterprises, especially in the United Kingdom, was another part of this reformist philosophy.

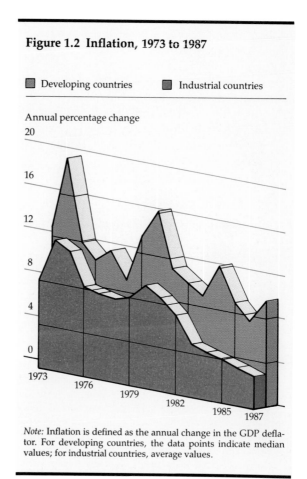

Figure 1.2 Inflation, 1973 to 1987

▣ Developing countries   ▣ Industrial countries

Annual percentage change

Note: Inflation is defined as the annual change in the GDP deflator. For developing countries, the data points indicate median values; for industrial countries, average values.

Effects of the new macroeconomic policies

The new policies had rapid and profound effects. On the positive side, with the help of the drop in dollar oil prices after 1981, they successfully re-

Table 1.1 Fiscal balances in major industrial countries, 1979 to 1987
(percentage of GNP)

Fiscal entity and country or country group	1979	1980	1981	1982	1983	1984	1985	1986	1987
Central government									
United States	−1.1	−2.3	−2.4	−4.1	−5.6	−5.1	−5.3	−4.8	−3.4
Japan	−6.1	−6.2	−5.9	−5.9	−5.6	−4.7	−4.0	−3.3	−3.8
Germany, Federal Republic of	−1.9	−1.9	−2.5	−2.4	−1.9	−1.6	−1.3	−1.2	−1.4
G-7[a]	−2.8	−3.3	−3.6	−4.6	−5.4	−5.0	−4.9	−4.3	−3.6
General government[b]									
United States	+0.5	−1.3	−1.0	−3.5	−3.8	−2.8	−3.3	−3.5	−2.4
Japan	−4.7	−4.4	−3.8	−3.6	−3.7	−2.1	−1.0	−0.6	−0.8
Germany, Federal Republic of	−2.6	−2.9	−3.7	−3.3	−2.5	−1.9	−1.1	−1.2	−1.7
G-7[a]	−1.8	−2.5	−2.7	−4.0	−4.1	−3.4	−3.4	−3.2	−2.6

Note: (+) indicates a surplus and (−) a deficit.
a. Canada, France, Federal Republic of Germany, Italy, Japan, United Kingdom, and the United States.
b. Includes central, state, and local governments.
Source: IMF data.

duced inflation. For industrial countries as a group inflation dropped from a peak of 9.4 percent in 1980 to 4.8 percent in 1983 and declined further to 2.9 percent in 1987 (Figure 1.2).

On the debit side the recession speeded the rise in unemployment that had already started in the 1970s. In many countries this contributed to wage restraint, which in due course helped to restore business confidence and corporate profitability.

Worryingly, though, unemployment shows no sign of declining in many industrial countries; in Europe the average rate of unemployment has remained above 10 percent since 1983. That is a heavy social cost, and it has contributed to a resurgence of protectionism (see Box 1.1). Political tension associated with high unemployment may also account for the industrial countries' reluctance to expand their aid programs.

Box 1.1   The rising costs of protectionism

Protectionism broadly declined up to 1974 as tariffs were cut under successive agreements of the GATT (General Agreement on Tariffs and Trade). GATT is based on three principles: first, nondiscrimination, which requires that tariffs be equal for all trading partners of a given country; second, transparency, which favors explicit tariffs rather than nontariff barriers (NTBs); and third, reciprocity, so that if country A lowers its tariffs on imports from country B, country B should reciprocate. Through the adoption of these standards, average import tariffs on manufactures fell from about 40 percent in the early 1950s to less than 10 percent in 1974. Agricultural products and textiles—two major developing-country exports—remained the biggest exceptions to the trend toward more liberal trade.

The revival of protectionism

Liberal trade has been seriously threatened since the mid-1970s, and especially since 1980. Manufacturing has seen a resurgence of protectionism, especially in the guise of NTBs such as Voluntary Export Restraints (VERs) and import quotas. Between 1981 and 1986 the proportion of imports to North America and the European Community (EC) affected by NTBs rose by more than 20 percent. Trade between industrial and developing countries is increasingly affected by NTBs. Roughly 20 percent of developing-country exports were directly covered by such measures in 1986. One form of growing and systematic protectionism involves the successive Multifibre Arrangements. These have created a worldwide system of managed trade in textiles and clothing, and severely curtail developing-country exports. For politicians in industrial countries NTBs are attractive because of their popular appeal and because in the short term they seem to safeguard employment in declining industries.

In farming, large subsidies and import barriers are common, especially in Europe, Japan, and—to a lesser degree—North America and appear to have been rising in recent years. The growth of the Common Agricul-

tural Policy (CAP), which heavily subsidizes EC agriculture and discriminates against all agricultural imports into the EC, is one of the developments that underlie this trend.

Of course protectionism is not restricted to industrial countries. Developing countries, particularly those with more inward-oriented policies, often use NTBs and import tariffs. Lack of data makes it difficult to judge the extent of protectionism in developing countries. However, numerous countries have in recent years lowered the effective rates of protection on manufactured goods as part of their structural reforms.

The costs of protectionism

Estimates of the costs of industrial countries' protection against developing countries range from 2.5 to 9 percent of the developing countries' GNP. For industrial countries the costs of their own protection range from 0.3 to 0.5 percent of GNP. The cost of protecting particular subsectors can be extremely large. For example, the cost of protecting agriculture ranges from 3 percent of total farm output in the United States to 16 percent in the EC. In the United States it is estimated that in 1983 every dollar paid to preserve employment in the steel industry cost consumers $35 and amounted to a net loss of $25 for the U.S. economy. In the United Kingdom the cost of preserving one job in the car industry was equivalent to four times the average industrial wage in 1983.

NTBs are usually much more damaging than tariffs. VERs are estimated to cost the importing country up to three times as much as the equivalent tariff protection. For example, the cost to the U.S. economy of protecting the steel industry alone was nearly $2 billion in 1985. NTBs also reduce the effectiveness of exchange rates as a way of influencing the balance of payments because trade regulations, not relative prices, determine the volume of trade. It has been demonstrated that the responsiveness of the U.S. trade balance to changes in the value of the dollar has been significantly reduced by the growing use of NTBs. Since foreign

Moreover the switch to anti-inflationary monetary policy raised interest rates sharply, especially in the United States, where it coincided with fiscal expansion. Real yields on U.S. Treasury bonds rose from an average of 2 percent in 1980 to a peak of 8 percent in 1984 (see Figure 1.3). On this account alone the developing countries would have had to carry a far heavier burden of debt service costs. The diverging paths of the industrial countries' fiscal policies—stimulation in the United States and budgetary consolidation elsewhere—sowed the seeds of persistent financial disequilibrium and the present external payments imbalances.

Emergence of macroeconomic imbalances among industrial countries

In the wake of the Mexican debt crisis of 1982 the U.S. government strongly expanded the money supply to avert the collapse of a banking system already weakened by recession. This was the catalyst for a strong economic recovery, further propelled by fiscal expansion and the "supply-side friendly" tax reform of 1981. The combination of lower tax revenues and higher public spending caused U.S. general and federal budget deficits, as a proportion of GNP, to rise considerably above past trends (see Table 1.1). The rate of private saving fell to its comparatively low postwar average, and private investment increased, partly as a result of the 1981 tax reform (see Box 1.2). The private saving-investment balance therefore moved from a surplus of 3.2 percent of GNP in 1982 to a deficit of 1.2 percent in 1987. Combined with a rising general government deficit, this resulted in a negative overall saving-investment balance, which was reflected in a spiraling current account deficit. In contrast, Japan and the Federal Republic of Germany followed a path of more restrictive fiscal policy. Against a background of high private saving, this led to mounting current account surpluses (see Table 1.2 and Figure 1.4).

These diverging trends of saving and spending prompted rising interest rate differentials between the dollar and other major currencies and a prolonged appreciation of the dollar (see Figure 1.5). This worsened the growing trade imbalances. The newly industrialized economies (NIEs) in East Asia were able to greatly expand their exports to the United States. By 1987 the United States' external imbalance had reached an unprecedented scale.

The capital flows that are the counterpart of these protracted payments imbalances have altered the creditor positions of the main industrial countries. The United States—long the world's largest creditor and capital exporter—is now the largest debtor. Its estimated net foreign debt was already equivalent to 6.5 percent of GNP at the end of 1986. In the same year Japan and Germany had already become the principal creditor countries, with net foreign assets of 8.5 and 10.5 percent of their respective GNPs.

producers enjoy swollen profits as a result of VERs, they can afford to keep dollar prices unchanged as the dollar depreciates and thus protect their market share.

Protectionism can also involve direct budgetary costs, especially when it takes the form of subsidies. For example, it has been estimated that direct agricultural subsidies in the United States amounted to roughly $25 billion in fiscal 1987, or approximately 17 percent of the federal budget deficit. Agricultural subsidies under the CAP amounted to $33 billion in 1987 and have been a significant source of friction between members. NTBs could be replaced by revenue-earning tariffs. The revenue forgone is a hidden budgetary cost.

Finally, large agricultural subsidies and import barriers in industrial countries have led to overproduction and have pushed agricultural export prices below production cost. This has been one of the important factors explaining depressed agricultural commodity prices in recent years. Protection has harmed agricultural commodity exporters in developing countries and has reduced the income of agricultural producers and rural labor.

The Uruguay Round

The current round of GATT negotiations ("the Uruguay Round") is an opportunity to address these issues and return to more liberal international trade in manufacturing, agriculture, and services. A particularly important breakthrough would emerge from a successful negotiation of U.S. proposals for a phased elimination of farm subsidies. Developing countries have an important stake in the Uruguay Round, especially in agriculture and industry. Progress toward reduced protectionism in industrial countries and in the developing countries could be a major factor in improving the world economic outlook and the development prospects of the Third World. (See *World Development Report 1986* and *World Development Report 1987* for discussions of agricultural and industrial protectionism, respectively.)

Figure 1.3 Real interest rates in major industrial countries, 1979 to 1987

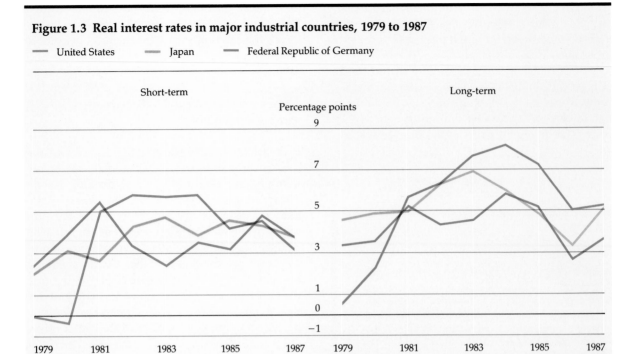

Notes: All rates are annual averages. The real interest rate is the nominal rate deflated by the CPI (for short-term rates) or by the GDP deflator (for long-term rates). The short-term nominal rates used are: United States, three-month bank certificates of deposit; Japan, unconditional call money before 1981 and two-month private bills for 1981-87; and Germany, three-month interbank loans. The long-term nominal rates used are: United States, ten-year treasury bonds; Japan, central government bonds with maturities of ten years or longer (OTC sales yield); and Germany, public authorities bonds with three years or more remaining to maturity.
Sources: IMF and World Bank data.

Box 1.2 Tax policy, the balance of payments, and international capital flows

Tax policy influences the balance of payments and international capital flows in many ways. It helps to determine the saving-investment balance, for example, and it affects the return on capital. These influences have become more pronounced as barriers to international capital mobility have declined. Against this background, many industrial country governments have recently adopted major tax reforms.

The structural effects of the U.S. tax reforms on the balance of payments and on international capital flows have received less attention than its effects on the federal budget deficit. The 1981 reform included investment tax credits, accelerated depreciation, and liberalized provisions for leasing capital equipment. These help to account for strong private investment in 1983 and 1984, despite high real interest rates. At the same time tax reform had an ambiguous effect on private savings; in fact private saving rates declined during the early 1980s from their high levels of the 1970s. The net effect of the 1981 tax reform on private investment and saving thus provides an added explanation for the growing saving-investment gap, the resulting current

account deficit, and the international capital requirements of the United States. The 1986 U.S. tax reform weakened the investment incentives introduced in 1981 by broadly equalizing effective tax rates for all forms of income. This should help to narrow both the U.S. saving-investment gap and the current account deficit.

Another aspect of tax policy is the treatment of income earned abroad. The United States, like most other industrial countries, uses a resident-based system, which taxes the income of residents even if it is earned outside the United States, but does not tax interest income paid to foreigners. In contrast, many developing countries, including most Latin American countries, use a source-based approach to taxation, which attempts to tax only income having its source within their boundaries and does not attempt to tax the income of their citizens originating in the rest of the world. The interaction of tax policies in industrial and developing countries can thus create incentives for capital outflows from developing countries, while discouraging inward foreign investment.

Table 1.2 Current account and saving-investment balances in major industrial countries, 1975 to 1987
(percentage of GNP)

Country	Average, 1975–84	1985	1986	1987
United States				
Current account and overall saving-investment balance	−0.4	−2.9	−3.3	−3.6
Government saving-investment balance	−1.9	−3.3	−3.5	−2.4
Private saving-investment balance	1.5	0.4	0.2	−1.2
Gross private saving	17.8	16.9	16.5	14.8
Gross private investment	16.3	16.5	16.3	16.0
Japan				
Current account and overall saving-investment balance	0.7	3.7	4.3	3.6
Government saving-investment balance	−3.8	−1.0	−0.6	−0.8
Private saving-investment balance	4.5	4.7	4.9	4.4
Gross private saving	29.3	28.4	32.4	33.3
Gross private investment	24.8	23.7	27.5	28.9
Germany, Federal Republic of				
Current account and overall saving-investment balance	0.3	2.6	4.2	3.9
Government saving-investment balance	−3.1	−1.1	−1.2	−1.7
Private saving-investment balance	3.4	3.7	5.4	5.6
Gross private saving	19.8	19.9	23.1	23.3
Gross private investment	16.4	16.2	17.7	17.7

Note: The saving-investment balance is defined as gross saving minus gross investment. The overall saving-investment balance is the sum of the government and private saving-investment balances; it is by definition equal to the current account.
Source: IMF data.

Initial steps toward international macroeconomic policy coordination

Between late 1981 and early 1985 the dollar appreciated in real terms by 35 percent against the main currencies. This trend was reversed in March 1985, when it began to decline because of changing perceptions of the sustainability of the U.S. external deficit. Policymakers of the five leading industrial countries (the G-5) initially supported this adjustment. In September 1985 the G-5 reached the Plaza Agreement, which set in motion concerted intervention in currency markets to maintain an orderly decline of the dollar.

However, the U.S. current account deficit continued to widen, despite a cumulative depreciation of 34 percent in the real effective value of the dollar from its peak in early 1985 through the end of 1987. Several factors account for this.

• Important trading partners of the United States—especially Canada, the Latin American countries, and the Asian NIEs—have either pegged their currencies to the dollar, devalued against it, or appreciated their currencies only recently and to a limited extent. In addition the real appreciation of the German mark has been slowed by its link to other major European currencies in the European Monetary System (EMS); its cumulative rise was only 12 percent between March 1985 and December 1987. Due to these various factors

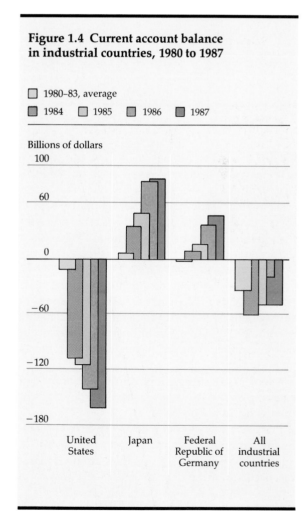

Figure 1.4 Current account balance in industrial countries, 1980 to 1987

☐ 1980–83, average
■ 1984   ☐ 1985   ■ 1986   ■ 1987

Billions of dollars

Figure 1.5 Real effective exchange rates of key currencies, 1978 to 1987

Dollars — Yen — German marks

Index (1980 = 100)

Notes: All index values are averages for December of each year. The "real effective" exchange rate is the trade-weighted exchange rate index (effective exchange rate) adjusted for relative inflation. An increase in the index indicates an appreciation of the currency.
Source: IMF data.

the dollar and the German mark returned to their real 1980 trade-weighted levels only in late 1987 (see Figure 1.5).

• Nominal trade balances take time to adjust. After a currency devaluation, prices respond faster than volumes, so current-price trade deficits tend to increase in the short run. This is known as the J-curve effect.

• Protectionist measures such as Voluntary Export Restraints (VERs) have reduced the price sensitivity of imports to exchange rate movements by encouraging foreign suppliers to reduce profit margins rather than accept quantity adjustments (see Box 1.1).

• Major U.S. corporations continue their foreign sourcing in low-cost labor markets, which adds to the rigidity of import volumes.

• Import compression after 1982 in several highly indebted developing countries—many of which, especially in Latin America, are major trading partners of the United States—accounts for a large part of the decline of U.S. exports after 1982.

• Last, but not least, the reduction of the U.S.

external deficit was impeded by the persistence of the fiscal deficit. The fiscal deficit, a key element in the overall U.S. saving-investment imbalance, is not significantly affected by exchange rate realignments. Thus, as long as the general government deficit remains at or close to its 1987 level (2.4 percent of GDP), the burden of adjustment must fall on the private sector; the private saving-investment deficit will have to become a sizable surplus if the U.S. current account is to improve. This would mean a big fall in private consumption or private investment or both. To achieve such a correction solely through exchange rate adjustments would probably call for a further depreciation of the dollar.

Recognizing the importance of convergent macroeconomic policies in correcting payments imbalances, the six largest industrial countries took a further step toward coordination in early 1987. The Louvre Accord of February 1987 marked a commitment by the countries with external surpluses to stimulate domestic investment and consumption so as to reduce their savings surplus. The United States, for its part, agreed to fiscal contraction to reduce its external deficit. These commitments were reiterated by the heads of state of the G-7 at the Venice Summit of June 1987 and in the G-7 statements of December 22, 1987, and April 13, 1988.

The parties to the Accord also agreed to "cooperate closely to foster stability of exchange rates around current levels," on the grounds that a further devaluation of the dollar would be counterproductive. Japan and Germany were concerned that a further drop of the dollar would erode the international competitiveness of their exports and precipitate a slowdown in their economies. U.S. authorities were similarly concerned that it would boost domestic inflation, sap foreign confidence in dollar assets, and deter further inflows of private capital.

In line with its commitment of February 1987, Japan adopted several expansionary fiscal measures. A supplementary budget allocation of ¥5 trillion (approximately $40 billion) for additional public investment expenditure and major public works programs was announced in May 1987. The Japanese authorities have also launched a major initiative to recycle a part of the country's surplus in favor of developing countries during the next three years (see Box 1.3).

The German federal government announced steps to stimulate its economy through a tax reduc-

Box 1.3 Recycling Japan's funds

In 1987 the Japanese government pledged to recycle up to $30 billion in the form of completely untied public and private funds to developing countries, in two tranches of, respectively, $10 and $20 billion.

The first tranche consists of three parts: the creation of the Japan Special Fund of about $2 billion in the World Bank, Japanese government lending to the IMF of 3 billion SDR, and the Japanese government's $2.6 billion contribution to IDA-8 and $1.3 billion contribution to the Asian Development Fund. The Japan Special Fund will comprise grants of ¥30 billion mainly for technical assistance in connection with World Bank-supported projects and programs as well as for cofinancing World Bank-supported sectoral and structural adjustment loans. It also provides for expanded access for World Bank borrowings in the Japanese capital market, in an amount of ¥300 billion (a total of about $2 billion), to be spread over three years.

The second tranche will be provided to the developing countries during a three-year period, ending in 1990. Of this $20 billion, about $8 billion represents the additional fund raising by the World Bank in the Tokyo market in accordance with the agreement between the Japanese government and the World Bank, the establishment of Japan Special Fund for the Asian Development Bank and the Inter-American Development Bank similar to that already established in the World Bank, and contributions to multilateral development banks; more than $9 billion is for expanded cofinancing with the World Bank and other multilateral development banks by the Export-Import Bank of Japan, the Overseas Economic Cooperation Fund (OECF), and Japanese commercial banks, and/or additional OECF direct loans in support of developing countries' adjustment programs; and about $3 billion is for expanded direct loans to the developing countries through the untied-loan scheme of the Export-Import Bank of Japan.

Finally, Japan also intends to advance by at least two years its target to double its official development assistance (ODA) to developing countries under its Third Medium-Term ODA Expansion Program and to have ODA disbursements exceed $7.6 billion in 1990. In 1986 Japan's ODA rose to $5.6 billion; it replaced France as the second largest provider of ODA after the United States. Japan has traditionally extended much of its aid to developing countries in Asia, but in recent years has increased its grants to Sub-Saharan Africa.

---

tion program to be phased over three years. It provides for a reduction in projected 1988 tax revenue of up to DM14 billion (0.7 percent of GNP), by bringing forward parts of a reform planned for 1990.

As a complement to fiscal stimulation in Japan and Germany, the U.S. government reaffirmed its commitment to significant public spending cuts, in line with the revised targets of the Gramm-Rudman-Hollings Amendment aiming at budget balance by 1993. The federal deficit was already set to fall by more than 1 percent of GNP in fiscal 1987 because of the nonrecurring revenue effect of the 1986 tax reform and the prospect of high revenues from capital gains taxes.

The financial crisis of October 1987

While consensus on the need to correct payments imbalances now exists among the governments of the leading industrial nations, progress has been limited. Aligning economic policy to international objectives rather than domestic ones is difficult. The German government's reluctance to add to inflationary pressures with fiscal stimulation or to jeopardize its medium-term goal of budget consoli-

dation is likely to preclude further fiscal expansion in the short term. Similarly, the United States has so far been unable to commit itself to a credible path of fiscal contraction. Moreover, even when governments agree on their joint goals, they often differ over ways and means.

The apparent stalemate contributed to a loss of confidence in financial markets. The G-7 decision to try to stabilize exchange rates before the announced fiscal measures proved damaging. In the United States it meant tightening credit after two years of modest monetary expansion. This caused a steep rise in interest rates between February and early October 1987. As a result the yield gap between bond and equity portfolios widened to more than 2 percent, well above past differentials. Allied to the perception that speculation had already driven equity prices too high, the yield gap induced a massive shift in international portfolios from stocks to higher yielding bonds. This was probably one of the triggers of the New York stock market collapse of October 19, 1987. The increasingly integrated global capital market transmitted New York's price falls to stock markets around the world.

The U.S. Treasury and Federal Reserve reacted

promptly, ensuring that liquidity in banking and financial markets was adequate to prevent a full-scale financial crisis. These steps restored some stability to the stock market, but they also provoked a temporary run on the dollar by rekindling fears of rising inflation. In late November and December 1987 the dollar dropped precipitously. In nominal terms it reached postwar record lows against the yen and German mark. This turbulence has added greatly to the complexity of the problem and has narrowed policy options. To date, negative wealth effects associated with the stock market losses appear to have been overestimated. But uncertainty remains for the longer term, although forecasts of GNP growth for 1988 have generally been revised upward after favorable growth statistics were announced for late 1987 and early 1988.

The brightest note in the international economy is Japan's shift to domestically led growth. In 1987 its domestic demand and GNP growth accelerated to 5.0 and 4.1 percent, respectively; they are expected to decline only moderately in 1988. Japan's current account surplus declined to 3.6 percent of GNP in 1987 from a peak of 4.3 percent in 1986; the volume of exports is declining moderately, and imports are surging.

Recent trends in Europe are less favorable. High unemployment continues to restrain domestic demand and hold growth below potential in most countries of the European Community (EC). Exports and investment have been harmed by the recent currency appreciations against the dollar. Meanwhile the Federal Republic of Germany, Western Europe's largest economy, remains committed to a path of relatively restrictive fiscal policy despite real GDP growth of only 1.7 percent in 1987.

Policy options for macroeconomic adjustment in industrial countries

The risk of renewed weakness of the dollar puts policymakers in a quandary. A further rapid depreciation could push up U.S. inflation, raise domestic interest rates, and—if international investors become reluctant to hold dollar assets at prevailing yields—cause instability in financial markets. Alternatively, stabilizing the dollar might require continued currency intervention, monetary tightening in the United States, or a combination of both. This course, too, has its drawbacks. Heavy intervention might result in unwanted monetary expansion. Tighter credit and rising U.S. interest rates would increase the risk of a domestic

recession and of a further disruption of the stock market. Concerted policy action by the main industrial countries therefore seems the only way to reduce payment imbalances to sustainable levels, avoid a recession in the United States, and set the stage for steady growth worldwide during the next decade.

The United States' low private saving rate means that it cannot safely maintain fiscal deficits as large relative to GNP as those of the other main industrial countries. Further fiscal action would reduce its aggregate domestic demand and its overall saving-investment deficit. To maintain adequate liquidity in financial markets and stimulate domestic investment, especially in export industries, the U.S. government should avoid tightening its monetary stance. With sufficient fiscal restraint it should be possible to achieve lower real interest rates and still contain inflationary expectations.

Fiscal contraction will be difficult. But without it tight money and the attendant risk of a domestic recession may be the only way to prevent further weakness of the dollar and stem an acceleration of inflation in the United States. Budget cuts amounting to $76 billion for fiscal years 1988 and 1989 were announced in November 1987 in the wake of the stock market crash. They are a step in the right direction. However, they may not suffice to cut the federal budget deficit to less than its 1987 level of $151 billion. Further reduction of the deficit is therefore needed.

Firm action along these lines can reduce the United States' external deficit, stabilize its ratio of net foreign liabilities to GNP, and gradually restore stability in currency markets. But rapid fiscal contraction and lower U.S. imports would depress the world economy. Unless a slowdown in domestic demand in the United States can be offset by increased demand in the countries with external surpluses, the correction of imbalances will be protracted and the risk of recession will increase. Under these circumstances Japan should maintain, and Germany accelerate, the growth of domestic demand by using a combination of monetary accommodation, fiscal expansion, and structural reform.

An accommodating monetary stance in both countries would help to keep down their interest rates, ease further downward pressure on the dollar, and permit a more flexible U.S. monetary policy. Fiscal stimulation will continue to be limited by domestic policy concerns. In Japan the need to reduce the existing burden of government debt is seen as paramount; Germany is unwilling to jeopardize its successful reduction of fiscal deficits. As a minimum, however, both should refrain from further procyclical fiscal tightening. In Germany additional stimulation of investment—and improved investment efficiency—through tax cuts and reduced market rigidities would also be desirable. Appropriate steps include eliminating domestic subsidies, improving the flexibility of labor markets, and deregulating domestic trade and distribution. Finally, both countries could reduce barriers to trade, which combined with stronger domestic demand would also create new and much needed export opportunities for developing countries.

In contrast to Germany, several countries in Europe already face considerable pressure on their current accounts and are likely to incur deficits in 1988 and 1989. Since they also face rising domestic inflation, they are ill placed to offset the effect of U.S. contraction. However, smaller European countries with a strong external position—the Benelux group and Switzerland—could also contribute to the international adjustment process by increasing domestic demand, increasing imports, and improving the efficiency of their markets through structural reforms.

Finally, the two largest Asian NIEs could increase the momentum of global adjustment by reducing their current account surpluses. Lower import barriers and further currency appreciation in these countries would reinforce the benefits of increased domestic demand growth and of concurrent fiscal contraction in the United States.

These combined steps could translate into significant benefits for the global economy: a gradual reduction of international payment imbalances, greater financial stability, and falling unemployment would move the world economy to a higher growth path for the next decade. The benefits for developing countries would also be important. Strong growth in industrial countries would assist them directly through greater demand for their exports. In addition lower U.S. trade and budget deficits would lessen U.S. dependence on foreign savings and result in lower interest rates. This more favorable external environment would make it easier for developing countries to service their debt. If combined with measures to restore the creditworthiness of problem debtors and to facilitate new lending, the improvement in the global economy would also permit a reduction in the net resource transfers by developing countries. This, in turn, would enhance their prospects of sustained adjustment with growth.

Developing countries in the world economy

Until the end of the 1970s GDP growth in developing countries remained generally strong, continuing the trend of the 1960s (see Table 1.3). After 1980 their growth rates dropped from an average of 5.4 percent a year during 1973–80 to 3.9 percent for 1980–87. China and India were important exceptions because of major growth-promoting policy reforms during the 1980s (see Box 1.4). The decline can be traced in part to unforeseen changes in the world economy. These changes not only had a direct adverse effect; they also exposed the unsustainability of the macroeconomic policies that many developing countries had adopted during the 1970s. Those most profoundly affected had four things in common:

Table 1.3 Growth of real GDP, 1965 to 1987
(annual percentage change)

Country group	Average, 1965–73	Average, 1973–80	Average, 1980–85	1986	1987
Industrial countries	4.5	2.8	2.4	2.7	2.9
Developing countries	6.5	5.4	3.2	4.7	3.9
Low-income	5.5	4.6	7.4	6.4	5.3
Excluding China and India	3.4	3.4	3.0	4.8	4.5
China and India	6.1	4.9	8.6	6.8	5.4
Low-income Africa	3.6	2.0	0.7	3.7	3.0
Middle-income	7.0	5.7	1.6	3.9	3.2
Oil exporters	7.0	5.9	0.9	0.3	0.8
Exporters of manufactures	7.4	6.0	5.8	7.2	5.3
Highly indebted countries	6.9	5.4	0.1	3.5	1.7
High-income oil exporters	8.7	8.0	−2.5	−8.1	−2.9

Note: Data for developing countries are based on a sample of ninety countries.

- High levels of external debt
- Major macroeconomic imbalances, such as large fiscal deficits and high inflation
- Distorted and inflexible markets
- Unresponsive policies.

External factors impinged on these highly vulnerable economies in two main ways: through trade and through finance.

International trade

A healthy international trading environment is important for strong economic growth in developing countries. Most have small domestic markets that make them highly dependent on trade. Moreover their foreign exchange earnings can be volatile; exports often comprise only a small number of primary commodities, such as grains, tropical beverages, vegetable oils, or minerals. In 1985 primary commodities accounted for 72 and 51 percent of the total exports of low- and middle-income countries (excluding China and India), respectively. The proceeds from these exports are needed to pay for

imports of manufactures, which are vital for continuing industrialization and technological progress. Shifts in the relative prices of commodities and manufactures can therefore change the purchasing power of the developing countries' exports dramatically, often with major repercussions for growth.

Between 1980 and 1986 the real prices of primary commodities fell sharply (see Figure 1.6). Several factors were at work. Slower growth in industrial countries had depressed demand. Over the longer term, shifts in technology continued to reduce the demand for industrial raw materials. Meanwhile supply had expanded. Growing subsidies and trade protection—as provided, for example, by the EC's Common Agricultural Policy—caused overproduction in the industrial countries. Output had also expanded in developing countries in response to the high prices of the early 1970s. Past investment in infrastructure, new techniques, and improved domestic policies also contributed.

Crude oil prices fell even more sharply than those of other primary commodities (see Figure 1.6). This posed serious adjustment difficulties for

Box 1.4 Economic progress and policy reforms in India and China

Among low-income countries India and China stand out with strong growth despite the worsening environment of the early 1980s. China, whose GDP had grown an average of 5.4 percent between 1973 and 1980, grew at 10.3 percent between 1980 and 1987; growth peaked at 12.7 percent in 1985. Average annual population growth remains relatively low at 1.6 percent, and the long-term per capita GDP is growing unusually quickly for the developing world. In some areas deep poverty persists. However, China's health, literacy, and life expectancy place it on a par with many middle-income countries. India suffered from declining terms of trade in the 1970s because of rising oil prices. Agricultural output also fell due to bad weather. GDP growth recovered in the early 1980s and averaged 5.0 percent during 1980–87. But population growth remains high, so per capita income growth averaged only 2.8 percent a year, and nearly half of India's population continues to live in poverty. Nutritional deficiency, infant mortality, and illiteracy also remain extremely high in many areas.

Considering their low income levels, both countries have uncommonly high saving rates and relatively low per capita external debt. China stands out with gross domestic savings of 34 percent of GDP in 1986, compared with 21 percent in India in 1987. For 1987 estimated long-term external debt as a share of GDP stood

at 7 percent for China and 15 percent for India. In both cases this debt is predominantly from official bilateral and multilateral sources. Finally, both countries have achieved growth with low current account deficits: India's has averaged less than 2 percent of GDP since 1980, and China's has declined from a post-1980 peak of 4.2 percent of GDP to a small surplus in 1987.

Economic policies and internal reform in China

China owes much of its recent success to wide-ranging domestic reforms and sound economic management. It is undertaking a delicate transition from a strictly centrally planned economy to one where market forces are increasingly brought into play. The thrust of the most recent reforms was provided by the Central Committee of the Chinese Communist Party at its meeting of October 1984 and confirmed at the Thirteenth Party Congress in October 1987. The "command economy" is giving way to indicative planning, with the focus on long-term guidance, and reliance on free market transactions is increasing. These reforms build on those begun in 1979.

Following the gradual opening of the economy and the revitalization of agriculture after the communes were disbanded, economic reforms have been extended to industry and the towns. Price reform is a key

Figure 1.6 Real commodity prices, 1970 to 1987

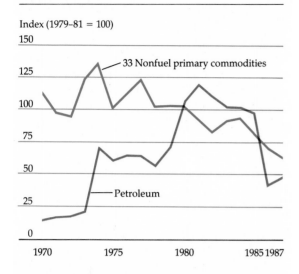

Index (1979–81 = 100)

Note: Real prices are annual average nominal prices in dollars, deflated by the annual change in the manufacturing unit value index (MUV), a measure of the price of industrial country exports to developing countries.

all oil exporters, including the high-income, oil-exporting countries. Growth in the latter group declined by an average of more than 3 percent from 1980 to 1987, compared with strong growth of 8 percent during 1973 to 1980. This abrupt shift in economic fortunes resulted directly from falling oil prices.

Starting in mid-1987, a better balance of supply and demand for non-oil commodities led to a small rise in the composite index of real commodity prices. Despite this improvement real commodity prices at the end of 1987 were still some 32 percent below the average for 1980–84.

Developing countries have differed greatly in their ability to respond to these changes. After the last significant peak in non-oil commodity prices in the late 1970s East Asia offset the decline in prices by stepping up the volume of primary commodity exports; the purchasing power of these exports therefore remained approximately unchanged (see Figure 1.7). In contrast, in Latin America and South Asia the volume growth of commodity exports was insufficient to compensate for declining prices, and their purchasing power declined. In

element. Macroeconomic management—including fiscal, credit, and pricing policies—is taking on a greater role. For example, a profit tax system has replaced the remittance of all enterprise profits to the state budget. Similarly, forced agricultural procurement has been replaced by contracts negotiated between farmers and procurement agencies. After a reform and decentralization of the banking system, interest rates are beginning to reflect the scarcity of capital. Management procedures are being reassessed at all levels. Foreign investment in joint ventures has been stimulated through tax and cost incentives, special economic zones, and special status for certain coastal cities. In January 1988 the government announced that it was aiming for export-led growth. The program has had its problems, however. Price reform has greatly increased the supply of food and consumer goods, but high inflation followed the fiscal and credit expansion after 1985.

Economic policies and internal reform in India

As well as striving for greater efficiency, competitiveness, and productivity, India's main challenge is to alleviate poverty and provide employment. The Seventh Plan, for 1985–90, addresses these problems directly. Overall it calls for maintaining the growth achieved under the Sixth Plan and aims for real GDP growth of 5 percent a year. In agriculture the plan gives the highest priority to completing irrigation schemes; in industry it emphasizes improvements in productivity. The plan stresses the need to keep food supplies up and prices down, both to protect the real income of the poor and to raise employment and productivity. It also emphasizes changes in economic policy. Unlike its predecessors the Seventh Plan calls for a greater role for the private sector and promises to provide the incentives needed to encourage private industrial investment. Measures taken during the Sixth Plan have already given entrepreneurs greater freedom. The Seventh Plan envisages further progress by easing licensing requirements and introducing more flexibility into pricing. It also calls for continued trade liberalization and emphasizes the promotion of exports.

In line with this plan several major initiatives have been undertaken to reform trade, industry, and public finance, for example by liberalizing imports of high technology products. Joint ventures with foreign investors are also being encouraged. The government is promoting exports by simplifying procedures, reducing export taxes, and facilitating forward cover of foreign exchange receipts.

25

Figure 1.7 Volume and purchasing power of exports by developing regions, 1965 to 1987
(index 1970 = 100)

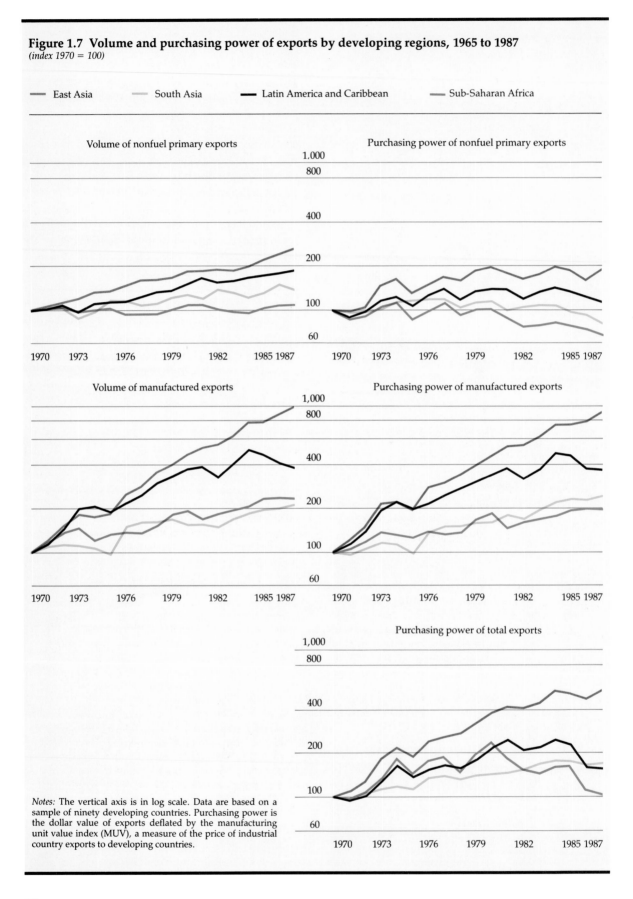

Notes: The vertical axis is in log scale. Data are based on a sample of ninety developing countries. Purchasing power is the dollar value of exports deflated by the manufacturing unit value index (MUV), a measure of the price of industrial country exports to developing countries.

Sub-Saharan Africa purchasing power declined sharply as commodity export volumes stagnated. All these regions faced similar trends in prices. The differences between trends in purchasing power must therefore be attributed to varying degrees of flexibility in supply response. That response, in turn, depended in no small measure on the domestic policy environment (see *World Development Report 1986*).

The growth in the value of manufactured exports from developing countries also slowed considerably after 1980, from an average of 25 percent during the 1970s to 9 percent after 1980, while the rate of growth in the volume of exports declined from 13 to 9 percent during the same period. Again these declines were most pronounced in Latin America and Sub-Saharan Africa, where they compounded the loss in the purchasing power of non-oil commodity exports. However, even the best performers experienced a decline in the growth of exports of manufactures during the early 1980s, mainly caused by the recession and rising protectionism in industrial countries (see *World Development Report 1987*, chapter 8).

Changes in the purchasing power of total exports capture the overall effect of these changes in prices and trade volumes (see Figure 1.7). The four major country groups discussed above fared quite differently after 1980. The purchasing power of East Asia's exports rose by 45 percent from 1980 to 1987, after doubling during the preceding five years. In South Asia purchasing power of exports improved moderately, while in Latin America it fell by 26 percent. Sub-Saharan Africa fared worst. The purchasing power of its exports was cut by more than half between 1980 and 1987; this fully reversed the gains of the 1970s. The divergence can only be partly accounted for by differences in the structure of trade. Economic flexibility in responding to essentially similar external forces is the major factor. However, GDP growth in almost all developing countries has been retarded since 1980 by the slowdown in international trade (see Table 1.3).

To sum up, growth and trade policies in industrial countries have a direct bearing on export opportunities for developing countries. Steady growth and more liberal trade policies in industrial countries have benefits for the wider world economy. But the developing countries' own policies help to determine how vulnerable they will be to such external factors. Prudent macroeconomic policies and outward-looking trade strategies give developing countries greater resilience and flexibility.

Box 1.5 illustrates the scope and need for domestic adjustment in Sub-Saharan Africa. With sound policies in place developing countries can generally preserve domestic growth, even in periods when the external environment deteriorates. In contrast, failure to adjust makes growth less certain.

External finance

Besides trade, the cost and availability of international finance are the other main external determinants of the economic performance of developing countries. The debt crisis has had a profound impact. One of the most urgent tasks facing the international community is to find ways of reducing the drag exerted by the continuing debt overhang on economic growth in the developing world.

DETERIORATION IN THE AVAILABILITY AND COST OF EXTERNAL FINANCE. Developing countries have traditionally been net importers of capital; their domestic savings are generally insufficient to meet their investment needs. The availability and cost of such external finance depend mainly on the overall size of the pool of exportable savings in capital-surplus countries and on the competing claims on that pool. During the 1980s both moved against the developing countries.

Between 1974 and 1982 the two oil price shocks had created a temporary savings surplus in high-income, oil-exporting countries. Their surplus funds were recycled to developing countries. This process is now well understood. In addition to increasing their development aid, high-income, oil-exporting countries placed much of their surplus oil revenue with international commercial banks in the form of short-term Eurodollar deposits. This contributed to raising liquidity in the international banking system because credit demand in the industrial countries had been depressed by the oil price shocks. Liquidity and monetary expansion in the industrial countries drove real interest rates down. It also prompted banks to compensate for the slack in their traditional markets by lending more to developing countries.

Commercial lending to developing countries—along with official lending and aid—grew very rapidly during this period. As a result the total medium- and long-term debt of developing countries rose fourfold in nominal terms, from about $140 billion at the end of 1974 to about $560 billion in 1982. In real terms it more than doubled (see Figure 1.8). Loans to central governments and

Box 1.5 Policy reform in Sub-Saharan Africa

In contrast to other developing regions, Sub-Saharan Africa has shown consistently weak economic performance over an entire generation. To make matters worse, during the 1980s per capita income has fallen to about three-quarters of the level reached by the end of the 1970s. Rapid population growth and external shocks have contributed to this, but weak economic management was a major cause. Africa's poor economic performance has now begun to erode the region's productive base and human resources. By the mid-1980s gross investment levels in many countries were too low to maintain the capital stock, and health care and education are now deteriorating.

However, many African governments have started to improve past policies. Their reform efforts can best be described as a slow process of important policy change that is gaining momentum. Changes cover a broad range of policies in many countries. Although reform was initially prompted by the austerity of the early 1980s, many African leaders now recognize that further reforms are essential for improved economic performance. At the U.N. Special Session on Africa in 1986, African governments submitted a Program of Action for African Economic Recovery and Development. That program recognizes the failures of past policies and stresses the need for sustained reform.

Commitment and action vary among countries. On balance, however, about half of the countries in Sub-Saharan Africa are already committed to serious reform. In some areas, especially where institutional and managerial changes are involved, progress is difficult to quantify. In other areas, such as fiscal and monetary policies and price incentives—where better data are available—the signs of progress are clear (see Box table 1.5). A number of countries have made positive adjustments. These include lowering real exchange rates, reducing fiscal deficits, and raising export crop prices. Policy reform has been greatest in countries whose ad-

justment programs have been sufficiently strong and sustained to be supported by World Bank program lending. Other countries have sometimes allowed policies to worsen.

Most adjusting countries have also taken steps to restructure public employment; rationalize and improve management in public enterprises; lift price and trade controls, both domestically and externally; and strengthen government economic management—especially in public investment programming.

The severity of Africa's structural economic imbalances and the vulnerability of African economies to the external environment often obscure the impact of reform efforts on economic performance. Moreover it takes considerable time to increase growth, and progress is often spread unevenly across countries and sectors. Although comparisons between countries with and without strong reform programs can be made difficult by the uneven effects of exogenous factors such as export prices and weather, evidence shows that adjustment is generally conducive to growth. For example, excluding countries recently affected by strong external shocks (both positive and negative), growth in reforming countries accelerated from an average of 1 percent during 1980–85 to nearly 4 percent during 1986–87. By contrast, growth in nonreforming countries, also 1 percent in the earlier period, barely increased during 1986–87. In most cases reform has helped to alleviate poverty by raising agricultural incomes and improving the efficiency of public spending on infrastructure and key social services.

Reform efforts in Africa are impressive. But given the uncertain global prospects and severe constraints such as high population growth, countries with adjustment programs must deepen existing reforms. Others still need to adopt and implement adjustment programs. Industrial countries and multilateral financial institutions, in turn, must persevere in their support of African adjustment through increased aid and debt relief.

Box table 1.5 Key reform indicators

Indicator of reform	Period	Countries with strong reform programs	Countries with weak or no reform programs
Fiscal deficit	1980–82	8.2	7.4
(percentage of GDP)	1987	5.2	8.1
Real effective exchange rate			
(1980–82 = 100)	1987	69	79
Inflation	1980–82	19	16
(annual percentage)	1987	15	38
Commercial bank lending rates	1980–82	−3.5	−2.2
(real)	1987	4.7	−11.6
Agricultural incentives			
Export crop prices			
(real, 1980/81–82/83 = 100)	1986/87	153	114
Food crop prices			
(real, 1980/81–82/83 = 100)	1986/87	122	94

Note: Depending on available data, twelve to seventeen countries have been included in the group of reforming countries and six to ten in the group of nonreforming countries, depending on the indicator. Averages are unweighted.

state-owned enterprises were especially favored by commercial banks. Because of their sovereign status these entities were considered to be low risk. Developing countries were happy to take advantage of this unaccustomed access to cheap loans with few strings attached. They stepped up their commercial borrowing. This enabled them to maintain domestic growth and to finance major public investment programs, especially in the energy sector. With hindsight it is clear that lending and borrowing decisions were often imprudent and resulted in excessive indebtedness in a number of countries. New funds were often channeled into low-yielding investments. And in a number of countries borrowings fueled a flight of capital that drained the pool of resources for investment even as the burden of foreign debt mounted.

The early 1980s were a turning point. The shift toward anti-inflationary macroeconomic policies in industrial countries led to a rapid rise in nominal interest rates. Developing countries with large for-

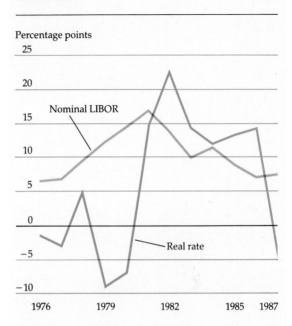

Figure 1.9 Interest rates on external borrowings of developing countries, 1976 to 1987

Note: The nominal rate is the average six-month dollar LIBOR during each year; the real rate is the nominal LIBOR deflated by the change in the export price index for developing countries.

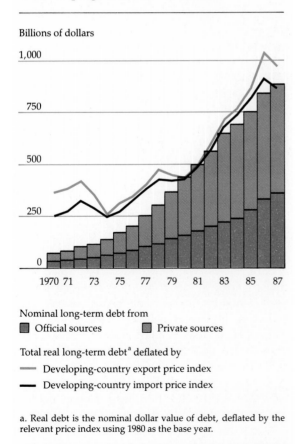

Figure 1.8 Long-term external debt of developing countries, 1970 to 1987

Nominal long-term debt from
■ Official sources   ■ Private sources

Total real long-term debt[a] deflated by
— Developing-country export price index
— Developing-country import price index

a. Real debt is the nominal dollar value of debt, deflated by the relevant price index using 1980 as the base year.

eign debts were hit hard. The combination of higher interest rates and lower export prices for non-oil commodities led to soaring real costs for all forms of new and existing debt (see Figure 1.9). The Mexican debt crisis of August 1982, triggered in part by these factors, precipitated an abrupt loss of confidence in the creditworthiness of many highly indebted countries. Voluntary lending to most of them came to a standstill. Finally, from 1982 onward, the rapid deterioration of the U.S. saving-investment balance caused the United States to stake a bigger claim on the world's savings at a time when the savings surplus of the high-income oil exporters was falling along with the price of oil.

IMPLICATIONS OF THE DETERIORATION IN EXTERNAL LENDING. Rising debt service and the cut in lending led to a reversal of net resource transfers to developing countries. In the five years to 1982 developing countries received positive net resource transfers of $147 billion through long-term lending (including concessional loans). Since 1982 resource transfers have become negative, totaling $85 billion. The shift in resource transfers was especially

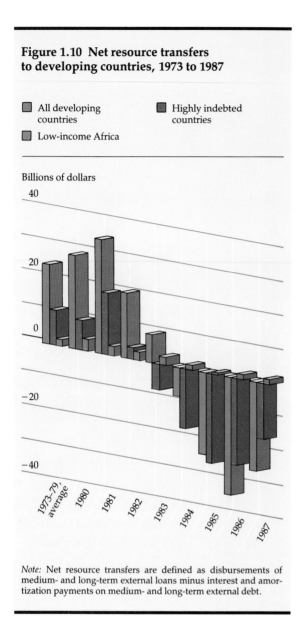

Figure 1.10 Net resource transfers to developing countries, 1973 to 1987

☐ All developing countries ■ Highly indebted countries

☐ Low-income Africa

Billions of dollars

Note: Net resource transfers are defined as disbursements of medium- and long-term external loans minus interest and amortization payments on medium- and long-term external debt.

pronounced for the highly indebted, middle-income countries. Their net resource transfers of $61 billion in 1978–82 became a net loss of $93 billion—or more than 2 percent of their aggregate GDP—in the next five years (see Figure 1.10). In addition, as interest costs soared and export revenue stagnated, the cost of servicing their long-term external debt increased as a proportion of exports of goods and services from 27.1 percent in 1980 to 38.8 percent in 1982 (see Table 1.4).

The drain of resources forced many countries to undertake rigorous domestic adjustments. Limited access to foreign financing meant that current account deficits had to be cut back after 1982 (see

Table 1.5). This in turn meant that trade balances had to move strongly into surplus. For the seventeen highly indebted countries, for example, an aggregate trade surplus of only $2 billion in 1982 had to be turned into an average annual trade surplus of $32 billion during 1983–87. This could be achieved only through import compression, lower investment, and reductions in per capita consumption; between 1980 and 1987 the imports of the highly indebted countries declined at an average annual rate of 6.3 percent, investment at 5.3 percent, and per capita consumption at 1.6 percent. In the twenty-two debt-distressed, Sub-Saharan African countries per capita consumption dropped by about 3.2 percent a year and investment by 2.6 percent a year between 1980 and 1986. The debt crisis of the 1980s thus dealt a double blow to the more vulnerable developing countries. Reductions in per capita consumption lowered economic welfare immediately, while large cuts in investment threatened the potential for future growth.

THE DEBT OVERHANG PERSISTS. The outright financial collapse that many had feared has not happened. It was averted through a combination of debt reschedulings by private and official creditors, expanded lending by international agencies, and substantial adjustment efforts in the debtor countries themselves. At the same time commercial banks have managed to reduce their exposure to debtor countries and build up their reserves and capital. More recently, substantial loan loss provisions have further strengthened the banks against possible defaults or debt moratoria. Finally, regulatory changes governing capital adequacy and portfolio risk have made a return to the excessive lending of the 1970s less likely. In many important ways, therefore, the past few years have seen considerable success in averting what might have been a deeper crisis.

However, the debt overhang remains an obstacle to growth in the debtor countries and a threat to the world economy. The outstanding long-term debt of developing countries has continued to increase since 1982 (see Figure 1.8); the total external debt of highly indebted countries rose from $390 billion in 1982 to an estimated $485 billion at the end of 1987. Valuation effects caused by the decline of the dollar account for most of the increase since 1985. The rest reflects increased official lending—especially in support of stabilization and adjustment programs—and, to a lesser extent, involuntary bank lending as part of debt reschedulings.

Most indicators of creditworthiness continued to

Table 1.4 Debt indicators in developing countries, 1975 to 1987
(percent)

Country group and debt indicator	1975	1980	1981	1982	1983	1984	1985	1986	1987[a]
All developing countries									
Debt service ratio	13.7	16.2	17.9	21.0	19.7	19.5	21.8	22.6	21.0
Debt-GNP ratio	15.7	20.7	22.4	26.3	31.4	33.0	35.9	38.5	37.6
Highly indebted countries									
Debt service ratio	24.0	27.1	30.7	38.8	34.7	33.4	33.9	37.7	32.7
Debt-GNP ratio	18.1	23.3	25.6	32.4	45.4	47.5	49.5	54.1	55.9
Low-income Africa									
Debt service ratio	10.2	13.6	14.6	14.2	14.2	15.1	17.9	19.9	34.7
Debt-GNP ratio	25.2	39.8	44.2	48.0	55.1	62.0	68.9	72.1	76.2

Notes: Data are based on a sample of ninety developing countries. The debt service ratio is defined as the dollar value of external debt payments (interest and amortization) on medium-and long-term loans expressed as a percentage of the dollar value of exports of goods and services. The debt-GNP ratio is defined as the dollar value of outstanding medium-and long-term debt expressed as a percentage of dollar GNP.
a. Estimated. Ratios do not assume further buildup of arrears. This accounts for the sharp increase in the debt service ratio for low-income Africa in 1987.

deteriorate until 1986. Despite a modest improvement in 1987 they are still worse than in 1982. In other words, despite drastic cuts in the growth of aggregate domestic demand (from an annual average increase of 5.8 percent between 1973 and 1980 to less than 1 percent during the next seven years), the highly indebted countries have seen little improvement in exports and a severe decline in economic growth. Poverty is on the rise (see Box 1 in the Overview). In several countries the economic and social costs of prolonged retrenchment are causing adjustment fatigue.

Negotiations between creditors and debtors have gradually become more confrontational. In 1985 Peru announced that it would limit the servicing of its long-term public debt to 10 percent of its export revenues. In 1986 it applied the ceiling to

private sector debt as well. In February 1987 Brazil suspended debt service payments on medium- and long-term debt owed to commercial banks; after protracted negotiations with its creditors it started to clear up its payment arrears in early 1988. In November 1987 U.S. bank examiners came close to declaring Brazilian debt "value impaired," which would have required large write-offs by creditors. Unilateral restrictions on debt service threaten economic performance in the longer term because they inevitably disrupt access to short-term trade finance and to longer term development funds.

Future defaults and moratoria might yet occur. This danger remains a potential threat to the stability of the international financial system. Moreover, import compression in the highly indebted coun-

Table 1.5 Current account balance, 1973 to 1987
(billions of dollars)

Country group	Average, 1973–79	Average, 1980–82	1983	1984	1985	1986	1987
Industrial countries	−5.1	−34.9	−23.3	−60.8	−50.4	−19.7	−50.3
Developing countries	−27.5	−82.2	−44.7	−18.5	−23.5	−21.3	2.1
Low-income	−3.4	−9.7	−2.7	−4.2	−22.4	−16.6	−9.6
Excluding China and India	−3.6	−8.5	−4.9	−4.2	−5.7	−5.3	−5.9
China and India	0.1	−1.1	2.2	0.0	−16.8	−11.2	−3.6
Low-income Africa	−2.3	−5.8	−3.5	−2.9	−2.9	−3.2	−4.4
Middle-income	−24.1	−72.5	−42.1	−14.3	−1.1	−4.7	11.7
Oil exporters	−5.8	−15.6	−5.9	3.2	0.1	−18.5	−8.8
Exporters of manufactures	−10.2	−25.9	−5.8	5.2	−4.7	10.3	25.9
Highly indebted countries	−14.2	−43.4	−13.9	1.0	0.6	−11.4	−7.2
High-income oil exporters	22.7	53.6	−0.2	1.7	7.4	2.7	1.0

Notes: The total current account balance for industrial, developing, and high-income, oil-exporting countries is less than zero primarily because of counting and measurement discrepancies in the balance of payments reporting, especially on trade in services and on the income of foreign assets.

tries is hampering the export growth of the industrial countries—especially the United States. From 1980 to 1986 the U.S. trade balance with Latin America turned from a surplus of around $2 billion to a deficit of $13 billion. As long as debt service continues to absorb a large part of the debtors' export revenues, their imports will not revive and global economic growth will suffer.

Dealing with the debt overhang:
the need for a comprehensive framework

There can be no simple, single solution to the debt problem: a comprehensive framework is needed. Its main objectives should be, first, to enable debtor countries to allocate more resources to investment and consumption and, second, to strengthen their creditworthiness, thus eventually permitting a resumption of voluntary commercial lending. Debtors and creditors alike stand to gain from such an approach. As creditworthiness is restored, the secondary-market discounts on outstanding debt—which exceed 50 percent for many of the highly indebted countries—would drop. Moreover the debtors' improving growth prospects would enable them to import more from the industrial countries. That would assist in the global correction of external imbalances.

A framework to reduce the burden of debt must have two elements. First, the debtors need to grow faster and export more. Second, the cost of debt service must fall. With the right policies in both industrial and developing countries, these elements can go hand-in-hand.

STRUCTURAL ADJUSTMENT. The key to faster growth and better export performance is the more efficient use of domestic resources in both the public and private sectors. Macroeconomic stabilization needs to be supported by sectoral policy reform in trade, agriculture, industry, energy, and human resources. This affects the use of public resources directly and influences the use of private resources through improved incentives of taxes, subsidies, and regulation. Countries such as Colombia, Indonesia, Republic of Korea, and Thailand were able to avoid major debt problems mainly because of their relatively sound economic policies. In other countries, though, once access to foreign capital was lost, investment dropped. As a result those countries found it harder, economically and politically, to reform domestic policies. The programs of structural adjustment that are now being pursued in several highly indebted

countries are therefore designed to permit faster economic growth by improving the economies' supply response.

NEW EXTERNAL CAPITAL INFLOWS. Capital inflows from official and commercial sources can help to finance new productive capacity and provide support for policy reform and growth. This has been the rationale for the balance of payments support provided by the IMF and the World Bank. For the foreseeable future, however, new lending is likely to remain scarce. In any case it will help only if used efficiently. Turkey shows that a combination of good policies, ample supplies of external funds—including aid—and a favorable external environment can successfully restore creditworthiness through growth. For low-income countries, new external capital, especially from official sources, is essential. Unfortunately, many low-income countries have suffered a decline in lending from industrial country governments. For example, disbursements of long-term bilateral official loans to low-income African countries declined from $2.1 billion in 1981 to $1.2 billion in 1986, reinforcing the fall in net resource transfers. Japan's recent initiative to increase grants and concessional flows to developing countries is, therefore, most welcome (see Box 1.3).

A BETTER TRADING ENVIRONMENT. As discussed above, favorable prices for developing-country exports and unimpeded access to growing markets in industrial countries can greatly strengthen the effectiveness of both domestic policy and external finance. Slower growth and increased protection in the industrial countries have narrowed export markets and depressed commodity prices for the debtors. The industrial countries should reverse the trend of rising protectionism—for their own benefit, as much as for that of the developing countries.

LOWER INTEREST RATES. Long-term solvency depends directly on the cost of debt. A simple rule of thumb is that if the real interest rate exceeds the rate of growth of exports, the debt service ratio will tend to rise. Between 1981 and 1986 this condition held for the developing countries in general, and for the highly indebted countries in particular. Conversely, lower interest rates can significantly reduce the debt service burden over time. For the highly indebted, middle-income countries, at their present level of external indebtedness, every percentage point decrease in the cost of debt service would lower their interest burden by an estimated $5 billion and reduce their debt service ratio by about 4 percentage points. Economic policies in the industrial countries—especially the stance of U.S. fiscal and monetary policy—determine interest rates worldwide. A return to low and stable interest rates would significantly improve the prospect of a gradual release from the debt overhang.

DEBT RESTRUCTURING AND DEBT RELIEF. Another approach is to alter the profile of debt service through debt restructuring. Depending on its terms, restructuring may involve nothing more than a deferral of debt service, leaving the discounted present value of total debt service unchanged. Alternatively it may involve an element of debt relief. This, in turn, might be either "nonconcessional," in the case where a trade in debt instruments lets the debtor share in a market discount, or "concessional," in the case where it involves the provision of public funds or explicit forgiveness of debt.

The need for alternative forms of debt restructuring—and their feasibility—will vary from country to country and over time. At its outbreak the debt crisis was commonly viewed as a problem of lack of liquidity; debt restructuring emphasized rescheduling with generally little relief. Subsequently awareness grew that the debt problems of some countries involved more fundamental issues of solvency, and a secondary market developed for the debt instruments of highly indebted developing countries. The development of this market resulted in a range of nonconcessional instruments for debt restructuring and relief, generally known as the "menu approach." It includes transactions such as debt-equity swaps, securitization, and interest capitalization (see Box 1.6). For some of the highly indebted countries these instruments have been used effectively in combination with domestic policy reforms and new money packages from commercial and official sources. The World Bank is actively supporting these developments (Box 1.7).

Concessional debt relief usually follows the recognition by creditors that a country's limited prospects for growth and expanded exports will limit its ability to regain solvency, even with effective domestic policy reform, injections of new money, or changes in the timing and structure of debt. Precedents for concessional debt relief exist. One example is the United States' cancellation of large war debts after World War II. This contributed to the successful postwar reconstruction of Europe. In contrast, the debts and reparation obligations

after World War I were among the factors that led to protracted economic difficulties. Moreover bilateral official debts of some low-income developing countries have been forgiven by many industrial countries. Expanded programs of concessional debt relief for the poorest countries, complementing domestic policy reform and supported by additional aid, are undoubtedly needed, especially for Sub-Saharan Africa. The debt of these countries consists mostly of official claims, so decisions about debt relief lie squarely with industrial country governments. The Venice economic summit of June 1987 endorsed the principle of concessional relief for the poorest countries. Recent progress and further options in this area are discussed in the World Bank's *World Debt Tables 1987–88*.

The issue of debt relief for the highly indebted, middle-income countries is more complex because prospects for medium-term growth are reasonable for some countries, assuming satisfactory domestic policies. Moreover some countries have succeeded in significantly expanding their exports with realistic exchange rate regimes and appropriate incentive frameworks. The bulk of their debt is owed to commercial creditors. Because of the substantially better economic prospects and higher per capita income of the middle-income countries, most official donors have not been willing to provide concessional financing in face of the growing demands of low-income countries and the scarcity of aid resources. Under these circumstances restructuring and nonconcessional relief (that is, debt reductions not exceeding market discounts) have been seen as the appropriate course of action for addressing their debt problems, with few exceptions. There nevertheless are a few highly indebted, middle-income countries whose per capita income figures are misleading because they reflect an enclave economy based on mineral exports. In such countries the debt is so great, compared with the productive potential of the nonmineral part of the economy, that with the nonconcessional instruments available a return to creditworthiness and growth remains very far off. If the international environment were to deteriorate substantially, many more countries could fall into this category. There is the challenge for creditors, debtor countries, regulators, tax authorities, and multilateral financial institutions to find new financial options, including ways to pass on current market discounts on debt to the debtor countries under case by case, market-based approaches.

In sum, progress is needed simultaneously on many fronts. Measures to improve the interna-

Box 1.6 Comparing alternative financial options to reduce the debt overhang

The Baker Initiative of September 1985 proposed a change of course in dealing with the debt overhang. It emphasized the importance of resumed lending to support growth and adjustment in highly indebted countries. Despite its merits this initiative has fallen short of its objective to date. Commercial lending failed to reach projected levels because of the banks' perception that "defensive" lending may not improve the value of loans already in their portfolio. Large discounts in the secondary market for developing-country debt play a crucial role in this respect: lenders assume that the market will value new loans at much less than book value.

Under these circumstances commercial banks have divergent long-term interests in their dealings with the developing countries because of the varied size and composition of their loan exposure. This stands in contrast with the period immediately after 1982, when most commercial lenders shared an interest in concerted lending to protect the financial system and gain time to reduce their individual exposures to developing countries. Now that both objectives have largely been accomplished, many smaller banks are trying to leave the debt-restructuring process—even at the cost of substantial write-offs—to redirect their lending to more traditional activities. The core of concerted lending now comprises the major international banks that have established branch networks in debtor countries or whose corporate clients are also active in those countries. Thus, depending on their business strategies, banks are eager to explore new options to reduce the risk of participating in "new money" packages, to improve the quality of existing exposures, or to seek "exits" to eliminate or reduce such exposures. Some of these options—which make up the so-called "menu approach"—are reviewed below. They can be attractive to borrowers as well as lenders. They can be a source of new funds for reducing exchange rate risk on existing debt and a means of reducing the debt burden through debt relief. All depend on voluntary cooperation between debtors and creditors.

• *Foreign direct investment (FDI)* can generate inflows of new capital. As distinct from loans, the return on FDI varies with the quality of the investment and the state of the economy; by definition investors share these risks. But potential political unrest and the unfavorable economic climate in most highly indebted countries may lead prospective foreign investors to seek appropriate risk coverage before committing themselves. The Multilateral Investment Guarantee Agency sponsored by the World Bank could play a useful role in this context. Even so the volume of investment flows is unlikely to make up for the current shortfall in lending or to provide a positive net inflow of resources. As investments bear fruit, foreign profit re-

mittances through dividend transfers could exceed normal servicing of interest-bearing debt and thus put additional strain on the current account of debtor countries.

• *Debt-equity swaps* are a variation on FDI. They convert foreign currency debt into domestic currency investment, rather than serve as a channel for new money. Such swaps alter the debtors' obligation and reduce their interest-bearing external debt. As discussed in the *World Development Report 1987*, debt-equity swaps have covered substantial amounts of debt, especially in Chile and Mexico. They could become vehicles for the repatriation of flight capital. However, since domestic currency is usually offered at a discount to investors, swaps can distort the allocation of resources: investments of marginal economic return may be undertaken. In addition the increase in the domestic money supply resulting from the conversion of foreign currencies may prove inflationary. On balance, though, debt-equity swaps are a useful item on the "menu." If used carefully, they can help to revive the momentum of productive investment. They can be used as "exits" by existing creditors if the original loan is sold to a third party before the swap, and they can provide a vehicle for repatriating flight capital.

• The *conversion of existing loans into local currencies* is a variety of swap. It too can be a vehicle for repatriating flight capital, as well as alleviating the drain on foreign currency resources. The most serious drawback is that since domestic interest rates in the debtor countries are usually high, increased debt-servicing costs may exacerbate domestic fiscal problems.

• Other forms of noninterest-bearing capital include instruments such as *performance bonds* or *commodity-indexed bonds*. Service is conditional and tied to the debtor's economic growth, or to an export price index for major commodities. Innovations of this sort are unlikely to reduce the debt overhang significantly, but they can be another source of "new money."

• *Financial engineering and liability management* are techniques that aim to cushion interest rate and currency shocks to debtor countries through hedging. For instance, interest rate swaps and interest rate caps reduce the interest rate sensitivity of existing liabilities by converting floating-rate borrowings into fixed-rate liabilities or by putting a ceiling on future interest rates. Similarly currency swaps can hedge currency exposure and alter the currency mix of a debt portfolio to match the composition of the debtor's export revenues. Financial hedges of this type involve a risk for the provider of the hedge that the purchaser—in this instance the debtor country—will not fulfill his obligations when the contract matures. This restricts use of these techniques to borrowers that have remained creditworthy, unless the risk can be guaranteed by a creditworthy third party.

• *New contractual arrangements* between debtors and lenders are another possibility. Debt-equity swaps and the renegotiation of interest spreads over LIBOR (London Interbank Offered Rate) and of loan maturities in debt reschedulings have set the legal precedents. One idea is to subordinate existing debt to future loans, thus giving the latter senior status. This could prevent new credits from being marked down in line with secondary-market prices and thus make it easier to attract new lenders. But current creditors might object if this practice became widespread. *Securitization*, which transforms traditional bank loans into negotiable securities, is another legal variant. It can be a channel for debt relief if the exchange of securities for loans reflects market prices and passes the discount on to the debtor. Mexico's novel scheme of December 1987 was a hybrid. It combined the features of securitization (by exchanging existing loans for tradable securities) and subordination (by deeming the collateralized securities "senior" to the remaining old loans). In this case "seniority" stems from the fact that the collateral (a zero-coupon U.S. Treasury bond with a present value equal to that of the new securities) guarantees the repayment of principal, although not of the interest on the new bonds. Despite its limited success this scheme sets a precedent for market-based debt relief: it passed some of the market discount to the debtor.

• In the same vein *partial write-offs* of existing loans could be an effective way of sharing the burden between debtors and creditors as well as providing debt relief. But write-offs raise delicate operational, accounting, and regulatory problems. Views differ over the banks' contention that partial write-offs are incompatible with existing accounting practices because these require an "all or nothing" approach. Clarification of these rules is essential. Partial write-offs recognize that the book value of developing-country loans is at odds with their market value, and they secure tax deductions. If set between existing secondary market value and nominal principal, they can provide an equitable formula for limited debt relief. They can thereby improve the borrowers' creditworthiness and debt-servicing capability, as well as improve the market value of existing loans.

• Finally, *partial or complete interest capitalization* is a constructive alternative to accumulating new loans to finance interest due. However, under U.S. banking regulations capitalization is currently tantamount to nonpayment: the loans involved would be declared nonperforming. A change in regulations will be needed to make this approach viable. Moreover, automatic interest capitalization may prove unacceptable to commercial creditors, most of whom will prefer to keep the refinancing of interest a matter for negotiation.

tional outlook, domestic policy reform, new money, and creative debt-restructuring approaches are all necessary. The right mix of ingredients will vary from case to case. Prospects for the next decade will depend on how effectively the broad policy framework outlined above can be implemented by all those concerned: industrial and developing country governments, commercial banks, and multilateral financial institutions. The next section examines the outlook for the world economy under alternative policy scenarios.

The outlook for the world economy until 1995

Growth in the world economy to the mid-1990s will largely depend on the extent to which governments in industrial countries address the policy issues identified above. This section presents alternative growth paths: a "base case," which assumes that the industrial countries will leave their policies broadly unchanged, and a "high case," which assumes that they will change them to conform with the guidelines spelled out in this chapter.

The base case

The assumptions underlying the base case scenario are as follows.

• Driven by circumstance as much as by design, fiscal policy in the United States will gradually, but fitfully, become more restrictive. The federal budget deficit will follow the broad targets set by the amended Gramm-Rudman-Hollings Act.

• Fiscal action in Japan and Germany will be confined to preventing a significant decline in domestic demand.

• Monetary policy in the major industrial countries will avoid increases in real interest rates.

• Industrial countries will pursue no major structural reforms, and protectionism will persist at roughly its present level.

• The world economy will encounter no shocks, such as a sharp change in the price of oil.

• Developing countries will continue their adjustment efforts at a pace similar to that in the recent past.

Under these conditions exchange rates and financial markets are likely to remain highly volatile. The threat of further stock market crashes, rising inflationary expectations, and the restrictive influence of U.S. fiscal contraction would depress domestic demand in the United States. This would be

Box 1.7 How the World Bank supports the highly indebted, middle-income countries

The World Bank's strategy for assisting the highly in-debted, middle-income countries is based on the prem-ise that the resumption of growth is an essential condi-tion for their return to creditworthiness. The resumption of growth, in turn, hinges both on domes-tic policy reforms and on the adequacy of external fi-nance. It also requires a supportive, international eco-nomic environment—above all, access to growing export markets and favorable interest rates.

More specifically the Bank's strategy calls for:

- Policy analysis and dialogue with member govern-ments to identify the needed structural changes and to gain agreement on the required reforms
- Financial support for implementing structural re-forms, often in the form of fast-disbursing, policy-based operations
- Sustained investment financing, refocused as nec-essary on rehabilitating and restructuring projects, en-terprises, and investment programs, as well as expand-ing productive capacity
- Continued efforts to alleviate poverty, including measures to cushion the effect of adjustment on the poorest groups
- Assistance in mobilizing financial support from commercial and official lenders.

The difficulties faced by the debtor countries require a sustained policy effort and continuing external assis-tance as part of a medium-term adjustment framework. The Bank's support is tailored to specific country cir-cumstances and problems. The pace of lending and the mix between adjustment and project lending varies among countries and depends on a variety of factors, such as the borrower's efforts to reform, project lend-ing opportunities, and the Bank's own guidelines on prudential exposure levels. Typically lending plans are made up of a series of operations, each intended to address specific adjustment and investment requirements.

The Bank plays a catalytic role by mobilizing the needed new financing from commercial banks (and other sources) or by encouraging other forms of finan-cial relief, including debt conversion and reduction. The Bank's efforts have focused particularly on com-mercial lenders. These provided by far the largest fi-nancing to the middle-income countries in the past but have reduced their net lending precipitously in recent years. As a result reforms in many countries are in danger of being underfunded.

The Bank's catalytic influence has traditionally been achieved through the example of its own lending and the signal of its confidence in the policy reforms under-taken by the debtor. Beyond this the Bank can—and does—play a more specific role on a case-by-case basis, by making use of formal linkages between its own lending and that of other lenders and, more rarely, by providing partial guarantees on commercial financing.

Changing priorities within the banking industry have widened the possibilities for providing cash flow relief both through new money and through the con-sensual debt reduction schemes summarized in Box 1.6. Consistent with its charter and policies, the Bank will seek to foster these market developments as a means of financial relief for its borrowers. For example, the Bank and its affiliate, the International Finance Cor-poration, have supported debt conversion by their as-sistance for policy reforms aimed at privatizing public enterprises. The Multilateral Investment Guarantee Authority will further enhance these schemes. The Bank has also supported market-based debt reduction schemes, as in Mexico, by agreeing to the establish-ment of a collateral trust by the debtor.

In performing a catalytic role, the Bank seeks to en-sure, on a case-by-case basis, that the financing plan it supports is well designed and reflects an adequate level of burden sharing by commercial banks. Credit enhancement is provided only when it is seen as essen-tial to close the transaction and when the added expo-sure that it entails for the Bank is acceptable in light of the Bank's overall country exposure.

---

only partly offset by increases in export demand resulting from the recent depreciation of the dollar. Growth in the other industrial countries and in the East Asian NIEs would also slow down, because of the slump in exports to the United States and the instability of financial markets. The U.S. current account deficit might fall to around 2 percent of GNP in the early 1990s, or roughly half its level in 1987. The ratio of U.S. net external liabilities to GNP would stabilize by the early 1990s. The cur-rent account surpluses of Japan and Germany would be correspondingly smaller.

This reduction of imbalances, although painful in the short term, would avoid a major world re-cession. For the longer term the scenario can be regarded as cautiously optimistic, since it sets the stage for somewhat faster growth in the early 1990s. If, subject to the assumptions above, macro-economic policies in industrial countries are rea-sonably well managed, a modest economic recov-ery could follow in the early 1990s. Investor and consumer confidence might improve, and, in re-sponse to more stable financial markets, real inter-est rates would decline. As capital stocks were rebuilt, the capacity for noninflationary growth and reduced unemployment would also improve. Under these circumstances real GDP growth in industrial countries should eventually return to rates similar to those of the turbulent 1970s and 1980s. Between 1987 and 1995, however, average industrial country growth would be 2.3 percent, or slightly less than that for 1980–87 (see Table 1.6).

For many developing countries, especially the highly indebted, middle-income countries and the low-income countries of Sub-Saharan Africa, this base case is decidedly unpromising. The prospect is for the demand for developing-country exports to slow down and for the real cost of servicing foreign debt to remain close to its 1987 level. Their economic growth will therefore be weak at best. For the most vulnerable countries—Sub-Saharan Africa, the highly indebted countries, and the oil-exporting countries—per capita incomes would stagnate or increase only slowly from their current

depressed levels (see Table 1.7). The countries' debt service burden would remain high (see Table 1.8). The tensions in the international financial system would remain, and the willingness of both creditors and debtors to search for cooperative solutions to the debt problem would continue to be strained.

This is a fragile situation—one that could rapidly deteriorate. For example, a tightening of U.S. money supply intended to stabilize the dollar might trigger a world recession instead. The process might begin as a repetition of the events of late 1987: a steep drop in stock markets worldwide followed, after a lag, by a further substantial fall in the dollar as international investors flee to other currencies. This could damage investment and consumption worldwide, enough to induce a deep recession. Dollar interest rates would rise as the flow of foreign capital to the United States dried up. The developing countries might therefore si-

Table 1.6 Growth of real GDP, 1973 to 1995
(average annual percentage change)

Country group and indicator	1973–80	1980–87	1987–95 Base	1987–95 High
Industrial countries	2.8	2.5	2.3	3.0
Developing countries	5.4	3.9	4.2	5.6
Low-income countries	4.6	7.4	5.4	6.5
Middle-income countries	5.7	2.4	3.6	5.1
Oil exporters	5.9	1.0	2.7	3.7
Exporters of manufactures	6.0	6.3	5.0	6.5
Highly indebted countries	5.4	1.1	3.2	4.8
Sub-Saharan Africa	3.3	0.2	3.2	3.9
Memo items				
Inflation rate[a]	8.2	4.1	4.0	3.2
Real interest rate[b,c]	1.3	5.6	2.6	2.1
Nominal interest rate[c]	9.3	10.5	8.1	7.7

Note: All growth rates for developing countries are based on a sample of ninety countries.
a. Weighted average of industrial countries' GDP deflators expressed in local currency.
b. Average six-month U.S. dollar Eurocurrency rate deflated by the GDP deflator for the United States.
c. Average annual rate.

Table 1.7 Growth of real GDP per capita, 1973 to 1995
(average annual percentage change)

Country group	1973–80	1980–87	1987–95 Base	1987–95 High
Industrial countries	2.1	1.9	1.8	2.6
Developing countries	3.2	1.8	2.2	3.6
Low-income countries	2.5	5.5	3.5	4.6
Middle-income countries	3.2	0.1	1.5	3.0
Oil exporters	3.2	−1.6	0.2	1.3
Exporters of manufactures	4.0	4.6	3.4	4.9
Highly indebted countries	2.9	−1.3	1.0	2.5
Sub-Saharan Africa	0.5	−2.9	0.0	0.7

Note: All growth rates for developing countries are based on a sample of ninety countries.

Table 1.8 Current account balance and its financing in developing countries, 1987 and 1995
(billions of dollars)

Item	All developing countries			Highly indebted countries			Sub-Saharan Africa		
		1995			1995			1995	
	1987[a]	Base	High	1987[a]	Base	High	1987[a]	Base	High
Net exports of goods and nonfactor services	27.6	−24.4	−41.0	25.3	35.0	30.8	−3.0	−4.3	−3.7
Interest on long-term debt	55.9	73.3	75.4	30.1	36.3	35.9	3.7	5.8	5.6
Official	17.0	26.6	26.5	6.7	9.0	8.8	2.1	3.5	3.4
Private	38.9	46.7	48.9	23.4	27.3	27.1	1.5	2.4	2.2
Net official transfers	16.0	21.7	23.2	1.1	2.3	2.2	3.7	7.6	7.8
Current account balance	2.1	−40.6	−52.1	−7.2	1.3	−1.6	−7.2	−5.0	−4.0
Long term loans, net	30.4	43.8	64.8	14.3	−7.7	−4.4	5.2	4.4	3.3
Official	19.6	35.3	36.9	6.9	5.6	5.0	3.3	7.3	6.8
Private	10.8	8.6	27.9	7.5	−13.3	−9.4	1.9	−2.9	−3.5
Debt outstanding and disbursed[b]	886.0	1,113.8	1,184.7	441.4	447.1	456.9	92.9	129.7	125.7
As a percentage of GNP	37.7	23.9	22.5	53.6	28.9	25.9	73.1	58.9	53.0
As a percentage of exports	145.3	94.5	85.4	300.4	172.8	155.3	263.3	215.9	190.6
Debt service as a percentage of exports[b]	20.2	15.6	13.7	35.2	37.3	33.0	25.5	24.5	22.5

Notes: Data are based on a sample of ninety developing countries. Subcategories may not add to totals because of rounding. Net exports plus interest does not equal the current account balance because of the omission of private transfers and investment income. The current account balance not financed by loans is covered by direct foreign investment, other capital (including short-term credit and errors and omissions), and changes in reserves. Ratios are calculated using currrent price data.
a. Estimated.
b. Based on long-term debt only.

multaneously have to face deteriorating exports, commodity prices, terms of trade, and debt service costs. The magnified risk of debt defaults would then feed back on prospects for the broader world economy. In short the risk of a severe setback for the global economy is real. The steps necessary to avoid it are well worth taking.

The high case

The best way to avoid these risks is for the industrial economies to adopt the economic policies that lead to the "high-case" scenario.

• Prompt and convincing steps to reduce payments imbalances, as suggested here, would rapidly restore confidence and equilibrium to financial markets worldwide. In the short term, private investment and consumption would rise, and inflation and real interest rates could be held within reasonable bounds.

• Renewed efforts at structural reform—through higher and more efficient private investment, the elimination of bottlenecks in labor markets, and the reduction of protectionism and agricultural subsidies—would greatly improve the industrial economies' potential for growth. Steps toward further integration and internal liberalization are currently envisaged in the EC by 1992. This too could

make an important contribution to longer term economic revival in the industrial countries.

Under these conditions it should be possible to achieve real annual growth rates of around 3 percent during 1987–95 in the industrial world (see Table 1.6) and perhaps even higher rates toward the end of the decade. The principal obstacle to achieving this result appears to lie not in the task of identifying the appropriate policies, but in finding ways to overcome political opposition to them.

An improved medium-term outlook for the industrial countries would greatly help the developing countries, too. By combining the direct effect of a more favorable external environment (higher export demand, improved commodity prices, and lower interest rates) with its indirect benefits (greater acceptability of domestic policy reform, improved access to external capital, and lower net resource outflows), the high case projects better economic performance in the developing world (see Tables 1.6 to 1.8). As in the past these improvements will be unevenly spread across countries. Highly indebted countries and exporters of manufactures would see substantial improvements in growth of per capita incomes. In contrast, even in this optimistic case, Sub-Saharan Africa would recoup the losses of the past only very slowly. Continued high population growth and the ongoing effect of existing structural rigidities mean that even apparently modest improvements pose a challenge.

The outlook for the developing countries depends critically on their own domestic policies. Whatever the international environment, they must seek to adjust in ways that minimize the effect of any deterioration in that environment on their growth and to maximize the benefits from any improvements. The rest of this Report discusses the role public finance can play in supporting effective adjustment over the short and medium term and in setting the stage for successful long-term development.

II

Public Finance in Development

2

The role of public finance in development

Most developing countries have faced a fiscal crisis of one sort or another during the past decade. Until 1982 public sector deficits rose to unsustainable levels almost without regard to economic structure and income level: oil exporters, oil importers, middle-income countries, low-income countries, commercial debtors, aid recipients, and planned and market economies all followed the same course. When the external economic shocks of the early 1980s made it impossible to finance these deficits, a period of severe fiscal retrenchment became inescapable (see Figure 2.1). The reduction in deficits since then has been remarkable, but many countries—still deprived of external financial resources—need to do more. For them the dilemma is how to cut deficits further without sliding even deeper into recession.

The urgency of this problem has distracted attention from the broader role of public finance in development. The short-term imperative has been to contain fiscal deficits through some mixture of reduced expenditure and higher revenues. The concern for the longer term is that such changes be carried out in ways that promote, rather than hamper, growth. Indeed prudent control of fiscal deficits is just one aspect of sound public finance in the widest sense. Among other things this means confining (or extending) public expenditure to those areas in which the public sector can act efficiently; it also means raising the necessary revenues in ways that distort prices as little as possible. This chapter introduces the broad perspective within which deficit reduction should be viewed.

Governments everywhere play an essential role in allocating resources—in influencing what gets produced, how it is produced, who receives the benefits, and who pays. They do so both directly and indirectly. For instance, all *directly* provide defense and social infrastructure; most supply power and telephone services; a few produce industrial and agricultural goods. Often governments create state-owned enterprises (SOEs) to carry out these functions. But governments also *indirectly* influence the production and allocation of privately produced goods through subsidies, taxes, and a wide range of regulatory tools such as price controls and quantitative restrictions. In centrally planned economies governments rely mainly on direct intervention; in market economies they tend to favor the indirect approach. Both modes of intervention involve public spending and revenue and are thus equally subject to the strictures of sound public finance.

Public finance affects economies in many different ways. Revenue, expenditure, and the public sector deficit they imply are essential tools for macroeconomic stabilization: they help to determine the inflation rate, the current account deficit, the growth of the national debt, and the level of economic activity. They also affect adjustment and growth by influencing the rates of consumption, savings, and investment in both physical and human capital. At the microeconomic level, taxes, subsidies, and government purchases of commodities encourage the production and consumption of some goods and discourage the production and consumption of others. Public finance policies can, in principle, affect all sectors of the economy, and they typically do so in developing countries as in industrial countries.

Figure 2.1 Public sector deficits in selected developing countries, 1979 to 1985

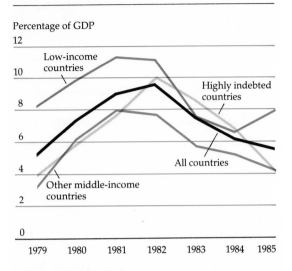

Percentage of GDP

Notes: Data are unweighted annual averages. The low-income sample includes Bangladesh, India, Kenya, Malawi, Zaire, and Zambia. The highly indebted sample includes Argentina, Bolivia, Chile, Colombia, Côte d'Ivoire, Dominican Republic, Ecuador, Jamaica, Mexico, Nigeria, Peru, and Venezuela. The other middle-income sample includes Indonesia, Malaysia, Poland, Thailand, and Turkey. The twenty-three countries were selected on the basis of available data.

However, three factors complicate any analysis of public finance policies, whether in developing or industrial countries.

• The dividing line between "public" and "private" is unclear. This is especially true for SOEs. For example, does an enterprise that is jointly owned by both the government and private individuals fall into the public or the private sector? What about a publicly owned enterprise that operates on commercial principles? Two criteria can help distinguish public from private activities: whether profits and losses accrue to the state and whether the state directly controls the allocation of resources of the enterprise. Even these tests are of only limited use, because ownership and control by the state vary in degree and over time. The definition of what is part of the public sector thus remains a matter of judgment. By necessity this Report relies on the conventions of each country to distinguish between the public and private domains.

• Governments are not monolithic entities, but consist of many agencies with varying degrees of autonomy. The structure of the public sector has both vertical and horizontal dimensions. The vertical dimension includes the central, state or provincial, and local government levels. The horizontal dimension reflects the division between government, SOEs, and other autonomous or semiautonomous entities, often grouped under the heading of "off-budget" accounts or agencies. The relations between these different branches of the public sector are usually complex.

• There is a lack of accurate public finance data for developing countries. For most developing countries consistent data are available only for the past decade or two and often cover only the central government. Comparable data on state and local governments and on SOEs are patchy across countries and over time (see Box 2.1). Because of this, much of the cross-country analysis in this Report focuses on central government finances. Where possible the analysis is extended to include state and local governments and SOEs, but conclusions based on data for the entire public sector have to be treated with caution. The weakness of public finance data has complicated the design and implementation of public finance policies. This is all the more troublesome in view of the rapid increase of the public sector worldwide.

Patterns of public finance

The pervasive growth of the public sector in the past half century represents a fundamental struc-

Table 2.1 Share of government spending in GNP or GDP in selected industrial countries, 1880, 1929, 1960, and 1985
(percent)

Year	France	Germany[a]	Japan	Sweden	United Kingdom	United States
1880	15	10[b]	11[c]	6[d]	10	8
1929[e]	19	31	19	8[d]	24	10
1960	35	32	18	31	32	28
1985	52	47	33	65	48	37

Note: Includes central, state, and local expenditure except where noted. For 1880 and 1929 data are the share of GNP; for 1960 and 1985 the share of GDP.
a. For 1960 and 1985, Federal Republic of Germany.
b. 1881.
c. 1885.
d. Central government only.
e. The year 1929 was chosen as a representative year before the disruptions of the Great Depression and World War II.
Sources: For 1880 and 1929: France, André and Delorme 1983, p. 723; Germany, Andic and Veverka 1964, p. 244; Japan, Ohkawa and others 1965–79, vol. 1, p. 200, and vol. 7, pp. 170-71; Sweden, Mitchell 1975, pp. 699 and 782; United Kingdom, Peacock and Wiseman 1961, p. 164; United States, Peltzman 1980, p. 239. For 1960: Saunders and Klau 1985, p. 29. For 1985: OECD 1987, *Economic Outlook* 42 (December), p. 187.

Box 2.1 Sources and limitations of public finance statistics

To be effective, public finance policies must be based on accurate and comprehensive statistics on the financial transactions of public agencies. For intercountry analysis, fiscal data also need to be compiled on a comparable basis across countries. Although much progress has been made during the past three decades in improving both national and international statistics, public finance analysis is still hampered by serious data limitations.

Public finance statistics are currently assembled on an internationally comparable basis in two systems: the *Government Finance Statistics* (GFS) of the IMF and the *System of National Accounts* (SNA) of the United Nations. The GFS focuses solely on government transactions, whereas the SNA considers government transactions as a component of the economy as a whole.

The GFS compiles national public finance statistics according to the standard specifications of the IMF's *Manual of Government Finance Statistics*. It distinguishes among the central government account, social security and other extra budgetary accounts, state and local accounts, and state-owned enterprises (SOEs). The first two accounts are grouped together in the "consolidated central government" account. When data for the first three groups are available, the accounts are consolidated in the "general government" account. Because of the difficulty of collecting consistent and accurate SOE data, only data on transactions between the general government and SOEs are currently recorded in the GFS. The GFS does not report asset or liability positions of the government, nor does it report depreciation for fixed assets owned by the government. Accounts are recorded on a cash, not an accrual, basis. GFS coverage is most complete for central government accounts, but more limited for general government accounts.

The SNA framework is designed to measure income, production, consumption, savings, and investment to aid economic analysis. The SNA accounts are recorded on an accrual basis and include depreciation. For national aggregates the SNA consolidates transactions between all sectors and eliminates intersectoral transactions, so that only final demand and value added are aggregated. (The GFS framework, in contrast, eliminates only transactions between parts of government.) National accounts data compiled within the SNA framework lack the detail required for many aspects of public finance analysis. The consolidated accounts omit some important financial flows, such as all domestic transfers, including interest. Moreover up-to-date national accounts data are not available in many developing countries.

These limitations of international statistics mirror the weaknesses of national data sources. Delays in auditing, weak administrative systems, and incomplete reporting of subnational government and SOE accounts combine to make it very difficult to get a timely, complete, and accurate picture of the main sources and uses of public funds. Therefore it is generally difficult to assess recent trends in major fiscal aggregates or to project and plan future financial flows. Fiscal planning, consistent fiscal policy design, and financial accountability by decisionmakers are thus significantly impeded. Improving the national and international fiscal data systems deserves a high priority in developing countries.

Lack of data has hampered the analysis of public expenditure, revenue, and financing in this Report. The discussion relies mostly on GFS data but for selected countries adds data from national sources for the total public sector, including available SOE statistics. Inferences drawn from these data need to be treated with caution, because the sample of countries is small and not necessarily representative, the coverage of SOEs may be incomplete and may differ across countries, and definitions may not always be strictly comparable.

---

tural change comparable in scope with such other basic transformations as industrialization and urbanization. The long-term evolution of public finance in the industrial countries provides a reference point for the experience of the developing world.

Industrial countries

The scale of public finance has increased dramatically in the industrial countries during the past century. Table 2.1 shows trends in government spending for six of them. In 1880 the (unweighted) average of their public expenditure as a share of GNP was about 10 percent. By 1985 the average share had reached 47 percent. Much of the increase occurred after World War II. Although the overall trend has been common to all six countries, some of the differences are significant. For example, Japan's share tripled during the century, while that of Germany and the United Kingdom increased almost fivefold.

Historically the growth of public revenue kept pace with that of public spending, but during the past two decades expenditures have tended to grow more rapidly than revenues. So govern-

Table 2.2 Central government total expenditure, current revenue, and deficit as a share of GNP, 1972 and 1985

(percent)

Country group	Total expenditure		Current revenue		Deficit[a]	
	1972	1985	1972	1985	1972	1985
Developing countries	18.7	26.4	16.2	22.7	−3.5	−6.3
Low-income[b]	..	20.8	..	15.4	..	−5.1
Middle-income	21.7	27.5	19.1	24.0	−3.3	−5.8
Industrial countries	22.2	28.6	21.6	24.1	−1.8	−5.1

Note: Data are based on a sample of ninety countries.
a. Deficits are defined as current and capital revenue and grants received, minus total expenditure, minus lending minus repayments.
b. Excluding China and India.

ments increasingly have become net borrowers. By the early 1980s sizable budget deficits prevailed in most industrial countries. Many have since made efforts to cut spending. These efforts have been motivated by the inflationary pressures that fiscal deficits can generate, by the perception that private sector activity was being displaced by public intervention, and by concern over the distortions resulting from efforts to raise more revenue. Gov-

ernments have largely failed to lower the absolute level of public spending in real terms, but they have managed to slow or reverse the trend of rising spending as a share of GDP.

Developing countries

Before 1940 public finance in the developing world was in a similar condition to that of the now-industrialized countries during the latter half of the nineteenth century. According to one study, colonial administrations and independent governments alike raised about 5 percent of GNP in taxes, spent the same amount on government consumption, and made only limited public investments, mostly in transport infrastructure (especially railways). After World War II the situation changed dramatically. Central government spending alone rose to 19 percent of GNP by 1972 and to 26 percent by 1985 (see Table 2.2).

The trend has not been uniform, however. In at least ten developing countries (such as Burma, Chile, the Dominican Republic, Peru, and Yugoslavia) central government expenditure as a share of GNP was substantially lower in 1985 than in 1972, and reductions in real government spending (often following rapid increases) have been quite common during the past decade. Some of these reductions reflect shifts in responsibility for expenditure from central government to state and local governments; more often they have been genuine cuts, prompted by economic crises or changes in political regime.

The most striking feature of public spending in developing countries is the variation in the share of government expenditure in GNP (see Figure 2.2). For example, in 1985 the central government shares for developing countries ranged between 7 percent (Yugoslavia) and 64 percent (Nicaragua). The correlation between central government expenditure shares and per capita income explains

Figure 2.2 The relation between per capita GNP and the share of central government expenditure in GNP, 1985

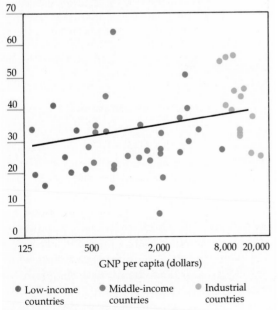

Central government expenditure/GNP (percent)

GNP per capita (dollars)

● Low-income countries   ● Middle-income countries   ● Industrial countries

Note: The horizontal axis is in log scale.
Source: IMF, *Government Finance Statistics,* 1987.

only about 10 percent of this variation. Even when total public spending is considered (that is, including the expenditures by state and local governments and SOEs) the variation remains (see Figure 2.3).

Despite this some general conclusions may be drawn. First, in most developing countries the share of central government spending in GNP remains below that of the industrial countries. Much of the difference, though, is due to the industrial countries' higher level of transfers for social security and welfare. Excluding these expenditures, central government spending as a percentage of GNP is higher in low- and middle-income countries than in the industrial countries (see Chapter 5).

Second, in developing countries the public sector tends to play a greater role as an investor than in industrial countries. The share of total public investment (including investment by SOEs) in total investment was higher for a sample of twelve developing countries than the average for a sample of thirteen industrial countries (see Table 2.3). This may in part be explained by the fact that developing countries tend to need more investment in infrastructure than the industrial countries—and government investment is bound to play a large role in infrastructure development.

Third, in most developing countries SOEs account for important shares both of total public spending and of GDP. Data are limited, and the variation is again large. For the sample of thirteen developing countries shown in Figure 2.3, the capital outlays of SOEs (that is, their spending on final

Figure 2.3 Total public sector expenditure as a share of GDP in selected developing countries, 1985

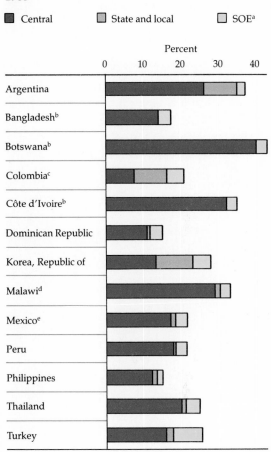

Notes: Except where noted, the expenditure figures represent total spending by central, state, and local governments minus transfers, plus fixed capital outlays by SOEs. Countries were chosen on the basis of available data.
a. SOE capital expenditure.
b. State and local data are not available.
c. State and local data include SOEs operating at the state and local levels.
d. 1982.
e. State and local data cover only the Federal District of Mexico.

Table 2.3 Public sector investment as a percentage of total investment for selected developing countries, averages for 1980 to 1985

Turkey[a]	68	Peru	29
Egypt[b]	65	Philippines[b]	26
Côte d'Ivoire	61	Dominican Republic	24
Argentina	58		
Botswana	45	*Average* (unweighted)	
Colombia	40	Twelve developing	
Korea, Republic of[c]	35	countries	43
Thailand	33	Thirteen industrial	
Mexico	31	countries[d]	30

Note: Data include investment by central, state, and local governments and SOEs.
a. 1983–85.
b. 1981–85.
c. 1982–85.
d. 1980.
Sources: Industrial countries, adapted from Saunders and Klau 1985; developing countries, World Bank data.

demand) was typically in the range of 5 to 7 percent of GDP in 1985. Since the coverage of SOEs and off-budget funds is incomplete, these figures understate the role of nongovernmental public entities. By comparison, in industrial countries the (unweighted) average share of SOE capital spending in GDP was only 3.6 percent during the late 1970s; in the United States it was as low as 0.9 percent.

Fourth, state and local governments appear in

general to have a smaller role in developing countries than in the industrial world—although, again, data are incomplete. Subnational governments are important in some developing countries, however, including Argentina, Brazil, Colombia, India, Republic of Korea, and Nigeria (see Chapter 7).

Public expenditure is only one aspect of public finance; revenue also needs to be considered. The ratio of central government current revenue to GNP in developing countries increased from 16 percent in 1972 to 23 percent in 1985 (see Table 2.2). Despite this, spending has tended to outstrip revenue, and the prevailing methods of collecting revenue have often resulted in unnecessarily severe losses in economic efficiency. Chapter 4 examines the costs of revenue raising and how to reduce them.

The excess of expenditure growth over revenue growth has led to fiscal deficits in developing countries, just as in industrial countries (see Table 2.2). Because developing countries have less scope for domestic financing, however, their fiscal deficits have tended to spill over more readily into domestic inflation or external imbalances (see Chapter 3).

One consequence of the fiscal deficits has been the public sector's contribution to the accumulation of foreign debt. Public and publicly guaranteed foreign debt tripled as a percentage of GDP between 1973 and 1986 for all developing countries and nearly quadrupled for the highly indebted, middle-income countries (see Figure 2.4). Moreover, in 1986 medium- and long-term public debt accounted for some three-quarters of total foreign debt in middle-income developing countries and for 89 percent of total foreign debt in low-income countries. The current debt overhang in developing countries is thus in part due to past fiscal policy failures and is at the core of the current fiscal crisis in the developing countries (see Chapter 3).

Expenditure, revenue, and deficit shares in GNP provide an incomplete picture of the public sector. They do not measure the full extent to which governments affect the private sector because they ignore regulations and other controls. Such policies, widely applied in developed and developing countries, are difficult to quantify. Scattered evidence suggests that the developing countries saw an increase in regulations and controls in the 1970s, although some of these were reduced as part of the adjustment efforts of the 1980s. Overall, however, there is little doubt that the role of the public sector has greatly expanded in the developing world during the past four decades.

Evolving views of the public sector

Since World War II the growing importance of the public sector has been seen by many development

Figure 2.4 Growth of public debt and the composition of total external debt
(percent)

Public and publicly guaranteed debt/GDP, 1973 and 1986

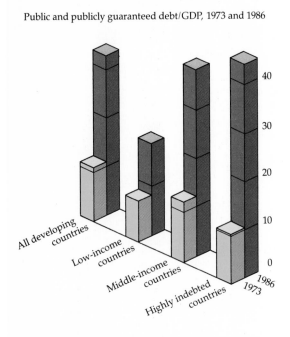

Composition of total external debt, 1986[a]

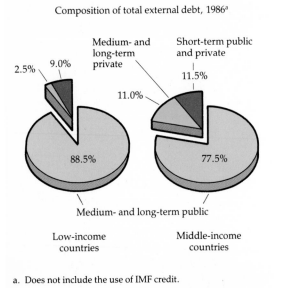

a. Does not include the use of IMF credit.

economists and policymakers as a natural and even necessary ingredient of development. In what can be called the "public interest" view, governments must intervene to foster development: the unmodified interaction of private agents will not achieve the goals of economic efficiency, growth, macroeconomic stability, and poverty alleviation.

According to this view, free markets underprovide "public" goods such as national defense, law and order, primary education, basic health, infrastructure, and research and development—goods that benefit people other than the producers or consumers. Equally, markets can overproduce goods that impose costs beyond those borne by the producer: traffic congestion, pollution, the depletion of natural resources, and so on. In addition the existence of monopolies, the lack of fully developed markets (especially for capital and insurance), and gaps in the supply of information may result in inefficient resource allocation and yield savings and investment rates that are less than optimal. Market mechanisms may thus produce insufficient growth as well as macroeconomic imbalances, such as balance of payments deficits and unemployment. According to the public interest view, these market failures need to be corrected by governments—through public provision of goods and services, through public savings and investment, and through taxes, subsidies, and regulations.

This approach reserves a special place for government in influencing the distribution of income and alleviating poverty. Some argue that the incidence of poverty determined by the market is not usually just or appropriate, so that government may—and should—step in. It might do so through the degree of progressivity of taxes and through expenditures targeted to the poor. Governments often design poverty programs to ensure that the poor are able to consume a minimum level of certain "merit" goods, such as food or shelter.

In the developing economies the unmet backlog of physical and social infrastructure, the low levels of savings and investment, the need to foster economic growth through modernization, and the availability of concessional foreign funding for public projects explain the rapid expansion of public finance that is consistent with the public interest view. While considering the growth of government to be appropriate in general, the public interest view also recognizes that the growth in government spending may at times have been excessive. Mistakes by government are seen as a serious

problem in practice, but not as inevitable or irreversible. Policy and administrative reforms have commonly been proposed to correct such "government failures."

During the late 1970s and 1980s concern about the expansion of the public sector arose in the industrial and developing countries. Slow growth, lagging private savings and investment, high inflation, balance of payments deficits, heavy debt burdens, continued poverty, and unemployment began to be seen, at least in part, as the result of the excessive growth of the public sector. Even when external events beyond the control of individual countries were the immediate cause of many of the difficulties, the actions of governments were often blamed for having left the developing countries poorly prepared. The late 1970s also marked an important turning point in the centrally planned economies, where reliance on direct command by government was increasingly seen as a drag on economic growth; during the 1980s several of these countries have increased the role of markets.

These concerns found an intellectual underpinning in the reemergence of what can be called the "private interest" view of the public sector. Tracing its roots back to the classical liberal economists, especially Adam Smith, the private interest view starts with the presumption that individuals, whether in or out of government, use the resources and influence at their disposal to further their private interests, rather than any abstract notion of the public interest. Although the pursuit of private interests allocates resources efficiently in competitive markets, this generally does not occur when individuals use the monopolistic powers of government to their own advantage. Politicians, bureaucrats, and many private interests gain from a growing government and greater government expenditure. So, it is argued, the government's necessary role as provider of public goods needs to be carefully circumscribed. Otherwise, inefficient public and private provision of goods and services is sure to follow.

The emergence of persistent fiscal imbalances and the difficulties of implementing effective stabilization and adjustment programs in developing countries have also been explained by the private interest view (see Box 2.2). Exponents of the private interest view commonly suggest balanced budget laws to prevent the emergence of fiscal deficits. Experience with such laws in developing countries suggests, however, that they are unlikely to be effective (see Box 2.3).

In their extreme versions the public interest and

Box 2.2   Political interests and economic reform

Effective stabilization and structural adjustment programs require political support. This is especially true of public finance policies, because they generally affect the distribution of income. A recent study by Stephan Haggard and Robert Kaufman highlighted four main aspects of the political process.

Interest groups

Economic policies are heavily influenced by the balance of power among competing interest groups, especially business, labor, and agriculture. Reforms are unlikely to succeed without the backing of some of these groups. For example, the support of business groups—and their confidence that reforms will be sustained—is vital for a successful reallocation of resources. Labor unrest over wage restraint, for instance, can undo reforms, as has been demonstrated in several developing countries, including Argentina, the Dominican Republic, Egypt, and Jamaica.

Type of regime

Authoritarian regimes have not always been better at imposing economic austerity than democracies. A distinction between different types of democracies and authoritarian regimes is more useful. Strong democracies, such as Costa Rica, have a tradition of consultation with business and labor; this facilitates acceptance of economic programs. In contrast, where policymaking is conducted by technocrats behind closed doors, reform may succeed in the short term but may be difficult to sustain. Strong authoritarian governments—characterized by continuity in leadership, insulation from societal pressures, well-established and integrated interest groups, and the power to enforce decisions—tend to be relatively successful in imposing the short-term costs of economic reform. The Republic of Korea in the early 1980s has been cited as an example. Weak authoritarian governments, which maintain political authority through personalistic patron-client relations, tend to be bad at economic reform. Several of the small, ethnically fragmented, Sub-Saharan states fall into this category. Here the maintenance of political power often depends on the discretionary use of public funds, and the reform of public finances, while economically rational, becomes politically irrational. Such regimes are likely to have greater difficulty imposing

reform than either strong authoritarian regimes or consultative democracies.

Political cycles

The time horizon of a government may influence its decisions. This will differ according to whether countries have a stable electoral system. In a stable system the period before elections is characterized by expansionary policies, the period after by retrenchment—as in Mexico during the past twenty years. In contrast, when transitions are insecure, uncertainty affects policy choices. New democratic governments are likely to pursue expansionary programs early in office—as in Argentina in the early years of Alfonsín, Brazil under Sarney, and Turkey after the succession of the civilian government. New authoritarian regimes tend to follow the opposite path. Typically the military seizes power in the midst of a crisis and attempts to restore order and rationalize the economic system. Although circumstances differed, Argentina (1966 and 1976), Bolivia (1971), Brazil (1964), Chile (mid-1973), Indonesia (1966), Turkey (1971 and 1980), and Uruguay (mid-1970s) all serve as illustrations.

The bureaucracy

The government's administrative capacity is crucial to its ability to organize and carry out a program of economic reform. In some countries, such as Korea, this capacity is well developed. In others, including many low-income African countries, it is not. Moreover, in most developing countries the bureaucracy forms an influential interest group that may oppose stabilization and structural reform. Economic reform often requires reducing the size of the public sector through government employee layoffs and privatization of SOEs. Such policies are at odds with the interests of the bureaucrats.

Politics and ''first-best'' policies

Political factors are important in developing a program of economic reform. ''First-best'' policies may not always be achievable because of political constraints. Indeed, failed attempts to pursue first-best policies without considering the political dimensions may make matters worse. ''Second-best'' policies will prove more successful if they respond better to political reality and thus are sustainable in the long term.

---

private interest views of the public sector are irreconcilable. It is therefore only natural to seek an empirical validation of either view. One approach is to ask whether the growth of government has helped or hurt economic growth: the former finding would tend to support the public interest view;

the latter would buttress the private interest view. At the simplest level a scatter diagram for a sample of countries shows a lack of any significant correlation between the growth of GDP and the share of government spending in GDP (see Figure 2.5). Some researchers, after allowing for other factors that may influence growth, have found that economic growth and the *share* of government spending in GDP are negatively related; others have found that economic growth and the *growth* of government spending are positively related. In any case serious questions remain about the analytical approaches and data used. The evidence is thus inconclusive.

A pragmatic approach to public policy

Rather than pursuing this line of inquiry, it is more fruitful to consider the public and the private views as contributing complementary perspectives to an understanding of the public sector and public finance. The public interest view stresses the potential benefits of government intervention when it is effectively deployed to correct market failures. It also provides a framework for identifying the conditions under which market failure is likely to occur and for designing the appropriate policies to offset these failures. The private interest view emphasizes the potential for failure and cautions against an overly sanguine view of government as the impartial guardian of the public interest. Box 2.4 provides an example of how the correction of market failures must be accompanied by efforts to minimize government failure in the environmental field.

Pragmatic policy design can draw on the strengths of both the public interest and private interest view by:

• Considering both the benefits and costs of government involvement

• Asking which groups in society are likely to receive the benefits and which to bear the costs

• Recognizing the institutional and political constraints that are likely to be encountered in implementing a particular policy

---

Box 2.3   Balanced budget laws

Some developing countries have adopted laws that require the national budget to be balanced. The economic rationale for these laws is shaky. What is intended is a budget consistent with targets for inflation, public debt, and private sector growth (see Box 3.2). A budget to achieve these targets need not necessarily be balanced. Experience has also shown that these laws are very hard to implement. A principal difficulty is defining "budget balance." To do this one must first define the "government." This is not straightforward, because most countries have a multiplicity of state-owned enterprises (SOEs) and extra-budgetary accounts. Then one must decide what constitutes revenue and expenditure for the purposes of the budget. For example, it is sometimes difficult to distinguish between asset sales, loans, and genuine revenue items. Finally, one must specify the period over which the budget is to be balanced.

Balanced budget laws in Colombia and Indonesia illustrate these difficulties. In both countries governments are required by law to prepare a balanced budget for each fiscal year. Colombia has an additional restriction that revenue must not increase by more than 10 percent over the level of the previous year. In both countries "revenue" is defined to include aid and loans already contracted by the government. "Expenditure" is defined to include debt amortization payments. The budget balance does not correspond, therefore, to the economic definition of government surplus or deficit (where loans are treated as financing items), and it provides little insight into the significance of the budget for inflation and debt. Colombia and Indonesia have run significant central government deficits and surpluses in recent years when defined in economic terms.

Other problems arise. It is relatively easy to keep important public sector agencies out of the budget and thus achieve the required balance. In Colombia, SOEs and other off-budget entities receive earmarked taxes directly and can borrow and spend without the sanction of the budget. Indonesia also has many SOEs that are not covered by balanced budget requirements.

Balanced budget laws can complicate fiscal planning. In Colombia supplemental budgets have had to be prepared during every fiscal year as extra revenue becomes available. These supplemental budgets disrupt expenditure planning, because little effort is made to check for consistency with overall spending goals. As many as five supplemental budgets have been prepared in a year. This increased the original budget by up to 50 percent.

Although balanced budget laws are in practice easy to evade, they can be useful to fiscally conservative governments. They allow the finance ministry to invoke the constraint of the "balanced budget" when resisting calls for more spending. Indeed, Colombia and Indonesia have on balance followed prudent fiscal policies since the laws have been in force. But balanced budget laws are more often a symbol of a fiscally conservative state than an effective restraint on a spendthrift one.

Figure 2.5 Relation between central government expenditure as a share of GDP and the growth of GDP in developing countries
(percent)

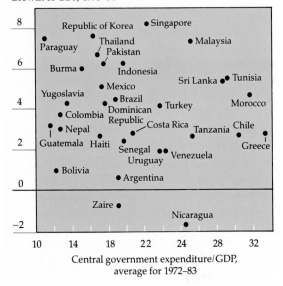

Growth of GDP, 1973–84

Central government expenditure/GDP, average for 1972–83

Sources: IMF, *Government Finance Statistics*, 1987, and World Bank data.

• Searching for ways to ensure that the public sector operates efficiently within these constraints.

A pragmatic approach to public policy analysis might begin by ranking areas of economic activity according to the extent to which government intervention is desirable. Plausible criteria for ranking would be the scope for government to promote efficiency, growth, poverty alleviation, and stabilization. Accordingly a stronger case can be made for government involvement in some areas than in others.

First, governments have certain core areas of responsibility. The public goods that only the public sector can effectively provide include defense, diplomacy, macroeconomic management, and a legal and institutional system that defines and enforces the rules of justice, property, and commerce. Second, governments need to help provide social, physical, and information infrastructure: education, health, transport networks, public utilities, technology development and dissemination, and environmental protection. Market failures are common in these areas, and many of the merit goods required to meet basic needs are

found there. Elsewhere the case for government involvement is weaker on economic or equity grounds, and the costs of intervention threaten to outweigh the benefits. For example, in agriculture, industry, energy, mining, and many services—although some support may be needed—governments are generally not well equipped to play a major role.

Where exactly the line should be drawn between government involvement and private sector responsibility depends in principle on an evaluation of the costs and benefits of government intervention. Where the system for collecting revenue allows additional resources to be raised with little distortion of private sector activity, greater government involvement may be appropriate—perhaps because market failures and poverty problems are especially severe or because the civil service is effective in providing the needed public goods. Elsewhere the same level of involvement may be too high because the revenue collection is already highly distortionary, because private markets are operating efficiently, or because the bureaucracy is ill equipped to intervene.

This suggests that what matters is the quality of government, more than its size as such. Quality might be defined broadly to cover five factors.

• *Prudent fiscal policy.* The need to improve fiscal policy has already been pressed upon most developing countries. Excessive fiscal deficits and the resulting financing requirements of the public sector have often been at the root of macroeconomic imbalances. Bringing expenditures more closely in line with revenues to ensure that the resulting deficits are consistent with other macroeconomic policies and objectives is an essential element of improving the quality of government (Chapter 3). The harder question is how to go about this. The goal is to raise additional revenue in the most cost-effective way and to cut spending, where necessary, in the least damaging way

• *Efficient revenue mobilization.* The cost associated with raising a given level of public revenue can generally be lowered by reforming the tax system so as to reduce the distortions and inefficiencies that taxes generate. Revenue can also be raised efficiently by raising prices or user charges for publicly provided goods and services when these are set below cost, as is frequently the case. Tax systems and user charges may be structured so as to minimize the burden on the poor without causing significant efficiency losses (Chapters 4 and 6).

• *Priorities for public expenditures.* For a given size of government as measured, for example, by the

Box 2.4 Public finance and the environment

Economic activity depends heavily on the natural resource base in most developing countries. Countries must increase the productivity of that base if their growing populations are to attain substantially higher living standards. Public finance policies designed to promote stable economic growth and to alleviate poverty have an important role in this effort. Without government intervention individuals may not adequately consider the long-term environmental effects of their collective actions. But inappropriate government interventions have sometimes aggravated environmental problems.

Lack of protection by free markets

Most resource degradation results from the cumulative activities of farmers, households, and industries, all trying to improve their economic well-being. There are several reasons why their efforts may actually work against them. First, people may not completely understand the long-term consequences of their activities on the natural resource base. Second, ill-defined or badly enforced property rights may result in environmental losses. For example, vaguely defined rights over communal grazing lands, tree crops, or water resources have discouraged soil, forest, and water conservation, because individuals are not certain they will benefit from their investment in conservation. Third, poverty can undermine the efficiency of market processes in accounting for long-term environmental concerns. In many cities around the world, in order to reduce housing costs and travel time, many people live in the shadow of factory walls where they are constantly exposed to pollution or industrial accidents.

In combination with other policies public finance instruments can be used to change the economic incentives to promote sustainable productive uses of natural resources. On the revenue side, taxes, subsidies, and price interventions can be designed to ensure that the private costs of resource use accurately reflect long-term economic costs. Education, family planning programs, and the enforcement of property rights can encourage people to think further ahead.

Well-designed environmental policies can add to government revenue while conserving natural resources. Between 1979 and 1982, for example, the Philippine government collected only about $140 million of a potential $1.5 billion in timber royalties; it left the remainder to favored concession holders. Because of such policies productive virgin forests in the Philippines have been reduced by nearly 90 percent, and

the logging of upland forests has contributed to severe erosion.

Failure of public finance policy

Many countries follow policies that aggravate rather than correct the market failures described above. Inefficient incentives may result from public finance policies that were designed without adequate recognition of environmental effects. The link between policy and the environment is often difficult to trace; sometimes the problem is a lack of influential environmental interest groups. In these cases there is no tradeoff between increasing efficiency and preserving the resource base.

In some cases there are tradeoffs between long- and short-term considerations. This is particularly true when economic problems are extreme and urgent. Often, however, the policies that accelerate resource degradation and reduce economic productivity also increase the fiscal burdens on government, distort short-term efficiency, and benefit relatively well-off groups at the expense of the disadvantaged.

The environmental effects of poorly designed public finance policies are well illustrated in the energy sector. In most developing countries energy prices have until recently failed to reflect opportunity costs. At the same time low prices have reduced returns to investments in energy conservation, perpetuated inefficient fuel use, and, in turn, caused environmental problems. For example, in countries where coal is an important fuel, prices have often been below economic costs, so that many mines operate at a loss and require government subsidies. Yet each step in using coal (mining, washing, transporting, and burning) also involves potential damage to land, water, and air quality. Similarly, subsidized electricity prices intended to promote industrialization in many developing countries (including Bolivia, China, Peru, and Uganda) have led to uneconomic growth in electricity demand and inefficient levels of public investment in power-generating capacity. This, in turn, has led to excessive or premature development of hydro resources and unnecessary pollution from oil or coal-fired power plants.

Limiting the risks for the future

Economic activities are bound to have environmental side effects. Public finance policies provide a set of effective instruments to limit the damage and reduce the risks, often without having to confront major tradeoffs between economic growth and poverty alleviation.

share of public spending in GDP, government spending may be devoted to sectors or activities of low priority, while high-priority sectors or activities get insufficient attention. Shifting public resources from low- to high-priority areas can significantly improve the effectiveness of the public sector in supporting long-term growth and poverty alleviation (Chapters 5 and 6).

• *Appropriate structure of government.* The quality of the public sector hinges on the effectiveness of its constituent parts—central, state, and local governments and SOEs. A combination of excessive control by the central government, poor accountability of decentralized agencies, and unclear fiscal relations among the different parts of the government have often contributed to an ineffective mobilization and use of public resources in developing countries. Improving the structure of government can significantly increase its quality (Chapters 7 and 8).

• *Good administration.* The administrative capabilities of government are an important constraint on its ability to design and implement high-quality expenditure and revenue programs. Improving the quality of administration is an essential part of improving the quality of government. (Public administration reforms are addressed in this Report only insofar as they relate directly to public finance.)

Placing stress on the quality of government is compatible with the view that the public sector in many developing countries in recent years has become overextended and has taken on responsibilities it is ill equipped to handle. As a result expenditures and available resources have been balanced poorly. The challenge for governments is to examine their priorities and policies in the light of experience and limited resources. Often this will point to a reduced role for government and a greater reliance on private initiative. In some countries or sectors, however, more public spending may be appropriate—especially where protracted fiscal austerity has led to deep, across-the-board cuts in public spending. The rest of this Report explores these choices and indicates ways to improve the quality of public finance so that developing countries can respond to their present fiscal emergency without seriously harming the prospects for long-term growth. Although the focus is on public finance policies in developing countries, there is no doubt that many of the lessons for policy apply with equal force to industrial countries. The main difference is that developing countries can even less afford to waste their extremely scarce resources than can the better-off industrial countries.

3

Fiscal policy for stabilization and adjustment

The fiscal crisis facing most developing countries—and the related problems of external debt, inflation, and recession—have called new attention to the importance of sound fiscal policy. Although country circumstances vary greatly, fundamental principles of fiscal management apply everywhere. This chapter describes these principles and then applies them to three different issues: the debt troubles of the middle-income countries, the problem of cycles in commodity-exporting economies, and the task of adjustment in the severely resource-constrained economies of Sub-Saharan Africa.

One of the most important aspects of fiscal policy is the management of the public sector's deficit—the excess of its spending over its revenue (see Box 3.1). Deficits in themselves do not automatically imply macroeconomic problems. If the use of public resources is sufficiently productive, future income can be generated to cover the servicing costs of any debts incurred. If expenditures rise owing to temporary factors, such as wars or natural disasters, then deficits may be justified as a way to spread the cost over several years. Deficits can be more easily absorbed by countries with high rates of domestic private saving and well-developed capital markets. Thus a relatively high deficit need not cause problems in an efficient, high-saving economy, whereas in a low-saving, highly distorted one, even a small deficit might be destabilizing. A prudent fiscal policy can therefore be defined as one that maintains the public deficit at a level that is consistent with other macroeconomic objectives: controlling inflation, promot-

ing private investment, and maintaining external creditworthiness.

Fiscal policy and macroeconomic performance

The extent to which any given public sector deficit can be reconciled with broader macroeconomic goals depends largely on the way it is financed. A deficit must be funded by the private sector lending the government some of the excess of its savings over its own investment, by foreigners lending part of their savings, by printing money, or by some mixture of the three (see Box 3.2). Too great a strain on any of these sources of finance can create macroeconomic imbalances. Overreliance on domestic borrowing may mean high real interest rates and falling private investment. Overreliance on foreign borrowing can cause appreciating real exchange rates, widening current account deficits, unsustainable external indebtedness, and dwindling foreign exchange reserves. Overreliance on money creation may prompt higher inflation. Viewed from the alternative perspective of production and expenditure, an increased fiscal deficit is an additional claim on the supply of goods. The only ways to meet this extra claim are by importing additional goods from the rest of the world (that is, increasing the current account deficit), by driving up domestic inflation and interest rates to make the private sector buy fewer goods, or by increasing domestic production.

Figure 3.1 illustrates the link between fiscal deficits and current account deficits in four countries. Since the surplus of private saving over invest-

Box 3.1 Measuring the public deficit

The correct way to measure the public sector deficit depends on the purpose. The most obvious objective is to measure the net claim on resources by the public sector; this in turn influences the external deficit, inflation, domestic interest rates, and employment.

A useful indicator would then be the public sector's net use of financial resources, the *public sector borrowing requirement* (PSBR). The PSBR represents the total excess of expenditure over revenue for all government entities, all of which must be financed by new borrowing net of repayment of previous debts. It is also called the "consolidated public sector deficit." Expenditure includes wages of public employees, spending on goods and fixed capital formation, interest on debt, transfers, and subsidies. Revenue includes taxes, user charges, interest on public assets, transfers, operating surpluses of public companies, and sales of public assets. Expenditure does not include amortization payments on government debt or accumulation of financial assets, while revenue does not include the drawdown of cash reserves.

The PSBR is the most comprehensive deficit measure, but it can be misleading in some circumstances. In countries with a high rate of inflation, part of the borrowing by the public sector is offset by the decline in the real value of their existing debts. A fraction of the interest payments by the public sector then compensates creditors only for the loss in the real value of the debts; it does not represent a real interest cost to the government. Sometimes the debt principal is explicitly indexed to inflation, in which case the indexation inflates the PSBR. Another measure of the public sector deficit for these cases is the change in real debt. The *operational deficit* is defined as the PSBR minus the inflation correction part of interest payments; it is sometimes called the "inflation-corrected" deficit. The difference can be significant. In 1985 in Brazil the inflation correction component of the indexed domestic debt was so large that the PSBR was 27.1 percent of GDP, while the operational deficit was only 3.5 percent of GDP.

The interest paid on debt is a result of past deficits rather than current behavior. A measure of the current policy stance might therefore exclude all interest payments, yielding the *primary deficit*, also called the "non-interest deficit." The primary deficit measures how current actions improve or worsen the public sector's net indebtedness, and it is important for evaluating the sustainability of government deficits. Although fiscal deficits can be run indefinitely, the primary balance must eventually become positive to cover at least part of the interest on current debt. If public revenue and the economy as a whole grow faster than the real interest rate, then even the primary balance can remain in deficit. However, it is generally not possible in the long run to always grow faster than the interest rate. The relation between these deficit concepts is shown in Box figure 3.1.

The public sector should include the central government, provincial and municipal governments, decentralized agencies, and state-owned enterprises. Conventional deficit measures often include only the central government. This can give a very misleading picture when other public entities are running large deficits or surpluses. Even in comprehensive measures the public financial intermediaries are often excluded because of their special role as financing agents. On occasion these intermediaries, especially the central bank, have run large losses. These are sometimes called the "quasi-fiscal deficit." They usually arise because the central bank assumes the exchange rate or portfolio losses of private banks (see Box 3.3) or because the central bank directly engages in subsidized lending. The deficit of public financial intermediaries has macroeconomic effects similar to the deficits of other public entities; they should therefore be included in the overall PSBR. Measurement difficulties are formidable, however. Such losses are often omitted unless they are too large to ignore.

Another correction to the deficit is to remove the effect of temporary factors: the deviation of domestic income, commodity prices, and interest rates from their long-run values, and events such as tax amnesties. Sales of government assets could also be excluded,

ment often cannot cover additional public deficits, these spill over in varying degrees as bigger current account deficits. Higher international interest rates and lower commodity prices also add directly to both types of deficit in many countries. So while foreign borrowing permits the fiscal deficit to expand without undue pressure on domestic inflation and interest rates, the buildup of external debt makes countries more vulnerable to external events such as global recession, falling commodity prices, and sudden changes in the cost and availability of new foreign lending. If fiscal expansion is unsustainable, the continued accumulation of external debt only delays an adjustment that is all the more severe for being postponed.

Fiscal deficits and inflation

Governments can choose to finance their fiscal deficits by creating money, that is, by printing and

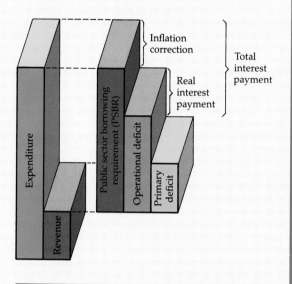

Box figure 3.1 The relation between different deficit concepts

Inflation correction

Real interest payment

Total interest payment

Expenditure

Revenue

Public sector borrowing requirement (PSBR)

Operational deficit

Primary deficit

since they are really financing deficits rather than contributing revenue. The result would be the *structural deficit*, that is, the deficit likely to persist unless corrective measures are taken.

All of these deficit measures provide their own insight into the economic impact of government finance. The PSBR measures the need for domestic or external financing (see Box 3.2). The operational deficit removes some of the distortions caused by high inflation. In debtor countries the primary deficit indicates the public sector's current contribution to debt difficulties. During times of abnormal commodity prices or domestic income, the structural deficit gives a picture of the long-run position.

spending currency. By issuing currency, governments are able to claim real resources; this claim is known as seignorage. The sum of currency holdings by the public and by banks is known as the money base, since it is the basis for monetary transactions performed with cash, checking accounts, savings accounts, and other types of monetary assets. Because the demand for monetary assets keeps increasing in a growing economy, the government can to a limited extent finance itself

through expanding the money base without causing inflation. When the rate of new money creation exceeds the growth in demand for money, however, inflation can result. (In countries where the currency is freely convertible, foreign exchange reserves might also be lost as people exchange the unwanted domestic money for foreign currency.) Individuals are, in effect, taxed by inflation because the real value of their money holdings falls: part of the government's seignorage then becomes an implicit "inflation tax." Banks holding reserves against deposits also face this tax, which they usually pass on to depositors in the form of lower interest rates on deposits. Inflation created by the printing of money may carry an extra fiscal benefit because it reduces the real value of domestic government debt. (When inflation is anticipated, however, nominal interest rates rise in advance to compensate bondholders for the inflation tax.)

Seignorage—the government's ability to claim resources in return for issuing currency—is usually limited by the demand for real money balances, which typically falls as inflation rises. Beyond a certain point an increase in money creation, and thus in the rate of inflation, may actually decrease seignorage if the demand for money falls sharply enough in response. Countries that have relied frequently on money creation as a form of public finance typically have a very low rate of money holdings. Brazil and Israel, for instance, have had modest levels of seignorage on currency—thanks to their low ratios of currency holdings to GDP—despite very high inflation (see Table 3.1). Only countries with extremely high rates of inflation—for example, Argentina and Bolivia—have temporarily generated seignorage on currency of more than 3 or 4 percent of GDP, but such seignorage rates are not sustainable.

Inflation, therefore, is often a fiscal phenomenon: it is caused by governments with no alternative source of deficit finance resorting to money creation at a higher rate than the growth in money demand. Any hope of controlling inflation without reducing government deficits is then in vain. Excessive reliance on money creation is particularly risky if the inflation itself worsens the deficits, because expenditures keep pace with rising prices while revenues do not. This means that still more money creation becomes necessary—further worsening the inflationary spiral.

To counteract the inflationary pressures of money creation, governments sometimes raise the reserve requirements on bank deposits. This in effect requires banks instead of the general public to

Box 3.2 What is a "prudent" fiscal deficit?

One way to decide whether a public deficit is "prudent" is to determine whether financing it is consistent with the government's other macroeconomic objectives—external creditworthiness, growth of private investment, and control of inflation, for example. To do this, financing must be broken down into its components. A good starting place is the identity stating that the sum of all investment in the economy must be equal to the saving available from both residents and foreigners (see Box figure 3.2, top). Foreign saving is the excess of foreigners' income from the domestic economy over their spending in it. This is equal to the current account deficit in the balance of payments. Private saving is equal to GNP minus taxes and private consumption, which gives the private component of gross national saving. Public saving is the excess of public current revenues over current spending, and the public deficit can therefore be defined as public investment minus public saving. The first identity can thus be rewritten as shown in Box figure 3.2, bottom. *A public deficit must be balanced by a domestic private sector that saves more than it invests and/or by an external current account deficit.* The "prudence" of the public deficit depends on the level of private saving, the desired level of private investment, and the desired current account deficit.

The financial flows corresponding to both the external current account deficit and the private surplus are also important. The amount and type of foreign and private lending will determine whether the public deficit is consistent with other macroeconomic goals, as described below.

External creditworthiness is sometimes defined as maintaining an acceptable ratio of gross external debt to exports. This is because exports determine the ability to service debt; a permanently increased debt-export ratio could impair creditworthiness. This suggests that public external debt should grow at the same rate as exports over the long run. Temporary increases in commodity exports should not lead to more public borrowing for the reasons discussed in the section on commodity export cycles in the text. If access to voluntary foreign lending has already been interrupted because of excessive borrowing in the past, then it makes sense to aim for a lower debt-export ratio, implying that the growth of debt should be held below the growth of exports.

The usual objective in managing foreign exchange

Box figure 3.2 The savings–investment identity and the financing of a public deficit

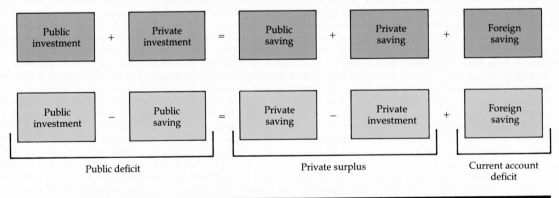

hold currency, so that the money base—but not the overall supply of money—expands. Alternatively, the financial system may be required to hold large amounts of government bonds in its portfolio at artificially low interest rates. While increased reserve or portfolio requirements avoid the inflationary effects of monetary expansion, the resulting increase in the spread between deposit and loan rates hinders domestic financial intermediation. Savers react to the poor returns on deposits by storing their wealth in property or by taking it abroad. The squeeze on bank loans restricts domestic investment and forces investors to turn abroad for funds.

reserves is to maintain an adequate ratio of reserves to imports of goods and services. Deficits can be prudently financed by running down reserves only to the extent that reserves remain over this target. As imports grow, additional reserves have to be accumulated; the financing available from this source could therefore be negative.

Printing money to finance a deficit can result in inflation to the extent that it exceeds the growth in demand for money at the current level of prices. Higher reserve requirements are one way to avoid that result, but they widen the spread between deposit and loan rates, and can therefore be inconsistent with other objectives of efficiency in domestic financial markets and greater private investment.

Nonmonetary domestic borrowing from the banking system or from the nonbank private sector should be consistent with the macroeconomic objective of promoting private sector investment. One guideline is to avoid an increase in the share of public borrowing in domestic credit provided by the banking system. Another approach would be to target public domestic borrowing at a level consistent with the desired level of domestic real interest rates.

Delaying payments on debt service or on goods purchases—that is, increasing arrears—is an important source of finance in some countries. Arrears are implicit credits that have similar macroeconomic consequences to other forms of public borrowing, as well as jeopardizing future financing. A common objective is to reduce arrears either in absolute terms or as a proportion of GDP.

These criteria can be used to judge what level of fiscal deficit is prudent. Higher growth in exports, real demand for money, and overall financial savings means a higher deficit can be financed without violating the objectives of external creditworthiness, low inflation, or reasonable real interest rates. In general, faster economic growth brings bigger deficits within the bounds of prudence, because it usually implies faster growth of exports and demand for money. In a slowly growing economy with low financial savings and stagnant exports, the prudent fiscal deficit is likely to be low.

Sustainability of fiscal deficits

Fiscal deficits have implications for the future as well as for the present. The debts created by borrowing have to be serviced. The public sector must generate the necessary resources through receipts from public investment, through additional taxes

or spending cuts, or through money creation. Although governments can borrow indefinitely, in the long run they must claim enough resources to pay at ___ ___rt of the interest; otherwise the level of det ___ without limit as a proportion of GDP. ___ that the so-called "primary defici ___ d public sector deficit excluding ___ (see Box 3.1)—must eventually ___ ___pensate for past deficits. The on__ ___ ___ement is if resources are used ___ ___rowth rate of the economy—__ ___s— persistently exceeds the rea__ ___ debt.

The sustainability of fiscal policy ___ stract concern. The private sector takes __ count, for example, when deciding whethe__ vest. If deficits are perceived to be unsustaina__ then the private sector will expect future tax in__ creases or money creation. If it predicts the latter, it will also expect higher inflation and currency devaluation. Savers can avoid this threat of implicit or explicit taxation by taking their capital abroad; this itself accelerates the breakdown of the unsustainable policies. The moment of truth for imprudent fiscal policy often comes with a financial or balance of payments crisis.

Stabilization versus structural adjustment

In analyzing the fiscal crisis in developing countries, a distinction must be made between macroeconomic stabilization and structural adjustment. Stabilization addresses short-term problems that need to be dealt with urgently: inflation, loss of foreign exchange reserves, capital flight, and large current account deficits. Structural adjustment addresses obstacles to longer term growth: distortions in the incentives for production (for example, overvalued real exchange rates); controls on prices, interest rates, and credit; burdensome tariffs and import restrictions; and excessive taxes and subsidies. These tasks must be undertaken together. Careless structural adjustment can make the problem of stabilization more difficult, because the distortions are often a source of revenue to the government. For example, high tariffs provide public revenue as well as protection to domestic industry. Equally, structural reforms are unlikely to command credibility unless stabilization policies are in place. Investors will expect trade liberalization to be short lived if fiscal deficits imply an eventual balance of payments crisis. And fiscal stabilization can hamper structural adjustment. For

Figure 3.1 Public deficits and current account deficits in four countries, 1977 to 1986
(percentage of GDP)

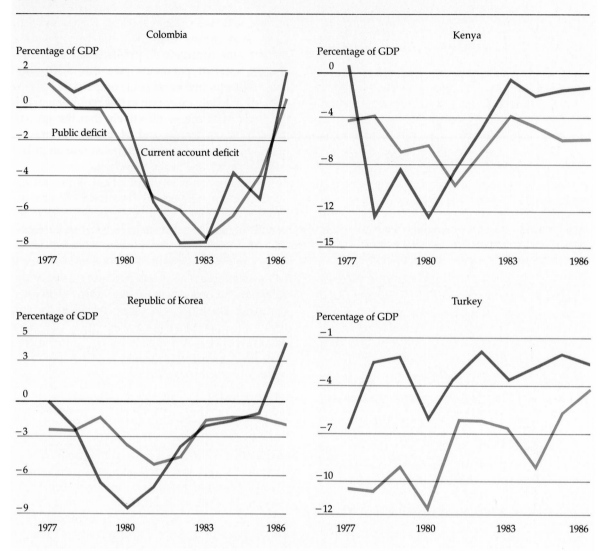

Notes: The public deficit for Turkey includes only central government and state-owned enterprises. The public deficit for Kenya includes only central and local governments. The 1986 public deficit figure for the Republic of Korea is a budget estimate. Other public deficit figures are for the consolidated public sector.

example, cuts in public infrastructure spending to reduce the deficit may cause private investment to fall. Raising tariffs to increase public revenues may distort relative prices.

Stabilization is often associated with a domestic recession characterized by rising unemployment, sharply contracting imports, and falling real wages and living standards. Lower living standards are unavoidable when the previous level has been artificially raised by unsustainable policies. But the re-

cession can be damaging to future growth if it is too deep or too prolonged. The blow to the confidence of domestic investors may inhibit necessary new investment. The decline in the economy can also strain the financial system and impair its ability to finance new growth. Excessive cuts in spending risk a downward spiral of continually falling output. These risks make it vital to team contraction of demand induced by fiscal retrenchment with structural adjustment to increase output.

Some waste of resources can be eliminated with little effect on growth; other forms of fiscal restraint can be damaging. Incentives to expand exports reduce the contraction of imports necessary to restore external balance, and steps to promote savings lessen the fall in investment required to finance the fiscal deficit. Additional external financing can buy time for new supply incentives to take effect.

Stabilization and structural adjustment face different institutional constraints. Stabilization is often postponed, but it can usually be implemented when a crisis forces events. In contrast, structural adjustment seldom carries the same sense of urgency; its results are less obvious and more gradual. It often requires the support of a broader circle of policymakers than stabilization, which is typically undertaken at the behest of the central bank and finance ministry. Structural reforms are difficult, too, because they inflict visible damage on a few and bring less obvious benefits to many. These difficulties reinforce the tendency to pursue short-run stabilization to the exclusion of structural adjustment during crises.

The interdependence of fiscal, monetary, and exchange rate policies

Fiscal policy needs to be judged alongside the other main tools of macroeconomic policy: monetary policy and exchange rate policy. Macroeconomic imbalances are often addressed by tightening monetary policy. However, the governments of developing countries find it more costly to control the money supply than do their counterparts in the industrial countries. To tighten monetary conditions, they are usually forced to impose higher reserve requirements on banks or to induce the banking system to hold more government bonds. In their shallow financial markets this often provokes a bigger rise in interest rates than would be the case in the industrial countries. Private borrowers must therefore reduce their demands for credit more drastically by decreasing capital investment or by going abroad for foreign loans. Higher interest rates on existing private debt are also more likely to cause financial distress for private enterprises and thus to weaken the banking system in developing countries. Interest rate controls are

Table 3.1 Revenues from seignorage on currency in selected countries, average for 1980 to 1985

Level of seignorage revenues and country	Seignorage revenues (increase in currency as a percentage of GDP)	Ratio of currency holdings to GDP (percent)	Currency growth (percent per year)	Inflation (percent per year)
High				
Argentina	4.0	3.8	269	274
Bolivia	6.2	6.1	438	506
Ghana	2.2	6.1	45	54
Sierra Leone	2.4	7.7	35	43
Moderate				
Brazil	1.0	1.4	129	147
Israel	1.1	1.3	165	181
Mexico	1.5	3.7	50	58
Peru	1.9	3.1	92	97
Turkey	1.2	3.8	38	46
Low				
Bangladesh	0.6	4.0	16	12
Colombia	0.8	4.7	18	22
Côte d'Ivoire	0.7	9.2	8	7
Dominican Republic	0.7	4.6	16	15
Korea, Republic of	0.5	4.3	13	9
Nigeria	0.8	7.2	13	16
Venezuela	0.4	4.5	8	12

Notes: This table measures only the seignorage corresponding to currency held by the public, since seignorage on banks' holding of currency reserves is difficult to measure for some countries. The first column is calculated as the end-of-year currency outside banks (IFS line 14a) minus the end-of-year value of the previous year, divided by the current year GDP. The second column is the ratio of the average of beginning-of-year and end-of-year currency outside banks to current GDP. The third column is the percentage change in currency outside banks from end-of-year to end-of-year. The final column is the percentage change in the consumer price index (IFS line 64) from December to December. The geometric average of growth rates is used for columns three and four; the arithmetic average of ratios is used for columns 1 and 2.
Source: IMF, *International Financial Statistics.*

Figure 3.2 Real effective exchange rate indexes for selected countries

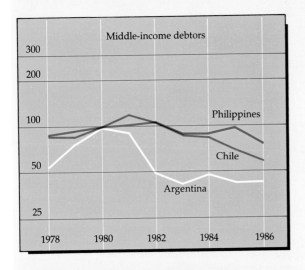

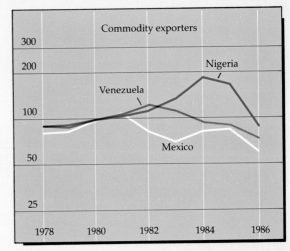

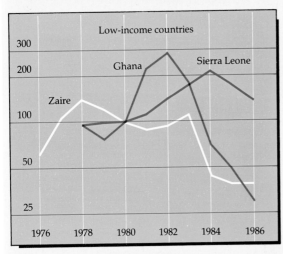

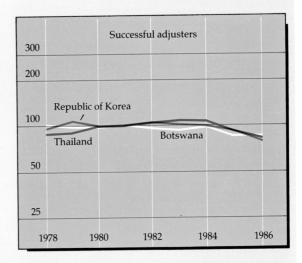

Notes: The vertical axis is in log scale. The real exchange rate is an index of relative domestic and international prices expressed in a common currency. (In technical terms it is defined as the domestic price index times the exchange rate–expressed as units of foreign currency per unit of domestic currency–divided by an international price index in foreign currency.) An increase in this index signifies that the foreign currency equivalent of the domestic price index is increasing faster than the international price index. This is referred to as a real appreciation of the domestic currency, which implies that the country exporters are less competitive in international markets, while foreign producers are more competitive in the domestic market. The real exchange rate index is often expressed in "effective" terms, which take into account the relative importance of inflation and exchange rate movements in each trading partner.

sometimes used to counteract these pressures, but this often leads to credit rationing and capital flight. So, more than in industrial countries, tight money is a poor substitute for fiscal discipline.

Exchange rate policy on its own is also unlikely to be successful at stabilization. Public deficits often result in real exchange rate overvaluation because the additional pressure on domestic demand

drives up wages and prices. Tight monetary policy reinforces this tendency by raising domestic interest rates and attracting capital inflows. Devaluations of the currency without an accompanying fiscal correction will eventually be offset by increases in domestic prices and affect the real exchange rate only temporarily. Equally, when wages and domestic prices do not fall readily in nominal terms, a fiscal contraction without a nominal devaluation is also unlikely to change the real exchange rate.

Figure 3.2 shows the pattern of real exchange rate movements for a sample of twelve countries representing middle-income debtors, commodity exporters, low-income countries, and countries that avoided debt-servicing difficulties through successful adjustment. The countries that stayed out of trouble had remarkably stable real exchange rates, thanks partly to stable fiscal policies. The other three groups saw expanding fiscal deficits in the late 1970s and early 1980s, and their real exchange rates appreciated during this period. After 1982 fiscal austerity accompanied by nominal devaluation began in these countries. The result was a sharp depreciation of the real exchange rate.

Nominal devaluations have an immediate effect on public sector accounts because they revalue foreign currency income and expenditure in domestic currency. Whether the effect on the fiscal deficit is negative or positive depends on whether the public sector's spending on debt service and imports exceeds its income from exports and trade taxes and on how producer prices and public sector wages change. For example, an oil exporter would likely gain additional public revenue from a devaluation, while a debtor without significant public sector exports would more likely find that its extra expenditure was greater than its additional revenue. So the degree of fiscal squeeze needed to achieve a given reduction in the budget deficit following a devaluation varies according to whether the public sector is a net earner of foreign exchange.

Figure 3.3 Overall and primary public balances for four middle-income debtors, 1977 to 1985

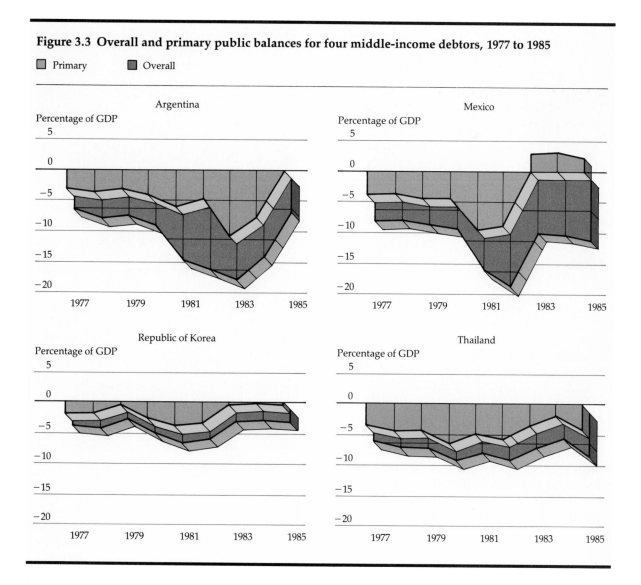

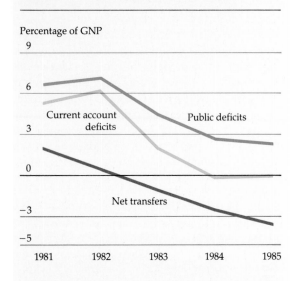

Figure 3.4 Net transfers, current account deficits, and public deficits for seventeen highly indebted countries, 1981 to 1985

Percentage of GNP

Current account deficits

Public deficits

Net transfers

1981   1982   1983   1984   1985

Notes: Net transfers are defined as disbursements of medium- and long-term external loans minus interest and amortization payments on medium- and long-term external debt. Public deficits refer to the consolidated public deficit, except for Costa Rica, Morocco, Uruguay, and Yugoslavia, where central government deficits are used. For Mexico and Brazil, two countries with high internal debt and high inflation, the "operational deficit" measure was used.

The fiscal dimension of the external debt crisis

Fiscal deficits were a principal cause of the international debt crisis—both directly, because they meant greater public borrowing, and indirectly, because they encouraged the private sector to send its capital overseas. Most developing countries have recognized that fiscal discipline will help both to prevent future debt problems and to resolve the present ones. But the debts already incurred make fiscal adjustment all the more difficult.

Fiscal management and external borrowing

With a few exceptions the countries that developed debt-servicing problems in the early 1980s were those that had significantly increased their fiscal deficits in the late 1970s and early 1980s. Figure 3.3 shows the overall public sector balance and the primary balance for four middle-income countries. Two of these (Argentina and Mexico) developed debt problems, the other two (Republic of

Korea and Thailand) did not. The problem debtors allowed their primary deficits to rise before 1982. These inflows of debt were used partly to finance an increase in public consumption and transfers. The governments of many debtor countries also greatly expanded their capital spending. But the quality of these projects—and the corresponding rates of return—declined, so that many projects were unprofitable once international interest rates rose.

The aggregate current account deficit of the seventeen highly indebted countries widened in step with their aggregate fiscal deficit (see Figure 3.4). This growing external imbalance was supported by a huge flow of financial resources. Real exchange rates appreciated. Then in August 1982 the capital inflow came to an abrupt halt. Mexico announced that it could not service the principal on its debt, which precipitated a sudden loss of confidence in the creditworthiness of all the indebted developing countries. Voluntary commercial lending to most of them ceased, and they were forced to reschedule their debt service payments. Thanks to the fall in new lending and the increase in international interest rates, the net flow of resources to the seventeen highly indebted countries was actually reversed. The turnaround in net transfers was equivalent to almost 6 percent of GDP from 1981 to 1985.

Some countries managed to avoid debt-servicing difficulties altogether or recovered quickly from earlier debt troubles. Korea and Thailand maintained uninterrupted access to commercial bank loans, even though their borrowing was heavy both in absolute terms and relative to their GNP (see Table 3.2). Turkey recovered vigorously from a debt crisis after 1980 and managed to regain access to commercial borrowing. In these cases the key to avoiding or recovering from the crisis was sound fiscal management, stable real exchange rates, and export-oriented trade policy. Korea had two years of high deficits in 1981–82 but recovered quickly to a sustainable deficit ratio of less than 2 percent of GDP (see Figure 3.3). Thailand had somewhat higher deficits, but benefited from low initial indebtedness and high growth. Turkey lowered its fiscal deficit after 1980, then managed to absorb the deficits that remained by promoting private saving. Relative fiscal restraint stabilized real exchange rates in Korea and Thailand and enabled Turkey's to depreciate gradually. This helped to fuel vigorous export expansion. As a result Thailand's debt-exports ratio was held to a manageable rate of increase; in Korea and Turkey it fell.

Table 3.2 External debt statistics for successfully adjusting debtor countries and highly indebted countries, 1980 and 1986

Country or country group	Total external debt (billions of dollars)		Debt-GNP ratio (percent)		Debt-export ratio (percent)		GDP growth rate, 1980–86
	1980	1986	1980	1986	1980	1986	
Successfully adjusting debtor countries							
Korea, Republic of	29.7	45.1	49.3	47.4	131.8	107.5	8.2
Thailand	8.3	18.0	25.1	44.7	96.3	148.4	4.8
Turkey	19.0	31.8	34.1	56.5	517.9	293.6	4.9
Seventeen highly indebted countries	287.6	471.7	32.8	60.8	175.6	364.1	0.7

Most of the highly indebted countries responded to the cessation of lending by tightening their fiscal policies. This austerity helped them to avoid a general suspension of payments, but it was insufficient to solve their debt problem. By 1985, Argentina, Colombia, the Dominican Republic, Mexico, and the Philippines had all achieved primary fiscal surpluses. However, this improvement fully offset neither the earlier deterioration in fiscal deficits nor the decline in external financing. The interest on foreign debt accumulated in the earlier fiscal expansion significantly added to the fiscal burden. For example, in Argentina interest on the external debt was equivalent to 17.1 percent of current public revenues in 1985, while in Mexico it was 12.9 percent in the same year. As a result the consolidated public deficit improved by far less than the primary deficit. In Mexico, for example, large public deficits remained although the primary balance reverted to surplus.

Almost all the debtors supported their fiscal contractions by devaluing their currencies. Depreciated real exchange rates made debt service more burdensome, although for many governments this was more than offset by the rise in trade taxes and export revenues. The devaluations were generally associated with lower real wages. The real wage fell in Mexico by 38 percent between 1981 and 1986, in Brazil by 21 percent between 1982 and 1984, and in Turkey by 45 percent between 1981 and 1986. Lower incomes were necessary to compress demand and improve the external balance. But this decline placed a heavy burden on the poorest members of society at a time when social spending was already being sharply cut.

To reinforce the effect of devaluation and fiscal contraction on the external balance, many countries also tightened import restrictions after 1982. This interrupted attempts at import liberalization, which had been embarked upon earlier when foreign debt was freely available. In Mexico quantita-

tive restrictions were imposed on all imports, in contrast to an average of 60 percent of imports in the 1970s. (After 1984 the country moved toward import liberalization.) Argentina subjected all imports to permits in 1984 and imposed a surcharge of 10 percent on imports in 1985. Chile raised import duties and imposed surcharges during 1982–84. Colombia increased tariffs and import restrictions in 1983–84 and imposed an import surcharge of 8 percent in 1984.

Fiscal policy and private capital flows

The fiscal imbalances of the late 1970s and early 1980s contributed to the external debt crisis in several ways—not merely through direct public borrowing. Unsustainable fiscal policies and the accompanying overvalued exchange rates helped to stimulate an exodus of private capital from the heavily indebted nations. The inconsistency of fiscal policy and exchange rate targets also led in some countries to large-scale external borrowing by the private sector.

Unsustainable fiscal deficits provoke capital flight because domestic savers anticipate a coming crisis that is likely to involve a major devaluation and new taxes on income and consumption. All estimates of capital flight are highly uncertain and controversial, but one recent study argued that it has been a significant factor in the debt accumulation of some countries. The estimate of cumulative capital flight from Argentina during 1974–82 was $31.3 billion. Nearly half of Venezuela's external debt is estimated to be due to capital flight. The total for seven highly indebted countries was $92 billion, compared with an aggregate debt of $307 billion. Most of the countries that suffered from severe capital flight had free currency convertibility at the time it occurred; countries with strict capital controls, such as Brazil and Colombia, were less badly affected. Countries that maintained pru-

Box 3.3   Fiscal deficits and financial crises

The public expenditures associated with subsidizing banking systems or resolving financial crises are often not included in the conventional measure of the public deficit. Such spending became important after the onset of the external debt problem in 1982, when several middle-income countries faced a banking system crisis. Highly leveraged enterprises in the debtor countries were unable to repay their debts. The banks that had been borrowing abroad on behalf of the enterprises were forced to absorb the losses. Some domestic banks had many of their liabilities denominated in foreign currencies, with the corresponding assets in domestic currency. Currency devaluations then meant sizable exchange rate losses. In Yugoslavia, for example, the foreign exchange losses of the commercial banking system averaged almost 2 percent of GDP between 1981 and 1983, and the banking system's equity dropped from 3 to −0.5 percent of total assets.

When a financial crisis occurs, policymakers face a dilemma: they need to stabilize the economy, which calls for a smaller fiscal deficit. But they also need to make substantial transfers to maintain the viability of the financial system, which implies a bigger deficit. In virtually all cases the central bank has borne the losses and financed them by printing money or by exchanging its bonds for the bad debts. Financial emergencies have not caused budget deficits, conventionally defined, to rise by much. A more meaningful measure of the public deficit, however, should include the losses of the central bank. Their economic consequences—including the impetus they give to inflation—are the same.

In Yugoslavia public sector entities, including the federal government, have been prohibited from borrowing from the banking system to finance their revenue shortfalls. Consequently public sector revenue has normally equaled or slightly exceeded expenditure. Some public expenditures, however, were financed by large contributions from enterprises, many of which were already incurring losses. These losses were financed, in turn, by credit from the banking system. Thus monetary growth was rapid despite fiscal restraint, mainly because the National Bank of Yugoslavia bore the banking system's portfolio and foreign exchange losses during the past few years. In 1986, for example, the government budget remained virtually balanced, but the losses of the National Bank of Yugoslavia were about 13 percent of national income. This led to substantial money creation and inflation of around 70 percent in that year.

In Chile the government response to financial crisis was more transparent. The private sector was given a preferential exchange rate for the repayment of external debt, and the central bank bought the nonperforming assets of the commercial banks in exchange for bonds under a repurchasing agreement. Under this agreement the central bank made large transfers to the banks in 1983 to support their liquidity. If the measured public sector deficit had included these transfers, it would have been 9 percent of GDP, not 3 percent as conventionally measured.

Argentina's fiscal deficit was relatively low in 1986, at about 2 percent of GDP. But the central bank was also posting annual losses of about 2 percent of GDP. These resulted mainly from the difference between the interest rate the central bank paid on deposits from banks and the preferential rate it charged on loans given to the troubled commercial banks. Furthermore, since the recipients of these preferential rates are not servicing their debt with the central bank, the loans could be thought of as a fiscal transfer. If such transfers were included, the overall deficit would have exceeded 7 percent of GDP in 1986. This helps to explain Argentina's difficulties in servicing public debt. In Bolivia the government still has to address a grave problem: the banks suffered foreign exchange losses when the government converted the foreign currency debts of nonfinancial firms to local currency. The government has suspended foreign debt service, and it has not decided how those losses are to be allocated.

Financial crises led to similar problems in other middle-income countries. In Mexico the losses associated with exchange rate differences between dollar assets and liabilities of the nationalized banks added 4 percent to the consolidated public deficit in 1982. This contributed to the burst of inflation in that year. In Costa Rica, where the conventional fiscal deficit was only 1.8 percent of GDP in 1985, central bank losses were about 5.3 percent of GDP. This helps to explain that year's current account deficit of 5 percent of GDP.

Transferring the burden of financial losses to the central bank does not eliminate the effects of public spending arising from a financial crisis. Such transfers simply make the conventional definition of the fiscal deficit misleading.

dent fiscal policies, such as Thailand, were able to avoid severe capital flight even without capital controls.

Flight capital has largely failed to return since 1982. This indicates continued uncertainty about policy sustainability and thus about the investment climate. Fiscal contraction has been more painful as a result; a return inflow would have increased the domestic savings available for productive investment. Capital flight also meant that the costs of stabilization were often inequitably distributed. The rich protected their income and wealth from devaluation and inflation by shifting assets abroad, while the poor suffered real wage declines.

Capital flight began in many cases because stabilization was postponed too long. Another contributing factor was lack of consistency in policy. Some countries tried to control inflation by fixing exchange rates or by depreciating them in real terms at a preannounced rate, but they could not sustain this policy alongside fiscal expansion. Argentina faced this problem during 1979–81; inconsistent policies led to massive capital flight and an exchange rate crisis in 1981, followed by a rapid real depreciation of the currency.

The interaction of fiscal policy with monetary and exchange rate policy also affected private borrowing. In Argentina private external debt grew from $3.1 billion to $11.2 billion between 1978 and 1982, while in Chile it rose from $1.6 billion to $8.7 billion. Tight money and insufficiently contractionary fiscal policy drove up domestic interest rates, while the comparatively low rate of currency depreciation made foreign loans seem cheap to private borrowers. Liberalized capital markets facilitated the inflow of foreign credits. The Chilean government ran a modest surplus until 1982, but even this was not contractionary enough to sustain a fixed exchange rate in the face of wage indexation, inflation inertia, and a deterioration in the terms of trade.

One oddity concerning the debt crisis, it might seem, is that large-scale capital flight and private foreign borrowing continued side by side. If the private sector expected a breakdown of policy and large devaluations, why did it keep borrowing? A partial answer is that many governments implicitly subsidized private borrowing. Argentina, Chile, Mexico, and Venezuela subsidized private debt repayment after the crisis broke, either through differential exchange rates or by explicitly taking on private foreign debt (see Box 3.3). To the extent that the private sector anticipated these subsidies, it was willing to keep borrowing. Distortions in financial markets also help to explain simultaneous capital flight and private borrowing. Where governments relied on large reserve requirements to finance deficits while maintaining strict monetary policy, the resulting interest rate spread between deposits and loans drove both savers and borrowers offshore. In effect the government's "tax" on

financial intermediation led the private sector to shift its financial intermediation abroad.

Inflation and internal debt management

After 1982 the highly indebted countries had to rely much more on internal financing of their public deficits. The fall in net external finance (that is, in their current account deficits) was greater than the reduction in their public deficits. That in turn meant greater reliance on monetary finance and internal debt accumulation. In some countries reduced foreign finance combined with devaluation led to domestic financial crises (see Box 3.3). Some governments assumed private foreign debt to preserve the country's international credit standing—sometimes under pressure from commercial banks—or to bail out private borrowers. Others made substantial public transfers to keep their financial systems afloat. Such operations further increased the public sector deficit and the need for additional internal financing.

Large exchange rate depreciations and growing reliance on monetary finance caused inflation to accelerate in many of the debtor countries during their stabilization programs, despite falling fiscal deficits. Faster money creation led to increased revenues from the "inflation tax," which helped to finance the remaining public deficit. The behavior of this "tax" was quite unstable, however. Capital flight and more rapid turnover of the money stock had diminished the share of the money base in GDP; accelerating inflation was therefore needed to maintain the required financing. Governments resorted to conventional and unconventional ways of stopping inflation, with mixed results (see Box 3.4). Bolivia and Chile managed to stop runaway inflation through fiscal austerity, although both suffered recessions in the process. Argentina and Brazil tried an unconventional ("heterodox") mixture of price controls, wage policies, and monetary reform but failed to halt inflation for lack of supporting ("orthodox") fiscal measures.

The highly indebted countries were aware of the inflationary consequences of printing money. Some used higher reserve requirements on domestic bank deposits to raise seignorage revenues without loosening their monetary stance. This was important in Mexico in 1982, in Peru during 1984–85, in the Philippines in 1986, and in Venezuela in 1983. Government borrowing from the banking system also increased, either through forced bond purchases or through borrowing at market rates.

Box 3.4 Stabilizing inflation: experiences in Latin America

Recent experience in Latin America gives some insight into the role of fiscal policy in fighting inflation.

"Orthodox" stabilization

Bolivia. Inflation accelerated in Bolivia when the government printed money to compensate for the abrupt decline in external financing in the early 1980s. This inflation itself worsened the fiscal deficit. As prices rose, people delayed paying taxes so that their tax liability would be lower in real terms. Revenues of the nonfinancial public sector dropped from more than 11 percent of GDP in 1981 to less than 5 percent by 1984. The consolidated public sector deficit exploded from 8 percent of GDP in 1981 to more than 27 percent in 1984. To cover this, the government printed money even faster. Even the suspension of debt service payments in 1984 could not arrest the spiraling inflation. In the twelve months preceding August 1985 prices rose by 24,000 percent.

A newly elected government unveiled a far-ranging stabilization program in August 1985. This ended controls on most prices, wages, and interest rates and tightened fiscal and monetary policies. Public sector revenues were increased by reforming the tax system and raising public sector prices (for oil, gas, electricity, and transport), while public sector wage costs were reduced through cuts in employment and wages. The program stopped inflation almost instantly. Because the inflation was so severe, peso prices were being set by converting dollar prices into pesos at the parallel market exchange rate. Once the exchange rate had been stabilized, which was possible because of fiscal and monetary austerity, the peso inflation rate rapidly converged to the dollar inflation rate prevailing in the world markets. However, the program has had limited success so far in restoring output and incomes.

Chile. Another successful anti-inflation program has been implemented in Chile. With some reversals, persistent fiscal and monetary austerity has gradually lowered inflation from triple-digit rates in the 1970s to around 20 percent at present (see Box table 3.4). A failed attempt at curbing inflation through a fixed exchange rate led to a large devaluation in 1982, followed by a recession and financial crisis. But fiscal restraint was broadly maintained, so inflation remained lower. The adoption of a flexible exchange rate policy and the abolition of formal wage indexation, along with a restrained monetary policy, allowed fiscal austerity to have the desired anti-inflationary effect. However, per capita income declined by 18 percent during 1982–83, partly because of the ill-fated exchange rate experiment and the decline in Chile's terms of trade. Growth has since resumed, with per capita income rising by 10 percent between 1983 and 1986.

"Heterodox" stabilization

The costs believed to be associated with conventional anti-inflation policies have led to a search for new methods. In 1985–86 Argentina and Brazil adopted an innovative policy mix of wage and price controls, monetary reform, fixed exchange rates, and fiscal adjustment. These programs—the Austral and Cruzado plans, respectively—were called "heterodox" in contrast to the "orthodox" mix of fiscal and monetary stringency.

Argentina. After the Austral Plan was introduced, inflation fell from monthly rates of 25 percent in May 1985 to 2 percent in the second half of the year. The fiscal deficit fell substantially because falling inflation and improved tax administration meant additional real revenues (equal to about 6 percent of GDP). The pro-

---

In some cases public bonds were also sold to nonbank institutions or individuals.

Greater reliance on domestic finance and higher reserve requirements drove up real domestic loan rates. As shown in Table 3.3, real loan interest rates reached extreme levels in many countries in 1985 or 1986. Often abrupt shifts in policy also led to great variability in real interest rates. In many cases domestic interest rates were higher than international rates—even when corrected for currency depreciation. So the substitution of internal for external debt—far from alleviating the debt crisis—has actually increased the public debt burden. In Mexico public domestic interest payments reached 24 percent of current public revenues in 1985. In Brazil domestic public debt more than doubled in real terms from 1981 to 1987. Without further fiscal adjustment some countries risk being trapped in a spiral of rising real interest rates, growing domestic debt service and fiscal deficits, or faster money creation and inflation.

Even countries with lesser external debt problems—Thailand and Turkey, for instance—have faced a growing pressure on domestic interest rates from domestic financing of public deficits. Thailand chose to forgo the inflation tax by follow-

Box table 3.4 Inflation in selected heavily indebted countries, 1971 to 1987

(CPI percent December-over-December)

Country	Average, 1971–80	1981	1982	1983	1984	1985	1986	1987
Argentina	121	131	210	434	688	385	82	175
Bolivia	20	25	297	328	2,176	8,170	66	11
Brazil	38	101	102	178	209	249	64	321
Chile	131	10	21	23	23	26	17	23

Source: 1971–86, IMF, *International Financial Statistics;* 1987, World Bank data.

gram was accompanied by new loans and debt rescheduling from both private and official external creditors. The economy began to grow again by the last quarter of 1985, when growth of 5.7 percent was achieved. In 1987, however, unfavorable movements in interest rates and export prices caused the external balance to deteriorate. Public spending had increased; when revenues again declined, the fiscal deficit grew. Inflation accelerated, although it remains below the pre-Austral rate. In retrospect the failure to reform taxes and cut public spending prevented the needed adjustment in public deficits.

Brazil. The Cruzado Plan was a failure. Inflation was even higher after the breakdown of the plan than before. Fiscal deficits significantly exceeded projections after price controls were put in place. The controls themselves contributed to the deficits of public enterprises, whose prices fell in real terms. The deficit was contained in the short run only because of a large fall in domestic debt service thanks to the "de-indexation" of government bonds. Real wages were increased by 8 percent at the beginning of the plan and continued to rise gradually thereafter. Fiscal stimulus and higher

wages led to a private consumption boom. This rapidly eroded the trade surplus required for external debt service and created shortages of domestic goods. In 1987 inflation accelerated, a new price freeze was imposed, and payments of interest on commercial external debt were suspended.

The necessity of fiscal correction

The attempts to stabilize prices through "heterodox" measures were based on a misreading of the causes of inflation. It was assumed that inflation was largely "inertial," meaning that it was caused by spiraling wage and price increases arising from indexed labor contracts. This undoubtedly explained some of the persistence of inflation in Argentina and Brazil (in contrast to Bolivia, which did not have indexed contracts). However, the financing requirements of the public sector were the more fundamental cause. The lack of sufficient external finance and continued high deficits meant that money creation had to continue in Argentina and Brazil. Although "heterodox" measures might speed the fall in inflation in the presence of fiscal correction and may help in building political consensus for reform, they are of little use by themselves.

Table 3.3 Real loan interest rates for selected countries, 1980 to 1986

(percent)

Country	1980	1981	1982	1983	1984	1985	1986
Argentina	26.8	8.7	−43.2	−22.5	−27.1	−9.2	19.6
Brazil	−2.5	4.9	29.8	−3.7	23.7	26.1	−7.8
Indonesia	..	..	10.5	9.5	16.5	20.0	17.5
Malaysia	1.0	−1.1	2.8	7.1	7.2	11.2	9.3
Mexico	3.5	5.2	−23.5	−23.0	2.5	9.2	15.4
Philippines	..	4.5	7.0	6.0	−19.7	21.1	17.0
Thailand	−4.0	2.9	8.4	13.3	19.2	15.2	15.2
Turkey	−38.0	−3.0	5.0	15.0	0.0	6.0	17.0
Uruguay	−8.4	9.3	26.4	14.5	8.9	2.4	0.3

Note: Calculated as the average nominal lending rate for each year minus the consumer price inflation for that year. Countries were selected on the basis of availability of data.

Figure 3.5 Aggregate production and expenditure in highly indebted and successfully adjusting countries, 1980 to 1986

— GDP — Expenditure — Consumption

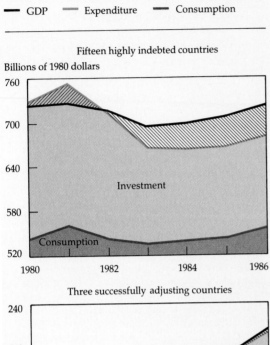

Fifteen highly indebted countries

Billions of 1980 dollars

Investment

Consumption

1980   1982   1984   1986

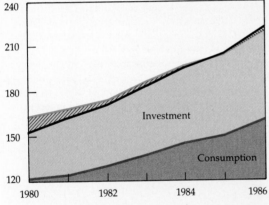

Three successfully adjusting countries

Investment

Consumption

1980   1982   1984   1986

Notes: The aggregate for highly indebted countries excludes Brazil and Colombia because of the atypical adjustment pattern in those countries. The three successfully adjusting countries are Republic of Korea, Thailand, and Turkey. The aggregate is computed by converting the domestic currency value in 1980 prices into dollars using the 1980 exchange rate, and then summing all dollar values. The difference between domestic production (GDP) and expenditure (total consumption plus investment) represents the net resource balance, which is the same as the net resource flow from the domestic economy to foreigners. An excess of expenditure over GDP represents a resource deficit (net resource inflow) ▨ , while a surplus of GDP over expenditure is equivalent to a resource surplus (net resource outflow) ▧

ing tight monetary policies. Interest rates increased, and public domestic interest payments reached 13 percent of current revenues in 1985 as

the cautious external borrowing policies of the government led to greater reliance on internal financing. Turkey experienced both high domestic interest rates and inflation as a result of moderately high fiscal deficits. In both cases the effect of high interest rates was cushioned by continuing access to international borrowing and by steady economic growth. Their mix of policies averted financial crisis. Nonetheless, the combination of tight monetary policy and moderately high fiscal deficits cannot continue indefinitely without causing internal or external debt difficulties.

The dynamics of growth and debt

As discussed above, stabilization programs have set back structural adjustment and growth in many highly indebted countries, despite well-meaning efforts to the contrary. Tariffs and quotas have been used to cut imports. Some countries liberalized later, but revenue requirements left little room for widespread tariff reductions. Financial liberalization has been set back by increased government demands on the banking system, higher reserve requirements on deposits, and financial crises. The only significant change in supply incentives has been the real devaluation of domestic currencies. Output has declined sharply during these stabilization programs. Per capita incomes in the seventeen highly indebted countries fell 9 percent during 1980–87. Despite the need to generate current account surpluses, the aggregate exports of the seventeen countries actually contracted in value terms, from $167 billion in 1981 to $147 billion in 1987. Lack of success in expanding domestic supply meant that the response to the cutoff of lending was heavily focused on contracting aggregate demand. Real domestic expenditure (the sum of total investment and consumption, public and private) fell precipitously after 1981 in the heavily indebted countries in order to generate a surplus of output over expenditure to make the required resource transfer (see Figure 3.5).

Investment bore the brunt of this cutback; consumption stayed roughly constant in absolute terms. High and volatile domestic interest rates against an uncertain economic background discouraged private investment. Public investment was cut sharply as a fiscal austerity measure. To the extent that productive investments were cut or delayed, growth of output suffered. If resource outflows could have been avoided, it would have been possible to keep investment at its level of the early 1980s. Countries that did not need to generate a resource outflow were able to maintain investment, in some cases slowing consumption to do so. Partly through strong supply incentives, countries such as Republic of Korea, Thailand, and Turkey have maintained reasonable debt ratios through strong income growth, without cutting total spending. Figure 3.5 shows the contrast between the steadily rising output, expenditure, and consumption of these three countries and the unhappy experience of their highly indebted counterparts.

Why has the private sector in many highly indebted countries responded weakly to the export incentives implied by the depreciation in the real exchange rate? Although the fall in commodity prices partly explains the poor export performance, another factor is the great variability of fiscal policy, real exchange rates, and real interest rates during the past five years (see Figure 1.7 on the export volume performance of Latin American countries). That degree of uncertainty makes investors reluctant to commit themselves, even if incentives are (temporarily) favorable. The more successful economies generally pursued more stable macroeconomic policies.

To sum up, many middle-income countries developed debt problems because of excessive fiscal expansion and overvalued currencies, which made them vulnerable to the rise in global interest rates and the fall in export prices after 1981. Responding to the cutoff of commercial lending, they have achieved considerable fiscal adjustment by cutting spending and generating additional revenue. Growth has been severely curtailed, however, because of the reliance on investment cutbacks, import rationing, and distortionary revenue increases. Inflation has accelerated in many cases because of large nominal devaluations and increased reliance on monetary finance of the remaining budget deficits. Heavy burdens of internal debt have also developed where governments have relied on nonmonetary domestic finance. Real wages have fallen, and the incidence of poverty has risen.

There are no easy remedies. The experiences of the more successful countries illustrate that prudent fiscal policy and timely adjustment are essential before a crisis becomes too severe. This is an important lesson for countries that have not yet reached the crisis stage. However, the lesson comes too late for most highly indebted countries. The challenge for them is to continue shrinking fiscal deficits without further contracting domestic demand. Cuts in public spending should prefera-

bly be selective rather than across-the-board. New revenues might come from increased user fees and tax reforms to close loopholes and expand tax bases. Lower deficits would allow less reliance on domestic financing and thus lower inflation and interest rates, which would permit renewed growth of the private sector. Redirecting spending away from import-intensive uses and providing incentives to expand exports would reduce the need to restrict demand. Moderate capital controls will probably remain necessary in most countries to restrain short-term capital outflows, at least until full stabilization is achieved. The adjustment task would be far easier if the international environment improved. Lower international interest rates, improved flows of financing to highly indebted countries, or selective debt relief would enable public and private investment to recover and would allow the indebted countries to grow out of their debt problems if appropriate domestic policies are pursued.

The fiscal management of commodity export cycles

Many developing countries rely on one or two primary commodity exports as their major source of foreign exchange. Often these exports also contribute revenue to the government budget, either through direct state ownership or through export taxes. Cyclical swings in commodity prices have had a large effect on both external and fiscal accounts. The price increases of the 1970s and the later unexpected collapses created fiscal crises in many countries. With hindsight it is clear that resources generated by the "booms" (periods of high export prices and volumes) were managed in a way that left countries vulnerable to the coming collapse. As a result some countries may even be worse off for having experienced a boom.

Country experience with commodity booms

Figure 3.6 shows the behavior of public spending and revenue before and after commodity booms in selected countries. It shows a remarkable regularity. In most countries public revenue accelerated dramatically during the boom. This was sometimes due to direct state ownership of the enterprise producing the export commodity, as in oil exporting countries such as Indonesia, Mexico, and Nigeria. Elsewhere it resulted from the increased profits of publicly owned marketing boards or stabilization funds. When world prices

Figure 3.6 Public revenues and expenditures during commodity booms

—— Revenues   ▬▬ Expenditures

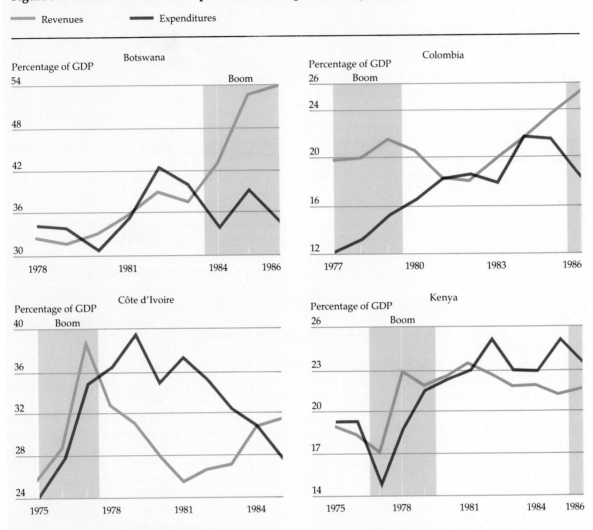

Note: Both revenues and expenditures exclude transfers, so their difference is not equal to an overall public sector balance. Figures for Kenya are for central government only.

went up, the marketing boards did not raise the prices they paid to producers proportionately. Marketing board revenues in Côte d'Ivoire, for example, reached a remarkable 16.5 percent of GDP at the peak of the cocoa and coffee boom of 1977. Even in countries where the profits of the commodity boom remained mostly with the private sector, the boom indirectly increased government revenue. For example, in Kenya the coffee sector is in private hands, and producer price increases more or less matched world price increases. Yet government revenue increased from 17 to 23 percent of GDP during 1977–78 thanks to increased

trade flows and higher export and import tax revenue.

When the boom ended, government revenue declined sharply. Commodity-producing state enterprises suffered sharply lower earnings. In other countries the marketing boards absorbed some of the decline in prices, which led to substantial losses. For example, public revenue in Côte d'Ivoire fell from 37 percent of GDP in 1977 to only 25 percent in 1981. Revenue from trade taxes fell as trade flows slowed.

Public spending also went up in the boom—in many cases by more than revenue. In Kenya government expenditure rose from 15 percent of GDP in 1977 to more than 21 percent in 1979. Public spending in Côte d'Ivoire shot up from 28 percent of GDP to 35 percent in only one year, from 1976 to 1977. Increases in both current and capital spending were often of dubious economic merit. Government payrolls expanded, consumer subsidies increased, and ambitious new investment projects began. In the Dominican Republic, for example, profits from sugar in the 1970s were used to subsidize consumer purchases of petroleum products. In many of the oil-exporting countries profits from oil exports were used to keep oil prices artificially low at home. Later evaluation of many of the public investments begun during the boom shows that they had very low rates of return. They were plagued by cost overruns and delays. For example, an analysis of a sample of investment projects in seven oil-exporting countries showed that the largest third of the projects had cost overruns averaging 109 percent. A quarter of these suffered delays of three to four years. Some were abandoned before completion; others were rendered uneconomical by changed world market conditions. Mexico, Trinidad and Tobago, and Venezuela began major public investments in large steel plants in the 1970s, not long before the prolonged glut on world markets. Far from paying the interest on the debt that was raised to finance them, these projects became a heavy drain on public budgets.

Even as the boom was ending, spending was maintained or increased (see Figure 3.6). This led to a jump in public deficits. Mexico's, for example, rose from 7.9 percent of GDP in 1980 to 17.5 percent in 1982. The Nigerian public deficit rose from 1.1 percent of GDP in 1979 to 9.1 percent in 1981. After a delay of several years most countries did cut spending or raise revenue; in many cases they were forced to do so because voluntary foreign commercial lending stopped.

External debt had grown rapidly during the boom in many countries; net capital flows were reduced or even reversed during the bust. Foreign commercial banks were eager to lend to commodity-exporting countries during the boom because of the apparent security provided by commodity revenue, while public sector borrowers wanted to leverage their commodity revenues into even greater spending growth. After revenue fell sharply, nervous lenders were reluctant to make new loans. For example, net flows of long-term public external debt to Nigeria were $1 billion a year as oil prices soared in 1979–80. During the disastrous oil price slump of 1986, however, the corresponding flow was only $20 million. Contrary to the principle that debt should be used to smooth such cycles, it exacerbated them.

The macroeconomic effects of the mismanaged booms were similar in most countries. Real exchange rates appreciated excessively (see Figure 3.2). Exports of other goods declined, while import growth accelerated under pressure from high aggregate demand, overvalued exchange rates, and the ready availability of foreign exchange. Nigeria's imports increased from $9.7 billion in 1977 to $19 billion in 1981; Mexico's more than quadrupled in value between 1977 and 1981. After the boom, imports contracted sharply in Nigeria, from $19 billion in 1981 to $4 billion in 1986, and in Mexico, from $24 billion in 1981 to $12 billion in 1986.

During the boom, export revenues and capital inflows led to a surge in central bank holdings of foreign exchange reserves. This in turn led to rapid monetary growth and higher inflation. In both Côte d'Ivoire and Kenya, for example, money growth accelerated to more than 43 percent in 1977, and inflation reached 21 percent in both countries. Inflation in Nigeria rose from 6 to 34 percent during the first oil boom, then from 14 to 44 percent during the second. Although most economies became overheated, higher export prices did not cause GDP growth to increase significantly above its long-run trend. For example, in Côte d'Ivoire growth was 7.0 percent during the boom years of 1975 to 1980 compared with 7.9 percent during 1965 to 1975.

Not all countries fell into the commodity cycle trap. Botswana, Cameroon, and Indonesia managed their boom revenues cautiously, by minimizing macroeconomic imbalances and easing adjustment in the downswing. Spending did increase in Cameroon and Indonesia in the boom, but the increases were comparatively modest. Indonesia avoided public deficits during the boom itself in 1979–81, and the downward adjustment in spending was rapid once the boom ended; in 1986–87 the government responded promptly to another fall in oil prices by cutting spending. In Cameroon up to 75 percent of the revenue generated during the 1979–81 oil boom was saved abroad, in part through the repayment of public external debt. In the aftermath of the boom, revenue continued to grow faster than expenditure—partly thanks to further growth in the volume of oil exports—so that deficits were avoided until recently. Botswana is an even more dramatic case. Its public spending fell as a share of GDP during the diamond boom after 1983. During the coffee boom of 1986 Colombia also showed exceptional fiscal restraint by cutting expenditures while revenue was increasing sharply.

Careful fiscal management greatly reduced the macroeconomic side-effects of these countries' commodity booms. Inflation either stayed level or increased only slightly in Botswana, Cameroon, and Indonesia. During the boom the real exchange rate actually depreciated modestly in Cameroon and Botswana, while in Indonesia the appreciation was moderate compared with elsewhere. Exports of other goods were satisfactory in all three cases, and import growth remained within bounds.

Principles for managing commodity export cycles

One commonly stated principle for managing commodity price movements is that the revenue from temporary price increases should be saved, whereas income from permanent increases can be spent. Usually this precept was disregarded, or else price increases were erroneously assumed to be permanent. In one sense, though, the principle misses the point, which is that all commodity prices have been extremely volatile during the past decade. Classifying a particular shift as "permanent" or "temporary" in such an environment is uncertain. Policymakers therefore have to ask which sort of mistake is more costly. The cost of assuming a temporary price increase to be permanent is probably higher than that of assuming a permanent increase to be temporary. As the examples of Mexico, Nigeria, and others illustrate, it is often difficult to rein back spending that increased during a supposedly permanent boom—especially if boom revenue was leveraged through borrowing into even higher spending. Delays in adjustment to the fall in export prices lead to further debt accumulation. When the adjustment finally comes, it is more difficult because countries have to cope not only with lower commodity revenue, but also with increased debt service and reduced flows of new lending. A prudent strategy, therefore, is for the public sector to save a large portion of its commodity revenue.

The use to which these additional savings are put determines how quickly the government can respond to changed circumstances. The main alternatives are increasing the country's net foreign asset position (either through repaying debt or accumulating foreign deposits), reducing public domestic debt, or raising public domestic investment. Besides the drawbacks of increased public spending described above, public investment suffers from the defect that it is difficult to reverse: new investment spending is hard to stop for projects under way, and it is usually difficult and time-consuming to sell physical assets once they have been acquired. All this suggests that any additional public investment financed by commodity revenue should be limited to highly profitable projects.

Although not completely without risk, foreign assets are highly liquid and thus can be sold quickly during bad times. Botswana has protected itself against downturns in the diamond market by increasing its foreign exchange reserves to cover two years' worth of imports. Repayment of debt reduces the public sector's exposure to unstable revenues and avoids the monetary pressures caused by reserve accumulation at the central bank. Cameroon (after 1978) and Colombia (in 1986) used their commodity revenues to repay public external debt. Reducing the government's net debt to the central bank would also reduce monetary expansion by offsetting ("sterilizing") the increase in foreign exchange reserves; Colombia used this method in 1986.

In addition many countries could usefully reconsider the balance between public and private saving during commodity booms. If governments save a high proportion of boom revenues, this can help the country to save enough in good times to provide resources for consumption in bad times. As discussed above, however, governments have often spent too much in booms. It may be better in many cases to allow private producers to retain more of the boom revenue, so that they can themselves save during good times to prepare for bad times. If private saving is thought to be inadequate, it may be due more to controls on financial markets, such as low deposit interest rates, than to any inherent defect in private savings behavior. Wise policy would try to facilitate both public and private saving during booms.

Adjustment in low-income Sub-Saharan Africa

In the 1980s low-income countries have faced economic problems similar to other developing countries. These problems include fiscal and external deficits, excess public indebtedness, overall economic contraction, and inflation. However, the problems in low-income countries have been particularly severe. The external debt problem has become even more serious than in the highly indebted middle-income countries, with little prospect for full debt servicing in the foreseeable future. In 1986 the ratio of all external debt to GNP in low-income Africa was 88 percent, compared with 61 percent for the seventeen highly indebted middle-income countries.

The special difficulties of low-income economies arise from their limited flexibility, particularly in the financing of public expenditure. Yet the need to build up social and physical infrastructure makes heavy demands on budgets. External financing is mostly limited to official sources, domestic financing is restricted because of thin financial markets, and the tax base is usually narrow. These countries depend heavily on official development assistance: in low-income Sub-Saharan Africa official development assistance amounted to 12.2 percent of GNP in 1986. However, the way the aid flows were managed may have contributed to the severe adjustment problems that became apparent in the 1980s. The inflow of foreign exchange supported an appreciation of real exchange rates, excessive imports by urban consumers, and a resulting decline of export- and import-competing sectors in the late 1970s and early 1980s. The mismanagement of aid may also have contributed to low rates of domestic saving.

The scarcity of public financing has led these countries to rely on some highly distortionary means of financing, including heavy taxes on the main commodity export. These are usually implemented through low producer prices paid by the commodity marketing board or through differential exchange rates that penalize producers. Import tariffs are another important source of revenue. Low-income countries derive 38 percent of government revenues from international trade taxes, compared with 19 percent in middle-income countries. The revenue system of low-income countries is thus very fragile and subject to wide swings as external conditions change. Their high commodity taxes have also encouraged the growth of black markets and smuggling.

Fiscal and external deficits in Africa

Low-income African countries borrowed heavily in the late 1970s and early 1980s to finance consumption and domestic capital formation in the face of declining export prices and volumes. The fall in export revenues was the result both of their own bad policies, such as heavy taxation of export commodities, and of weak growth in export demand from the industrial countries. High fiscal deficits led rapidly to external borrowing because the level of domestic savings is low in most low-income

countries. In 1986 the average rate of gross domestic saving in all low-income countries besides China and India was only 8 percent of GDP, compared with 23 percent in middle-income countries. In Burkina Faso, Lesotho, Mozambique, and Somalia saving was negative in 1986. The corresponding levels of public and private consumption were unsustainable without external financing.

After 1980 official and private creditors and the countries themselves realized that the rate of public borrowing needed to be cut. The debt troubles of the highly indebted middle-income countries also contributed to a drop in lending to low-income countries. Total net lending to Sub-Saharan low-income countries fell from more than $4 billion in 1980 to less than $2 billion in 1985 (see Figure 3.7). Repayments of principal on past official credits, as well as a drop in new disbursements, were to blame.

The countries were forced to cut deficits sharply. In Kenya the primary deficit (that is, excluding interest) fell from 7.4 percent of GDP in 1981 to near zero in 1985, while in Malawi it dropped from 11.8 percent of GDP in 1981 to 1.0 percent in 1985. Interest payments increased in Kenya from 2.4 to 4.4 percent of GDP during the same period, however, while in Malawi they rose from 4.6 to 6.3 percent of GDP. This meant that the overall deficit improved about 2 percent of GDP less than the primary balance. As with middle-income debtors, external debt service (including both interest and amortization) was a large burden on the budget and amounted to 34 percent of current public revenue in Kenya and 44 percent in Malawi in 1985. Debt service was also a heavy burden on the balance of payments, although severe import restriction allowed current account deficits to improve in line with improved fiscal balances.

Negative rates of economic growth and more realistic exchange rates have dramatically increased the ratio of outstanding and disbursed debt to GNP in many low-income countries, despite the drop in net flows of new debt. In Malawi the ratio of public debt to GNP increased from 56 percent in 1980 to 71 percent in 1985, while in Kenya it increased from 32 to 51 percent, in Zaire from 43 to 112 percent, and in Zambia from 61 to 133 percent. Unfortunately adjustment to date has been at best a matter of running harder to stay in place.

Exchange rate management in Africa

Overvalued real exchange rates have been particularly common in Sub-Saharan Africa. They are at

Figure 3.7 Net flows of medium- and long-term debt financing to Sub-Saharan Africa, 1980 to 1986

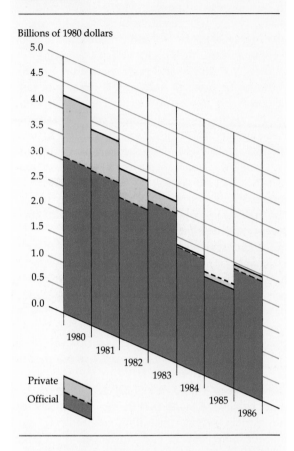

Billions of 1980 dollars

Notes: Net flows are disbursements minus amortization of concessional and nonconcessional lending; figures do not include grants or short-term lending. The deflator used to convert to 1980 dollars is the manufacturing unit value index, which measures the average price of manufacturing exports by the five largest industrial countries. The solid line indicates the level of total net flows, and the dotted line indicates total net official flows. For 1985, net private flows are negative.
Source: World Bank 1987d.

and requiring commodity exporters to sell foreign exchange at this rate to the central bank. Alternatively the government sets domestic producer prices with reference to the official rather than the parallel rate. The official exchange rate is also often used to subsidize certain sectors through the administrative allocation of foreign exchange to these sectors at the official rate. If the government's purchases of foreign exchange exceed its sales, then the tax implicit in the differential between the official and parallel exchange rates exceeds the subsidy to the private sector. The tax is distortionary because it discourages exports. Attempts to evade the tax lead to the growth of parallel markets in smuggled goods and foreign exchange.

Since 1982 many countries have sharply devalued their official exchange rate (see Figure 3.2). Official and parallel rates have converged, which has reduced the export tax and improved production incentives. However, the devaluations can be destabilizing: where other revenue sources are not found to replace the lost export tax, the result may be bigger fiscal deficits and an inflationary increase in money creation. Fiscal reform therefore needs to happen along with exchange rate reform (see Box 3.5).

The need for fundamental reform

As has happened elsewhere in the developing world, fiscal restraint in low-income countries has often damaged the prospects for long-term growth. Spending cuts have fallen disproportionately on public capital formation, as in the middle-income countries. Social services have been cut from already inadequate levels. A more selective way to reduce expenditure must be found, by eliminating subsidies to better-off consumers in favor of priority areas such as transport maintenance, primary education, and basic health. Chapters 5 and 6 discuss these issues in more detail.

The tension between stabilization and structural adjustment runs in both directions. Stabilization has sometimes made the task of structural reform all the harder—for example, when it has meant cutting productive investment. But structural reform can also set back efforts at stabilization. Low-income countries face this problem in a particularly acute form. They find it hard to reduce distortionary taxes, for instance, since the lost revenue is difficult to replace. Without a doubt these countries need to reduce the massive protection that they grant to inefficient industries, but the revenue role of tariffs cannot be lightly dismissed. No alter-

the center of the macroeconomic management problems that many countries in the region have faced. The official exchange rate is used as a fiscal instrument in many low-income African countries, although not in the francophone countries, where the individual authorities do not control the exchange rate. Lacking an adequate tax base to finance desired spending, governments resort to taxing the mineral and agricultural export commodities, which account for a large share of the formal sector. Often this is done by maintaining an official exchange rate below parallel market rates

native revenue source could immediately compensate for the loss of revenue that would result from a sweeping liberalization effort. The implication is that trade liberalization must proceed in stages, accompanied by matching fiscal reforms. Replacing quotas by tariffs and adopting more uniform tariff structures are two ways to reconcile liberalization and revenue goals in the short term.

Box 3.5 Exchange rate unification and fiscal balance

The effect on the fiscal balance of closing the gap between the official and parallel exchange rates can be seen in the experience of Ghana and Sierra Leone. Before 1983 Ghana had large fiscal deficits financed by printing money, strict foreign exchange rationing, high inflation, and a strong demand for foreign currency as a hedge against inflation. The black market exchange rate was a more accurate measure of the true value of the local currency (the cedi) than the official rate. The purchase and allocation of foreign exchange at the official rate levied an implicit tax on exports and granted an implicit subsidy on imports. The black market premium was generally more than 500 percent and reached more than 2,000 percent in 1982. Production of the key exports, cocoa and gold, fell sharply during 1970–82 in response to the prohibitive rate of implicit export taxation; real per capita incomes fell 30 percent. Because of the fall in exports and the lack of external financing, imports were severely compressed.

In April 1983 the Ghanaian government initiated its Economic Recovery Program. In October 1983 the official exchange rate was increased from 2.75 cedis/dollar to 30 cedis/dollar, at a time when the black market rate was roughly 90 cedis/dollar. The black market received formal recognition: special import licenses were granted to those who wished to bring imports in through the black market, provided the appropriate taxes were paid. Noncocoa exporters were allowed to retain a fraction of their foreign exchange earnings for debt service and approved imports. The Cocoa Board also had a retention account from 1983 to early 1987. In January 1986 the currency was devalued again to 90 cedis/dollar. The market was split into two tiers in September 1986. Only cocoa exports, debt service, and petroleum imports were to go through the official market, while raw materials and inputs were to pass through an auction market for foreign exchange; consumer goods were excluded. In February 1987 the markets were unified at the auction rate. Consumer goods were subsequently integrated into the auction except for a few prohibited items.

The stepwise devaluation of the official exchange rate was accompanied by fiscal reform to reduce the deficit, thus lessening the need for the export tax implied by the previous difference between the official and black market exchange rates. The fiscal deficit was reduced from 2.7 percent of GDP in 1983 to 0.7 percent in 1986. This was accomplished mainly by dramatically increasing tax revenue, from only 5.5 percent of GDP in 1983 to 13.6 percent in 1986. This allowed the government to decrease its use of the "inflation tax." Wholesale price inflation fell from 81 percent in 1984 to 30 percent in 1986, despite the huge changes in the official exchange rate. Overall the Ghanaian experience is one of successful devaluation accompanied by fiscal reform.

Sierra Leone encountered greater difficulties with exchange rate unification. The local currency (the leone) was floated in June 1986, at a time when the black market rate was five times the official exchange rate. Inflation immediately accelerated from 57 percent for the twelve months preceding the float to 259 percent for the following twelve months. The monetary base increased by 151 percent from June 1986 to June 1987. In reaction, the official exchange rate was artificially fixed one year after the initial float. Since then few transactions have been occurring at the official rate.

The disappointing outcome reflected an underlying fiscal imbalance. During the preceding five years revenue had been greatly eroded; it fell from 16.1 percent of GDP in 1978–79 to 6.0 percent in 1985–86. The sharpest decline was in international trade taxes, reflecting the shrinkage of reported trade flows as goods moved into the parallel market, but domestic tax collections also fell. This chronic inability to collect taxes caused the deficit to increase to 14 percent of GDP in 1985–86. The deficit was financed through a combination of money creation and the implicit tax on exports arising from the difference between the official and black market rates. The effective elimination of the difference led to a drop in the export tax, so the rate of money creation had to rise. Maintaining consumer subsidies on staple foods and petroleum in the face of increased inflation and depreciation increased the deficit further. Thus for fiscal year 1987 the fiscal deficit was about $6.7 million a month. The average monetary base for the fiscal year was the equivalent of $44 million, so that inflation of about 15 percent a month was necessary to generate the "inflation tax" to finance the deficit. This was close to the actual inflation rate of about 11 percent a month for this period.

The experience of Sierra Leone illustrates that floating the official exchange rate by itself does not solve a macroeconomic imbalance—indeed, without accompanying fiscal reform it may actually make it worse. The Sierra Leonean float was implemented when the fiscal balance was out of control. Fiscal reform is often a prerequisite to unify dual exchange rates.

In summary, the fiscal problems of the low-income African economies are even more severe than those of the middle-income debtors and commodity exporters. Past fiscal deficits have left a legacy of debt that complicates their present adjustment efforts. Impressive reductions in fiscal deficits have been achieved, but they have by necessity focused on unsustainable short-term measures. The scarcity of public revenue sources is cramping attempts to correct structural distortions, such as large gaps between official and parallel exchange rates, high tariffs, and low producer prices for commodities. Fiscal reform is a way to resolve the dilemma. Broader revenue bases would make it possible for the low-income countries to reduce or eliminate some of their most distortionary taxes. A greater flow of external finance, together with selective debt relief, would help support reform.

Fiscal policy and the growth imperative

The developing countries face a fiscal dilemma. On the one hand, departures from prudent fiscal policy have helped to create economic crises involving excessive debt and high inflation. Fiscal austerity in these circumstances was unavoidable. On the other hand, it is essential to restore growth, incomes, and employment. Several of the worst affected countries are in depressions as severe as the Great Depression of the 1930s.

One of the most important lessons from this situation is that overspending and unsustainable growth carry a high cost. Countries that followed stable macroeconomic policies were hurt far less by the turbulence of the 1980s. For example, Thailand surpassed the Philippines, and Colombia outpaced Peru in per capita income in the 1980s, although the pairs were closely matched in the 1970s. The poor also fared much better in the stable economies, although the excessive public spending that helped to destabilize the other economies was sometimes carried out in their name.

The only way to resolve the tension between austerity and growth is to combine fundamental fiscal reform with other measures in trade, industry, agriculture, and finance. The recent progress toward short-term stabilization can now be supplemented with structural adjustment to restart growth. The contribution that sound public finance can make to this task is described in the following chapters. The narrow public revenue base in many developing economies can be expanded through improved tax administration and collection, new broadly based taxes such as the value added tax, and increased reliance on user charges for public services. This would make it possible to rely less on the "inflation tax," excessive trade taxes, and parallel exchange rates, all of which can do great economic harm. Public expenditure can be shifted toward infrastructure and away from subsidies for consumption and ill-chosen capital spending. Reforms in local government and state enterprises can also help to make public spending more effective and revenue less costly to raise. In these ways sound public finance—more perhaps than any other area of policy—offers opportunities to reconcile lower public deficits with long-term economic growth.

4

Reforming tax systems

Reducing the fiscal deficits analyzed in the previous chapter will require some combination of lower public spending and higher public revenue. The following chapters discuss lowering and redirecting public spending. This chapter examines the scope for increasing and restructuring public revenues.

Ultimately public spending is limited by the ability of the public sector to transfer resources from the private sector through taxes or charges on *current* economic activities, or to issue public debt secured by taxes or charges on *future* economic activities. Other sources of finance are either temporary or corrosive, as in the case of money creation in excess of real economic growth, or of minor importance, as is income from public property, licenses and fines, and other nontax revenues (see Figure 4.1). This Report focuses, therefore, on taxes and user charges (or public prices) as the primary means of financing public spending.

Taxes are unrequited, compulsory payments collected primarily by the central government. In contrast, user charges are payments in exchange for specific publicly provided goods and services and are collected primarily by state-owned enterprises and local governments. The relative importance of these two sources of public revenue is difficult to establish because the financial accounts of state-owned enterprises or local governments are rarely available on an aggregate, nationwide basis. Rough estimates exist for a few countries, however. In Thailand during 1977–83 the gross revenue of state-owned enterprises was estimated to be of the same order of magnitude as the central govern-

ment's tax revenue. In Bangladesh gross revenue from state-owned enterprises in fiscal 1985–86 was estimated to be almost double central government tax revenue. The importance of user charges varies from country to country and depends on the number of publicly provided goods and services outside the budget. Nevertheless, user charges are an important component of public revenue—even though only a fraction of the funds they generate is passed to the central government as income tax or as a transfer of the operating surplus of state-owned enterprises.

In principle the criterion for choosing between taxes and user charges is straightforward. Charges should be used wherever a publicly produced good or service can be sold and should reflect some measure of the cost—preferably the incremental cost—of production (see Box 6.1). This is an efficient way to fund necessary public expenditures. Tax financing should be reserved for cases where user charges are not appropriate: to pay for public goods whose costs or benefits cannot be assigned to individuals, to compensate for market failures (such as externalities), or to achieve a distributional goal (such as alleviating poverty).

User charges can provide substantial revenue. A recent study on Sub-Saharan Africa put the proceeds from modest increases in charges at roughly 20 to 30 percent of central government revenue or 4 to 6 percent of GDP (see Box 4.1). In practice, though, taxes remain the principal source of income for central governments. Tax reform has therefore become an increasingly important aspect of structural adjustment and stabilization. Indeed,

Figure 4.1 Share of tax and nontax revenue in central government current revenue, 1975 and 1985

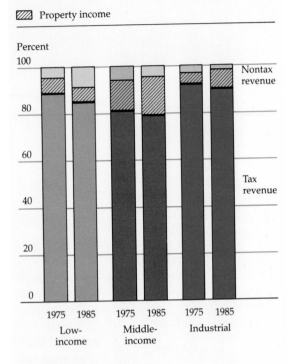

Notes: Figures are unweighted and represent the average pattern for countries in the sample. The low-income sample includes seventeen countries. The middle-income sample includes thirty-three countries; the larger role of nontax revenues in middle-income countries reflects the classification of oil royalties. The industrial sample includes seventeen countries.
Source: IMF, *Government Finance Statistics,* 1987.

to be successful, tax reform must serve both these goals at once. However, this may not always be the case: lower international trade taxes in pursuit of structural adjustment can run afoul of revenue and other constraints; higher taxes aimed at reducing budget deficits can hinder the efficient allocation of resources or make the poor worse off.

This chapter examines the scope for reforming the main central government taxes. User charges are discussed in more detail in Chapters 6, 7, and 8. Price ceilings, quantity restrictions, and other devices analogous in some ways to taxes are not covered; nor are taxes that generate little revenue (poll taxes and stamp duties, for instance). Taxes on property, which are often important at the local level, are discussed in Chapter 7.

Patterns of taxation

Patterns of taxation differ from country to country both in level and composition. These are considered in turn.

Tax levels

On average, taxes have risen slightly as a proportion of GDP since 1975 in all broad country groups (see Figure 4.2, top). However, this disguises wide variation from country to country. The tax-GDP ratios for Botswana, Italy, and Yemen Arab Republic grew much faster than the average of their groups, while the ratios for Sri Lanka, Venezuela, and Zimbabwe fluctuated sharply from year to year, and those for Brazil, Canada, and Turkey were lower in 1985 than in 1975.

Tax-GDP ratios appear to rise with per capita income, but the wide variation across countries suggests that income growth is only a partial explanation. For example, the average tax-GDP ratio for countries in Sub-Saharan Africa, which are primarily low-income, is similar to that for countries in Latin America and East Asia, which are primarily middle-income—and higher, than the average ratio of South Asia's low-income countries (see Figure 4.2, bottom).

Tax composition

Tax revenue is usually considered under two headings: direct taxes on individuals and firms, and indirect (commodity) taxes on goods and services.

Direct taxes include taxes on personal and company income as well as other direct taxes, consisting mainly of social security contributions, payroll taxes, and taxes on property and wealth. Indirect or commodity taxes include domestic taxes, such as broadly based taxes on turnover, value added, and sales, as well as excises on specific goods; and taxes on international trade, namely import duties, export taxes, and cesses.

Difficulties over definitions and lack of data make it hard to compare tax patterns across countries. Nonetheless two important points seem clear. First, trade taxation is insignificant in industrial countries; second, developing countries rely very heavily on commodity taxes (see Figure 4.3). Low-income countries collect almost three-fourths of their tax revenue, and middle-income countries almost one-half, through commodity taxes. Excises and import taxes account for approximately two-thirds of this.

The growing experience with user charges in developing countries suggests that their benefits have been understated and their costs exaggerated (see Chapter 6). The main advantages are efficiency, equity, and revenue, as discussed below.

Efficiency

Unlike taxes, most user charges do not involve a trade-off between revenue and efficiency. Setting the price of a publicly produced good or service equal to marginal cost is often efficient (for some qualifications see Box 6.1). Charging less than marginal cost leads to excess demand and the need to generate funds from other activities, which can create distortions elsewhere in the economy. These economic costs must be added to the efficiency loss associated with expanding underpriced public services. Setting prices correctly generates revenue while ensuring an efficient allocation of resources.

Equity

The tradeoff between efficiency and equity may be overstated for user charges. At present there are many subsidized services in developing countries that disproportionately benefit the better-off. Rationing is required when production of subsidized goods is curtailed by the lack of financial resources. In these circumstances the poor often do not gain access to rationed public goods and services. By charging marginal cost prices to most users or beneficiaries while targeting limited subsidies to poor consumers (for example, through lifeline or multiblock pricing arrangements for water and power services, as described in Box 6.1), it is possible to improve efficiency and relieve poverty at the same time.

Revenue

User charges are also a potentially important source of revenue. The public revenue aspect of user charges is not readily apparent in standard fiscal statistics be-cause this revenue is not transferred to the central budget directly. At best, net not gross, revenue is transferred to the revenue account of the budget or subject to profit taxes. More often the services concerned fail to generate a surplus. In such cases higher user charges will reduce the need for borrowing or transfers from the budget to pay for such expenditures.

A recent study on Sub-Saharan Africa has linked the limited use of user charges for infrastructure services, such as electricity, water, roads, and telecommunications, to revenue shortfalls that worsen the central government's budget deficit, undermine the quality of service, and restrict the provision of services to low-income groups and regions. The study estimates gross investments in infrastructure (water, electricity, telecommunications, and roads) at $6 billion in 1987 in the region's oil-importing countries. Suppose the value of these assets is twelve times current investment, then a 5 to 6 percentage point increase in the financial rates of return on the capital stock could generate more than $3.6 billion, or approximately 20 to 30 percent of current central government revenue.

Raising prices and user charges to levels closer to marginal supply costs could generate additional revenue to reduce, and possibly eliminate, deficits in the consolidated enterprise accounts—the primary source of budget deficits in many Sub-Saharan African countries. Greater reliance on user charges might also reduce instability in public revenue, because demand for services is much less volatile than revenue from trade taxes—particularly on primary commodities—a major source of current revenue. Finally, revenue from user charges could finance an expansion of services. In this case the reduction in net deficits may be small, but welfare would increase.

In spite of qualifications and limitations to the estimates above, the revenue potential is large enough to suggest that user charges are worth exploring in other developing countries as well.

In industrial countries income and other direct taxes account for 69 percent of total tax revenue. The weight placed on personal income (27 percent) and social security taxes (31 percent) in industrial countries is feasible because the necessary administrative apparatus exists. (Even so, other factors are evidently at work; among this sample of industrial countries the revenue share of personal income taxes ranges from Norway's low of 9 percent to Australia's high of 56 percent.)

Personal taxes are hard to collect in predominantly rural, agricultural economies, where people are widely dispersed. Taxes on company income—including taxes levied on the profits of commodity exporting firms, especially mining and agricultural estate operations—present fewer administrative difficulties. Company taxes are therefore relatively more important in the revenue structure of developing countries.

Cultural and historical factors also influence tax composition in developing countries. On average low- and middle-income countries raise roughly 10 percent of their tax revenue through personal income taxes. Surprisingly, however, the richer Latin

Figure 4.2 Trends in ratios of tax revenues to GDP, 1975 to 1985

(percent)

■ Industrial   ■ Middle-income   ■ Low-income

□ Middle East and   □ Latin America
North Africa   and Caribbean
■ Sub-Saharan Africa   ■ East Asia   □ South Asia

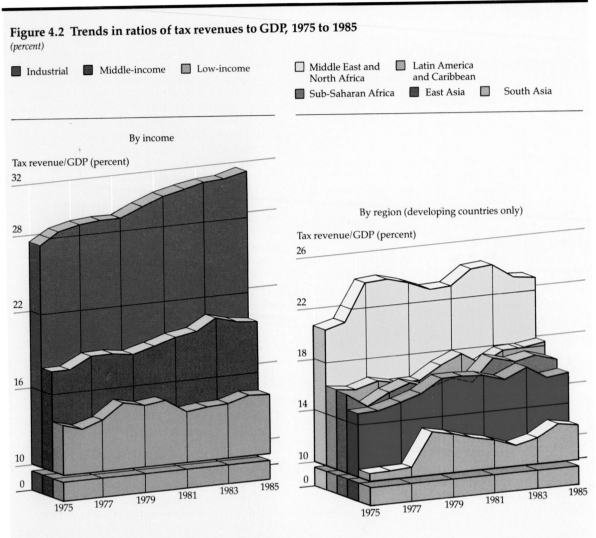

Notes: Figures are unweighted and represent the average pattern for countries in the sample. The sizes of the low-income, middle-income, and industrial samples are given in Figure 4.1. The Middle East and North Africa sample includes seven countries; the East Asia sample, six countries; the Latin America sample, twelve countries; the Sub-Saharan Africa sample, seventeen countries; and the South Asia sample, four countries. Data are for central government tax revenue. Inclusion of state tax revenue in federal systems, such as in Brazil and India, will change the absolute magnitudes but not the trends or relative rankings.
Sources: IMF, *Government Finance Statistics*, 1987, and World Bank data.

American countries raise a smaller share of revenue from personal income taxes than do the poorer countries of Sub-Saharan Africa, where the personal tax base is limited to public employees and employees of large firms, particularly multinational firms. In contrast, Latin American countries are the dominant users, within developing countries, of social security taxes, which fall primarily on wage income (see Figure 4.4).

The revenue shares of general commodity taxes (that is, taxes on sales, value added, and turnover) are similar across three of the four developing country groupings. Again this masks important differences. General commodity taxes in Latin America are usually value added taxes (VATs); in Africa, Asia, and the Middle East they are usually taxes on turnover or manufacturer's sales. (In industrial countries general commodity taxes are typically retail sales or comprehensive VATs.) Governments in Asia and Latin America collect excises on a wide variety of goods and services; in Africa and the Middle East excises apply to comparatively few products. Reliance on import taxes also varies by region. Sub-Saharan Africa depends on them most, followed by the Middle East, Asia (particularly South Asia), and Latin America. Export taxes matter more in Sub-Saharan Africa, Asia, and Latin America than in the Middle East; overall, however, their role is small and declining (see Figure 4.4).

In summary, there is a clear difference in the composition of taxes between industrial and developing countries and to a lesser extent between groups of developing countries. The differences between industrial and developing countries mainly reflect the difficulties of taxing informal sectors (such as subsistence agriculture, and informal production and distribution) with the limited administrative capacity available in the developing world. The differences between groups of developing countries are partly a matter of varying stages of development and partly a reflection of historical and cultural factors.

Objectives and constraints in tax reform

Governments attempt to use tax systems to achieve many goals; raising revenue is only one of them. To facilitate compliance and collection, however, a tax system must be administratively feasible. For the same reason, but also as an end in itself, it must spread its burden equitably. To avoid misallocating resources, it must not upset the patterns of production, trade, consumption, saving, and investment. All these aims can rarely be satisfied simultaneously, so tax reform is a matter of tradeoffs.

The need for revenue

Over the long term, revenue cannot lag behind expenditure. So unless public spending is expected to grow at the same rate as national income, the government should ideally choose tax bases that will expand in tandem with spending, not GDP. Since spending plans can change, tax revenue should be generated by a few broadly based instruments. Changes in a few tax rates will then be all that is required to adjust the revenue total.

It makes little sense to seek a norm for tax-GDP ratios. The opportunity cost of raising more revenue, the benefits to be derived from extra public spending, and the cost of servicing public sector debt all change over time and differ across countries. Decisions on public spending, borrowing, and revenue are highly interrelated; if they are to be set, they must be set jointly.

Higher tax-GDP ratios may be necessary in some

Figure 4.3 Variations in tax composition, by income group, 1975 and 1985
(percentage of tax revenue)

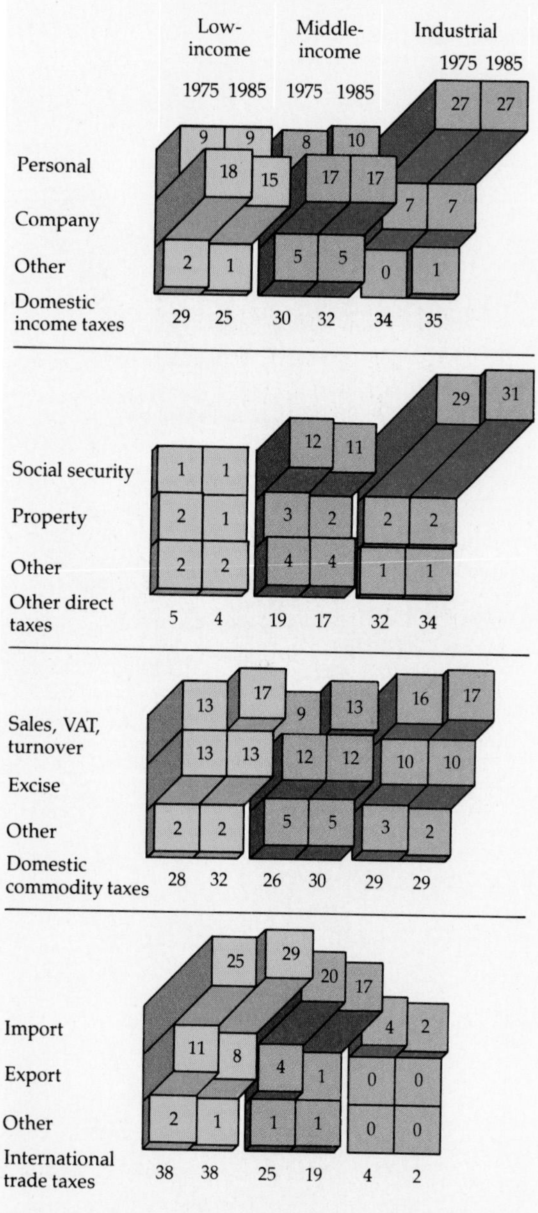

Notes: Figures are unweighted and represent the average pattern for countries in the sample. Totals may not add to 100 because of rounding. The sample sizes are given in Figure 4.1.
Sources: IMF, *Government Finance Statistics*, 1987, and World Bank data.

countries where public deficits are high and unsustainable and where feasible public spending cuts cannot reduce the deficit as required. What matters is how any such increase is brought about. Experi-

Figure 4.4 Variation in taxes, by regional group, 1985
(percentage of tax revenue)

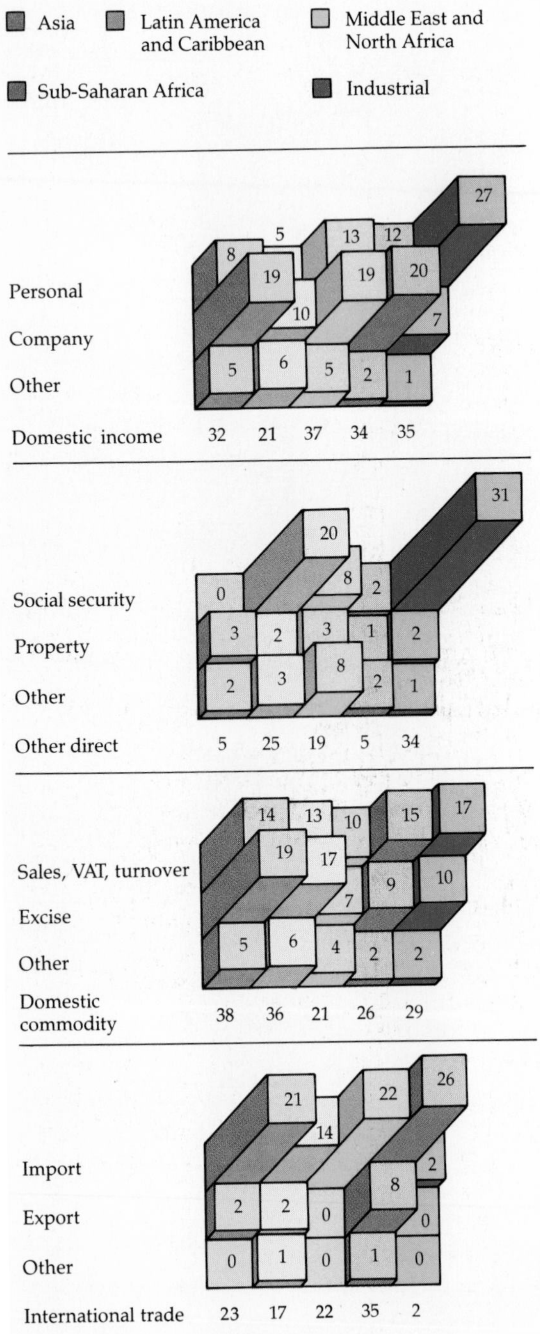

Asia ■ Latin America and Caribbean ■ Middle East and North Africa ■
Sub-Saharan Africa ■ Industrial ■

	Asia	Latin America	Middle East	Sub-Saharan	Industrial
Personal	8	5	19	13	12
Company		19		19	20
			10		7
Other	5	6	5	2	1
Domestic income	32	21	37	34	35

			20		31
		0		8	2
Social security	3	2	3	1	2
Property			8		
Other	2	3		2	1
Other direct	5	25	19	5	34

	14	13	10	15	17
		19	17		
Sales, VAT, turnover			7	9	10
Excise					
Other	5	6	4	2	2
Domestic commodity	38	36	21	26	29

		21		22	26
			14		
Import				8	2
Export	2	2	0		0
Other	0	1	0	1	0
International trade	23	17	22	35	2

Notes: Figures are unweighted and represent the average pattern for countries in the sample. Totals may not add to 100 because of rounding. The sample sizes are given in Figure 4.1.
Sources: IMF, *Government Finance Statistics*, 1987, and World Bank data.

ence suggests that increases in tax-GDP ratios should be gradual. During the late 1970s and early 1980s some countries (Kenya, Malawi, and Senegal, for example) increased their tax-GDP ratios by 3 to 4 percentage points in the short span of five or six years. The increases were soon eroded. Even if tax-GDP ratios can be increased, domestic saving may fall if public saving rises by less than private saving falls, as happened in Senegal.

In the short run the urgency of deficit reduction will generally necessitate the use of easily activated taxes. In developing countries this has often meant increasing international trade taxes, as in Argentina, Kenya, the Philippines, and Thailand in the early or mid-1980s (see also Chapter 3). However, these taxes are among the most damaging for the efficient allocation of resources. Since quick fixes have a tendency to become permanent, the cumulative effect of repeated short-term measures can seriously distort the system of taxation. In such circumstances there is a strong case for fundamental reform. Jamaica, Malawi, and the Philippines implemented such reforms in the mid-1980s.

The concern for efficiency and growth

Any intentional change in tax revenue will require a change in the base or rate of some tax. Firms and households will then shift resources from heavily taxed activities to lightly taxed ones. When market prices reasonably reflect social costs and benefits, this poses a tradeoff between revenue and efficiency. Sometimes market prices may not reflect social costs and benefits. Taxes can then improve the allocation of resources, but only if the market imperfections can be quantified so as to guide the design of the tax structure. Such cases are rare. A safer course is to aim for a tax structure that is relatively neutral: one that generates the necessary revenue with the least effect on the allocation of resources.

As a rule the economic cost of taxation increases more than proportionately with the rate of taxation. In other words, the economic cost of a tax levied at 15 percent is likely to be substantially more than three times those of a tax levied at 5 percent. The narrower the base, the higher the tax rate will have to be to generate a given amount of revenue. This is one of the strongest arguments in favor of broadly based taxes.

Evidence on the efficiency losses resulting from taxation in developing countries is sparse. Studies of the tax structure in India, Kenya, and Pakistan in the early 1980s suggest, however, that the efficiency or economic cost of increasing trade taxes is higher than that of increasing domestic taxes and that the economic cost of taxes on all sales (that is, turnover taxes) is higher than that on the sale of final goods only (that is, retail sales taxes and VATs). A recent study on the Philippines focused on the economic cost of trade taxes versus domestic commodity taxes; its results are shown in Figure 4.5. The study found that the marginal (incremental) economic cost of trade taxes is higher than that of domestic taxes and that this cost rises with the rate of the tax. While the magnitudes are case-specific and reflect the prevailing structure of taxes and assumptions about their interactions, the direction and pattern of these findings are consistent with those of other studies.

The pursuit of equity

Tax reform raises questions of equity. This has many dimensions. Equity in the distribution of household expenditure may matter more than in the distribution of personal income. Attention has traditionally focused on income distribution, however, and on the distinction between horizontal and vertical equity. Horizontal equity asks how those with similar incomes are treated: it is concerned, in other words, with fairness. Vertical equity refers to the scope for reducing income inequality by taxing the rich more heavily than the poor.

Taxes in developing countries often fail badly in terms of horizontal equity because the coverage of tax instruments is spotty and arbitrarily enforced. The tax net may capture income in some formal activities, but not its equivalent in informal or hard-to-tax formal activities, such as professional services. This undermines the system's credibility and the average taxpayer's willingness to pay. Even in terms of vertical equity, tax systems in developing countries are not notably successful, despite the fact that they would generally be highly progressive if their rate structures were fully applied. But that is rarely so. A 1978 study of income tax in Argentina found that 80 percent of gross income was not reported and that only 30 percent of 1.6 million people eligible to pay taxes on nonwage income did so.

In practice it seems that taxes do little to change the overall distribution of income. Their important role in the pursuit of equity is to raise the revenue needed to pay for distributive spending, particularly to alleviate poverty. So it is public finance broadly defined—taxes and spending together—

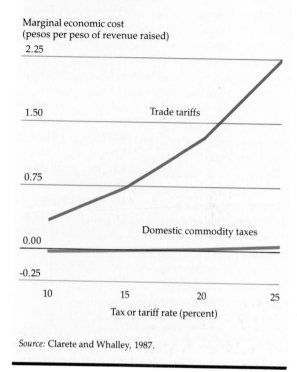

Figure 4.5 Marginal economic costs of raising revenue from tariffs and domestic commodity taxes in the Philippines

Marginal economic cost
(pesos per peso of revenue raised)

Trade tariffs

Domestic commodity taxes

Tax or tariff rate (percent)

Source: Clarete and Whalley, 1987.

that matters for equity, not the structure of taxation alone.

Consistency with administrative capacity

Lack of trained administrative personnel and the accounting sophistication of taxpayers prevent many developing countries from applying broadly based income or consumption taxes. Instead they have to rely on taxes on trade, production, and company income. These can be collected from relatively few sources. Given the staffing and resource limitations in developing countries, tax reform must give preference to taxes that are simple and enforceable. But this preference is not unlimited. Sometimes simplicity can conflict with fairness because it means that taxes pay no heed to the varying circumstances of the taxpayers. Sometimes it can lead to inefficiency, too.

For example, the *administrative* costs of trade and excise taxes normally range from 1 to 3 percent of revenue collected. The corresponding figure for VATs can be as high as 5 percent; for personal income taxes it can reach 10 percent. However, the *economic* costs of trade and excise taxes are often higher than those for income taxes and VATs. Reform of the tax structure must try to weigh these two types of cost. The resulting tradeoff may suggest different systems for different countries according to the existing tax structure, the effectiveness of the administrative apparatus, and the structure of the economy. In Papua New Guinea trade taxes are low, and the administration of an income tax or VAT would be extremely difficult, so the government has been advised to increase revenue from trade taxation. In Thailand, by contrast, trade taxes are high and have created serious distortions; the government has been advised to shift toward a simple VAT.

The next two sections examine the options for improving the design of commodity and income taxes. However, ultimately it is the *interaction* of the different taxes that determines revenue and influences economic behavior. For example, increasing domestic or trade taxes on inputs used in production may reduce the revenue collected from taxes on company profits. It is important that tax reforms also take account of these interactions.

Commodity taxation

Commodity taxes are taxes on the transaction of goods and nonfactor services. They include the array of taxes on domestic production and consumption, as well as those on international trade. Reducing the distortionary effects of commodity taxes can be important for two reasons. First, they currently account for 50 to 70 percent of all tax revenue in most developing countries (see Figure 4.3). Second, in the early stages of development governments often rely heavily on the least desirable sort of commodity taxes, namely turnover taxes on domestic production and taxes on international trade. These latter taxes are often used because they generate revenue with limited administrative costs. As economic and administrative conditions change, however, it is useful to reassess the tradeoff between the administrative and economic costs of these tax instruments.

Taxes on domestic production and consumption

Production taxes are levied on goods before they enter the distribution chain. Often they fall on transactions between producers, such as the sale of an intermediate good. As such they affect production decisions and feed through the system of production to affect consumption decisions also. In contrast, taxes on the sale of final goods only—consumption taxes—do not generally affect the efficiency of domestic production. They are therefore a better way to raise revenue. Commodity taxes, whether on domestic production or consumption, can be general or selective.

GENERAL COMMODITY TAXES. The most common general tax on production is the turnover tax. Its base is every sale—whether between firms or between firms and consumers. As such it is a multistage tax, activated at every stage of the production-distribution chain. Turnover taxes are relatively easy to administer because they do not require tax authorities to differentiate between different kinds of transactions. This simplicity is bought at the expense of distorting transactions between producers. In addition this tax ''cascades'': tax liabilities accumulate as each succeeding transaction adds tax to that already paid at previous stages of production and distribution. This increases the price of outputs that use taxed inputs, as in exports, and it generates differential taxation of consumption even when the turnover tax is applied at a single rate.

Under a pure consumption tax all domestically consumed goods, whether imported or produced locally, would be taxed at the retail stage. Rates may vary for different consumer goods, but similar goods would be subject to the same tax rate independent of origin. All inputs into production—intermediate products, raw materials, and capital goods—and all exports would not be taxed. As a result consumption taxes have some general advantages over other broadly based taxes. Unlike production taxes they do not interfere with producers' choices between intermediate inputs, or between the latter and factors of production (capital, land, and labor). Consumption taxes also do not cascade through the production process and do not create incentives for firms to avoid tax liabilities through vertical integration. In contrast to taxes on international trade, they do not favor production of import-substitutes or reduce incentives to produce for export.

Commodity taxes on consumption are of two types. The first is a general sales tax on final goods imposed at the retail level. This ensures that all consumed goods are taxed, but leaves other goods tax free. The second is a value added tax (VAT). In its most popular version the VAT is a tax on consumption. Applied to all transactions in the production-distribution chain up to and including the retail stage, it has the same final tax base as a retail sales tax. Each intermediate purchaser in the chain is able to credit taxes paid on purchases against taxes due on sales. All inputs are therefore, in effect, tax free. The final purchaser—the consumer—has no means of crediting, and thus all sales at this stage are taxed. The rate is set to zero for exports. Thus, both general sales taxes and comprehensive VATs have the economically desirable properties of commodity taxes on consumption.

Retail sales taxes are rare in developing countries because of the prominence of informal distribution networks. Instead, single stage manufacturer's sales taxes are commonly used, as in the Philippines (before 1986) and Kenya. In some developing countries the pattern of sales taxes and excises resembles a turnover tax—the sales taxes in Zambia and Tanzania, for example, or the excises in the Republic of Korea (before 1976) and India (before 1986).

The VAT has made consumption-type taxes more accessible to developing countries (see Box 4.2). Some distortions between sectors will remain because the VAT, although a high yield tax, can be costly to administer for producers in agriculture and services and for small enterprises generally. However, a movement toward a VAT is likely to promote efficiency while also generating a substantial amount of tax revenue.

India is a case in point. Until 1986 its extended system of excise taxes covered a wide range of goods, including intermediates. It thus resembled a turnover tax. Because of cascading, export prices included a 5 to 7 percent tax. This was only partly offset by rebates. In addition the prices of goods such as cereals and edible oils—especially important to the poor—contained a 5-to-10-percent tax, although they were nominally exempt. India sharply reduced excises on intermediate goods in 1986 by implementing a modified VAT through the manufacturing stage. A higher rate is required to raise the same revenue as before, because the tax base shrinks from gross output to net output. However, the new tax will interfere less with production and trade decisions.

SELECTIVE COMMODITY TAXES. Some taxes, by their nature, cannot be broadly based. Taxes to correct for specific market failures, such as externalities, are best restricted to a few goods only, because a great deal of information is needed to determine the appropriate rate structure. Taxes to cover specific spending programs—fuel taxes to re-

cover road use costs, for instance—are sometimes necessary, but the rates cannot deviate significantly from taxes on close substitutes. Studies on the Philippines, Thailand, and Tunisia found that petroleum taxes led producers and consumers to switch to other fuels. Other selective taxes include traditional excises on demerit goods such as alcohol and tobacco, and luxury excises on goods such as cars or jewelry.

Governments generally set the base and rates for these selective taxes for ease of collection; thus the taxes are often not well integrated with the broadly based taxes. This is of greatest concern for excise taxes, which are an important source of revenue in most developing countries. In contrast to broadly based taxes, many excise rates are specified per unit of quantity rather than as a proportion of the price. Therefore excises can be regressive and not insulate revenues against inflation. Where inflation proofing is desired, the tax rates should be set relative to prices rather than quantities. For excises on goods such as tobacco and alcohol, it is also possible to retain specific rates, provided there is periodic adjustment for inflation and the rate structure is differentiated to reflect distributional considerations.

The case for some progressivity in commodity taxes is strengthened by the limited coverage of personal income taxes and the scale of evasion by the highest income groups. So, for example, governments that collect the bulk of their domestic commodity tax revenue from a general tax, such as a single rate VAT, can supplement this with a selective luxury or excise tax with a few rates. The base of such a tax should be goods whose share in household expenditure increases with income—motor vehicles in Indonesia, for instance, or entertainment and recreational services in Korea. Such a tax can be outside the VAT crediting system if it is restricted to final consumer goods. This distinguishes the combination of the VAT plus a luxury excise tax used in Korea and Indonesia from the multirate VAT used in the EC. The latter attempts to promote equity within the rate structure of the VAT and therefore within the crediting system. This increases the administrative burden of the VAT and may be premature for many developing countries.

International trade taxes

International trade taxes generate about a third of the tax revenue in developing countries and are among the easiest taxes to administer.

Box 4.2   The value added tax in developing countries

In 1967 Brazil imposed the first comprehensive value added tax (VAT) extending to the retail stage and applying to all states of the federation. It was designed to ensure greater tax coordination among the states and to overcome the defects of the turnover tax. The Brazilian VAT is based on the destination principle, which focuses on the use of the product. As such it is a tax on consumption or final sales. It is this comprehensive form of the consumption-type VAT that the European Communities adopted in the late 1960s. An alternative type of VAT is based on the origin principle, which focuses on the income generated by an activity. It is used in Argentina and Peru, and some of its features are found in the VAT introduced in Turkey in 1985. The consumption-type VAT is easier to implement and has become by far the most popular version of the VAT in developing countries.

VATs generally replace a multitude of small taxes and can greatly simplify the system of commodity taxation. The consumption-based version has three main advantages. First, by not taxing inputs used in production (for example, through a system of credits), it simultaneously avoids the distortion of choices between inputs; the cascading of taxes, which can lead to inefficient vertical integration; and the presence of multiple effective tax rates in consumer prices. Second, it does not discriminate between imports and domestic production in domestic markets. Third, exports are not taxed. Together these provisions ensure that the tax does not interfere with production or trade.

VATs have become an important source of revenue in many countries. They yield more than 20 percent of tax revenue in about thirty industrial and developing countries. Some twenty developing countries, primarily in Latin America, now have comprehensive VATs through the retail stage. Many others, including some in Sub-Saharan Africa, have taxes with VAT-like characteristics through the manufacturer-importer stage.

VATs at the retail stage are more feasible in middle-income developing economies, such as the Republic of Korea, than in low-income ones, because the formal distribution network is more developed in the former. VATs through the manufacturer-importer stage are increasingly common in lower middle-income countries such as Côte d'Ivoire and Indonesia, since they are easier to implement. Even these VATs can cover large-scale distributors, agricultural estates, and other activities beyond manufacturing. Because of its relatively

high administrative costs, a VAT is often implemented at a rate of at least 10 percent. Where the tax base is narrow, particularly when the tax does not go to the retail stage, it is likely that the VAT will have to be imposed at 15 percent or more to generate sufficient revenues. Despite initial skepticism about high rates, experience (in Brazil and Chile, for example) has shown that rates of about 17 to 20 percent can also be enforced, even for VATs that extend to the retail stage.

A valuable feature of the VAT is its potential for self-enforcement through a system of credits. However, an important requirement for successful VAT administration is to minimize problems of implementation. From an administrative point of view a single rate is preferable to a multirate VAT. To reduce regressivity, the VAT can be supplemented by a luxury tax with two to three rates. Exemptions complicate administration because the distinction between what is exempt and what is taxed is often tenuous or arbitrary. Nevertheless, distributional objectives have led many countries to exempt some basic commodities (such as some unprocessed foods and selected medical items). Zero-rating, a more complex form of exemption that requires refunds and therefore burdens the administration, has been limited to exports by most countries. The need to provide special treatment for small businesses under a VAT is much more pressing in developing than in industrial countries. Various methods for dealing with small taxpayers are used, but all methods present technical and practical problems.

Successful introduction of a VAT depends largely on whether the country has had previous experience with multistage taxes or general sales taxes, the nature of the taxes that the VAT will replace, the lead-in time, and the structure of rates and exemptions, including provisions for small taxpayers. Indonesia and Korea introduced a VAT after two to three years of preparation, whereas Turkey successfully implemented a VAT within two months of its enactment, following a relatively long period of analysis. Administrations with few resources often stress enforcement for large taxpayers and practice restrictive refunds. Such administrative practices weaken the broadbased and neutral features of an ideal VAT. Most successful tax reforms, however, have introduced some form of a VAT, both to reduce distortions in production and trade, and to generate adequate revenues to compensate for revenues lost through rationalizing other tax instruments.

IMPORT TAXES. In principle, taxes can be collected from imports at the border without driving a wedge between the price of imports and competing domestic products, provided the tax on imports has a counterpart on domestic production. In

practice, however, import taxes are used not only to raise revenue but also to protect domestic production and to promote equity in consumption.

In view of these multiple objectives it is not surprising that the typical import tax regime is complex. For imported goods that have no domestic competition, tariff rates are determined by the need for revenue or adjustments in the exchange rate rather than the need to achieve a desired degree of protection. But for competing imports, where protection is the primary concern, rates are often differentiated, with goods for production subject to lower rates than goods for consumption. Rebates or duty drawbacks are often introduced to avoid increasing the cost of production for exporters and for firms that have been granted investment incentives. For equity reasons some basic goods are either exempt from tariffs or subject to very low rates, whereas luxuries are subject to high rates. In some countries strategic or priority imports, including government and parastatal purchases, are exempt from duties. Finally, where high rates do not stem the volume of selected imports, quantitative restrictions or prohibitions are introduced, but these entail a loss of tariff revenue.

The incentives generated by such complex systems are often not transparent. It would be preferable to transfer as much as possible of the revenue function of tariffs to broadly based domestic consumption taxes, such as the VAT, and of the equity function to selective taxes. Quantity restrictions on trade are best replaced by tariffs, and "specific" rates (per unit quantity) should be changed to ad valorem rates (per unit price). These changes would make it easier to rationalize the protective functions of tariffs.

As noted above, a tax on domestic production can also be collected from imports at the border. This will fulfill the revenue function of a tariff and be equally easy to administer without protecting domestic producers. Similarly, if the objective is to restrict the consumption of imported luxuries rather than to stimulate their domestic production, it is better to subject them to a domestic luxury tax rather than a higher rate tariff. In the absence of a retail-level consumption tax, the luxury tax on imports can be collected at the border, with its domestic counterpart collected at the factory gate—as in Indonesia.

In rationalizing tariffs there is a general consensus that protection should be reduced in the long run because it penalizes consumers and promotes inefficient patterns of production. In practice it is hard to cut tariffs quickly because of revenue losses and opposition from the protected sectors.

Moreover statutory tariff rates are a poor measure of the protection provided to domestic producers because of interactions with other taxes. If the domestic producer is subject to a domestic excise or turnover tax and the competing import is not, then the nominal rate of protection is not the statutory tariff, but the difference between the statutory tariff rate and the domestic tax. If, in addition, domestic production uses imported inputs, then the nominal rate of protection is unlikely to be a good measure of the protection afforded to domestic value added. A better measure is the effective rate of protection (ERP). This takes into account the interaction between tariffs on output and inputs. The dispersion of ERPs is often large—larger than for statutory rates—and can include negative rates of protection (see Table 4.1). When calculating ERPs, taxes on domestic inputs must also be taken into account, so restructuring the pattern of protection generally requires a joint review of taxes and tariffs.

Import tariffs also implicitly tax exports. An increase in import tariffs can result in an exchange rate appreciation and the preferential treatment of import-substituting industries. This reallocates resources toward import-substituting industries and away from all other industries, including exports. This is so even when imported inputs are not subject to tariffs; where imported inputs also face tariffs, the distortion against exports can be greater

Table 4.1 Distribution of effective rates of protection for selected countries in East Asia
(percent)

Item	Indonesia, 1987	Republic of Korea, 1982	Malaysia, 1982	Philippines, 1985	Thailand, 1985
Selected sectors					
Textiles	−11–155	..	54	106	118
Intermediates	4–280	40–62	17	15–125	45–60
Machinery	75–82	31	37	116–201	18–37
Transport equipment	6–220	124	74	118	60–90
Summary measures					
Import competing sectors	−30–380	..	27	25	..
Export sectors	−23–11	..	5	−3	..

Box 4.3 Integrating trade and domestic taxes in Malawi

In the early 1970s the tax-GDP ratio in Malawi was relatively low (11 percent), and trade taxes applied primarily to consumer imports. By the late 1970s revenue pressures forced the government to introduce new tax measures annually to generate additional revenue and reduce its budget deficit. During the same period imports were constrained to reduce the trade deficit. Import priority was given to government, aid-financed projects, and necessities–all of which were duty free. As a result the taxable import base shrank. To compensate, tariff rates were first increased on consumer goods, particularly luxuries, and then extended to intermediate and capital imports; finally, taxes were imposed on exports.

By 1984–85 the tax-GDP ratio had reached approximately 20 percent, and it was clear that the ad hoc approach to generating revenue had relied too heavily on easily administered instruments, even though they were likely to have adverse incentive effects. Increasing tariffs and excises on intermediate goods raised the cost of exports—making Malawi less competitive, especially in nontraditional exports such as textiles and even in traditional agricultural exports. The tax rebate system was not functioning well because of administrative problems and restrictive interpretations of the definition of inputs qualifying for rebates. In addition, increasingly high tax rates on imported luxuries and exemptions for imported necessities were creating a protective structure inconsistent with the objectives of industrial development. Finally, increased import tariffs and excises on intermediate goods caused the tax content in consumer prices to cascade and to reduce the already limited progressivity of indirect taxes.

On the basis of a 1985 tax study the government initiated a comprehensive tax reform in 1986–87 to broaden the tax base and simplify tax procedures. The first phase was to eliminate the export tax and reduce taxes on intermediate goods. Revenue losses were to be offset by increasing the rate of the surtax. However, the surtax—essentially a consumption tax at the manufacturer and importer level and less distortive of production and trade decisions—had to be increased by 5 percentage points to 35 percent to offset revenue losses associated with the declining import tax base and the elimination of the export base. This unusually high rate demonstrated the narrowness of the domestic tax base.

Expanding the base to include additional producers and distributors will take a few years and will include, among other things, the introduction of a crediting system within the surtax. This new feature will reduce tax pressure on exports, which results from the taxation of inputs used in production. It will also indirectly tax the informal sector producers and traders who would not be eligible for a credit unless their output is taxed. Distributional concerns in the reformed surtax are addressed by introducing two or three luxury rates, which will apply equally to domestic and imported goods. This will enable import tariff rates on luxuries to be lowered and restructured so as not to inadvertently stimulate their production relative to necessities. The joint determination of domestic and trade taxes will allow improvements in trade tariff incentives without losing revenue. However, revenue needs will still set limits on the extent to which the tax structure can be rationalized in the short run.

---

still. Many developing countries have tried to deal with this using export subsidies, export rebates, or duty drawback systems. Their record of success is mixed. When there is no paper trail of taxes and tariffs paid, it is difficult to avoid over- or undercompensating different exports, although well-administered schemes, as in Korea, have been reasonably successful. Linking information about tariffs and the VAT may improve such crediting schemes, because the VAT provides a fuller record of taxed transactions. The standard design of a VAT automatically eliminates the need for a separate export rebate for taxes on domestic inputs.

During a fiscal crisis trade liberalization can falter for revenue reasons. Import tariffs on inputs are, in effect, also a tax on export production. This weakens the case for increasing tariffs on inputs to

compensate for revenue losses when tariffs on output are cut. Joint reform of tariffs and taxes then becomes desirable, as in Malawi (see Box 4.3). Restructuring trade tariffs and domestic taxes to produce a broadly based consumption tax should be the primary objective of tax reform in countries that do not already have one. Such a tax can become an important source of revenue.

Where rudimentary taxes on consumption are already in place, their role as a source of revenue should be increased at the expense of tariffs. This could be achieved by an increase in the tax rate with a compensating reduction in tariff rates. In the long run an increasing amount of revenue can be generated from taxing domestic activities. The development of the manufacturer's stage VAT in Côte d'Ivoire illustrates this. In 1960 the tax accounted for 15 percent of total revenue, with 70 percent of its contribution coming from the taxation of imports. By 1982 the corresponding figures were 30 and 40 percent. Thus the tax generated more revenue, with an increasing share coming from the taxation of domestic activities.

EXPORT TAXES. Many countries levy export taxes on primary products. The use of export taxes in mining is less frequent than in agriculture primarily because economic rents in mining can often be captured through company taxation, such as the resource rent taxes in Papua New Guinea. Export taxes are on occasion used, as in Liberia and Zambia, to supplement the company tax. Such use of export taxes is justified to the extent they substitute for royalties. They should not, however, be

greater than the royalties, otherwise they are likely to interfere with the time profile of extraction.

The use of export taxes is more common in agriculture. A 1987 study of seventy-four developing countries found that export taxes were used in at least fifty-three of these countries. In general these taxes did not account for more than 5 percent of tax revenue, but there were exceptions to this observation in selected periods (see Figure 4.6). Export taxes are inadvisable because they reduce the incentive to produce for export. This is inappropriate in view of the slow rates of growth in agriculture and the importance of trade in agricultural products to many of the countries that use this form of tax. Under some circumstances these taxes can be justified as imperfect substitutes for other forms of taxation, but for a limited period only (see Box 4.4).

Box 4.4   Export taxes and agriculture

Export taxes are commonly used in agriculture because traditional taxes on income and profit are hard to administer in this sector. In principle land taxes are an attractive alternative. Where land is in fixed supply, a land tax is collected from economic rent and leaves production decisions unchanged. However, with a few exceptions, such as Ethiopia, Kenya, Paraguay, Peru, and Somalia, land taxes generate less than 1 or 2 percent of total revenue. The low yield reflects the inadequacy of land registration and valuation. In many African countries and the Pacific islands it is difficult to establish ownership because land tenure is based on customary arrangements. In other countries rural land transactions are infrequent, which restricts the use of market prices to determine the value of land. There are also limitations on the use of presumptive measures to link land values to the productivity of land, because data on land quality and the variations in productivity between seasons are generally inadequate.

Some export taxes are implicit and result, for example, from the price-setting activities of marketing boards, such as the Cocoa Board in Ghana and the Agricultural Development and Marketing Corporation in Malawi. These boards act as distributor and exporter of a few important smallholder crops and usually set farmgate prices below border prices, thereby implicitly taxing smallholders.

Evidence on the level of taxation suggests that in some countries producers of agricultural exports may be overtaxed. If export taxes substitute for income taxes, it is possible to compute a rate of tax on exports that will generate the same amount of revenue as a tax on the smallholder's income. A simple calculation for a

typical cocoa farmer in Ghana in the early 1980s reveals that an export tax of 4 percent of the farmgate price would have yielded as much revenue as if the farmer's profits had been subject to income tax. The prevailing export tax was more than 100 percent, which suggests that to the extent export taxes substituted for income taxes, rates could have been reduced substantially. Even as a tax to capture excess profits, the export tax would be only 12 percent.

More important, export taxes create an incentive to shift production to other crops. Given the ample empirical evidence that smallholders respond to prices, the economic costs of export taxes are likely to be substantial. Where feasible, presumptive taxes on agricultural income may be preferable, as in Uruguay.

Other arguments favoring export taxes include the desire to manipulate the terms of trade and the need for revenue. The former should be treated with caution.

Inelasticity of world demand in the short run can lead quickly to loss of markets in the long run because of changes in both world demand and supply. This happened to Ghana and Nigeria's world market share of cocoa and to Nigeria's and Zaire's share of palm oil in 1961–63. Given the large budget deficits in many countries, the need for revenue cannot be ignored in the short run, especially if there is a case for export taxes as a cess or proxy user charge. In the long run extending broadly based commodity and income taxes to also include the agricultural sector is necessary to reduce and eventually eliminate agricultural export taxes.

Figure 4.6 Countries in which agricultural export taxes provide more than 5 percent of tax revenue for selected years

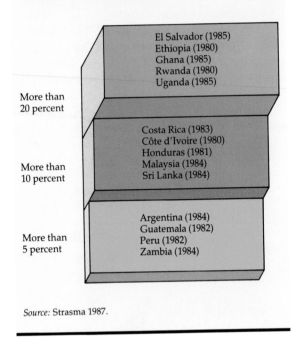

More than 20 percent
El Salvador (1985)
Ethiopia (1980)
Ghana (1985)
Rwanda (1980)
Uganda (1985)

More than 10 percent
Costa Rica (1983)
Côte d'Ivoire (1980)
Honduras (1981)
Malaysia (1984)
Sri Lanka (1984)

More than 5 percent
Argentina (1984)
Guatemala (1982)
Peru (1982)
Zambia (1984)

Source: Strasma 1987.

Income taxes

Income taxes have long been the principal means of taxation in industrial countries. With relatively few distortions they can generate a great deal of revenue and leave scope for income redistribution. Experience in developing countries, however, suggests that personal income taxes are difficult to administer, raise little revenue, are weak in redistribution, and are often unfair. Recent reforms have therefore stressed the role of commodity taxes. Nonetheless, the reform of taxes on personal and company income will often be necessary to enhance the revenue and efficiency of a tax system.

Company income taxes

Reform of taxes on company income is especially important because they account for about a third of revenue in developing countries and have a greater potential for misallocating new investments.

BASE AND RATE STRUCTURE. Company taxes are designed to collect revenue from a firm's economic profits. In practice, the tax base is net accounting profits: gross revenue less operating costs and cap-

ital adjustments. Often a single statutory rate is used and is usually most desirable, particularly when there are administrative constraints. However, a few developing economies use an explicitly progressive rate structure with two to three brackets and a moderate range of 15 to 35 percent. Fewer still use more than three brackets: Guatemala's and Mexico's rates ranged between 5 and 42 percent up to 1987. Finally, some have an implicitly progressive rate structure through the use of differentiated surcharges, as in Brazil.

The statutory rate of the company tax is often a poor indicator of its effect on revenue or investment behavior. Rates apply to financial income not economic income; inflation, for instance, drives the two apart. For policy, therefore, effective tax rates are more important. The average effective tax rate (AETR) is the ratio of total revenues collected through the company income tax to the company's economic profits. For revenue purposes this rate should be high. By contrast, the marginal effective tax rate (METR) measures the effect of taxes on investors' rate of return for an incremental addi-

Figure 4.7 Asset-specific marginal effective tax rates in Malawi, 1974 and 1984

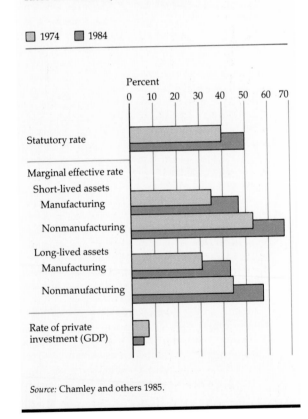

☐ 1974 ■ 1984

Percent
0   10   20   30   40   50   60   70

Statutory rate

Marginal effective rate
Short-lived assets
Manufacturing
Nonmanufacturing

Long-lived assets
Manufacturing
Nonmanufacturing

Rate of private investment (GDP)

Source: Chamley and others 1985.

tion to their activities. To avoid interfering with investment decisions, the METR should be low. The main tasks of company tax design should be to achieve a high AETR while keeping the METR low, or preferably zero, and to avoid large variations in METRs across different types of investment.

Differences between METRs and statutory rates arise from provisions that allow the recouping of invested capital, deduction of interest incurred on investment debt, credits for investment, corrections for inflation, and so forth. As a result a single rate company tax can mean many different METRs across assets and sectors.

A 1985 study of taxes in Malawi found that when statutory rates changed, METRs changed in the same direction (see Figure 4.7). However, METRs in manufacturing were substantially lower than in nonmanufacturing. At a subsectoral level the

METR of an investment project varied according to the economic lifespan of its assets. Since METRs are so hard to observe, it is difficult to use company taxes to steer investment in a particular direction.

It is possible to compare company taxes across countries as well, as in Table 4.2, by positing a hypothetical standard project with a fixed asset composition and a common pretax rate of return, investment horizon, and other relevant parameters. As a result the figures do not show actual after-tax rates of return, which will be affected by variations in the asset composition of projects and by tax enforcement practices. However, they are useful for highlighting on a comparable basis the wide variation between statutory rates and METRs. As is apparent in the table, METRs are equal to statutory rates only by chance. Countries

Table 4.2 Marginal effective tax rates for a hypothetical project investment, circa 1985
(percent)

Economy[a]	Statutory tax rate (1)	All equity financing with loss carried forward		50 percent debt financing with loss carried forward		50 percent debt financing with full loss offset[b]	
		5 percent inflation (2)	50 percent inflation (3)	5 percent inflation (4)	50 percent inflation (5)	5 percent inflation (6)	50 percent inflation (7)
Hong Kong	18.5	18.4	29.5	16.4	17.4	9.6	7.3
Ecuador	20.0	13.5	27.9	10.1	12.8	10.1	9.4
Yemen, Arab Republic	25.0	32.2	62.2	30.5	47.4	30.5	45.4
Colombia	30.0	28.5	47.4	36.9	43.0	14.5	35.1
Korea, Republic of	30.0	33.2	48.0	32.8	52.3	24.6	42.8
Egypt	32.0	37.0	73.9	31.2	56.8	29.2	48.7
Argentina	33.0	31.7	51.0	29.7	42.5	11.2	29.8
Jamaica	33.3	40.6	59.0	35.3	37.1	33.7	28.4
Brazil	35.0	54.4	68.1	45.9	62.9	45.9	62.9
Indonesia	35.0	41.6	81.4	36.0	63.1	34.1	54.1
Philippines	35.0	40.5	81.0	40.2	66.1	31.9	53.3
Thailand	35.0	24.9	68.6	20.0	48.9	18.6	42.6
Jordan	38.0	37.4	64.2	27.3	37.8	25.1	34.6
Tunisia	38.0	24.5	23.0	19.8	20.1	4.9	−60.9
Malaysia	40.0	31.7	62.7	24.2	34.0	20.5	20.9
Portugal	40.0	45.5	79.1	28.7	51.4	28.7	46.5
Singapore	40.0	29.5	46.5	23.2	20.5	15.2	1.9
Guatemala	42.0	10.7	40.3	2.8	39.1	−13.6	39.1
Mexico	42.0	19.6	24.0	10.3	6.9	−20.5	−22.9
Turkey	46.0	45.5	81.5	27.7	47.9	25.6	30.0
Morocco	48.0	44.0	65.3	24.0	65.3	22.9	60.4
Greece	49.0	20.0	68.3	10.6	40.5	10.6	34.1
Ireland	50.0	5.8	11.5	5.5	5.6	−65.9	−54.0

Note: The asset composition of the hypothetical project consists of 40 percent building, 40 percent machinery and equipment, 10 percent vehicles, and 10 percent land. Replacement investment is at the rate of economic depreciation for ten years. Real rate of return before taxes is fixed at 10 percent. Calculations are based on tax code provisions, not actual enforcement. Ireland is included as an example of a tax code with 100 percent depreciation in the first year but no adjustment to nominal interest deductions.
a. Ranked by statutory income tax rates.
b. Refers to the use of negative tax liabilities in the project to offset positive tax liabilities on income from other investments. This can arise either from legal provisions in the tax code, allowing the filing of consolidated returns for a firm or holding company, or through transfer pricing schemes when consolidated returns are not allowed.
Sources: Pellechio and Dunn 1987, and Pellechio and others 1987a and 1987b.

with equivalent statutory rates—such as Brazil, Indonesia, the Philippines, and Thailand at 35 percent or Malaysia, Portugal, and Singapore at 40 percent—can have dramatically different METRs because of other company tax provisions. Equally, differences in statutory rates may not reflect differences between METRs. For example, Ireland's METRs are lower than Hong Kong's despite a much higher statutory rate.

In most cases debt financing lowers the METR for a given level of inflation (columns 4 and 5 against 2 and 3, respectively, in Table 4.2). This creates a bias in favor of debt financing—increasingly so for higher rates of inflation. However, the interaction of inflation and the mode of financing can vary. In Ecuador high inflation increases the METR for equity financing relative to the statutory rate and lowers it for debt financing; in Argentina, Brazil, and Colombia high inflation increases the METR relative to the statutory rate regardless of the mode of financing and despite indexing provisions. If the tax code allows negative tax liabilities in a project to be offset against positive tax liabilities on income from other investments, the METR will be lowered (columns 6 and 7, Table 4.2). It can even become negative, as in Mexico and Tunisia, which suggests an implicit investment subsidy at the expense of the treasury for activities submitting consolidated returns.

The treatment of depreciation, debt, and inflation greatly affects the METR. Valuing assets at historic cost and spreading depreciation allowances over more than one year ensure that tax depreciation will diverge from economic depreciation in the presence of inflation; the recouping of the initial investment is understated and taxable income overstated. When this is combined with full deductibility of nominal rather than real interest on debt, it is likely that the company tax will skew the firm toward debt, as the deductibility of nominal interest rates overcompensates for the real cost of borrowed funds. The firm's reduced capitalization may then increase its vulnerability to external shocks.

There is no single answer to this interlocking set of problems. When inflation is low, the overcompensation of financing costs (due to nominal interest deductions) may just offset the undercompensation of depreciation values based on historic cost. The effect of inflation on revenues would then be limited. Although the incentive in favor of debt finance remains, it is likely to be small and unlikely to justify the administrative complications of schemes to convert financial income into economic income. In such cases the METR can be reduced by lowering the statutory rate. This approach, however, also lowers the AETR, which means a windfall to past investments and a revenue loss for the treasury whether or not new investments materialize. The revenue loss can be partially offset by reducing asset-specific investment incentives. The combination of a lower statutory tax rate and streamlined investment incentives—as in Jamaica and Indonesia, as well as in the recent U.S. tax reform—will reduce tax differentiation between taxed sectors. (It may reduce the difference between the taxed and untaxed sectors.) However, the METR remains positive.

When inflation is high, other measures may be needed. Indexation of historic cost or periodic revaluations are an important step toward bringing depreciation allowances in line with economic depreciation. Periodic revaluation of assets, as in Africa, or various indexing schemes, as in Latin America, have a mixed record. Revaluations are costly and infrequent; indexation is often insufficiently comprehensive to avoid generating distortions between assets or sectors. For example, a move toward economic depreciation must be accompanied by the use of real interest rates, yet nominal interest deductions are rarely adjusted for inflation. Such a correction was recently introduced in Mexico and has been proposed for Turkey.

A simpler alternative is "full expensing." Under this approach, when calculating taxable profits, firms can treat investment expenses like other business costs at the time they are incurred. This relatively new approach has not been applied frequently in practice, but it is similar to the treatment of exploration and development expenses for mining in developing countries. It is also used for the manufacturing sector in Ireland and as an option in the tax codes of Bangladesh and Zimbabwe. Full expensing eliminates the need for indexing, for special rules about inventories, and for estimates of depreciation rates for different types of assets. It would also make it easier to withdraw explicit investment incentives, many of which have the same purpose, that is, to reduce the taxation of returns to new investment.

If expensing is allowed, however, the cost of debt should *not* be allowed as a tax deduction. If an interest deduction is granted, the firm would be receiving a double deduction for assets financed by debt. This can result in a negative METR, as in Ireland. It is appropriate only if there is a strong case to subsidize overall investment and if other activities can generate the revenue to finance such a subsidy.

Full expensing without interest deductions provides, in effect, a zero METR and does not interfere with an investor's rate of return. It also reduces intersectoral differences in incentives and eliminates the bias toward debt finance and thin capitalization. It can be difficult to introduce in some sectors—financial institutions, for instance—and initially it can be costly in revenue foregone, because the invested capital is recouped in the early years rather than over the life of the asset. However, income in later years will not be reduced by depreciation allowances, and tax revenue will then increase—although not to the levels associated with a positive METR. In the ore and hydrocarbon mining sectors in many countries (for example, Cameroon and Nigeria) revenue from company taxes is high because of high economic profits. The taxes imply AETRs of 70 to 80 percent, even though METRs may be negative because of the combined immediate write-off of most investments and the full deductibility of nominal interest. Transition problems make hybrids—with partial expensing, positive METRs, and a lower initial loss of revenue, as in Malawi—attractive. This is an area that warrants further research.

INVESTMENT INCENTIVES. Governments often use explicit investment incentives in addition to those implicit in the tax treatment of depreciation, interest, and so forth. Where market failures can be quantified, there may be a case to use tax instruments to promote efficiency. Special investment incentives include exemptions, tax allowances, tax credits, or special tax reliefs designed to assist particular groups or activities in specified industries or locations. These incentives serve either to reduce or defer tax liability; the latter corresponds to an interest-free government loan over the deferment

---

Box 4.5 Reform of Indonesia's investment incentives

The government of Indonesia adopted a major tax reform in late 1983. Here the focus is on only one aspect of the reform—namely the wholesale elimination of tax incentives for investment.

Before 1983 the tax structure was inordinately complex. Hundreds of ad hoc amendments had been adopted, which created a law that was incomprehensible to taxpayers and tax collectors alike. Many amendments resulted from changing trade and business conditions, and many more were for special nonrevenue purposes, with predictably negative consequences for revenues and unforeseen results on equity and development.

The massive array of incentives in the investment code was designed to favor specific industries, promote exports, develop remote regions, promote technology transfers, strengthen the stock exchange—and even to encourage firms to be audited by public accountants. The numerous and often contradictory tax incentives created an excessively complicated system unable to fulfill its revenue function or to serve the special purposes originally intended.

Investors and the Investment Coordinating Board (BKPM) negotiated many incentives as part of an overall package. These incentives, and the relatively rapid change in both their design and their structure, meant that firms in the same industry were taxed under different rules and that the same firm faced a different tax regime at various times. Such incentives created effective tax rates that varied both between and within sectors and thus misallocated the capital stock. For example, the tax rules created incentives to change the composition of investment toward short-term projects that, in extreme cases, never paid taxes, such as "hit-and-run" projects, particularly in textiles and light manufacturing.

Because of a lack of communication with the BKPM, auditors in the tax department did not know what incentives were available to firms, which resulted in audit conflicts. In addition some firms did not file returns during the tax holiday period, or simply filed blank returns, which made it difficult to audit returns once the holiday period ended.

Finally, nonuniform tax holidays created the impression of discrimination against certain industries, which would then seek extended tax holidays or alternative incentives to offset the perceived discrimination. Problems similar to these existed for every incentive. Tax incentives are difficult to administer, and thus the gains from incentives must be weighed against the increased administrative costs.

The principles underlying the tax reform were administrative simplicity, transparency, and minimum distortion of economic behavior. As a result all special tax incentives—tax holidays, investment allowances, and accelerated depreciation other than double-declining balance—were eliminated. The expected revenue gains from eliminating incentives allowed the tax rate to be reduced. The simplified incentive system is expected to minimize tax-induced intersectoral preferences, while the lowered company tax rate is expected to benefit all investors.

Figure 4.8 Income level at which personal income tax liability begins and the subsequent structure of the marginal tax rates during 1984 and 1985

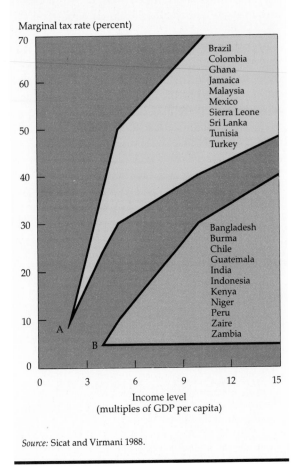

Marginal tax rate (percent)

Brazil
Colombia
Ghana
Jamaica
Malaysia
Mexico
Sierra Leone
Sri Lanka
Tunisia
Turkey

Bangladesh
Burma
Chile
Guatemala
India
Indonesia
Kenya
Niger
Peru
Zaire
Zambia

Income level
(multiples of GDP per capita)

Source: Sicat and Virmani 1988.

new firms. But costs and profits must then be divided between old and new operations, thus causing problems of internal transfer pricing and cost allocation. It makes sense to reduce the number of investment incentives; Indonesia has eliminated them altogether (see Box 4.5).

Personal income taxes

Personal income taxes account for about a tenth of total tax revenue in developing countries. The low yield reflects limited coverage and poor design. Improving the yield requires changes in the base and rates to make the tax easier to administer, without adverse effects on incentives to work and save.

BASE AND RATE STRUCTURE. The typical personal income tax is levied on net taxable income, derived by deducting allowances and exemptions from gross personal income. A schedule of rates is applied to determine tax liability. Tax credits are then subtracted from this tax liability to generate the final tax obligation.

The design of personal income taxes varies considerably across countries. In some countries, such as Ghana in 1984, very low levels of income are legally subject to tax; in others, such as India, exemption rates are quite high. In some the marginal rate increases very rapidly—as in Jamaica before tax reform. In others the rate schedule is relatively flat—as in Côte d'Ivoire. Finally, the highest marginal rate and the level of income to which it applies vary significantly.

Figure 4.8 shows two groups of countries, based on their legal or intended tax structures, not the tax structures as actually enforced. In the group A countries low levels of income are subject to tax, and the marginal tax rate increases rapidly. This structure is difficult to administer since large numbers of small taxpayers are caught in the tax net and subject to high rates. The higher exemptions and more gradual increase in marginal tax rates of the group B countries are better suited to the administrative capacity of most developing countries.

Figure 4.9 shows that many countries have maximum rates above 50 percent. These rates often affect only a handful of individuals—those with incomes in excess of fifty times per capita GDP. High rates on narrow bases generate little revenue and, if not enforced, damage the credibility of the system.

period. Tax incentives for special purposes, however, are often ad hoc and poorly integrated into the overall tax structure.

In general the effectiveness of a tax is inversely related to the number of goals it is meant to achieve. Tax incentives overload tax instruments with multiple objectives. They complicate compliance and prompt unproductive efforts to obtain their benefits. If the incentives are small, the economic gains are likely to be limited. If they are large, the erosion of the tax revenue base is likely to be significant.

Investment incentives are also difficult to administer. Consider tax holidays, for instance. To be consistent, they would have to be granted to existing firms making new investments as well as to

The revenue share of personal taxes has grown slowly in the past two decades. Their base had been expected to expand more rapidly than GDP as more and more activities entered the formal sector. The ability to fine-tune tax rates according to ability to pay was another reason to expect the share of personal taxes to rise. But these factors have been outweighed by the difficulties of enforcement and collection. In many countries personal income taxes are collected from less than 15 percent of the population; in South Asia and Sub-Saharan Africa the figure is less than 5 percent. Almost everywhere the potential revenue from personal taxes is further eroded by avoidance through loopholes and tax shelters, as well as outright evasion. A 1981 study of Bolivia estimated that 75 percent of the revenue due from labor income was collected primarily because of withholding taxes on wages, whereas the equivalent figure for capital income was 20 percent.

Many of the same features that limit the revenue yield of personal income taxes also limit the equity features of these taxes in practice. In developing countries personal income taxes are not the mass taxes they are in industrial countries. The progressivity of the rate structure is therefore less important when 80 to 90 percent of the population, primarily the lowest income groups and those in subsistence or informal activities, are outside the personal income tax net. With the difficulty of enforcing this tax on high-income recipients in agriculture, trade, and the professions, plus the prevalence of a multitude of allowances and provisions benefiting wealthier groups in society, it is not surprising that in many countries it is now recognized that the personal income tax does not significantly improve the distribution of income. However, a less ambitious distributive objective can be attained. Legally excluding the poor from the tax base altogether is a more powerful way to protect them than incorporating lower rates in a multirate structure. Revenue lost from more exemptions at the bottom of the income scale can be largely offset by eliminating loopholes for those at the top. This

Figure 4.9 Maximum marginal tax rate (MTR) and the level of personal income at which it becomes effective during 1984 and 1985

Maximum MTR (percent)	Multiples of per capita GDP at which the maximum rate becomes effective		
	Less than 30	30 to 50	Greater than 50
Greater than 70	Portugal	Republic of Korea Zambia	Burma Morocco Côte d'Ivoire Niger Egypt Tanzania Ethiopia Tunisia Liberia
50 to 70	Ghana Mali Greece Pakistan Jamaica Sri Lanka Malaysia Sudan	Argentina Brazil India Sierra Leone Zaire Zimbabwe	Benin Mexico Chile Nigeria Chad Peru Kenya Senegal Madagascar Thailand Malawi Turkey
Less than 50	Hong Kong Yemen Arab Republic	Burkina Faso Ecuador	Colombia Jordan Guatemala Philippines Indonesia Singapore

Source: Sicat and Virmani 1988.

will also improve the equity features of the tax.

Horizontal equity requires that all sources of income (from agriculture, trade, manufacturing, and services) and all types of income (wages, interest, rent, profits, and so forth) be treated equally. This favors a global income tax over schedular taxes for different sources or types of income. A global tax, however, entails a tradeoff between equity and savings. Personal income taxes can affect the volume of private saving by reducing both the income of would-be savers (usually higher income households) and the returns to savings. The second effect depends on the openness of capital markets and the extent of financial intermediation—that is, the availability of nonbank institutions to attract savings through insurance schemes, social security schemes, pension plans, and so forth.

Some governments have tried to exclude the returns to savings from the income tax base. They have exempted interest from certain types of deposits, for example, small post office deposits in India and Malawi, or interest income up to a ceiling, as in Jamaica. In other countries schedular income taxes are used to tax different sorts of income—such as interest from savings deposits—at a lower rate. Such taxes are used, as in West Africa, because they are considered easy to administer.

There is some evidence, however, that in developing countries changes in the returns to savings may have a greater effect on the composition of savings than on the level. Taxes on the return to financial savings can reallocate savings between different types of assets—for example, between stocks and bonds in middle-income countries (if capital gains and dividend income is treated differently from interest income) or between financial and real assets in lower income countries. These switches can disturb the efficiency of intermediation between savings and investment. Some have therefore argued that personal taxes based on expenditures are preferable to personal taxes based on income; expenditure taxes do not tax income that is saved. However, such taxes applied to individuals, as opposed to transactions, have not yet been implemented anywhere.

It makes better sense to ease the tasks of administration and enforcement by simplifying personal income taxes. Most allowances can be eliminated. Instead the threshold should be set high enough—say up to incomes three times per capita GDP—to exclude most low-income earners, and the maximum rate should be set low enough—say 30 to 40 percent—to reduce the incentive for tax evasion.

Revenue would in any case be low from the very lowest income groups and from those subject to confiscatory rates. A multitude of brackets can be replaced by a few brackets. Even a single rate tax with the fewest number of loopholes and a high threshold can still be reasonably progressive, as, for example, in Jamaica (see Box 4.6).

PRESUMPTIVE INCOME TAXES. One way to improve the income tax is to supplement it with a presumptive tax—a tax assessed not on income itself but on indicators of income—for evasion-prone groups such as self-employed professionals and those employed in agriculture and trade. Income tax assessment has evolved from presumptive to exact methods as indicators of income have gradually been replaced by measures of actual income received. In practice, however, income tax assessment for large numbers of taxpayers in both industrial and developing countries is still largely presumptive.

The francophone countries of West Africa rely on presumptive or "forfeit" taxes more than other developing countries. However, this kind of tax is also used elsewhere. In the early 1980s Turkey's tax authorities noted that 85 percent of taxpayers filing income declarations claimed to be in the lowest tax bracket; audits of cases of suspected evasion found that approximately 50 percent of income was undeclared. The government introduced a system of presumptive taxation in 1983. Indicators of living standards are used to assess taxpayers filing regular tax declarations. A presumptive assessment of certain minimum tax amounts is made for activities in agriculture, trade, and professional practices. Further, specified amounts of income are presumed to be associated with, for instance, ownership of residential property (both owner-occupied and rental), automobiles, boats, airplanes, and racehorses; foreign travel; and employment of personal servants. Tax is levied on the income determined by a presumptive assessment or the taxpayer's declaration, whichever is greater. This system increased tax collections; 84 percent of those who filed declarations in 1985 had their tax liability based on the presumptive assessment.

These methods can also be applied to taxes on goods and services or on wealth, where valuation is difficult. However, experience in countries as different as Colombia and Korea suggests that a considerable administrative effort is still required for any type of presumptive tax to ensure it is based on realistic criteria and applied fairly.

Tax administration

Tax administration in industrial countries by and large carries out the intent of tax legislation; in developing countries tax administrators often make their own tax policy by selective administration.

As a result steps to simplify the task of tax administration are likely to make tax policy more ef-

---

Box 4.6   Reform of Jamaica's personal income tax

The government of Jamaica embarked on a comprehensive tax reform in 1985. It includes changes in the personal income tax, the company tax, and indirect taxes. The reform of the personal income tax is unique. A complicated, narrowly based individual income tax levied under a progressive statutory rate structure—commonly found in developing countries—was replaced by a broadly based, single-rate tax in 1986.

Before the reform the highest marginal tax rate of 60 percent (including payroll taxes) was reached at the relatively low annual income level of less than three times per capita GDP. The provisions in the tax code were complicated. There was no standard deduction, but taxpayers qualified for sixteen separate credits. These credits had been added to the system over the years for purposes that ranged from personal allowances to stimulation of savings and home ownership, and even to employment of helpers in the home. In addition employers could grant nontaxable allowances to employees. These allowances were negotiated between employer and employee, and the results did not have to be reported to the income tax commissioner. The ratio of nontaxable allowance to taxable wage was estimated to average 40 percent.

The tax was difficult and costly to administer. Important disincentives were inherent in the rate structure. Capital gains and interest income were tax free, but dividends were taxed twice. The pay-as-you-earn (PAYE) tax ensured that formal sector labor income was taxed at a high rate but that self-employed income went virtually untaxed. In addition Jamaicans with higher incomes, many outside the pay-as-you-earn system, tended to avoid or evade a substantially higher percentage of the tax liability than did lower income families. This evasion and avoidance all but negated the progressivity of the statutory rate structure. A taxpayer survey suggested that the tax net did not cover about half of the potential individual income tax liability. The complexities of the system contributed to poor enforcement, which compounded the inequities.

The primary objective of the tax reform was to simplify the tax and minimize adverse incentives. This led to several changes in its design: the sixteen tax credits were replaced with a standard deduction equal to two times per capita GDP, the present rate structure was replaced with a single rate of 33 1/3 percent, most nontaxable allowances were incorporated into the tax base, and interest income was included in the tax base.

The tax reform was enacted after a committee of citizens from the private sector spent several months scrutinizing and amending the proposals before recommending its adoption. Another committee of representatives from union, business, and public interest groups also reached a consensus that the revised and streamlined tax seemed fairer than the previous system. From 80 to 90 percent of the population would not pay income tax as a consequence of the relatively high standard deduction. By eliminating loopholes, the tax base would expand, which enabled the maximum statutory tax rates to be lowered. This would in turn reduce the incentive for evasion or avoidance at higher income levels and would facilitate enforcement and collection.

It now appears that the combination of a higher standard deduction, a broadened base, and a lower flat rate has improved administration and increased the progressivity of the tax system. Revenues from company and personal income taxes are also running 18 percent higher in the twelve-month period after introduction of the reform, in part because of improved administration of the streamlined tax.

Perhaps the best indicator that the program has been accepted is the lack of public discontent with the new reform. However, the reform has three significant problems. First, the potential exists for abuse in the few allowances that remain; if the numbers or significance of these allowances grow, they could compromise the fairness of the new structure and necessitate a rate increase to compensate for the narrowing of the base. Second, the standard deduction has not yet been indexed, and this could become another policy problem if the rate of inflation were to increase again. Finally, to avoid burdening lower income savers, there is no tax on the interest from bank deposits below a certain ceiling, which could encourage higher income depositors to split their holdings. All these problems can, in principle, be dealt with by a continuing policy review.

The Jamaican case shows that comprehensive tax reform can occur in a weak economic setting. Jamaica restructured its tax system at the same time it faced a serious exchange rate disequilibrium and a substantial government deficit. The tax system had become so onerous, obviously unfair, and out of control administratively, that there was substantial public support for a major overhaul. This support also reflected the realization that tax rates would have to be increased significantly under the old system because of the country's serious fiscal and external imbalances. In many ways, therefore, the time was right for tax reform.

fective. Administrative reforms can improve the tax structure by bringing reality in line with intentions. But they can also magnify distortions that were dormant when the structure was badly administered. Setting goals for long-term tax policy—broadening the base, say, or shifting the tax base from production and trade toward consumption—can identify needed improvements in administration. So, even though present administrative resources limit the scope for tax reform, thinking about reform helps to set administrative priorities.

In the 1960s and 1970s comprehensive tax reforms focused on instruments rather than on the system as administered. Some of these comprehensive reforms were only partially implemented, as in Colombia, and some not at all, as in Ghana. Some partial reforms paid attention to administrative difficulties (as in Korea, for instance) and were successful. In the 1980s, in contrast, comprehensive reforms placing a greater weight on administration have become more common (such as the reforms in Indonesia, Jamaica, and Malawi). Administrative reforms must try to address the following problems.

Compliance and enforcement

Poorly drafted tax forms, long queues, rude officials, and cumbersome appeals procedures all reduce compliance. Slow—or no—refunds of legitimate claims can foster reluctance to pay taxes in the first place. High tax rates increase the benefits of evasion, particularly if the tax authorities are known to lack the resources to track down the offenders. In most developing countries the sanctions on fraudulent taxpayers are neglible.

For obvious reasons evasion is hard to measure. Defining avoidance and evasion also raises conceptual problems. As a result there are few country-specific or comparative studies on the subject. A 1980 study of the income tax in Indonesia before reform found that, depending on the year, tax evasion ranged from 84 to 94 percent of taxes due on personal income tax, and 76 to 93 percent of taxes due on corporate income. These high evasion rates were blamed on rates too high to be enforceable even by a relatively efficient administration. Realism in tax laws is important.

A 1985 study estimated India's black, or unrecorded, economy to account for roughly a fifth of GDP. Not only was the treasury losing revenue, but evasion was also blunting the allocative and distributive features of the system. For example, tax rates could not be lowered to reduce tax-related

distortions without a loss in revenue given that the tax base had been narrowed by evasion. Other, older studies in the 1960s and 1970s for Chile, Colombia, Kenya, and Nigeria all found similar high rates of evasion.

Poor system design promotes corruption. Reform can reduce the opportunities for taxpayers to bribe rather than pay taxes. One way to do this is to reduce the number of discretionary elements in the tax code (as was done in Indonesia and Jamaica). Another partial solution is to separate assessment and collection (as in Malawi), while ensuring that assessments are not made without regard for what is collectible.

Other measures are also often needed, including reasonable salary levels and more trained officials, particularly those able to audit company and personal accounts and to design and operate computer procedures. A greater capacity to gather and process data would enable administrators to identify assessment and collection problems more easily. Ultimately, though, political backing is necessary for successful enforcement.

Improving collection

The revenue yield of the tax system cannot readily be increased unless ways are found to improve collection.

TAX AMNESTIES. It serves no purpose to have a tax assessed but not paid. In some countries the problem of tax arrears has become so critical that governments have taken emergency measures such as tax amnesties and provisions for rescheduling tax payments. These may make it easier to collect delinquent taxes, but they can also undermine voluntary compliance if used frequently.

WITHHOLDING. The scant auditing resources available in the tax administrations of most developing countries make it impractical to audit more than a small percentage of taxpayers. A system to withhold money from current income is therefore one of the most efficient techniques for preventing deliquency and evasion. Withholding is most commonly applied to wage income, as in the pay-as-you-earn (PAYE) systems in Jamaica, Malawi, and other countries. Withholding is also applied to interest and dividends in some countries, such as Colombia and Indonesia. An effective withholding scheme, however, requires a relatively small number of easily identifiable payers of income. Withholding is hard to apply to rental income, professional income, and small business income, where there are as many payers as receivers.

INFORMATION EXCHANGE. Another approach is for tax-collecting agencies to exchange information. In many developing, as well as industrial, countries import duties and taxes on domestic transactions are administered by separate departments, with little or no exchange of information. In other countries sales and income taxes are administered by separate departments. The exchange of information between these revenue departments is highly advisable because gross sales figures are important in determining income tax liabilities, and valuations of sales for income tax purposes make it easier to implement ad valorem excises and duties.

SELF-ENFORCEMENT AND CROSS-CHECKING. The availability of personal and minicomputers makes the use of self-enforcing taxes–based on matching information from different sources–more feasible than it was a decade ago. It is now possible for information furnished by one taxpayer to reveal the receipts and gains made by other taxpayers, as, for example, in a VAT. The ultimate goal of a linked, self-checking system of taxes, however, is still far away.

COMPUTERIZATION. Automated data processing (ADP) can improve the administration of taxes. ADP systems that perform multiple functions require an integrated master file system. The usefulness of master files depends mainly on a reliable and up-to-date system of *unique* taxpayer identification numbers to distinguish one taxpayer's records from another's. Despite the technical problems, automation may eventually offer the most effective way to deal with expanded workloads in customs departments (with the growing volume and complexity of international trade), income tax departments (with the growing number of taxpayers), and treasuries (which need to forecast and monitor revenues). Such systems are currently being set up in Indonesia, Jamaica, Malawi, and Morocco. They are already partially or fully operational in Brazil, Ecuador, Honduras, Korea, and Nigeria. Experience suggests that ADP can increase the efficiency of well-run operations, but it can exacerbate problems if superimposed on badly organized administrations.

Tax analysis units

Better collection and administration can improve the implementation of tax policy. However, it is also important in most developing countries to strengthen the treasury's ability to analyze revenue options. A tax analysis unit can support policymakers by analyzing the revenue consequences of changes in exchange rates, interest rates, and trade and industrialization policies—all of which affect tax bases and interact with tax rates. It can also weigh the implications of new revenue measures for other policies and forecast revenue to assist in fiscal planning. Such units feature in many of the comprehensive tax reform programs currently under way.

The scope for tax reform

With fiscal deficits high and access to new borrowing limited, there is little scope for deliberate reductions in taxation in the near future. Whether taxes can be raised to cut fiscal deficits depends on the existing structure of taxes and the period over which the deficit reduction is to occur. Where tax bases are narrow, a rapid increase in revenue will call for higher rates. But in some cases higher rates will erode the tax base through evasion. In other cases they will cause inefficiencies in economic behavior, especially if the changes rely on administratively convenient measures such as trade taxes. In contrast, carefully designed tax reform can reduce the cost of raising additional revenue and ensure that tax policy complements other policies. Such reforms take time.

Even in the absence of fiscal deficits, tax reform may be necessary, especially when price regulations and barriers to market competition are being removed, or when there is a case for rectifying an accumulation of ad hoc distortionary tax measures. Recent tax reforms in developing countries have focused on reducing tax-induced distortions and on simplifying tax administration. Reforms are long term but not permanent. Significant changes will be needed periodically to take account of shifting external circumstances or internal needs. (See Box 4.7 on Colombia's reforms.)

No system of taxation can be perfectly neutral with respect to allocation. Nor can tax policy ignore distributional concerns. The balance between the various taxes is a matter of changing priorities and constraints. Where the growth of income is adequate, equity can be given greater weight through expansion of taxes on income. However, where slow income growth and limited administrative capacity are of greater concern, taxes on consumption may need to be given preference.

In spite of the complexity of these issues, some

Box 4.7 Periodic tax reform in Colombia

At the start of the twentieth century Colombia relied almost exclusively on trade tariffs for public revenue. The collapse of international trade in the 1930s sharply curtailed revenues from customs duties and prompted a reform that established the basis of the present tax system, including full-fledged taxes on income, net wealth, and inheritance. This early reform was intended to strengthen public revenues weakened by the effects of the Depression and to increase the importance of direct taxes, especially on capital income.

Since then Colombia has had major tax reforms in 1953, 1960, 1974, and 1986. The objective of the 1953 reform was broadly the same as in 1930: to increase revenue and taxes on capital income, both by raising income tax rates and by taxing dividends. The reforms were carried out in the face of strong opposition by some political groups and were successful in large part because of support from other political groups. By the end of the 1950s taxes on income and wealth were more important, and probably more progressive, in Colombia than elsewhere in Latin America.

Though it set out to increase revenue and impose taxes on capital income, the 1960 reform had the opposite effect in both respects because a wide range of tax incentives was simultaneously introduced to foster investment in manufacturing and exports. These incentives were so heavily used, however, that both the revenue and the progressivity of the income tax declined.

A series of ad hoc reforms, mainly income tax surcharges, were implemented in an effort to close the revenue gap; by far the most important reform was the introduction of a general sales tax in 1963. As a result of strong opposition aroused by fears that the sales tax would be regressive, its implementation was delayed

until 1965. Serious administrative problems soon caused the tax to be transformed into a value added tax at the manufacturing level, and it came to be second only to the income tax as a revenue producer. Administrative problems with income taxation, particularly tax evasion due to high and rising marginal tax rates, also resulted in the introduction of a system of wage withholding and current payments in the late 1960s. These measures helped the income tax retain its importance in Colombia's fiscal system.

The next major tax reform in 1974 reflected Colombia's extensive experience with such reforms. Not only was this reform intended to strengthen revenue as in previous years, but it represented a return to the pre-1960 emphasis on taxation as an instrument of social policy rather than the use of tax incentives as an instrument of economic policy. Ineffective tax incentives were substantially reduced. Additionally, a minimum presumptive income tax was introduced to ensure more adequate taxation of income from capital. Other changes were made to reinforce the role of income (and wealth) taxation. At the same time, however, the rates of the sales tax with value added features were substantially increased, and its base was expanded.

The immediate effect of the 1974 reform was to increase income tax revenue substantially, largely as a result of the new presumptive tax regime. These effects were not permanent, however. The courts had decided that some critical administrative changes included as part of the reform package were beyond the power of the legislative authority. This greatly weakened the ability to enforce the minimum tax. Moreover, a series of rate reductions and amnesties in the late 1970s, intended in part to offset the effects of inflation, not only

---

general prescriptions for tax design can be gleaned from recent experience. Clearly their application will vary from county to country.

- Simplify the design of tax instruments, with fewer rates and fewer adjustments to the base; in particular, eliminate or streamline special tax incentives for investment, production, and trade.
- Strengthen tax administration to improve collection and facilitate the shift in the tax structure from reliance on higher tax rates to reliance on broader tax bases.
- Avoid taxing the poor.

Simplify the design of tax instruments

Simplification of tax instruments applies primarily to the definition of the base and adjustments to it.

This in turn has a bearing on the number of tax instruments and their rate structure.

Commodity taxes could be consolidated into three or four instruments with the following characteristics.

- A shift from the taxation of production to the taxation of consumption. This could be achieved with two instruments. The first is a broadly based, general tax on consumption (such as a retail VAT or a manufacturer's VAT), which does not tax transactions between industries, does not differentiate commodities by source of production (import versus domestic), and does not tax exports (implicitly or indirectly); this tax could have a single rate if equity concerns can be met with a luxury tax. The second instrument is a selective commodity tax for demonstrable and quantifiable externalities and for

eroded the capacity of the income tax to keep up with inflation but, in effect, eliminated the capital gains tax. In 1983 the changes of the previous years were to some extent offset both by regularizing the system of inflationary correction and by strengthening the presumptive tax. At the same time the sales tax was considerably altered and became in effect a full-fledged, value added tax through the retail level.

Tax reform continued to be high on the Colombian political agenda, however, leading to significant changes in income taxation in 1986. This reform lowered tax rates on business income, freed dividends from taxation at the individual level, and abolished the inheritance tax. To some extent this reform reversed the 1974 reform, just as that in 1960 had reversed part of the 1953 reform. Unlike in 1960, however, the 1986 reform was intended more to unify the marginal effective tax rates on different types of investment than to favor some types of investment over others. At present still further changes along these lines in business taxation are being considered. An especially interesting feature of the current wave of tax reform in Colombia, however, is that it is the first designed primarily to improve the tax structure rather than to increase revenue.

The more than fifty years of tax reform in Colombia point to several lessons.
• Except for the reforms of 1986 and (to a lesser extent) 1974, all have been motivated primarily by economic crises. These in turn were frequently caused by external shocks and required new efforts to raise revenue.
• The influence of changing intellectual fashions on tax reform is as obvious in Colombia as in most countries. The reforms of the 1930s and 1950s, like those of 1974, reflected the dominant "progressive" view of most tax experts in this century, while the 1960 reform reflected the transitory popularity of "incentive-directed" growth policies, and the 1986 reform reflects the renewed interest in "market-directed" growth.
• Despite the strong influence of outside forces—whether economic or intellectual—Colombia's fiscal system, and the timing and manner in which it has developed, is peculiarly its own. It reflects both the balance of forces in its rather stable political system and what has been called "fiscal inertia," or the tendency of fiscal institutions to persist and change gradually rather than radically.
• A continuing undercurrent has been the inability of tax administration to cope with direct taxes in a distorted inflationary environment; hence the growing importance of both the sales tax and presumptive income taxes.

Above all, the Colombian experience suggest that tax reform is inherently neither a continuous nor a once-for-all process, but a periodic one. The almost-annual minor changes in tax bases and rates common in many countries are not usually enough to accommodate fundamental changes in the economic and political environment of developing countries. Circumstances change, and tax systems must change with them. The Colombian case shows that such adaptive efforts are inevitably affected by external circumstances, the political context, and administrative constraints. They are not always successful. However, Colombia's relative success in maintaining government revenue, and even a moderate degree of progressivity, in the face of considerable adversity also suggests that tax reform is not beyond the reach of a developing country.

purposes of equity. In the latter case the base should be luxuries (defined as those final consumption goods whose share of expenditure increases with income). Again there should be no distinction between sources of production (imports versus domestic producers); exports should be excluded and the number of rates limited.

• A shift from the taxation of international trade to the taxation of domestic transactions. Domestic taxes on goods and services—restructured as described above—can be collected at the point of import for administrative convenience without being confused with tariffs. It is then possible to restructure taxes on international trade so that the level and variation of protection rates are reduced. Export rebates or duty drawback schemes would have to be strengthened if production inputs faced tariffs. Export taxes should be phased out or redesigned in light of their primary function—for example, as a proxy for taxing income, profits, or economic rent.

Income taxes could be simplified as follows.

• A restructuring of company taxes so that average effective rates are high for revenue purposes and marginal effective rates low for investment purposes. This can be achieved through some combination of better approximations of annual economic depreciation rates, elimination of sector- and asset-specific allowances, lower statutory tax rates, and adjustments for inflation where inflation rates are high (say more than 10 to 15 percent). Eliminating double taxation of dividends and improving the links between personal and company taxes is also desirable.

- A restructuring of personal taxes to include all sources of income, with lower maximum rates, fewer brackets, higher exemptions, and the elimination of most existing special allowances. Indexing will be important where inflation is high.

Strengthen tax administration

Administrative procedures, capabilities for data processing and analysis, and staff training must be improved in all types of tax reform. A reform that eliminates multiple adjustments to the base of a tax and reduces the number of rates can go a long way toward improving administration. Increased administrative costs, however, may sometimes be justified to lower economic costs, for example, by shifting from trade taxes to a VAT.

In the abstract there is no reason to prefer comprehensive over partial reforms. Country-specific needs will determine the reform required. Comprehensive reforms need not be avoided on the grounds of overloading administrative capacity. The elements of a comprehensive reform can be introduced simultaneously or in stages in light of revenue and administrative constraints. New tax instruments have been introduced successfully, as in Colombia and Korea. Implementing a tax change, however, is likely to be easier if the reform builds on existing tax instruments, as in India and Malawi. The benefits of tax reform take time to become apparent.

Avoid taxing the poor

The equity characteristics of actual tax systems can be improved by incorporating moderate progressivity in both income and commodity taxes and by simplifying tax instruments to free administrative resources for collection, auditing, and enforcement. The progressivity of the tax system can be enhanced by exempting the income *and* essential purchases of the poor from the tax net, by eliminating most of the income tax deductions and allowances that primarily benefit the rich, and by subjecting luxury purchases to higher rates of taxation. The revenue loss resulting from high exemptions in the personal income tax can largely be offset by eliminating most allowances.

Improving the resource allocation aspects of a tax can also improve its equity aspects. For example, eliminating taxes on production inputs ensures that nominally exempt basic goods are not inadvertently taxed. Efforts at fine-tuning the tax structure to achieve income redistribution objectives, however, are not likely to be successful in practice. Poverty alleviation can better be served through coordination with other policies, especially on the spending side of the budget.

Careful reform of revenue instruments can enhance their contribution to revenue and minimize their social and economic costs. But the remaining costs of raising revenue, in effect, set a floor to the benefits required from public spending. Accordingly, revenue should be planned jointly with spending: cost-benefit considerations apply to both parts of the budget. The next chapter turns to the expenditure side of this equation.

5

Improving the allocation of public spending

Public spending plays a critical role in development. Through spending, governments preserve and promote national identity, supply infrastructure for development, influence both the course of economic growth and the distribution of its benefits, and provide social services to meet the basic needs of the population. Yet rapid growth in public spending unmatched by domestic revenue has led many developing countries into fiscal crisis, and in many cases spending has been ineffective in promoting growth and equity. Governments throughout the developing world face the need to trim expenditures and to improve their allocation. It is a formidable challenge. The technical and institutional problems involved in planning, budgeting, implementing, and monitoring expenditures are very great.

This chapter addresses three questions:
- How do governments spend their resources?
- How might governments best spend their resources?
- What institutional and technical reforms might improve the allocation of public spending?

Although the quality of budget execution is also critical in determining the ultimate impact of public spending, this and other issues of public management and administration were the focus of *World Development Report 1983* and are not dealt with in detail here.

Patterns and trends in government spending

How do governments spend their resources? This section looks at both longer term trends in central

government spending and patterns of recent spending cutbacks in selected developing countries.

Long-term patterns and trends

Central government spending as a share of GDP grew substantially in many developing countries until 1982 but then tended to decline until a renewed rise in 1985 (see Figure 5.1). As noted in Chapter 2, government spending as a share of GDP is smaller on average in developing countries than in industrial ones, but the exclusion of transfer payments (which are controlled by government but do not represent direct public claims on GDP) eliminates that gap. Generalizations about government spending patterns in the developing countries need to be treated with caution because of the wide variation among countries even at similar levels of income and because of the lack of comprehensive data on the public sector.

The countries of the Middle East and North Africa have, on average, the largest central governments in the developing world. This reflects in part the relatively expansive view of the public sector's role in countries such as Algeria, Egypt, Syria, and Tunisia and in part the region's heavy military spending (see Box 5.1). Central governments are smallest in South Asia, but state governments are unusually prominent in India and Pakistan. Central governments are of intermediate size in East Asia, Latin America, and Sub-Saharan Africa, with Africa's somewhat larger than those in the other two regions.

Figure 5.1 Central government spending as a share of GDP by region, 1975 to 1985

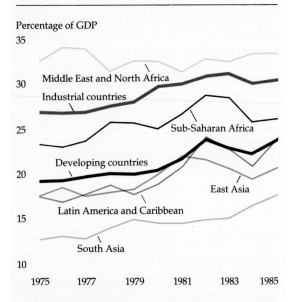

Percentage of GDP

Note: Figures represent group averages weighted by GDP. Because of the lack of comparable data, China, Japan, Nigeria, and several relatively small countries are excluded from the samples in this figure and in Figures 5.2 through 5.7.
Sources: IMF, *Government Finance Statistics*, various years, and World Bank and IMF data.

comes rise; it expands in composition, coverage, and quality in response to demand pressures. It also becomes increasingly influenced by demographic trends as social services take on the character of entitlements (see Box 5.3).

Classifying expenditures is problematic (see Box 5.2), but Figures 5.2 through 5.5 present some broad comparisons of the allocation of central government spending in low-income, middle-income, and industrial countries. In 1980 capital spending accounted for 16 percent of total central government spending in low-income countries and 23 percent in middle-income countries, compared with only 6 percent in industrial countries. (The year 1980 was chosen because data were available for more countries for that year than in later years.) This contrast between developing and industrial countries partly reflects their different priorities. Governments tend to emphasize infrastructural investment in the early stages of development. Basic infrastructure—such as roads, water, electric power, and telecommunications—is essential for developing a national market and an industrial base. Furthermore, the demand for such infrastructure rises rapidly with income at low levels of per capita income and tapers off as incomes reach a middle range. Spending on social services and income transfers takes on added importance as in-

Box 5.1   Military spending

An estimated 6 percent of the world's total public spending goes for military purposes: more than $900 billion in 1985 alone. Industrial countries spend by far the most in absolute and per capita terms (heavily weighted by the relatively high spending in the United States), while developing countries spend more on the military as a share of their GNP (see Box figure 5.1). Most of the growth in military spending in recent years, both absolutely and as a share of GNP, has occurred in industrial countries. (These data exclude the Soviet Union and Eastern Europe. Their total military spending is equivalent to that of the industrial countries; as a share of GNP it is significantly higher.)

On a regional basis, Latin America devotes the smallest share of its GNP—about 1.5 percent—to military spending. Military spending as a share of GNP is highest in the Middle East and North Africa, where it accounted for 11 to 14 percent between 1974 and 1985. Military spending is also relatively high in East Asia (more than 7 percent of GNP), mainly because of high spending in China. It is less than 4 percent of GNP in South Asia and Sub-Saharan Africa.

The data are not necessarily reliable, however. Governments often deliberately understate and conceal military spending. They may categorize military-related construction as public works, combine military pensions with civil service ones, or classify interest on military debt with other debt service. Or they may not account for military spending at all and pay for it with export earnings that are never repatriated or entered into official trade accounts. If a bias exists, it is likely to lean toward understatement rather than overstatement of total military expenditure.

The goals of military spending are noneconomic ones—primarily defense against external threat and internal instability. However, some have also justified military spending by claiming it can contribute to economic development. A controversial 1973 study by Emile Benoit found that higher spending was positively associated with economic growth. This and subsequent studies have argued that military spending can have positive spinoff effects, such as fostering technological innovation, training personnel who later move into civilian work, providing employment opportunities, building domestic institutions, stimulating a county's tax effort, and promoting more intensive use of existing resources. Furthermore, military industries can be a focus of industrialization activities. Although

Although these data cover only central government spending, the addition of data for state and local government and for state-owned enterprises (SOEs) would probably only heighten the differences among country groups. SOEs are most prominent in developing countries, where they concentrate on infrastructure and other economic services and typically account for a large share of public investment. State and local governments are more prominent in industrial countries, where

military spending in developing countries has traditionally been for personnel and imported weapons, in recent years several developing countries—including Argentina, Brazil, China, India, the Republic of Korea, and Pakistan—have developed arms export industries of their own. Brazil is now the world's sixth largest arms exporter.

These positive effects appear to be more than offset by the long-term negative impact of military spending, however. Research in the past decade, although not conclusive, points to a negative relation between military expenditure and economic growth. The most basic criticism is the high opportunity cost of military spending, that is, the diversion of scarce resources from more productive civilian uses. As seen in Figure 5.4, low-income countries spend much more for military purposes than for social services. The true difference is likely to be much greater, because IMF data appear to understate military spending. Moreover, the military has typically been the sector most protected from spending cuts (see Figure 5.8). A 1982 study of sixty-nine developing countries indicated that growth of military spending during the 1950s and 1960s significantly reduced overall investment, agricultural production, and economic growth. Other studies have found negative relations between military spending and spending on social development (including education and health) and between military spending and savings. Critics of military spending have argued that the spinoff effects are overstated—for example, that the linkages with civilian industries are small or that the benefits of military training to the civilian economy are few in countries with professional armed forces. Moreover, defense spending often has a high import content. In developing countries as a whole, arms imports represent about 5 percent of total imports. Payment for such imports can add considerably to balance of payments problems and to the debt burden.

In sum, although the controversy over the relation between military spending and economic growth is by no means resolved, evidence increasingly points to high military spending as contributing to fiscal and debt crises, complicating stabilization and adjustment, and negatively affecting economic growth and development. Whatever benefits might arise from such spending must be carefully weighed against these heavy costs.

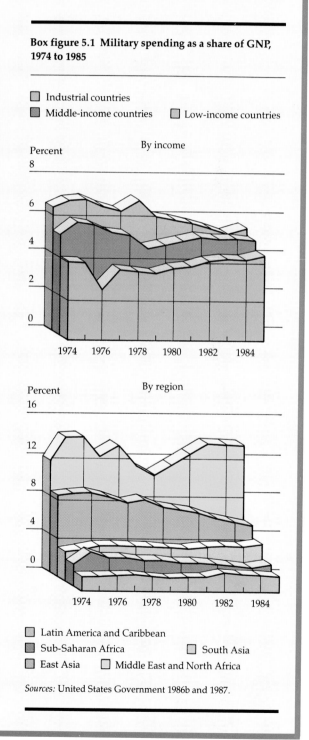

Box figure 5.1 **Military spending as a share of GNP, 1974 to 1985**

☐ Industrial countries
■ Middle-income countries   ☐ Low-income countries

Sources: United States Government 1986b and 1987.

Box 5.2 Alternative classifications of public expenditures: their uses and abuses

Government spending can be classified in a variety of ways. For purposes of national accounting it is usually classified by presumed effect on the economy: consumption, investment, or transfer payments. For government budgeting purposes it can be classified either by "economic" type (wages and salaries, other goods and services, interest, subsidies and transfers, investment in fixed assets, and so forth) or by "function" or sector (general administration, defense, education, health, infrastructure, and so forth), or by some combination of both. Budget classifications vary enormously among countries, and many budget reforms during the past forty years—including moves toward "performance" or "program" budgeting discussed later in this chapter—have primarily been attempts to improve budget structures.

The most important distinction in a budget is between current and capital transactions. Separate budgets for each are common. Dual budgets grew from the idea that originated in the 1930s that current spending is equivalent to current consumption and should be financed by taxation. Capital spending, in contrast, is investment that will generate returns in the future and that should—on grounds of efficiency and intergenerational equity—be financed by borrowing or other capital revenues. Borrowing to build assets is acceptable, because assets increase in line with liabilities, while borrowing to fund consumption is not. The balance on the current account, called "public savings," can also be used for investment and is an important indicator in its own right.

The dual budget system has advantages and disadvantages. On the positive side, the distinction between current and capital spending gives a clear picture of the extent of both borrowing and capital formation and assumes a link between them that does have an underlying economic rationale. Because a current surplus is seen as a positive indicator, the distinction also helps to impose discipline on current spending while implicitly favoring investment.

On the negative side, however, if capital spending is defined as spending on tangible assets with a life span of more than one year, the distinction can introduce a bias, toward investment in physical capital at the expense of current operations and maintenance. Such a bias can, in turn, lead to a bias toward "hard" sectors, such as infrastructure, and away from social sectors, for which physical capital investment is a small share of total spending. To overcome this bias, some countries have altered the traditional split between current and capital spending and have distinguished instead between "developmental" and other spending. Under this distinction the developmental budget includes current expenditures that either constitute investment in human resources or enhance the productivity of physical investment. While perhaps avoiding the bias toward tangible assets, this variant introduces difficult definitional problems that can make the distinction in the two budgets seem quite arbitrary.

In addition to the problem of bias, an emphasis on the current balance alone may be misplaced. For macroeconomic stabilization the important variables are the overall budget balance and its means of financing. Furthermore, borrowing may need to be limited not only for stabilization but also because public investment may not always yield long-term returns as high as the cost of debt service. Low returns on the investment of borrowed capital have contributed significantly to the current international debt crisis.

Finally, the existence of two budgets is often institutionalized in two budget-making bodies. For example, in developing countries ministries of finance often have responsibility for current budgets, while ministries of planning are in charge of capital budgets. Lack of coordination between the two can lead to serious inefficiencies and biases in the allocation of overall spending.

---

they are major providers of social services such as education.

Current government spending is divided among subsidies and transfers, wages, other goods and services, and interest. Subsidies and transfers comprise the largest category, accounting for more than 40 percent of current spending in developing countries. Interest is the smallest category, although its size has been growing rapidly in recent years, especially in the highly indebted countries (see Figure 5.6). Spending on wages and other goods and services is a larger share of government spending in developing—particularly middle-

income—countries than in industrial countries. As a share of GDP, however, the difference is much smaller (see Figure 5.3). Similarly, central government interest payments command a greater share of the budget in low-income countries but as a share of GDP are higher in the industrial world. As discussed earlier, perhaps the most striking difference between the spending patterns of developing and industrial countries is the large share of GDP that the latter devote to subsidies and transfers.

The severity of the resource constraint facing developing countries comes into sharper focus in comparing spending per capita (see Figure 5.7).

Central government spending per capita was only $44 in low-income countries in 1984, compared with $298 in middle-income countries and $3,429 in industrial ones. The disparities are even more pronounced in the social sectors. The low-income countries spent only $1 per capita on education and health, against levels more than a hundred times greater in the industrial world, especially if state and local government spending are included. Different levels of spending do not translate fully into different levels of inputs, because wage rates are lower, and thus purchasing power higher, in developing countries. Nonetheless input (and thus presumably output) differences are clearly huge. Big increases in spending are not possible for these countries; they lack the resources. Their task is to use the few resources they have more efficiently.

Figure 5.2 Allocation of central government spending by economic category, 1980

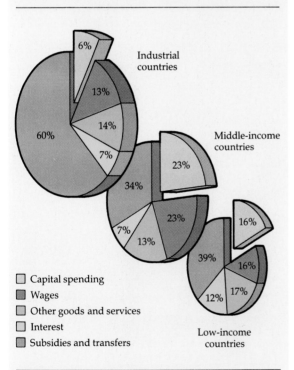

Note: The areas of the circles represent the relative shares of total spending in GDP; the figures in the circles represent group averages weighted by GDP.
Source: IMF, Government Finance Statistics, 1987.

Figure 5.3 Shares of GDP allocated by the central government to various economic categories, 1980

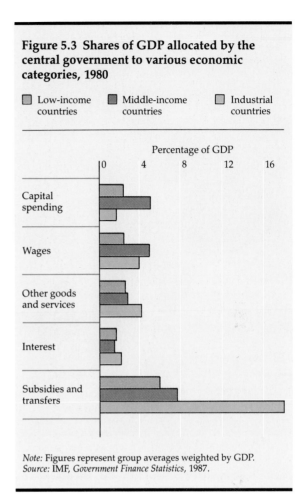

Note: Figures represent group averages weighted by GDP.
Source: IMF, Government Finance Statistics, 1987.

Patterns of recent spending cutbacks

In the early 1980s many developing countries reduced the share of government spending in GDP as international banks curtailed their lending and recession squeezed domestic revenues. Which public sector activities were worst hit by the new austerity? Figure 5.8 shows the average reduction in real central government spending in fifteen (mainly highly indebted) countries during the early 1980s. Total real expenditure fell on average by 18.3 percent. Capital spending suffered a 35.3 percent decline, while current spending fell only 7.8 percent. This may reflect the greater flexibility of capital spending; it is easier to cancel or postpone a few large projects than to lay off government workers, reduce civil service pensions, or delay or renegotiate interest payments. Among categories of current spending, lower payments for goods and services and for subsidies were partially offset by sharply higher interest payments. Analyzed by sector, infrastructure spending—

109

Figure 5.4 Allocation of central government spending by functional category, 1980

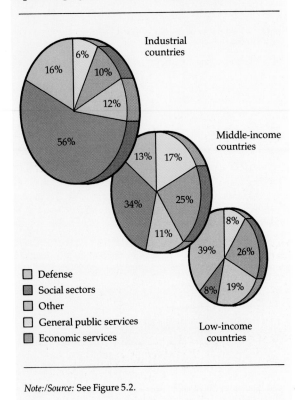

Industrial countries

6%
16%
10%
12%
56%

Middle-income countries

13% 17%
34% 25%
11%

8%
39% 26%
8% 19%

Defense
Social sectors
Other
General public services
Economic services

Low-income countries

Note:/Source: See Figure 5.2.

much of it capital spending—suffered the deepest cut. Social spending fell by somewhat less, military spending by much less.

Although the pattern of cuts is clear, interpreting it is difficult. First, the data show the decline in total spending as deflated by a general GDP deflator—not necessarily the decline in the actual quantity of government activity. If prices in some sectors rose faster than in others, the decline in services rendered would have been greater than indicated. Second, prior spending levels were not necessarily optimal; certain cuts should have been made anyway. Many cases of spending reduction in fact followed periods of rapid spending expansion. Finally, each cut needs to be judged in the context of the country where it happened. If the private sector is active in certain sectors, greater private sector activity may readily offset reduced government spending. In many cases, however, domestic recession hit private sector activity at the same time that public spending was falling.

Detailed case studies confirm that in many countries public investment dropped dramatically dur-

ing recent periods of austerity. In Mexico, for example, total public sector investment fell from almost 11 percent of GDP in 1982 to less than 6 percent in 1986. In the Philippines it declined from 8 percent of GDP in 1981 to less than 4 percent in 1985. In addition, the cut in public investment was often exacerbated by lower private investment. Gross private investment in the Philippines, for example, fell from 23 to less than 13 percent of GDP between 1981 and 1985. An even more extreme case is Argentina, where gross private investment plummeted from 14 percent of GDP in 1980 to less than 3 percent in 1985, and net private investment (after depreciation) was negative—in other words, the capital stock was shrinking. In cases such as these it is clear that a revival of efficient investment spending, both public and private, is needed.

Figure 5.5 Shares of GDP allocated by the central government to various functional categories, 1980

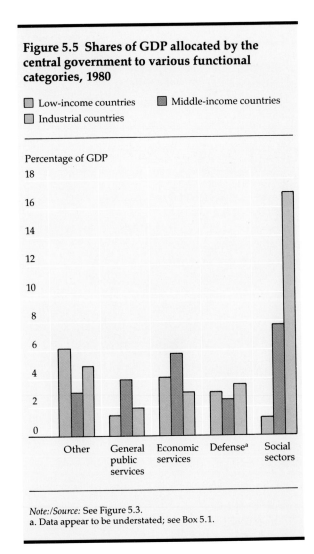

Low-income countries   Middle-income countries
Industrial countries

Percentage of GDP

Note:/Source: See Figure 5.3.
a. Data appear to be understated; see Box 5.1.

Box 5.3   Demographic trends and public spending

Population trends affect spending in the social sectors. This is particularly true in industrial countries, where many social services in education, health, and social security are considered to be entitlements mandating universal coverage. The predominant demographic trend expected during the next forty years in these countries is the rapid growth of the elderly population, both in absolute terms and as a share of total population. This trend implies higher spending on pensions and health care, offset only partially by savings on education, unemployment insurance, and other social programs.

Demographic trends are very different in developing countries. Most of these countries experienced high birth rates and declining infant and child mortality in the 1960s and 1970s, and many are still experiencing these trends. The result is rapid growth in the population as a whole and particularly among the young. In some countries, such as Kenya and Rwanda, school-age populations will double by 2000 and put added pressure on spending for education.

The demand for additional public spending resulting from these demographic trends must confront the reality of severe resource constraints. Many developing countries have not achieved universal coverage in such areas as education, health, and social security, so coverage and quality—rather than spending—may unfortunately be the variables that must adjust when populations increase. If a country has set a goal of achieving a particular level of coverage, higher population growth will make that achievement more expensive. Cutting costs and improving efficiency in the near term and moderating population growth over the medium term are both critical to expanding the coverage and quality of social services in developing countries.

Fertility rates in some countries, such as China, Colombia, and the Republic of Korea, have declined significantly since the 1960s. Perhaps the most extreme example is China, where, as a result of the one-child policy, the school-age population will fall during the next fifty years not only as a proportion of the total population but in absolute size as well. The working-age population is projected to grow from 64 percent of the total population in 1980 to 68 percent in 2000, and then fall again to 65 percent in 2030. The elderly population is projected to grow from 4 percent in 1980 to 7 percent in 2000 and to 14 percent in 2030. Pressures for social spending will ease in the next decade as dependency ratios fall, and China can emphasize improving the quality of services and access to them. Only well into the next century will the dependency ratio increase from today's levels, as current and future workers reach old age. Long-range planning is needed to adapt to the changing balance of needs of young and old generations.

The risks and challenges of austerity

In sum, the data point to a steadily increasing role for the public sector in the economies of most countries in the world until the early 1980s. Increasing demands on governments have not been met, however, with the flow of resources needed to fund their activities. Adjustment programs, often mandated by fiscal crises, have forced cutbacks in public spending in some developing countries in the 1980s. Public sector investment has been particularly prone to cutbacks. Spending on wages and on subsidies and transfers has been reduced less, while spending on interest has increased dramatically because of rising debt burdens. Such changes in spending patterns hold considerable risk. Although curbing overall expenditure growth may be necessary to maintain or restore fiscal stability, governments must be increasingly concerned about the allocation of spending among activities and the quality of each activity. These will determine the longer run effect of public spending on development goals.

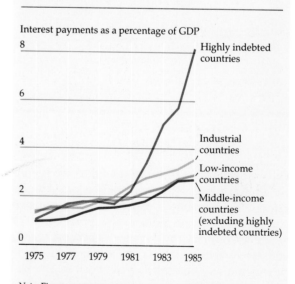

Figure 5.6 Trends in central government interest payments, 1975 to 1985

Interest payments as a percentage of GDP

Highly indebted countries

Industrial countries

Low-income countries

Middle-income countries (excluding highly indebted countries)

Note: Figures represent group averages weighted by GDP.
Source: IMF, *Government Finance Statistics*, various years.

Figure 5.7 Central government spending per capita, 1975 and 1984
(constant 1984 dollars)

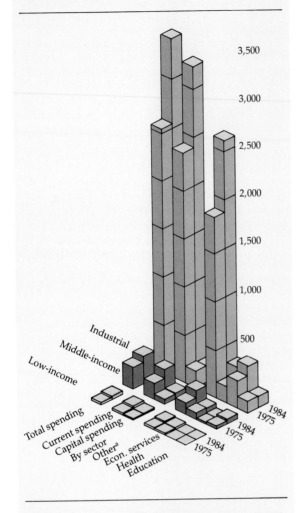

Note: Figures represent group averages weighted by population.
a. Includes social security, general public services, defense, housing, and other miscellaneous spending for which detailed data were not available in certain countries.
Sources: IMF, *Government Finance Statistics*, various years.

Priorities for public spending

Governments must set priorities if they are to control the total level of spending and allocate it efficiently. These priorities should be based on two considerations. The first is an appreciation of where government involvement is necessary and, conversely, where markets can be counted upon to provide the same output as well or better. The second is an understanding of how limited resources can be spent most efficiently and effectively in the areas in which public involvement is called for.

As discussed in Chapter 2, both economic theory and practical experience suggest that governments should concentrate their spending in certain areas where their participation is necessary for a well-functioning market, for economic growth, and for the alleviation of poverty. Decisions on public spending should be grounded in an understanding of these basic principles and in the recognition of the fact that spending is not costless. All funds have alternative uses, or opportunity costs (see Box 5.1), and governments create economic burdens in the process of raising revenues to finance spending (see Chapter 4). In addition the public provision of goods and services may affect market prices or behavior (such as an individual's work effort or tendency to save or consume). It may thus have far-reaching effects beyond its direct benefits.

Unfortunately, many governments are not allocating their limited resources efficiently or effectively. Too much is being spent in the wrong areas, and too little is being left for the critical tasks that only governments can perform. Misallocation is occurring both within and between capital and current spending.

Public investment

Governments must plan their public investment programs by jointly considering both their overall priorities for the economy and the appropriate division of responsibility between public and private activities. Intersectoral priorities will depend on economic structure, natural resource endowment, and development strategy. No clear techniques exist to guide intersectoral choices, although identifying bottlenecks in an economy and comparing rates of return to different activities may provide some clues. Intersectoral spending allocations are inevitably based largely on intuitive judgments, recognizing the need for overall balance between sectors.

Within any sector the principles discussed above can help to guide public investment decisions. The general goal of public sector investment should be to complement and support—rather than compete with—market-determined activities. The priority areas of public sector involvement in education, health, urban services, and rural infrastructure are discussed in Chapter 6. Both primary education and preventive health care provide broad benefits to society in addition to those received by the direct beneficiaries and would tend to be undersupplied without government involvement. There is room for government involvement in higher education and curative health care, but more of the costs of these services should be borne directly by the beneficiaries through user charges. In both urban and rural infrastructure, governments have an important role in road construction, water supply, electricity generation and distribution, and solid waste disposal. Less justification exists for public involvement in bus service and housing construction, which can be provided efficiently by private companies. Unfortunately, many governments are not observing these priorities (see Chapter 6).

The roles for government investment in agriculture and industry were discussed in the past two *World Development Reports*. Government investment in these sectors should concentrate on providing basic complementary infrastructure, including electricity, water, transport, communications, and flood control. Basic research is also an important area for government involvement. Public investment in direct production or marketing of agricultural or industrial products is rarely justified on economic grounds. The involvement of SOEs in these activities has been widespread, however, often for historical reasons. Although SOEs can be as dynamic and efficient as privately owned enterprises if they are run by competent, autonomous managers, often SOEs are sheltered from competition or are subjected to intrusive political interventions, the appointment of unqualified managers, or the expectation that they will meet a variety of often conflicting social objectives (see Chapter 8).

Although setting priorities for public investment is a first important step in using the government's limited resources most effectively, an equally important concern is the quality of investment. Several characteristics of investment projects contribute to quality and are important determinants of success (see Box 5.4). The investment needs to be not only economically attractive, but also technically, administratively, and financially feasible. The objectives of the investment should be clearly stated and acceptable to the main parties concerned. Finally, the policy environment should be stable and predictable and should create incentives that encourage efficiency. Government officials and project managers respond to input and output prices, interest rates, and the international trade regime in selecting and implementing investments. If these signals are significantly out of line with true opportunity cost, investments are unlikely to promote long-term growth. In Sierra Leone, for example, government price controls on the output of SOEs have led to a squeeze on SOE profits and thus on investment and maintenance.

Capacity has not expanded enough to meet demand, and the quality of services has suffered. Furthermore, SOEs are being decapitalized and require large government subsidies in many cases. Sierra Leone is not unique. SOEs in many other countries face similar problems because of price controls. It is clear that the success of public investment is being seriously hampered by the skewed policy environments in those countries.

Operation and maintenance of investment

Part of current public spending on goods and services goes for the operation and maintenance (O&M) of capital investment and is critical for the

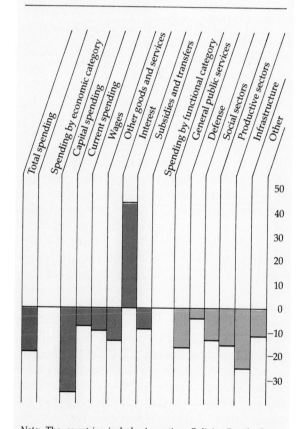

Figure 5.8 Real reduction in central government spending in fifteen countries, early 1980s
(unweighted average percentage change)

Note: The countries include Argentina, Bolivia, Brazil, Costa Rica, Dominican Republic, Indonesia, Liberia, Mexico, Morocco, Paraguay, Senegal, Sri Lanka, Togo, Uruguay, and Venezuela.
Source: Hicks 1988.

Box 5.4 An example of successful investment: cotton projects in West Africa

The success of seven cotton projects in three West African countries illustrates the positive effect of good public sector investment and some of the characteristics that lead to success. These seven projects have led to dramatic increases in the yields, the area planted, and the number of growers in cotton during the past fifteen to twenty years and have resulted in major production gains (see Box table 5.4).

Several characteristics of the projects account for this success. First, the objectives were clear and had strong support from the government. These included the provision of farm inputs, credit, and extension support for cotton and foodcrops; assistance to the project authority; the construction of feeder roads and village wells; and the establishment of a seed multiplication system. Second, the technical packages were well adapted to local socioeconomic conditions and were adjusted periodically to new developments at the international, national, and farm levels. The cotton companies, which

had monopolies on seed production and distribution, maintained close links with the cotton research institute and were able to introduce homogenous and better-performing varieties resistant to insects and disease. Third, the institutions running the projects were autonomous and effective, and the extension agents, who lived in the villages and spoke the local languages, were motivated and well trained. Both the delivery of inputs to farmers and the payment for farmers' seedcotton were timely, in part because of government-provided input subsidies that helped to insure the parastatals' financial health. This contrasted sharply with the unreliable input supply and late crop payments of similar crop parastatals elsewhere, particularly those in financial trouble. Fourth, the financial arrangements were adequate. Future project costs were taken into account, cash flow was sufficient, and project authorities had both a strong incentive and the ability to recover the costs of crop inputs from farmers. The financial arrangements did entail government subsidies on input use, however, that were quite expensive. Since 1984 all three countries have eliminated or considerably reduced input subsidies while increasing producer prices, thus maintaining adequate differences between output and input prices to provide good incentives for farmers. The overall economic environment for the projects has deteriorated somewhat, however, because of drastically lower world market prices. Even successful rural development efforts are vulnerable to unfavorable external economic conditions.

Box table 5.4 The positive effect of cotton projects in West Africa

| Country | Percentage increase in project areas | | | |
	Seedcotton production	Yields	Area	Number of growers
Burkina Faso (1965–86)	700	240	280	230
Côte d'Ivoire (1967–86)	450	140	330	190
Togo (1971–86)	800	160	660	590

success of such investment in promoting economic growth and development. Inadequate spending on operations (whether supplies or personnel costs) can lead to low levels of effectiveness in areas such as education and health and result in a poorly educated, less healthy population. In Zambia, for example, a 1975 evaluation of health clinics found large shortfalls in drugs and medical supplies, with some key drugs (such as chloroquine, penicillin, and oral rehydration salts) out of stock for up to seven months in some areas. Inadequate spending on maintenance can lead to rapid deterioration of physical capital. In Indonesia, for example, inadequate maintenance of irrigation facilities has led to breakdowns and inefficiency in water delivery. It has lowered the productive life of irrigation systems by up to 50 percent.

Often a choice must be made between investment and maintenance. The latter is frequently the more cost-effective use of resources. For example, developing countries have lost road infrastructure

worth billions of dollars through insufficient maintenance. In eighty-five developing countries with a main road network of 1.8 million kilometers, a quarter of the paved roads and a third of the unpaved roads outside urban areas need to be rebuilt. The cost of restoring these deteriorated roads—estimated at $45 billion—is three to five times greater than the bill would have been for timely maintenance. Furthermore, the cost of operating vehicles on deteriorated paved roads can be 20 to 50 percent higher than the cost on roads in good condition. If the road is unpaved, this difference can be more than 100 percent. Because operating costs constitute a large share (75 to 95 percent) of total road transport costs, except when the traffic is extremely low, insufficient road maintenance exacts hidden costs several times the cost of restoring road infrastructure. These hidden costs, borne primarily by road users, can become a heavy drag on economic growth.

Unfortunately, spending on O&M (particularly

spending on materials and supplies as opposed to personnel) is generally undervalued and underfunded in developing countries. It is undervalued because the benefits are often hard to measure precisely and may lack political visibility. The benefits of increased operational spending in education and health, for example, tend to be subtle ones relating to quality rather than quantity, once the bare minimum necessary to keep schools and clinics open has been allocated. The benefits of maintenance—particularly routine as opposed to periodic maintenance—are often not clearly visible at all. They consist merely of costs avoided in the relatively distant future. O&M is underfunded not only because it is undervalued, however, but also because other spending demands—interest, subsidies, civil service wages, investment projects, and so on—exert stronger pressure on decisionmakers or lead to more visible disruption if not met. Furthermore, bureaucratic incentives may provide few rewards for efficient O&M once funds have been allocated. This leads managers to spend more on administrative overheads than on the delivery of services or supplies. More attention must be given to O&M in budget allocation and execution, and incentives must be changed to make this spending effective.

Public pay and employment policies

Among the most important issues surrounding spending on general government administration, as well as wage-related spending on O&M, are those involving public pay and employment policies. These policies differ considerably among developing countries. In Sub-Saharan Africa, for example, not only has the growth of public employment differed markedly among countries (see Figure 5.9), but the salary structure—including differentials in wages between skilled and unskilled workers and between public and private sectors—has also varied greatly. Salary differentials between senior (undersecretary level) and unskilled civil servants are twenty-five to one in Malawi but only seven to one in Zambia. The ratio of an unskilled civil servant salary to per capita GNP is greater than four in Liberia but less than one in Sudan and between one and two in Malawi, Sierra Leone, and Zambia. One consistent pattern among African countries and several other developing countries around the world is the decline from the mid-1970s to the mid-1980s both in real compensation levels—whether cash or fringe benefits—and in pay differentials between skilled

Figure 5.9 Growth in central government employment
(percentage annual rate of growth)

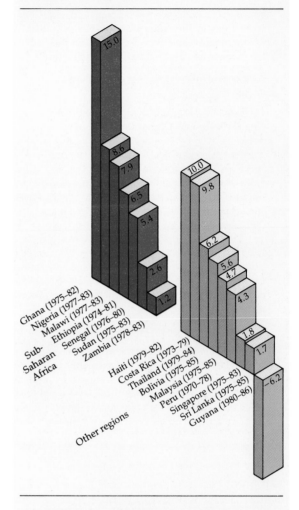

Sources: Lindauer (background paper) and World Bank data.

and unskilled workers. Extreme cases include Ghana and Uganda, where real basic starting salaries had fallen to below subsistence level by 1983, and Sudan, where these salaries fell by four-fifths between 1970 and 1983.

Public pay and employment policies not only have important implications for the total level of public spending, but they also affect the development effort in other ways. First, employment and wage policies help to determine the mix of inputs going into the production of public goods. If the wage bill is too large and other expenditure categories are relatively underfunded, too much labor will be employed relative to nonlabor inputs. Com-

Box 5.5 Controlling the wage bill of the public sector

Many countries recognize that government pay and employment policies need reform, and some have taken steps in that direction. The following list describes some avenues for reform; the first five address employment and the last two the wage structure.

Civil service censuses and the elimination of "ghosts"

The most blatant abuse of government employment policy is the so-called "ghost" or "phantom" worker—somebody who receives government wages but either does not exist or is not employed in the position for which the payment is made. To isolate and delete "ghost" workers from the payroll often requires a civil service census that matches payroll data with budgeted and actual employment. Ghana and Zambia have carried out such censuses. Efforts to eliminate "ghosts" in the Central African Republic and Guinea identified 1,300 and 7,000 "ghost" workers, respectively, equivalent in both cases to roughly 7 percent of civil service employment. Once "ghosts" are eliminated, it is important to establish payroll mechanisms that prevent them from materializing again.

Elimination of vacancies and temporary positions

Audits of government employment in The Gambia led to the dismissal of 2,625 temporary and daily wage employees and 764 permanent employees and the elimination of 848 out of 10,700 civil service posts. Jamaica has also dismissed temporary workers. The significance of reducing expenditures on temporary labor

should not be overlooked. In Zambia, for example, temporary workers account for roughly one-fifth of total government expenditure on wages. Such workers are often easier and less expensive to release than permanent staff, because they possess fewer legal claims.

Freezes on recruitment and suspension of employment guarantees

Employment can be reduced over time by freezing general recruitment, with some limited provision to replace essential staff. Retirements and other attrition will then reduce total employment. Costa Rica froze public sector employment for three years beginning in 1984. The Central African Republic limited recruitment with a rule permitting the hiring of one functionary for every three dismissed. This proved expensive because a higher level person was commonly recruited when three lower level ones were fired. Recruitment was subsequently limited to a ratio of one franc of hiring for every three francs of saving.

Suspending "employer-of-last-resort" practices can also reduce government hiring. Sudan abolished its employment guarantees for secondary school graduates during the 1970s. In general such guarantees are becoming less common, except perhaps for teacher colleges.

Automatic and voluntary retirement

Costa Rica and Senegal have imposed automatic retirement upon reaching retirement age or requisite years of service. Guinea is offering voluntary retirement.

---

plaints of teachers without textbooks, public health workers without vaccines, and agricultural extension workers without fuel for their vehicles are manifestations of this problem; the crowding out of investment by an excessive wage bill is another indicator. Alternatively, the combination of labor skills may be inefficient; corridors full of idle messengers outside the offices of overworked senior administrators point to this. Public employment programs initiated in part to combat unemployment, combined with the political difficulty of dismissing civil servants, appear to have led in many developing countries to an excess of workers compared with the availability of nonlabor inputs and to an excess of unskilled workers relative to skilled ones.

Second, civil service compensation creates incentives that affect performance. Rapid erosion in real compensation can reduce work effort (if em-

ployment is considered secure), because workers will turn to other activities—such as moonlighting, petty corruption, and the pursuit of nongovernment work during official working hours—to supplement their declining salaries. Maintaining staff morale and honest, efficient government under such conditions is difficult. Furthermore, while wage costs may decline, if services decline more than proportionally, the unit costs of government goods and services will rise.

Wage differentials between grades are important too. The severe wage compression that is occuring in many countries not only diminishes the incentive to work hard, but it also encourages better qualified staff to leave and lesser qualified staff to stay. Most efforts to reduce the public sector wage bill, although important in helping to achieve fiscal balance, have overlooked the critical importance of wage differentials (see Box 5.5).

While reducing the total work force, such schemes provide governments with little control over who actually leaves public service, and governments risk losing staff they would prefer to retain. In addition, voluntary retirement schemes may require expensive inducement mechanisms, such as severance pay, to be effective.

Dismissal of workers

The most difficult form of retrenchment politically is outright dismissal of redundant or (even more difficult) incompetent workers. Severance pay for redundant workers can ease the transition. However, only those workers with a legitimate claim to public employment as an acquired right, rather than a recent windfall, should be eligible for severance pay. A public education program can ease the political costs of a dismissal program. In Guinea, French technical assistance financed an information campaign that publicized and explained the government's retrenchment plan, and apparently increased the public's acceptance of the austerity measure.

Wage cuts, caps, and freezes

The most common form of salary action is an across-the-board wage freeze. In 1982 Togo imposed a 5 percent cut in wages, referred to as the "solidarity tax," and a multiyear freeze on salaries. These policies led to virtually zero growth in the wage bill from 1983 to 1986. Nigeria also froze its salary structure until recently. In addition it reduced fringe benefits, lowered transport allowances, cut cash leave grants in half, and eliminated subsidized lunches.

Wage freezes may relieve budget pressures only temporarily if governments acquiesce to built-up wage demands when the freeze is lifted. Furthermore, because freezes are applied to the salary structure and not to individual compensation, promotions may offset intended budgetary savings. A 7 percent increase in the real wage bill followed a wage and employment freeze in 1980 in Senegal.

Wage differentials

Salary reforms to improve the pay of senior staff are especially difficult to implement despite the clear need for them in many cases. Budgetary constraints and political pressures are significant barriers. Nonetheless, improving the overall performance of government may require such reforms. After sustained periods of wage compression both Ghana and Sri Lanka have increased the differentials in their salary structure. From 1984 to 1986 the ratio of top to bottom salaries in Sri Lanka increased from about 4:1 to about 12:1.

Creating supergrades for upper management, like the senior executive service in the United States, is one way to offer higher compensation to senior government officials. Ghana has seconded staff to several important government posts from more remunerative positions in SOEs or the private sector. Such secondment is currently eligible for financing through a World Bank technical assistance credit.

Subsidies

Subsidies fall into two main types. The first, which may include export or credit subsidies, is designed to encourage the private sector to undertake activities that generate external benefits. Subsidies of this type are intended to promote growth through more efficient allocation of resources. The second, which includes food or housing subsidies and subsidies to SOEs to support government-imposed price controls, is intended mainly to provide income support. Some such subsidies—those for food, health, or education, for example—can also be justified because of their social benefits.

Although subsidies can contribute to efficiency, the relief of poverty, and growth, their benefits must be carefully weighed against their costs—which can be very substantial. If a government's revenue-raising capacity is severely constrained by administrative limitations, as is true in many developing countries, using scarce revenues to subsidize private activities will mean that fewer resources are available for other uses. The investments or O&M spending forgone must be seen as a major cost of subsidies in such cases. If a government's revenue-raising capacity is not so limited—as in more advanced countries—a major cost of subsidies is the burden incurred in raising the revenue to finance them (see Chapter 4).

Still further costs of subsidies arise from the changes in private behavior they induce. Credit subsidies designed to spur investment, for example, cheapen capital relative to labor and can lead to excessive capital-labor ratios in production and thus exacerbate unemployment. In Thailand credit subsidies to agriculture in the late 1970s encouraged excessive mechanization and have since been scaled back. Similarly, subsidies on certain forms

Box 5.6 How agricultural subsidies affect the environment

Countries generally subsidize agricultural inputs to promote agricultural growth. However, the subsidies can promote wasteful, careless, or excessive applications of these inputs and lead to significant environmental damage. For example, many countries–including Colombia, Ecuador, Egypt, Ghana, Honduras, and Indonesia–have heavily subsidized sales of agricultural pesticides to overcome farmers' misperception of risk in adopting an unfamiliar technology, or in some cases to offset implicit taxes on farm output. Such subsidies ignore the negative effects of pesticide use on human health, other species, and the resistance and future resurgence of the pest itself. In addition, heavy irrigation subsidies in developing countries have encouraged low-return investment and caused or aggravated flooding and salinization, exposure of the population to waterborne diseases, and productivity losses in fisheries. Subsidies to chemical fertilizers have depressed the use of organic manures essential to long-term soil productivity, discouraged investments in soil conservation, and increased chemical

runoff into surface and groundwater. Economic analysis of these programs has rarely considered their environmental effects.

Environmentally costly subsidies also exist on the output side. Several Latin American countries have subsidized livestock production on large estates through a variety of tax incentives, low-interest loans, and other means. As a result ranchers have cleared millions of hectares of tropical forest despite rapid pasture deterioration, low carrying capacity, and long distance from markets. Such subsidies have made investments that are questionable on both economic and environmental grounds highly profitable to private entrepreneurs, only few of whom are poor smallholder farmers. Brazil has subsidized ranching investments so heavily in some parts of the country that, although they lose more than one-half the capital invested, they yield positive returns to the private investors as high as 250 percent of their equity input. As with input subsidies, fiscal policymakers have rarely considered the environmental cost of these production subsidies.

---

of energy or food can lead to overconsumption and waste, as well as to inefficient use of the subsidized product in unintended ways. The use of subsidized kerosene rather than unsubsidized diesel or fuel oil in industry and the use of subsidized bread as animal feed are two examples. Furthermore, in some cases subsidies can have harmful environmental side effects (see Box 5.6). Finally, the mere existence of subsidies can divert the private sector away from productive pursuits while it lobbies for a share of the subsidies.

Although the exact magnitude of the costs associated with subsidies is difficult to measure, in most cases costs are likely to rise faster than benefits as the subsidy scheme grows. Careful targeting of benefits to those most in need can go far in increasing the benefit-cost ratio of such a scheme (see Box 5.7).

Public spending to alleviate poverty

Experience has revealed that certain characteristics of subsidies and other spending intended to relieve poverty help determine whether resources reach the poor efficiently and effectively. Assuming a service is needed by the poor, the first important characteristic is the level or standard at which the service is delivered, as indicated by the unit

cost of the service per beneficiary. Poor people cannot afford expensive services, and no developing country government can afford to provide expensive services to large numbers of people free of charge. Therefore, programs that offer basic low-cost services are most likely to be of greatest help to the poor. Furthermore, such schemes are in a sense self-targeting, because higher income groups often seek higher standards of service.

For example, spending on low-cost, broadly based primary education is more likely to reach the poor than spending on expensive primary education or on higher education. In São Paulo, Brazil, low-cost approaches to preschool childcare, which use existing community buildings and mothers as teaching assistants, can reach five times as many preschool children for a given budget as high-cost approaches, which use new buildings and only fully qualified primary teachers. Similarly, investment in basic health clinics is more likely to assist the poor than investment in fancier clinics or hospitals. The same is true for upgrading slums as opposed to building new housing or for providing water through standpipes as opposed to individual house connections. Food subsidies can also be targeted to the poor by choosing less expensive foods to subsidize. A study in Brazil in the early 1980s showed that subsidies on bread or milk would benefit the relatively well-off more than the poor, while a subsidy on cassava flour, a cheap food consumed primarily by the poor, would be highly progressive.

A second factor affecting a program's effect on the poor is location; the poorest tend to be concentrated in certain regions, in rural areas, and in urban slums. For example, subsidies—whether for food, health care, education, credit, or housing—are unlikely to reach the poorest segments of the population if they are available exclusively in urban areas. Unfortunately, isolation—the very characteristic that tends to exacerbate poverty—also heightens the administrative difficulty and cost of projects designed to reach the poor in rural areas.

An urban bias in public spending programs has often been alleged but is hard to prove. One reason is the difficulty of tracing the spatial impacts of particular spending programs. For example, a bus terminal or port facility located in a city may benefit primarily rural dwellers. Another reason is that investments in urban infrastructure, whether for safe water, electricity, health, or education, tend to involve lower unit costs than their rural counterparts and thus may be justified on efficiency grounds. Although rural development should never be neglected, neither should the demands of urbanization that inevitably accompany economic development and growth. The main issue is not so much the distribution of spending, but rather how it is financed. Avoiding subsidies to urban services through increased reliance on local taxes and user

---

Box 5.7 An example of expenditure targeting: food subsidies in Mexico

Until 1986 the Mexican government offered global subsidies on most staple foods. Most subsidies were administered by the state-owned National Basic Foods Company, CONASUPO, through one of two mechanisms: either by selling the products at reduced prices to processors (who themselves were subject to price controls on output) or by reimbursing processors directly for costs not covered by sales revenue. These subsidies rose substantially in the early 1980s as the government increased guaranteed producer prices to stimulate domestic production and held down consumer prices to avoid upward pressure on domestic wages. In 1983 the total cost to the government of these food subsidies alone exceeded 1 percent of GDP.

By the mid-1980s subsidies of this magnitude were no longer sustainable. Mexico faced high fiscal deficits, rapid inflation, a rising debt service burden, and declining access to international resources. As part of an effort to reduce the fiscal deficit, policymakers reduced global subsidies in 1985 and phased most of them out in 1986. This more than doubled the real prices of both tortillas and bread. By the end of 1986 the remaining subsidies administered by CONASUPO amounted to less than 0.2 percent of GDP.

Because of the precarious nutritional status of the poor in Mexico, where more than 30 percent of preschoolers suffer from malnutrition, the elimination of all food subsidies for the poor could cause great suffering and undermine support for the government's austerity program. The government addressed this problem by beginning a program of food coupons for tortillas, while continuing its existing program of milk distribution in poor urban areas. CONASUPO had long operated special stores that sold staple foods at subsidized prices in poor rural areas. However, all of these efforts were underbudgeted and ineffectively monitored. The government, supported by an agricultural sector loan from the World Bank, has recently expanded the food coupon and milk programs by increasing the number of urban families covered. It is also strengthening supervision and monitoring to reduce diversion of the subsidies to nontarget populations. If targeted to the poorest 20 percent (16 million persons), a funding level of $250 million would be approximately sufficient to compensate them for the global subsidies that were eliminated.

Targeted subsidies are a more efficient use of resources than are global ones, but they face difficult administrative challenges in Mexico and elsewhere. The first challenge is minimizing leakage to nontarget populations. Three types of targeting are possible: by location, if the poor are concentrated geographically; by food, if certain foods are consumed primarily by the poor; and by individual income or income indicator. The last, although the most exact in defining the target population, is the most difficult to administer because of the individual screening required. The Mexican food coupon system is officially targeted by income level; coupons are available only to families with total income less than twice the legal minimum wage. But CONASUPO's outlets are concentrated in lower income urban areas, thus implicitly also targeting by location.

The second challenge is reaching the poorest and most malnourished, who in Mexico, as in many developing countries, live in rural areas and have limited interaction with formal markets. The rural CONASUPO stores already offer low-priced staples in many poor areas. Special efforts will be needed to improve their operation without crowding out efficient private wholesalers and retailers.

charges is the key to achieving both efficiency and equity.

A third characteristic that determines the effect of public spending on poverty is the program's ability to reach the informal sector. Government programs that touch only employees in the formal sector, such as social security and other public pension schemes, subsidized employee health insurance, or civil service housing assistance, are not likely to alleviate the worst conditions of poverty in developing countries.

Finally, the effect of public spending on poverty can be increased through an explicit focus on employment and poverty alleviation in project design. Labor-intensive rural works programs, such as rural road maintenance, can efficiently create many jobs for the poor. Attempts have been made in recent years to bring a poverty focus into rural development projects. Of 192 World Bank projects approved between 1974 and 1979, for example, the cost for each beneficiary family was $1,104 for the 112 targeted projects, as compared with almost $1,400 for the 80 untargeted ones. Targeted projects could therefore reach more families for equal cost. The rates of return on poverty-oriented projects were not significantly different from those of the untargeted ones, which suggests that efficiency and equity can be compatible goals.

An agricultural project just beginning in Bangladesh provides a good example of appropriate public investment well designed to reach the poor. The project will finance basic complementary infrastructure, in particular new construction and rehabilitation of flood-control, drainage, and irrigation schemes. In addition to reducing crop losses and boosting yields by about 160,000 metric tons a year, it will generate employment equivalent to almost 5 million days of work. The project is expected to benefit more than 200,000 poor rural families, many of them landless laborers and sharecroppers.

Emerging lessons

Several lessons emerge from the above discussion. First, public investment should in general be complementary to, rather than directly competitive with, private investment. Second, public investment planners should concentrate on all aspects of project design. Projects should be not only economically viable, but also technically, administratively, and financially feasible, and set in a policy environment that provides signals to encourage efficiency. Third, adequate funding for continued O&M must be provided for the life of an investment. Fourth, developing-country governments must put greater emphasis on attracting and motivating qualified staff. They cannot afford to be employers of last resort for the entire labor force. Finally, efficiency and equity are not necessarily incompatible goals. Government programs that provide low-cost services or subsidies that are rigorously limited in scope and targeted to those most in need can help alleviate poverty at reasonable cost while building the human skills so important to growth. Untargeted subsidies have generally proven to be too costly and inefficient to be justified, given the tight resource constraints now facing governments.

Three important tasks face governments as they plan, budget, and implement public spending decisions: they must control the overall level of spending, set priorities for its allocation, and ensure quality within each spending category. The challenge of planning and budgeting public spending is the focus of the rest of the chapter.

Planning and budgeting public spending

The two primary tools typically used in controlling and allocating public spending are the medium-term plan and the annual budget. The medium-term plan promotes careful consideration of spending alternatives, facilitates the phasing of lumpy investments over several years, and provides some indication of the sustainability of proposed revenue and expenditure patterns over the medium term. The annual budget is the authoritative legal document for allocating resources. It is not the best vehicle for medium-term planning because its time horizon is short, it provides little scope for proposing and evaluating options, and it is typically prepared under significant time pressure.

The continuing need for fiscal planning

The practice of planning has varied immensely in developing countries during the past thirty years. On one end of the spectrum are countries, such as China and Hungary, which have attempted comprehensive central planning and direction of both public and private investment. On the other end are economies, such as Hong Kong, in which little or no emphasis has been placed on central planning and in which investments have been guided essentially by price signals arising from a relatively freely functioning market. Between these two extremes are countries (including India, the Republic of Korea, Malaysia, and Singapore) that have used planning actively to guide public spending and set a framework for private sector decisionmaking, and countries (including Indonesia, Thailand, and much of Sub-Saharan Africa) that have regularly prepared central plans but have used them primarily as general policy statements and often have only nominally adhered to them.

Comprehensive central planning for the economy as a whole has lost favor in both government and academic circles in recent years. Many countries, including China and Hungary, have put growing emphasis on market forces and individual incentives. In part this follows a change in the emphasis of development theory. Although economists once thought structural rigidities in developing countries were a major barrier to growth, emphasis is now placed more on the harm done by distortionary price signals. This reflects the growing belief that resources are more mobile than once thought and that producers and consumers in developing countries do respond readily to price signals. Previous theories called for direct government intervention in resource allocation, while the newer view stresses the primary importance of well-functioning markets and correct price signals.

A further reason for growing skepticism with comprehensive central planning is the widespread disappointment with its results in practice. Centralized decisionmaking has proved inflexible and inefficient and has resulted in a growing array of state institutions and large public projects, some of which remain costly burdens. Planning has suffered, particularly in the 1980s, as financial crises have forced many governments to resort to short-term crisis management, crowding out almost any attempts to take a medium-term view.

The move away from comprehensive economywide planning should not signal, however, a move away from all planning. A danger exists that the current economic crisis may obscure the virtues of a medium-term plan for the public budget. Another danger is that ideological stereotypes will block reform, with comprehensive economywide planning linked to interventionist approaches to development and lack of planning to noninterventionist, market approaches. That would be regrettable, because the case for better management of public expenditure is not an ideological one. Fiscal prudence is needed in both capitalist and socialist economies.

The goal of fiscal planning should be to forecast and program public spending over a three- to five-year period and to take into account both likely resource constraints and the linkages of such spending with the economy. A comprehensive medium-term expenditure plan to accomplish such a goal contains several components. First, it sets out a macroeconomic framework linking the growth of national income, savings, investment, and the balance of payments to public expenditure and revenue. Second, it projects current spending obligations on debt service, public administration, defense, the operation and maintenance of investment, and so on. Although few if any items of spending are completely inflexible, some types of current spending (such as debt service on existing debt, civil service pensions, and certain portions of spending on O&M) are less flexible than others. Third, it defines a multiyear phased public investment program, divided between high-priority projects and those with lower priority that will be undertaken only if resources are sufficient. Finally, it projects revenue from tax and nontax sources and resources needed from domestic and external borrowing and grants. Such a plan is formulated on an iterative basis under alternative assumptions concerning the tax system, the level of user charges, policies toward SOEs, and the macroeconomic environment. It thus helps to achieve consistency between expenditures and macroeconomic assumptions, and stresses the role of public spending as a policy instrument.

Although few countries have the capacity to formulate such a comprehensive medium-term plan, the concept is a useful prototype toward which to strive. Progress on individual components is possible in many cases, as illustrated in some of the country examples cited below.

Using budgets as policy instruments

The annual budget is usually the legal authority for public spending. It is ideally a one-year slice of a medium-term expenditure plan, although in practice this link between planning and budgeting has often been tenuous. The role and form of the budget process varies markedly among countries and depends in large part on tradition. While the exact process may vary, certain key characteristics are important if the budget is to be an effective policy instrument.

First, the budget should be comprehensive. It should include all spending of the central government, whether financed by general taxes, earmarked sources of revenue, borrowing, or grants. Major investment projects of subnational levels of government and of SOEs should definitely be subject to central review and might also be included in the budget or a related document. Although these entities need autonomy in managing their day-to-day operations, the central government should retain the right of approval over significant new investments or new borrowings.

Such comprehensiveness is more the exception than the rule, even at the national level. Extra-budgetary accounts flourish in many countries, both developed and developing. Furthermore, the investments, and in some cases even the borrowing, of state and local governments or SOEs are often excluded from central review. Some countries are exceptions. Core ministries in Chile and Panama, for example, are able to exert effective budgetary and administrative control over all public sector expenditure, and Thailand has established adequate monitoring of all public sector borrowing.

An important reason for the existence of extra-budgetary accounts and the earmarking of revenues is the desire to avoid cumbersome and often highly politicized budgetary procedures in funding essential services. Such accounts may be inevitable in the short-run when budgetary processes are severely dilapidated. The longer term goal should be to improve these processes, however, and to consolidate revenues and expenditures into the budget.

Turkey has experienced rapid growth in the use of extra-budgetary funds; more than eighty are believed to exist, about a dozen of which are large and fully operational. They accounted in 1985 for about 20 percent of central government budget revenue (up from only 8 percent in 1983), or 3.5 percent of GNP. Financed primarily through earmarked levies, the funds are used for such diverse purposes as promoting exports and investment, funding high-priority public investments, subsidizing agricultural inputs such as fertilizer and livestock feed, and financing miscellaneous social programs. They were created both to avoid cumbersome budgetary and disbursement procedures and to ensure protection from general budget cutbacks. However, their independence has undermined overall budgetary control, put added pressure on those items of spending that are included in the budget, and exacerbated inefficiencies and inconsistencies in the allocation of public resources. The government of Turkey recently announced plans to place up to 30 percent of the revenue of these funds into the consolidated budget.

In addition to being comprehensive, meaningful links should exist between government objectives (as laid out in programs and projects) and traditional budget categories such as salaries, equipment, and supplies. Traditional line-item budgets, useful in tracking spending in a narrow accounting sense, cannot provide an adequate picture of the extent to which public objectives are being achieved.

Several countries, both developing and industrial, have reformed their budgeting procedures in the direction of "program" or "performance" budgeting. Such reforms not only reclassify the budget to reflect objectives and programs, but also attempt to monitor government performance by relating inputs to outcomes. They have proved hard to implement because of institutional and informational difficulties in programming and in measuring performance. The outcome has been mixed. For example, Sri Lanka attempted to introduce performance budgeting in 1969 but abandoned it after 1976. A more sustained effort has produced a working system in India, but it is cumbersome, and the detailed information it produces (more than 2,000 pages) is not well adapted to the needs of the legislature or ministries. Performance budgeting reforms in Malaysia have had a deep and lasting effect in only two or three ministries. Despite these problems, the efforts in all three cases have improved performance measurement and auditing, have broadened managerial attitudes, and have indirectly improved resource allocation. In sum, although the term "performance budgeting" has lost favor because of the difficulties of implementation, its elements—the categorization of spending by program, the emphasis on monitoring performance, and the view of the budget as a planning and policy instrument—remain central to better public budgeting.

Improving expenditure planning and budgeting

Few countries—developing or developed—engage in such thorough decisionmaking processes as those described above. In fact, planning and budgeting systems in many developing countries have deteriorated markedly in recent years because of heightened economic instability. Some of the more common problems—inadequate basic accounting, the lack of an economic framework, uncoordinated decisionmaking, uneconomic investment choices, and failure to consider the lifetime cost of projects, to plan for contingencies, or to anticipate the effects of inflation on the budget—are considered below.

REHABILITATING BASIC ACCOUNTING. The correct and timely recording of expenditures as they occur is an integral part of proper fiscal control. Whether, and after what delay, government accounts appear, and their credibility when they do, are the most basic indicators of the health of a fiscal system. Some developing countries fail in this elementary requirement for fiscal control. Accounts are often so late or so unreliable that they cannot serve as the basis for rational public expenditure planning or monitoring. Their absence can jeopardize the discipline of the entire planning and budgeting regime.

The example of one West African country is illustrative. Although the basic accounting system used to work reasonably well, in recent years it has disintegrated. The data needed to prepare and evaluate budgetary requests are no longer available, and the discipline of the budget timetable has been lost. Managers at all levels either disregard requests for budget estimates for the next fiscal year or submit estimates far in excess of what is possible. They reason that the government cannot fail to allocate some resources to their activities, that whatever they might submit is unlikely to be reflected in the ultimate budget, and that the actual release of funds will not match the budget anyway. Yet unrealistic budget submissions in turn destroy confidence among those who receive them. All phases of the process lose credibility in a cycle of mutually reinforcing skepticism.

Rehabilitation of basic accounting functions is a prerequisite for improving public expenditure management in cases such as this. Improvements in recording spending as it occurs should receive top priority. Computerization of government payrolls can be one significant improvement. Simple and systematic monitoring of the investment program can be another. Recent efforts to improve monitoring of the investment program in several African countries, including Ghana and Uganda, have focused on preparing simple project profiles. The standardized profiles contain five components: a concise description of project content and objectives, an unambiguous identifying title and project number, an estimate of total investment costs, a proposed annual phasing of investment costs, and an estimate of recurrent costs arising from the project. If regularly prepared and updated, these simple standardized profiles can be very useful in tracking project spending.

SETTING THE ECONOMIC FRAMEWORK. In addition to knowing what was spent in the past, an assessment and projection of the macroeconomic outlook for the coming three to five years is important in estimating available resources. Yet governments often lack either the skilled personnel to do such macroeconomic analysis or the institutional incentives that ensure such analysis is properly considered when plans and budgets are formulated. As a result revenue forecasts and spending estimates may not exist or, if they do exist, may have little basis in reality. In addition, without central guidance the spending ministries and SOEs may make different assumptions concerning macroeconomic variables such as expected inflation or exchange rates that lead to inconsistencies that resurface at later stages of the expenditure cycle. Building up both macroeconomic and sector-specific microeconomic skills should be a high priority.

COORDINATING DECISIONMAKING. Responsibility for planning and budgeting is often dispersed among several institutions without effective coordination. While the organizational structure will depend in large part on history and tradition, and while a variety of structures can work in practice, coordination is essential.

Perhaps the most obvious example of this problem is the tension that often exists between the ministries of finance and planning; a common institutional question is whether the two should be merged. There are many examples of mergers and almost as many of subsequent separations. A number of countries, including Kenya and Sierra Leone, have been through several rounds of this process. Only rarely is there a genuine fusion. More often a single minister simply presides over both institutions. An exception is Botswana, where the merger of the Finance and Planning Ministries was a genuine merger of roles.

The question of whether to have one ministry or two, or a budget office separate from both, is perhaps not of central importance—reconciling the two functions is. Short-term budgets need to reflect a well-considered, longer term perspective, and medium-term plans need the accountability and relevance provided by direct links with the budget. The medium-term expenditure planning process discussed earlier can provide the vital link between the two.

Unfortunately, few countries have managed to integrate the planning and budgeting functions well. For several reasons the plan is often disregarded as the budget is prepared. First, plans may not be sufficiently detailed to provide guidance in budgeting. Second, the budget process is often rushed and subject to many short-term pressures, not allowing adequate time to consider plan input. Third, planners may have less influence than budgeters, because the budget is the authoritative legal document, while the plan does not typically have the force of law. Frequent organizational changes can also diminish the influence of planners. In Argentina, for example, the planning function has undergone five major organizational changes and several minor ones since 1973, which has undermined its credibility. Finally, traditional stereotypes have sometimes acted as a wedge. Budgeters are often depicted as being concerned with short-term expenditure control more than long-term development, while planners are depicted as being overly concerned with economic aggregates over which the government has little practical control.

Chile and Thailand are two countries that have tackled the integration of plans and budgets quite successfully. Thailand has accomplished this through procedural measures rather than organizational ones. No project can be included in the annual budget unless it is first fully appraised according to methods approved by the planning agency and then reviewed by that agency. Chile, in contrast, does not have a separate planning agency in the traditional sense. Both annual budgeting and medium-term planning are the responsibility of the Finance Ministry and are carried out simultaneously. ODEPLAN, the central project review agency, assists the Finance Ministry in long-term planning and must fully appraise each project before it can be included in the budget. In both countries the planning and budgeting agencies have traditionally been well staffed, fully supported by the political leadership, and respected for their competence and professionalism.

Problems of coordination can also exist between core ministries and spending agencies, whether sectoral ministries, subnational levels of government, or SOEs. As discussed further in Chapters 7 and 8, in all of these cases the goal is to maintain coordination and accountability without losing the benefits of decentralized decisionmaking. With regard to sectoral ministries, the role of the central ministries (finance or planning) should be to set binding overall expenditure ceilings and to establish guidelines reflecting national priorities for the allocation of total resources among broad categories of activities. For example, the ministry of education might be allocated 10 percent more than the previous year's spending limit, but told to hold higher education spending constant while increasing expenditure on primary education. Within

these guidelines (and probably with restrictions on overall recruitment), the ministry could determine the best allocation of resources within each activity, subject to normal central review. Only the spending agencies have the specialized knowledge to make detailed allocations of resources within a subsector.

As a corollary to this division of responsibilities, the spending agencies should not be allowed to submit spending requests in excess of target—and thus force the central ministries, who are in a worse position to judge priorities, to take the responsibility for cutting the sector budget. In 1979 the Canadian government took an innovative step to reinforce this division of responsibilities when it introduced the "envelope" system into its budgeting process. Before 1979 ministers could approve policy ideas without explicitly considering their fiscal implication. Under the envelope system each policy committee in the cabinet is given an expenditure limit ("resource envelope") for which it is responsible and within which it must fit all spending in its policy area. Both intrasectoral allocation authority and fiscal responsibility are thus delegated downward to those in charge of spending. While developing countries may perceive a greater need for central direction of public investment than industrial ones, the insistence on "hard" budget constraints at all levels and the devolution of fiscal responsibility represented by the envelope system can strengthen budget control in all countries.

Coordination can also break down during implementation. In theory, spending agencies (sector ministries or SOEs) should generally be responsible for implementing a spending plan once decisions about allocation have been made through the plan and the budget. Central ministries should monitor expenditures to ensure that the allocated amounts are spent for the assigned purposes (within some range of flexibility) and to assess the effect of spending choices on development. However, central ministries often react to tight budget constraints, overprogrammed budgets, or simple mistrust of spending agencies by slowing the disbursement of funds or by erecting unnecessarily cumbersome procedures in areas such as procurement, land acquisition, or contractor eligibility. Often these are politically easier ways of controlling a budget than denying funding requests as plans and budgets are formulated. Such indirect forms of control slow the implementation of projects and restrict managerial flexibility in the sectoral ministries and the SOEs. They may be better than no control at all, but they have costly implications for institutional development in planning and budgeting; they affect the morale, the staffing, and the managerial capabilities of the implementing agencies. Governments should instead foster accountability (particularly in SOEs) by giving financial and managerial autonomy while implementing a system of performance evaluation (see Chapter 8).

Of course adverse events may force a government to cut spending below originally budgeted amounts. Ideally the ministry of finance should amend the original budget by negotiating new ceilings with individual agencies, but in the short run slowing disbursements may be the only feasible way to make the necessary cuts.

CHOOSING BETWEEN INVESTMENTS. Decisionmakers typically face a staggering array of choices when designing or updating a public investment plan. First, they must choose between alternatives for new investment, including rough ideas to be further investigated as well as projects with designs already worked out in detail. In addition they must consider the stock of ongoing projects, some funded by foreign aid and others not.

Preparing and updating a public investment program should be seen as a matter of screening, in which projects are accepted on the condition that they meet satisfactory appraisal criteria at appropriate stages in their life cycle. Projects at early stages of development would receive a less detailed screening; firm proposals for new projects should be subject to full-scale economic analysis before construction begins (see Box 5.8). Ongoing projects should not be exempt from continued eco-

---

Box 5.8   The role of cost-benefit analysis in project selection

Few public investment projects are selected on economic criteria alone. Other concerns, including national security or the political or personal interests of policymakers, often play a role. Economic analysis can, however, indicate the potential effect of proposed projects on growth or poverty alleviation and can help prevent costly mistakes.

The basic technique of economic appraisal is cost-benefit analysis. It consists of adding up all the benefits and costs of the project to society, discounting them to reflect the opportunity cost of the invested funds, and calculating the absolute amount of discounted net benefits expected from the project (the "net present value"). The discount rate should reflect either the preference society has for consumption today over consumption tomorrow, or the amount that could have been earned if the funds had been invested elsewhere, or (if they are different) some combination of both. Social costs and benefits are intended to represent not financial costs and benefits to any particular individual, but the true opportunity (or "shadow") cost of inputs and outputs (such as goods, labor, or foreign exchange) to an economy.

Techniques of cost-benefit analysis originated more than fifty years ago in the United States and have become increasingly sophisticated since then. Analysts have devised methods to take into account such considerations as the distribution of costs and benefits of a project among income groups or regions, the net contribution of the project to national savings, the riskiness of the project and its correlation with other risks in an economy, and the economic costs of raising the funds necessary to finance the project. At the same time, however, inherent difficulties remain in such fundamental tasks as measuring costs and benefits and choosing the appropriate discount rate. How does one measure, for example, the benefits of constructing a national monument, building a prison, helping to create a more educated or more healthy population, investing in agricultural research, or controlling population growth? For a large class of public expenditures in which benefits are difficult to measure, "cost effectiveness" analysis—that is, trying to minimize the costs of an agreed-upon output or to maximize such output with given cost—is often more useful than cost-benefit analysis. Cost-effectiveness techniques cannot be used to compare the economic returns on investment in different sectors or between returns of different activities within a sector (such as primary and university education). Even though intersectoral comparisons of rates of return are possible with cost-benefit analysis, however, such comparisons are usually too uncertain to do more than indicate which activities might usefully receive greater priority.

The most important consideration in individual project analysis is not which specific type of economic analysis is used, but that some attempts are made to bring rational, objective, and, to the extent possible, quantitative analysis into the decisionmaking process. Systematic attempts at objective project appraisal will not always prevent poor investments, but if given sufficient weight in the allocation process, they are likely to provide some defense against the largest and most costly investment mistakes. They can also help in choosing among various alternatives for the size, location, components, timing, or technology of a proposed project.

nomic scrutiny merely because costs have been incurred. Their economic rationale may disappear as conditions change.

Unfortunately, economic criteria are often neglected, partly because many core and spending ministries lack the capability to appraise projects thoroughly. In addition, other considerations may take precedence over economic return: the power of interest groups, tied financing, the desire for prestige projects, the unwillingness to forget sunk costs and stop bad projects, ministerial lobbying, corruption, or simple inertia. Requiring that a team (possibly a centralized one such as ODEPLAN in Chile) carry out a simple and consistent project appraisal for every major project (including those of SOEs and subnational levels of government)—and then adopting procedures that ensure the results receive attention—can help to avoid the most costly mistakes (see Box 5.9).

CONSIDERING THE LIFETIME COSTS OF A PROJECT. One way spending agencies try to preserve or enlarge their claims on the central budget is to submit a funding request for only the first phase of a large project without specifying what later phases will cost. Because projects are difficult to cancel once begun, the best way to avoid ballooning costs is to require that no project begin without a full picture of projected future costs.

It is important to emphasize here that ''costs'' include not merely capital costs but all recurrent resources needed to complete and operate the project. Although this point is now widely appreciated, the recurrent cost implications of investment decisions are often understated or overlooked. The problem is partly procedural. Recurrent and development budgets are often drawn up by separate processes, even by different groups of people, with little or no account taken of

---

**Box 5.9   Economic analysis makes a difference:
Thailand's Eastern Seaboard Development Program**

An example of the importance of economic analysis in designing an investment program is Thailand's Eastern Seaboard Development Program. The Fifth Five-Year Plan (1982–86) selected the eastern seaboard region of Thailand as a major new center for industrial development. The region was one of the most rapidly growing in the country and had several advantages: proximity to Bangkok and to raw material and labor supplies; excellent road, port, and communications infrastructure; and direct access to natural gas. The plan proposed large investments in heavy and light industry both to contribute to employment and export growth and to shift economic activity from Bangkok. Total investment for the program was projected to be $4.5 billion (in constant 1981 prices).

The government initiated a major study in 1981 to assess the feasibility and economic implications of this program. It concluded that:

• The economic rate of return for the overall program would be 9.7 percent, which meant a negative net present value using a 12 percent discount rate; but selected components had returns as high as 50 percent.
• The effect on employment would be relatively small, and the program's cost for each job created would be very high—more than ten times the average for new industrial investment in Thailand in 1981.
• The financing requirements would place significant burdens on the Thai financial system; the program

would require about one-third of the average new equity capital generated annually in the country.
• The program would contribute significantly to the country's international indebtedness; it would require loans equal to about 10 percent of total medium- and long-term disbursements to Thailand in 1981.
• The program would impose substantial burdens on public finances by absorbing 6.5 percent of total public investment during the plan period and by reducing total revenues by 5 to 10 percent because of declining trade taxes.
• The net foreign exchange savings from the program could be substantial because of import substitution in heavy industry.

The doubts raised by the study, together with the subsequent deterioration of Thailand's fiscal position, prompted the government to adopt a cautious approach to the program's implementation. It subjected major components, especially the large-scale industrial projects, to further in-depth evaluation and scaled down the program significantly. Total investment during the 1980s will probably amount to only about one-half of that originally projected. All parts of the program continue to be subject to economic and financial analysis. Such analysis is clearly making a difference, not only in the way public spending is allocated, but also in its effect on economic growth and development.

the complementarities between the two. The problem can also be one of inadequate information. Country-specific norms, established through empirical investigation of ongoing projects, can be useful as a rough guide in forecasting recurrent costs.

Botswana's planning and budgeting system is exemplary in its attention to the recurrent cost implications of investment spending. In preparing the most recent (the sixth) National Development Plan (covering fiscal 1985–86 to 1990–91), each sector ministry was asked to list the programs that it needed to carry out its sector policies. The programs were presented in summary form with a brief description of each project, its purpose, and its cost in both capital and recurrent expenditures. The investment ceilings were then determined from the overall targeted growth of recurrent spending, itself reflecting ceilings for use of skilled employees. The historical relation between recurrent and capital spending was an additional guide. The system allowed investments in excess of the ceilings only if a ministry could demonstrate that such investments would require no further allocations from the recurrent budget.

PLANNING FOR CONTINGENCIES. Because of their inability or unwillingness to make difficult decisions, planners and budgeters often overprogram and pay too little attention to priorities, resource constraints, or phasing. In addition unexpected shortfalls can make a well-programmed fiscal plan obsolete. In the squeeze caused by an overprogrammed budget, the tendency is to cut or delay all spending rather than to define priorities. As a result funding for many programs is likely to fall below the minimum effective level. For these reasons setting priorities and developing contingency plans for unexpected shortfalls should be a part of any planning or budgeting exercise. This can be accomplished in part by formulating a "core" investment program—a group of projects that should receive funding under all circumstances—together with a list of standby projects to be funded only when additional resources are available. The common practice of partially funding all or most projects should be abandoned.

ADJUSTING FOR INFLATION. Plans and budgets are often drawn up in constant prices. Forecasting inflation is technically difficult, especially during periods of economic instability. Moreover, providing explicitly for inflation is often regarded as a self-fulfilling prophecy. Yet inflation can play havoc

with forecasts made in constant prices, especially if spending rises faster than revenue when inflation accelerates. This is likely to be true if, for example, government wages and transfer payments are fully indexed to inflation while taxes are not. If fiscal deficits are to be properly managed, inflation must be taken explicitly into account in planning and budgeting. Medium-term spending plans, although generally drawn up in constant prices, should consider the likely consequences of alternative inflation scenarios. Annual budgets should be formulated in current terms, with contingencies built in for unexpected price movements. The problem is not unique to developing countries. The British government recognized the need to consider inflation in its 1981 shift from the use of constant to current prices in medium-term expenditure planning. Under the previous system automatic adjustments were made to spending allocations in response to price movements, which led to constant upward pressure on total spending. Under the new system of "cash planning," in contrast, binding cash limits are imposed on departmental spending, which allows greater discipline in budgetary control.

COORDINATING DONOR ACTIVITIES. Donors finance a large portion of the investment budget in many developing countries—up to 100 percent in parts of Sub-Saharan Africa. Their involvement has both good and bad effects on the allocation of spending.

On the positive side, in addition to providing concessional funds, some donors carry out relatively comprehensive economic evaluation and demand thorough recordkeeping. Their skills in economic analysis and in project appraisal and monitoring may be higher than those of the borrowers. They can influence not just the selection of individual projects, but borrowers' standards more generally (see Box 5.10). Furthermore, they help to educate governments, citizens, and the private sector in the industrialized world about the problems of development and the urgent need for continued international capital transfers.

Balanced against this, however, are potential drawbacks. First, donors can complicate policymaking. In many countries each sector ministry deals directly with donors. This can lead to duplicate efforts and, more important, can impede central control of the budget. Lack of a central viewpoint makes intersectoral tradeoffs difficult to judge and overall spending hard to contain. In the extreme an investment program may be no more

Box 5.10   The World Bank's evolving role in public expenditure reviews

The World Bank has made a significant commitment in the past few years to carrying out extensive analyses of the public investment and public expenditure programs of its borrowers. Aside from studies incorporated directly into general country economic reports, more than thirty public investment reviews (PIRs) or public expenditure reviews (PERs) have been produced. These reviews provide recommendations to governments on the size and composition of their spending programs and on ways to strengthen local institutions to enhance the countries' own abilities to design such programs.

A typical review begins by laying out a feasible macroeconomic framework, which usually includes projected borrowing requirements of both the central government and the public enterprises. It may present alternative macroeconomic scenarios to illustrate the favorable consequences of policy reform or the unfavorable consequences of excessive spending. PERs then consider the adequacy of operation and maintenance expenditure and the appropriateness of the level of wages, employment, transfers, and subsidies. Both PERs and PIRs recommend a core public investment program based on a review of priorities for eight to ten sectors, including agriculture, industry, energy, transport, telecommunications, housing, water, education, and health. They consider ongoing and newly proposed projects in light of the sector strategy, the appropriate role of the public sector, and specific project se-

lection criteria. They also consider financing alternatives, including cost recovery.

The role of these World Bank reviews has expanded and evolved in recent years. Earlier reviews looked mainly at investment priorities; more recent reviews have looked more broadly at the economic and institutional dimensions of managing public expenditure. Increasingly PERs are also used to examine particular types of government expenditure. For example, current expenditure and public social expenditure are being reviewed for Senegal and Brazil, respectively, in 1988. Recommendations on spending priorities are frequently incorporated into structural adjustment lending—at either the sectoral or economywide level. The reviews are also often discussed at meetings of aid donors, where concessional loans and grants are sought, and as an element of conditionality in IMF adjustment lending.

This process of public expenditure review faces two challenges in the future. First, so far the reviews have been very costly. The growing experience of Bank staff in conducting such reviews and the accumulation of country-specific knowledge should help improve cost-effectiveness. Second, ultimately the country's own policymakers and economic staff should carry out the reviews, preferably on a continuous basis. Without this latter goal no lasting contribution can be made to the country's institutional development.

than a list of projects that donors choose to fund, without any centralized consideration of the economic merits of each project or the balance between them. Furthermore, donor representatives may be under pressure from their own organizations to lend and disburse, which may lead them to seek special treatment. This could include separating counterpart funds from the budget or exempting projects from the normal procedural checks.

In addition, donors sometimes place restrictions on project funding that can lead to greater cost, heighten domestic budgetary pressures, or reduce effectiveness. One example is the requirement that aid be tied to the purchase of goods and services from the donor country, even if the cost is higher than it would be under competitive bidding. Another is the common refusal of donors to fund current spending on O&M. This means that budgetary pressures mount later, because countries must provide not only matching capital funds but also

continued recurrent funding. It also reinforces the underlying bias against spending on O&M.

Aside from the need for changes in some donor policies and practices, all of these problems can be tackled through better coordination of foreign aid by borrower governments. Donor projects and financing should be incorporated into the central budget, and donor projects should be subject to at least the same standards of central review as domestically financed ones. The willingness of donors to fund should not be the decisive factor in allocating resources to investment. Efforts at better coordination of aid have increased in recent years, but the difficulties are great.

Indonesia provides an example of effective aid coordination. Donor activities enter into the normal planning and budgeting process, so that spending priorities drive funding rather than vice versa. The Planning Ministry coordinates the total size of the aid program and major policy decisions relevant to it, while donors work with individual spending ministries on detailed project objectives and design. Although constant interaction among individual donors, sector ministries, and core ministries occurs throughout the year, donor representatives and senior economic ministers meet annually as a group. At this meeting the parties review recent economic developments, the ministers brief participants on upcoming policy initiatives, and donors indicate the size and provisional allocation of their funding for the coming year. A spirit of cooperation pervades the process, primarily because all parties see the government as both responsible for coordinating aid and effective in carrying it out.

Box 5.11   The importance of process in budget reform: the Kenyan task force on budget issues for agriculture

The problem was familiar, the causes baffling: Kenya's overall agricultural program in the mid-1970s was performing poorly. Projects were stalled, disbursements lagging, and overall results disappointing. What was going wrong?

Some of the difficulties clearly resulted from weak technical packages, from distortionary policies (such as credit or marketing systems), and from poor project management. But the budget process also emerged as a source of problems. Officials of the Ministry of Agriculture insisted that funds were insufficient because of arbitrary budget cuts and slow disbursements of authorized funds by the Ministry of Finance. Finance officials, however, argued that fault lay with the Ministry of Agriculture and its poor use of the resources it received. It was clear that sector plans were vague, that project screening techniques were undefined, and that the many projects on the books did not together form a coherent investment program. Too much was spent on recurrent costs, especially salaries, and on financial support of parastatal institutions. Mistrust and failure to coordinate decisionmaking characterized the planning, budgeting, implementation, and monitoring systems. The budgeting process was not well linked with either planning or with final budget allocations, and funds took months to reach spenders.

Attempts were made to redress the problems through studies, technical assistance, and incremental changes in procedures and institutions, but to no avail. The root causes were simply too complex and involved too many actors and basic government procedures to be susceptible to simple, one-shot solutions, especially where these rested primarily on outside assistance.

The government finally decided to focus first on the process of reform rather than on detailed solutions. A task force, composed of top officials from the Ministries of Agriculture and Finance, was established in 1981 for two years (later extended) to recommend and implement improvements in planning, budgeting, spending, accounting, and project management. The work program entailed four formal meetings a year, which were geared to the major phases of the resource management cycle: the plan (forward budget estimates),

the budget estimates for the year, the release of funds, and the evaluation of annual results.

Meetings were well attended and well prepared. Papers prepared by Kenyan government staff and consultants (mostly from Kenyan institutions) set the substantive agenda, which was eventually expanded to include the broader effect of budget issues on the work of the Ministry of Agriculture. The meetings focused increasingly on specific issues. Practical proposals and results followed. The process was linked with, and reinforced throughout by, exercises supported by the World Bank, including a public expenditure review, an agricultural sector loan, other agricultural projects, and technical assistance.

The effort was considered a great success. It helped to spotlight budget issues, promoted changes, and led to steady and visible improvement in the resource management process. For example, disbursements sped up dramatically, with the time required for funds to reach a project manager in the field falling from seven months to three weeks. A much stronger, policy-oriented budget proposal was prepared, with priorities clearly defined, and the Ministry of Agriculture was able to defend its budget more successfully. A sound project management system was launched. Overall the Ministry of Agriculture developed better management tools and information systems, aided by the introduction of microcomputers. The overall quality of agricultural programs improved markedly during this period. After four years the Ministry of Finance decided to begin a similar reform process.

Several lessons emerged from this experience. First, the "process" approach is a precondition for success. The outcome in this case was not, and could not be, precisely specified in advance. The direct involvement of participants in forging solutions was critical. Second, the budget is central to the policy process and is a good vehicle for promoting institutional change. Government policy is reflected directly in how funds are spent and how effectively. Finally, change in this field is likely to be quite slow and incremental. One-shot efforts or complex blueprints for change are unlikely to succeed.

Directions for reform

The tasks of containing and allocating spending call for medium-term plans and shorter term budgets that set clear priorities and ceilings. But developing countries face shortages of skills and information, fragile political systems, and unstable macroeconomic conditions—exacerbating the difficulties that all governments face in these matters.

Although improvement is certainly possible, reforms in planning and budgeting will be slow and incremental, as Kenya's budget reform suggests (see Box 5.11). Along with a continuing need for training to improve civil service skills, experience indicates some directions for reform. The starting point is basic accounting. Governments must develop ways to track spending in a timely and accurate way. The next step is routine economic analysis—as part of the planning process—of both the macroeconomic environment and proposed investments. The first should tell governments approximately how much they will have to spend; the second should prevent at least the most flagrant mistakes of investment selection, while alerting decisionmakers to the future capital and recurrent cost implications of their choices.

Another basic concern is the coordination of decisionmaking among planners, budgeters, spending agencies, and donors. Budgets cannot be properly controlled and directed without it. All of these decisionmakers have important roles to play. In turn, each should be directly responsible for operating within clear limits—that is, within ''hard'' rather than ''soft'' budget ceilings. Furthermore, such ceilings should be in the form of cash limits on spending to prevent inflation from eroding budgetary discipline. Priorities within these ceilings should be as explicit as possible (for example, through the specification of a core investment program) to permit a flexible, efficient response to unforeseen circumstances. Finally, once allocations have been made, they must be followed up by monitoring, with the proper incentives in place to ensure that implementation proceeds as intended. Chapter 8 returns to this issue. It shows that many governments are already trying to improve the incentives for efficient performance of SOEs through innovations such as performance contracts and an expanded role for market forces in public provision.

6

Spending priorities and revenue options in selected sectors

Public finance policies to meet the goals of stable long-term growth, economic efficiency, and poverty alleviation vary from sector to sector. Despite these differences all sectors confront the same fiscal dilemma: tightening financial constraints make it impossible to maintain large subsidies across a wide range of public services and still provide adequately for priority needs and target groups. This chapter complements the earlier discussion by focusing jointly on spending, revenue, and the role of government in certain specific sectors. It has three recurring themes.

- *Setting priorities.* Spreading resources across low-priority tasks is common. Spending and subsidies need to be selective in the types of services covered and to be directed toward target beneficiaries.
- *Mobilizing financial resources.* User charges and other benefit-related fees can improve economic efficiency as well as raise revenue. Charging provides incentives for efficiency in production and use (see Box 6.1). Distributive goals need not suffer if charges are levied on services used primarily by the rich and are differentiated by income.
- *Decentralizing provision.* Shifting more administrative and financial responsibilities to those in closer touch with local conditions and needs may both improve efficiency and raise revenue.

The sectors examined are those in which public finance has traditionally had a major role—human resources and urban and rural infrastructure. Other important sectors, such as industry, agriculture, and national infrastructure (for example, transport and telecommunications) are not dis-

cussed, but examples drawn from some of them appear in other chapters. Public policies toward agriculture and industry were examined in the 1986 and 1987 *World Development Reports.*

Education and health

For historical, economic, and political reasons, government has had a dominant role in education and health in most countries. Schools are usually owned, administered, and financed by central governments. As shown in Table 6.1, the average regional percentage of students in public schools exceeds 83 percent at the primary level and 74 percent at the secondary level. The direct cost of public schooling is borne almost entirely by the government. In a survey of thirty-six developing countries in 1980, more than 30 percent obtained no fee revenue at primary or higher levels. Of those with fees, the amount collected was small—about 8 percent of cost.

Although private activity in the health sector is greater than in education, the government accounts for a major share of total health expenditure in all regions except Asia. Government activities include free or low-cost curative care in public health institutions or social security facilities, specialized hospitals for certain diseases, and other public programs for immunization, water purification, sanitation services, and the like.

What's wrong with present financing arrangements?

Government activity in education and health has produced dramatic improvements in the indicators

Box 6.1 Pricing public services

What price should public providers charge to induce the amount of consumption that is best for society as a whole? If efficiency is the principal goal of price setting, the marginal cost rule generally applies. According to this rule, price should be set equal to society's cost of providing the last, or marginal, unit. Since the price the consumer is willing to pay measures the benefit of another unit of consumption, when price exceeds marginal cost, society can be made better off by a lower price and more consumption. By the same argument, at a price that is lower than marginal cost, society gains from a higher price and less consumption.

Evaluating benefits and costs is difficult

As with most rules the exceptions and qualifications are as important as the rule itself. Finding the right price is complicated for many goods and services. When a state-owned enterprise operates in a competitive market, such as in traded goods like steel, copper, or rice, the appropriate reference point is generally the prevailing market price (see Chapter 8). For nontraded goods, such as water, electricity, or other utilities, however, the incremental cost of resources used in production must be considered in relation to the benefits. This raises difficulties.

Externalities. When one individual's consumption of a publicly provided good affects others, the individual should be induced to consider the social rather than the private costs and benefits of his or her behavior. For example, because individuals may primarily consider only their own well-being, fewer of them are willing to pay the cost of being immunized against a contagious disease than would be socially desirable. A price below marginal cost is thus required. But how much lower? In some cases, as in immunization or family planning programs, it is almost impossible to estimate the price that

will promote the desired behavior, and the service is best provided free. In other cases a fee to "internalize" the externality is feasible, as when toll roads charge a premium for congestion during peak periods. In all cases it is important not to generalize across a wide range of services, even within a sector.

Lumpy investments. In some sectors, such as ports, telecommunications, and power, system expansion requires a few large investments rather than a series of small ones. Setting price to short-run marginal cost results in considerable price instability. Price rises as the system approaches full capacity and falls immediately after a new facility is built, usually with excess capacity. One way to avoid this problem is to use average incremental cost, a formula that provides an inexact but more stable approximation of marginal cost. A further problem is that since unit cost drops as the scale of operation increases (that is, there are scale economies), charging marginal cost will fail to cover operating cost. A two-part pricing scheme—a fee for connection plus a fee equal to the marginal cost of consumption—is sometimes the answer.

Budget constraints and economic distortions. Many countries face tight budgetary constraints because the cost of generating revenue from general sources is high. In many cases, therefore, a price above marginal cost may be warranted.

Price influences the consumption and production of substitutes and complements. In addition misaligned prices and taxes elsewhere in the economy can cause economic distortions. Where feasible, prices should compensate for these effects.

Incomplete markets. Some public services, such as higher education or a hospital stay, would require large payments, albeit over relatively short periods, to cover marginal cost. Where financial markets cannot provide

---

of human well-being during the past thirty years. But risks lie ahead because of three basic problems.

- In a time of rising demands and tightening financial constraints, many governments cannot financially sustain these rates of improvement.
- Many public programs are inefficiently run.
- The distribution of education and health subsidies is not equitable.

INSUFFICIENT SPENDING ON COST-EFFECTIVE ACTIVITIES. Despite improvements in literacy, child mortality rates, and other human resource indicators during the past three decades, more investment in education and health is still socially profitable. Studies based on wage employment data show

that the social rate of return to education, as calculated by comparing the higher lifetime productivity of educated workers with the social cost of education, generally exceeds that of most alternative investments. This finding is corroborated by evidence that educated farmers are considerably more productive: the crop yields of farmers with four years of education are up to 9 percent higher than those of farmers with no education. Health investments, too, have been shown to contribute to development through improvements in the productivity of the labor force, although returns here are more difficult to quantify.

Moreover, much remains to be done for purely humanitarian reasons (see also Box 1 in the Over-

educational credit or health insurance, as is generally the case in developing countries, a price equivalent to marginal cost would be beyond the means of most of the population. Until such markets can be developed, their failure serves as a practical constraint on higher prices.

Administrative costs. For some goods or services (for example, a malarial spraying program to eliminate mosquitoes), it may be extremely costly to identify individual beneficiaries. It may not be feasible to charge at all. In many cases, however, there are alternatives to charging individuals, such as levies within a geographic area. Another problem is that it may be costly to monitor consumption (such as urban road use) or to administer the collection of fees. If fees are collected and kept by the public facility that provides the service, collection may be easier: beneficiaries are often willing to pay more when they know that their money will go toward improved access or quality. Even a high collection cost may not justify free provision. The inefficiency and administrative cost of generating revenue from general taxes may exceed that of mobilizing revenue through prices.

Poverty alleviation. Many public services are provided free so that the poor have access to them. In practice, however, poor people often fail to get these services anyway. Because of budget constraints, public services must often be rationed. When that happens, poor people are likely to be at a disadvantage. Subsidized water and electricity consumption benefits heavy users, such as the rich or industry. Subsidized universities are open only to students, mostly from rich families, who have finished secondary education and who can pass the entrance examination. Subsidized urban transport often bypasses the poorest neighborhoods.

Generating revenue by charging users can improve the distribution of income if the revenue then subsidizes services used by the poor, such as rural health care, primary education, and maintenance of feeder roads. In addition fees can be designed so that subsidies are targeted to the poor rather than dispersed across the entire population. For example, a "lifeline charge" for water allows for free consumption up to a threshold amount and then charges at marginal cost thereafter.

Bureaucratic incentives and political constraints. Basing price purely on cost may limit the incentives for public providers to minimize cost. To ensure efficient operation in the absence of competition, public providers should be evaluated according to rigorous performance criteria and should be made responsive to users who lobby for better and cheaper public services. Political constraints are important because, once subsidies have become entrenched, beneficiaries see them as an entitlement and will object vigorously to any reductions. Subsidy cuts are more easily implemented if they are combined with a credible commitment to improve quality and cut costs.

Apply pricing rules carefully . . . but apply them all the same

Because of the many objectives and constraints, charging for publicly provided goods and services almost always involves some tradeoffs. As the sectoral examples of this chapter demonstrate, however, the tradeoffs are generally less dramatic than often thought. Against a background of clear spending priorities, appropriate prices improve investment decisions and the operational efficiency of public agencies—and often reduce inequities, too.

---

view). In developing countries infant mortality rates are still about eight times higher, and female life expectancy about a third shorter, than in industrial countries. Investment in human resources is critical for poverty alleviation. Without access to basic education or health care the poorest in developing countries have little chance of improving their prospects.

Unfortunately the outlook is bleak for increased resources to improve education and health care. As many developing countries adjust to recent macroeconomic setbacks, human resource sectors have been adversely affected because they rely heavily on the central government budget. Between 1972 and 1985 education's share in central government budgets in all developing countries dropped from 13 to 10 percent; health's share also fell slightly. More important, for many of the poorest countries the falling shares meant real declines in spending and even larger declines in spending per capita. Between 1975 and 1983 in Sub-Saharan Africa, for example, real expenditure for each pupil in primary education declined in seventeen out of the twenty-five low-income countries. Almost all the countries in which such spending fell had lower per capita incomes than those where the spending rose. These trends mean that the enormous gap in per capita spending on human resources between industrial and developing countries has been widening rather than closing.

Table 6.1 The role of the public sector in educational enrollment and health expenditure in developing countries, by region

Region	Percentage of public school students in total enrollment, 1980		Percentage of public spending in total health spending, 1975–80
	Primary	Secondary	
Sub-Saharan Africa	84	80	63
Francophone	90	83	..
Anglophone and others	78	78	..
Asia	87	78	32
Latin America and the Caribbean	84	75	49
Middle East and North Africa	92	91	42

Note: Unweighted averages are used for each country group.
Source: Unesco data and de Ferranti 1985, table 2.

A fundamental problem is that the limited resources are badly used. Too little goes to relatively cheap and cost-effective services. In education, there is a pressing need to expand and improve primary education, the socially most profitable form of investment, particularly in the poorest countries. In twenty-six African countries surveyed by Unesco in 1982, more than half of all adults were illiterate; among women the proportion was much higher. Yet, in a quarter of the countries in Sub-Saharan Africa, primary school enrollment in 1982 was less than 50 percent of the school-age population. In health, most current public spending goes to nonessential drugs and expensive curative services provided largely by hospitals (see Figure 6.1). Inexpensive health measures (in terms of the cost of each death averted), such as immunizations and prenatal care, are not as well financed.

The problem of resource allocation for health and education is partly the result of large across-the-board subsidies and the lack of any pricing mechanism, particularly in centralized systems. The large share of the health budget going to hospitals is a response to demand stimulated by subsidies. Much more of the burden of hospital spending could be borne by the beneficiaries, especially in urban areas. The direct and implicit annual public cost of university students in developing countries is on average twenty-six times that of primary school students. The gap is largest for Sub-Saharan Africa (see Figure 6.2). Much of this cost is in living allowances. In some of the poorest African countries, including Benin, Burkina Faso, Cameroon, and Niger, these living allowances—paid directly to students regardless of need—amounted in 1982 to about one-half of the average salary in the public sector. Because of subsidies such as these the private rate of return to higher education for all developing countries exceeds 20 percent, about twice the social rate of return to higher education.

INTERNAL INEFFICIENCY OF PUBLIC PROGRAMS. Evidence indicates that the mix of inputs in publicly

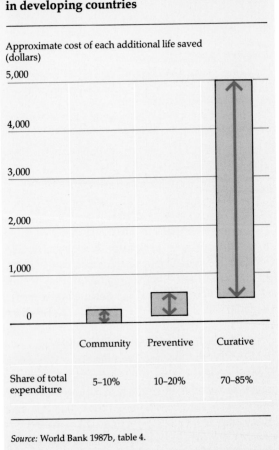

Figure 6.1 Range of approximate cost of each additional life saved by various health services in developing countries

Approximate cost of each additional life saved (dollars)

	Community	Preventive	Curative
Share of total expenditure	5–10%	10–20%	70–85%

Source: World Bank 1987b, table 4.

provided services is often inefficient—that is, the same funds could achieve more if they were reallocated. One problem is that administrators of centralized tax-supported systems have to set norms on budgetary allocations for key inputs; for example, they must balance labor inputs (such as teachers', doctors', and nurses' salaries) against nonlabor inputs (such as drugs and school books). These norms may not match the institution's needs or the community's preferences, but school or health administrators have neither the financial power nor any incentive to change them.

This problem has worsened in recent years because centralized systems have been slow to adjust to aggravated resource scarcities. A common response has been to underfund nonlabor recurrent costs. Central authorities find it extremely difficult to cut the wage bill in favor of operation and maintenance. This creates an imbalance that reduces the efficiency of spending. For example, the scarcity of learning materials in the classroom, such as books and pencils, is the most serious impediment to educational effectiveness in Africa. In health, drug shortages are common in public facilities; Zambia's "free" government health services simply ceased for lack of basic supplies.

Another sort of inefficiency arises when, for lack of an appropriate price signal, demand fails to match supply. When demand cannot be met, institutions resort to rationing by queue. In health, this means long waiting times in government facilities: up to eight hours in Nigeria and five hours in Uganda, according to some studies. Not only is time wasted, but services could be unintentionally and inefficiently rationed, because people with relatively minor ailments are induced to use health facilities more often when the facilities are heavily subsidized.

Inequitable distribution of public subsidies. Uniformly low prices throughout the education and health sector imply that high-cost services are much more subsidized than low-cost ones. The relatively poor have little access to those high-cost services, however. Contrary to policy, the poorest are not only denied a greater share, but they often get less than their proportionate share.

In education, subsidies for higher education are much greater than at lower levels. Thus the very small percentage of the population able to gain access to higher education receives a large share of the education budget. Moreover, among these few, the rich are overrepresented. In the sample of countries shown in Table 6.2, the bottom 40 per-

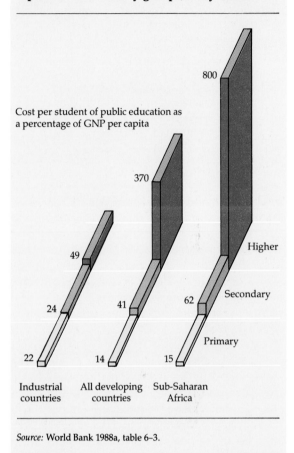

Figure 6.2 Cost per student of different levels of public education as a percentage of GNP per capita in three country groups, early 1980s

Cost per student of public education as a percentage of GNP per capita

Source: World Bank 1988a, table 6–3.

cent of the population obtains from 2 to 17 percent of all higher education subsidies. In Colombia, the Dominican Republic, and Indonesia, this poorest group obtains less than 10 percent of the subsidies. The evidence for Africa suggests that only 39 percent of students in higher education have parents with poor rural backgrounds, although farmers make up 76 percent of the population.

The distribution of public health expenditures is also skewed in many countries. Most health facilities are in urban areas, where household incomes are on average higher. Because 70 to 90 percent of hospital clients live within ten kilometers of the facility they use and public hospitals are generally free, health subsidies disproportionately benefit higher income households. The average health sector subsidy for urban households in China, Colombia, Indonesia, and Malaysia, for example, is up to five times that for rural households.

Table 6.2 Share of higher education subsidies received by different income groups in selected countries in Asia and Latin America
(percent)

Country	Year	Income group		
		Lowest 40 percent	*Middle 40 percent*	*Highest 20 percent*
Argentina	1980	17	45	38
Chile	1982	12	34	54
Colombia	1974	6	35	60
Costa Rica	1982	17	41	42
Dominican Republic	1980	2	22	76
Indonesia	1978	7	10	83
Malaysia	1974	10	38	51
Uruguay	1982	14	52	34

Note: Rows may not add to 100 because of rounding.
Sources: Colombia, Indonesia, and Malaysia, World Bank 1986a, table 10; all other countries, Petrei 1987.

Toward more efficient and equitable delivery of human resource services

What can governments do to alleviate these problems? Specific policy options will vary, but the overall direction of change is clear. Public involvement should be more selective, both in the type of service to be subsidized and the beneficiaries to be targeted.

SELECTIVE USER CHARGES. Public facilities that are used mostly by high-income households and have large private benefits (but few additional benefits to society at large) should carry charges, with some protection for the poor. Higher education is an obvious candidate. It is usually heavily subsidized, and in many countries excess demand is so great that fees would have little effect on enrollment. Such fees should initially be small (perhaps taking the form of reduced allowances). Further improvements in cost recovery will depend partly on the development of scholarship and student loan schemes. In health, fees set at cost are generally undesirable unless insurance is widely available (as discussed below), but outpatient fees and more modest inpatient charges would discourage inappropriate resort to hospital care. Alternatives are charges in public hospitals for patients of doctors in private practice, hospital charges payable directly by insurance providers for insured patients, and charges for drugs.

The allocation of services will be improved if the revenue generated from charges is used to supply more of those services with the highest social benefit. For many of the poorest countries this means improving access to primary education, which should continue to be subsidized. The budget for primary education in some African countries—for

example, Côte d'Ivoire, Mali, Senegal, Tanzania, and Togo—could be increased by more than 20 percent if the stipends for living expenses paid to higher education students were terminated. For other developing countries in which enrollment in primary education is already high, the best policy would be to improve its quality and to expand secondary education or even some selected disciplines in higher education where graduates are in short supply.

Similar considerations apply to health. Revenue from user charges would allow underfunded, cost-effective basic health services to expand. Modest fee increases could cover a substantial part of non-salary costs, the component of expenditure that tends to be squeezed.

Charges to users could also make delivery of government services more efficient. In health, a small charge proportional to the service cost would tend to make clients avoid unnecessary services. Different charges for different services could be used to signal priorities. For example, a clinic could charge nothing for prenatal care but a fee for regular outpatient care. In education, too, fees induce students, their parents, and administrators to scrutinize costs.

Modest charges for some services used by the bulk of the population, such as drugs and school materials, also appear to be affordable. In surveys of several countries the current level of spending by households indicates a willingness to pay for both education and health services. This willingness is greater if households feel they are receiving better services in return. In the Philippines visits to private facilities and traditional practitioners remain popular, despite the fact that their charges averaged twenty-eight times those of government clinics.

Can social goals such as poverty alleviation still be met? Increased charges need not reduce the poor's access to health and education facilities. Charges for universities and tertiary-level hospitals have a negligible effect on the poor. If spending on services used by the poor expanded at the same time that charges for services used by the rich increased, the distribution of subsidies could be significantly improved at no additional cost. For example, in developing countries 71 percent of people leave their school-age years with either no schooling or at most only primary schooling. These people, who tend to be poor, receive only 22 percent of public spending on education. Their share would rise to 64 percent if user charges were introduced to recover the entire public cost of higher education and the savings were then used to finance additional primary school places for those now denied access. The funds could also be used to stimulate the demand for education, particularly in rural areas, through reimbursement for out-of-pocket expenses, feeding programs, and other initiatives. Although full cost recovery is generally neither economically appropriate, for reasons explained below, nor politically feasible, this rough calculation illustrates the potential redistributive gains to introducing or increasing fees.

These policies do not preclude safeguarding the poor's access to higher education or hospital care, or the access of the very poor—who cannot afford even modest fees—to services at every level. Differential pricing is needed. One option would be to base fees on residence, so that people living in poor areas pay less. In Mali, for example, cost recovery in hospitals began in 1983. The fee for a day's stay in a small-town health center is less than 20 percent of the fee at a main urban hospital. Adult consultation at rural health posts costs half that at an urban health post. In Thailand, where insurance is available only in urban areas, rural coverage is provided through the sale of health cards, which entitle the bearer to a specified number of treatments. In education, one approach is to make greater use of scholarships based on need as well as merit. More sophisticated schemes, such as student loans, need to be developed if cost recovery is going to be used extensively for the most expensive services.

AN ADEQUATE FINANCIAL ENVIRONMENT. The development of educational credit and health insurance systems is critical in determining how much governments should recover of costs. Educational loans can serve the goals of cost recovery, effi-ciency, and equity. Particularly in the middle-income countries of Latin America and Asia, it is possible to recover a substantial part of current subsidies through loans, while keeping the repayment burden relatively low. Such schemes increase the competition for places by opening higher education to a larger pool of applicants—including good students with no funds—thus increasing efficiency and equity.

Few developing countries have capital markets that enable individuals to borrow for education, however, even though the returns on such investments are high. Education is a particularly long-term investment. Risks are high because few students have acceptable collateral, and many countries lack the legal or administrative framework to enforce financial contracts. Governments can therefore play an important role. Whether they lend the money themselves or insure commercial loans, governments are big enough to absorb risks that private lenders will not bear. Many countries in Latin America have been able to maintain a long-standing educational credit system with a relatively low incidence of default and late repayment. Administrative problems remain, however; some of the present systems fail to be self-financing because of low interest rates. If a subsidy is desired, a financially viable loan scheme should be complemented by scholarships targeted to needy students.

In health, where large individual expenditures are unpredictable, risk-sharing through insurance is desirable. Health insurance programs generally cover only a small proportion of low-income households, despite government sponsorship. Coverage is often restricted to urban areas or to employees of agricultural estates. One reason for this is that many governments have opted to offer free services, making insurance unnecessary. Another is that the administrative cost of organizing and operating a risk-sharing program tends to be high. The government can play an important role in setting up these schemes by encouraging increased participation and, for example, by mandating that only high-cost services be covered. Such schemes—like any others—should use techniques such as deductibles and copayments to encourage beneficiaries to take care of themselves and encourage providers to compete with each other. In Uruguay, for instance, the social security system funds health care organizations in which members pay a participation fee plus small charges for services used. Such schemes pool risk without eliminating the incentive to minimize cost.

Many health schemes are part of the national social security systems existing in most developing countries; old age pensions are usually the other main element. Although most such systems are recently established and are not yet a burden on public finance, experience from older schemes in both industrial and developing countries shows that financial problems can easily arise. In many developing countries the fiscal cost of new and expanded schemes may outweigh the benefits (see Box 6.2). Countries that already have such systems can try to improve their design.

DECENTRALIZING RESPONSIBILITIES. User charges will improve efficiency if public institutions such as clinics or schools are given greater responsibility for collecting them and choosing how to spend the proceeds. Decentralization means greater flexibility in responding both to local demands and to tightening financial constraints. Incentives for fee collection and efficiency should also improve, since users are more willing to pay when they can hold the providers accountable for the cost.

However, the central government must retain an important role in areas such as training policy, overall facilities planning (particularly of large institutions, such as hospitals and universities), research funding, the setting of national education standards, and the provision of information about the benefits and costs of services.

Public transfers can ensure that equity is not sacrificed. Ideally these should be given directly (based on need and, for education, on merit) to individuals to spend the funds at the facility of their choice—public or private. These schemes are still at the experimental stage in some developing countries, such as Chile and Thailand. A more modest approach is to distribute subsidies according to the economic need of localities or neighborhood groups. But funding should be set to maintain the local community's incentive to collect its own revenue (see Chapter 7).

INCREASING THE USE OF NONGOVERNMENTAL RESOURCES. As Chapter 2 made clear, there is no uniquely "correct" balance between public and private activity. However, governments reduce their ability to broaden access to education and health when they discourage private initiatives. For example, Congo, Ethiopia, Nigeria, and Pakistan banned or tried to ban private schools through legislation in the late 1970s. In Benin, Cameroon, and Togo, private health care is frowned upon. Private schemes elsewhere face un-

Box 6.2   Financing social security

Most developing countries have social security systems; that is, public programs that provide financial support if people lose their source of income (caused by retirement, disability, death of a primary earner in a family, illness, maternity, work-related injury, or unemployment) and often if they need medical care or help with the expense of raising children. These programs provide social insurance by sharing the risk against individual income loss among the population. As of 1985, twenty-four out of thirty-seven low-income economies and fifty-two out of sixty middle-income economies had programs that cover at least work-related injury and provide pensions for those retired because of age or disability. Many of these systems apply only to urban workers in the formal sector and are small. In urbanized middle-income countries such as Brazil, Chile, Cyprus, Hungary, Malaysia, Portugal, Singapore, Uruguay, and Yugoslavia, however, social security covers much of the labor force, and receipts exceed 5 percent of GDP.

Issues in social security finance

Solvency, distribution, and efficiency of social security are critical issues in public finance.

Solvency. Current mandatory contributions from workers and their employers finance disability, unemployment, and maternity benefits. Pensions may be operated on a pay-as-you-go basis, where current contributions pay for current benefits, or on a fully funded one, where reserve funds equal the value of future benefit payments, or some combination of the two. In most developing countries benefit payments are still substantially below revenues, particularly for recently established systems where there are few beneficiaries relative to contributing workers. For a sample of twenty-nine developing countries, only four with older systems—Mexico, Peru, Portugal, and Uruguay—had deficits in 1983 (Box figure 6.2). These deficits amounted to less than 10 percent of revenues for all sampled countries except Uruguay, which is discussed further below.

However, social security systems can easily become insolvent and have broader public finance implications. First, surpluses generated in the early stages of these systems can be quickly dissipated if they are used to fund general government activities with low financial returns. Once the social security system matures and ceases to run surpluses, governments that rely on it may not redeem the bonds held in the social security reserve fund. A more subtle, and more common, means by which a government escapes its obligation to its social security reserve fund is through high inflation, which erodes the value of nominally fixed assets such as government bonds. This has happened in Turkey (in the late 1970s and early 1980s) and in many Latin American systems. Second, the soundness of social security finance can also be altered by demographic factors. An unexpected rise in life expectancy, decline in the birth rate, or increase in emigration raises the "dependency ratio"—the number of pension beneficiaries for each contributing worker—and worsens the system's financial status. For example, the old age and survivors components of Uruguay's social security system, which is now being reformed, required subsidies in 1983 amounting to more than 3 percent of GDP partly due to low retirement ages (sixty for men, fifty-five for women), high life expectancy (seventy-two years at birth), and a high rate of emigration among the

Box figure 6.2 Financial status of social security systems, 1983

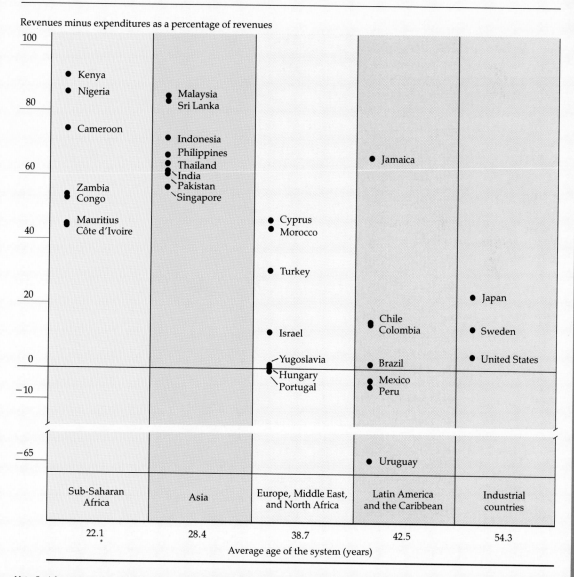

Revenues minus expenditures as a percentage of revenues

Note: Social security systems include public programs that provide benefits for old age, disability, death, work injury, and unemployment. Some of these programs also provide health and family allowance benefits.
Sources: Puffert (background paper), U.S. Government 1986, and World Bank data.

young. Third, financial problems can arise unless a pragmatic balance is reached between the objectives of social assistance, which call for an adequate benefit financed by redistribution from rich to poor, and individual equity, which provides benefits based solely on an individual's contributions. For example, Turkey's use in 1984 of general revenue to finance the government's social assistance objective for the civil service pension will soon have a substantial effect on the budget deficit.

Distribution. The use of general funds to subsidize social security can be inequitable. Coverage is limited in most developing countries. Only in industrial countries and several middle-income countries in Latin America (Argentina, Brazil, Chile, Costa Rica, Uruguay, and Venezuela) and a few other countries (such as Israel, Mauritius, and Singapore) are most of the labor force and population covered. In most other countries less than 10 percent of the population, primarily in urban areas, is covered. Coverage is highly correlated with income, work skills, and the power of pressure groups. If social security is funded from general revenues, it can be a mechanism for a regressive redistribution.

Efficiency. Social security reserve funds may not be directed toward investments with the highest economic returns. As a readily available and large source of long-term financing, such funds are often used for projects that turn into "white elephants." In the 1970s the Philippine Government Service Insurance Systems (GSIS) devoted a large share of its investment portfolio to developing a series of first-class hotels in Manila. These hotels were never used at full capacity and have had a mixed record of profits. The present government plans to turn them over to the private sector.

Social security may also distort savings and labor markets. People may reduce their own savings because their expected social security benefits serve as a replacement. Social security systems can affect the labor market both by inducing earlier retirement and by introducing distortionary marginal taxes on wage payments. In practice, the net effect on savings and labor markets varies across countries and depends on the responsiveness of private transfers and labor supply to social security taxes.

What can be done?

For the poorest countries the financial, economic, and administrative costs of establishing a publicly funded social security system, or of significantly expanding existing systems, can be substantial. The risk that such schemes may eventually be a substantial drain on general revenue and distort resource allocation will generally outweigh the benefits of serving only a limited and already privileged segment of the population.

Countries that have already implemented extensive systems have several policy options.

Sustainable benefit bases. First, where low retirement ages are partly responsible for financing problems, an increase in the age at which workers can receive benefits is appropriate. Second, social security programs should be structured so that the growth of benefits is tied to the growth of revenue. If benefits are indexed for inflation, then the revenue base should also be indexed. Third, social security benefits are often much higher than an actuarial return on contributions. This happens, in part, because benefits are frequently based on the last few years of a person's earnings, when they peak, while contributions are drawn from a much longer earnings history. To bring benefits in line with contributions, benefit levels could be more closely related to an individual's full earnings history.

Financially autonomous systems. One efficient method of safeguarding against insolvency is through autonomous social security funds. Current contributions for disability, work-related injury, unemployment, and maternity benefits should thus equal the actuarial premiums. Managers of such funds would be responsible for providing actuarially fair benefits based on explicit principles of social insurance and would be accountable to the beneficiaries. They should be subject to oversight and incentives to promote investments with high economic returns (see Chapter 5).

Targeting social assistance. Providing social assistance for redistributive purposes through social security poses risks for financial solvency and autonomy. Social assistance is best provided through programs financed from general revenue and kept separate from social security funds.

---

duly harsh restrictions on fees and on the hiring of professionals such as teachers and health workers, as well as overly high requirements for quality.

Relaxing these restrictions can mobilize new resources. In Pakistan in 1983, five years after a nearly complete ban on private schools was lifted, enrollment at the primary and secondary levels had increased significantly. Private schools ac-

counted for at least 10 percent of total enrollment. With assistance in training and coordinating activities, private voluntary organizations can also contribute.

Again, the central government retains an important role. It must balance incentives and regulation to ensure that services are provided efficiently. In health, the government must ensure that the private market for individual health services is as competitive as possible. This involves spreading information on the prices charged by alternative providers, on the appropriate treatment for various ailments, and on the importance of insurance coverage. Cost control through prepayment plans or capitation (set fees per patient) is crucial in privately provided health care. For example, the Brazilian government encourages prepaid health organizations by allowing social security contributions to be used as payment. In education, this informational role might mean displaying the results of systemwide examinations. The government can also withhold accreditation from institutions that attempt to defraud students.

The scope for reform

These measures could be combined into a program that would make spending on education and health more efficient and more equitable. They would do so by making public spending more selective, both in the services covered and in the beneficiaries targeted. They include: charging for publicly provided curative hospital care, drugs, and university education; increasing public subsidies for basic services, such as preventive care and primary education; providing an adequate financial environment for both private consumers and providers through effective insurance and credit systems; decentralizing government services to foster management accountability; and encouraging the use of nongovernmental resources with an appropriate balance of incentives and regulation.

Such a package may be difficult to implement. In some countries it would upset the long-established traditions, often inherited from developed countries, of free education and health. Institutional limitations may also complicate the administration of some policies, such as the loan schemes or the insurance systems. For these reasons reform will take time and is bound to vary from country to

---

Box 6.3 Implementing educational reform in Ghana

Until the mid-1970s Ghana had one of the most developed and effective educational systems in Western Africa, with enrollment rates at all levels among the highest in the region. As the country's economy declined during the 1970s, however, the quality of education deteriorated, and school enrollments stagnated or fell. With some international assistance the present government started in 1987 to rehabilitate its educational system. The overall objectives of the six-year reform are to improve teaching standards, to make education financing more efficient and equitable, and to ensure that the reformed system is fiscally sustainable.

The reform is concerned with both the primary and the secondary levels. It calls for savings from eliminating nonexistent staff from the rolls, from reducing the number of nonteaching staff (universities had more than one nonteaching member of staff for each student), and from avoiding duplication in programs. Moreover the public share of postprimary education costs will be reduced by gradually eliminating boarding subsidies and by introducing fees for the use of books. At both the secondary and tertiary levels, loan and scholarship schemes are being developed to make education more accessible to poorer students.

In 1971 an effort to reduce the cost of higher education by introducing maintenance fees along with student loans provoked strong opposition. Within a year the government was overthrown, and its successor withdrew official support for the proposal. The present government, recognizing the importance of gaining broad public support for the current reforms, drew up a plan. The early signs are that it is enjoying some success. It has two main elements.

• *Cost recovery linked with improved quality.* Secondary school boarding subsidies will end at the same time that new science equipment and textbooks for secondary students arrive. At the university level, to minimize opposition to the announced reduction of boarding subsidies, the policy promises to make books and equipment more easily available, to rehabilitate educational facilities, to offer land on which students can grow food, and to introduce student loans to cover the cost of textbooks and, eventually, boarding.

• *Public education campaign.* Since it was first announced, the education reform program has dominated the media and been a major topic of public debate in Ghana. Through leaflets, meetings, and speeches by high officials, the government has stressed the disparities in the cost for each student at different levels of education (unit costs in Ghanaian universities are 120 times those in primary education); the high cost of subsidizing the boarding of university students and secondary students, when the funds could provide places for many more students; the fact that the cost of food and lodging for one university student is enough to educate fifteen primary school pupils; and the savings to be achieved through improved quality and effectiveness.

country. Improvements in public administration, management, and institutions are also generally needed to complement the reforms in financing mechanisms. A hopeful sign is that many governments have already begun reform (see Box 6.3 on Ghana). Even if it is only partial, reform can produce worthwhile improvements.

Urban services

Governments usually play a large role in the provision of urban services. A traditional justification for this is that private providers find it hard to make profits from some urban services. For example, it is usually impractical to charge individuals for road use. Economies of scale in water provision imply that a service may be economical only if run or regulated by government. For almost all urban services the government's role is also important because of congestion and environmental externalities: one person's consumption affects the well-being of others. Moreover the provision of urban services has a distributional dimension. Although urban residents are, on average, better off than their rural counterparts, a significant proportion of a country's poor lives in urban slums with no access to safe water and other basic services.

Despite the great diversity between and within

Box 6.4 The public finance of power: issues and options

With few exceptions electric power in developing countries is provided by a single, publicly owned, vertically integrated utility. In many countries this is the largest state-owned enterprise (SOE). Its prices are regulated by the government. This public involvement is usually justified by the argument that electric power is a natural monopoly. Power production and transmission have high fixed costs and low marginal costs that make it both expensive for a newcomer to enter the market and cheap for the established firm to add another customer.

The financial and management autonomy of power utilities varies. Often they have little of either. This leads to budgetary difficulties and to inefficient use of resources.

Financial and fiscal issues

A well-managed power utility that sets tariffs at long-run marginal costs should generally be able to cover all of its operating expenses and debt service and to contribute substantially to its investment program out of its own resources. Its effect on the government budget would be neutral or even positive if it were subject to corporate income taxes. Unfortunately, however, a recent study by the World Bank concluded that since 1965 the financial performance of power utility companies in developing countries has declined. The self-financing ratio—internal funds as a proportion of the enterprise's investment requirements—has fallen on average from 25 percent during 1966–73 to 17 percent during 1980–85. Financial rates of return are also falling (see Box figure 6.4).

The poor financial state of many power utilities has been blamed on the failure of governments to permit timely and sufficient rate increases. Collecting tariffs is a problem in itself. Accounts receivable increased from an average of 77 days in 1966–73 to 112 days in 1980–85,

a trend that reflects difficulties over metering, billing, and collection. In many countries governments and SOEs are among the most delinquent customers (see Chapter 8).

As a result many utilities depend on government for investment financing at preferential interest rates, for the waiving of debt, and sometimes even for subsidies toward operating costs. In turn, these subsidies in-

Box figure 6.4 Financial rate of return of power utilities, 1965 to 1984
(percent)

Source: Munasinghe, Gilling, and Mason 1988, figure 5.

---

countries, most urban services are provided by local governments and financed from local taxes, user charges, or transfers from higher level governments (see Chapter 7). Infrastructure, such as water, transport, and solid waste disposal, takes up a substantial share of the municipal budget in many cities. Some of these lower tier decisions can also have decidedly national repercussions, however, especially in the power sector (see Box 6.4).

Issues in public finance

Urban services are best examined as a whole. The major components—urban transport, water sup- ply, power, and housing—confront the same issues of allocation, internal efficiency, and equity. More- over consumers, private and public providers, and regulators typically make decisions about several services jointly. For example, residents do not buy or rent housing without considering the availabil- ity of local infrastructure.

UNDERPROVISION OF BASIC SERVICES. Efficient ur- ban services are a precondition for economic growth. Urban-based firms need transport and communications to do business with each other, sanitary services to dispose of their waste, and power to make their capital productive. Their

crease the national debt and deprive other sectors of the economy—where user charges may be inappro- priate—of budgetary resources. In Colombia, for exam- ple, an ambitious investment program, which raised power's share in total public investments from 24 per- cent in 1980 to 38 percent in 1985, was not matched by new revenues. As a result the combined deficits of the country's power utilities amounted to 345 million dol- lars, or 1 percent of GDP, by 1986.

Efficiency issues

Electricity is efficiently supplied in very few developing countries. In Colombia excessive public investments in power, made when growth in demand was falling, con- tributed not only to the public deficit but also to excess capacity, which is expected to be about 20 to 25 percent of installed capacity during 1987–89. A comprehensive energy reform is now being planned. Even in a country such as the Republic of Korea, where operational stan- dards are high, reforming investment policies and set- ting less ambitious targets for reliability could save $200 million a year.

Weak planning, high transmission losses, excessive staffing, inefficient operation, and inadequate mainte- nance are common and growing problems. In some cases the size and sophistication of the power sector has increased dramatically in the past decade without a corresponding improvement in management. In many other cases these problems can be blamed on regula- tions that take away managerial incentives to be inno- vative and efficient, such as rules regarding pricing, coverage of service, the use of inputs, and pay.

Inefficiency on the demand side is a worry, too. Effi- ciency requires that in principle the prices that guide the decisions of producers and consumers reflect true economic costs. Unsatisfied demand at those prices also indicates the need to expand production; under

these conditions it is clear that consumers are willing to pay for the expansion. When the principle is violated, consumption is distorted, and the utility may face a serious financial handicap, leading in turn to a deterio- ration in service.

Policy options

Appropriate pricing is critical for allocational and inter- nal efficiency in the absence of effective competition. Because investments in power are large and lumpy, the level of revenues needed to ensure financial viability will not necessarily coincide with that produced by short-term marginal cost pricing (see Box 6.1). In that case alternatives such as multipart pricing may need to be considered.

From a macroeconomic perspective the net fiscal ef- fect of efficient electricity prices would generally assist programs of stabilization and structural adjustment. Rough estimates based on data from six African coun- tries indicate that raising user charges closer to long- run marginal cost could add 5 to 10 percent to central government revenue.

Manipulating prices to redistribute income often goes wrong. Subsidizing the unit cost of electricity encourages waste and fails to aid the small consumer, who has few appliances, let alone the majority of poor households, which lack access altogether. If subsidies are used, they should be targeted. For example, the utility might charge ''lifeline rates'' for low levels of consumption. Alternatively, selective rebates on the connection charge to allow easier access are more visible and efficient than cuts in the unit price of consumption.

Pricing policy reform in power should be comple- mented by more transparent and accountable manage- ment practices, increased training, and a greater reli- ance on private sector (see Chapter 8).

Table 6.3 Comparative operating conditions and costs of private and public bus services in selected cities in developing countries, 1985

City, country	Ownership	Fleet utilization (percent)	Staff-operating bus ratio	Cost per passenger (km/U.S. cent)	Revenue-cost ratio
Ankara, Turkey	Public	65	6.0	2.5	0.67
	Private	95	2.6	1.2	1.70
Bangkok, Thailand	Public	80	6.2	1.9	0.74
	Private	80	..	1.2	1.10
Calcutta, India	Public	64	20.7	1.9	0.46
	Private	86	4.0	0.7	1.10
Istanbul, Turkey	Public	60	7.5	2.0	0.88
	Private	..	..	1.7	1.10
Jakarta, Indonesia	Public	59	14.5	1.8	0.50
	Private	76	7.3	0.9	1.20
Karachi, Pakistan	Public	40	12.4	2.8	0.49
	Private	72	6.4	1.0	1.15
Khartoum, Sudan	Public	65	18.1	1.5	0.80
	Private	80	4.5	0.6	1.10

Note: Only data for comparable large bus types are included.
Source: Armstrong-Wright and Thiriez 1987, table 1.

workers need all these services and housing, too. Yet, despite heavy subsidies, many urban services are underprovided. Most recent World Bank estimates indicate that 23 percent of the urban population in developing countries has no potable water within 200 meters; the figure rises to 35 percent in Sub-Saharan Africa. Road congestion is spreading, and escalating transport costs have reduced productivity. Housing shortages are common in many cities.

Both sides of the public finance equation—revenue and spending—have contributed to this underprovision. Municipalities face tight budgetary constraints (see Chapter 7). Traditional ways of

---

Box 6.5 How do Nigerian manufacturers cope with inadequate infrastructure services?

Nigerian manufacturers face frequent interruptions of publicly provided services such as water, electricity, telecommunications, transport, and waste disposal. When available, the services are often of poor quality. This is a waste of public funds that also adds significantly to the cost of manufacturing.

Nigerian manufacturers therefore make capital investments in services such as electricity and water for themselves. According to the Nigerian Industrial Development Bank (NIDB), frequent power outages and fluctuations in voltage affect almost every industrial enterprise in the country. To avoid production losses as well as damage to machinery and equipment, firms invest in generators. A milk processing firm, for example, needed its own generators because voltage surges or gaps in supply could threaten vital equipment. One large textile manufacturing enterprise estimates the depreciated capital value of its electricity supply investment as $400 per worker. If extrapolated to all 6,000 Nigerian manufacturing firms, such an amount (at current prices) could pay for capital equipment to improve transmission and distribution for the entire country,

including the residential sector. Similarly companies invest in boreholes and water treatment plants. Typically as much as 20 percent of the initial capital investment for new plants financed by the NIDB is spent on electric generators and boreholes.

The cost of poor telecommunications is reflected in numerous small expenditures, such as motorcycles for couriers and radio systems, and in time wasted, as managers and sales people travel to deliver messages or hold conversations that would take moments over a working phone line. In Lagos long commuting times caused by inefficient bus services have led firms and workers to rely on private transport as much as possible.

Although necessary, many of these self-provided infrastructure investments are inefficient, because they are too small. Since possibilities for input substitution are limited, firms that make capital expenditures to provide their own services have higher production costs. Better public provision of infrastructure would reduce the losses; policy options are already being studied and developed.

raising revenue are becoming increasingly costly. Transfers from higher tiers of government are unreliable, and many local authorities have neither the authority nor the know-how to coax more out of the property tax. Services that rely heavily on general funding sources are therefore bound to suffer.

The problem is aggravated because spending in many cities is not directed toward the appropriate services. In some cases, as in bus transport, large subsidies to public providers have squeezed out more efficient private providers. Table 6.3 shows that in cities where both types operate simultaneously, the cost per passenger is lower for private operators compared with subsidized public operators. Also public transit authorities often favor expensive schemes. The new metros in Caracas, Venezuela, and São Paulo, Brazil, cost (at 1983 prices) $1.44 billion and $2.34 billion, respectively. They serve a small percentage of the urban population, place a considerable and continuous burden on the cities' financial resources, and displace improvements elsewhere.

At the same time basic services are being neglected. The cost of this neglect is particularly high when alternative private sources are either unavailable or too small to be efficient. This is true for the provision of water and electricity. Private water vendors, who have an inefficiently small volume of business, operate in congested cities where the unit cost of piped water would be low. A water carrier's average charge was at least three times higher than the average incremental cost of publicly provided piped water in Nairobi, Kenya, in 1977 and two times higher in Lomé, Togo, in 1981. In Lagos, Nigeria, low-income families buy potable water from vendors at a price at least four times the marginal cost of piped water and must carry it long distances. Private manufacturing firms in Lagos have also found it necessary, at great cost, to provide almost all basic services themselves (see Box 6.5).

Public regulatory policies have inhibited private providers. Although not explicitly part of the public budget, these policies can have large effects akin to taxation and spending. The situation in housing illustrates this problem. In many cities private housing markets have been overly restricted by rent control, which has often produced results exactly opposite to those intended. Roughly 40 percent of the world's urban dwellers are renters. Most are subject to some form of rent control. Studies in industrial as well as developing countries show that the benefits of such restrictions to present renters are low. Some restrictions are simply not effective because of side payments. Effective restrictions, however, inhibit maintenance and new construction—as in Kumasi, Ghana, where controls have contributed to a nearly complete shutdown of the housing market. In addition rent control reduces property taxes and, thus, the government's ability to improve those services that cannot be privately provided.

Another constraint on the supply of private housing is housing finance. In many countries credit to finance investment in housing is limited. In some cases this is the result of financial policies that repress the efficient flow of capital in general and housing investment in particular. These policies act very much like distortionary taxes, with effects throughout the economy as well as the sector (see Box 6.6).

THE HIGH COST OF SOME SERVICES. Heavily subsidized public providers often produce urban services inefficiently. They have little incentive to be cost-effective or to respond speedily to changing conditions. In Calcutta, India, the public bus corporation requires a subsidy of around $1 million a month, since revenues cover only about one-half of the system's operating cost. Yet it has a lower fleet utilization rate, a higher staffing ratio, and a greater incidence of fare evasion than private sector competitors that are not subsidized (see Table 6.3).

FAILURE TO SERVE THE POOR. Heavy subsidies in urban infrastructure often fail to reach the poor. The poorest members of urban society do not use the most expensive forms of urban transport. For example, the Caracas metro, due to be completed in 1990, will not directly serve the lowest income groups; they demand few of the longer trips that the metro will provide, and they neither live nor work on the main line. Middle-income groups are expected to benefit the most.

As noted above, one-quarter of the developing world's urban population has no access to safe water. These are the city's poorest; many have to buy water from private vendors at rates from 4 to 100 times higher than those paid by the more fortunate, who have access to piped water (see Table 6.4).

Improving the delivery of urban services

The direction of reform depends on the service. Where a competitive private market is viable, such

Box 6.6 Hidden fiscal dimensions of housing policies

Fiscal policy has a significant effect on the housing sector even though, on average, housing accounts for only about 2 percent of central government expenditure in developing countries. One reason is that the intermediaries that finance and build housing in many countries are state-owned enterprises, which are regulated and financed in part by budgetary transfers that are not classified under the housing category. Another reason is that these intermediaries, whether private or public, are subject to implicit taxes and subsidies through government regulation. Interest ceilings and portfolio restrictions on banking institutions have tax-like effects that are magnified in inflationary environments. They significantly affect the ability of financial institutions to intervene efficiently in housing markets.

In Argentina implicit subsidization of housing finance for low-income dwellers and households that already own their homes has been costly. During the most recent macroeconomic downturn the only institutions lending for housing were FONAVI, a government wage tax fund, and BHN, a national mortgage bank. Both recover only a small percentage of their loans. The former pays extraordinarily large subsidies to a fraction of the eligible households. The latter has been decapitalized by a loan forgiveness program for previous borrowers. Other lenders have no access to government subsidies and have withdrawn from the market because of financial policies that make it impossible to mobilize resources and on-lend profitably. Access to housing finance is thus severely limited. Those most

badly affected by the recent macroeconomic downturn are low-income renters, whose real rents doubled, and middle-income savers, who are either not eligible for, or have been denied, FONAVI and BHN funds.

In Poland public subsidies for housing, combined with restrictions on the ability of private providers to enter the market, have led to a severe housing shortage. High subsidies have stimulated the demand for government and cooperative housing programs. However, the large amounts being spent (off-budget interest subsidies and explicit government housing programs claim 6 and 13 percent of current government spending, respectively) have been insufficient to meet the growing demand. At the same time restrictions on prices and sales, the centralized allocation of housing materials, limitations on homeownership, and other regulations have removed the incentive for private finances to enter the sector. Thus, despite the obviously high rates of return to investment, shortages persist. In 1980 there were roughly 18 percent more households than dwellings, a very high figure compared with other countries.

Removing these distortions would bring substantial benefits. Reducing off-budget subsidies would alleviate pressure on the overall rate of inflation by slowing the rate of money creation. In the longer term there are also implications for growth, because housing is the single most important repository of household savings, and because efficient housing markets would increase labor mobility.

---

as in urban transport and housing, narrowing public involvement will release resources for better use elsewhere. This might mean shifting from direct provision to financial and regulatory policies that mitigate externalities and breakdowns in capital

Table 6.4 Ratio of the price charged by private water vendors to the price charged by the public utility in selected cities, mid-1970s to early 1980s

City, country	Price ratio
Kampala, Uganda	4:1 to 9:1
Lagos, Nigeria	4:1 to 10:1
Abidjan, Côte d'Ivoire	5:1
Lomé, Togo	7:1 to 10:1
Nairobi, Kenya	7:1 to 11:1
Istanbul, Turkey	10:1
Dhaka, Bangladesh	12:1 to 25:1
Tegucigalpa, Honduras	16:1 to 34:1
Lima, Peru	17:1
Port-au-Prince, Haiti	17:1 to 100:1
Surabaya, Indonesia	20:1 to 60:1
Karachi, Pakistan	28:1 to 83:1

markets. Where direct provision is most efficient—as in water, power, and roads—the public provider should apply user charges or cost-covering benefit taxes.

PRIORITIES FOR URBAN TRANSPORT. Governments can do much to improve urban transport in developing countries. The most pressing task is to upgrade and extend the urban road network. Experience shows that such activities offer high rates of return through faster journeys, reduced fuel consumption, and fewer breakdowns. Maintenance, in general, is a cost-effective form of spending (see Chapter 5). But some developing countries could make it more so. Studies in Argentina, Brazil, and Kenya, for example, have shown that roads can be maintained more effectively by private contractors than by public agencies. In Ponta Grossa, Brazil, in the mid-1970s road maintenance cost 59 percent more when done by municipal workers rather than by private contractors.

Governments also have a role in traffic regulation and management, vehicle licensing, the setting of safety and environmental standards in mass transit, and, where feasible, road pricing. These policies can serve as cheap, congestion-relieving alternatives to new transport investments. For example, in San José, Costa Rica, intense commercial development in the business district increased on-street parking and slowed average car speeds to ten kilometers an hour. Peak-hour parking restrictions (especially on bus routes), parking meters, and formal designation of loading areas greatly improved the traffic flow. Thus funds for new roads could be shifted to other priority areas in the overall highway system.

Efficient private providers should be allowed to enter the market for bus services. Transport services, whether publicly or privately provided, work best with a minimum of control on the setting of fares. Aside from balancing supply and demand, competitive fares create a favorable climate for efficient investment. Equally, they discourage investment that is unlikely to be profitable—such as capital-intensive subway systems in poor, densely populated cities.

In most cases a greater reliance on competitive provision of bus services will not hurt the very poor, since they tend to live in areas that are not served by subsidized bus routes. Indeed, competitive provision may even increase access by extending service to areas not covered by subsidized public providers. In Bangkok, Thailand; Istanbul, Turkey; and Kingston, Jamaica; for example, bus routes that public operators deemed "unprofitable" were contracted out to competitive private operators who earned profits without changing the fare structure.

PUBLIC PRIORITIES IN HOUSING. Housing means shelter, the lot on which the shelter stands, and the surrounding infrastructure. By itself public shelter construction can rarely meet the housing needs of the poor, let alone that of the entire population. Public housing projects frequently fail to give the poor what they want. Subsidies intended for the poor are often captured by high- and middle-income households. Instead of building shelter, the public sector could try to make the private market work better. That could mean, for example, rationalizing land tenure; liberalizing financial markets; easing restrictions, such as rent control; and providing basic infrastructure, such as water, sewerage, and electricity.

Housing finance has been particularly neglected.

The scope for housing finance to stimulate supply is admittedly limited in low-income developing countries. In middle-income countries, however, appropriate reforms could readily free additional resources. In many countries interest rate ceilings and restrictions on new lenders have increased the public deficit (since many financial institutions are publicly owned) and have acted as distortionary taxes on the housing sector (see Box 6.6). Such subsidies are bad vehicles for relieving poverty. A liberalized financial sector would enable most of the population to finance its housing needs privately.

For the very poor, direct public intervention in housing will continue to be needed. However, such intervention is better focused on providing basic services and security of tenure rather than on dwellings. Where ill-defined property rights increase the risk of buying and selling a site, security of tenure makes squatters better off. One study in the Philippines estimated that it increases the value of dwellings by 18 percent. It also encourages squatters to improve their buildings. The provision of basic urban services is essential, too. For example, the *kampung* (neighborhood) improvement program in Indonesia—which emphasizes the provision of service roads, footpaths, drainage, and improved water supply and sanitation—has been extended into a national program covering 220 towns during the past fifteen years. Studies have concluded that this has greatly assisted a large proportion of poor neighborhoods without imposing too much of a fiscal burden. The lessons are being applied in slum-upgrading projects elsewhere in the world.

EFFICIENT PRICING OF WATER AND SEWERAGE. Water and sewerage systems are generally managed at the local level by autonomous or semiautonomous agencies. Spending on these services is usually a big part of total local government expenditure; user charges generate additional revenue to finance such spending and can also improve efficiency.

Cities in developing countries differ greatly in their policies toward pricing water services. Efficient pricing in the absence of externalities means setting the price at marginal cost and using the proceeds to provide the service. For water supply the marginal costs of different levels of service may differ. Thus efficient pricing would include three components: a consumption charge related to the quantity consumed and roughly equal to the marginal cost of producing, treating, and pumping water; a connection charge to reflect the marginal capital cost of connection, metering, and billing; and a development charge to cover the capital cost of the distribution network. Further refinements might take account of geographical and seasonal variations in cost.

Most cities face rising long-run costs because supplies of clean water are hard to find. In such cases the efficient price exceeds the average cost. Some cities have put this rule into practice. As a result, in Jakarta the local water company was able to pay surplus revenues to the local government in the early 1970s, and in Nairobi water surpluses were used to fund other city spending. What matters is that user charges should be set with efficiency—not merely short-term financing needs—in mind.

Falling long-run costs occur only rarely, as in Lahore, Pakistan, which has a plentiful supply of ground water. Marginal cost may sometimes fall below average cost temporarily, as a result of excess capacity following expansions of the system. In these cases efficient pricing would entail a deficit and would run counter to the objective of financial self-sufficiency. So in balancing efficiency with financial objectives, governments must also take account of the cost of raising revenue in other ways (that is, through taxation).

Urban water tariffs often reflect equity considerations. Some such price structures are consistent with efficiency and financing objectives, while others are not. Rising block rates (that is, higher unit prices at higher levels of consumption) have been used in cities as diverse as Belo Horizonte, Brazil; Bujumbura, Burundi; Cartagena, Colombia; and Jakarta, Indonesia. These might appear to meet efficiency and equity objectives. Water demand may be more sensitive to household size than income, however. If this is so, such schemes could hit poor families harder. A better way to ensure access for low-income households would be to charge according to the consumer's characteristics—according to property values, for example, or to the type and size of connection. Another possibility is to charge "lifeline" rates for very low levels of consumption (see Box 6.1). Because the poor may have no access at all, it is usually better to subsidize connection charges first and then consumption, if at all, later.

PRICING OF OTHER URBAN SERVICES. In principle, road pricing is an attractive approach to the urban transport problem. Charges could ideally be related to the amount of travel through congested areas. In practice, such schemes can be expensive

to run. A scheme in Singapore, however, where low-occupancy vehicles pay a charge for entering congested areas during rush hours, has been working since 1975. Where such charges are impractical, another option may be to use benefit taxes, such as lump sum charges to recoup costs from beneficiaries (see Chapter 7).

Subsidies for refuse disposal are required because of the externality of pollution and the difficulty of controlling unauthorized disposal. Still, it may be useful to levy different charges for industrial and commercial waste, as opposed to residential waste; to enforce refuse charges by collecting them jointly with water or electricity charges; or to levy a flat monthly fee according to area.

The pace of reform

Ultimately the public sector must decide which services to provide or to subsidize. Housing and urban mass transit are subsectors in which private providers can be efficient—especially if policy facilitates both free entry by new providers and a flow of private financing. Government can then focus its financial and administrative resources in areas where intervention is essential: road maintenance, traffic management, and urban land tenure. Where a competitive market does not exist because of economies of scale, as in water supply, cost recovery through consumption and development charges is desirable.

Administrative and political factors pose obstacles, however. Coordinating the activities of different tiers of the public sector is difficult (see Chapters 7 and 8). Once in place, subsidies are hard to remove, because they come to be perceived as entitlements, even if they were conceived as temporary measures to ease adjustment. City dwellers are particularly vocal in protecting their entitlements. Urban demonstrations forced the Philippine government to cancel a planned doubling of gasoline prices in August 1987. Rights to subsidies are also sometimes implicitly traded, since the price of land reflects the value of the surrounding infrastructure. Highly visible improvements in the quality of service, publicity campaigns, support from popular leaders, and gradual rather than sudden increases in user fees can reduce political inertia. These were part of the successful effort in Bangkok to increase the public water company's revenues during the mid-1980s.

Rural infrastructure

The importance of rural infrastructure in productivity has long been recognized. Rural roads allow inputs and outputs to be more efficiently transported between farms and market. Irrigation increases the yield from agricultural land. Rural electrification expands the area under irrigation through the use of pumps and offers power for rural nonfarm enterprises. Residential water supply may bring health benefits and, hence, a more productive labor force.

In most cases the central or provincial government—either directly or through state-owned enterprises (SOEs)—is the main provider of infrastructure in rural areas. Most services are provided either free or at highly subsidized rates. According to a recent study in Asia, tariffs covered only a small percentage of the economic costs of electrification. User charges for residential water are well below cost. In six Asian irrigation systems revenues collected from farmers as a percentage of capital and recurrent costs ranged from a high of 25 percent to a low of 1 percent. It is impractical to charge directly for access to rural roads, although vehicle and gasoline taxes might be considered as user charges to recover the cost of road maintenance.

Arguments of efficiency and equity have been used to justify this pattern of provision. Many of the benefits of rural infrastructure accrue to society at large. For services such as potable water the individual consumer might not be aware of all the benefits—especially improved health—and would consume too little at competitive prices. In addition subsidizing agricultural infrastructure is one way to target government spending toward the poor.

Issues in present financing arrangements

Although the arguments above justify public intervention in rural infrastructure in some form, the precise manner of intervention will depend as before on the criteria of allocation, internal efficiency, and equity.

UNDERINVESTMENT IN WATER AND ROADS. The need for more infrastructure is becoming pressing partly because of the continuing rise in rural populations. Despite recent improvements, access to potable water has fallen short of what had been hoped for. More than 1.5 billion people—roughly a third of the world's population—are estimated to be without access. In many low-income countries more than half of all villages remain unconnected to any all-weather road.

The cost of distributing rural services is high because the beneficiaries are scattered. Economies of scale in the production and transmission of power and water, for example, are offset by the high cost of serving far-flung communities. Extending coverage will be increasingly costly, since those easiest to reach have already been served.

Better allocation of resources is one way forward. Few rural electrification programs are part of an integrated plan based on the costs and benefits of alternatives. In residential water supply, misallocation has resulted from central governments (and external funding agencies) taking too great a role in deciding what to install and how to operate it. Projects tend to fail when users have no sense of responsibility for the service. The Thai government dug wells, installed handpumps, and committed itself to maintaining them, only to find that the people continued to use their traditional surface water sources. Another cause of failure is lack of maintenance. In Tanzania better access to potable water was provided without support for recurrent costs. The people wanted the new facilities, but the systems rapidly fell into disrepair.

Similar problems face investment in irrigation. Programs tend to be biased toward big new projects at the expense of cheaper solutions, such as improving existing systems, developing smaller community-controlled facilities, and improving rainfed farming methods. Studies conclude that irrigation agencies, which get most of their resources from central treasuries, support farmers' demands for costly and subsidized investments. This is in line with their traditional role of expanding water supplies, and it enables the agencies to preserve high levels of staffing and spending. Cost-benefit analysis may sometimes screen out bad investments, but the system's incentives still encourage bigger and more expensive alternatives. If water diverted for irrigation were used more efficiently, partly through appropriate maintenance, the need for costly new irrigation projects would diminish. In Pakistan, where waterlogging and salinity problems are widespread, reducing water losses in the Indus Canal system from 50 to 30 percent would match the contribution to irrigation supply of three dams the size of Tarbela, the largest in the country, each costing $3 billion.

INEFFICIENT SUPPLY AND CONSUMPTION. Rural access roads tend to be constructed by the roads departments of national or provincial ministries. These departments do not like to contract out. They claim that small contractors have little experience or are generally inefficient. Yet, according to World Bank surveys in Latin America and West Africa, the performance of road maintenance agencies has been generally poor. Equipment is under-used because of lack of spare parts, poor training, lack of preventive maintenance, operator abuse of equipment, and inadequate workshop facilities. Government regulations make it difficult for roads departments to attract the right personnel, hire and fire staff, and provide incentives. Private contractors or highly decentralized rural construction units—as in Benin and Kenya—have been more cost effective. Ghanaian contractors now undertake regraveling and routine maintenance.

The pattern of consumption is often inefficient as well, because prices are set too low. In fully irrigated areas, for example, farmers closer to the main water source, where water is abundant, typically waste more than those further away. To avoid such waste, prices need to confront users with true economic costs. Underpricing also makes it harder to plan investments.

INEQUITABLE ACCESS BY THE POOR. Heavy public spending on rural infrastructure is often justified as a measure to help the poor. Incomes in rural areas are indeed lower on average than those in urban areas, but the range is wide. In many countries poverty alleviation is not well served by the current system of rural subsidies.

Highly subsidized rural electrification does not mean that all village families have equal access to electricity. Findings from a survey of ninety villages in India indicate that about 15 percent of the population was connected during the first few years of electrification and only 45 percent after twenty years. The poorest often live far from the main electricity lines and can rarely afford to connect to them. Data for 1974 show that nearly 65 percent of the highest income groups in Malaysian rural areas had electricity compared with 20 percent of the lowest income groups; in Colombia only 29 percent of those connected were in the lowest 40 percent of rural income groups. Thus the uniform distribution of subsidies within rural areas (for example, through low prices for all) may mean that the poorest do not get their share.

There is also evidence of a regressive distribution of subsidies for rural water supply. For example, the proportion of the poorest families with connections to rural water services was about one-half that of higher income households in Colombia, Kenya, and the Republic of Korea in the late 1970s. The alternative to piped or well water is very expensive. Without access in their local community, families must walk and queue for their supplies. This claims 15 percent of women's time in some areas.

The distribution of benefits from spending on rural roads and irrigation is more difficult to judge. Some studies have found that the rural poor tend to live outside areas affected by new roads and are neglected by publicly financed rural development programs. Subsidies for irrigation can be regressive if instituted in response to political pressure, and the larger landowners are experienced at exerting such pressure. Land values rise in irrigated areas, but these economic rents are generally not shared with labor. Thus free (or nearly free) public provision of rural infrastructure may not serve the poorest: landless farm workers and smallholders of irrigated upland farms.

Policy options

Policymakers first have to set priorities and decide which services will be provided centrally rather than locally. The central government can shift responsibility for decisionmaking, investing, maintaining, and overseeing some rural infrastructure services to local communities and in so doing improve efficiency. This is particularly so for rural roads and the distribution-related services of water supply, where economies of scale and technical difficulties pose fewer problems. The center can then focus on training, regulating, and targeting subsidies toward selected impoverished communities. Having set priorities, the next task is to arrange for appropriate financing of the services that will continue to be centrally provided.

DECENTRALIZING PUBLIC RESPONSIBILITY. Although the argument for centralizing "natural" monopolies is strong for services that require heavy capital spending, it may not hold when the source of supply is local. Many irrigation facilities are supplied by national networks, but even in such cases a community-level service might still be the most efficient system for distribution to individual users. Programs with community participation coordinated by village-level officials or private associations have been shown to be generally more successful than those without such participation.

Such programs provide the services that are in demand, provide them at the appropriate standard, and do so effectively. Decisions made with little local consultation often result in low use. In northeast Thailand, for example, five years after handpumps and communal standpipes were installed, only one-quarter of the systems were still operating. Communal facilities were then converted to individual yard taps; after another five years about 90 percent were functional and well-

Box 6.7 Cooperation in irrigation: the Philippines

In the Philippines the National Irrigation Administration (NIA) is responsible for constructing and operating the national irrigation system and smaller pump systems. The NIA is a semiautonomous public corporation that finances the capital costs of the projects from foreign assistance, capital stock subscriptions of the government, and general government appropriations. It covers operation and maintenance costs with supplementary income (equipment rental, funds on deposit, and fees charged for managing the construction of new projects) and water charges.

At its inception the NIA was authorized to collect user fees directly from the beneficiaries. Until 1980 the NIA remitted the entire collection to the national treasury. From 1980 onward, however, the NIA was given authority to retain the collection for operation and maintenance, and the government gradually reduced subsidies. To counter an initial shortage of funds, the NIA began promoting water users' organizations (WUOs) among farmers' groups to share responsibility for constructing, operating, and maintaining of irrigation systems. The NIA converted some of the marginal irrigation schemes (those that generate revenues less than operation and maintenance costs) into communal systems. In some cases it transferred the responsibility for managing entire systems to groups of WUOs. In other instances it turned over responsibility for operating and maintaining a portion of a project (such as the area served by a lateral canal) to WUOs with no cash payment in return. Sometimes WUOs were contracted to maintain sections of lateral canals at a fixed fee

and at lower cost than if the job were done by NIA personnel.

The NIA relies on WUOs for better cost recovery. It encourages farmers to form user groups to collect charges among the group members and to pay a lump sum to the NIA. As an incentive the farmers' groups are allowed to retain some of their collection. In cases where the NIA collects charges directly from individual farmers, it provides cash incentives to collectors. In all cases it tries to raise the farmers' willingness to pay for irrigation services by improving them. Within the farmers' groups, farmers pay either in cash or in kind to the groups. The NIA negotiates with each group over the quantity of water delivered, and the group members in turn allocate water and costs among themselves.

The results are promising. The NIA has reduced its personnel, improved cost recovery, and reduced operation and maintenance costs. A case study on the Angat-Maasim River irrigation system showed that the collection of irrigation fees increased by 15 percent after the farmers' groups were formed. Fee collections as a percentage of spending on operation and maintenance increased from 69 percent in 1979 to 75 percent in 1984. The ratio of collections to collectibles improved from about 45 percent in the late 1970s to more than 60 percent in 1984. The expenditure on operation and maintenance per hectare declined 38 percent between 1981 and 1984. At the same time the ratio of personnel costs to total costs declined from 90 to 78 percent, indicating significant cuts in personnel.

---

maintained, despite relatively high metered consumption charges. Water systems in Kenya built as part of *harambee* (self-help) efforts have proved more reliable than those installed by the water ministry, which were hampered by lack of funds, poor organization, and failure to design according to the communities' needs. In Malawi a carefully administered water supply program has tried to maximize local participation by making committees responsible for construction of local branches, cleanliness around the taps, enforcement of rules on water use, and minor maintenance. The systems have received a high rating for reliability. Informal users' associations can play an important role in such programs (see Box 6.7).

Central governments can rarely provide heavy subsidies indefinitely, especially during periods of fiscal adjustment. Self-financed community schemes, in contrast, match needs to available resources.

Paying for the service also gives users an incentive to consume economically and to monitor the efficiency of provision. If development as well as operational costs are recovered, the bias in favor of expansion over maintenance is reduced. Farmers in the Philippines, although responsible for only a modest fraction of the cost of developing their irrigation system, lobbied successfully against the use of expensive components that they considered unnecessary for good service.

Some have argued that it is impossible to make user charges for rural services cost-effective, particularly when metering is required. Egypt offers a counterexample. The cost of metering irrigation there is estimated to be only about $1 to $7 an acre—less than 3 percent of the full cost of supplying irrigation water. In many cases, however, metering is indeed uneconomical, and other methods of cost recovery have to be relied upon. In water supply, for example, charges for connection and

Box 6.8 Local village cooperation in India

Robert Wade's recent study of thirty-one villages in upland South India suggests that local initiatives can thrive in an appropriate setting. Within the sample many villages have autonomous institutions to provide public goods and services. Only a few miles may separate a village with a substantial amount of "corporate" organization from others with none.

The "corporate" villages have a village council (distinct from the officially designated but moribund village council, the *panchayat*), maintain a village fund, and hold a general meeting of all the village's cultivators at least once a year. They employ a group of "common irrigators" to distribute water between and below the outlets of the government-run irrigation canal, to which all the sampled villages have access, and another work group of village field guards to protect the crops from livestock and thieves. In addition to paying the irrigators' and field guards' salaries, the village fund is used to hire laborers to repair access roads, wells, and primary school buildings; to provide matching grants for the construction of animal clinics and primary schools; and to hire professional monkey catchers. Money for the fund is raised by the sale of franchises, which the council creates and sanctions. For example, the council auctions the right to sell liquor in the village and sells the right of access to the village's stubble grazing to groups of outside shepherds. Some villages also auction the right to catch fish in the village pond and to collect a commission on all bulk grain sales.

Why do some villages have this kind of organization while others close by do not? One answer is that production conditions in the corporate villages make the net collective benefit of concerted action substantially higher than in other villages. The corporate villages tend to be located toward the tailends of irrigation distributories (which may be from five to twenty miles long). Because of their location, their water supply is more at risk than villages higher up. The function of the common irrigators is to reduce the risk by obtaining more water from higher up and by distributing water equitably between and beneath the outlets. The government's irrigation department is meant to control all water allocation in the canal above each outlet, but deficiencies in the quality of control prompt villagers lower down to compensate through collective action.

The corporate villages also face a greater risk of crop damage by animals. Because they are in lower-lying locations, they tend to have a higher proportion of black soils, which are especially suitable for growing stubble for a long period after the harvest. As a result there is a higher density of livestock in the villages at the same time that some rainfed crops are still standing and therefore vulnerable to livestock. Organized villages can charge an entry fee to outside shepherds and thus have a larger village fund.

So where the risks of crop loss and conflict caused by water shortage and straying animals are high, villages tend to organize. Once set up to handle these problems, they can go on to organize village infrastructure at little additional cost.

---

development can be used instead of consumption charges. Betterment levies or access charges of this kind are analogous to urban benefit taxes. Connection charges can be subsidized for the poor.

Even where neither connection charges nor user charges are feasible—as in roads—remedies do exist. Many of them are better handled by local organizations than by central ones. In India local village funds have successfully provided basic services (see Box 6.8). Local benefit taxation (for example the valorization scheme discussed in Chapter 7) can be costly to implement in village areas but has sometimes proved feasible. In Kenya local residents have formed rural road crews to ensure effective maintenance.

These policy recommendations do not imply complete decentralization—nor even a diminution of the central government's role. Rather they suggest a change in that role, away from directly providing many local services and toward helping local communities to organize themselves. Unlike in urban municipalities, formal government in rural areas is generally weak. Often at the village level traditional household groupings must be relied upon. In some cases individuals have little incentive to plan communal services (see Box 6.8). Central governments can play a crucial role in organizing rural communities, motivating them, and curbing the influence of self-serving local elites.

Further roles for the central or regional government are as educator, regulator, and financial intermediary. Rural residents will generally be unaware, for example, of the latest techniques for maintaining irrigation canals. National or provincial authorities can provide technical assistance, spread information about the benefits of innovation, design educational materials, and develop standards of service. Since local communities may find it hard to get loans for rural infrastructure, governments might provide financial guarantees or even funds. Experience has shown, however, that such credit schemes can be sustained only if they are not used to distribute subsidies through distorted interest rates.

The higher tier of government must regulate the use of common resources that cut across localities, such as water and roads. It must also provide those services for which only a systemwide approach is economical, such as trunk irrigation lines and large-scale power generation and distribution.

EFFICIENT MANAGEMENT AND FINANCIAL AUTONOMY OF CENTRALIZED PROVIDERS. In some countries and for some services it may be neither desirable nor feasible to decentralize. However, national institutions need to become more efficient, too. The managerial and administrative improvements discussed in *World Development Report 1983* would be important elements of reform.

Managerial reforms would be more effective if central institutions had greater financial autonomy (as in power, see Box 6.4). The tendency for publicly subsidized irrigation authorities to invest anew when it may be more cost-effective to maintain or improve existing systems can be partly countered by making them more financially accountable to users—local communities or individual farmers. One approach would be to set up public utilities under the supervision of a regulatory body. Another would be to establish water districts empowered to impose fees or betterment levies. In either case the goal should be to establish a closer link between user and provider.

Such schemes hinge on the pattern of user charges. Traditional arguments that water systems are subject to large economies of scale and externalities in consumption do not justify low levels of cost recovery (see Box 6.1). Economies of scale in production are often offset by the rising cost of finding new sources. Efficiency pricing would then require full cost recovery. The externality argument correctly cites the health benefits of water supply, but without cost recovery there may be no service at all.

Decentralizing financial responsibility to local communities and to semiautonomous agencies does not mean that government subsidies from general sources are no longer needed. In some cases central subsidization is necessary to protect the interests of the poor or because the cost of raising revenue from beneficiaries is too high. But even when subsidies from general sources are necessary, governments can devise ways to ensure that they are distributed efficiently. What is important is that subsidized consumers are, as far as possible, given an incentive to choose the most efficient alternative. Similarly, public providers must be free to choose efficient suppliers. For example, governments could establish relatively autonomous road maintenance departments with the freedom to contract out to private providers.

Prospects for change

In summary, a gradual devolution of financial and administrative responsibility to the local level would improve efficiency and equity for services with few economies of scale—residential water supply, the distribution of local irrigation services, and the building and maintenance of rural roads. The central government's roles would shift from those of primary decisionmaker, investor, maintainer, and overseer to those of regulator, technical adviser, and dispenser of information. For services with economies of scale—rural electricity generation and main trunk line construction, for instance—a higher tier of government must remain the provider. In such cases the focus must be on appropriate pricing policies.

Decentralizing public activity must be done in stages, because built-in incentives lead the system to perpetuate itself. Some of the clearest lessons in the political economy of subsidies come from industrial countries, not developing ones. Irrigated water in the United States is a case in point. In 1985 the value of the total subsidy to the 146,000 farms that use water provided by the U.S. Bureau of Reclamation amounted to nearly $15 billion—or 56 percent of the average market value of irrigated land. The 6 percent of all farmers who receive the subsidy are among the richest in the nation. Farm groups, politicians, and the irrigation agencies all support this largely wasteful scheme. Reform is always possible—in the developing countries as well as in the United States—but the risks of doing nothing are far greater in the developing countries. It is indeed encouraging that many of the reforms discussed above are already being implemented.

7

Financing local government

State and local governments play an important role in providing public services. Decentralizing both spending and revenue authority can improve the allocation of resources in the public sector by linking the costs and benefits of local public services more closely. To the extent possible, subnational government should charge for services, but, where such charges are not feasible or desirable, spending must be financed from local general revenue, loans, or grants from higher levels of government. This chapter examines subnational government finance and focuses on reforming local revenue systems to allocate resources efficiently.

Patterns of subnational government finance

The role of subnational government varies from country to country—for political and historical reasons as much as for economic ones. The relative importance of the subnational level of government is indicated by its share of total government spending. For a sample of eighteen developing countries for which comparable data are available, this share ranges from 2.5 percent in The Gambia to 74.9 percent in Yugoslavia (see Figure 7.1). To capture longer run patterns, all figures reported in this section are averages of data available for 1974 through 1986. The sample is diverse. India and Yugoslavia conduct more than half of government spending at the subnational level, while for seven other countries this share is less than one-tenth. India, Yugoslavia, and, to some extent, Brazil have high subnational spending because they are large countries with strong state governments. The subnational

shares of total government revenue—not including intergovernmental grants–also vary widely, ranging from 2.2 percent for Tunisia to 72.1 percent for Yugoslavia.

The figures show that subnational governments tend to be more important as providers of public services than as collectors of revenues. China—not in the sample—is an exception and relies heavily on subnational governments to collect revenue (see Box 7.1). In every sample country the revenue raised by subnational government from its own sources falls short of its spending. These shortfalls range from 0.1 percent of GDP in Costa Rica, The Gambia, and Sri Lanka to 4.2 percent of GDP in India and are more than 2 percent of GDP in six sample countries. In several countries the combined state and local fiscal imbalance was more than the total government deficit, which means that central governments operated in surplus before intergovernmental grants were disbursed.

In most countries own-source revenues at the subnational level fail to cover even current spending (see Figure 7.2). When grants are included, however, subnational government achieves fiscal balance or surplus in most sample countries. Accordingly, net borrowing, which is equal to the difference between total spending and total revenue, is a relatively minor source of funds for subnational governments.

Fiscal imbalances do not necessarily indicate inappropriate fiscal policies at the subnational level. A grant may really be a shared tax, as in Brazil, or a compensatory grant for the central government's repeal of a local tax, as in Bangladesh, or a transfer

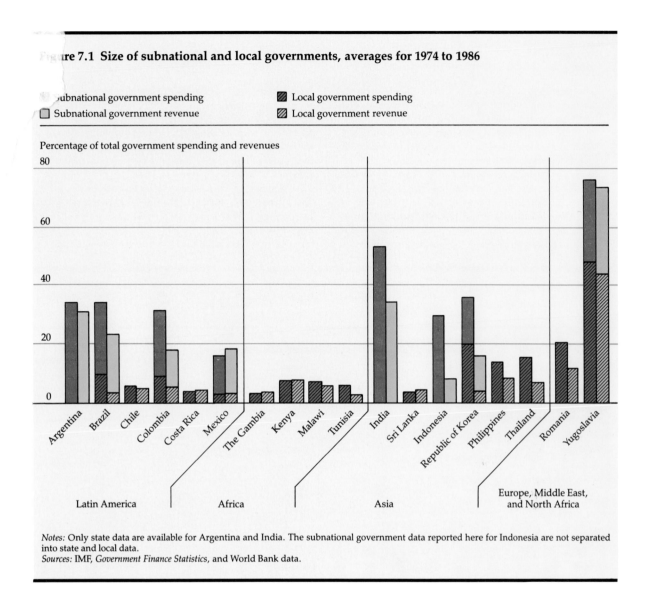

Figure 7.1 Size of subnational and local governments, averages for 1974 to 1986

Subnational government spending   Local government spending
Subnational government revenue   Local government revenue

Percentage of total government spending and revenues

Argentina · Brazil · Chile · Colombia · Costa Rica · Mexico · The Gambia · Kenya · Malawi · Tunisia · India · Sri Lanka · Indonesia · Republic of Korea · Philippines · Thailand · Romania · Yugoslavia

Latin America | Africa | Asia | Europe, Middle East, and North Africa

Notes: Only state data are available for Argentina and India. The subnational government data reported here for Indonesia are not separated into state and local data.
Sources: IMF, *Government Finance Statistics,* and World Bank data.

to finance some centrally mandated expenditure such as teachers' salaries, as in Kenya. Nonetheless, the allocation of spending and revenue responsibilities, and the resultant transfers between levels of government, may induce an inefficient use of resources that contributes to total government deficits.

Expenditure and financing measures can be combined to indicate the degree of fiscal decentralization. The share of state and local governments in total government spending reveals their importance as providers of public services. The extent to which they are self-financing indicates their fiscal autonomy, because outside financing may come with conditions that limit local discretion in the use of funds. Figure 7.3 looks at both aspects for the sample of eighteen countries. Yugoslavia's posi-

tion in the upper right-hand corner indicates a highly decentralized government sector. Not only do the state and local governments account for a large share of total government spending, but they are largely self-financing. The Gambia is autonomous in the financing of subnational government, yet the size of its subnational government is only a small fraction of the government sector. Colombia, Indonesia, and the Republic of Korea display the opposite pattern: the subnational government has a large role in the provision of services, but its financing comes largely from central government grants and revenue sharing.

Expenditure and financing measures, however, provide only a partial indication of decentralization. Central governments that want to exert control over local finance usually have many instru-

Figure 7.2 Spending and revenue of subnational governments, averages for 1974 to 1986

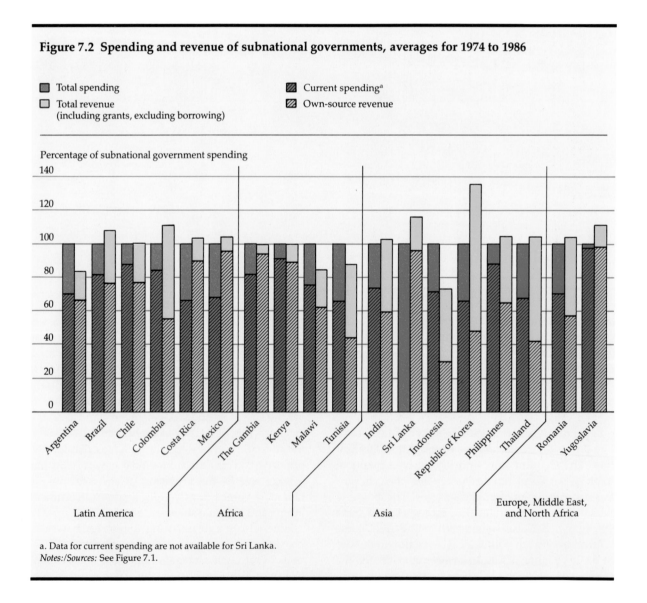

a. Data for current spending are not available for Sri Lanka.
Notes:/Sources: See Figure 7.1.

sales. This is a structural problem, possibly exacerbated by weaknesses in the tax administration system. The high tax rates may induce tax avoidance by enterprises and perhaps even by the local governments that own them. The lack of borrowing and self-financing mechanisms creates a bias against infrastructure investments because the full cost is shifted onto the general public. Options presently under discussion include reform of the company tax, introduction of autonomous local taxes, and, in particular, the institution of a local government property tax.

ments, such as approval of budgets, spending requirements, restrictions on the use of tax bases, limits on tax rates, and other fiscal constraints. Many developing countries are actively exploring ways to increase local fiscal autonomy to improve public sector efficiency and reduce total government deficits.

Fiscal decentralization and the role of subnational government

State and local governments usually provide a range of public services that contribute substantially to raising living standards and growth. These include basic health and education; street lighting and cleaning; water, sewerage, and power; public markets and refuse collection; major transport networks; and land development for business and residential purposes. Subnational government must decide how much to spend for these public services and how to finance them. Ideally each subnational government provides both the level and mix of public services and the means of financing these services that most closely meet the preferences of individuals in its jurisdiction. In this way decentralization promotes efficiency by allowing a close match between public services and the multiplicity of individual preferences, and it promotes accountability and equity by clearly linking the benefits of services with their costs. This is the rationale for establishing state and local governments that are responsive to the wishes of their citizens and not simply the instruments of central government.

Decentralization faces certain practical problems. First, local governments often lack the administra-

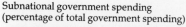

Figure 7.3 Fiscal decentralization to the subnational level, averages for 1974 to 1986

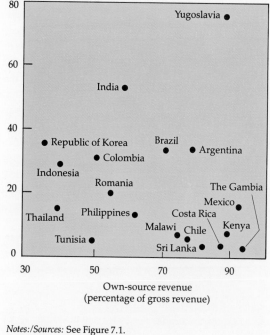

Subnational government spending (percentage of total government spending)

Own-source revenue (percentage of gross revenue)

Notes:/Sources: See Figure 7.1.

tive capacity to collect revenue and prepare budgets and investment plans. In Tunisia, because municipal staff lacked expertise in project design and implementation, municipalities used only a portion of the capital resources available to them. Second, improving local government's administrative capacity can unnecessarily duplicate the number and skills of staff at the central and local levels. Decentralization should not inefficiently expand public employment. Third, the fact that public services provided by one jurisdiction produce benefits or costs for other jurisdictions calls for involvement by higher levels of government. However, these problems can be addressed through appropriate grant policies and other mechanisms for strengthening local administration, as discussed below.

Assigning responsibility for services among levels of government should be as clear and simple as possible for decentralization to work. Vagueness in the division of responsibility can undermine local accountability. In Brazil, because of an unclear division of functions between state and municipal government, mayors can garner support for favored municipal projects from state governors instead of pushing for increased local taxes. This diminishes the incentive for generating local revenue.

A common feature of government in developing countries is joint responsibility at different levels for providing the same service in a particular jurisdiction. In Turkey, for example, something as apparently local in nature as street lighting involves all levels of government. The central government shares responsibility for funding; a national agency is mainly responsible for planning, execution, and operation and maintenance; and local governments have the main responsibility for funding and secondary responsibility for planning. In some cases—education and health, for example—the structure of service delivery is unavoidably complex. But for services that are clearly local, such as water and street lighting, it can generally be simple.

Many countries would benefit from periodic reviews of the assignment of functions and finances to different levels of government. A review of intergovernmental fiscal relations in Colombia was the basis for comprehensive local fiscal reform and showed that such reform is feasible (see Box 7.2). The rest of this chapter focuses on reforming local revenue instruments and overcoming problems in local administration.

Strengthening local government finance

Strengthening local government finance can improve the efficiency of the public sector and reduce the need for transfers from central to local government, particularly in urban areas. Certain revenue sources, such as user charges and property taxes, are more easily administered by local government. Strengthening these revenue sources is important for stabilization and structural adjustment in developing countries such as Indonesia and Pakistan, where inadequate reliance on subnational government finance has caused a heavy financial drain on the central government.

The principles discussed in previous chapters suggest four criteria for efficiency in raising local revenue:

Box 7.2 Fiscal decentralization in Colombia

Concerns about the assignment of fiscal responsibilities among central, departmental, and municipal governments in Colombia led to the appointment of the Mission of Intergovernmental Finance in 1980. The mission concluded that local resources should be relied on more for local purposes. Subsequent legislation to strengthen local government institutions and to decentralize both functions and finances marked a historic point in Colombia's fiscal and institutional development.

The finances of subnational governments were strengthened by expanding their traditional revenue sources. The most important changes were those relating to the property tax, in particular those relating to the tax base. First, all cadastral values were updated to a 1983 base by applying an annual increase of 10 percent for each year (up to a maximum of fifteen years) since the last official valuation. Thereafter, in years when properties were not revalued, their cadastral values were to be adjusted automatically each year by a price index. Although political considerations have kept the rate of adjustment consistently below the rate of inflation, the adjustment has nonetheless slowed the erosion of this important source of local revenues.

Property tax rates were also changed. The basic municipal rate can now be set between 0.4 and 1.2 percent, compared with the previous fixed rate of 0.4 percent. This change was important because it introduced an element of local discretion in rate-setting for the first time.

The base and rates of the industry and commerce tax were also reformed. Before 1983 this tax—although important as a revenue source, particularly in the larger municipalities—was levied on a wide variety of bases, generally with large variations in rates depending on the type and size of the business. The reforms established a uniform tax base (based on gross sales) and reduced the variation in rates.

The flow of national transfer payments to the small municipalities has substantially increased. The share of the sales tax allocated to the subnational level is to rise from 30 percent in 1986 to 50 percent by 1992. Moreover, for the first time in Colombia, the distribution formula was changed to give a bigger share to small municipalities that tried to raise their own resources. A new law provided that the additional funds for municipalities above the 1986 share are to be spent solely on investment, including maintenance and debt service. Finally, the national government was given one year to transfer functions to the municipal level so as to match the transfer of additional revenues by 1992.

Table 7.1 Comparison of local public spending and revenue shares by major categories in selected cities
(percentage of total spending)

Spending and associated revenue category	Brazil, São Paulo, 1984	Colombia			Kenya		Republic of Korea, Seoul, 1983	India			Pakistan	
		Bogotá, 1972	Cali, 1974	Cartagena, 1972	Nairobi, 1981	Mombasa, 1981		Ahmedabad, 1981	Bombay, 1981–82	Calcutta, 1982	Gujranwala, 1983	Karachi, 1982
Spending on general urban services[a]	30.2	17.3	22.6	37.2	10.3	7.9	34.0	23.2	12.4	42.2	33.1	16.8
Local tax revenue	68.7	14.0	16.9	27.1	34.1	75.6	44.2	61.4	47.0	61.3	98.4	85.9
Spending and debt service for public utilities[b]	36.3	69.1	74.5	61.2	53.0	28.0	29.1	48.9	69.8	46.4	55.4	52.3
User charges and borrowing	30.8	72.0	80.4	60.1	52.1	−7.8	33.8	30.1	52.2	−16.2	−8.7	11.1
Spending on social services[c]	33.6	13.7	2.9	1.6	36.8	64.0	36.9	27.8	17.8	11.4	11.5	30.8
Grants received	0.4	14.0	2.8	12.8	13.7	32.2	22.0	8.6	0.7	54.9	10.3	3.0

Note: For each city, spending shares (including debt service) add to 100 percent, except for rounding errors; likewise all revenue shares (including borrowing) add to 100 percent.
a. Includes refuse collection, parks and recreation, industries, fire protection, law enforcement, general administration, employee pensions and health care, grants and transfers, and other miscellaneous services. Local taxes include other miscellaneous revenues.
b. Includes water supply, sewerage and drainage, electricity, telephones, housing, markets and abattoirs, highways and roads, and public transport. User charges include revenues from development charges, housing schemes, and so forth.
c. Includes education, health, and social welfare.
Source: Bahl and Linn, forthcoming.

• The cost of providing local services should be recovered, to the extent possible, from charges on the beneficiaries. Such charges should be related to individual consumption or, where this is not possible, to a measure of individual benefit received.

• Services whose costs cannot be recovered from charges can be financed from general taxes—property taxes, business taxes, and sales taxes—levied within the relevant jurisdictions.

• If the benefits of local services spill over into other jurisdictions or produce nationwide benefits, then grants from higher level governments should finance such services in proportion to their outside benefits.

• Borrowing is an appropriate way to finance at least some local capital investment, provided macroeconomic fiscal balance is maintained.

As these criteria indicate, the appropriate use of local revenue instruments depends on the spending responsibilities assigned to local government. Equity can dictate modifications of these criteria, such as avoiding the imposition of user charges on low-income households.

In the absence of detailed nationwide information, public finance data for a sample of cities provide some insight into the composition of spending by sector, and of revenue by source, for particular local jurisdictions (see Table 7.1). These data make it possible to relate broad categories of spending with revenue sources. The four efficiency criteria suggest that general urban services

should be financed by local taxes, public utilities should be self-financing, and social services should be supported by grants.

In Bogotá and Cali spending and revenue have closely matched the efficiency criteria. In Cartagena grants from other levels of government have tended to support the nonsocial services. All the other sample cities collected a surplus of local taxes to help finance public utilities and social services. Calcutta has received a large share of grants, apparently mostly to support public utilities.

Increasing local revenues—especially through user charges—is often desirable, but it is difficult when local governments do not have revenue authority commensurate with their spending responsibilities. Central government usually lets local government use only a few revenue sources, and even these are subject to limits. In Thailand, for example, the proportion of local expenditure financed from local sources declined between 1977 and 1982 because of central restrictions on the rate at which local taxes and charges could be levied. Local authorities could, and should, be encouraged to raise more revenue locally. This might be done through user charges, local taxes, borrowing, and grants.

User charges

User charges can be of two types: consumption related and benefit related. They account for about one-third of all locally raised revenue in a sample

Box 7.3 Benefit financing: land readjustment in the Republic of Korea and the valorization system in Colombia

In Korea urban land readjustment schemes involve the consolidation of numerous small parcels of raw land at the urban periphery. Nothing is paid to the owners. This land is serviced and subdivided for urban use and then returned to the original owners in proportion to the value of their land contribution. Some of the land is retained by the public authority, in part to meet the needs of urban infrastructure (especially roads and green spaces) and in part to provide a source of finance to defray the cost of development. The land retained for this latter purpose is sold at market prices in commercial transactions or auctions.

The scale of Korea's land readjustment program has been impressive. By 1985 some 43 percent of Seoul's total built-up area was covered by completed or ongoing schemes. The system has opened up new land for urban uses and thus has helped to increase the supply of housing and raise public funds. While it appears to have conveyed its direct benefits mainly to middle- and high-income landowners, some trickle-down effect may have occured. The large scale of the program probably reduced general urban land prices and rents below the levels that would have occurred in its absence.

Land readjustment programs require fairly sophisticated methods of public land management, including effective land registration and cadastral records and land redistribution formulas. Nevertheless the administrative feasibility of the schemes has been amply demonstrated in Korea.

In contrast to land readjustment programs, which have been used mainly to develop new areas at the fringe of cities and towns, the valorization system often applied in Latin American countries has principally been used to finance improvements in infrastructure in built-up areas. Street improvements, water supply, and other services have been financed by this system of taxation, in which the cost of public works is allocated to affected properties in proportion to the benefits conferred. Valorization charges are designed to recover project costs, not to recapture all the benefits the project is expected to confer. The system is intended to make urban services largely self-financing and thus re-

duce municipal tax burdens.

The valorization system has been used most extensively in Colombia, and its application in the capital city, Bogotá, has been carefully studied. At the height of its use in 1968 it contributed 16 percent to the financing of all local public expenditures, including spending by local state-owned enterprises. Subsequently its relative importance has decreased, but it has retained a role in the financing of urban infrastructure in Bogotá.

One of the practical problems encountered in the application of the system has been its dependence on large financial transfers from the city's general revenue. In practice, valorization charges have not fully recovered the costs of all projects. An important reason for this is that some projects have been designed to improve living conditions in low-income areas, and the beneficiaries have not been expected to pay valorization charges. If a valorization program is to be maintained while pursuing subsidization of low-income neighborhoods, the resulting need for transfers from local general revenues should be recognized, explicitly calculated, and met.

Arrears in the collection of charges have been another reason why valorization charges have failed to recover costs. For projects undertaken from 1968 to 1986, arrears amounted to 16 percent of project costs. The collection problem has arisen mainly from lack of payment by public agencies and by a few large properties. The introduction of interest charges on late payments after 1981 reduced the recovery period for project costs.

Finally, Bogotá has demonstrated that the valorization system depends heavily on the quality of investment planning and project preparation. In years in which infrastructure planning was weak, the system receded in importance even though requirements kept growing. Projects for which benefits were uncertain or not clearly concentrated among the properties bearing the valorization charge often created the greatest collection problems. The participation of beneficiaries in planning and managing the project made the resulting charges more acceptable to them.

of twenty-five cities in developing countries. User charges are especially important at the local level because, being closer to beneficiaries, local public services are more amenable to such charges than services provided by higher levels of government. User charges reduce the pressure to raise revenue from general local taxes; this can improve efficiency because the costs of public services and in-

frastructure are borne by its beneficiaries. Of course, when the imposition of such charges is expressly not desired for equity reasons, as in subsidized improvement of poor neighborhoods, general taxes or grants can provide the necessary finance.

A major benefit-related charge is the development charge or "betterment tax": a lump sum charge designed to recover the cost of infrastructure development from beneficiaries. A development charge may cover only a limited project—for example, a neighborhood paving scheme or the construction of a sewage canal—or it may cover the full development of a new area. It is usually imposed on the owners of property in the areas that are improved by public action, and it represents a tax on the increase in land values that results from new local infrastructure. It can be an equitable tax because those who benefit from development pay for its cost. Two particularly successful systems of development charges—land readjustment in East Asia and the valorization system in Latin America—indicate their potential (see Box 7.3).

The main difficulty with development charges lies in administration and collection. Jakarta's betterment tax suffered from late notification of the tax department that an area would be improved and, hence, late notification of landowners; difficulties in tracing landowners because of unregistered land transactions; and a lack of data on land values. A properly functioning property tax (discussed below) makes administering development charges far more straightforward.

User charges are especially well suited to local government finance, but they have often been underutilized. Colombian cities, such as Bogotá, Cali, and Cartagena, were an exception because of their relatively limited dependence on local taxes and grants and much heavier reliance on user charges. Two main factors account for this. First, in the larger Colombian cities local governments provide the important public utility services (water, sewerage, electricity, and telephones), whose cost can be recovered through user charges. Second, local governments in Colombia have placed a relatively heavy emphasis on benefit charges to finance infrastructure.

When not relying on user charges, local governments often require inefficient transfers from central government that strain central budgets. For example, in Pakistan increasing dependence on federal grants to finance provincial services is attributed, in part, to the provinces' low reliance on user charges. In Mexico municipalities have not had the incentive to recover the cost of investments made with grants from states or the federal government.

Local taxes

As the efficiency criteria indicate, another way to raise revenue locally is through local taxes. These can be either property taxes or other local taxes, such as those on industry, commerce, and the professions.

PROPERTY TAX. The property tax has several advantages as a local revenue source. First, all municipalities have some taxable real estate within their boundaries. Unlike taxes on business and trade, whose bases are concentrated in major cities, the property tax can produce revenue in small outlying local governments as well as in large cities. Second, within small towns the property tax base is broad; thus the burden of such a tax can be distributed across a large segment of the population, and significant revenue can be raised at low tax rates. Third, because property values are enhanced by the provision of local government services, property taxation based on accurate property valuation can recover the cost of services directly from the beneficiaries. Relatively little of the tax on residential property will be shifted from property owners to others, whereas the tax on commercial property can be shifted to consumers. Finally, the burden of the property tax on the poor can be reduced or eliminated by reducing or exempting taxes on properties below a certain value.

Despite these theoretical advantages, data for urban local governments in selected developing countries indicate that property taxes account for only 5 to 25 percent of recurrent receipts of local government, except in Africa, where reliance on property taxation is generally higher. Moreover, the performance of the property tax over time has been mixed. Property tax revenues have declined in real terms in more than half of the Asian and Latin American countries. The countries experiencing the greatest revenue erosion were generally those with high rates of inflation, particularly in Latin America. In most of Africa, however, property tax revenues have grown in real terms.

An obvious way to increase property tax yields is to raise the tax rate. This is often a bad approach, however. It exaggerates inequities by increasing the burden on taxpayers whose properties are on the tax rolls and who pay their taxes in full. A better approach is to raise more revenue from delinquent taxpayers by collecting more efficiently. Examining payment records to identify major delinquents, introducing a systematic method of chasing them (such as reminders and warnings), and conspicuous enforcement of penalties can together significantly increase collected arrears and produce longer term improvements in the system. In Delhi, for example, better property tax collection—including rebates for timely payments, penalties for late payments, better facilities for making payments, and an improved management information system—increased revenue by 16 percent in 1985–86 and 96 percent in 1986–87. Another major reason for improved collections was that taxpayers had to pay their assessment before being able to appeal it in court.

Improving collections works best when the tax rolls are reasonably complete and valuations are accurate—at least in relative terms. Otherwise, increases in the efficiency of collection may exaggerate existing inequities. More basic reforms may then be necessary. The maintenance of accurate property tax records, usually termed the fiscal cadastre, is a particularly important step in basic reform, because the tax base is constantly changing in developing countries because of rapid urban growth and high inflation. An accurate cadastre also aids in planning and providing local services, especially infrastructure, and in administering and collecting development charges.

Valuation is a critical step in basic property tax reform. One approach is to use the annual rental value, which in many developing countries is determined by asking renter occupants how much they pay in rent and extrapolating from that to owner-occupied property. The method is simple, but open to inaccuracy and misrepresentation, especially for owner-occupied structures. A second approach is based on the capital value, which is calculated either by estimating the value of the land and the cost of replacing the structure or by extrapolating from recent sales of comparable property. (A fundamental policy decision must be made on whether to tax only land or buildings and improvements as well.) In practice a pragmatic mix of the two approaches will be needed depending on the availability of rental and sales data. Valuations also require technical expertise and time. To economize on scarce skills, local governments can draw on a central valuation agency for information and technical assistance, as was done in Malaysia.

Setting the property tax rate is the next key step in basic reform. The rate should be high enough to make the property tax worth collecting, and local governments should be allowed some flexibility in setting it, as in Colombia's fiscal reform (see Box 7.2). Flexible rates can ensure that property tax revenues are maintained between valuations: by adjusting rates, local governments can keep property taxes constant in real terms. When property is revalued, the rate can be reset to where it was at the previous valuation.

Once established, a well-functioning property tax system needs continual updating. General revaluation of properties, which can be very expensive, can be done at five-year intervals if changes in property characteristics are recorded promptly and price increases are captured by indexing the tax base or increasing the rate.

Experience with fundamental property tax reform in Brazil and the Philippines demonstrates the need to address all aspects of the problem (see Box 7.4). Brazil, especially, shows that an efficient property tax can be achieved only if intergovernmental fiscal relations provide the right incentives—an important general rule for all countries.

OTHER LOCAL TAXES. Taxes on industry, commerce, and the professions are usually another important source of local revenue. These taxes may take several different forms, including a turnover (gross sales) tax, a tax on the value of gross business assets, or specific levies tailored to the type of enterprise. Local taxes on industry, commerce, and services have accounted for more than 80 percent of local revenue in San Salvador and more than one-half in La Paz. In the Philippines, business license taxes are the second largest source of locally raised revenue. The revenue from business taxes can grow substantially, because with urbanization the number and size of business establishments increase and the taxable base grows. A flat charge or exemption eliminates the need to assess small firms.

Few local governments in developing countries levy broadbased sales taxes partly because central governments prohibit it and partly because sales taxes are difficult to administer. To avoid administrative problems, a higher tier of government might assess and collect a sales tax and then remit part or all of it to the local authority. For example, the sales tax could be a local surtax on the central government tax, with the central government acting as collector. The local government could set the rate, determine special exemptions and other details, and pay the central government a collection charge. Local autonomy would be sacrificed only in choosing the tax base and determining collection efficiency. One problem with this approach—and the reason it is rarely adopted—is that central governments are generally unwilling to let the local authorities share in so lucrative a revenue source because it may limit the national government's ability to raise revenue from the base. Another is that such a tax might be less visible and thus make local governments less accountable to their taxpayers.

Some local governments use personal income

Box 7.4 Fundamental property tax reform in the Philippines and Brazil

The Philippine Real Property Tax Administration (RPTA) Project was designed to address the problems of a weak property tax system. The project's approach was to change the system of valuation from one based on owners' declarations to one based on a government inventory. The project aimed to compile in each jurisdiction a comprehensive inventory of all land parcels, which would incorporate missing parcels, eliminate duplicate claims, and include an accurate measurement of all land and building characteristics to be used in valuation.

The project was successful within its narrowly defined objectives. Average valuations increased by 50 percent. This was largely due not to the discovery of missing parcels, but to the revaluation of existing parcels, based on property characteristics gathered in the field. Contrary to the government's original diagnosis, property owners were in the habit of declaring all parcels under their ownership. Owners did, however, understate the dimensions and quality of each parcel and the improvements they had made to it.

The RPTA left several problems, however. First, the calculation of individual valuations remained highly arbitrary. Although the RPTA yielded more accurate data on the characteristics of individual properties, the method used by valuers to convert that data into estimates of value was not improved. Second, property tax liabilities remained low. The RPTA did not reform rate setting and related policies. The central government in the Philippines fixes the maximum tax rate on property, mandates fixed assessment ratios (as low as 15

percent on low-value residential property), and fixes the date on which new general revaluations become effective. Interim indexation of values is not permitted. As a result, effective tax rates before and after RPTA were as low as 0.3 percent. Finally, the RPTA did not improve collection. On average revenue collections increased by only 1 percent in the year after the project began.

Brazil's property tax reform (known by the acronym CIATA) was designed, like the RPTA, to address the technical defects of a system producing very little revenue. The objectives of the CIATA were to revise the fiscal cadastre, in order to incorporate missing parcels and improve the accuracy of valuations, and to devise a better system for monitoring collection and financial reporting.

The short-run effect of the CIATA on municipal revenues was dramatic. Municipalities typically reported increases of 100 to 200 percent in revenues in the year following implementation. Most of this increase was due to improvements in the fiscal cadastre: missing parcels were discovered, and values were recalculated using more accurate data on the physical characteristics of individual properties.

Intergovernmental relations in Brazil were an obstacle to property tax reform. Unconditional transfers provide 80 percent of the recurrent revenues of local government. Because local governments could draw on outside finances to deliver services, they had little incentive to raise property taxes for their constituents.

---

taxation as an alternative to business taxes. Local income taxes have the same characteristics and face the same problems as those at the national level, as described in Chapter 4: that is, they tend to be narrow in coverage and often quite primitive in administration. Thus most local "income taxes" are really poll (head) taxes, wage taxes, or procedures for limited income tax sharing with higher authorities. As with sales taxation, a local surtax on the national personal income tax may be the best way for local governments to raise revenue from the base of individual income.

Taxing the ownership and use of urban motor vehicles can be an important source of local revenue—and a reasonably efficient and equitable one. Automobile use is growing rapidly in developing countries and is concentrated in urban areas and among the better off. The increase in use has been accompanied by greater traffic congestion and air and noise pollution, as well as by rapidly

rising demand for investment in, and maintenance of, street infrastructure and traffic management. The case for recouping these costs with a tax is strong. Unfortunately not all urban governments in developing countries are authorized to tax automobiles. For instance, local authorities in Manila have been told not to levy taxes or fees on motor vehicle registration. Furthermore, even where local governments can impose taxes, they generally have not made a significant effort to tap this revenue source to its full potential. Jakarta and Seoul are among the few exceptions. Jakarta proves that automotive taxation, if turned over to local authorities and given sufficient attention, can make a large contribution to local revenue; it accounted for 37 percent of local current revenue in 1983–84. In Seoul automobile tax revenue more than doubled between 1982 and 1986, while total local tax revenue increased 64 percent.

One of the most striking features of local government taxation in developing countries is the proliferation of minor revenue sources, including selective excise taxes and a variety of license taxes, fees, stamp, and poll taxes. While any one of these adds little revenue, they may jointly make a significant contribution. For example, local taxes and fees account for more than 20 percent of total local revenue in Indonesia. Often, however, their administrative and compliance costs are considerable, and they are subject to wide discretion by tax collectors. Fewer such taxes would be appropriate in most jurisdictions.

Borrowing

As mentioned earlier, borrowing is generally a minor source of local government revenue in developing countries. This reflects both the conservative financial policies of central and local governments and their limited sources of loan finance. In principle, however, there is no reason why local governments should not borrow to finance at least a portion of capital project costs. Debt service payments can be linked to user charges for local services generated by the capital projects for which the debt was incurred. In this manner greater reliance on borrowing favors self-financing projects. This need not imply an increase in aggregate public sector borrowing. Instead it would usually mean replacing intergovernmental capital grants with internal loans from central to local government. Grant financing places the burden on central governments and general taxpayers, rather than on local decisionmakers and beneficiaries where it properly belongs.

One way to provide local access to loans while ensuring some central control to preserve macroeconomic balance is to create a municipal development fund (MDF). Typically, MDFs have two broad objectives. The first is to raise additional resources for public investment. This usually begins with an initial injection of funds from a donor and a counterpart contribution, usually larger, from central or state government. In addition domestic financial markets may be tapped through bond and debenture issues. But ultimately most of these programs aim to extract additional resources from municipalities themselves through better revenue administration and cost recovery.

The second objective is to improve the use of resources. This can be done by developing appraisal criteria and enlarging local capacity for sound financial analysis of the projects financed by MDFs (as proposed in Brazil and Mexico), by as-

sisting municipalities with the design and execution of their investment programs (as in Turkey and Venezuela), and by improving the operation and maintenance of local infrastructure (as in Jordan, which is discussed below).

MDFs are not new. In the past thirty years they have spread rapidly through Africa, Asia, and Latin America. Historically, few have developed a capacity for sustained assistance and funding for municipal government on the scale needed. They have tended to play a narrow and passive financing role by providing little technical or financial appraisal to the investments they have funded and offering little assistance to municipalities other than capital finance. Furthermore repayment discipline has sometimes been weak. MDFs in Honduras, Kenya, and Morocco, for example, have experienced (and tolerated) substantial arrears, and the latter two made new advances to borrowers in default.

Jordan's MDF has been notably successful. In 1979 the government established an autonomous Cities and Villages Development Bank to provide investment finance and assistance to municipal and village councils, with the aim of extending access to infrastructure and employment. The bank played a role in financing the spread of urban physical and social infrastructure (for example, paved roads, schools, clinics, piped water, and electricity) to virtually all settlements, however small and remote. It has also been instrumental in maintaining and improving the quality of infrastructure investment through its standards, appraisal, and monitoring. The bank has taken on an increasingly active role in financial and technical advice and in training for municipal authorities. It has introduced new criteria that will allow municipalities to forecast their debt service capacity more accurately.

Efforts are under way in many developing countries to strengthen existing MDFs or to set up new ones. To succeed the local governments concerned will need a buoyant revenue base to support debt service. If MDFs are allowed to recover debt service from central government transfers to local governments, they will be tempted to induce local authorities to borrow more than they can afford.

Intergovernmental grants

Central government transfers to subnational governments through shared taxes and grants are a critical link in distributing expenditure responsibility and taxing authority between the two tiers.

Box 7.5 Effects of intergovernmental grants: the experience of Nigeria in the late 1970s

Nigeria embarked on a nationwide reform of its local government system in 1976. It was intended to reverse the deterioration in the treatment of local governments by the states after the country achieved independence. Specifically, many states had cancelled their grants.

Under the reform, grants from both the federal and the state governments were to be substantially increased. In the first year local governments received in grants from the federal government roughly five-and-a-half times the amount they had received in the previous year. This increase followed from sharp increases in revenue from oil exports and the reformed grant allocation rules. The budgeted revenue of some local governments increased 1,000 to 2,000 percent. As a result local governments greatly expanded their provision of social services and economic infrastructure. Some serious problems arose, however. State administrations sit between federal and local governments; all but one of them failed to pay its full allocation to the local governments. In many cases federal transfers were diverted to other uses without consultation. In addition virtually all the state governments approved large salaries for state-appointed local government officials—increases, in some cases, of more than two-thirds.

Federal grants to states depended in part on the number of localities under state jurisdiction and thus led to a widespread demand for more local government units. The number of local governments increased from 301 to 781 between 1979 and 1983, which led to a severe shortage of skilled managerial and technical staff.

Furthermore the criteria for distributing transfers placed too great an emphasis on the equality of revenue across jurisdictions, rather than on the generation of local revenue. The transfers served as a disincentive to local revenue effort. Local taxes, such as the property tax, remained grossly underdeveloped, and some states decided to suspend or abolish important revenue sources. Various explanations were given to justify abolition, but they all rested on the supposition that federal transfers made collection of local taxes unnecessary. So the cumulative effect of Nigeria's dramatic increase in transfers to local government was to reduce local governments' own contribution to local finance in relative and absolute terms. For example, the number of property tax payers in Ibadan City dropped from 27,000 persons in 1975 to 8,650 in 1979. Other cities experienced similar declines.

The administrative burdens on local government increased as a result of the 1976 reform. The distribution of increased transfers through states brought local governments under stricter control. Local budgets had to be approved by the states, which often caused severe delays in program execution. In one case the budget process had to go through eight stages of approval with state officials before final approval by the state's chief executive. The substantial increase in transfers to local governments in Nigeria in the late 1970s—in the wake of the steep rise in oil revenue—did not enhance local governments' autonomy or ability to act.

Grants are needed because the benefits or costs of public services provided by local governments can spill over to other jurisdictions. For example, a highway constructed through one jurisdiction is likely to benefit residents in neighboring jurisdictions, or one jurisdiction's education services contribute to a productive labor force that can migrate to other jurisdictions. Some local public services, especially social services, may have national and regional benefits as well.

Another objective of grants is to adjust for disparities in fiscal capacity among local jurisdictions caused by variations in resources, tax bases, and population. Grants can equalize local fiscal capacities, although obtaining adequate data to do this by formula can be difficult.

Excessive reliance on grants, or unexpected increases in them, can result in poor use of public finances. Nigeria's grant system expanded greatly

in the late 1970s, and this had severely detrimental effects on local government finance and intergovernmental relations (see Box 7.5). Grants can encourage recipients to be less efficient. For example, grant systems in Indonesia and Sri Lanka have paid the salaries and allowances of virtually all local government employees, including primary school teachers. This cost reimbursement grant guarantees a uniform pay scale for local government employees without regard for the financial health of any single locality; its lack of cost sharing can encourage local governments to employ inefficiently large numbers of people.

The experience of several developing countries, including Colombia, Ecuador, and Mexico, reveals that increasing reliance of local governments on grants can decrease the fiscal autonomy of local jurisdictions. Local governments come to view grants as substitutes for local taxes and user charges. Many intergovernmental grants are simply central government subventions of local activities. They have many undesirable qualities: they are a drain on central revenue, they encourage inefficiency and worsen regional and urban-rural disparities, and they reduce the accountability of local government while giving it no assured access to funds.

A formula-based grant system addresses these problems by simultaneously meeting central government objectives and providing local governments with some degree of autonomy. Formula-based allocations require the granting government to decide on the factors that are to be used in determining grant amounts. These may include, for example, indicators of need, such as population or miles of road, or indicators of local revenue capacity, such as local income or taxable economic activity. The grants may be block grants, that is, general-purpose, lump-sum transfers that provide local governments with considerable autonomy, as in the Philippines. Alternatively they may be categorical, that is, restricted to particular uses, sometimes requiring approval by the central government. Categorical grants give the central government more control over the allocation of funds between sectors.

Categorical grants can be designed to cover only part of the total spent locally in a sector, in which case grant funds are said to "match" local funds. The matching rate can be set to achieve an efficient level of local spending. If a matching grant is used to support spending that has spillover benefits, the matching rate should ideally equal the ratio of spillover benefit to total benefit, although the information needed to compute matching rates precisely is very difficult to obtain. A single grant cannot accomplish all objectives. For example, if the principal objective is to equalize fiscal capacity across jurisdictions, the goals of stimulating local government tax effort and promoting local fiscal autonomy are not likely to be well served. This problem can be addressed by including different types of grants in the system, for example, pure shared taxes to provide adequate revenues for large urban areas, formula grants to equalize across jurisdictions, and matching grants to stimulate tax effort. Balancing the merits of shared taxes and formula grants is a central issue in designing grant systems.

Grant systems should be kept as simple as possible. Complex systems lack transparency, are likely to introduce mutually offsetting incentives, are difficult to implement effectively, and are open to abuse or ad hoc political bargaining.

Local government administration

Decentralizing spending responsibility and revenue authority can assist development, provided local administrative capacity is adequate to the tasks. An important reason for past shortcomings was the failure to deal with the difficulties of planning and implementation.

Many of the reforms recommended for public spending in Chapter 5 apply at the local level also. In particular, local governments should prepare both a medium-term fiscal plan and a comprehensive annual budget. These force local governments to evaluate the needs of their jurisdictions and to make strong arguments for spending programs, either current or capital, which then serve as the foundation for strong fiscal efforts. They also help central governments to coordinate municipal development and provide a clearer picture of required intergovernmental transfers.

Effective local administration is hampered by lack of finance and accounting skills because skilled personnel frequently would rather work for the central government. One approach to local staffing is to assign central civil servants temporarily to local authorities. Also technical agencies at the center can provide direct services to local governments. Malaysia's central government lends assistance in public health, sanitation, and food inspection, especially in rural areas, and has assigned accountants to state governments. Technical assistance to local governments may be provided with either loan or grant finance. Municipal development funds can enlarge the local capacity for financial analysis and implementation of investment programs.

Training local officials is essential for better local administration. Several Indonesian cities have pilot programs for local training to improve tax administration and financial management. In Nepal local officials have attended training workshops on techniques of financial analysis, current and capital budgeting, and tax collection procedures (including records systems). As a result, at least initially, locally raised revenues have increased.

Another option for local governments with staffing shortages is to buy services from the private sector. Many services can be provided this way. Contracting reduces staff requirements and gives local governments the flexibility to provide a changing mix of services.

Toward more efficient local government

The structure of government in many developing countries is inefficient. Often fiscal relations are opaque because of political expediency rather than lack of knowledge or skill. This makes reform much more difficult. Nonetheless more open and transparent systems are urgently needed. Responsibility for many services can be devolved to local government. Local government should rely on the revenue sources that they are best equipped to use, such as property taxes and user charges. A properly designed system of grants can encourage efficient provision of local services. Local governments must be held responsible for their use of public resources to those who provide them: for user charges, the beneficiaries; for locally raised revenue, the general public; for grants, the central government; and for borrowed funds, the creditors.

8

Strengthening public finance through reform of state-owned enterprises

In almost every developing country the public sector undertakes a significant share of its production and investment through state-owned enterprises (SOEs). SOEs are financially autonomous and legally distinct entities wholly or partly owned by central or subnational governments. Unlike government departments that generally depend on taxes, SOEs can earn most of their revenue by selling goods and services. The output of SOEs can be a substantial share of GDP, although it varies widely from country to country (see Figure 8.1). SOEs have an even greater share of total investment; they accounted for more than 20 percent in thirteen of the nineteen developing countries shown in Figure 8.1. In Zambia, Burma, and Venezuela their share of total investment was more than half in 1984.

SOEs produce a wide variety of goods and services, many of which are also produced by the private sector. They range from power generation, water supply, telecommunications, and transport to manufacturing, mining, agricultural marketing, and finance. Varying degrees of state control and different legal forms further underscore the diversity of SOEs. However, the pricing and borrowing practices of SOEs have much in common; so do their financial implications for government budgets. As a result SOEs have been a major element in public finance in developing countries. In the past their fiscal effect was often hidden by a lack of consolidated financial data on their operations, opaque budgetary procedures, extrabudgetary financing, implicit subsidies, and protection from

competition. More recently tight budget constraints, limits on domestic and external financing, and the effects of devaluation and trade liberalization have exposed the weakness of SOE finances and their worrying effect on the fiscal stability of many developing countries.

SOE contributions to rising public sector deficits and growing foreign indebtedness are increasingly recognized as key issues in public finance. Moreover, during the past twenty years many governments have added dramatically more SOEs to the utilities, marketing boards, and other enterprises they inherited at independence. More than half of Africa's SOEs were established between 1967 and 1980; during the same period the number of SOEs grew rapidly in many other countries, including Mexico, Peru, the Philippines, and Portugal. By establishing a wide array of largely manufacturing and service-oriented SOEs, governments have sought to localize ownership of assets, to control strategic resources, and to foster infant industries. More recently, this trend has led to mounting concern over possible displacement of private initiative in areas where the public sector does not have a clear advantage. This chapter focuses on the issues of public finance common to many SOEs and explores the scope for reform.

How SOEs interact with public finances

As an integral part of the public finance system, SOEs both affect and are affected by public finance policies and institutions. Direct transfers to SOEs from government budgets are the most obvious sign of this. Others are harder to see: interagency arrears and government guarantees of SOE debts do not appear by name in the budget. Through these interactions SOEs have added to public sector deficits and to a lack of transparency in public finance.

SOEs have imposed direct budgetary burdens

The budgetary effect of SOEs is the balance between central government financing of SOE operations through subsidies, net lending, and equity injections, on the one hand, and SOE contributions to the budget in the form of dividends and interest payments, on the other. In eight developing countries with suitable data the net budgetary transfers to SOEs ranged from more than 1 percent of GDP in the Dominican Republic to more than 5 percent in Sri Lanka during 1983–85 (see Figure 8.2). In a few cases—most notably Turkey—these transfers have fallen in recent years, through reforms in pricing and management and cuts in investment. In 1984 the net budgetary transfers to the SOEs among six of the countries shown in Figure 8.2 ranged from one-tenth of the overall central government deficit in Turkey to twice the deficit in the Philippines.

Some SOEs do make sizable positive contributions to the budget. In Egypt, for example, SOEs in the construction and services sector—as well as the Suez Canal and petroleum authorities—made positive net contributions. Persistently weak performance elsewhere, however, meant that Egyptian SOEs as a whole were a drain on government finances.

Transfers to SOEs can sometimes be justified by economies of scale, externalities, or attempts to relieve poverty. As discussed below, such goals might be achieved if SOE transfers were evaluated in advance, appropriately targeted, and closely monitored. Too often, however, such controls have been lacking. Budgetary transfers have thereby been the unintended outcome of poor decisions in investment, pricing, and management.

Interagency arrears have grown

SOEs also affect government finances through the buildup of interagency arrears and cross-debts. Sizable arrears can impede effective financial management because they obscure the true pattern of financing within the public sector. This situation has been especially common in Egypt, Morocco, Portugal, and many Sub-Saharan African countries. In several instances unpaid government bills from state-owned utilities producing power, water, and telecommunications services have amounted

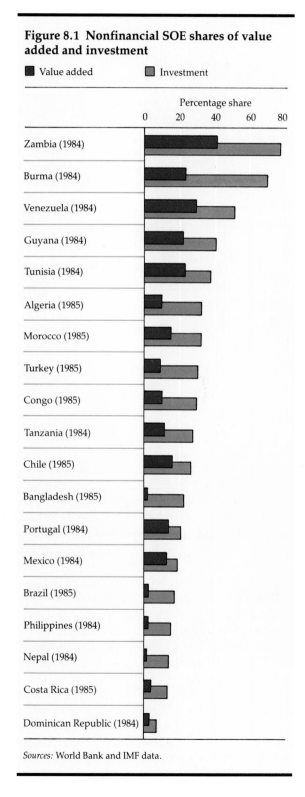

Figure 8.1 Nonfinancial SOE shares of value added and investment

Sources: World Bank and IMF data.

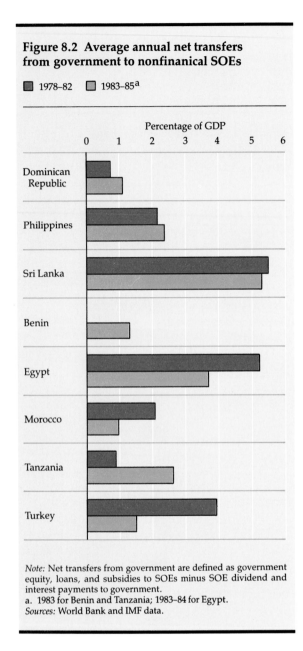

Figure 8.2 Average annual net transfers from government to nonfinanical SOEs

■ 1978–82   ▨ 1983–85[a]

Percentage of GDP

Dominican Republic

Philippines

Sri Lanka

Benin

Egypt

Morocco

Tanzania

Turkey

Note: Net transfers from government are defined as government equity, loans, and subsidies to SOEs minus SOE dividend and interest payments to government.
a. 1983 for Benin and Tanzania; 1983–84 for Egypt.
Sources: World Bank and IMF data.

to the equivalent of one year or more of the government's consumption of the relevant SOE output. Governments sometimes fail to hand over promised capital grants or subsidies; these become obligations for future fiscal years. If capital grant arrears had been counted in Morocco's central government budget in 1984, they would have added two and a half percentage points of GDP to the net budgetary transfers shown in Figure 8.2.

Sometimes, however, SOEs do not pay their obligations to governments: taxes, dividends, debt service, and so on. Often this happens after governments have failed to meet their financial obliga-

tions toward the SOEs; mutual arrears are a short-term answer for all concerned. The Gambian state power company owed the treasury an equivalent of 16 percent of current government revenue in 1984; its own unpaid claims on the government amounted to one-quarter of these arrears. At the same time interlocking arrears accumulated among other Gambian SOEs and municipalities. In extreme cases chain reactions may occur that seriously undermine the financial discipline of the entire public sector. For example, Egypt's publicly run railway company refused to pay state-owned engineering industries because of mounting government arrears. In turn the engineering industries did not pay the state-owned steel industries; the steel industries then refused to pay the state power company.

Government guarantees of SOE debt can be risky

SOEs have borrowed significantly in domestic and foreign credit markets. Governments have commonly guaranteed substantial parts of their debt and have often assumed the debts of SOEs in financial difficulties even where there were no formal guarantees. Explicit or implicit guarantees of this kind create contingent liabilities, but lack of accounting discipline means that often they do not appear in government budgets or accounts. Recent experience in many countries has made it painfully clear that the government's contingent liabilities can have serious repercussions if the financial situation of one or more major SOEs deteriorates. For example, when the former state agricultural marketing board in Senegal was liquidated in 1980, the government assumed bank debts equivalent to 15 percent of GDP.

Partly because of government guarantees SOE borrowing has added significantly to foreign debt. The direct foreign borrowings of SOEs accounted for more than one-fifth of total foreign debt in ninety-nine countries as a group and grew faster than the foreign debt of private borrowers during 1970–86 (see Figure 8.3). The total contribution of SOEs to external indebtedness is greater than this suggests, because governments passed much of their own foreign borrowing on to SOEs. SOEs have accounted for more than half of the outstanding external debt of Brazil, Mexico, the Philippines, Portugal, Zambia, and other countries. In most cases overambitious investment programs explain the rapid rise in foreign borrowing. Foreign interest rates often were, or at least appeared to be, lower than domestic rates; foreign lenders preferred lending to SOEs rather than to private enterprises because of explicit or implicit guarantees.

Government backing of SOE borrowing is all the more risky when public ownership is extensive in the financial sector. Credit granted to SOEs by government-owned banks poses the well-known risks of any financial institution lending to borrowers connected with its owners. Standard lending criteria may not be applied, so that loans are made for unsound investments, and foreclosures, where called for, are too long delayed. When SOEs perform badly, this can then mean a sharp rise in the banking sector's nonperforming assets, as in Cameroon, Madagascar, and Mali, for instance. In such cases public capital is required to recapitalize the banking system, which implies heavy future claims on the budget. In Benin, for example, SOEs created central government contingent liabilities to the domestic banking sector ten times larger than the direct budgetary transfers shown in Figure 8.2. Moreover most of their borrowing—which accounted for more than one-third of outstanding domestic bank credit and 13 percent of GDP in 1986—became nonperforming. This virtually paralyzed the country's banking system and put heavy demands on future budgets. The total effect of SOEs on public finance is understated when they contribute to financial crises. This is because public

expenditure associated with resolving financial crises is usually not included in the public sector deficit (see Box 3.3).

SOEs contribute to public sector deficits

The aggregate effect of SOEs on public finance shows up in the overall deficit of the public sector. For some of the years shown in Figure 8.4, SOEs realized deficits larger than the overall public sector deficit in Brazil, the Dominican Republic, Ecuador, Egypt, Turkey, and Venezuela. In other words, the rest of the public sector would have generated a fiscal surplus without the net transfers to the SOEs. In the Philippines and Costa Rica, SOE deficits on average accounted for one-half of the overall public sector deficit during 1981-84. In many other countries such calculations are impossible for lack of data. Most countries fail to monitor the financial position of their public sector as a whole, even though macroeconomic management and stabilization policies call for control of public sector deficits, broadly defined. What accounts for this weakness in fiscal management?

SOEs have diminished the transparency and accountability of public finances

Traditionally, public finance analysts and policymakers have focused their attention on the central government budget as the main determinant of fiscal policy. Analysis of SOE finances had largely been left to sectoral experts. Thus few systematic attempts have been made to monitor SOE financial performance in the aggregate or to compile fiscal data for all levels of the public sector. In Brazil, for example, where SOEs were the fastest growing part of the public sector during the 1970s, the government had no consolidated statistics on their earnings, spending, or debt until 1979. Where efforts have been made to gather information, the rapid growth of SOEs has often outpaced the analysts' ability to collect and evaluate it. In Tanzania in 1986, where the number of SOEs had increased tenfold since the mid-1960s, almost a third were more than two years behind in submitting accounts for audit. SOEs often do not follow uniform accounting standards, so their financial statistics are difficult to consolidate with other public sector statistics. Unforeseen budgetary claims can also arise from failing private enterprises in which public holding companies and state-owned banks had acquired portfolio interests. These indirect and minority state shareholdings have rarely been subject

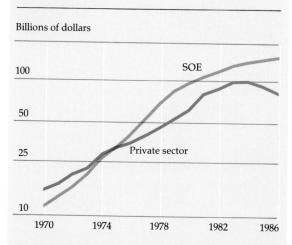

Figure 8.3 SOE contributions to the growth of external debt in developing countries, 1970 to 1986

Billions of dollars

SOE

Private sector

Notes: The vertical axis is in log scale. Data are from a sample of ninety-nine countries and include only direct SOE and private sector medium- and long-term debt.

Figure 8.4 Trends in SOE and public sector balances

(percentage of GDP)

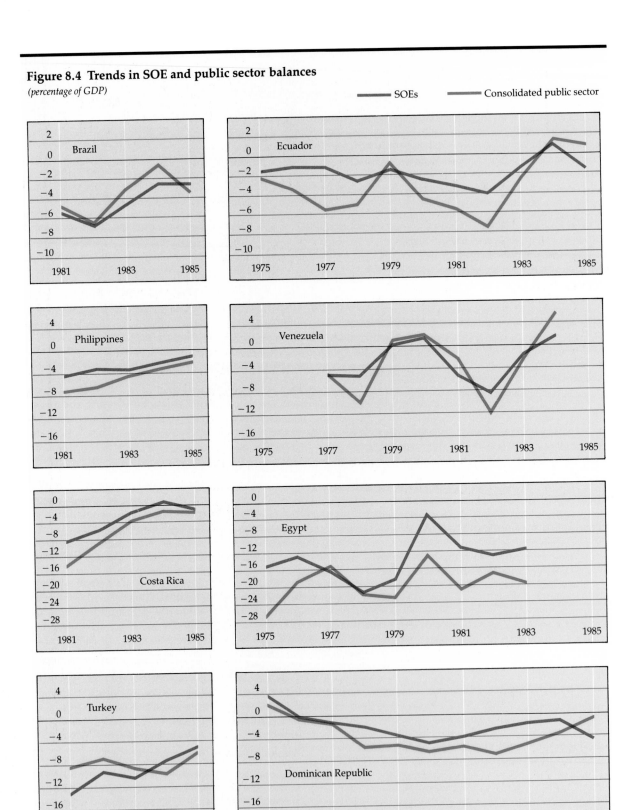

Notes: SOE balances are calculated after taxes and before net transfers from government. Public sector balances are defined as total public revenue minus total public expenditure and are based on consolidated government and nonfinanical SOE accounts. The years covered vary because of differing data availability for individual countries.
Sources: World Bank and IMF data.

either to strict investment criteria or to central monitoring.

However, the failure to view public finances comprehensively is not entirely caused by a lack of data. SOEs were often set up or enlarged precisely because they were largely exempt from fiscal control. Where strict legal or administrative rules limited the creation of new SOEs, ways were often found to circumvent them. For example, in the Philippines during the 1970s and early 1980s some sectoral ministries were able to avoid legal restrictions on the establishment of new SOEs by forming subsidiaries of existing ones. This practice has been widespread elsewhere, as in Brazil, where the creation of SOE subsidiaries was largely uncontrolled until 1979.

SOEs have therefore been both a cause and a symptom of weak fiscal discipline and lack of transparency. Transparency—the ability to assess the financial implications of public sector activities in advance, to evaluate them after the fact, and to identify who bears the costs and who receives the benefits—is necessary if decisionmakers are to be accountable for their actions. Of course, developing countries are not alone in these difficulties. A recent study has documented the growth of off-budget SOEs and agencies at all levels of government in Japan, the United Kingdom, and the United States—"underground public sectors" not subject to the usual fiscal and political controls. Even in the United States, where SOEs have traditionally had only a limited role, off-budget enterprises borrowed an estimated $50 billion in private capital markets in 1982; this sum was implicitly or explicitly guaranteed by the federal government. However, lack of transparency has been particularly disruptive in developing countries. The SOE sector has often been the source of unexpected fiscal crises when the economic or political fortunes of a country worsened, which exposed the weaknesses of substantial segments of the economy that had directly or indirectly come under public control.

Recent fiscal crises have forced the governments of developing countries to reconsider the role and management of SOEs. Official reports in India, Kenya, and Tanzania, for example, have drawn attention to poor management of the SOE sector and to its budgetary implications. More than thirty governments have undertaken studies to identify weaknesses in the sector and in its relations with government. More than ten developing countries have begun comprehensive reforms as part of broader efforts to improve resource mobilization,

allocation of public expenditures, and overall fiscal management. One approach is to reform the traditional instruments of fiscal policy: pricing, taxation, subsidies, and expenditure allocation. Another is to enhance fiscal discipline within the public sector. A third is to increase the role of the private sector.

Strengthening SOEs through fiscal instruments

SOEs finance their spending in three main ways: through revenues from the sale of goods and services, through transfers from the government (including receipts from earmarked taxes, subsidies, and equity contributions), and through borrowing. For commercial SOEs the first of these three sources of finance is generally by far the most important.

Rationalizing SOE pricing policies

Better pricing can have many benefits. It can make SOE operations and investments self-financing, thus reducing the SOE contribution to the overall public sector deficit. This facilitates the pursuit of sound public finance policies. For example, it alleviates the pressures on central government to raise taxes, which are often costly in terms of administration and economic distortions (see Chapter 4). It also alleviates pressure to raise financing through inflation, crowding out, and foreign debt (see Chapter 3). In addition, it helps to limit the overall imbalance between savings and investment in the economy, thus reducing pressures on the balance of payments. The scope is substantial. In Argentina in 1985 the sale of SOE outputs accounted for roughly one-third of public sector revenue. Pricing adjustments in Costa Rica helped move the SOE overall deficit from more than 5 percent of GDP in 1982 to a small surplus in 1984 (see Figure 8.4).

As discussed earlier, raising revenue from the sale of publicly provided goods and services can also improve the efficiency of resource allocation, provided prices or user charges are set to reflect economic cost (see Boxes 4.1 and 6.1). Where SOEs produce internationally traded goods, prices in international trade—also called "border prices"—are generally the appropriate reference point. The coal industry provides an example. In many countries its domestic price was often set below border prices. The implicit subsidy to users was met by grants, equity contributions, or loans from governments to coal-producing SOEs. This encouraged inefficient use and excessive expansion of capacity. Tighter budgets then forced deep cuts in investment, in some cases compromising longer term energy plans. This happened in Indonesia and the Philippines during the 1970s; since 1980 both have taken steps to align domestic coal prices with border prices.

For SOE outputs not traded internationally—for example, power, water, and telecommunications—the long-run marginal cost of production is the basis for efficient pricing. The principles were discussed and illustrated for the water and power sectors in Chapter 6. Underpricing leads to overexpanded capacity, unnecessary burdens on government budgets, and excessive foreign borrowing by the SOEs concerned. Often it happens because cumbersome centralized mechanisms for revising utility tariffs delay price increases after costs have gone up. Political difficulties can then cause further delay. Small but frequent price increases, in line with broad factors affecting costs (such as inflation or devaluations), have successfully avoided these problems in some countries.

Limiting SOE subsidies

Setting SOE prices with reference to economic cost will go a long way toward limiting both the call on central government transfers and SOE borrowing. Experience has shown that for most SOEs efficient prices will be compatible with financial viability. However, subsidies will still be appropriate in some cases, most notably for the relief of poverty or on the grounds of declining costs, since efficient prices will then not cover financial costs.

In principle, to ensure financial viability and transparency, SOEs should be explicitly reimbursed from the budget for the cost of financially unviable, but socially desirable, projects. Otherwise they may have an incentive to underprovide such services or may encounter financial difficulties. The costs and benefits of such subsidies should be evaluated according to standard investment criteria, and a budgetary provision should be made in advance. In some instances, though, it may be more effective to subsidize low-income consumers by charging them less than cost and charging better-off consumers more. Some countries have applied this approach to water, power, and rural telephone services. Cross-subsidies are particularly suitable where the obstacles to raising general taxes are insurmountable.

Rather than receive subsidies, commercial SOEs should pay taxes just as private enterprises do.

This will put them on an equal footing with private competitors and thus encourage efficiency. Where SOE prices act as taxes, as in commodity boards, surpluses should be transferred to the treasury. In areas such as telecommunications and natural resource extraction, efficient SOE prices may lead to financial surpluses. In these cases it is better to tax away some of the surplus to finance other high-priority public investments than to plough it all back into the same sector, pass it on to SOE clients through insufficient charges, or pay SOE employees higher wages. In several oil-producing countries, for example, much of the income generated by state-owned oil companies was wasted in excessive domestic consumption of oil, gas, and electricity.

Controlling SOE borrowing

Borrowing is justified as a way of allocating part of the financial burden of large-scale, lumpy investments to future users. However, it should not become a substitute either for justified increases in user charges or for injections of equity by the government.

It is also important that SOEs bear the full marginal cost of borrowing—especially foreign borrowing. The marginal cost will exceed the nominal cost if the loan has been provided on concessional terms or if access to foreign lenders is rationed. To ensure adequate discipline, some central control of borrowing will be needed in most countries. SOEs in Brazil and Côte d'Ivoire, for example, became subject to such controls in the late 1970s. Thailand has a strict ceiling on total public sector borrowing from abroad that also applies to government-guaranteed SOE loans. In addition, there are regulations that require SOEs to satisfy certain self-financing ratios and to remit a prescribed amount of profit to the government in order to be eligible for government loan guarantees.

Government guarantees on SOE borrowing should be given sparingly and mainly for public works and infrastructure that could spur private investment. They should not be used for commercial projects or joint ventures where unguaranteed credit on market terms is available. Informal or implicit guarantees are to be avoided; this can be done only with strict, pre-established limits on government exposure to SOEs, clear bankruptcy laws for SOEs, and the willingness of governments to liquidate insolvent enterprises. In the interest of fiscal discipline two socialist countries—China and Yugoslavia—have recently begun to apply their bankruptcy laws to SOEs. Another remedy is to pass laws that clearly excuse governments from liability for SOE debts that are not formally guaranteed.

Improving the allocation of SOE spending

SOEs often operate in areas of special concern to the government; their investments are seen as crucial for development. In allocating their resources, they may not be subject to a direct market test. Moreover, in financing their expenditures, they often draw on subsidies, loans, or guarantees from government. Accordingly their spending—and especially their investment—should face an evaluation as rigorous as that applied to direct government transactions (see Chapter 5). Much of this can be properly carried out within the enterprise by applying standard criteria for project appraisal and operational cost-effectiveness. Central government agencies, in particular the planning and finance ministries, should restrict themselves to ensuring that the broad directions of SOE investment fall within national planning parameters, that the SOE carries out the appropriate analysis, and that SOE managers are accountable for the resources they use. However, the precise dividing line between central and delegated responsibility will vary from enterprise to enterprise.

In practice governments and SOEs everywhere—not just in developing countries—have deviated from these principles. The demands on public managers could be reduced by excluding from public sector planning those activities in which SOEs could compete among themselves or with private enterprises for banking credit—in manufacturing, for example, and many services. Financing in these cases would then be independent of government subsidies, loans, or guarantees. The point is also relevant for socialist countries that have begun to move away from central planning. Since 1984 the profits of SOEs in China, instead of being remitted to the government budget, have been taxed and the balance retained by the enterprises. SOEs in China have thus increasingly financed their investments from internal resources and bank loans rather than from government budgetary grants.

Enhancing fiscal discipline

Fiscal discipline is more than a matter of controlling borrowing and allocating spending more efficiently. This section highlights three further aspects: eliminating interagency arrears, improving the transparency of the financial reporting and monitoring of SOEs, and increasing the accountability of SOE managers. Experience in several developing countries has shown that after progress has been made in these areas, sound public finance becomes much more feasible.

Eliminating interagency arrears

Clearing government arrears to SOEs can be a laborious and expensive exercise, but it can greatly strengthen SOE finances. In 1982, using the proceeds of a special bond issue equivalent to 6 percent of GDP, the Ethiopian government settled its unpaid bills to SOEs and strengthened their capital base. Eliminating government arrears in Portugal has improved the financial ratios of several SOEs. Once arrears have been settled, government consumption of SOE outputs must be rigorously budgeted to prevent the problem from recurring. By reducing waste and by making civil servants pay the cost of utilities in government housing, the Moroccan government reduced its consumption of water, power, and telecommunications services— all provided by SOEs—by 4 percent, although its arrears remain substantial. An integrated government cash control system in Jamaica allows adequate budgetary provision and timely payment for SOE outputs.

The arrears of SOEs to governments also deserve attention. They are often settled by being converted to equity. But as long as SOEs do not pay dividends, such conversions are akin to government grants: they provide no incentive for fiscal discipline. Conversions should therefore be complemented by reforms in SOE taxation and pricing. Government auditing should monitor financial balances between individual SOEs and guard against the accumulation of arrears, which hamper efficient financial management in individual enterprises.

Improving financial reporting and monitoring

Improving the transparency of SOE finances calls for up-to-date data. These should include data on actual and planned spending and revenues and on changes in assets and liabilities, organized in a systematic accounting framework, and assembled regularly by a central agency. Most utilities in developing countries that receive foreign assistance or loans already apply standards of this kind; in principle they can be adapted for other commercial

SOEs without much difficulty. The use of a common fiscal year for all public bodies facilitates the consolidation of public sector accounts. Once established, such a reporting system is an invaluable tool of fiscal analysis and policy. In Thailand the central bank compiles SOE financial data in a comprehensive and timely manner. In 1979 Brazil created a federal body (SEST) charged with centrally monitoring SOE finances; it permitted the government to exercise better control over the creation, expansion, and liquidation of SOEs, as well as over their foreign and domestic credit operations. Kenya recently established a debt-reporting system, and it is already beginning to improve the management of SOE debt (see Box 8.1).

It is often useful to separate commercial and noncommercial public entities. Noncommercial activities are usually best integrated into the budget, as in Brazil, where 200 noncommercial agencies were removed from the oversight of SEST and put into the government budget. Separating these two kinds of public bodies (which is also being planned in the Central African Republic and Malawi) allows enterprises that are able to finance themselves to be overseen in a different way from those that must continue to depend on budgetary transfers.

Competent auditing is one of the keys to accurate financial reporting. It is also essential for creating or maintaining good internal financial management and for ensuring public confidence that funds collected by SOEs are not misused. Where public audit institutions and the domestic audit profession are too weak to carry out a radical reform of SOE audit procedures, it may be necessary to bring in foreign firms on a temporary basis, both for initial rounds of audits and to train local staff.

Increasing the accountability of managers

Reliable and timely information on the operations of SOEs improves the accountability of SOE managers. At the same time data collection and monitoring systems are of little help unless they are part of a broader effort to give managers incentives for efficiency. Recently some developing countries have introduced incentive systems based in part on indicators of financial performance. In Pakistan an evaluation system provides managers and employees with bonuses based on performance; these have led to better cost control (see Box 8.2). In Senegal the government and six major SOEs signed contracts that established objectives and performance indicators and set out the reciprocal obligations of the government and the enterprises. Compared with others in the first three years of the experiment, these enterprises had greater sales growth and lower personnel costs. However, continued restrictions on SOE managers and the government's inability to honor financial commitments have reduced the effectiveness of these experiments. Similar experiments have recently started in other developing countries, including Bangladesh, Guyana, Mexico, and Morocco; others are being considered in Argentina, Egypt, and India. Agreements on pricing, subsidies, loan and equity financing, and investment programs should feature in performance contracts or evaluation systems.

Box 8.1 Improving the monitoring of SOE debt in Kenya

During the 1970s and early 1980s Kenya's SOE sector was plagued by poor debt reporting. No clear indication existed whether funds provided by the government to its SOEs were loans, equity, or grants, and the interest and amortization schedule for loans were often unspecified.

In 1984 the government began to assemble data on all outstanding loans to SOEs. The Kenya Internal Debt Reporting System (KIDRES) became operational in 1986. The system computes amounts due from SOEs according to banking principles, with penalty interest accruing on overdue balances. Retroactive agreements are sought where no loan records exist. If an SOE does not pay, the Treasury will not approve its budget.

During implementation several weaknesses in the system became apparent. KIDRES cannot legally enforce debt servicing. It does not cover commercial bank lending to SOEs and thus presents an incomplete picture of debt-servicing obligations. Inadequate administrative resources have handicapped the smooth running of the system.

Nonetheless KIDRES has achieved progress in several areas in a short time. First, better information is now available for judging existing as well as new debts of SOEs. Second, a standard agreement is now completed before any new government funds are released to an SOE. KIDRES has also enabled the government to recover loan repayments from SOEs with above-average financial performance. In the past these SOEs had been unwilling to repay their loans.

Box 8.2   Evaluating SOE performance in Pakistan

In 1980 an Experts Advisory Cell (EAC) was established in the Ministry of Production in Pakistan to administer an oversight system for industrial SOEs. The system consists of enterprise information, performance evaluation, and incentive components. By evaluating SOEs on the basis of financial after-tax profits as well as indicators measuring physical production and energy consumption, the EAC focuses on increasing SOE production and sales while minimizing costs. Each SOE is required to provide cost-accounting data in a standard format. Targets based on budgetary proposals presented by SOEs are officially agreed on in a contract between the EAC and SOE managers, subject to approval from the ministry. A comprehensive weighted indicator based on agreed criteria and weights is used to grade the performance of each SOE into one of five categories. Managers receive bonuses ranging from three months of base salary down to nothing on the basis of this performance evaluation.

The new system appears to have induced managers to increase after-tax financial profits, which rose for most of the SOEs evaluated. By linking performance evaluation to bonuses, the new system also provided incentives for improved SOE accounting. Audited reports, which previously were delivered one to three years after the fiscal year, are now received within five to seven months. SOE managers more readily understand and accept performance targets, because these are negotiated with them rather than set from above. Required periodic meetings organized by the EAC between SOE managers and the heads of their holding companies have increased motivation and communica-

tion of problems.

Several constraints have, however, limited the ability of SOE managers to increase operating efficiency. Among them are the inability to reduce labor to cut costs, lack of control over compensation decisions, inability to close certain product lines, inflexibility in procurement decisions, and constraints on the choice of product mix, markets, and suppliers. In addition credit and foreign exchange ceilings are allocated as part of the budgetary process through negotiations between SOE holding companies and the Ministries of Production and Finance. There is no reason why these ceilings would tend to favor the more efficient firms, especially since price distortions make it hard to judge efficiency. Finally, the system's profit measure appears to provide incentives to SOE managers to minimize taxes, undertake interest arbitrage, underprovide for depreciation, and focus on nonoperating income that does not reflect operating efficiency.

These problems could be mitigated by reducing restrictions on managers in employment and production policies as well as by lowering barriers to domestic and foreign competition with SOEs. Further improvements might result from using the indicator originally proposed when the system was first considered. Performance was to be evaluated using "public profits" in constant prices based on private profits plus taxes, interest costs, and depreciation minus nonoperating income. These adjustments were designed to discourage SOE managers from activities that do not directly enhance the efficiency of their operations.

Although performance monitoring can bring improvements, the scarcity of managerial skills in most developing countries severely limits the number of SOEs that governments can oversee effectively. Improved SOE performance demands a balance between autonomy and accountability that is especially difficult to achieve when the number of SOEs and parent ministries is large. Evaluating SOEs that encompass utilities, manufacturing enterprises, transport companies, marketing boards, and financial institutions requires skill and resources. Where such expertise exists, it is usually captured by the enterprises, so governments often depend on the SOEs themselves for technical evaluation. As long as the number of SOEs remains large, measures to avoid arrears and to monitor financial flows will severely strain public resources. Where possible, therefore, SOEs should

accept competition and involvement by the private sector.

Reappraising the environment and the scope of SOEs

In recent years several industrial and more than fifty developing countries have begun to reduce the administrative and financial burden of the public sector by liberalizing and narrowing the SOE sector. These efforts have meant more competition and a smaller role for the government in the management and ownership of the enterprises. Because the span of effective government oversight is limited, such avenues should continue to be explored through periodic reviews of government shareholdings. These should assess the benefits of privatization, broadly defined as increased private

Box 8.3 Performance of public bus companies in two Indian cities

Comparing the performance of public bus companies in two Indian cities illustrates how prudent management, financial independence, and competition can combine to produce efficient and commercially viable public systems.

The Calcutta State Transport Corporation (CSTC) has a fleet of some 1,100 buses, of which usually less than 700 are in operation, mainly for want of repair and maintenance and sometimes because of lack of drivers. It has a high staffing ratio of 20.7 per operational bus. The CSTC has also been plagued by fare evasion estimated at more than 15 percent of revenue. The resulting combination of low productivity with fare inadequacies and evasion necessitates a subsidy of about $1 million a month. By contrast, the city's 2,200 private buses—operated mainly by small companies or individual owners grouped into several route associations—have been able to survive financially without subsidy and to maintain low staffing ratios and high fleet availability. The drivers and conductors of private buses receive a percentage of revenue, which gives them a strong incentive to combat fare evasion. As a result the fare losses of private bus operations are extremely low, and their operating costs are about half those of the CSTC and are more than covered by revenues.

The Cheran Transit Corporation (CTC) in Coimbatore, a city of about 1 million inhabitants, is one of fourteen publicly owned bus corporations in the state of Tamil Nadu—all of which are financially viable and efficient. The CTC does not have an exclusive franchise but operates in direct competition with private buses. The corporation operates with a very high level of efficiency: more than 95 percent of the fleet is regularly in service, and the staffing ratio of 7.3 per operating bus is comparatively low for public bus corporations. Despite very low fares ($0.04 for a five-kilometer trip), the CTC is able to make a profit ($750,000 in fiscal 1984–85), which enables it to expand its fleet in line with demand. Much of the success of the CTC must be attributed to its dynamic and accountable management and to relatively consistent state government support for adequate and timely fare revisions. Also the CTC pursues prudent commercial policies, comprehensively monitors and costs its services, and has incorporated staff incentives that are common among its private competitors, including bonuses based on revenue gains and savings that result from a higher rate of bus use and better fare collection as well as an annual bonus for accident-free driving.

sector participation in the management and ownership of activities and assets controlled and owned by the government. Leases, management contracts, and divestiture are the principal modes of privatization. Among 600 documented privatizations completed worldwide since 1980, nearly 400 have occurred in developing countries and more than 160 in Sub-Saharan Africa alone. This excludes the divestiture of government shareholdings in many nationalized enterprises that were once in private hands, as in Bangladesh, Chile, and Uganda.

Reducing SOE protection

In many areas, exposing SOEs to domestic and foreign competition would promote economic efficiency. This means, as a rule, removing several forms of protection, including budgetary subsidies. In India public bus companies have performed better in cities where they are fully exposed to competition without subsidy than in cities where subsidies and inappropriate incentives have fostered inefficiency (see Box 8.3).

SOEs are also be protected by regulated domestic markets that keep out private competitors. This has occurred in agricultural marketing, where SOEs have been especially inefficient because of the geographical dispersion of their operations under diverse market conditions and rapidly changing circumstances. Eliminating state marketing monopolies in China led to big gains in agricultural efficiency and drew greater output from private farmers and collectives. Replacing SOE monopolies with private trading networks to import, export, and distribute crops and fertilizers can also improve the distribution of income. By using decentralized modes of transport instead of the capital-intensive systems generally employed by SOEs, private sector marketing can generate higher productivity while favoring unskilled workers and small entrepreneurs.

Tariffs or import quotas protect SOEs from foreign competition and make their inefficiencies less transparent. Tanzania's industrial SOEs were profitable in terms of domestic prices, but, when their inputs were valued at world prices, more than one-third of the enterprises (compared with one-tenth of private industrial firms) were producing negative value added. In other words the output of the enterprise was worth less than its inputs. Removing protection brings inefficiencies into the open: in Turkey, for example, eliminating the trade monopoly of a giant meat-processing SOE in 1980 led to fewer subsidies and to the closing of inefficient slaughterhouses. Private agents generally adapt more quickly to the removal of trade distortions than SOEs, unless the government removes its budgetary and banking support for SOEs at the same time.

Using private management

In sectors where the domestic and foreign private sector have strong technical and management skills, governments can use management contracts and leases to increase the operating efficiency of its SOEs while retaining ownership. Management contracts for state-owned hotels in several countries including Egypt, Jamaica, Sudan, and Zaire have proved to be politically acceptable and commercially successful. In Sri Lanka management contracts transformed the financial performance of state-owned textile mills. Water and sewerage services of a high standard are provided in Côte d'Ivoire by a joint venture company comprising local and foreign interests. Where private operators might be unable to manage an entire SOE, it is often feasible to hive off certain parts. For a port,

for instance, these might include stevedoring, transit, container, and other activities. The Kelang Port Authority in Malaysia initially arranged for private management of its container terminal through a lease.

Nonetheless leases and management contracts can be difficult to draw up and can pose the same dilemmas as enterprises run by public managers. Contracted managers can be efficient only if they are given autonomy in day-to-day operations. At the same time management fees may be payable regardless of performance. Incentives rewarding managers for increased profitability are therefore useful. Governments need to avoid depending on a single contractor if the service is not provided competitively. With a lease the business risk is borne by the lessee. Although governments might shed their immediate financial burdens, they need safeguards to ensure that a viable asset is returned at the end of the lease. Leases are often used as an intermediate step toward eventual transfer of ownership from the public to the private sector.

Divesting SOEs

To alleviate the burdens of a large public portfolio of commercial enterprises, several governments in industrial countries and an even larger number in developing countries have begun to divest part or

---

Box 8.4 An SOE public offering in an undeveloped capital market

In December 1986 the Jamaican government sold 51 percent of its equity in the National Commercial Bank (NCB), the country's largest bank. Although this was not the first privatization undertaken by the government, it was by far the largest and the first to involve a public share offering on the Jamaican Stock Exchange. The NCB, which had been a private bank before it was nationalized in 1977, had a record of moderate profitability and had not created any financial burden on the government. The government decided that the most important objective of the public offering was to promote broad share ownership and to demonstrate the merits of privatization rather than to maximize government revenues.

Supported by a major media campaign explaining share ownership, the offering attracted tens of thousands of new Jamaican shareholders, none of whom was allowed to acquire more than 7.5 percent of the voting shares. Oversubscription at the end of the offering led the government to use a sliding scale to allocate proportionately more shares to small buyers. The larg-

est single group of new shareholders were the NCB's own employees, who were offered a special share purchase scheme; they controlled almost 13 percent of the voting shares after the offering.

As with similar offerings in industrial countries with substantially more sophisticated capital markets, getting the "right" price was difficult; in accordance with common practice the issue was priced at a discount from the share price of the NCB's closest competitor, a publicly quoted private bank. Because of heavy oversubscription NCB shares traded at a substantial premium after the offering. Since the government retained a 49-percent stake in the NCB, it will be able to sell shares in the future at market prices. The NCB's privatization demonstrates that a developing country with a relatively low per capita income can mobilize domestic savings from a broad spectrum of the population; can channel these funds through a small, undeveloped stock market; and can shift control of a major SOE to the shareholding public.

all of their ownership in several SOEs. In the few industrial countries such as France and the United Kingdom where divestiture has been extensive, it has sometimes proved difficult. Appropriate valuation of SOEs, resistance from public employees and interest groups, and the dangers of substituting private monopolies for public ones have been significant problems even where capital markets are well developed, where public debate has been open and extensive, and where regulatory mechanisms are strong. The constraints are far more severe in developing countries, where capital markets are thin, where deep fears prevail of economic domination by foreigners or by ethnic minorities, and where the regulatory capacity of governments is limited.

Nonetheless divestiture is being actively pursued in several developing countries. Where SOEs are financially sound and can attract a large number of local investors, some governments have made public offerings partly to develop domestic capital markets (see Box 8.4). Private offerings are, however, likely to remain the primary form of divestiture in most developing countries. They include the outright sale of assets of SOEs (see Box 8.5).

Along with divestiture the government needs to decide on whether to continue providing protection and subsidies to the newly private enterprise. Generally this will not be desirable, especially where SOE reform is part of a broader adjustment in trade and fiscal regimes. Some SOEs are unsuitable for divestiture because they are not financially viable once protection and subsidies are removed. In these cases liquidation may be the only feasible course of action. Many small unviable SOEs have been closed or liquidated in several countries, including Guinea, Mali, Mexico, and Venezuela.

Agenda for SOE reform

Some SOEs in developing countries have been able to operate as successful commercial ventures without burdening public finances (see Box 8.6). In most countries, however, many have drained budgetary resources, contributed to overall public sector deficits, weakened fiscal management, and made negative contributions to value added. Such problems, although they may vary across countries and SOEs, suggest common areas for reform.

A few key SOEs in developing countries, especially those concerned with infrastructure, are likely to remain under public ownership, as in several industrial countries. Strengthened account-

---

Box 8.5   Divestiture of state-owned textile mills in Togo

Like many other African countries, Togo undertook an ambitious state-led industrial development program in the 1970s using the windfall from short-lived commodity booms and substantial foreign borrowing. By the early 1980s the country was left with several ailing SOEs, including its two largest textile mills. One of these textile mills, designed to produce knitted and woven garments for exports, was completed by the government in 1980 at a cost of $50 million. It was closed shortly after start-up, however, because of inadequate management, faulty equipment, lack of technical expertise and working capital, and insufficient knowledge of the market. The second mill, built by a private concern that went bankrupt in 1981, had been taken over by the government. Although it was in fair condition, it required extensive rehabilitation.

On the basis of proposals from several interested groups, the government decided to sell to private investors the assets of the mills but to retain their liabilities. Three independent audits confirmed a sale price of about $10 million. A Korean group with U.S. financing was selected.

The resulting privatized concern was established in mid-1987 and engaged 120 Korean technicians and managers to supervise the rehabilitation of the existing plant. Overall, a $20 million investment in rehabilitation and additional equipment is envisioned. At full capacity the two plants are expected to employ about 5,000 Togolese workers and to produce more than 24 million garments for export and 12 million yards of printed fabric.

In early 1988 a U.K.-based investment group acquired a majority interest in the operating company to cover a shortfall in the U.S. financing. The original Korean and U.S. investors remained as minority shareholders. The shareholders plan to be operating both plants on a significant scale by late 1988. By creating a private concern that will substantially increase employment, maximize the use of existing equipment, and assume significant financial risk with no direct subsidy, this transaction has provided a favorable impetus for further privatizations that are planned by the Togolese government.

Box 8.6 Malaysia's power utility: a financially viable SOE

Malaysia's National Electricity Board (NEB) is an example of an SOE that is well run and financially sound. Through appropriate pricing policy, investment planning, financial discipline, and adequate autonomy, it has avoided the debt-servicing difficulties and dependence on government budgets of commercial SOEs in many other countries. After adjusting its tariffs to fully reflect the effect of fuel price increases in the late 1970s, the NEB maintained those high rates until 1985. In its 1986 financial year the NEB tariffs were adjusted twice. The NEB has no significant problems with accounts receivable (arrears).

Through maximizing its use of internally generated cash to finance investment, the NEB has been able to maintain a strong capital base and to finance 50 percent of its investment from its own resources. Although 40 percent of NEB total capital was provided in foreign exchange, prudent management had led to a relatively small financial risk based on its existing loan portfolio. By introducing a foreign exchange stabilization reserve in its accounts in 1986, the NEB will be able to adjust its investment program or its financing patterns quickly in response to any changes in exchange rates.

The government of Malaysia reviews tariff changes and the financial performance of the utility, but it does not interfere in operational matters or investment decisions. As natural gas (managed by another SOE) and large-scale hydropower (purchased from another domestic utility) have recently become attractive options for power generation, the government has become more involved with the NEB. However, it has been providing mostly advice and arbitration rather than imposing decisions.

---

ing, incentive-based performance evaluation, and rigorous investment appraisal are essential if these SOEs are to contribute to development rather than burden public finances. It is also vital for governments to define, and then follow, pricing, taxation, and oversight policies to permit cost recovery, proper accounting, and a balance between autonomy and accountability.

The degree of state ownership does not itself determine the performance of an enterprise. However, a large portfolio of SOEs can severely burden public administrative and financial resources. Many governments in industrial, as well as developing, countries have halted and even reversed their earlier policies of extending public ownership. Governments should continually review the costs and benefits of maintaining public management and ownership in individual SOEs and consider, where feasible, divestiture to private hands. For many activities, notably manufacturing and services, it is often possible to use management contracts and leases as intermediate steps in that direction.

Such reforms demand substantial adjustments by the public and private sectors alike. Often they also encounter serious financial, managerial, and political constraints. To help overcome political resistance, greater transparency is needed to demonstrate the costs of unviable or poorly managed SOE operations. The transfer of management or ownership to private agents should occur according to explicit criteria and without additional protection. Since better performance is the strongest argument for privatization, governments should ensure that private agents operate within a macroeconomically sound framework and without the distortionary pricing and subsidies that produced inefficiency in SOEs. The challenge calls for government commitment and adequate resources to support adjustment.

9

Directions for reform

The public sector has grown rapidly in almost all countries during the past few decades. This Report has shown how the poor conduct of fiscal policy has contributed to serious economic problems in parts of the developing world. Unsustainable budget deficits have led many countries into heavy foreign borrowing, high inflation, and stagnant private investment. Public revenues have failed to match spending. They have also been costly and inequitable, relying too much on trade, excise, and turnover taxes and not enough on broadly based domestic commodity and income taxes or user charges. Too many public funds have been spent on unwise investment, costly subsidies, and excessive public employment; too few have been spent on investment to support development.

The Report has pointed to many examples of sound public finance policy. Some developing countries have managed to avoid serious fiscal problems. Others have taken bold steps toward reform. Reform is clearly possible, although institutional change is difficult and takes time. The experience of the past few decades suggests five broad policy prescriptions. These are not unattainable ideals, but practical goals. Some countries have already taken steps in their direction.

- Adopt prudent budget policies.
- Reduce the cost of raising revenue.
- Increase the efficiency and effectiveness of public spending.
- Strengthen the autonomy and accountability of decentralized public entities.
- Design public finance policies consistent with poverty alleviation goals.

Prudent budget policies

Moderate and sustainable public deficits, with some allowance for cyclical ups and downs, are far preferable to successive phases of rapid fiscal expansion followed by sharp fiscal contraction. Debt accumulation, capital flight, and loss of confidence during the expansion ensure that the ensuing contraction will be all the more severe. The poor then bear the greatest burden. They are unable to shield income by moving assets abroad, and they are often the first to lose their jobs in times of recession. What then are "moderate and sustainable" public deficits? They are deficits at levels consistent with low and stable inflation, an acceptable external debt service burden, and reasonable real interest rates. A higher rate of domestic saving and more productive use of public resources will permit higher deficits consistent with prudent fiscal management.

Countries that depend on commodity exports face a particularly difficult fiscal environment. Their safest strategy is to treat commodity revenue as inherently volatile. Mistakenly treating a temporary boom in revenue as permanent carries heavy long-term costs, because it can take years to cut spending and reverse the accumulation of debts incurred during the boom. By contrast, erring on the side of caution—treating a permanent boom as temporary—is easily put right later. Boom revenue can then be used to accumulate external assets or repay debt, thus avoiding the risk of inflation and an appreciating exchange rate.

If a deficit becomes unsustainable, macroeconomic stabilization is a top priority. Structural economic adjustment cannot happen alongside major macroeconomic imbalances. At the same time stabilization without structural measures to support growth may itself prove unsustainable. Stabilization and structural adjustment must therefore be coordinated to avoid inconsistency in policy. Adjustment that relies on lowered tariffs and import barriers, unified exchange rates, and deregulated financial markets can be destabilizing because of its fiscal implications. Adjustment should therefore allow for complementary fiscal reform to replace any lost revenue. Conversely, stabilization that relies on higher tariffs, restricted imports, and reduced public and private investment can stifle structural reform and growth. In fiscal retrenchment the choice between higher revenue and lower spending will vary; it will depend on the size of the public sector and the efficiency of both its revenue gathering and its spending. Regardless of that choice, special short-run measures may be needed to cushion the effect of stabilization on the poor.

Reduced costs of raising revenue

Raising public revenue is expensive. The costs include not just the direct costs of administration, but also the indirect costs that arise from distortions in economic activity. Some methods, though, are far costlier than others. Certain principles should guide governments in reforming their revenue systems.

As far as possible the costs and benefits of public services should be linked through user charges. These might be charges related to consumption (public pricing) when specific consumers can be identified or charges related to benefits (such as valorization schemes in Latin America) when the benefits of a public service are concentrated in a particular area. User charges can promote greater economic efficiency by making beneficiaries weigh the economic cost of a good or service against its benefit. Users are also more likely to oversee the performance of suppliers when they have to pay. Many public services for which charges are both feasible and appropriate are often provided free or at highly subsidized prices to all users. As a result there is significant scope for raising additional public revenue from higher user charges—especially for services such as higher education, hospital care, electricity, water supply, and urban transport. Far from hurting the poor, evidence shows that cost recovery can help them by producing the

financial resources necessary to expand the supply of basic services. Subsidies can still be targeted to the poorest groups to alleviate poverty and to meet basic needs for education, health, and sanitation.

Even though user charges can often be increased, general taxes will continue to be necessary to finance public goods that benefit the citizenry at large. Although some tradeoffs among objectives remain unavoidable, taxes can be reformed to raise revenue while reducing economic distortions and the burden on the poor. Simplicity in tax design is essential, because developing countries have severely limited administrative resources. Thus administrative feasibility and better tax administration should be basic concerns of any tax reform.

Tax systems satisfying these criteria will typically include more streamlined company and personal income taxes, a value added tax (often at the manufacturer's level only, for simplicity), and a few excise taxes on luxury or socially undesirable goods. Where import duties are judged to be necessary, they should be low and more uniform. Marginal tax rates should be low to minimize distortions and to promote compliance. Taxes should be simply structured, with few rates and few exemptions. Extensive use of tax incentives to achieve particular social goals rarely works in practice, since it tends to create or exacerbate economic distortions and severely complicates tax administration. High threshold exemptions in the individual income tax and exemption of unprocessed products from the VAT will go far toward reducing taxes on the poor while concentrating administrative resources where they are most productive in raising revenue.

Efficient and effective public spending

A guiding principle for public investment is that it should complement, rather than compete with, private investment. Government involvement is clearly needed to supply public goods, such as defense and law and order. It is also needed where the private sector would undersupply goods or services that benefit society at large, such as primary education, basic preventive health care, transport infrastructure, and agricultural research. Public intervention can also be appropriate for utilities that monopolize a single source of supply or that face large economies of scale. But governments need not spend scarce, costly resources on activities that the private sector—if allowed to—can do better. For example, they need not try to produce or market most agricultural and industrial goods, nor to provide services such as urban bus transport.

Spending needs to follow sound priorities. Priorities emerge more forcefully when all parties are aware of their specific resource constraints. Setting overall spending limits means balancing needs against the cost of raising revenue. It is best achieved through a coordinated process of medium-term fiscal planning, annual budgeting, and regular monitoring of revenue and expenditure. Binding spending limits should apply not just to finance and planning ministries, but also to sector ministries, subnational levels of government, and SOEs.

The effectiveness of each item of spending is critical in determining its effect on development. Each major project should be carefully appraised, not only for economic viability (using cost-benefit or cost-effectiveness analysis), but also for technical, administrative, and financial feasibility. A distorted policy environment may cause even the best projects to fail. They need the support of appropriate pricing, trade, and credit policies.

Among recurrent expenditures, adequate allocations for operations and maintenance are essential for efficient use of the existing capital stock. Governments often face a tradeoff between maintenance and new investment, but the former is usually the more efficient. The cost of rebuilding roads can be three to five times that of timely maintenance. Adequate civil service salaries are also needed to attract and motivate qualified policymakers and administrators. The common practice of cutting salaries and narrowing pay differences while expanding total employment is bound to produce poor administration. Developing-country governments cannot afford to be employers of last resort for the entire labor force. Finally, subsidies for poverty alleviation should be aimed at those most in need.

Strengthened autonomy and accountability of decentralized public entities

Decentralized decisionmaking and accountability can help to link costs and benefits, and thus improve efficiency. Local decisionmakers can be more flexible and responsive to the needs and preferences of their constituents; equally, citizens can better watch over local entities than over central ones. The extent of feasible decentralization varies

from sector to sector. Urban infrastructure—roads, water, and sewerage—is best handled by local governments and financed as far as possible through user charges. In rural infrastructure a greater role can also be played by village-based community groups, such as water user associations in irrigation. Social service providers, such as schools and clinics, can usually be given greater responsibility for delivery and for cost recovery, although some degree of central control is needed to maintain standards and to provide targeted subsidies where necessary. SOEs should be granted the autonomy to cover costs through pricing, with managers held accountable for the quality of services and for the financial viability of their enterprises.

Local entities and SOEs will require financing other than user charges if they supply public goods or subsidies. Local governments can streamline their tax systems and—through more accurate property valuation and better administration—broaden the base and improve the collection of property taxes. Borrowing by local governments or SOEs may be warranted for capital spending whose benefits occur in later years, but major borrowing throughout the public sector should be subject to central approval, especially when government guarantees are given. Central government grants and subsidies are often justified, usually on equity grounds, but they should be designed to provide incentives for efficient cost recovery. Regular and reliable auditing by central authorities can increase local accountability for the use of borrowed funds, grants, or subsidies.

Financial flows within the public sector are usually complex and often confusing. Transparency in these transactions can be increased by accounting explicitly for all subsidies, equity injections, dividends, taxes, payments for goods and services, borrowing, or debt guarantees. Financial obligations between agencies should be enforced. Arrears in one account jeopardize the financial stability of the creditor and often lead to compensating arrears in other accounts. This causes greater confusion and lack of control.

Like most of the other reforms suggested in this Report, strengthening local government requires improved administration and management. Efforts to upgrade the quality of public sector employees through recruitment, training, and performance incentives will always be critical in fiscal reform. For many commercial SOEs greater competition from private providers or increased private sector involvement—through private management contracts, leasing, or outright divestiture —can help to reduce inefficiency as well as the budgetary burden.

Public finance policies consistent with poverty alleviation

Reducing poverty remains the ultimate challenge of development policy. Public finance can be a powerful tool for this purpose if the prescriptions described above are borne in mind. Fiscal prudence sets the groundwork for growth—the precondition for defeating poverty in the long run. Moreover the poor often bear the biggest direct burden of imprudent policies.

On the revenue side the poor can be exempted from income and property taxes. Exemption of unprocessed products (particularly food) from sales taxes softens the effect of such taxes on the poor. Targeted subsidies can be used to exempt the poor

from user charges. In some cases modest user charges on higher cost services may actually help the poor by permitting increased investment in, and thus expanded access to, publicly provided essential services, such as potable water, primary education, and basic health care.

The most important instrument for directly relieving poverty is public spending. Expanding the resources devoted to low-cost urban and rural infrastructure can lead to immediately improved living standards, even if they are financed through user charges. Strengthening local governments is crucial because they are usually the main providers of urban services. Subsidies targeted for the poor can be maintained even in times of fiscal austerity. In the long run, investment in human resources— including basic health care and nutrition, primary education, and family planning—can significantly improve the lot of the poor and support growth in developing countries.

Statistical appendix

The tables in this statistical appendix present data for a sample panel of ninety developing countries, along with information for industrial countries and high-income oil exporters where available. The tables show data on population, national accounts, trade, and external debt. Readers should refer to the technical notes to the World Development Indicators for definitions and concepts used in these tables. For Tables A.13, A.14, and A.15 readers should refer to the Chapter 1 text for further explanation of the base and high case scenarios.

Table A.1 Population growth, 1965 to 1986, and projected to 2000

Country group	1986 population (millions)	Average annual growth (percent) 1965–73	1973–80	1980–86	1986–90	1990–2000
Developing countries	3,528	2.5	2.1	2.0	2.1	1.9
Low-income countries	2,374	2.6	2.0	1.9	2.0	1.8
Middle-income countries	1,154	2.5	2.4	2.3	2.2	2.0
Oil exporters	475	2.6	2.6	2.6	2.5	2.3
Exporters of manufactures	2,081	2.5	1.8	1.6	1.7	1.5
Highly indebted countries	570	2.6	2.4	2.4	2.3	2.2
Sub-Saharan Africa[a]	399	2.7	2.8	3.1	3.3	3.2
High-income oil exporters	20	4.8	5.5	4.2	4.0	3.4
Industrial countries	742	1.0	0.7	0.6	0.5	0.4
World[a]	4,290	2.2	1.9	1.8	1.8	1.7

a. Excludes nonmarket industrial economies.

Table A.2 Population and GNP per capita, 1980, and growth rates, 1965 to 1987

Country group	1980 GNP (billions of dollars)	1980 population (millions)	1980 GNP per capita (dollars)	Average annual growth of GNP per capita (percent) 1965–73	1973–80	1980–84	1985	1986[a]	1987[a]
Developing countries	2,096	3,130	670	3.9	3.1	0.7	3.3	3.1	1.8
Low-income countries	573	2,124	270	2.9	2.6	5.1	7.2	4.2	3.1
Middle-income countries	1,523	1,006	1,510	4.5	3.1	−1.4	1.1	2.3	1.1
Oil exporters	523	407	1,290	4.8	3.1	−2.4	1.3	−1.7	−1.3
Exporters of manufactures	949	1,889	500	4.7	3.9	3.4	6.4	5.8	3.5
Highly indebted countries	876	494	1,770	4.5	2.8	−3.7	1.7	1.9	−0.5
Sub-Saharan Africa	198	331	600	3.7	0.7	−4.9	2.9	−0.2	−4.6
High-income oil exporters	227	16	14,540	4.2	5.6	−7.7	−8.2	−10.1	5.7
Industrial countries	7,701	716	10,760	3.6	2.1	1.3	2.4	2.0	2.2

a. Preliminary.

Table A.3 Population and composition of GDP, selected years, 1965 to 1987
(billions of dollars, unless otherwise specified)

Country group and indicator	1965	1973	1980	1983	1984	1985	1986[a]	1987[a]
All developing countries								
GDP	339	759	2,135	2,103	2,149	2,158	2,244	2,403
Domestic absorption[b]	342	764	2,180	2,120	2,135	2,151	2,237	2,379
Net exports[c]	−3	−5	−46	−17	14	6	6	24
Population (millions)	2,211	2,700	3,130	3,328	3,392	3,457	3,528	3,605
Low-income countries								
GDP	148	260	574	603	604	621	634	691
Domestic absorption[b]	149	259	597	617	618	651	657	706
Net exports[c]	−1	0	−23	−13	−14	−31	−24	−15
Population (millions)	1,509	1,847	2,124	2,249	2,289	2,328	2,374	2,424
Middle-income countries								
GDP	192	499	1,561	1,500	1,545	1,537	1,610	1,712
Domestic absorption[b]	193	504	1,584	1,504	1,517	1,500	1,580	1,673
Net exports[c]	−1	−5	−23	−4	28	37	30	39
Population (millions)	702	854	1,006	1,078	1,103	1,129	1,154	1,181
Oil exporters								
GDP	51	138	539	506	531	546	466	452
Domestic absorption[b]	50	137	523	495	510	530	468	447
Net exports[c]	0	1	16	11	21	16	−2	4
Population (millions)	277	339	407	440	452	463	475	488
Exporters of manufactures								
GDP	166	368	961	963	979	1,014	1,119	1,245
Domestic absorption[b]	168	373	993	963	968	1,013	1,105	1,219
Net exports[c]	−2	−5	−32	0	11	1	15	26
Population (millions)	1,365	1,660	1,889	1,987	2,017	2,047	2,081	2,118
Highly indebted countries								
GDP	117	292	898	775	800	803	812	809
Domestic absorption[b]	115	291	906	755	764	769	793	777
Net exports[c]	2	1	−8	20	36	35	19	32
Population (millions)	341	419	494	531	543	556	569	584
Sub-Saharan Africa								
GDP	26	60	203	180	178	177	160	127
Domestic absorption[b]	26	59	205	187	178	175	165	129
Net exports[c]	0	1	−2	−7	0	2	−5	−3
Population (millions)	221	273	331	364	376	386	399	414
High-income oil exporters								
GDP	8	28	224	214	198	184	..	..
Domestic absorption[b]	5	17	148	190	192	..	..	..
Net exports[c]	2	11	76	24	6	..	..	..
Population (millions)	7	11	16	18	19	19	20	21
Industrial countries								
GDP	1,397	3,297	7,661	7,927	8,284	8,680	10,613	12,224
Domestic absorption[b]	1,390	3,284	7,713	7,920	8,311	8,702	10,590	12,206
Net exports[c]	6	12	−52	7	−27	−23	23	18
Population (millions)	632	681	716	730	734	738	742	745

Note: Components may not add to totals because of rounding.
a. Preliminary.
b. Private consumption plus government consumption plus gross domestic investment.
c. Includes goods and nonfactor services.

Table A.4 GDP, 1980, and growth rates, 1965 to 1987

Country group	1980 GDP (billions of dollars)	Average annual growth of GDP (percent)					
		1965–73	1973–80	1980–84	1985	1986[a]	1987[a]
Developing countries	2,135	6.5	5.4	3.0	5.1	4.7	3.9
Low-income countries	574	5.5	4.6	7.1	9.2	6.4	5.3
Middle-income countries	1,561	7.0	5.7	1.4	3.3	3.9	3.2
Oil exporters	539	7.0	5.9	0.5	3.7	0.3	0.8
Exporters of manufactures	961	7.4	5.9	5.2	7.9	7.2	5.3
Highly indebted countries	898	6.9	5.4	−0.7	3.8	3.5	1.7
Sub-Saharan Africa	203	6.6	3.3	−1.5	5.8	2.6	−1.4
High-income oil exporters	216	8.8	8.0	−2.1	−5.9	−8.1	−2.9
Industrial countries	7,661	4.5	2.8	2.0	3.0	2.7	2.6

a. Preliminary.

Table A.5 GDP structure of production, selected years, 1965 to 1987
(percentage of GDP)

Country group	1965		1973		1980		1984		1985		1986[a]		1987[a]	
	Agriculture	Industry	Agriculture	Industry	Agriculture	Industry	Agriculture	Industry	Agriculture	Industry	Agriculture	Industry	Agriculture	Industry
Developing countries	30	29	24	32	19	37	20	35	19	35	19	35	19	35
Low-income countries	41	27	38	32	34	35	34	33	32	33	31	33	32	33
Middle-income countries	22	30	17	32	14	37	14	36	14	36	14	35	13	36
Oil exporters	24	28	19	32	15	41	17	38	17	38	18	35	16	37
Exporters of manufactures	34	31	27	35	21	39	21	37	20	37	18	37	18	37
Highly indebted countries	20	32	16	33	13	37	15	36	15	36	14	35	13	36
Sub-Saharan Africa	44	19	34	24	29	32	37	25	36	27	37	25	34	27
High-income oil exporters	4	62	2	68	1	74	2	58	..	..	..	..	..	..
Industrial countries	5	40	5	38	3	36	3	34	3	34	3	34	3	35

a. Preliminary.

Table A.6 Sector growth rates, 1965 to 1986
(average annual percentage change)

Country group	Agriculture			Industry			Services		
	1965–73	1973–80	1980–86	1965–73	1973–80	1980–86	1965–73	1973–80	1980–86
Developing countries	3.3	2.6	3.6	8.6	6.4	3.7	7.0	5.9	3.2
Low-income countries	2.9	2.5	5.5	8.6	7.2	9.9	6.3	4.5	6.9
Middle-income countries	3.6	2.8	1.7	8.7	6.2	1.2	7.1	6.3	2.3
Oil exporters	3.9	1.9	1.3	9.9	6.4	0.2	6.1	7.0	1.5
Exporters of manufactures	3.2	2.7	5.7	10.0	7.9	6.7	8.6	6.1	5.1
Highly indebted countries	3.5	2.2	1.5	8.5	5.6	−1.1	7.1	6.1	0.6
Sub-Saharan Africa	3.4	0.2	0.2	13.7	4.7	−2.4	5.7	5.0	0.1
High-income oil exporters	..	..	..	13.2	3.9	−8.2	..	..	..
Industrial countries	1.7	0.4	2.5	5.0	2.0	2.5	4.7	3.4	2.6

Table A.7 Consumption, savings, and investment indicators, selected years, 1965 to 1987
(percentage of GDP)

Country group and indicator	1965	1973	1980	1983	1984	1985	1986[a]	1987[a]
All developing countries								
Consumption	79.7	76.9	75.8	77.8	76.5	76.6	76.7	75.6
Investment	20.8	23.6	26.6	23.2	22.9	23.6	23.4	23.8
Saving	19.3	23.0	23.4	20.3	21.4	21.3	21.5	23.6
Low-income countries								
Consumption	81.1	76.0	78.9	77.8	76.6	75.3	75.4	74.0
Investment	20.4	23.8	26.0	24.8	26.2	29.8	28.8	28.2
Saving	18.5	23.7	22.1	23.4	24.4	25.4	25.1	26.2
Middle-income countries								
Consumption	78.7	77.4	74.7	77.7	76.5	77.1	77.3	76.3
Investment	21.1	23.4	26.8	22.5	21.6	21.1	21.3	22.1
Saving	19.9	22.6	23.9	19.1	20.2	19.6	20.1	22.5
Oil exporters								
Consumption	80.2	76.6	70.5	76.0	75.0	77.3	79.8	76.1
Investment	19.4	22.6	26.4	21.8	21.0	21.2	21.2	23.2
Saving	17.3	21.6	26.6	19.4	20.3	18.3	15.9	20.0
Exporters of manufactures								
Consumption	77.9	75.4	75.6	75.1	73.0	71.9	71.3	71.9
Investment	22.5	25.9	28.4	25.2	26.2	28.1	27.7	27.3
Saving	21.6	25.4	24.5	24.2	26.2	27.3	28.1	27.7
Highly indebted countries								
Consumption	76.2	77.8	75.7	79.2	78.2	78.9	79.2	77.6
Investment	21.2	21.8	25.2	18.0	17.2	17.7	19.0	19.6
Saving	22.0	21.3	22.4	16.2	17.2	16.6	17.0	20.7
Sub-Saharan Africa								
Consumption	82.3	78.4	80.3	88.8	88.3	86.6	88.5	84.8
Investment	15.0	18.9	20.4	15.1	11.6	12.2	14.5	17.4
Saving	15.4	17.5	16.7	8.5	8.5	10.2	7.6	10.9
Industrial countries								
Consumption	76.5	74.6	77.7	80.0	79.0	79.5	78.9	78.8
Investment	23.2	25.0	23.0	19.9	21.3	20.7	20.9	21.2
Saving	23.9	25.8	22.7	20.3	21.3	20.7	21.2	22.0

a. Preliminary.

Table A.8 Growth of export volume, 1965 to 1987

Country group and commodity	Average annual change in export volume (percent)					
	1965–73	1973–80	1980–84	1985	1986[a]	1987[b]
By commodity						
Developing countries	4.9	4.7	4.7	3.3	5.7	5.9
Manufactures	11.6	13.8	9.5	3.3	4.9	9.5
Food	2.9	4.3	1.7	4.3	4.1	4.2
Nonfood	2.7	1.2	0.1	7.9	5.9	4.2
Metals and minerals	4.8	7.0	−0.2	7.8	11.1	1.2
Fuels	4.0	−0.8	1.8	0.7	6.8	0.0
World[c]	8.8	4.4	1.4	3.0	3.7	4.3
Manufactures	10.7	6.1	3.8	4.3	1.8	4.8
Food	5.0	6.6	0.8	0.9	4.4	8.2
Nonfood	3.1	1.0	0.6	8.1	−0.3	7.6
Metals and minerals	6.8	8.7	−0.7	3.9	3.6	10.6
Fuels	8.6	0.0	−5.0	−2.6	12.3	−2.9
By country group						
Developing countries	4.9	4.7	4.7	3.3	5.7	5.9
Manufactures	11.6	13.8	9.5	3.3	4.9	9.5
Primary goods	3.7	1.2	1.3	3.3	6.4	2.8
Low-income countries	2.0	4.7	5.4	7.7	10.4	6.2
Manufactures	2.4	8.2	9.6	0.7	15.0	9.3
Primary goods	1.7	2.8	2.4	13.7	6.9	3.6
Middle-income countries	5.3	4.8	4.6	2.7	5.0	5.8
Manufactures	14.9	14.8	9.4	3.6	3.5	9.5
Primary goods	3.9	1.1	1.2	1.8	6.3	2.7
Oil exporters	4.1	−0.9	0.4	0.0	3.2	−1.0
Manufactures	10.1	3.4	24.5	3.6	3.9	6.7
Primary goods	4.0	−1.0	−1.0	−0.4	3.1	−1.8
Exporters of manufactures	8.4	9.8	9.3	4.1	8.2	12.2
Manufactures	11.6	14.0	10.2	2.8	7.8	12.8
Primary goods	5.5	3.4	7.4	7.2	9.1	10.9
Highly indebted countries	3.1	1.1	0.9	0.5	−2.6	−0.4
Manufactures	13.4	10.2	5.6	−2.3	−11.5	3.4
Primary goods	2.4	−0.4	−0.3	1.3	0.2	0.4
Sub-Saharan Africa	15.0	0.1	−7.5	9.9	0.8	−6.8
Manufactures	7.5	5.6	2.9	12.5	2.3	−0.3
Primary goods	15.3	−0.1	−8.2	9.7	0.7	−7.4
High-income oil exporters	12.8	−0.6	−16.3	−15.4	24.9	−8.8
Industrial countries	9.4	5.4	2.5	4.2	1.9	4.6

a. Estimated.
b. Projected.
c. Excludes nonmarket industrial countries.

Table A.9 Change in export prices and terms of trade, 1965 to 1987
(average annual percentage change)

Country group	1965–73	1973–80	1980–84	1985	1986[a]	1987[b]
Export prices						
Developing countries	6.4	14.0	−3.2	−4.0	−6.4	12.2
Manufactures	7.2	8.1	−2.7	−1.1	12.0	10.9
Food	5.3	9.1	−2.3	−9.8	4.9	−4.3
Nonfood	4.5	10.3	−4.1	−13.8	0.1	23.8
Metals and minerals	2.5	4.7	−5.2	−5.5	−4.2	13.2
Fuels	8.0	27.1	−4.0	−3.5	−47.2	23.9
High-income oil exporters	7.6	26.9	−4.1	−2.6	−45.3	20.8
Industrial countries						
Total	4.8	10.4	−3.5	−0.6	13.9	8.4
Manufactures	4.6	10.8	−3.4	0.9	19.8	9.4
Terms of trade						
Developing countries	0.7	1.6	−0.9	−2.3	−7.3	0.6
Low-income countries	1.7	−2.5	0.0	−3.6	−2.0	0.5
Middle-income countries	0.6	2.2	−1.0	−2.1	−7.9	0.4
Oil exporters	0.0	10.0	−1.8	−3.1	−38.7	9.3
Exporters of manufactures	1.8	−2.7	0.3	−0.4	3.9	−2.4
Highly indebted countries	1.4	3.5	−0.7	−2.3	−14.3	−0.5
Sub-Saharan Africa	−8.4	4.8	−1.4	−5.9	−23.5	1.1
High-income oil exporters	0.3	13.4	−2.3	−2.2	−49.1	7.6
Industrial countries	−1.0	−3.0	0.1	1.7	9.5	−0.1

a. Estimated.   b. Projected.

Table A.10 Growth of long-term debt of developing countries, 1970 to 1987
(average annual percentage change, nominal)

Country group	1970–73	1973–80	1980–84	1985[a]	1986[a,b]	1987[a,c]
All developing countries						
Debt outstanding and disbursed	18.2	21.6	12.2	9.2	11.8	5.8
Official	15.8	17.4	9.9	15.1	20.9	8.8
Private	20.5	24.8	13.5	6.1	6.8	3.9
Low-income countries						
Debt outstanding and disbursed	13.0	16.4	8.2	18.0	19.2	11.0
Official	13.1	15.1	8.8	17.7	18.2	10.0
Private	12.6	22.7	5.9	19.1	22.7	14.7
Middle-income countries						
Debt outstanding and disbursed	19.7	22.8	12.9	7.8	10.6	4.9
Official	17.5	18.6	10.4	13.9	22.1	8.3
Private	21.1	24.9	13.9	5.6	6.0	3.3
Oil exporters						
Debt outstanding and disbursed	22.7	24.9	13.7	5.2	13.4	6.4
Official	16.9	19.6	7.6	12.0	29.4	13.1
Private	27.5	27.8	16.0	3.2	8.1	3.7
Exporters of manufactures						
Debt outstanding and disbursed	22.3	19.9	10.5	8.4	8.4	5.6
Official	15.3	13.5	8.6	10.7	19.0	8.0
Private	30.7	24.6	11.2	7.3	3.5	4.4
Highly indebted countries						
Debt outstanding and disbursed	17.4	22.1	15.4	4.7	11.2	5.2
Official	13.3	15.3	13.6	17.5	32.6	13.7
Private	19.1	24.2	15.7	2.0	6.0	2.6
Sub-Saharan Africa						
Debt outstanding and disbursed	20.4	24.5	10.0	13.8	22.6	6.7
Official	18.1	23.6	12.4	16.4	30.4	7.6
Private	24.2	25.9	6.9	10.0	10.6	5.0

a. The increase in debt outstanding and disbursed is caused in part by the effect of rescheduling.
b. Preliminary.   c. Estimated.

Table A.11 Saving, investment, and the balance on goods, services, and unrequited private transfers, 1965 to 1986
(percentage of GNP)

Country	Gross domestic investment			Gross national saving			Balance on goods, services, and unrequited private transfers		
	1965–73	1973–80	1980–86	1965–73	1973–80	1980–86	1965–73	1973–80	1980–86
Latin America and Caribbean									
*Argentina	19.8	23.8	15.2	19.9	22.7	10.4	−0.1	−0.6	−4.7
*Bolivia	25.4	25.3	7.0	22.4	18.4	−1.7	−3.0	−6.8	−8.7
*Brazil	21.2	23.7	20.6	19.2	19.1	17.2	−2.0	−4.6	−3.3
*Chile	14.3	17.4	17.4	12.5	11.8	6.8	−1.8	−5.5	−10.6
*Colombia	18.9	18.8	19.8	16.5	18.7	14.4	−2.5	−0.1	−5.4
*Costa Rica	21.8	25.5	24.4	13.0	13.4	12.7	−8.8	−12.2	−11.7
*Ecuador	19.0	26.7	22.9	14.6	21.0	18.0	−4.4	−5.7	−4.9
Guatemala	13.3	18.7	11.9	11.0	14.3	7.7	−2.2	−4.3	−4.2
*Jamaica	32.0	20.2	23.1	20.9	12.2	6.9	−11.1	−8.0	−16.2
*Mexico	21.4	25.2	25.3	19.2	21.2	23.4	−2.2	−4.0	−1.9
*Peru	27.7	28.9	26.7	27.1	24.6	22.3	−0.6	−4.3	−4.4
*Uruguay	12.0	15.7	13.3	11.5	11.3	10.0	−0.5	−4.4	−3.3
*Venezuela	29.5	32.5	20.0	30.3	35.2	24.3	0.8	2.6	4.3
Africa									
Cameroon	16.8	21.8	26.4	..	17.7	24.3	..	−4.1	−2.0
*Côte d'Ivoire	22.8	29.2	20.5	..	23.2	15.5	..	−6.0	−5.0
Ethiopia	12.8	9.5	11.3	11.8	6.0	2.2	−1.1	−3.5	−9.1
Ghana	12.3	8.7	4.7	11.4	6.9	−0.8	−0.9	−1.8	−5.5
Kenya	22.6	26.2	25.5	17.8	16.4	17.7	−4.9	−9.8	−7.8
Liberia	19.1	28.7	15.0	..	30.6	12.3	..	1.8	−2.7
Malawi	20.0	29.7	19.5	..	10.7	6.1	..	−19.0	−13.4
Niger	9.7	23.8	18.5	..	11.8	6.8	..	−12.0	−11.8
*Nigeria	17.5	22.1	14.5	15.3	24.0	13.2	−2.2	1.9	−1.4
Senegal	14.7	17.5	15.9	..	4.6	−2.7	..	−13.0	−18.6
Sierra Leone	13.8	14.1	13.6	9.7	−1.6	4.4	−4.2	−15.7	−9.2
Sudan	11.9	16.2	16.7	10.5	7.5	−0.7	−1.4	−8.7	−17.5
Tanzania	19.9	23.9	18.0	16.9	13.0	8.5	−3.0	−10.9	−9.6
Zaire	13.7	15.0	14.4	12.1	9.3	6.5	−1.6	−5.6	−7.9
Zambia	31.9	28.5	18.5	38.5	24.7	7.2	6.6	−3.7	−11.3
South Asia									
India	18.4	22.5	24.5	16.7	21.2	21.5	−1.7	−1.3	−3.0
Pakistan	16.1	17.5	17.5	..	6.4	4.6	..	−11.1	−13.0
Sri Lanka	15.8	20.6	28.0	12.7	12.5	11.9	−3.1	−8.1	−16.1
East Asia									
Indonesia	15.8	24.5	28.1	12.4	24.6	24.9	−3.5	0.1	−3.2
Korea, Republic of	23.9	31.0	30.6	16.2	25.0	27.6	−7.7	−6.0	−3.0
Malaysia	22.3	28.7	34.1	23.4	29.8	27.5	1.0	1.0	−6.6
Papua New Guinea	27.8	22.0	28.4	..	14.1	7.8	..	−7.9	−20.6
*Philippines	20.6	29.1	23.8	19.3	23.5	18.3	−1.3	−5.6	−5.5
Thailand	23.8	26.6	24.2	21.5	21.1	19.1	−2.3	−5.4	−5.1
Europe and North Africa									
Algeria	32.1	44.5	37.0	25.5	37.5	36.1	−6.6	−7.0	−0.9
Egypt	14.0	29.8	28.6	9.0	8.9	3.6	−5.0	−20.9	−25.0
*Morocco	15.0	25.6	23.1	12.5	11.2	6.4	−2.6	−14.4	−16.8
Portugal	26.6	29.7	30.6	..	16.5	14.5	..	−13.2	−16.0
Tunisia	23.3	29.9	30.2	16.9	19.9	17.9	−6.4	−9.9	−12.3
Turkey	18.5	21.8	22.0	16.1	14.9	14.7	−2.4	−6.9	−7.3
*Yugoslavia	29.9	35.6	38.8	25.6	26.9	31.8	−4.2	−8.7	−6.9

Note: An asterisk indicates a highly indebted country.

Table A.12 Composition of debt outstanding, 1970 to 1986

(percentage of total long-term debt)

Country	Debt from official sources			Debt from private sources			Debt at floating rates[a]		
	1970–72	1980–82	1986	1970–72	1980–82	1986	1973–75	1980–82	1986
Latin America and Caribbean									
*Argentina	9.5	6.7	11.4	65.5	68.3	88.6	4.9	21.9	74.4
*Bolivia	43.7	38.6	57.6	31.3	36.4	42.4	5.5	19.8	20.4
*Brazil	23.0	9.4	20.6	52.0	65.6	79.4	17.8	34.1	58.4
*Chile	35.3	8.2	16.4	39.7	66.8	83.6	5.9	17.8	69.7
*Colombia	51.2	34.5	49.4	23.8	40.5	50.6	4.0	25.3	38.1
*Costa Rica	29.8	27.4	43.5	45.2	47.6	56.5	11.1	32.2	53.3
*Ecuador	38.8	22.9	28.9	36.2	52.1	71.1	6.0	27.4	71.6
Guatemala	35.6	53.2	63.4	39.4	21.8	36.6	0.0	4.2	29.6
*Jamaica	5.5	51.3	81.3	69.5	23.7	18.7	3.3	13.0	20.4
*Mexico	14.6	8.1	12.6	60.4	66.9	87.4	22.4	46.5	66.0
*Peru	11.7	30.1	39.8	63.3	44.9	60.2	11.2	17.2	32.3
*Uruguay	33.1	15.8	17.8	41.9	59.2	82.2	7.5	21.4	68.0
*Venezuela	22.4	1.8	0.4	52.6	73.2	99.6	13.1	45.5	70.0
Africa									
Cameroon	61.7	42.9	66.8	13.3	32.1	33.2	1.4	8.3	6.6
*Côte d'Ivoire	38.6	17.3	33.3	36.4	57.7	66.7	13.8	27.0	34.2
Ethiopia	65.5	69.5	86.2	9.5	5.5	13.8	1.1	1.6	4.1
Ghana	43.8	68.6	95.1	31.2	6.4	4.9	0.0	0.0	0.0
Kenya	43.8	42.1	75.6	31.2	32.9	24.4	1.4	7.5	3.4
Liberia	60.8	56.5	81.8	14.2	18.5	18.2	0.0	11.7	12.3
Malawi	63.4	54.6	92.9	11.6	20.4	7.1	1.6	15.8	4.9
Niger	72.8	31.7	65.9	2.2	43.3	34.1	0.0	9.9	12.2
*Nigeria	51.6	15.3	40.1	23.4	59.7	59.9	0.5	36.4	53.4
Senegal	44.4	52.1	87.9	30.6	22.9	12.1	17.3	6.4	7.2
Sierra Leone	45.5	50.8	64.3	29.5	24.2	35.7	2.4	0.1	0.6
Sudan	64.7	55.8	80.1	10.3	19.2	19.9	1.6	7.6	22.9
Tanzania	45.7	57.0	89.7	29.3	18.0	10.3	0.3	0.2	4.0
Zaire	19.1	49.4	86.6	55.9	25.6	13.4	19.3	8.5	12.9
Zambia	16.4	52.8	83.7	58.6	22.2	16.3	14.7	7.5	34.8
South Asia									
India	71.4	68.4	77.9	3.6	6.6	22.1	0.0	2.5	10.0
Pakistan	68.0	69.7	93.1	7.0	5.3	6.9	0.0	2.3	5.1
Sri Lanka	61.2	60.5	77.7	13.8	14.5	22.3	0.0	8.9	8.4
East Asia									
Indonesia	54.1	38.8	50.9	20.9	36.2	49.1	3.6	11.3	24.2
Korea, Republic of	27.1	26.0	32.3	47.9	49.0	67.7	8.4	22.2	37.5
Malaysia	38.3	16.5	19.5	36.7	58.5	80.5	12.3	27.1	44.1
Papua New Guinea	4.6	19.2	24.5	70.4	55.8	75.5	0.0	17.7	19.6
*Philippines	17.0	24.3	38.0	58.0	50.7	62.0	5.3	17.5	48.8
Thailand	30.1	30.3	48.6	44.9	44.7	51.4	0.3	16.5	25.1
Europe and North Africa									
Algeria	34.4	14.0	21.2	40.6	61.0	78.8	24.5	18.2	30.0
Egypt	50.4	58.8	71.9	24.6	16.2	28.1	2.3	2.2	3.1
*Morocco	59.4	38.7	67.9	15.6	36.3	32.1	2.0	22.7	33.8
Portugal	29.3	18.9	16.2	45.7	56.1	83.8	0.0	25.7	44.0
Tunisia	53.9	45.8	66.5	21.1	29.2	33.5	0.0	10.0	16.4
Turkey	69.4	47.4	60.8	5.6	27.6	39.2	0.6	17.3	27.2
*Yugoslavia	28.7	17.9	31.4	46.3	57.1	68.6	2.3	7.6	50.7

Note: An asterisk indicates a highly indebted country.
a. Percentage of public long-term debt.

Table A.13 External financing for developing countries, by type of flow, 1980 to 1995
(billions of dollars)

Country group and type of flow	Level 1980	Level 1987	Level 1995 Base	Level 1995 High	Period average (mean value) 1981–87	Period average (mean value) 1988–95 Base	Period average (mean value) 1988–95 High
All developing countries							
Deficit on goods, services, and private transfers	71.2	13.9	62.3	75.3	56.0	37.0	39.4
Net ODA	23.6	27.5	47.6	50.1	24.3	38.3	39.1
Grants	12.1	17.3	21.7	23.2	14.5	17.9	18.5
Concessional loans	11.5	10.1	25.9	26.9	9.7	20.4	20.6
Direct private investment	10.0	11.3	19.5	21.2	11.8	15.3	16.1
Long-term nonconcessional loans, net	49.4	20.2	17.9	37.9	36.9	6.7	15.4
Official	8.8	9.4	9.4	10.0	10.4	6.3	6.6
Private	40.6	10.8	8.6	27.9	26.5	0.4	8.8
Other capital	−0.3	−5.0	−2.5	−1.2	−10.1	−5.5	−4.8
Highly indebted countries							
Deficit on goods, services, and private transfers	23.4	8.3	1.0	3.8	20.0	7.9	8.5
Net ODA	1.6	1.4	5.9	5.3	1.9	4.6	4.0
Grants	0.5	1.4	2.3	2.2	1.0	1.7	1.7
Concessional loans	1.1	0.0	3.7	3.0	0.9	2.9	2.3
Direct private investment	4.4	2.6	5.9	6.4	4.3	4.5	4.8
Long-term nonconcessional loans, net	27.5	14.4	−11.4	−7.4	19.3	−2.7	−1.0
Official	3.6	6.9	1.9	2.0	5.0	1.0	1.0
Private	23.9	7.5	−13.3	−9.4	14.3	−3.8	−2.0
Other capital	0.9	0.9	4.4	5.3	−9.6	2.8	3.3
Sub-Saharan Africa							
Deficit on goods, services, and private transfers	5.5	10.9	12.6	11.8	11.0	11.1	10.6
Net ODA	5.2	6.5	15.3	15.1	5.6	12.2	11.9
Grants	2.7	3.6	7.6	7.8	3.1	6.2	6.3
Concessional loans	2.5	2.9	7.7	7.3	2.5	6.0	5.6
Direct private investment	0.0	1.0	1.7	1.8	0.9	1.3	1.4
Long-term nonconcessional loans, net	5.5	2.3	−3.3	−4.0	3.3	−1.5	−1.6
Official	1.2	0.4	−0.5	−0.5	1.0	−0.7	−0.7
Private	4.3	1.9	−2.9	−3.5	2.2	−0.8	−0.9
Other capital	−1.4	−0.7	−0.1	0.0	−0.8	−0.3	−0.3

Note: All data are based on a sample of ninety developing countries. The deficit on goods, services, and private transfers not financed by ODA, direct investment, long-term loans, and other capital is covered by foreign exchange reserves.

Table A.14 Current account balance and its financing in developing countries, 1987 and 1995

(billions of dollars)

	All developing countries			Low-income countries			Middle-income countries		
		1995			1995			1995	
Item	1987[a]	Base	High	1987[a]	Base	High	1987[a]	Base	High
Net exports of goods and nonfactor services	27.6	−24.4	−41.0	−14.9	−33.2	−38.0	42.5	8.8	−3.0
Interest on long-term debt	55.9	73.3	75.4	4.9	14.5	15.4	51.0	58.8	60.0
Official	17.0	26.6	26.5	3.0	6.6	6.6	14.0	20.0	19.9
Private	38.9	46.7	48.9	1.9	7.9	8.8	37.0	38.7	40.1
Net official transfers	16.0	21.7	23.2	5.3	7.6	8.1	10.7	14.1	15.1
Current account balance	2.1	−40.6	−52.1	−9.6	−27.7	−31.4	11.7	−13.0	−20.7
Long-term loans, net	30.4	43.8	64.8	9.1	35.9	42.9	21.3	8.0	21.9
Official	19.6	35.3	36.9	7.4	16.7	17.7	12.2	18.6	19.2
Private	10.8	8.6	27.9	1.7	19.2	25.2	9.1	−10.6	2.7
Debt outstanding and disbursed	886.0	1,113.8	1,184.7	137.7	320.8	344.5	748.3	793.0	840.2
As a percentage of GNP	37.7	23.9	22.5	21.9	22.8	22.2	43.4	24.4	22.7
As a percentage of exports	145.3	94.5	85.4	180.6	187.0	169.5	140.3	78.7	70.9
Debt service as a percentage of exports	20.2	15.6	13.7	17.5	18.2	16.3	20.6	15.2	13.2

Note: All data are based on a sample of ninety developing countries. Columns may not add to totals because of rounding. Net exports plus interest plus official transfers does not equal the current account balance because private transfers and investment income are omitted. The current account balance not financed by loans is covered by direct foreign investment, other capital (including short-term credit and errors and

Table A.15 Change in volume of trade in developing countries, 1973 to 1995

(average annual percentage change)

	Exports of goods				Exports of manufactures			
			1987–95				1987–95	
Country group	1973–80	1980–87	Base	High	1973–80	1980–87	Base	High
Developing countries	4.7	5.4	4.0	5.6	13.8	8.6	5.8	8.3
Low-income countries	4.7	6.8	5.2	6.7	8.2	8.9	7.4	9.9
Middle-income countries	4.8	5.2	3.9	5.5	14.8	8.6	5.6	8.1
Oil exporters	−0.9	1.6	2.2	3.2	3.4	17.3	8.3	11.3
Exporters of manufactures	9.8	9.3	5.1	7.1	14.0	9.6	6.0	8.5
Highly indebted countries	1.1	1.4	3.2	4.3	10.2	2.1	5.9	8.5
Sub-Saharan Africa	0.1	−1.6	2.7	3.4	5.6	4.7	4.6	7.0

Note: All data are based on a sample of ninety developing countries.

Oil exporters			Exporters of manufactures			Highly indebted countries			Sub-Saharan Africa		
	1995			1995			1995			1995	
1987[a]	Base	High	1987[a]	Base	High	1987[a]	Base	High	1987[a]	Base	High
9.0	25.2	25.8	20.8	−37.2	−51.0	25.3	35.0	30.8	−3.0	−4.3	−3.7
17.2	18.7	17.7	16.3	31.9	35.2	30.1	36.3	35.9	3.7	5.8	5.6
3.6	6.2	6.2	5.3	8.7	8.8	6.7	9.0	8.8	2.1	3.5	3.4
13.7	12.5	11.5	10.9	23.3	26.4	23.4	27.3	27.1	1.5	2.4	2.2
1.4	1.3	1.4	4.5	4.7	5.1	1.1	2.3	2.2	3.7	7.6	7.8
−8.8	0.5	2.9	25.9	−33.8	−47.2	−7.2	1.3	−1.6	−7.2	−5.0	−4.0
11.8	−5.3	−7.6	3.8	39.6	60.9	14.3	−7.7	−4.4	5.2	4.4	3.3
7.0	6.5	6.9	4.2	10.9	12.0	6.9	5.6	5.0	3.3	7.3	6.8
4.9	−11.8	−14.5	−0.4	28.7	48.9	7.5	−13.3	−9.4	1.9	−2.9	−3.5
255.8	247.7	240.6	262.8	451.7	523.4	441.4	447.1	456.9	92.9	129.7	125.7
59.8	32.4	28.4	22.1	17.5	17.7	53.6	28.9	25.9	73.1	58.9	53.0
253.6	143.4	124.5	80.4	65.5	62.9	300.4	172.8	155.3	263.3	215.9	190.6
35.3	30.8	26.9	11.3	10.5	9.5	35.2	37.3	33.0	25.5	24.5	22.5

omissions), and changes in reserves. Debt outstanding and disbursed, as well as debt services, is for long-term loans only. Ratios are calculated using current price data.
a. Estimated.

Exports of primary goods				Imports of goods				
		1987–95				1987–95		
1973–80	1980–87	Base	High	1973–80	1980–87	Base	High	Country group
1.2	3.1	2.2	2.8	5.9	1.1	4.6	6.3	Developing countries
2.8	5.3	2.9	3.4	5.6	6.4	5.0	6.6	Low-income countries
1.1	2.8	2.1	2.7	6.0	0.1	4.5	6.3	Middle-income countries
−1.0	0.5	1.3	2.0	10.3	−6.0	1.9	3.1	Oil exporters
3.4	8.4	2.8	3.2	5.6	5.8	5.8	7.9	Exporters of manufactures
−0.4	1.1	2.4	3.0	5.5	−6.3	3.3	4.9	Highly indebted countries
−0.1	−2.0	2.5	2.9	7.5	−6.9	2.6	3.0	Sub-Saharan Africa

Bibliographical note

This Report has drawn on a wide range of World Bank reports and numerous outside sources. World Bank sources include ongoing research, as well as country economic, sector, and project work on individual countries. Outside sources include research publications and reports from other organizations working on global economic and public finance issues. Staff of the IMF provided valuable comments and data in addition to the contributions specified here. The principal sources in each chapter are noted below. These and other sources are then listed alphabetically by author or organization in two groups: background papers commissioned for this Report and a selected bibliography. The background papers, some of which will be available through the Policy, Planning, and Research (PPR) Working Paper series, synthesize relevant literature and Bank work. The views they express are not necessarily those of the World Bank or of this Report.

In addition to the principal sources listed, many persons both inside and outside the World Bank helped prepare this Report by writing informal notes or by providing extensive comments. Among these were members of the Bank's Public Economics Division, as well as Roy Bahl, Bela Balassa, Richard M. Bird, Willem H. Buiter, Ramesh Chander, Raja J. Chelliah, Rudiger Dornbusch, Arnold C. Harberger, David Lindauer, Richard Musgrave, Jacques J. Polak, Sarath Rajapatirana, Vito Tanzi, and Herman G. van der Tak.

Overview

Box 1 of the Overview draws on numerous Bank reports as well as on Cornia and others 1987. Box 2 comes from Webber and Wildavsky 1986.

Chapter 1

The data used in this chapter were mainly drawn from IMF, BIS, and OECD publications and from World Bank sources. The discussion of recent macroeconomic issues in industrial countries has benefited especially from the background paper by Buiter and also draws on Baneth 1987, Hooper and Mann 1987, Marris 1987, Rohatyn 1987, Thurow and Tyson 1987, and Williamson and Miller 1987. The discussion of the debt overhang draws on de Carmoy 1987, Dornbusch 1987, Fischer (forthcoming), Lever and Huhne 1987, Loxley 1986, Sachs 1987b, and, in particular, on the *World Debt Tables 1987-88*. Box 1.1 relies on the 1986 and 1987 editions of *World Development Report* and also draws on Finger and Olechowski 1987. Box 1.2 draws on McLure 1987 and Sinn 1987. Box 1.5 was drafted by Charles Humphreys. Box 1.7 is based on inputs from Sanjivi Rajasingham. Jean Baneth and Richard Snape provided useful comments on earlier drafts.

Chapter 2

The discussion in this chapter draws on the background papers prepared by Balassa, Lindauer, and Musgrave. The fiscal data used are largely from the IMF, *Government Finance Statistics*. Figures 2.1 and 2.3 and Table 2.3, however, are based on World Bank and IMF country reports. The section on patterns of public finance uses material from Reynolds 1983 and 1985, and Saunders and Klau 1985. The discussion of evolving views of the public sector draws upon Buchanan 1987, Buchanan and Tollison 1984, Mills 1986, Mueller 1987, Musgrave 1959 and 1981b, and Stiglitz 1986. Ramesh Chander helped prepare Box 2.1. Box 2.2 is based upon Haggard and Kaufman 1987. Box 2.4 draws on the Development Committee Paper 14 and on work by Robert Repetto. Comments on earlier drafts by Jonathan Skinner were particularly helpful.

Chapter 3

The section on fiscal policy and macroeconomic performance draws on the background papers of Buiter and Taylor, as well as on Buiter 1985, Tanzi 1984, and Tanzi and Blejer 1983. The treatment of external borrowing and fiscal management draws on Edwards (forthcoming), Feldstein and others 1987, and Sachs 1987b and (forthcoming). The section on private capital flows benefits from Ize and Ortiz 1987, Khan and ul Haque 1987, Lessard and Williamson 1987, and van Wijnbergen 1985. The analysis on inflation and internal debt management draws on Blejer and Liviatan 1987, Kiguel and Liviathan 1988, Knight and McCarthy 1986, Williamson 1985, the study of East Asia by Kharas and Kiguel 1987, and on the background paper by Easterly. The section on growth and debt benefits from Corbo and others 1987, Dervis and Petri 1987, and van Wijnbergen 1988. The background paper of Martone on Brazil and country briefs by Ritu Anand and Sweder van Wijnbergen on Turkey, Michael Lav on Poland, F. Desmond McCarthy on Argentina, and Peter Miovic on Bolivia provided additional country perspectives.

The section on fiscal policy and commodity export cycles draws on the background paper of Cuddington, as well as on Auty and Gelb 1986, Bevan and others 1987, Devarajan and de Melo 1987, Gelb (forthcoming), and Pinto 1987. Country briefs by Patrick Clawson on Côte d'Ivoire and Cameroon, Ernesto May on Indonesia, and Joanne Salop on Nigeria helped fill in the country background. The analysis of fiscal policy in low-income Africa benefits from the background paper of O'Connell, as well as from Gulhati and others 1986 and Lancaster and Williamson 1986.

Box 3.2 draws on the framework set out in van Wijnbergen and others 1988. Box 3.3 draws on contributions by Manuel Hinds. Box 3.4 is based on the country briefs by Miovic and McCarthy, as well as on the background paper of Martone. It also draws on Cardoso and Dornbusch 1987 (Brazil), Edwards 1987 (Chile), Heymann 1987 (Argentina), and Sachs 1987a (Bolivia). Box 3.5 is based on the background paper by Pinto.

Data underlying the analysis are gathered from Bank and Fund country reports and from *International Financial Statistics*. The comments of Mario

Blejer, Homi Kharas, and Sweder van Wijnbergen on early drafts of the chapter were particularly helpful.

Chapter 4

The comparative data are based primarily on IMF, *Government Finance Statistics*, consolidated central government series (Table A) and material from the Bureau of International Fiscal Documentation. The discussion of the sections on commodity and income taxes draws on Shalizi and Squire 1987. The section on tax administration draws heavily on background notes prepared by the Fiscal Affairs Department of the IMF. Box 4.1 is based on Anderson 1987; Box 4.2 on a series of papers in Gillis and others (forthcoming); Box 4.3 on Chamley and others 1985; Box 4.4 on *WDR* background notes by Robert Wieland; Box 4.5 on Conrad 1986 and Gillis 1985; Box 4.6 on *WDR* background notes by Roy Bahl; and Box 4.7 on *WDR* background notes by Richard Bird. Background material was also provided by J. Gregory Ballentine, Christophe Chamley, Robert Conrad, Harvey Galper, Hafez Ghanem, Malcolm Gillis, Homi Kharas, Jonathan Skinner, Ruben Suarez-Berenguela, and P. T. Wanless. Useful comments on earlier drafts were provided by Robert Conrad, Charles E. McLure, Jonathan Skinner, and Lyn Squire.

Chapter 5

The data on patterns and trends in public spending are from IMF, *Government Finance Statistics*, consolidated central government series. Gertrud Windsperger assisted in gathering important data for Africa. The data on military expenditures in Box 5.1 are from the U.S. Arms Control and Disarmament Agency, and the box is based on the background paper by Bhatia. The discussion of recent spending cutbacks includes data from Buffie and Krauss 1987, Dohner 1987, Dornbusch and de Pablo 1987, and Hicks 1988. The section on priorities in public spending draws extensively on the many public investment and public expenditure reviews carried out by World Bank staff during the past several years. The discussion of operation and maintenance spending benefited from Peter Heller's work on Indonesia, and Asif Faiz contributed to the discussion of road maintenance problems; a more detailed analysis is provided in World Bank 1988b. The analysis of public pay and employment policies draws on the background paper by Lindauer. Boxes 5.5 and 5.6 are based on work by Barbara Nunberg and Robert Repetto, respectively. Robert Sadove prepared background material on the effect of investment on development goals. The section on planning and budgeting public spending draws heavily on the background papers by Lacey and Lister and on the Bank's public investment and public expenditure reviews. The discussion of performance budgeting is from Dean 1986. The background paper by Baldwin is the principal source for Box 5.8. Box 5.10 was prepared by Martha de Melo and Box 5.11 by Katherine Marshall. Peter Dean, Martha de Melo, Friedrich Kahnert, and Ajit Mazoomdar provided extensive comments on drafts of the chapter.

Chapter 6

The discussion of education and health finance draws mainly from Jimenez 1987 and World Bank 1986a, 1987b, and 1988a. The section on urban services draws on Bahl and Linn (forthcoming), Linn 1983, World Bank 1986b, and contributions by Stephen Malpezzi. The section on rural services is based on Briscoe and de Ferranti 1988, Repetto 1986, Small and others 1986, and a background paper by Mason. The Office of Statistics of Unesco, under the direction of Gabriel Carceles, provided the data used in compiling Table 6.1. Box 6.2 is based on the background paper by Puffert. Box 6.3 was drafted by Jan Leno and Peter Moock. Box 6.4 is taken from the background paper by Julius with contributions by Gabriel Sanchez-Sierra. Box 6.5 was drafted by Kyu Sik Lee. Box 6.6 is based on the background paper by Buckley and Mayo; Box 6.7 on Small and others 1986, other unpublished documents, and comments by Robert Y. Sin; and Box 6.8 on Wade 1988. Dennis Anderson, Nancy Birdsall, Dennis de Tray, and Fred Golladay commented on early drafts.

Chapter 7

This chapter uses data from the IMF, *Government Finance Statistics*, for the quantitative presentation of the role of subnational government. The discussion of fiscal decentralization was drawn in part from United States Government 1985 and World Bank reports on municipal finance. The discussion of local government finance, including the four efficiency criteria for raising local revenue and Table 7.1, draw on Bahl and Linn 1983 and forthcoming. Carmela Quintos provided revised and updated data for Table 7.1. Box 7.3 is based on Doebele and others 1979 and the background paper by Pineda. The background paper by Dillinger was the main

source of the presentation on the property tax and Box 7.4. The sections on borrowing and intergovernmental grants were based on the background papers by Davey and Schroeder, respectively. Boxes 7.1, 7.2, and 7.5 were drawn from the background papers by Bahl, Bird, and Olowu, respectively. Consultations with Kenneth Davey and William Dillinger were valuable at all stages of development of this chapter.

Chapter 8

The discussion of SOE problems and reforms is based primarily on the Bank's extensive operational experience. The data on SOE contributions to production, investment, net budgetary burdens, external debt, and public sector deficits are mainly from World Bank and IMF country reports. They are extensively discussed in the background paper by Nair and Filippides. Other work on the macroeconomic effect of SOEs is found in the collected papers by Floyd and others 1984. References to off-budget agencies and SOEs in Japan, the United Kingdom, and the United States are based on Bennett and DiLorenzo 1983. The chapter draws from the paper by Vuylsteke and others 1988 for the discussion on private management and ownership and for data on privatizations. Other references for this discussion include Bank papers by Berg and Shirley 1987, Hegstad and Newport 1987, and Vernon 1987. Boxes 8.1, 8.2, and 8.4 are based on work by Mustapha Rouis, Mary Shirley, and Roger Leeds, respectively. Elliot Berg, John Nellis, Mary Shirley, Raymond Vernon, and Charles Vuylsteke provided useful comments on earlier versions of the chapter.

Background papers

These papers are available from the World Development Report office, World Bank, Washington, D.C.

Bahl, Roy. "Local Government Financing in China."
Balassa, Bela. "The Adding Up Problem."
———. "Public Finance and Economic Development."
Baldwin, George B. "Cost-Benefit Analysis and the Allocation of Investment Resources."
Ballentine, Gregory J., and Harvey Galper. "The Practical Importance of Tax Distribution."
Bhatia, Anita. "Military Expenditure and Economic Growth."
Bird, Richard M. "Fiscal Decentralization in Colombia."

Buckley, Robert M., and Stephen K. Mayo. "Housing Policy in Developing Economies: Evaluating the Broader Costs."

Buiter, Willem H. "Some Thoughts on the Role of Fiscal Policy in Stabilization and Structural Adjustment in Developing Countries."

———. "The Current Global Economic Situation, Outlook, and Policy Options with Special Emphasis on Fiscal Policy Issues."

Conrad, Robert F. "Considerations for the Development of Tax Policy When Capital Is Internationally Mobile."

Cuddington, John. "Fiscal Policy in Commodity-Exporting LDCs."

Davey, Kenneth J. "Municipal Development Funds and Intermediaries."

Dillinger, William. "Urban Property Taxation in Developing Countries."

Easterly, William. "Fiscal Deficits, Real Interest Rates, and Inflation: A Consistency Approach."

International Monetary Fund, Fiscal Affairs Department. "Tax Administration as an Element of Fiscal Policy in LDCs."

Feltenstein, Andrew. "The Role of Fiscal Policy in Centrally Planned Economies: Three Countries in Transition."

Fleisig, Heywood W. "The International Consequences of the Macroeconomic Policy Mix in OECD Countries."

Gillis, Malcolm. "Lessons from Post-War Experience with Tax Reform in Developing Countries."

Julius, DeAnne. "Public Finance and the Energy Sector."

Kaminski, Bartlomiej. "Fiscal Policy as a Tool of Public Economic Policy in a Reformed Centrally Planned Economy."

Lacey, Robert. "The Management of Public Expenditures: An Evolving Bank Approach."

Lindauer, David L. "Government Pay and Employment Policy in Developing Economies."

———. "The Size and Growth of Government Expenditures."

Lister, Stephen. "Improving the Allocation and Management of Public Spending: Some Lessons of African Experience."

Martone, Celso L. "Fiscal Policy and Stabilization in Brazil."

Mason, Melody K. "Sectoral Perspectives of Public Finance: Rural Infrastructure."

Musgrave, Richard A. "The Role of the Public Sector and Public Sector Growth."

Nair, Govindan, and Anastasios Filippides. "State-Owned Enterprises and Public Sector Deficits in Developing Countries: A Comparative Statistical Assessment."

O'Connell, Stephen A. "Fiscal Policy in Low-Income Africa."

Olowu, Dele. "Nigeria: Federal and State Transfers to Local Governments, 1970–87."

Peters, R. Kyle. "Fiscal Policy in the Pacific Islands."

Pineda, José Fernando. "The Valorization System in Bogotá: An Assessment of Recent Trends."

Pinto, Brian. "Black Market Premia, Exchange Rate Unification, and Inflation in Sub-Saharan Africa."

Puffert, Douglas J. "Means and Implications of Social Security Finance in Developing Countries."

Schroeder, Larry. "Intergovernmental Grants in Developing Countries."

Sinn, Hans-Werner. "U.S. Tax Reform 1981 and 1986: Impact on International Capital Markets and Capital Flows."

Skinner, Jonathan. "Do Taxes Matter? A Review of the Incentive and Output Effects of Taxation."

Taylor, Lance. "Fiscal Issues in Macroeconomic Stabilization."

Versluysen, Eugene. "Financial Deregulation and the Globalization of Capital Markets: A Stabilizing Force or a Conduit of Volatility and Uncertainty?"

Wanless, P. T. "Tax Reform in Centrally Planned Economies."

Selected bibliography

Acharya, Shankar N., and others. 1985. *Aspects of the Black Economy in India.* New Delhi: Ministry of Finance.

Ahmad, Ehtisham, and Nicholas Stern. 1986. "Tax Reform for Pakistan: Overview and Effective Taxes for 1975–76." *The Pakistan Development Review* 25, 1: 43–72.

———. 1987. "Alternative Sources of Government Revenue: Illustrations from India, 1979–80." In David Newbery and Nicholas Stern, eds., *The Theory of Taxation for Developing Countries,* New York: Oxford University Press.

Ames, Barry. 1987. *Political Survival: Politicians and Public Policy in Latin America.* Berkeley: University of California Press.

Anand, Ritu, and Sweder van Wijnbergen. 1987. "Inflation and the Financing of Government Expenditure in Turkey: An Introductory Analysis." Washington, D.C.: World Bank. Processed.

Anderson, Dennis. 1987. *The Public Revenue and Economic Policy in African Countries: An Overview of Issues and Policy Options.* World Bank Discussion Paper 19. Washington, D.C.

Andic, Suphan, and Jindrich Veverka. 1964. "The Growth of Government Expenditure in Germany since Unification." *Finanzarchiv* 23, 2 (January): 169–278.

André, Christian, and Robert Delorme. 1983. *L'Etat et l'Economie.* Paris: Editions du Seuil.

Argy, Victor, and Joanne Salop. 1983. "Price and Output Effects of Monetary and Fiscal Expansion in a Two-Country World under Flexible Exchange Rates." *Oxford Economic Papers* 35 (July): 228–46.

Armstrong-Wright, Alan, and Sebastien Thiriez. 1987. *Bus Services: Reducing Costs, Raising Standards.* World Bank Technical Paper 68. Washington, D.C.

Atkinson, A. B., and Joseph Stiglitz. 1980. *Lectures on Public Economics.* New York: McGraw-Hill.

Auerbach, Alan J., and Martin Feldstein. 1985. *Handbook of Public Economics.* Vol. I. Amsterdam: North-Holland.

Auty, Richard, and Alan Gelb. 1986. "Oil Windfalls in a Small Parliamentary Democracy: Their Impact on Trinidad and Tobago." *World Development* 14, 9: 1161–75.

Bahl, Roy W. 1983. *Intergovernmental Grants in Bangladesh.* Interim Report 10. Zilla Roads/Local Finance Project. Metropolitan Studies Program, Syracuse University.

Bahl, Roy W., Daniel Holland, and Johannes F. Linn. 1983. *Urban Growth and Local Taxes in Less Developed Countries.* Papers of the East-West Population Institute 89. Honolulu, Hawaii.

Bahl, Roy W., and Johannes F. Linn. 1983. "The Assignment of Local Government Revenues in Developing Countries." In Charles E. McLure, Jr., ed., *Tax Assignment in Federal Countries.* Canberra: Australian National University Press.

————. Forthcoming. *Urban Public Finance in Developing Countries.* New York: Oxford University Press.

Bahl, Roy W., Jerry Miner, and Larry Schroeder. 1984. "Mobilizing Local Resources in Developing Countries." *Public Administration and Development* 4: 215–30.

Bahl, Roy W., and Matthew N. Murray. 1986. "Income Tax Evasion in Jamaica." Jamaica Tax Structure Examination Project Staff Paper 31. Syracuse, N.Y.: Maxwell School of Citizenship and Public Affairs, Syracuse University. Processed.

Bahl, Roy W., and S. Nath. 1986. "Public Expenditure Decentralization in Developing Countries."

Environment and Planning C: Government and Policy 4: 405–18.

Balassa, Bela. 1982. "Structural Adjustment Policies in Developing Economies." *World Development* 10, 1: 23–38.

Baneth, Jean. 1987. "The World Economy's Uncertain Future." *Canadian Business Review* (Summer): 25–27.

Bank of England. 1985. "Review of Economic and Financial Developments." *Quarterly Bulletin* 25, 1 (March): 163–211.

————. 1987a. "Developments in International Banking and Capital Markets in 1986." *Quarterly Bulletin* 27, 2: 234–46.

————. 1987b. "The Instruments of Monetary Policy." *Quarterly Bulletin* 27, 3 (August).

Bank for International Settlements. 1982–87. *Annual Report.* Basle.

————. 1986. *Recent Innovations in International Banking.* Basle.

Baum, Warren C., and Stokes M. Tolbert. 1985. *Investing in Development: Lessons of World Bank Experience.* New York: Oxford University Press.

Beckerman, Wilfred. 1986. "How Large a Public Sector?" *Oxford Review of Economic Policy* 2, 2: 7–24.

Bennett, James T., and Thomas J. DiLorenzo. 1983. *Underground Government: The Off-Budget Public Sector.* Washington, D.C.: Cato Institute.

Benoit, Emile. 1973. *Defense and Growth in Developing Countries.* Boston: Lexington Books.

Berg, Alan. 1987. *Malnutrition: What Can Be Done?: Lessons from World Bank Experience.* Baltimore, Md.: Johns Hopkins University Press.

Berg, Elliot, and Mary M. Shirley. 1987. *Divestiture in Developing Countries.* World Bank Discussion Paper 11. Washington, D.C.

Bevan, D. L., P. Collier, and J. W. Gunning. 1987. "Consequences of a Commodity Boom in a Controlled Economy: Accumulation and Redistribution in Kenya 1975–83." *World Bank Economic Review* 1 (May): 489–513.

Bird, Richard M. 1976. *Charging for Public Services: A New Look at an Old Idea.* Canadian Tax Paper 59. Toronto: Canadian Tax Foundation.

————. 1980. *Central-Local Fiscal Relations and the Provision of Urban Public Services.* Research Monograph 30. Canberra: Centre for Research on Federal Financial Relations, Australian National University.

————. 1984. *Intergovernmental Finance in Colombia: Final Report of the Mission on Intergovernmental Finance.* International Tax Program. Cambridge: Harvard Law School.

————. 1986. *Federal Finance in Comparative Perspective.* Toronto: Canadian Tax Foundation.

————. 1987a. "The Administrative Dimension of Tax Reform in Developing Countries." Rotterdam: Erasmus University. Processed.

————.1987b. "A New Look at Indirect Taxation in Developing Countries." *World Development* 15, 9: 1151–61.

Bird, Richard M., and B. D. Miller. Forthcoming. "Taxation and the Poor in Developing Countries." In Richard M. Bird and S. Horton, eds., *Government Policy and the Poor in Developing Countries.* Toronto: University of Toronto Press.

Blejer, Mario I., and Adrienne Cheasty. 1986. "Using Fiscal Measures to Stimulate Savings in Developing Countries." *Finance & Development* 23 (June): 16–19.

Blejer, Mario I., and Nissan Liviatan. 1987. "Fighting Hyperinflation: Stabilization Strategies in Argentina and Israel, 1985–86." *IMF Staff Papers* 34 (September): 409–38.

Blinder, Alan S., and Robert M. Solow. 1974. *The Economics of Public Finance.* Washington, D.C.: Brookings Institution.

Bradford, David F., and the U.S. Treasury Tax Policy Staff. 1984. *Blueprints for Basic Tax Reform.* 2nd ed. Springfield, Va.: National Technical Information Service.

Briscoe, John, and David de Ferranti. 1988. *Water for Rural Communities: Helping People Help Themselves.* Washington, D.C.: World Bank.

Bryant, Ralph C. 1988. *External Deficits and the Dollar: The Pit and the Pendulum.* Washington, D.C.: Brookings Institution.

Buchanan, James. 1987. *Public Finance in Democratic Process: Fiscal Institutions and Individual Choice.* Chapel Hill: University of North Carolina Press.

Buchanan, James, and Robert D. Tollison, eds. 1984. *The Theory of Public Choice-II.* Ann Arbor: University of Michigan Press.

Buffie, Edward F., and Allen Sangines Krauss. Forthcoming. "Mexico 1958–1986: From Stabilizing Development to the Debt Crisis." In Jeffrey D. Sachs, ed., *Developing Country Debt and the World Economy.* University of Chicago Press.

Buiter, Willem H. 1983. "Measurement of the Public Sector Deficit and Its Implications for Policy Evaluation and Design." *IMF Staff Papers* 30, 2 (June): 307–49.

————. 1984. "Allocative and Stabilization Aspects of Budgetary and Financial Policy." Inaugural lecture delivered to the London School of Economics and Political Science, November 1983. Processed.

————. 1985. "A Guide to Public Sector Debt and Deficits." *Economic Policy* 1 (November): 13–79.

Camdessus, Michel. 1987a. "Remarks before the Economic and Social Council of the United Nations." Speech delivered in Geneva, June 26. Washington, D.C.: IMF.

————. 1987b. "Remarks to the Banker's Association for Foreign Trade." Speech delivered in Boca Raton, Fla., April 28. Washington, D.C.: IMF.

Cardoso, Eliana, and Rudiger Dornbusch. 1987. "Brazil's Tropical Plan." *AER Papers and Proceedings* 77 (May): 288–92.

Casanegra de Jantscher, Milka. 1986. "Problems of Administering a Value-Added Tax in Developing Countries." IMF Working Paper 86/15. Washington, D.C. Processed.

Cassen, Robert M., and others. 1986. *Does Aid Work?* New York: Oxford University Press.

Chamley, Christophe, Robert Conrad, Zmarak Shalizi, Jonathan Skinner, and Lyn Squire. 1985. "Tax Policy for Malawi." Washington, D.C.: World Bank, Country Economics Department. Processed.

Chandler, William U. 1986. *The Changing Role of the Market in National Economies.* Worldwatch Paper 72. Washington, D.C.: Worldwatch Institute.

Chelliah, Raja J. 1971. "Trends in Taxation in Developing Countries." *IMF Staff Papers* 18, 2 (July): 254–331.

Chelliah, Raja J., and Narain Sinha. 1982. *State Finances in India. Vol. 3: The Measurement of Tax Effort of State Governments, 1973–1976.* World Bank Staff Working Paper 523. Washington, D.C.

Chenery, Hollis B., Montek S. Ahluwalia, Clive Bell, John H. Duloy, and Richard Jolly. 1974. *Redistribution with Growth.* London: Oxford University Press.

Chhibber, Ajay. 1985. "Taxation and Aggregate Savings: An Econometric Analysis for Three Sub-Saharan African Countries." CPD Discussion Paper 1985–35. Washington, D.C.: World Bank, Country Programs Department. Processed.

Churchill, Anthony A., and others. 1987. *Rural Water Supply and Sanitation: Time for a Change.* World Bank Discussion Paper 18. Washington, D.C.

Clarete, Ramon, and John Whalley. 1987. "Comparing the Marginal Welfare Costs of Commodity and Trade Taxes." *Journal of Public Economics* 33 (October): 357–62.

Claudon, Michael P., ed. 1986. *World Debt Crisis: International Lending on Trial.* Cambridge, Mass.: Ballinger.

Cline, William. 1987. *Mobilizing Bank Lending to Debtor Countries.* Policy Analyses in International Economics 18. Washington, D.C.: Institute for International Economics.

Cnossen, Sijbren. 1978. "The Case for Selective Taxes on Goods and Services in Developing Countries." *World Development* 6: 813-25.

———. 1987. "VAT and RST: A Comparison." *Canadian Tax Journal* (May–June): 559–615.

Cochrane, Glynn. 1983. *Policies for Strengthening Local Government in Developing Countries.* World Bank Staff Working Paper 582. Washington, D.C.

Conrad, Robert F. 1986. "Essays on the Indonesian Tax Reform." CPD Discussion Paper 86-8. Washington, D.C.: World Bank, Country Programs Department. Processed.

Conyers, Diana. 1983. "Decentralization: The Latest Fashion in Development Economics." *Public Administration and Development* 3, 2 (April–June): 97–109.

Corbo, Vittorio, Morris Goldstein, Mohsin Khan, eds. 1987. *Growth-Oriented Adjustment Programs.* Washington, D.C.: IMF/World Bank.

Cornia, Giovanni, Richard Jolly, and Frances Stewart, eds. 1987. *Adjustment with a Human Face.* Oxford: Clarendon Press.

Datta, Abhijit. 1987. "Case Study of Improvements in Property Tax Collection in Delhi." New Delhi: Indian Institute of Public Administration. Processed.

Davey, Kenneth J. 1983. *Financing Regional Government: International Practices and Their Relevance to the Third World.* Chichester: John Wiley and Sons.

Dean, Peter N. 1986. "Assessing the Performance Budgeting Experiment in Four Developing Countries." *Financial Accountability and Management* 2, 1 (Spring): 1–24.

de Carmoy, Hervé. 1987. "Debt and Growth in Latin America: A European Banker's Proposal." Working Paper 9. Madrid: Institute for European-Latin American Relations. Processed.

de Ferranti, David. 1985. *Paying for Health Services in Developing Countries: An Overview.* World Bank Staff Working Paper 721. Washington, D.C.

Dervis, Kemal, and Peter Petri. 1987. "The Macroeconomics of Successful Development: What Are the Lessons?" In *NBER Macroeconomics Annual 1987*: 211–54.

Devarajan, Shantayanan, and Jaime de Melo. 1987. "Adjustment with a Fixed Exchange Rate: Cameroon, Côte d'Ivoire, and Senegal." *World Bank Economic Review* 1, 3 (May): 447–87.

Development Committee. 1987. *Environment, Growth, and Development.* Pamphlet 14. Washington, D.C.: World Bank.

Doebele, William A., Orville F. Grimes, Jr., and Johannes F. Linn. 1979. "Participation of Beneficiaries in Financing Urban Services: Valorization Charges in Bogotá, Colombia." *Land Economics* 55, 1 (February): 73–92.

Doern, G. Bruce. 1984. "Canada's Budgetary Dilemmas: Tax and Expenditure Reform." In A. Premchand and Jesse Burkhead, eds. *Comparative International Budgeting and Finance.* New Brunswick, N.J.: Public Financial Publications, Inc.

Dohner, Robert S., and Ponciano Intal, Jr. Forthcoming. "Debt Crisis and Adjustment in the Philippines." In Jeffrey D. Sachs, ed., *Developing Country Debt and the World Economy.* University of Chicago Press.

Dornbusch, Rudiger. 1986. *Dollars, Debts, and Deficits.* Cambridge, Mass.: MIT Press.

———. Forthcoming. "Debt Problems and the World Macroeconomy." In Jeffrey D. Sachs, ed., *Developing Country Debt and the World Economy.* University of Chicago Press.

Dornbusch, Rudiger, and Juan Carlos de Pablo. Forthcoming. "Debt and Macroeconomic Instability in Argentina." In Jeffrey D. Sachs, ed., *Developing Country Debt and the World Economy.* University of Chicago Press.

Dornbusch, Rudiger, and Stanley Fischer. 1986. "Stopping Hyperinflation Past and Present." NBER Working Paper Series 1810. Cambridge, Mass.: National Bureau of Economic Research. Processed.

Economist, The. 1987. "The Limits to Cooperation: A Survey of the World Economy." Supplement to the September 26 issue.

Edwards, Sebastian. 1987. *Monetarism and Liberalization: The Chilean Experiment.* Cambridge, Mass.: Ballinger Publishing Company.

———. Forthcoming. "Structural Adjustment Policies in Highly Indebted Countries." In Jeffrey D. Sachs, ed., *Developing Country Debt and the World Economy.* University of Chicago Press.

Faini, R., P. Annez, and L. Taylor. 1984. "Defense Spending, Economic Structure and Growth: Evidence among Countries and over Time." *Economic Development and Cultural Change* 32, 3.

Feldstein, Martin, Hervé de Carmoy, Koei Narusawa, and Paul R. Krugman. 1987. *Restoring Growth in the Debt-Laden Third World.* A Task Force Report to the Trilateral Commission; Triangle Papers 33. New York.

Feltenstein, Andrew, and Ziba Farhadian. 1987.

"Fiscal Policy, Monetary Targets, and the Price Level in a Centrally Planned Economy: An Application to the Case of China." *Journal of Money, Credit and Banking* 19, 2 (May): 137–56.

Finger, J. Michael, and Andrzej Olechowski, eds. 1987. *The Uruguay Round: A Handbook on the Multilateral Trade Negotiations.* Washington, D.C.: World Bank.

Fischer, Stanley. 1987. "Stopping High Inflation: The Israeli Stabilization Program, 1985–86." *AER Papers and Proceedings* 77 (May): 275–78.

———. Forthcoming. "Resolving the International Debt Crisis." In Jeffrey D. Sachs, ed., *Developing Country Debt and the World Economy.* University of Chicago Press.

Floyd, Robert, Clive Gray, and Peter Short. 1984. *Public Enterprises in Mixed Economies: Some Macroeconomic Aspects.* Washington, D.C.: IMF.

Friedman, Irving S. 1983. *The World Debt Dilemma: Managing Country Risk.* Washington, D.C.: Council for International Banking Studies.

Gall, Pirie. 1976. *Municipal Development Programs in Latin America.* New York: Praeger.

Gelb, Alan. 1986. "From Boom to Bust: Oil Exporting Countries over the Cycle 1970–84." *IDS Bulletin* 17, 4 (October): 22–29.

———. Forthcoming. *Oil Windfalls: Blessing or Curse?* New York: Oxford University Press.

Gillis, Malcolm. 1985. "Micro- and Macroeconomics of Tax Reform: Indonesia." *Journal of Development Economics* 19: 221–54.

Gillis, Malcolm, Carl S. Shoup, and Gerardo P. Sicat. Forthcoming. *Value-Added Taxes in Developing Countries.* A World Bank Symposium. Washington, D.C.

Goode, Richard. 1984. *Government and Finance in Developing Countries.* Washington, D.C.: Brookings Institution.

Gray, Cheryl Williamson. 1982. *Food Consumption Parameters for Brazil and Their Application to Food Policy.* Washington, D.C.: Internatonal Food Policy Research Institute.

Griffith-Jones, Stephany. 1987. "Learning to Live with Crisis." *The Banker* 137, 739: 23–39.

Gulhati, Ravi, Swadesh Bose, and Vimal Atukorala. 1986. "Exchange Rate Policies in Africa: How Valid Is the Scepticism?" *Development and Change* 17 (July): 399–423.

Hafer, R. W., ed. 1986. *The Monetary versus Fiscal Policy Debate: Lessons from Two Decades.* Totowa, N.J.: Rowman and Allanheld.

Haggard, Stephan, and Robert Kaufman. Forthcoming. "The Politics of Stabilization and Structural Adjustment." In Jeffrey D. Sachs, ed., *Developing Country Debt and the World Economy.* University of Chicago Press.

Han, Seung Soo. 1987. "The Value Added Tax in Korea." DRD Discussion Paper 221. Washington, D.C.: World Bank, Development Research Department. Processed.

Haq, Khadija, ed. 1984. *Crisis of the '80s: World Monetary Financial and Human Resource Development Issues.* Washington, D.C.: North South Roundtable.

Harberger, A. C. 1963. "Principles of Efficiency: The Measurement of Waste." *American Economic Review* 76: 58–76.

Hegstad, Sven Olaf, and Ian Newport. 1987. *Management Contracts: Main Features and Design Issues.* World Bank Technical Paper 65. Washington, D.C.

Heian, Betty C., and Terry Monson. 1987. "The Value Added Tax in the Côte d'Ivoire." DRD Discussion Paper 227. Washington, D.C.: World Bank. Processed.

Heller, Peter S., Richard Hemming, Peter W. Kohnert, and others. 1986. *Aging and Social Expenditure in the Major Industrial Countries, 1980–2025.* IMF Occasional Paper 47. Washington, D.C.

Heller, Peter S., and Alan Tait. 1982. *International Comparisons of Government Expenditure.* IMF Occasional Paper 10. Washington, D.C.

Heymann, Daniel. 1987. "The Austral Plan." *AER Papers and Proceedings* 77 (May): 284–87.

Hicks, Norman L. 1988. "Expenditure Reductions in Developing Countries." Washington, D.C.: World Bank, Asia Country Department-II. Processed.

Hicks, Ursula K. 1961. *Development from Below: Local Government and Finance in Developing Countries of the Commonwealth.* Oxford: Clarendon Press.

Hirschman, Albert O. 1982. *Shifting Involvements: Private Interest and Public Action.* Oxford: Martin Robertson.

Hooper, Peter, and Catherine L. Mann. 1987. "The U.S. External Deficit: Its Causes and Persistence." International Finance Discussion Paper 316. Washington, D.C.: Board of Governors of the Federal Reserve System. Processed.

Humes, Samuel, and Eileen Martin. 1969. *The Structure of Local Government: A Comparative Survey of 81 Countries.* The Hague: International Union of Local Authorities.

India, Government of. 1985. *Long Term Fiscal Policy.* New Delhi: Ministry of Finance, Department of Economic Affairs.

Institute for International Economics. 1987. *Resolving the Global Economic Crisis: After Wall Street.* Washington, D.C.

International Labour Office. 1988. *The Cost of Social Security: Twelfth International Inquiry, 1981–83.* Basic Tables. Geneva.

International Monetary Fund. 1986a. *A Manual on Government Finance Statistics.* Washington, D.C.

———. 1986b. *International Financial Statistics.* Supplement on Government Finance. Supplement Series 11. Washington, D.C.

———.1987. *Annual Report.* Washington, D.C.

———. Various years. *Government Finance Statistics Yearbook.* Washington, D.C.

———. Various years. *International Financial Statistics.* Washington, D.C.

———. Various years. *World Economic Outlook.* Washington, D.C.

Ize, Alain, and Guillermo Ortiz. 1987. "Fiscal Rigidities, Public Debt, and Capital Flight." *IMF Staff Papers* 34, 2 (June): 311–32.

Jamaica, Government of. 1985. "White Paper on Comprehensive Tax Reform." Kingston: Revenue Board. Processed.

Jimenez, Emmanuel. 1984. "Tenure Security and Urban Squatting." *Review of Economics and Statistics* 66, 4: 556–67.

——— 1986. "The Public Subsidization of Education and Health in Developing Countries: A Review of Efficiency and Equity." *World Bank Research Observer* 1, 1: 111–30. Washington, D.C.

———. 1987. *Pricing Policy in the Social Sectors: Cost Recovery for Education and Health in Developing Countries.* Baltimore, Md.: Johns Hopkins University Press.

Julius, DeAnne, and Adelaida P. Alicbusan. 1986. "Public Sector Pricing Policies: A Review of Bank Policy and Practice." PPR Working Paper. Washington, D.C.: World Bank, Policy, Planning, and Research Department. Processed.

Kelly, Margaret. 1982. "Fiscal Adjustment and Fund-Supported Programs, 1971–80." *IMF Staff Papers* 29, 4 (December): 561–602.

Khan, Mohsin S., and Nadeem Ul Haque. 1987. "Capital Flight from Developing Countries." *Finance & Development* 24, 1 (March): 2–5.

Khan, Mohsin S., Peter Montiel, and Nadeem U. Haque. 1986. "Adjustment with Growth: Relating the Analytical Approaches of the World Bank and the IMF." Development Policy Issues Series VPERS8. Washington, D.C.: World Bank, Development Research Department. Processed.

Kharas, Homi, and Miguel Kiguel. 1987. "Monetary Policy and Foreign Debt." Paper presented at conference on Challenges to Monetary Policies in Pacific Basin Countries, April. Federal Reserve Bank of San Francisco. Processed.

Kiguel, Miguel A., and Nissan Liviatan. 1988. "Inflationary Rigidities and Stabilization Policies." PPR Working Paper 4. Washington, D.C.: World Bank; Policy, Planning, and Research Department. Processed.

Kindleberger, Charles. 1986. *The World in Depression, 1929–1939.* Berkeley/Los Angeles: University of California Press.

Knight, Peter, and Desmond McCarthy. 1986. "Escaping Hyperinflation." *Finance & Development* 23 (December): 14–17.

Krugman, Paul. Forthcoming. "Private Capital Flows to Problem Debtors." In Jeffrey D. Sachs, ed., *Developing Country Debt and the World Economy.* University of Chicago Press.

Lancaster, Carol, and John Williamson, eds. 1986. *African Debt and Financing.* Special Report 5. Washington, D.C.: Institute for International Economics.

Landau, David. 1986. "Government and Economic Growth in the Less Developed Countries: An Empirical Study for 1960–80." *Economic Development and Cultural Change* 35 (October): 35–75.

Leeds, Roger S. 1987. "Privatization of the National Commercial Bank of Jamaica: A Case Study." Working paper. Cambridge, Mass.: Harvard University, John F. Kennedy School of Government. Processed.

Lessard, Donald R., and John Williamson. 1987. *Capital Flight and Third World Debt.* Washington, D.C.: Institute for International Economics.

Lever, Harold, and Christopher Huhne. 1987. *Debt and Danger: The World Financial Crisis.* Harmondsworth: Penguin.

Lindauer, David L., Oey Astra Meesook, and Parita Suebsaeng. 1988. "Government Wage Policy in Africa: Some Findings and Policy Issues." *World Bank Research Observer* 3, 1 (January): 1–25.

Linn, Johannes F. 1977. *The Incidence of Urban Property Taxation in Developing Countries: A Theoretical and Empirical Analysis Applied to Colombia.* World Bank Staff Working Paper 264. Washington, D.C.

———. 1983. *Cities in the Developing World: Policies for Their Equitable and Efficient Growth.* New York: Oxford University Press.

Loxley, John. 1986. *Debt and Disorder: External Financing for Development.* Boulder, Col.: Westview Press.

Mahar, Dennis J., and William R. Dillinger. 1983. *Financing State and Local Government in Brazil: Recent Trends and Issues.* World Bank Staff Working Paper 612. Washington, D.C.

Marris, Stephen. 1987. *Deficits and the Dollar: The World Economy at Risk.* Washington, D.C.: Institute for International Economics.

McLure, Charles E. Jr., ed. 1983. *Tax Assignment in Federal Countries.* Canberra: Australian National University Press.

———. 1987. "U.S. Tax Laws and Capital Flight from Latin America." Stanford, Calif.: Hoover Institute, Stanford University. Processed.

———. 1988. "Fiscal Policy and Equity in Developing Countries." In Elliot Berg, ed., *Policy Reform and Equity.* San Francisco, Calif.: ICS Press.

Meerman, Jacob. 1979. *Public Expenditure in Malaysia: Who Benefits and Why.* New York: Oxford University Press.

Mehran, Hassanali, ed. 1985. *External Debt Management.* Washington, D.C.: IMF.

Meier, Gerald M., ed. 1983. *Pricing Policy for Development Management.* Baltimore, Md.: Johns Hopkins University Press.

Mills, Edwin S. 1986. *The Burden of Government.* Stanford, Calif.: Hoover Institution Press.

Mitchell, Brian R. 1975. *European Historical Statistics, 1750–1970.* New York: Columbia University Press.

Morgan Guaranty Trust Company of New York. 1987. *World Financial Markets* (August, September-October).

Mountfield, Peter. 1984. "Recent Developments in the Control of Public Expenditures in the United Kingdom." In A. Premchand and Jesse Burkhead, eds. *Comparative International Budgeting and Finance.* New Brunswick, N.J.: Public Financial Publications, Inc.

Mueller, Dennis. 1987. "The Growth of Government: A Public Choice Perspective." *IMF Staff Papers* 34, 1 (March): 254–331.

Munasinghe, Mohan, Joseph Gilling, and Melody K. Mason. 1988. "Review of World Bank Lending for Electric Power." Industry and Energy Department Working Paper, Energy Series Paper 2. Washington, D.C.: World Bank, Industry and Energy Department. Processed.

Musgrave, Richard. 1959. *The Theory of Public Finance.* New York: McGraw Hill.

———. 1981a. *Fiscal Reform in Bolivia: Final Report of the Bolivian Mission on Tax Reform.* Cambridge, Mass.: Harvard Law School.

———. 1981b. "Leviathan Cometh—Or Does He?" In Helen Ladd and T. Nicholaus Tideman, eds., *Tax Expenditure Limitations.* Washington, D.C.: Urban Institute Press.

Musgrave, Richard, and Alan Peacock. 1959. *Classics in the Theory of Public Finance.* New York: Macmillan.

Nellis, John R. 1986. *Public Enterprises in Sub-Saharan Africa.* World Bank Discussion Paper 1. Washington, D.C.

Newbery, David M., Gordon A. Hughes, William D. O. Paterson, and Esra Bennathan. 1988. *Road Transport Taxation in Developing Countries: Design of User Charges and Taxes for Tunisia.* World Bank Discussion Paper 26. Washington, D.C.

Newbery, David, and Nicholas Stern, eds. 1987. *The Theory of Taxation for Developing Countries.* New York: Oxford University Press.

Nunberg, Barbara. Forthcoming. "Public Sector Pay and Employment Policy Issues in Bank Lending: An Interim Review of Experience." PPR Working Paper. Washington, D.C.: World Bank, Country Economics Department. Processed.

Ohkawa, Kazushi, Miyohei Shinohara, and Mataji Umemura. 1965–79. *Estimates of Long-Term Economic Statistics of Japan since 1868.* Vols. 1 and 7. Tokyo: Toyo Keizai Shinposha.

Organisation for Economic Co-operation and Development. 1987. *National Accounts, 1973–85.* Paris.

———. Various issues. *Economic Outlook.*

Paul, Samuel. 1987. "Training for Public Administration and Management in Developing Countries: A Review." Course on Urban Finance and Management in East Asia. Kuala Lumpur, Malaysia: National Institute of Public Administration, Malaysia (INTAN). Processed.

Peacock, Alan, and Jack Wiseman. 1961. *The Growth of Public Expenditure in the United Kingdom.* Princeton, N.J.: Princeton University Press.

Peacock, Alan, and others. 1980. *Structural Economic Policies in West Germany and the United Kingdom.* London: Anglo-German Foundation for the Study of Industrial Society.

Pellechio, Anthony J., and David G. Dunn. 1987. "Taxation of Investment in Selected Countries in Europe, the Middle East, and Northern Africa." Provisional Papers in Public Economics 87–8. Washington, D.C.: World Bank, Development Research Department. Processed.

Pellechio, Anthony J., Gerardo P. Sicat, and David G. Dunn. 1987a. "Taxation of Investment in East Asian Countries." DRD Discussion Paper 261. Washington, D.C.: World Bank, Development Research Department. Processed.

———. 1987b. "Effective Tax Rates under Varying Tax Incentives." DRD Discussion Paper 262. Washington, D.C.: World Bank, Development Research Department. Processed.

Peltzman, Sam. 1980. "The Growth of Government." *The Journal of Law and Economics* 23, 2 (October): 209–87.

Penati, Alessandro. 1983. "Expansionary Fiscal Policy and the Exchange Rate: A Review." *IMF Staff Papers* 30, 3 (September): 542–69.

Petrei, A. Humberto. 1987. *El Gasto Publico Social y sus Efectos Distributivos: Un examen comparativo de cinco paises de America Latina.* Serie Documentos ECIEL 7. Rio de Janeiro: Programa ECIEL.

Pinto, Brian. 1987. "Nigeria during and after the Oil Boom: A Policy Comparison with Indonesia." *World Bank Economic Review* 1 (May): 419–45.

Prest, A. R. [1962] 1985. *Public Finance in Developing Countries.* New York: St. Martin's Press.

Prud'Homme, Remy. 1987. "Financing Urban Public Services." In E. S. Mills, ed. *Handbook of Regional and Urban Economics.* Vol. II. Amsterdam: North Holland.

Rakodi, Carole. 1988. "The Local State and Urban Local Government in Zambia." *Public Administration and Development* 8, 1 (January–March): 27–46.

Ram, Rati. 1986a. "Causality between Income and Government Expenditure: A Broad International Perspective." *Public Finance* 41, 3: 393–413.

————. 1986b. "Government Size and Economic Growth: A New Framework and Some Evidence from Cross-Section and Time-Series Data." *American Economic Review* 76, 1 (March): 191–203.

————. 1987. "Wagner's Hypothesis in Time-Series and Cross-Section Perspectives: Evidence from 'Real' Data for 115 Countries." *The Review of Economics and Statistics* 69, 2 (May): 194–204.

Reisen, Helmut, and Axel van Trotsenburg. 1988. *Developing Country Debt: The Budgetary and Transfer Problem.* Development Centre Studies. Paris: OECD.

Repetto, Robert. 1985. *Paying the Price: Pesticide Subsidies in Developing Countries.* Washington, D.C.: World Resources Institute.

————. 1986. *Skimming the Water: Rent-Seeking and the Performance of Public Irrigation Systems.* Research Report 4. Washington, D.C.: World Resources Institute.

Research Triangle Institute. 1986. *Management Support for Town Panchayats Project Pilot Phase: Final Report.* Research Triangle Park, N.C.

Reynolds, Lloyd G. 1983. "The Spread of Economic Growth to the Third World: 1880–1980." *Journal of Economic Literature* 21, (September): 941–80.

————. 1985. *Economic Growth in the Third World, 1850–1980.* New Haven, Conn.: Yale University Press.

Rohatyn, Felix. 1987. "On the Brink." *New York Review of Books.* (June 11): 3–6.

Rondinelli, Dennis A. 1983. "Implementing Decentralization Programs in Asia: A Comparative Analysis." *Public Administration and Development* 3, 3 (July–September): 181–208.

Rondinelli, Dennis A., John R. Nellis, and G. Shabbir Cheema. 1984. *Decentralization in Developing Countries: A Review of Recent Experience.* World Bank Staff Working Paper 581. Washington, D.C.

Roth, Gabriel. 1987. *The Private Provision of Public Services in Developing Countries.* New York: Oxford University Press.

Sachs, Jeffrey D., 1985. "External Debt and Macroeconomic Performance in Latin America and East Asia." *Brookings Papers on Economic Activity* 2: 523–64.

————. 1987a. "The Bolivian Hyperinflation and Stabilization." *AER Papers and Proceedings* 77 (May): 279–83.

————. 1987b. "Trade and Exchange Rate Policies in Growth-Oriented Adjustment Programs." In Vittorio Corbo, Morris Goldstein, and Mohsin Khan, eds., *Growth-Oriented Adjustment Programs.* Washington, D.C.: IMF/World Bank.

————, ed. Forthcoming. *Developing Country Debt and the World Economy.* University of Chicago Press.

Sachs, Jeffrey D., and Charles Wyplosz. 1984. "Real Exchange Rate Effects of Fiscal Policy." NBER Working Paper Series 1255. Cambridge, Mass.: National Bureau of Economic Research. Processed.

Saint-Etienne, Christian. 1984. *The Great Depression, 1929–1938: Lessons for the 1980's.* Stanford, Calif.: Hoover Institution Press.

Saunders, Peter, and Friedrich Klau. 1985. "The Role of the Public Sector: Causes and Consequences of the Growth of Government." Special issue. *OECD Economic Studies* 4.

Schroeder, Larry. 1984 *A Plan for Increased Resource Mobilization by Local Governments in Bangladesh.* Final report on the Zilla Roads/Local Finance Project. Vol. I: Executive Summary. Vol. II: Policy Recommendations. Syracuse, N.Y.: Metropolitan Studies Program, Syracuse University.

Selowsky, Marcelo. 1979. *Who Benefits from Government Expenditure?: A Case Study of Colombia.* New York: Oxford University Press.

Senge, Stephen V. 1986. "Local Government User Charges and Cost-Volume-Profit Analysis." *Pub-*

lic Budgeting and Finance (Autumn): 92–105.

Shalizi, Zmarak, Vasant Gandhi, and Jaber Ehdaie. 1985. ''Patterns of Taxation in Sub-Saharan Africa: Trends in 'Tax Effort' and Composition during the Period 1966–81.'' CPD Discussion Paper 1985–48. Washington, D.C.: World Bank, Country Programs Department. Processed.

Shalizi, Zmarak, and Lyn Squire. 1987. ''A Framework for Tax Policy Analysis in Sub-Saharan Africa.'' PPR Policy Brief 1. Washington, D.C.: World Bank; Policy, Planning, and Research Department. Processed.

Shirley, Mary M. 1983. *Managing State-Owned Enterprises.* World Bank Staff Working Paper 577. Washington, D.C.

Shoup, Carl S. 1986. ''Criteria for Choice among Types of Value-Added Tax.'' DRD Discussion Paper 191.Washington, D.C.: World Bank, Development Research Department. Processed.

Sicat, Gerardo P., and Arvind Virmani. 1988. ''Personal Income Taxes in Developing Countries.'' *World Bank Economic Review* 2, 1: 123–38.

Sinn, Hans-Werner. 1987. ''Der Dollar, die Weltwirtschaft, und die amerikanische Steuerreform von 1986.'' *Hamburger Jahrbuch für Wirtschafts- und Gesellschaftspolitik* 32: 9–23.

Sivaramakrishnan, K. C., and Leslie Green. 1986. *Metropolitan Management: The Asian Experience.* New York: Oxford University Press.

Small, Leslie, Marietta S. Adriano, and Edward D. Martin. 1986. ''Regional Study on Irrigation Service Fees: Final Report.'' Vol. 2. Report by the International Irrigation Management Institute. Manila: Asian Develoment Bank. Processed.

Smith, Gordon W., and John T. Cuddington, eds. 1985. *International Debt and the Developing Countries.* A World Bank Symposium. Washington, D.C.

Stiglitz, Joseph E. 1986. *The Economics of the Public Sector.* New York: Norton.

Strasma, John. 1987. ''Impact of Land Revenue Systems on Agricultural Land Usage.'' Burlington: Associates in Rural Development for USAID. Processed.

Streeten, Paul, Shahid Javid Burki, Mahbub ul Haq, Norman Hicks, and Frances Stewart. 1981. *First Things First: Meeting Basic Human Needs in Developing Countries.* New York: Oxford University Press.

Tanzi, Vito. 1977. ''Inflation, Lags in Collection, and the Real Value of Tax Revenue.'' *IMF Staff Papers* 24: 154–67.

————. 1984. ''Is There a Limit to the Size of Fiscal Deficits in Developing Countries?'' In Bernard P.

Herber, ed. *Public Finance and Public Debt.* Detroit, Mich.: Wayne State University Press.

————. 1985. ''Fiscal Management and External Debt Problems.'' In Hassanali Mehran, ed., *External Debt Management.* Washington, D.C.: IMF.

————. 1986a. ''Fiscal Policy Responses to Exogenous Shocks in Developing Countries.'' *AER Papers and Proceedings* 76, 2 (May): 88–91.

————. 1986b. ''Public Expenditure and Public Debt: An International and Historical Perspective.'' In John Bristow and Declan McDonogh, eds., *Public Expenditure: The Key Issues.* Dublin: Institute of Public Administration.

————. 1987. ''Quantitative Characteristics of the Tax Systems of Developing Countries.'' In David Newbery and Nicholas Stern, eds., *The Theory of Taxation for Developing Countries.* New York: Oxford University Press.

Tanzi, Vito, and Mario Blejer. 1983. ''Fiscal Deficits and Balance of Payments Disequilibrium in IMF Adjustment Programs.'' In Joaquin Muns, ed., *Adjustment, Conditionality, and International Financing.* Washington, D.C.: IMF.

Thirsk, Wayne R. 1987. ''Some Lessons from Colombian Tax Reform.'' Provisional Papers in Public Economics 87–14. Washington, D.C.: World Bank, Development Research Department. Processed.

Thurow, Lester, and Laura D'Andrea Tyson. 1987. ''The Economic Black Hole.'' *Foreign Policy* 67 (Summer): 3–21.

Tobin, James. 1980. *Asset Accumulation and Economic Activity.* University of Chicago Press.

Trebilcock, M. J., and others. 1982. *The Choice of Governing Instrument.* A study prepared for the Economic Council of Canada. Ottawa: Canadian Government Publishing Center.

United Nations. 1986. *Population Growth and Policies in Mega-Cities: Seoul.* Population Policy Paper 4. New York.

————. 1987. *World Economic Survey.* New York.

United States Government. 1975. *Historical Statistics of the United States: Colonial Times to 1970.* Bicentennial edition. Washington, D.C.: U.S. Department of Commerce, Bureau of the Census.

————. 1985. *Federal-State-Local Fiscal Relations.* Report to the President and the Congress. Washington, D.C.: Office of State and Local Finance, Department of the Treasury.

————. 1986a. *Social Security Programs throughout the World—1985.* Research Report 60 by the Department of Health and Human Services, the Social Security Administration, the Office of Policy, and the Office of Research, Statistics, and International Policy. Washington, D.C.: Government Printing Office.

———. 1986b and 1987. *World Military Spending and Arms Transfers.* Washington, D.C.: Arms Control and Disarmament Agency.

van Wijnbergen, Sweder. 1985. "Fiscal Deficits, Exchange Rate Crises, and Inflation." Washington, D.C.: World Bank, EMENA Technical Department. Processed.

———. 1988. "External Debt, Inflation, and the Public Sector: Towards Fiscal Policy for Sustainable Growth." Washington, D.C. World Bank, EMENA Technical Department. Processed.

van Wijnbergen, Sweder, Ritu Anand, and Roberto Rocha. 1988. "Inflation, External Debt, and Financial Sector Reform: A Quantitative Approach to Consistent Fiscal Policy." Washington, D.C.: World Bank, EMENA Technical Department. Processed.

Veloo, S. 1987. "Human Resources Management in Malaysia vis-à-vis Local Government." Course on Urban Finance and Management in East Asia. Kuala Lumpur, Malaysia: National Institute of Public Administration, Malaysia (INTAN). Processed.

Vernon, Raymond. 1987. "Economic Aspects of Privatization Programs." Washington, D.C.: World Bank, Economic Development Institute. Processed.

Versluysen, Eugene L. 1980. *The Political Economy of International Finance.* New York: St. Martin's Press.

Vogel, Ronald J. 1988. *Cost Recovery in the Health Care Sector: Selected Country Studies in West Africa.* World Bank Technical Paper 82. Washington, D.C.

Vuylsteke, Charles, Helen Nankani, and Rebecca Candoy-Sekse. 1988. *Techniques of Privatization of State-Owned Enterprises.* 2 vols. World Bank Technical Paper 88. Washington, D.C.

Wade, Robert. 1988. *Village Republics: Economic Conditions for Collective Action in South India.* London: Cambridge University Press.

Wallich, Christine. 1982. *State Finances in India.* 3 vols. World Bank Staff Working Paper 523. Washington, D.C.

Wasylenko, Michael. 1987. "Fiscal Decentralization and Economic Development." *Public Budgeting & Finance* 7, 4 (Winter): 57–71.

Webber, Carolyn, and Aaron Wildavsky. 1986. *A History of Taxation and Expenditure in the Western World.* New York: Simon and Schuster.

Whalley, John. 1984. "Regression or Progression: The Taxing Question of Incidence Analysis." *Canadian Journal of Economics* 17 :654–82.

Wildasin, David E. 1985. "Urban Public Finance." Bloomington, Ind.: Indiana University, Department of Economics. Processed.

Williamson, John, ed. 1985. *Inflation and Indexation: Argentina, Brazil, and Israel.* Washington, D.C.: Institute for International Economics.

Williamson, John, and Marcus H. Miller. 1987. *Targets and Indicators: A Blueprint for the International Coordination of Economic Policy.* Washington, D.C.: Institute for International Economics.

Wissenschaflicher Beirat beim Bundesminister für wirtschafliche Zusammenarbeit. 1985. *Wirtschaftsordnung und Entwicklungserfolg.* Forschungsberichte des Bundesministeriums für wirtschaftliche Zusammenarbeit 72. Cologne: Weltforum Verlag.

World Bank. 1983. *China: Socialist Economic Development.* 3 vols. Washington, D.C.

———. 1984. *Thailand: Managing Public Resources for Structural Adjustment.* Washington, D.C.

———. 1986a. *Financing Education in Developing Countries: An Exploration of Policy Options.* Washington, D.C.

———. 1986b. *Urban Transport.* A World Bank Policy Study. Washington, D.C.

———. 1987a. *Bangladesh: Promoting Higher Growth and Human Development.* Washington, D.C.

———. 1987b. *Financing Health Services in Developing Countries: An Agenda for Reform.* A World Bank Policy Study. Washington, D.C.

———. 1987c. *Social Indicators of Development 1987.* Washington, D.C.

———. 1987d. *World Debt Tables, 1987–88: External Debt of Developing Countries.* 2 vols. Washington, D.C.

———. 1988a. *Education in Sub-Saharan Africa: Policies for Adjustment, Revitalization, and Expansion.* A World Bank Policy Study. Washington, D.C.

———. 1988b. *Road Deterioration in Developing Countries: Causes and Remedies.* A World Bank Policy Study. Washington, D.C.

———. Various years. *World Development Report.* New York: Oxford University Press.

World Development Indicators

Contents

Key

In each table, economies are listed in their group in ascending order of GNP per capita except for those for which no GNP per capita can be calculated. These are italicized, in alphabetical order, at the end of their group. The reference numbers below reflect the order in the tables.

Figures in the colored bands are summary measures for groups of economies. The letter *w* after a summary measure indicates that it is a weighted average; *m*, a median value; *t*, a total.

All growth rates are in real terms.

Figures in italics are for years or periods other than those specified.

. . = not available.
0 and 0.0 = zero or less than half the unit shown.
Blank means not applicable.

Afghanistan	34	*Guinea*	36	Pakistan	28
Albania	121	Haiti	27	Panama	83
Algeria	86	Honduras	52	Papua New Guinea	50
Angola	122	Hong Kong	93	Paraguay	62
Argentina	84	Hungary	79	Peru	63
Australia	111	India	20	Philippines	44
Austria	108	Indonesia	42	Poland	80
Bangladesh	5	*Iran, Islamic Republic of*	95	Portugal	81
Belgium	107	*Iraq*	96	*Romania*	97
Benin	17	Ireland	103	Rwanda	21
Bhutan	2	Israel	92	Saudi Arabia	98
Bolivia	46	Italy	105	Senegal	33
Botswana	57	Jamaica	58	Sierra Leone	25
Brazil	74	Japan	115	Singapore	94
Bulgaria	123	Jordan	71	Somalia	18
Burkina Faso	3	*Kampuchea, Democratic*	37	South Africa	76
Burma	9	Kenya	23	Spain	102
Burundi	13	*Korea, Democratic People's*		Sri Lanka	31
Cameroon	59	*Republic of*	127	Sudan	26
Canada	117	Korea, Republic of	85	Sweden	116
Central African Republic	19	Kuwait	99	Switzerland	120
Chad	35	*Lao People's Democratic Republic*	38	Syrian Arab Republic	72
Chile	69	*Lebanon*	73	Tanzania	14
China	22	Lesotho	29	Thailand	55
Colombia	68	Liberia	40	Togo	15
Congo, People's Republic of the	61	*Libya*	101	Trinidad and Tobago	91
Costa Rica	70	Madagascar	11	Tunisia	65
Côte d'Ivoire	51	Malawi	6	Turkey	64
Cuba	124	Malaysia	75	Uganda	12
Czechoslovakia	125	Mali	8	*Union of Soviet Socialist Republics*	129
Denmark	114	Mauritania	32	United Arab Emirates	100
Dominican Republic	49	Mauritius	67	United Kingdom	106
Ecuador	66	Mexico	77	United States	119
Egypt, Arab Republic of	53	*Mongolia*	128	Uruguay	78
El Salvador	56	Morocco	45	Venezuela	87
Ethiopia	1	Mozambique	10	*Viet Nam*	39
Finland	113	Nepal	4	Yemen Arab Republic	43
France	110	Netherlands	109	Yemen, People's Democratic	
Gabon	88	New Zealand	104	Republic of	41
German Democratic Republic	126	Nicaragua	54	Yugoslavia	82
Germany, Federal Republic of	112	Niger	16	Zaire	7
Ghana	30	Nigeria	48	Zambia	24
Greece	89	Norway	118	Zimbabwe	47
Guatemala	60	Oman	90		

Note: For U.N. and World Bank member countries with populations of less than 1 million, see Box A.

Introduction

The World Development Indicators provide information on the main features of social and economic development. Most of the data collected by the World Bank are on its developing member countries. Because comparable data for developed industrial market economies are readily available, these are also included in the indicators. Additional information on some of these and other countries may be found in other World Bank publications, notably the *Atlas*, the *World Tables*, the *World Debt Tables*, and *Social Indicators of Development*. National accounts data for economies that are not members of the World Bank are not included in this report because they are not readily available in a comparable form.

Every effort has been made to standardize the data. However, full comparability cannot be ensured, and care must be taken in interpreting the indicators. The statistics are drawn from sources thought to be most authoritative, but many of them are subject to considerable margins of error. Variations in national statistical practices also reduce the comparability of data which should thus be construed only as indicating trends and characterizing major differences among economies, rather than taken as precise quantitative indications of those differences.

The indicators in Table 1 give a summary profile of economies. Data in the other tables fall into the following broad areas: national accounts, industry, agriculture, energy, external trade, external debt, aid flows, other external transactions, central government finances, monetary system, demographics, health, education, labor force, and urbanization.

Two new tables have been added this year. Table 33 provides indicators on women's comparative demographic status and access to some health and education services. Table 6 provides information on the structure of consumption. An earlier table on the origin and destination of merchandise exports has been discontinued (but a similar table for trade in manufactures has been kept). The table on life expectancy and related indicators has been discontinued, but most of its data can be found in other tables.

Data on external debt are compiled directly by the Bank on the basis of reports from developing member countries through the Debtor Reporting System. Other data are drawn mainly from the United Nations, its specialized agencies, and the International Monetary Fund (IMF), but country reports to the World Bank and Bank staff estimates are also used to improve currentness or consistency. In particular, national accounts estimates are obtained from member governments by World Bank staff on economic missions and are, in some instances, adjusted by Bank staff to conform to international definitions and concepts to provide better consistency.

For ease of reference, ratios and rates of growth are shown; absolute values are reported in only a few instances in the World Development Indicators but are usually available from other World Bank publications, notably the recently released fourth edition of the *World Tables*. Most growth rates are calculated for two periods, 1965–80 and 1980–86, and are computed, unless noted otherwise, by using the least-squares method. Because this method takes all observations in a period into account, the resulting growth rates reflect general trends that are not unduly influenced by exceptional values, particularly at the end points. In order to reflect real changes from year to year—that is, to exclude the effects of inflation—constant price economic indicators are used in calculating growth rates. Details of this methodology are given on page 288. Data in italics indicate that they are for years or periods other than those specified—up to two years earlier for economic indicators and up to three years on either side for social indicators, since these tend to be collected less regularly but change less dramatically over short periods of time. All dollar figures are U.S. dollars. The various methods used for converting from national currency figures are described, where appropriate, in the technical notes.

Differences between figures shown in this year's and those in last year's edition reflect not only updating but also revisions to historical series and methodological changes and changes to procedures for aggregation. In addition, the Bank also reviews methodologies in an effort to improve the international comparability and analytical significance of the indicators, as explained in the technical notes.

As in the *World Development Report* itself, the economies included in the World Development Indicators are grouped into several major categories. These groupings are analytically useful for distinguishing economies at different stages of development. Many of the economies are further classified by dominant characteristics. The major classifications used in the tables this year are 39 low-income developing economies with per capita incomes of $425 or less in 1986, 58 middle-income developing economies with per capita incomes of $426 or more, 4 high-income oil exporters, and 19 industrial market economies. For a final group of 9 nonreporting nonmember economies, paucity of data, differences in method for computing national

income, and difficulties of conversion are such that estimates of gross national product (GNP) per capita and other economic variables are not attempted.

Economies with populations of less than 1 million are not included in the main tables, but basic indicators for those that are members of the World Bank or the U.N. are in a separate table on page 289. One Bank member, Gabon, has moved into the main tables because its population now exceeds 1 million.

The summary measures are overall estimates: countries for which individual estimates are not shown, because of nonreporting or insufficient history, have been included by assuming they followed the trend of reporting countries during such periods. This gives a more consistent aggregate measure by standardizing country coverage for each time period shown. Where missing information accounts for a significant share of the overall estimate, however, the group measure is reported as not available.

Throughout the World Development Indicators, the data for China do not include Taiwan, China. However, footnotes to Tables 11–15 provide estimates of the international transactions for Taiwan, China.

The format of this edition follows that used in previous years. In each group, economies are listed in ascending order of GNP per capita except those for which no such figure can be calculated. These are italicized and are in alphabetical order at the end of the group deemed to be appropriate. This order is used in all tables except Table 21, which covers only OECD and OPEC countries. The alphabetical list in the *key* (page 215) shows the reference number for each economy; here, too, italics indicate economies with no estimates of GNP per capita.

In the colored bands are *summary measures*—totals, weighted averages or median values—calculated for groups of economies if data are adequate. Because China and India heavily influence the overall summary measures for the low-income economies, summary measures are shown for two subgroups, *China and India*, and *other low-income economies*. For analytical purposes, data for all developing economies are also summarized in the following overlapping groupings: oil exporters, exporters of manufactures, highly indebted countries, and Sub-Saharan Africa. Sub-Saharan Africa includes all African countries except South Africa and those with access to the Mediterranean. For definitions and lists of countries in the other groups, see page xi.

The methodology used for computing the summary measures is described in the technical notes. For these numbers, *w* indicates that the summary measures are weighted averages; *m*, median values; and *t*, totals. The coverage of economies is not uniform for all indicators, and the variation from measures of central tendency can be large; therefore readers should exercise caution in comparing the summary measures for different indicators, groups, and years or periods.

The technical notes and footnotes to tables should be referred to in any use of the data. These notes outline the methods, concepts, definitions, and data sources used in compiling the tables. The bibliography gives details of the data sources, which contain comprehensive definitions and descriptions of concepts used. It should also be noted that country notes to the *World Tables* provide additional expla-

Groups of economies

The colors on the map show what group a country has been placed in on the basis of its GNP per capita and, in some instances, its distinguishing economic characteristics. For example, all low-income economies, those with a GNP per capita of $425 and less (in 1986), are colored yellow. The groups are the same as those used in the 33 tables that follow, and they include only the 129 countries with a population of more than 1 million.

- Low-income economies
- Middle-income economies
- High-income oil exporters
- Industrial market economies
- Nonreporting nonmember economies

- Not included in the Indicators

nations of sources used, breaks in comparability, and other exceptions to standard statistical practices that have been identified by Bank staff on national accounts and international transactions.

The World Development Indicators includes three world maps and two charts. The first map shows country names and the main groups in which economies have been placed. The maps on the following pages show population and the share of agriculture in gross domestic product (GDP). The first chart illustrates the fertility and mortality indicators from Tables 28 and 33. The second reports the external balances of developing countries. While Table 15 reports these measures in nominal dollar terms for two years (1970 and 1986), the chart expresses each for three longer periods (1970–79, 1980–83 and 1984–86) as a percentage of GNP for the appropriate economy group.

The difference between the two measures is net official unrequited transfers (essentially foreign aid) which, for developing countries, tends to make current account deficits smaller than the financing requirement.

The Eckert IV projection has been used for these maps because it maintains correct areas for all countries although it slightly distorts shape, distance, and direction.

Comments and questions relating to the World Development Indicators should be addressed to:

Socio-Economic Data Division
International Economics Department
The World Bank
1818 H Street, N.W.
Washington, D.C. 20433.

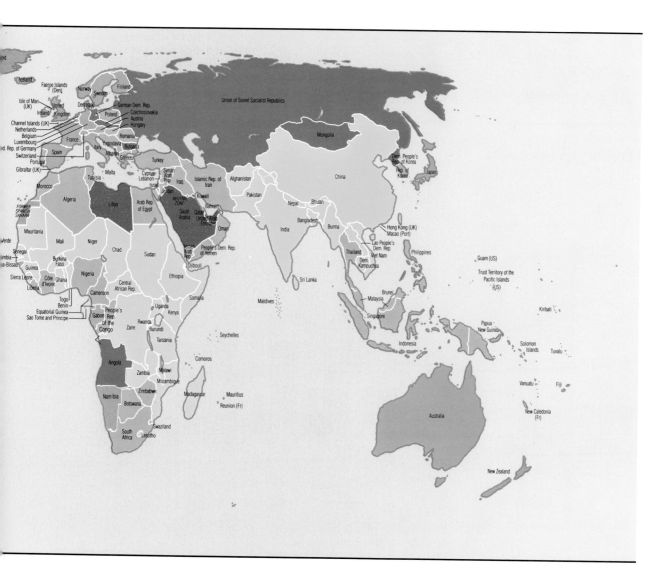

Population

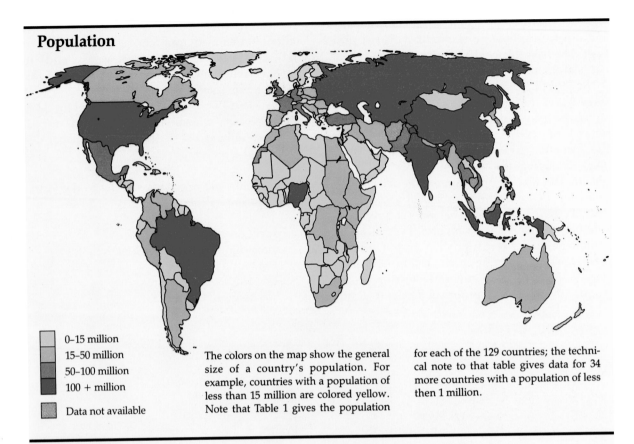

0–15 million	
15–50 million	
50–100 million	
100 + million	
Data not available	

The colors on the map show the general size of a country's population. For example, countries with a population of less than 15 million are colored yellow. Note that Table 1 gives the population for each of the 129 countries; the technical note to that table gives data for 34 more countries with a population of less then 1 million.

Fertility and mortality

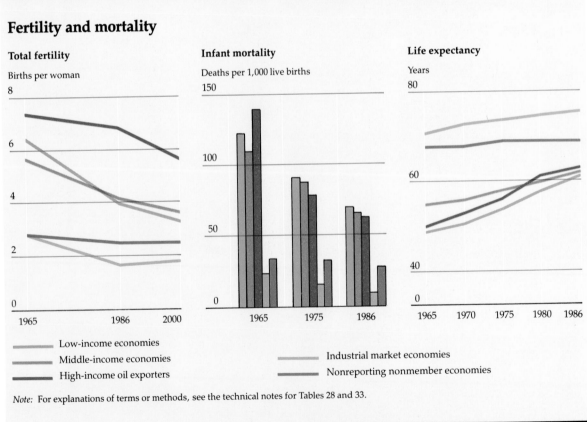

Total fertility

Births per woman

Infant mortality

Deaths per 1,000 live births

Life expectancy

Years

Low-income economies
Middle-income economies
High-income oil exporters
Industrial market economies
Nonreporting nonmember economies

Note: For explanations of terms or methods, see the technical notes for Tables 28 and 33.

Share of agriculture in GDP

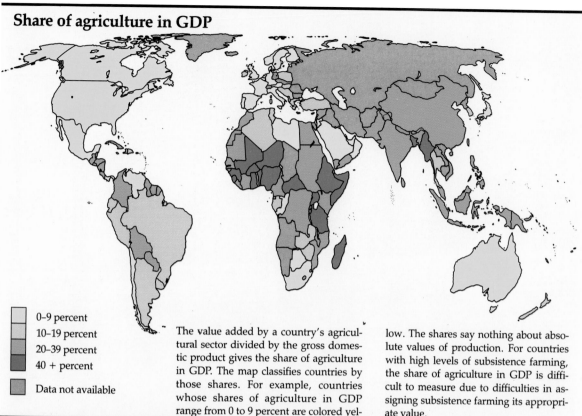

0–9 percent
10–19 percent
20–39 percent
40 + percent

Data not available

The value added by a country's agricultural sector divided by the gross domestic product gives the share of agriculture in GDP. The map classifies countries by those shares. For example, countries whose shares of agriculture in GDP range from 0 to 9 percent are colored yellow. The shares say nothing about absolute values of production. For countries with high levels of subsistence farming, the share of agriculture in GDP is difficult to measure due to difficulties in assigning subsistence farming its appropriate value.

External Balances of Developing Countries

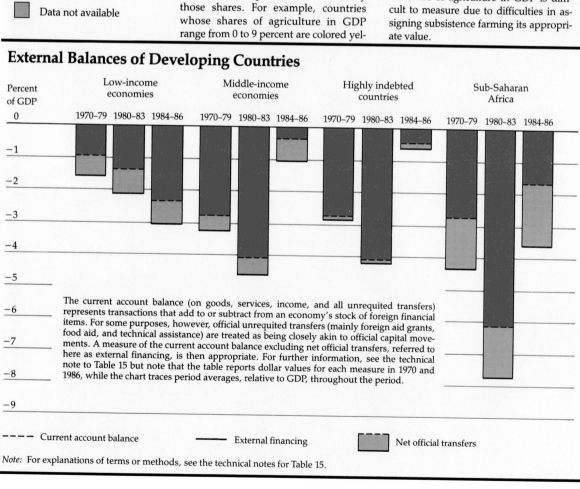

The current account balance (on goods, services, income, and all unrequited transfers) represents transactions that add to or subtract from an economy's stock of foreign financial items. For some purposes, however, official unrequited transfers (mainly foreign aid grants, food aid, and technical assistance) are treated as being closely akin to official capital movements. A measure of the current account balance excluding net official transfers, referred to here as external financing, is then appropriate. For further information, see the technical note to Table 15 but note that the table reports dollar values for each measure in 1970 and 1986, while the chart traces period averages, relative to GDP, throughout the period.

- - - - Current account balance   ——— External financing   Net official transfers

Note: For explanations of terms or methods, see the technical notes for Table 15.

Table 1. Basic indicators

	Population (millions) mid-1986	Area (thousands of square kilometers)	GNP per capita[a] Dollars 1986	GNP per capita[a] Average annual growth rate (percent) 1965–86	Average annual rate of inflation[a] (percent) 1965–80	Average annual rate of inflation[a] (percent) 1980–86	Life expectancy at birth (years) 1986
Low-income economies	**2,493.0 t**	**33,608 t**	**270 w**	**3.1 w**	**4.6 w**	**8.1 w**	**61 w**
China and India	**1,835.4 t**	**12,849 t**	**300 w**	**3.7 w**	**2.9 w**	**5.3 w**	**64 w**
Other low-income	**657.6 t**	**20,759 t**	**200 w**	**0.5 w**	**11.3 w**	**19.1 w**	**52 w**
1 Ethiopia	43.5	1,222	120	0.0	3.4	3.4	46
2 Bhutan	1.3	47	150	. .	. .	. .	45
3 Burkina Faso	8.1	274	150	1.3	6.2	6.3	47
4 Nepal	17.0	141	150	1.9	7.7	8.8	47
5 Bangladesh	103.2	144	160	0.4	14.9	11.2	50
6 Malawi	7.4	119	160	1.5	7.0	12.4	45
7 Zaire	31.7	2,345	160	−2.2	24.5	54.1	52
8 Mali	7.6	1,240	180	1.1	. .	7.4	47
9 Burma	38.0	677	200	2.3	8.7	2.1	59
10 Mozambique	14.2	802	210	. .	. .	28.1	48
11 Madagascar	10.6	587	230	−1.7	7.9	17.8	53
12 Uganda	15.2	236	230	−2.6	21.5	74.9	48
13 Burundi	4.8	28	240	1.8	8.4	6.4	48
14 Tanzania	23.0	945	250	−0.3	9.9	21.5	53
15 Togo	3.1	57	250	0.2	6.9	6.7	53
16 Niger	6.6	1,267	260	−2.2	7.5	6.6	44
17 Benin	4.2	113	270	0.2	7.4	8.6	50
18 Somalia	5.5	638	280	−0.3	10.3	45.4	47
19 Central African Rep.	2.7	623	290	−0.6	8.5	11.5	50
20 India	781.4	3,288	290	1.8	7.6	7.8	57
21 Rwanda	6.2	26	290	1.5	12.4	5.6	48
22 China	1054.0	9,561	300	5.1	0.0	3.8	69
23 Kenya	21.2	583	300	1.9	7.3	9.9	57
24 Zambia	6.9	753	300	−1.7	6.4	23.3	53
25 Sierra Leone	3.8	72	310	0.2	8.0	33.5	41
26 Sudan	22.6	2,506	320	−0.2	11.5	32.6	49
27 Haiti	6.1	28	330	0.6	7.3	7.7	54
28 Pakistan	99.2	804	350	2.4	10.3	7.5	52
29 Lesotho	1.6	30	370	5.6	8.0	13.1	55
30 Ghana	13.2	239	390	−1.7	22.8	50.8	54
31 Sri Lanka	16.1	66	400	2.9	9.6	13.5	70
32 Mauritania	1.8	1,031	420	−0.3	7.7	9.9	47
33 Senegal	6.8	196	420	−0.6	6.5	9.5	47
34 *Afghanistan*	. .	648	. .	. .	4.9	. .	. .
35 *Chad*	5.1	1,284	. .	. .	6.3	. .	45
36 *Guinea*	6.3	246	. .	. .	2.9	. .	42
37 *Kampuchea, Dem.*	. .	181	. .	. .	. .	. .	. .
38 *Lao PDR*	3.7	237	. .	. .	. .	. .	50
39 *Viet Nam*	63.3	330	. .	. .	. .	. .	65
Middle-income economies	**1,268.4 t**	**37,278 t**	**1,270 w**	**2.6 w**	**21.0 w**	**56.8 w**	**63 w**
Lower middle-income	**691.2 t**	**15,029 t**	**750 w**	**2.5 w**	**22.3 w**	**22.9 w**	**59 w**
40 Liberia	2.3	111	460	−1.4	6.3	1.1	54
41 Yemen, PDR	2.2	333	470	. .	. .	4.8	50
42 Indonesia	166.4	1,919	490	4.6	34.3	8.9	57
43 Yemen Arab Rep.	8.2	195	550	4.7	. .	13.1	46
44 Philippines	57.3	300	560	1.9	11.7	18.2	63
45 Morocco	22.5	447	590	1.9	6.1	7.7	60
46 Bolivia	6.6	1,099	600	−0.4	15.7	683.7	53
47 Zimbabwe	8.7	391	620	1.2	6.3	13.0	58
48 Nigeria	103.1	924	640	1.9	14.4	10.5	51
49 Dominican Rep.	6.6	49	710	2.5	6.8	15.9	66
50 Papua New Guinea	3.4	462	720	0.5	8.1	5.1	52
51 Côte d'Ivoire	10.7	323	730	1.2	9.3	8.3	52
52 Honduras	4.5	112	740	0.3	6.3	5.2	64
53 Egypt, Arab Rep.	49.7	1,001	760	3.1	7.5	12.4	61
54 Nicaragua	3.4	130	790	−2.2	8.9	56.5	61
55 Thailand	52.6	514	810	4.0	6.8	3.0	64
56 El Salvador	4.9	21	820	−0.3	7.0	14.9	61
57 Botswana	1.1	600	840	8.8	8.0	7.6	59
58 Jamaica	2.4	11	840	−1.4	12.8	19.8	73
59 Cameroon	10.5	475	910	3.9	9.0	11.0	56
60 Guatemala	8.2	109	930	1.4	7.1	11.3	61
61 Congo, People's Rep.	2.0	342	990	3.6	7.1	7.5	58
62 Paraguay	3.8	407	1,000	3.6	9.4	19.0	67
63 Peru	19.8	1,285	1,090	0.1	20.5	100.1	60
64 Turkey	51.5	781	1,110	2.7	20.7	37.3	65
65 Tunisia	7.3	164	1,140	3.8	6.7	8.9	63
66 Ecuador	9.6	284	1,160	3.5	10.9	29.5	66
67 Mauritius	1.0	2	1,200	3.0	11.4	8.1	66
68 Colombia	29.0	1,139	1,230	2.8	17.4	22.6	65

Note: For data comparability and coverage, see the technical notes. Figures in italics are for years other than those specified.

	Population (millions) mid-1986	Area (thousands of square kilometers)	GNP per capita[a] Dollars 1986	GNP per capita[a] Average annual growth rate (percent) 1965-86	Average annual rate of inflation[a] (percent) 1965-80	Average annual rate of inflation[a] (percent) 1980-86	Life expectancy at birth (years) 1986
69 Chile	12.2	757	1,320	−0.2	129.9	20.2	71
70 Costa Rica	2.6	51	1,480	1.6	11.3	32.3	74
71 Jordan	3.6	98	1,540	5.5	..	3.2	65
72 Syrian Arab Rep.	10.8	185	1,570	3.7	8.4	6.2	64
73 *Lebanon*	..	10	..	..	9.3	..	..
Upper middle-income	**577.2 t**	**22,248 t**	**1,890 w**	**2.8 w**	**20.5 w**	**72.0 w**	**67 w**
74 Brazil	138.4	8,512	1,810	4.3	31.3	157.1	65
75 Malaysia	16.1	330	1,830	4.3	4.9	1.4	69
76 South Africa	32.3	1,221	1,850	0.4	9.9	13.6	61
77 Mexico	80.2	1,973	1,860	2.6	13.1	63.7	68
78 Uruguay	3.0	176	1,900	1.4	57.8	50.4	71
79 Hungary	10.6	93	2,020	3.9	2.6	5.4	71
80 Poland	37.5	313	2,070	..	..	31.2	72
81 Portugal	10.2	92	2,250	3.2	11.5	22.0	73
82 Yugoslavia	23.3	256	2,300	3.9	15.3	51.8	71
83 Panama	2.2	77	2,330	2.4	5.4	3.3	72
84 Argentina	31.0	2,767	2,350	0.2	78.3	326.2	70
85 Korea, Rep. of	41.5	98	2,370	6.7	18.8	5.4	69
86 Algeria	22.4	2,382	2,590	3.5	9.9	6.1	62
87 Venezuela	17.8	912	2,920	0.4	8.7	8.7	70
88 Gabon	1.0	268	3,080	1.9	12.7	4.8	52
89 Greece	10.0	132	3,680	3.3	10.5	20.3	76
90 Oman	1.3	300	4,980	5.0	20.5	*3.6*	54
91 Trinidad and Tobago	1.2	5	5,360	1.6	14.0	8.6	70
92 Israel	4.3	21	6,210	2.6	25.2	182.9	75
93 Hong Kong	5.4	1	6,910	6.2	8.1	6.9	76
94 Singapore	2.6	1	7,410	7.6	4.7	1.9	73
95 *Iran, Islamic Rep.*	45.6	1,648	..	..	15.6	..	59
96 *Iraq*	16.5	435	..	..	..	..	63
97 *Romania*	22.9	238	..	..	..	..	71
Developing economies	**3,761.4 t**	**70,922 t**	**610 w**	**2.9 w**	**16.7 w**	**44.3 w**	**61 w**
Oil exporters	538.3 t	13,053 t	930 w	2.5 w	15.3 w	26.0 w	59 w
Exporters of manufactures	2,132.4 t	22,472 t	540 w	4.0 w	13.0 w	51.0 w	64 w
Highly indebted countries	569.5 t	21,213 t	1,400 w	2.3 w	26.5 w	91.6 w	63 w
Sub-Saharan Africa	424.1 t	20,895 t	370 w	0.9 w	12.5 w	16.1 w	50 w
High-income oil exporters	**19.1 t**	**4,011 t**	**6,740 w**	**1.8 w**	**16.4 w**	**-1.3 w**	**64 w**
98 Saudi Arabia	12.0	2,150	6,950	4.0	17.2	−1.3	63
99 Kuwait	1.8	18	13,890	−0.6	14.1	..	73
100 United Arab Emirates	1.4	84	14,680	..	..	*−1.4*	69
101 *Libya*	3.9	1,760	..	..	..	..	61
Industrial market economies	**741.6 t**	**30,935 t**	**12,960 w**	**2.3 w**	**7.6 w**	**5.3 w**	**76 w**
102 Spain	38.7	505	4,860	2.9	11.8	11.3	76
103 Ireland	3.6	70	5,070	1.7	12.2	10.7	74
104 New Zealand	3.3	269	7,460	1.5	9.6	11.0	74
105 Italy	57.2	301	8,550	2.6	11.2	13.2	77
106 United Kingdom	56.7	245	8,870	1.7	11.2	6.0	75
107 Belgium	9.9	31	9,230	2.7	6.6	5.7	75
108 Austria	7.6	84	9,990	3.3	5.8	4.5	74
109 Netherlands	14.6	41	10,020	1.9	7.6	3.1	77
110 France	55.4	547	10,720	2.8	8.0	8.8	77
111 Australia	16.0	7,687	11,920	1.7	9.5	8.2	78
112 Germany, Fed. Rep.	60.9	249	12,080	2.5	5.2	3.0	75
113 Finland	4.9	337	12,160	3.2	10.4	8.1	75
114 Denmark	5.1	43	12,600	1.9	9.2	7.3	75
115 Japan	121.5	372	12,840	4.3	7.8	1.6	78
116 Sweden	8.4	450	13,160	1.6	8.3	8.2	77
117 Canada	25.6	9,976	14,120	2.6	7.2	5.5	76
118 Norway	4.2	324	15,400	3.4	7.7	7.0	77
119 United States	241.6	9,363	17,480	1.6	6.4	4.4	75
120 Switzerland	6.5	41	17,680	1.4	5.3	4.2	77
Nonreporting nonmembers	**367.3 t**	**25,825 t**	**..**	**..**	**..**	**..**	**69 w**
121 *Albania*	3.0	29	..	..	..	..	71
122 *Angola*	9.0	1,247	..	..	..	..	44
123 *Bulgaria*	9.0	111	..	..	..	..	72
124 *Cuba*	10.2	115	..	..	..	..	75
125 *Czechoslovakia*	15.5	128	..	..	..	..	70
126 *German Dem. Rep.*	16.6	108	..	..	..	..	72
127 *Korea, Dem. Rep.*	20.9	121	..	..	..	..	68
128 *Mongolia*	2.0	1,565	..	..	..	..	64
129 *USSR*	281.1	22,402	..	..	..	..	70

Note: For U.N. and World Bank member countries with populations of less than 1 million, see Box A.

a. See the technical notes.

Table 2. Growth of production

	GDP		Agriculture		Industry		(Manufacturing)[a]		Services, etc.	
Average annual growth rate (percent)	1965-80	1980-86	1965-80	1980-86	1965-80	1980-86	1965-80	1980-86	1965-80	1980-86
Low-income economies	**4.8 w**	**7.5 w**	**2.7 w**	**4.9 w**	**7.5 w**	**10.6 w**	**7.6 w**	**11.2 w**	**5.1 w**	**6.6 w**
China and India	**5.3 w**	**8.6 w**	**2.9 w**	**5.7 w**	**8.0 w**	**11.3 w**	**7.9 w**	**11.7 w**	**5.7 w**	**7.8 w**
Other low-income	**3.1 w**	**2.9 w**	**1.9 w**	**2.0 w**	**4.6 w**	**4.2 w**	**4.8 w**	**4.8 w**	**3.8 w**	**3.3 w**
1 Ethiopia	2.7	0.8	1.2	-3.9	3.5	3.8	5.1	3.9	5.2	5.1
2 Bhutan[b]	..	..	..	..	..	..	..	..	..	..
3 Burkina Faso	3.5	2.5	..	2.7	..	2.1	..	..	..	2.4
4 Nepal	2.4	3.5	1.1	4.8	..	..	..	..	..	..
5 Bangladesh[b]	2.4	3.7	1.5	2.7	3.8	4.6	6.8	2.1	3.4	4.7
6 Malawi	6.1	2.4	..	2.5	..	1.5	..	..	..	2.8
7 Zaire[b]	1.4	1.0	..	1.7	..	2.7	..	-0.7	..	-0.7
8 Mali[b]	4.1	0.4	2.8	-2.3	4.2	4.0	..	..	7.0	3.8
9 Burma[b]	3.9	4.9	3.7	4.7	4.4	6.3	3.9	5.8	4.0	4.8
10 Mozambique	..	-9.0	..	-15.9	..	-13.3	..	..	..	0.2
11 Madagascar[b]	1.6	-0.1	..	2.1	..	-3.6	..	..	..	-0.7
12 Uganda	0.8	0.7	1.2	-0.1	-4.1	0.9	-3.7	-0.3	1.1	3.3
13 Burundi	3.6	2.3	3.3	1.3	7.8	4.9	5.9	6.9	2.7	3.2
14 Tanzania	3.7	0.9	1.6	0.8	4.2	-4.5	5.6	-4.6	6.9	2.9
15 Togo[b]	4.5	-1.1	1.9	1.7	6.8	-2.2	..	-2.6	5.4	-2.3
16 Niger[b]	0.3	-2.6	-3.4	2.8	11.4	-4.3	..	..	3.4	-8.0
17 Benin	2.3	3.6	..	3.0	..	10.2	..	4.6	..	1.8
18 Somalia	2.5	4.9	..	7.9	..	-5.1	..	-3.4	..	3.6
19 Central African Rep.	2.6	1.1	2.1	2.5	5.3	1.7	..	-0.6	2.0	-0.5
20 India	3.7	4.9	2.8	1.9	4.0	7.1	4.3	8.2	4.6	6.0
21 Rwanda[b]	5.0	1.8	..	0.9	..	4.8	..	4.1	..	1.1
22 China[b]	6.4	10.5	3.0	7.9	10.0	12.5	9.5[c]	12.6[c]	7.0	9.4
23 Kenya	6.4	3.4	4.9	2.8	9.8	2.7	10.5	4.1	6.4	4.2
24 Zambia[b]	1.8	-0.1	2.2	2.8	2.1	-0.7	5.3	0.6	1.5	-0.5
25 Sierra Leone	2.6	0.4	2.3	0.5	-1.0	-2.4	4.3	2.0	5.8	1.5
26 Sudan	3.8	0.3	2.9	0.4	3.1	2.1	..	0.0	4.9	-0.3
27 Haiti[b]	2.9	-0.7	1.0	-1.3	7.1	-2.4	6.2	-2.6	2.7	0.5
28 Pakistan	5.1	6.7	3.3	3.3	6.4	9.3	5.7	9.3	5.9	7.2
29 Lesotho	6.6	0.9	..	1.6	..	-3.9	..	16.1	..	2.7
30 Ghana[b]	1.4	0.7	1.6	-0.2	1.4	-2.4	2.5	-1.9	1.1	3.3
31 Sri Lanka	4.0	4.9	2.7	3.9	5.1	4.5	3.2	5.6	4.3	5.7
32 Mauritania	2.0	1.0	-2.0	1.2	2.2	5.4	..	..	6.5	-2.4
33 Senegal[b]	2.1	3.2	1.4	2.3	4.8	4.0	3.4	4.1	1.3	3.2
34 *Afghanistan*	2.9	..	..	..	..	..	..	..	..	..
35 *Chad*[b]	0.1	..	..	..	..	..	..	..	..	..
36 *Guinea*[b]	3.8	0.9	..	0.3	..	0.1	..	1.5	..	2.1
37 *Kampuchea, Dem.*	..	..	..	..	..	..	..	..	..	..
38 *Lao PDR*	..	..	..	..	..	..	..	..	..	..
39 *Viet Nam*	..	..	..	..	..	..	..	..	..	..
Middle-income economies	**6.6 w**	**2.3 w**	**3.4 w**	**2.3 w**	**7.0 w**	**2.1 w**	**8.2 w**	**2.5 w**	**7.6 w**	**2.6 w**
Lower middle-income	**6.5 w**	**1.8 w**	**3.4 w**	**2.1 w**	**8.4 w**	**1.2 w**	**7.4 w**	**3.0 w**	**7.5 w**	**2.3 w**
40 Liberia	3.3	-1.3	5.5	1.2	2.2	-6.0	10.0	-5.0	2.4	-0.8
41 Yemen, PDR[b]	..	1.7	..	..	..	..	..	..	..	..
42 Indonesia[b]	7.9	3.4	4.3	3.0	11.9	1.8	12.0	7.7	7.3	5.6
43 Yemen Arab Rep.[b]	..	4.3	..	0.2	..	8.3	..	16.5	..	5.2
44 Philippines[b]	5.9	-1.0	4.6	2.0	8.0	-3.5	7.5	-1.7	5.2	-0.6
45 Morocco[b]	5.4	3.3	2.2	3.9	6.1	1.1	5.9	1.1	6.5	4.4
46 Bolivia[b]	4.5	-3.0	3.8	-1.8	3.7	-7.5	5.4	-9.0	5.6	-0.8
47 Zimbabwe	4.4	2.6	..	3.4	..	0.8	..	1.3	..	3.7
48 Nigeria	8.0	-3.2	1.7	1.4	13.4	-5.1	14.6	1.0	8.8	-4.0
49 Dominican Rep.[b]	7.3	1.1	4.6	1.0	10.9	1.0	8.9	0.4	6.7	1.3
50 Papua New Guinea[b]	4.1	1.8	..	..	10.4	-1.9	9.1	..	9.4	-0.5
51 Côte d'Ivoire	6.8	-0.3	3.3	0.9	..	..	..	..	..	..
52 Honduras	4.2	0.6	1.6	2.2	5.7	-0.8	6.0	-2.1	5.4	0.3
53 Egypt, Arab Rep.	6.7	4.7	2.8	1.9	7.0	6.3	..	..	9.5	4.4
54 Nicaragua[b]	2.6	0.2	3.3	1.4	4.2	0.3	5.2	0.8	1.4	-0.4
55 Thailand[b]	7.4	4.8	4.9	2.9	9.5	5.0	10.9	5.2	8.0	5.6
56 El Salvador[b]	4.3	-1.0	3.6	-2.3	5.3	-0.7	4.6	-1.1	4.3	-0.4
57 Botswana[b]	14.3	11.9	9.7	-9.8	24.0	19.1	13.5	6.2	11.5	7.6
58 Jamaica[b]	1.3	0.0	0.5	1.4	-0.1	-1.3	0.4	1.1	2.7	0.7
59 Cameroon[b]	5.1	8.2	4.2	2.0	8.1	15.9	7.0	..	4.8	7.0
60 Guatemala[b]	5.9	-1.2	5.1	-0.4	7.3	-3.0	6.5	-1.6	5.7	-0.7
61 Congo, People's Rep.[b]	5.9	5.1	3.1	-0.6	10.3	8.4	..	2.9	4.7	3.7
62 Paraguay[b]	6.9	1.1	4.9	1.9	9.1	-0.7	7.0	0.5	7.5	1.6
63 Peru[b]	3.9	-0.4	1.0	2.2	4.4	-1.1	3.8	..	4.3	-0.3
64 Turkey	6.3	4.9	3.2	3.1	7.2	6.4	7.5	8.0	7.6	4.7
65 Tunisia	6.6	3.7	5.5	3.3	7.4	3.3	9.9	6.5	6.5	4.1
66 Ecuador[b]	8.7	1.8	3.4	1.0	13.7	3.5	11.5	0.2	7.6	0.6
67 Mauritius	5.3	4.4	..	5.3	..	6.1	..	7.8	..	3.4
68 Colombia	5.7	2.4	4.3	2.3	5.5	3.8	6.2	2.5	6.4	1.7

Note: For data comparability and coverage, see the technical notes. Figures in italics are for years other than those specified.

	GDP		Agriculture		Industry		(Manufacturing)[a]		Services, etc.	
	1965–80	*1980–86*	*1965–80*	*1980–86*	*1965–80*	*1980–86*	*1965–80*	*1980–86*	*1965–80*	*1980–86*
69 Chile[b]	1.9	0.0	1.6	3.1	0.8	0.7	0.6	−0.2	2.7	−0.9
70 Costa Rica[b]	6.2	1.3	4.2	2.2	8.7	1.1	..	..	6.0	1.1
71 Jordan	..	5.1	..	1.8	..	5.8	..	4.9	..	5.1
72 Syrian Arab Rep.[b]	8.7	*1.5*	4.8	−1.4	12.2	0.6	..	..	9.0	2.9
73 Lebanon[b]	−1.2	..	..	..	..	..	..	..	..	..
Upper middle-income	**6.7 w**	**2.5 w**	**3.4 w**	**2.4 w**	**6.5 w**	**2.5 w**	**..**	**2.4 w**	**7.7 w**	**2.7 w**
74 Brazil	9.0	2.7	3.8	2.0	9.9	1.6	9.6	1.2	10.0	3.8
75 Malaysia[b]	7.4	4.8	..	3.0	..	6.0	..	5.8	..	4.5
76 South Africa	4.0	0.8	..	−1.3	..	−0.5	..	−1.7	..	2.4
77 Mexico[b]	6.5	0.4	3.2	2.1	7.6	−0.1	7.4	0.0	6.6	0.4
78 Uruguay	2.4	−2.6	1.0	−0.7	3.1	−5.2	..	..	2.3	−1.6
79 Hungary[b]	5.6	1.6	2.7	2.8	6.4	1.3	..	..	6.2	1.4
80 Poland	..	1.5	..	..	..	..	..	..	..	..
81 Portugal	5.5	1.4	..	0.1	..	1.4	..	..	..	1.7
82 Yugoslavia	6.0	1.2	3.1	1.4	7.8	1.1	..	..	5.5	1.4
83 Panama[b]	5.5	2.6	2.4	2.2	5.9	−1.4	4.7	0.2	6.0	3.7
84 Argentina[b]	3.4	−0.8	1.4	2.3	3.3	−1.7	2.7	−0.4	3.9	−0.8
85 Korea, Rep. of[b]	9.5	8.2	3.0	5.6	16.5	10.2	18.7	9.8	9.3	7.2
86 Algeria[b]	7.5	4.4	5.8	3.2	8.1	5.2	9.5	..	7.1	3.6
87 Venezuela[b]	5.2	−0.9	3.9	2.3	3.4	−0.8	5.8	2.0	6.5	−1.2
88 Gabon[b]	9.5	1.5	..	..	..	..	..	..	..	..
89 Greece	5.6	1.5	2.3	0.3	7.1	0.4	8.4	0.2	6.2	2.5
90 Oman[b]	12.5	5.7	..	..	..	..	..	..	..	..
91 Trinidad and Tobago	*5.1*	−6.3	*0.0*	4.8	*5.0*	−9.1	*2.6*	−12.8	*5.8*	−3.2
92 Israel[b]	6.8	2.0	..	..	..	..	..	..	..	..
93 Hong Kong	8.5	6.0	..	..	..	..	..	..	..	..
94 Singapore[b]	10.4	5.3	3.1	−3.5	12.2	4.4	13.3	2.2	9.7	6.1
95 Iran, Islamic Rep.	6.2	..	4.5	..	2.4	..	10.0	..	13.6	..
96 Iraq	..	..	..	..	..	..	..	..	..	..
97 Romania	..	..	..	..	..	..	..	..	..	..
Developing economies	**6.1 w**	**3.8 w**	**3.1 w**	**3.6 w**	**7.2 w**	**4.6 w**	**8.0 w**	**5.9 w**	**7.1 w**	**3.4 w**
Oil exporters	**7.1 w**	**1.7 w**	**3.4 w**	**2.4 w**	**6.8 w**	**1.6 w**	**8.5 w**	**2.4 w**	**8.7 w**	**1.9 w**
Exporters of manufactures	**6.6 w**	**6.2 w**	**3.0 w**	**5.0 w**	**8.9 w**	**7.8 w**	**9.1 w**	**8.6 w**	**7.4 w**	**5.3 w**
Highly indebted countries	**6.6 w**	**0.7 w**	**3.0 w**	**1.8 w**	**7.3 w**	**−0.2 w**	**7.3 w**	**0.4 w**	**7.2 w**	**1.0 w**
Sub-Saharan Africa	**5.6 w**	**0.0 w**	**1.6 w**	**1.2 w**	**9.4 w**	**−1.6 w**	**8.5 w**	**0.3 w**	**7.5 w**	**0.1 w**
High-income oil exporters	**7.8 w**	**−3.3 w**	**5.7 w**	**..**	**6.5 w**	**..**	**9.6 w**	**..**	**11.1 w**	**..**
98 Saudi Arabia[b]	10.9	−3.4	4.1	10.3	11.6	−10.4	8.1	6.1	10.5	4.4
99 Kuwait[b]	3.1	−0.9	..	..	..	..	..	..	..	..
100 United Arab Emirates	..	−3.8	..	..	..	..	..	..	..	..
101 Libya	4.2	..	10.7	..	1.2	..	13.7	..	15.5	..
Industrial market economies	**3.6 w**	**2.5 w**	**0.9 w**	**2.5 w**	**3.2 w**	**2.5 w**	**3.7 w**	**..**	**3.6 w**	**2.6 w**
102 Spain[b]	5.2	1.8	3.0	2.8	5.8	0.8	6.7	*0.3*	4.6	2.3
103 Ireland	5.1	0.7	..	−6.2	..	−1.1	..	..	..	3.8
104 New Zealand[b]	3.1	2.6	..	2.1	..	3.8	..	..	..	2.0
105 Italy[b]	3.9	1.3	0.8	0.5	4.2	0.2	5.1	−0.2	4.1	2.1
106 United Kingdom	2.2	2.3	1.7	4.1	1.2	2.0	1.1	*1.2*	2.9	2.6
107 Belgium[b]	3.9	0.9	0.5	3.1	4.4	0.5	4.8	*1.6*	3.8	1.1
108 Austria	4.3	1.8	2.2	1.2	4.5	1.6	4.7	*2.1*	4.4	*1.9*
109 Netherlands[b]	3.7	1.0	*4.3*	4.5	*3.6*	0.5	*4.3*	..	*4.0*	1.9
110 France[b]	4.4	1.3	0.8	2.8	4.6	0.6	5.3	..	4.6	1.6
111 Australia[b]	4.0	3.1	2.6	6.1	2.9	2.0	1.2	..	5.4	3.5
112 Germany, Fed. Rep.[b]	3.3	1.5	1.4	3.1	2.9	0.7	3.3	*0.8*	3.7	2.1
113 Finland	4.1	2.7	0.1	0.2	4.4	2.8	5.0	*3.0*	4.8	2.4
114 Denmark	2.7	2.8	0.9	4.6	*1.9*	2.6	*3.2*	2.9	*3.1*	2.4
115 Japan[b]	6.3	3.7	0.8	1.0	8.5	5.0	9.4	7.8	5.2	2.9
116 Sweden	2.8	*2.0*	−0.2	2.5	2.2	2.5	2.3	*2.3*	3.3	0.5
117 Canada	4.4	2.9	0.7	2.8	3.4	2.9	3.8	3.6	5.5	2.9
118 Norway[b]	4.4	3.5	−0.4	3.0	5.6	3.8	2.6	*0.3*	4.2	3.4
119 United States[b]	2.8	3.1	1.1	3.1	1.9	3.2	2.7	4.0	3.4	*3.0*
120 Switzerland[b]	2.0	1.5	..	..	..	..	..	..	..	..
Nonreporting nonmembers	**..**	**..**	**..**	**..**	**..**	**..**	**..**	**..**	**..**	**..**
121 *Albania*	..	..	..	..	..	..	..	..	..	..
122 *Angola*	..	..	..	..	..	..	..	..	..	..
123 *Bulgaria*	..	..	..	..	..	..	..	..	..	..
124 *Cuba*	..	..	..	..	..	..	..	..	..	..
125 *Czechoslovakia*	..	..	..	..	..	..	..	..	..	..
126 *German Dem. Rep.*	..	..	..	..	..	..	..	..	..	..
127 *Korea, Dem. Rep.*	..	..	..	..	..	..	..	..	..	..
128 *Mongolia*	..	..	..	..	..	..	..	..	..	..
129 *USSR*	..	..	..	..	..	..	..	..	..	..

Average annual growth rate (percent)

a. Because manufacturing is generally the most dynamic part of the industrial sector, its growth rate is shown separately.   b. GDP and its components are at purchaser values.   c. World Bank estimate.

Table 3. Structure of production

	GDP[a] (millions of dollars)		Distribution of gross domestic product (percent)							
			Agriculture		Industry		(Manufacturing)[b]		Services, etc.	
	1965	1986	1965	1986	1965	1986	1965	1986	1965	1986
Low-income economies	146,330 t	621,260 t	42 w	32 w	28 w	35 w	21 w	24 w	30 w	32 w
China and India	111,850 t	475,670 t	42 w	31 w	31 w	39 w	24 w	27 w	27 w	30 w
Other low-income	34,480 t	145,590 t	43 w	38 w	18 w	20 w	10 w	11 w	41 w	41 w
1 Ethiopia	1,180	4,960	58	48	14	15	7	10	28	36
2 Bhutan[c]	. .	210	. .	. .	. .	. .	. .	. .	. .	. .
3 Burkina Faso	260	930	53	45	20	22	. .	. .	27	33
4 Nepal	730	2,200	65	. .	11	. .	3	. .	23	. .
5 Bangladesh[c]	4,380	15,460	53	47	11	14	5	8	36	39
6 Malawi	220	1,100	50	37	13	18	. .	12	37	45
7 Zaire[c]	3,140	6,020	21	29	26	36	16	. .	53	35
8 Mali[c]	. .	1,650	. .	50	. .	13	. .	7	. .	37
9 Burma[c]	1,600	8,180	35	48	13	13	9	10	52	39
10 Mozambique	. .	4,300	. .	35	. .	12	. .	. .	. .	53
11 Madagascar[c]	670	2,670	31	43	16	16	11	. .	53	41
12 Uganda	1,100	3,310	52	76	13	6	8	5	35	18
13 Burundi	150	1,090	. .	58	. .	17	. .	10	. .	25
14 Tanzania	790	4,020	46	59	14	10	8	6	40	31
15 Togo[c]	190	980	45	32	21	20	10	7	34	48
16 Niger[c]	670	2,080	68	46	3	16	2	4	29	39
17 Benin	220	1,320	59	49	8	13	. .	4	33	37
18 Somalia	220	2,320	71	58	6	9	3	6	24	34
19 Central African Rep.	140	900	46	41	16	12	4	4	38	47
20 India	46,260	203,790	47	32	22	29	15	19	31	39
21 Rwanda[c]	150	1,850	75	40	7	23	2	16	18	37
22 China	65,590	271,880	39	31	38	46	30[d]	34[d]	23	23
23 Kenya	920	5,960	35	30	18	20	11	12	47	50
24 Zambia[c]	1,060	1,660	14	11	54	48	6	20	32	41
25 Sierra Leone	320	1,180	34	45	28	22	6	4	38	33
26 Sudan	1,330	7,470	54	35	9	15	4	7	37	50
27 Haiti[c]	350	2,150	. .	. .	. .	. .	. .	. .	. .	. .
28 Pakistan	5,450	30,080	40	24	20	28	14	17	40	47
29 Lesotho	50	230	65	21	5	27	1	13	30	52
30 Ghana[c]	2,050	5,720	44	45	19	17	10	12	38	39
31 Sri Lanka	1,770	5,880	28	26	21	27	17	15	51	47
32 Mauritania	160	750	32	34	36	24	4	. .	32	42
33 Senegal[c]	810	3,740	25	22	18	27	14	17	56	51
34 Afghanistan	600	. .	. .	. .	. .	. .	. .	. .	. .	. .
35 Chad[c]	290	. .	42	. .	15	. .	12	. .	43	. .
36 Guinea[c]	520	1,980	. .	40	. .	22	. .	2	. .	38
37 Kampuchea, Dem.	. .	. .	. .	. .	. .	. .	. .	. .	. .	. .
38 Lao PDR	. .	. .	. .	. .	. .	. .	. .	. .	. .	. .
39 Viet Nam	. .	. .	. .	. .	. .	. .	. .	. .	. .	. .
Middle-income economies	202,630 t	1,740,010 t	22 w	15 w	33 w	36 w	19 w	22 w	45 w	48 w
Lower middle-income	65,950 t	504,440 t	30 w	22 w	25 w	30 w	15 w	17 w	43 w	46 w
40 Liberia	270	990	27	37	40	28	3	5	34	35
41 Yemen, PDR[c]	. .	930	. .	. .	. .	. .	. .	. .	. .	. .
42 Indonesia[c]	3,830	75,230	56	26	13	32	8	14	31	42
43 Yemen Arab Rep.[c]	. .	4,760	. .	34	. .	16	. .	7	. .	50
44 Philippines[c]	6,010	30,540	26	26	28	32	20	25	46	42
45 Morocco[c]	2,950	14,760	23	21	28	30	16	17	49	49
46 Bolivia[c]	710	4,180	23	24	31	23	15	13	46	52
47 Zimbabwe	960	4,940	18	11	35	46	20	30	47	43
48 Nigeria	4,190	49,110	53	41	19	29	7	8	29	30
49 Dominican Rep.[c]	890	5,280	23	17	22	30	16	16	55	53
50 Papua New Guinea[c]	340	2,530	42	34	18	26	. .	9	41	40
51 Côte d'Ivoire	760	7,320	47	36	19	24	11	16	33	40
52 Honduras	460	2,960	40	27	19	25	12	14	41	48
53 Egypt, Arab Rep.	4,550	40,850	29	20	27	29	. .	. .	45	51
54 Nicaragua[c]	570	2,900	25	23	24	33	18	27	51	44
55 Thailand[c]	4,050	41,780	35	17	23	30	14	21	42	53
56 El Salvador[c]	800	3,980	29	20	22	21	18	15	49	59
57 Botswana[c]	50	1,150	34	4	19	58	12	6	47	38
58 Jamaica[c]	970	2,430	10	6	37	40	17	22	53	54
59 Cameroon[c]	750	11,280	32	22	17	35	10	. .	50	43
60 Guatemala[c]	1,330	7,470	. .	. .	. .	. .	. .	. .	. .	. .
61 Congo, People's Rep.[c]	200	2,000	19	8	19	54	. .	6	62	38
62 Paraguay[c]	440	3,590	37	27	19	26	16	16	45	47
63 Peru[c]	5,020	25,370	18	11	30	38	17	20	53	51
64 Turkey	7,660	52,620	34	18	25	36	16	25	41	46
65 Tunisia	880	7,790	22	16	24	33	9	15	54	52
66 Ecuador c	1,150	11,510	27	14	22	42	18	19	50	45
67 Mauritius	190	1,160	16	15	23	32	14	23	61	53
68 Colombia	5,570	29,660	30	20	25	25	18	18	46	56

Note: For data comparability and coverage, see the technical notes. Figures in italics are for years other than those specified.

226

	GDP[a] (millions of dollars)		Agriculture		Industry		(Manufacturing)[b]		Services, etc.	
	1965	1986	1965	1986	1965	1986	1965	1986	1965	1986
69 Chile[c]	5,940	16,820	9	..	40	..	24	..	52	..
70 Costa Rica[c]	590	4,260	24	21	23	29	..	..	53	50
71 Jordan	..	4,000	..	8	..	28	..	14	..	63
72 Syrian Arab Rep.[c]	1,470	17,400	29	22	22	21	..	..	49	58
73 Lebanon[c]	1,150	..	12	..	21	..	..	..	67	..
Upper middle-income	**136,680 t**	**1,235,570 t**	**18 w**	**10 w**	**37 w**	**40 w**	**21 w**	**25 w**	**46 w**	**50 w**
74 Brazil	19,450	206,750	19	11	33	39	26	28	48	50
75 Malaysia[c]	3,130	27,580	28	..	25	..	9	..	47	..
76 South Africa	10,540	56,370	10	6	42	46	23	22	48	49
77 Mexico[c]	20,160	127,140	14	9	31	39	21	26	54	52
78 Uruguay	930	5,320	15	12	32	33	..	..	53	56
79 Hungary[c e]	..	23,660	..	17	..	41	..	..	..	43
80 Poland[c]	..	73,770	..	..	..	..	..	..	..	..
81 Portugal	..	27,480	..	10	..	40	..	..	..	..
82 Yugoslavia	11,190	61,640	23	12	42	42	..	..	35	51
83 Panama[c]	660	5,120	18	9	19	18	12	8	63	46
84 Argentina[c]	16,500	69,820	17	13	42	44	33	31	42	44
85 Korea, Rep. of[c]	3,000	98,150	38	12	25	42	18	30	37	45
86 Algeria[c]	3,170	60,760	15	12	34	44	11	13	51	44
87 Venezuela[c]	8,290	49,980	7	9	41	37	..	23	52	54
88 Gabon[c]	220	3,190	26	10	34	35	..	..	40	55
89 Greece	5,270	35,210	24	17	26	29	16	18	49	54
90 Oman[c]	60	7,320	61	..	23	..	0	..	16	..
91 Trinidad and Tobago	690	4,830	8	5	48	35	..	8	44	59
92 Israel[c]	3,590	29,460	..	..	..	..	..	..	..	..
93 Hong Kong	2,150	32,250	2	0	40	29	24	21	58	71
94 Singapore[c]	970	17,350	3	1	24	38	15	27	73	62
95 Iran, Islamic Rep.	6,170	..	26	..	36	..	12	..	38	..
96 Iraq	2,430	..	18	..	46	..	8	..	36	..
97 Romania	..	..	..	..	..	..	..	..	..	..
Developing economies	**348,960 t**	**2,361,370 t**	**30 w**	**19 w**	**31 w**	**36 w**	**20 w**	**..**	**38 w**	**46 w**
Oil exporters	**58,080 t**	**642,360 t**	**24 w**	**18 w**	**31 w**	**33 w**	**14 w**	**15 w**	**46 w**	**49 w**
Exporters of manufactures	**178,990 t**	**..**	**34 w**	**18 w**	**33 w**	**..**	**24 w**	**..**	**46 w**	**49 w**
Highly indebted countries	**111,120 t**	**713,560 t**	**20 w**	**15 w**	**34 w**	**36 w**	**22 w**	**..**	**31 w**	**47 w**
Sub-Saharan Africa	**26,440 t**	**165,990 t**	**45 w**	**36 w**	**19 w**	**25 w**	**9 w**	**10 w**	**37 w**	**36 w**
High-income oil exporters	**6,820 t**	**153,270 t**	**5 w**	**..**	**65 w**	**..**	**5 w**	**..**	**30 w**	**..**
98 Saudi Arabia[c]	2,300	78,480	8	4	60	50	9	9	31	46
99 Kuwait[c]	2,100	22,310	0	..	73	..	3	..	27	..
100 United Arab Emirates	..	25,280	..	..	..	..	..	..	..	..
101 Libya	1,500	..	5	..	63	..	3	..	33	..
Industrial market economies	**1,373,360 t**	**10,451,880 t**	**5 w**	**3 w**	**40 w**	**35 w**	**29 w**	**..**	**54 w**	**61 w**
102 Spain[c]	23,320	229,100	15	6	36	37	..	27	49	56
103 Ireland	2,340	21,910	..	14	..	45	..	..	..	41
104 New Zealand[c]	5,640	26,630	..	11	..	33	..	..	..	56
105 Italy[c]	72,150	599,920	11	5	41	39	23	22	48	56
106 United Kingdom	88,520	468,290	3	2	46	43	34	26	51	55
107 Belgium[c]	16,600	112,180	5	2	41	33	31	23	53	64
108 Austria[c]	9,480	93,830	9	3	46	38	33	28	45	59
109 Netherlands[c]	19,890	175,330	..	4	..	34	..	18	..	62
110 France[c]	99,660	724,200	8	4	39	34	28	..	53	63
111 Australia[c]	24,050	184,940	9	5	39	34	26	17	51	62
112 Germany, Fed. Rep.[c]	114,790	891,990	4	2	53	40	40	32	43	58
113 Finland	7,540	62,370	16	8	37	37	23	25	47	55
114 Denmark	8,940	68,820	8	6	36	28	23	20	55	66
115 Japan[c]	91,110	1,955,650	9	3	43	41	32	30	48	56
116 Sweden	19,610	114,470	6	3	40	35	28	24	53	62
117 Canada	45,940	323,790	6	3	40	36	27	..	53	61
118 Norway[c]	7,080	69,780	8	4	33	41	21	14	59	56
119 United States[c]	701,670	4,185,490	3	2	38	31	28	20	59	67
120 Switzerland[c]	13,920	135,050	..	..	..	..	..	..	..	..
Nonreporting nonmembers	**..**	**..**	**..**	**..**	**..**	**..**	**..**	**..**	**..**	**..**
121 Albania	..	..	..	..	..	..	..	..	..	..
122 Angola	..	..	..	..	..	..	..	..	..	..
123 Bulgaria	..	..	..	..	..	..	..	..	..	..
124 Cuba	..	..	..	..	..	..	..	..	..	..
125 Czechoslovakia	..	..	..	..	..	..	..	..	..	..
126 German Dem. Rep.	..	..	..	..	..	..	..	..	..	..
127 Korea, Dem. Rep.	..	..	..	..	..	..	..	..	..	..
128 Mongolia	..	..	..	..	..	..	..	..	..	..
129 USSR	..	..	..	..	..	..	..	..	..	..

a. See the technical notes. b. Because manufacturing is generally the most dynamic part of the industrial sector, its share of GDP is shown separately. c. GDP and its components are shown at purchaser values. d. World Bank estimate. e. *Services, etc.* includes the unallocated share of GDP.

Table 4. Growth of consumption and investment

	Average annual growth rate (percent)					
	General government consumption		Private consumption, etc.		Gross domestic investment	
	1965–80	1980–86	1965–80	1980–86	1965–80	1980–86
Low-income economies	**5.7 w**	**5.4 w**	**3.8 w**	**5.4 w**	**7.4 w**	**13.2 w**
China and India	**6.1 w**	**6.1 w**	**4.0 w**	**6.2 w**	**8.3 w**	**14.9 w**
Other low-income	**4.1 w**	**1.7 w**	**2.9 w**	**2.7 w**	**3.7 w**	**0.4 w**
1 Ethiopia	6.4	5.6	3.0	1.6	−0.1	2.0
2 Bhutan	..	..	..	..	..	..
3 Burkina Faso	8.7	*3.2*	*3.1*	*0.9*	8.8	*−3.2*
4 Nepal	..	..	..	..	..	..
5 Bangladesh	a	a	2.7	3.5	0.0	3.6
6 Malawi	5.7	3.7	4.3	−0.1	9.0	−7.9
7 Zaire	0.7	−13.0	−0.2	−0.4	6.7	−0.3
8 Mali	1.9	−0.5	5.6	*5.3*	1.8	−7.9
9 Burma	a	a	3.5	5.7	5.3	−2.8
10 Mozambique	..	−11.0	..	−5.3	..	−22.8
11 Madagascar	2.0	−1.1	0.6	−0.6	1.5	−6.1
12 Uganda	a	..	1.2	..	−5.7	..
13 Burundi	7.3	2.9	4.0	1.8	9.0	5.0
14 Tanzania	a	−7.0	4.6	1.0	6.2	1.8
15 Togo	9.5	−0.4	5.0	−1.8	9.0	−2.0
16 Niger	2.9	0.7	−0.6	−0.6	6.3	−20.4
17 Benin	0.7	3.8	2.6	1.8	10.4	−15.5
18 Somalia	12.7	*−9.1*	2.0	*3.4*	0.4	*21.5*
19 Central African Rep.	−1.1	−3.0	4.2	0.2	−5.4	12.5
20 India	6.3	8.2	2.8	5.2	4.9	4.6
21 Rwanda	6.2	6.1	5.1	1.8	9.3	10.1
22 China	6.0	5.3	5.3	6.8	10.5	19.3
23 Kenya	10.6	−0.1	5.7	2.8	7.2	−5.1
24 Zambia	5.1	−3.3	0.1	0.5	−3.6	−7.1
25 Sierra Leone	a	a	2.6	−4.6	−1.0	−6.3
26 Sudan	0.2	−3.2	4.3	0.3	6.5	−5.2
27 Haiti	1.9	1.7	2.3	−1.5	14.8	−1.8
28 Pakistan	4.7	8.9	4.7	5.0	2.6	7.5
29 Lesotho	12.3	..	8.6	..	17.3	..
30 Ghana	3.8	*0.1*	1.4	−0.6	−1.6	*−0.5*
31 Sri Lanka	1.1	6.7	3.8	7.1	11.5	−4.9
32 Mauritania	10.0	−9.0	1.8	5.8	19.3	−4.3
33 Senegal	2.9	2.9	1.8	2.2	3.9	0.3
34 *Afghanistan*	..	..	..	..	..	..
35 *Chad*	..	..	..	..	..	..
36 *Guinea*	..	−5.2	..	*1.1*	..	−7.6
37 *Kampuchea, Dem.*	..	..	..	..	..	..
38 *Lao PDR*	..	..	..	..	..	..
39 *Viet Nam*	..	..	..	..	..	..
Middle-income economies	**7.9 w**	**1.8 w**	**6.5 w**	**2.0 w**	**8.9 w**	**−2.3 w**
Lower middle-income	**8.7 w**	**2.2 w**	**6.0 w**	**2.4 w**	**9.2 w**	**−3.4 w**
40 Liberia	3.4	1.3	3.2	0.8	6.4	−16.7
41 Yemen, PDR	..	..	..	..	..	..
42 Indonesia	11.4	4.2	6.3	5.3	16.1	3.7
43 Yemen Arab Rep.	..	9.9	..	*1.5*	..	−12.9
44 Philippines	7.7	−0.3	5.0	1.7	8.5	−17.6
45 Morocco	11.0	4.1	4.5	2.9	11.1	−2.2
46 Bolivia	8.2	−2.3	4.0	−0.7	4.3	−17.3
47 Zimbabwe	a	8.4	*6.3*	−2.2	0.9	−4.7
48 Nigeria	13.5	−1.2	6.7	−2.2	14.7	−13.7
49 Dominican Rep.	0.3	−2.3	7.1	−0.4	13.5	−0.7
50 Papua New Guinea	0.1	−3.1	3.7	1.5	1.4	−3.0
51 Côte d'Ivoire	12.7	−4.0	7.8	0.9	10.4	−21.6
52 Honduras	7.3	*−0.1*	4.3	*−1.9*	6.7	−2.6
53 Egypt, Arab Rep.	a	5.3	5.6	2.4	11.5	−2.8
54 Nicaragua	6.6	*20.6*	2.0	−9.0	..	*0.2*
55 Thailand	9.3	4.0	6.7	4.2	7.5	0.8
56 El Salvador	7.0	2.2	4.1	−0.9	6.6	−0.8
57 Botswana	12.0	*12.8*	9.2	*4.2*	21.0	−6.9
58 Jamaica	9.8	0.7	2.0	−0.1	−3.2	0.8
59 Cameroon	5.0	8.3	4.1	3.8	9.9	10.0
60 Guatemala	6.2	*0.3*	5.2	−1.4	7.3	−9.8
61 Congo, People's Rep.	5.5	4.1	2.8	5.0	4.5	−5.7
62 Paraguay	5.1	2.6	6.4	2.8	13.9	−6.0
63 Peru	5.6	−1.2	4.7	0.8	1.0	−13.9
64 Turkey	6.1	2.9	5.7	4.9	8.9	5.1
65 Tunisia	7.2	5.2	8.3	4.2	4.6	−1.8
66 Ecuador	12.2	−1.9	6.8	1.2	9.5	−5.6
67 Mauritius	7.1	2.0	4.5	0.6	8.0	11.7
68 Colombia	6.7	1.1	5.9	2.5	5.8	0.1

Note: For data comparability and coverage, see the technical notes. Figures in italics are for years other than those specified.

	Average annual growth rate (percent)					
	General government consumption		Private consumption, etc.		Gross domestic investment	
	1965–80	1980–86	1965–80	1980–86	1965–80	1980–86
69 Chile	4.0	1.4	1.0	−2.0	0.6	−7.4
70 Costa Rica	6.8	−0.5	5.2	1.5	9.4	0.7
71 Jordan	..	5.0	..	9.3	..	−5.8
72 Syrian Arab Rep.	15.0	*4.8*	10.1	*0.2*	14.3	*3.1*
73 *Lebanon*	..	..	..	..	..	..
Upper middle-income	**7.6** *w*	**1.6** *w*	**6.9** *w*	**1.8** *w*	**8.7** *w*	**−1.9** *w*
74 Brazil	7.0	0.8	9.0	2.7	11.2	−2.7
75 Malaysia	8.5	2.7	5.9	1.2	10.4	0.8
76 South Africa	4.9	3.7	3.3	1.5	4.0	−8.2
77 Mexico	8.5	3.0	5.8	−1.0	8.5	−7.6
78 Uruguay	3.2	1.2	2.4	−3.9	8.0	−16.3
79 Hungary	a	0.4	3.5	0.1	7.0	−3.2
80 Poland	..	*3.5*	..	*−1.7*	..	*−0.8*
81 Portugal	8.1	3.0	7.2	−0.2	4.5	−6.2
82 Yugoslavia	3.6	0.0	8.1	−1.8	6.2	1.6
83 Panama	7.4	3.5	4.6	4.3	5.9	−5.2
84 Argentina	3.6	−2.4	2.9	0.6	4.5	−12.6
85 Korea, Rep. of	7.7	4.2	7.8	5.5	15.9	9.6
86 Algeria	8.6	*5.3*	9.0	4.8	15.9	0.0
87 Venezuela	7.3	−0.4	8.8	−1.2	8.4	−8.4
88 Gabon	..	..	..	..	..	2.4
89 Greece	6.6	2.9	5.2	3.1	4.5	−2.4
90 Oman	..	..	..	..	..	..
91 Trinidad and Tobago	8.9	−3.5	6.7	−8.8	12.1	−15.8
92 Israel	8.8	−1.2	6.0	3.7	5.9	0.2
93 Hong Kong	7.7	5.8	9.0	6.5	8.6	−0.6
94 Singapore	10.1	8.3	7.8	4.5	14.4	3.3
95 *Iran, Islamic Rep.*	14.6	..	10.0	..	11.6	..
96 *Iraq*	..	..	..	..	..	..
97 *Romania*	..	..	..	..	..	..
Developing economies	**7.3** *w*	**2.7** *w*	**5.7** *w*	**2.9** *w*	**8.5** *w*	**2.4** *w*
Oil exporters	**11.1** *w*	**1.4** *w*	**7.4** *w*	**1.5** *w*	**11.3** *w*	**−3.1** *w*
Exporters of manufactures	**6.3** *w*	**3.9** *w*	**5.9** *w*	**4.2** *w*	**8.8** *w*	**8.0** *w*
Highly indebted countries	**7.0** *w*	**0.6** *w*	**6.6** *w*	**0.7** *w*	**8.4** *w*	**−6.3** *w*
Sub-Saharan Africa	**8.1** *w*	**−1.0** *w*	**4.9** *w*	**0.7** *w*	**8.8** *w*	**−9.3** *w*
High-income oil exporters	..	..	..	..	**16.7** *w*	..
98 Saudi Arabia	a	..	20.0	..	27.5	..
99 Kuwait	a	..	8.4	..	11.7	..
100 United Arab Emirates	..	..	..	..	..	..
101 *Libya*	19.7	..	19.1	..	7.3	..
Industrial market economies	**2.8** *w*	**2.9** *w*	**4.0** *w*	**2.6** *w*	**3.0** *w*	**2.8** *w*
102 Spain	5.0	3.9	5.4	0.7	4.0	−0.2
103 Ireland	6.1	1.2	3.8	−2.4	6.8	−1.6
104 New Zealand	3.3	1.1	2.9	1.9	1.4	3.3
105 Italy	3.3	2.6	4.6	1.9	2.5	−1.1
106 United Kingdom	2.3	1.0	2.2	2.7	1.2	4.7
107 Belgium	4.6	0.3	4.3	0.6	2.9	−2.2
108 Austria	3.7	1.9	4.4	1.9	4.5	1.4
109 Netherlands	3.1	0.8	4.3	0.2	1.6	2.4
110 France	3.5	1.8	4.9	2.0	3.8	−0.2
111 Australia	5.1	3.9	4.1	2.9	2.7	0.9
112 Germany, Fed. Rep.	3.5	1.3	4.0	1.1	1.7	−0.1
113 Finland	5.3	3.7	3.9	3.1	2.7	1.0
114 Denmark	4.8	0.9	2.3	2.5	1.2	7.1
115 Japan	5.1	3.1	6.2	2.9	6.7	3.2
116 Sweden	4.0	1.5	2.4	1.1	0.9	1.2
117 Canada	4.8	1.8	5.0	2.6	4.7	1.6
118 Norway	5.5	3.7	3.8	3.4	4.4	2.9
119 United States	1.4	4.5	3.4	3.5	2.1	5.6
120 Switzerland	2.7	2.2	2.5	1.3	0.8	2.6
Nonreporting nonmembers	..	..	..	..	..	..
121 *Albania*	..	..	..	..	..	..
122 *Angola*	..	..	..	..	..	..
123 *Bulgaria*	..	..	..	..	..	..
124 *Cuba*	..	..	..	..	..	..
125 *Czechoslovakia*	..	..	..	..	..	..
126 *German Dem. Rep.*	..	..	..	..	..	..
127 *Korea, Dem. Rep.*	..	..	..	..	..	..
128 *Mongolia*	..	..	..	..	..	..
129 *USSR*	..	..	..	..	..	..

a. General government consumption figures are not available separately; they are included in *private consumption, etc.*

Table 5. Structure of demand

	General government consumption		Private consumption, etc.		Gross domestic investment		Gross domestic savings		Exports of goods and nonfactor services		Resource balance	
Distribution of gross domestic product (percent)												
	1965	1986	1965	1986	1965	1986	1965	1986	1965	1986	1965	1986
Low-income economies	12 w	13 w	73 w	62 w	20 w	29 w	17 w	25 w	7 w	10 w	−7 w	−4 w
China and India	13 w	13 w	66 w	57 w	22 w	32 w	21 w	30 w	4 w	9 w	−1 w	−3 w
Other low-income	10 w	12 w	78 w	78 w	15 w	15 w	12 w	7 w	19 w	14 w	−3 w	−8 w
1 Ethiopia	11	17	77	80	13	9	12	3	12	13	−1	−7
2 Bhutan	..	..	..	..	..	..	..	..	..	..	..	..
3 Burkina Faso	9	*15*	87	*91*	12	*20*	4	*−7*	9	*16*	−8	*−26*
4 Nepal	a	8	100	84	6	19	0	9	8	13	−6	−10
5 Bangladesh	9	8	83	90	11	12	8	2	10	6	−4	−9
6 Malawi	16	18	84	75	14	10	0	7	19	22	−14	−3
7 Zaire	9	7	61	81	14	12	30	13	36	33	15	0
8 Mali	..	13	..	83	..	21	..	4	..	15	..	−17
9 Burma	a	14	87	74	19	15	13	12	14	..	−6	−3
10 Mozambique	..	15	..	86	..	9	..	−1	..	3	..	−10
11 Madagascar	23	13	74	76	10	14	4	10	16	14	−6	−3
12 Uganda	10	a	78	89	11	14	12	11	26	12	1	−3
13 Burundi	7	12	89	79	6	17	4	9	10	12	−2	−8
14 Tanzania	10	8	74	89	15	17	16	2	26	10	1	−15
15 Togo	8	15	76	71	22	28	17	13	20	33	−6	−14
16 Niger	6	11	90	82	8	11	3	7	9	18	−5	−4
17 Benin	11	9	87	90	11	13	3	0	13	14	−8	−12
18 Somalia	8	*12*	84	*93*	11	*15*	8	*−5*	17	7	−3	*−21*
19 Central African Rep.	22	9	67	88	21	16	11	2	27	20	−11	−13
20 India	10	12	74	67	18	23	16	21	4	6	−2	−2
21 Rwanda	14	20	81	71	10	19	5	9	12	12	−5	−10
22 China	15	14	59	50	25	39	25	36	4	11	1	−3
23 Kenya	15	19	70	55	14	26	15	26	31	27	1	0
24 Zambia	15	25	45	62	25	15	40	13	49	46	15	−2
25 Sierra Leone	8	a	83	92	12	10	9	8	30	13	−3	−1
26 Sudan	12	14	79	83	10	12	9	4	15	9	−1	−8
27 Haiti	8	12	90	83	7	12	2	6	13	14	−5	−6
28 Pakistan	11	12	76	81	21	17	13	7	8	12	−8	−10
29 Lesotho	18	35	109	143	11	33	−26	−78	16	12	−38	−112
30 Ghana	14	*10*	77	*82*	18	*10*	8	8	17	*10*	−10	−2
31 Sri Lanka	13	9	74	78	12	24	13	13	38	23	1	−11
32 Mauritania	19	14	54	71	14	25	27	15	42	56	13	−11
33 Senegal	17	17	75	77	12	14	8	6	24	28	−4	−8
34 *Afghanistan*	a	..	99	..	11	..	1	..	11	..	−10	..
35 *Chad*	20	..	74	..	12	..	6	..	19	..	−6	..
36 *Guinea*	..	*14*	..	*73*	..	*9*	..	*13*	..	*25*	..	*4*
37 *Kampuchea, Dem.*	16	..	71	..	13	..	12	..	12	..	−1	..
38 *Lao PDR*	..	..	..	..	..	..	..	..	..	..	..	..
39 *Viet Nam*	..	..	..	..	..	..	..	..	..	..	..	..
Middle-income economies	11 w	13 w	68 w	63 w	21 w	23 w	21 w	24 w	17 w	22 w	0 w	1 w
Lower middle-income	11 w	13 w	73 w	69 w	17 w	19 w	16 w	17 w	15 w	21 w	−1 w	−2 w
40 Liberia	12	17	61	65	17	10	27	18	50	43	10	9
41 Yemen, PDR	..	..	..	..	..	..	..	..	..	..	..	..
42 Indonesia	5	12	87	64	8	26	8	24	5	21	0	−2
43 Yemen Arab Rep.	..	22	..	93	..	21	..	−15	..	5	..	−36
44 Philippines	9	8	70	73	21	13	21	19	17	25	0	6
45 Morocco	12	17	76	70	10	20	12	13	18	25	1	−7
46 Bolivia	9	10	74	85	22	8	17	5	21	16	−5	−3
47 Zimbabwe	12	19	65	62	15	18	23	20	..	26	8	2
48 Nigeria	7	12	76	78	19	12	17	10	18	14	−2	−2
49 Dominican Rep.	19	8	75	80	10	*18*	6	12	16	*30*	−4	−6
50 Papua New Guinea	34	22	64	63	22	24	2	15	18	45	−20	−8
51 Côte d'Ivoire	11	15	61	62	22	12	29	22	37	40	7	11
52 Honduras	10	*17*	75	*70*	15	*17*	15	*13*	27	27	0	*−4*
53 Egypt, Arab Rep.	19	19	67	72	18	19	14	9	18	18	−4	−11
54 Nicaragua	8	*45*	74	*57*	21	*19*	18	−2	29	*14*	−3	*−21*
55 Thailand	10	13	71	62	20	21	19	25	18	27	−1	4
56 El Salvador	9	14	79	79	15	13	12	7	27	23	−2	−6
57 Botswana	24	28	89	47	6	26	−13	26	32	63	−19	*−1*
58 Jamaica	8	15	69	65	27	19	23	19	33	53	−4	0
59 Cameroon	14	9	73	62	13	25	13	28	25	23	−1	4
60 Guatemala	7	*7*	82	*84*	13	*11*	10	*9*	17	*19*	−3	−2
61 Congo, People's Rep.	14	20	80	50	22	29	5	30	36	47	−17	1
62 Paraguay	7	7	79	87	15	24	14	7	15	15	−1	−17
63 Peru	10	11	59	71	34	20	31	18	16	13	−3	−1
64 Turkey	12	9	74	69	15	25	13	22	6	18	−1	−3
65 Tunisia	15	17	71	66	28	24	14	17	19	31	−13	−7
66 Ecuador	9	12	80	68	14	20	11	20	16	23	−3	−1
67 Mauritius	13	11	74	64	17	17	13	25	36	63	−4	7
68 Colombia	8	12	75	68	16	18	17	20	11	20	1	3

Note: For data comparability and coverage, see the technical notes.   Figures in italics are for years other than those specified.

	General government consumption		Private consumption, etc.		Gross domestic investment		Gross domestic savings		Exports of goods and nonfactor services		Resource balance	
	1965	1986	1965	1986	1965	1986	1965	1986	1965	1986	1965	1986
69 Chile	11	13	73	69	15	15	16	18	14	31	1	4
70 Costa Rica	13	17	78	59	20	23	9	24	23	33	−10	1
71 Jordan	..	27	..	81	..	24	..	−9	..	39	..	−33
72 Syrian Arab Rep.	14	25	76	62	10	24	10	14	17	11	0	−11
73 *Lebanon*	10	..	81	..	22	..	9	..	36	..	−13	..
Upper middle-income	**11 w**	**13 w**	**65 w**	**61 w**	**23 w**	**24 w**	**23 w**	**26 w**	**18 w**	**22 w**	**1 w**	**2 w**
74 Brazil	11	a	67	76	20	21	22	24	8	9	2	3
75 Malaysia	15	17	61	51	20	25	24	32	42	57	4	6
76 South Africa	11	19	62	51	28	19	27	30	26	33	0	10
77 Mexico	7	*10*	72	*64*	22	*21*	21	27	9	*16*	−1	5
78 Uruguay	15	14	68	73	11	8	18	13	19	24	7	5
79 Hungary	a	10	75	65	26	26	25	25	..	40	−1	−1
80 Poland	..	a	..	70	..	29	..	30	..	18	..	2
81 Portugal	12	14	68	66	25	22	20	20	27	34	−5	−2
82 Yugoslavia	18	14	52	46	30	38	30	40	22	24	0	2
83 Panama	11	22	73	57	18	17	16	21	36	34	−2	3
84 Argentina	8	12	69	77	19	9	22	11	8	11	3	2
85 Korea, Rep. of	9	10	83	55	15	29	8	35	9	41	−7	6
86 Algeria	15	a	66	69	22	32	19	31	22	16	−3	−1
87 Venezuela	12	13	54	66	24	20	34	21	31	24	10	1
88 Gabon	11	26	52	55	31	37	37	19	43	37	6	−18
89 Greece	12	19	73	66	26	23	15	14	9	22	−11	−8
90 Oman	..	..	..	..	..	..	..	..	..	..	..	..
91 Trinidad and Tobago	12	19	67	62	26	22	21	18	65	33	−5	−4
92 Israel	20	31	65	58	29	17	15	11	19	38	−13	−6
93 Hong Kong	7	8	64	65	36	23	29	27	71	112	−7	4
94 Singapore	10	12	80	48	22	40	10	40	123	..	−12	0
95 *Iran, Islamic Rep.*	13	..	63	..	17	..	24	..	20	..	6	..
96 *Iraq*	20	..	50	..	16	..	31	..	38	..	15	..
97 *Romania*	..	..	..	..	..	..	..	..	..	..	..	..
Developing economies	**11 w**	**13 w**	**68 w**	**63 w**	**21 w**	**24 w**	**20 w**	**24 w**	**13 w**	**19 w**	**−1 w**	**0 w**
Oil exporters	**10 w**	**14 w**	**69 w**	**63 w**	**19 w**	**23 w**	**21 w**	**22 w**	**18 w**	**16 w**	**2 w**	**0 w**
Exporters of manufactures	**13 w**	**12 w**	**65 w**	**60 w**	**23 w**	**29 w**	**22 w**	**29 w**	**8 w**	**18 w**	**−1 w**	**0 w**
Highly indebted countries	**10 w**	**11 w**	**67 w**	**67 w**	**21 w**	**19 w**	**23 w**	**22 w**	**14 w**	**16 w**	**1 w**	**2 w**
Sub-Saharan Africa	**11 w**	**13 w**	**73 w**	**74 w**	**15 w**	**14 w**	**15 w**	**11 w**	**23 w**	**19 w**	**1 w**	**−2 w**
High-income oil exporters	**15 w**	**..**	**30 w**	**..**	**20 w**	**..**	**54 w**	**..**	**63 w**	**..**	**35 w**	**..**
98 Saudi Arabia	18	40	34	43	14	27	48	18	60	36	34	−9
99 Kuwait	13	..	26	..	16	..	60	..	68	..	45	..
100 United Arab Emirates	..	..	..	..	..	..	..	..	..	..	..	..
101 *Libya*	14	..	36	..	29	..	50	..	53	..	21	..
Industrial market economies	**15 w**	**17 w**	**61 w**	**62 w**	**23 w**	**21 w**	**23 w**	**21 w**	**12 w**	**17 w**	**0 w**	**0 w**
102 Spain	7	14	71	63	25	21	21	23	11	20	−3	2
103 Ireland	14	19	72	58	24	19	15	23	35	57	−9	3
104 New Zealand	12	16	61	60	28	23	26	24	21	29	−2	1
105 Italy	13	16	60	61	24	21	26	23	14	20	2	2
106 United Kingdom	17	21	64	62	20	18	19	18	19	26	−1	−1
107 Belgium	13	17	64	64	23	16	23	20	43	69	0	4
108 Austria	13	19	59	56	28	24	27	25	25	37	−1	1
109 Netherlands	15	16	59	59	27	21	26	25	43	54	−1	4
110 France	15	19	57	61	26	19	28	20	13	22	1	1
111 Australia	13	19	61	61	28	22	26	21	15	16	−2	−2
112 Germany, Fed. Rep.	15	20	56	56	28	19	29	24	18	30	0	5
113 Finland	14	21	60	55	28	23	27	24	20	27	−2	1
114 Denmark	16	24	59	55	26	22	25	22	29	32	−2	0
115 Japan	8	10	59	58	32	28	33	32	11	12	1	4
116 Sweden	18	27	56	52	27	18	26	21	22	33	−1	3
117 Canada	14	20	60	58	26	21	26	22	19	27	0	1
118 Norway	15	20	56	54	30	29	29	26	41	38	−1	−3
119 United States	17	19	63	66	20	18	21	15	5	7	1	−3
120 Switzerland	11	13	60	60	30	26	30	27	29	37	−1	1
Nonreporting nonmembers	**..**	**..**	**..**	**..**	**..**	**..**	**..**	**..**	**..**	**..**	**..**	**..**
121 *Albania*	..	..	..	..	..	..	..	..	..	..	..	..
122 *Angola*	..	..	..	..	..	..	..	..	..	..	..	..
123 *Bulgaria*	..	..	..	..	..	..	..	..	..	..	..	..
124 *Cuba*	..	..	..	..	..	..	..	..	..	..	..	..
125 *Czechoslovakia*	..	..	..	..	..	..	..	..	..	..	..	..
126 *German Dem. Rep.*	..	..	..	..	..	..	..	..	..	..	..	..
127 *Korea, Dem. Rep.*	..	..	..	..	..	..	..	..	..	..	..	..
128 *Mongolia*	..	..	..	..	..	..	..	..	..	..	..	..
129 *USSR*	..	..	..	..	..	..	..	..	..	..	..	..

Distribution of gross domestic product (percent)

a. General government consumption figures are not available separately; they are included in *private consumption, etc.* .

Table 6. Structure of consumption

	Percentage share of total household consumption (range of years, 1980–85)										
	Food		Clothing and footwear	Gross rents, fuel and power		Medical care	Education	Transport and communication		Other consumption	Other consumer durables
	Total	Cereals and tubers		Total	Fuel and power			Total	Motor cars	Total	
Low-income economies											
China and India											
Other low-income											
1 Ethiopia	32	12	8	17	5	3	2	12	4	27	8
2 Bhutan	..	..	..	..	..	..	..	..	..	..	..
3 Burkina Faso	..	..	..	..	..	..	..	..	..	..	..
4 Nepal	..	..	..	..	..	..	..	..	..	..	..
5 Bangladesh	..	..	..	..	..	..	..	..	..	..	..
6 Malawi	55	28	5	12	2	3	4	7	2	15	3
7 Zaire	55	15	10	11	3	3	1	6	0	14	3
8 Mali	57	22	5	6	5	1	2	20	2	10	3
9 Burma	..	..	..	..	..	..	..	..	..	..	..
10 Mozambique	..	..	..	..	..	..	..	..	..	..	..
11 Madagascar	58	22	6	12	7	1	6	4	1	14	2
12 Uganda	..	..	..	..	..	..	..	..	..	..	..
13 Burundi	..	..	..	..	..	..	..	..	..	..	..
14 Tanzania	62	30	12	8	3	1	5	2	0	10	3
15 Togo	..	..	..	..	..	..	..	..	..	..	..
16 Niger	..	..	..	..	..	..	..	..	..	..	..
17 Benin	37	12	14	11	2	5	4	14	2	15	5
18 Somalia	..	..	..	..	..	..	..	..	..	..	..
19 Central African Rep.	..	..	..	..	..	..	..	..	..	..	..
20 India	52	..	10	8	5	3	4	11	..	12	..
21 Rwanda	29	10	11	15	6	4	4	9	4	28	9
22 China	..	..	..	..	..	..	..	..	..	..	..
23 Kenya	42	18	8	13	3	0	2	9	1	26	6
24 Zambia	50	13	7	10	2	5	6	2	0	21	2
25 Sierra Leone	47	18	4	12	4	2	1	10	0	24	1
26 Sudan	58	..	5	13	4	6	4	2	..	12	..
27 Haiti	..	..	..	..	..	..	..	..	..	..	..
28 Pakistan	54	17	9	15	6	3	3	1	0	15	5
29 Lesotho	..	..	..	..	..	..	..	..	..	..	..
30 Ghana	50	..	13	11	..	3	5[a]	3	..	15	..
31 Sri Lanka	48	21	5	6	2	3	3	11	1	24	6
32 Mauritania	..	..	..	..	..	..	..	..	..	..	..
33 Senegal	53	16	12	14	6	2	3	6	0	10	3
34 Afghanistan	..	..	..	..	..	..	..	..	..	..	..
35 Chad	..	..	..	..	..	..	..	..	..	..	..
35 Guinea	..	..	..	..	..	..	..	..	..	..	..
36 Kampuchea, Dem.	..	..	..	..	..	..	..	..	..	..	..
37 Lao PDR	..	..	..	..	..	..	..	..	..	..	..
39 Viet Nam	..	..	..	..	..	..	..	..	..	..	..
Middle-income economies											
Lower middle-income											
40 Liberia	..	..	..	..	..	..	..	..	..	..	..
41 Yemen, PDR	..	..	..	..	..	..	..	..	..	..	..
42 Indonesia	48	21	7	13	7	2	4	4	0	22	5
43 Yemen Arab Rep.	..	..	..	..	..	..	..	..	..	..	..
44 Philippines	47	..	6	11	..	4	8	3	..	21	..
45 Morocco	48	14	10	14	3	3	6	5	0	13	5
46 Bolivia	33	..	9	13	1	5	7	12	..	21	..
47 Zimbabwe	43	9	11	13	5	0	8	6	1	19	6
48 Nigeria	52	18	7	10	2	3	4	4	1	20	6
49 Dominican Rep.	46	13	3	15	5	8	3	4	0	21	8
50 Papua New Guinea	..	..	..	..	..	..	..	..	..	..	..
51 Côte d'Ivoire	38	10	12	9	2	1	5	17	2	18	4
52 Honduras	39	..	9	21	..	8	5	3	..	15	..
53 Egypt, Arab Rep.	36	7	4	5	1	14	11	3	1	26	2
54 Nicaragua	..	..	..	..	..	..	..	..	..	..	..
55 Thailand	34	..	11	6	3	6	6	13	..	24	..
56 El Salvador	33	12	9	7	2	8	5	10	1	28	7
57 Botswana	35	13	8	15	5	4	9	8	2	22	7
58 Jamaica	38	..	4	16	7	3[a]	..	17	..	22	..
59 Cameroon	26	8	15	11	3	7	4	16	4	22	8
60 Guatemala	36	10	10	14	5	13	4	3	0	20	5
61 Congo, People's Rep.	31	12	3	6	2	22	2	16	1	19	3
62 Paraguay	30	6	12	21	4	2	3	10	1	22	3
63 Peru	35	8	7	15	3	4	6	10	0	24	7
64 Turkey	40	..	15	13	7	4	1	5	..	22	..
65 Tunisia	42	10	9	20	3	3	7	6	1	14	5
66 Ecuador	31	..	11	6[b]	1[b]	5	5[a]	11[c]	..	31	..
67 Mauritius	20	4	8	10	3	13	5	12	1	33	5
68 Colombia	29	..	6	13	2	7	5	13	..	27	..

Note: For data comparability and coverage, see the technical notes. Figures in italics are for years other than those specified.

	Food			Gross rents, fuel and power				Transport and communication		Other consumption	
	Total	Cereals and tubers	Clothing and footwear	Total	Fuel and power	Medical care	Education	Total	Motor cars	Total	Other consumer durables
69 Chile	29	7	8	13	2	5	6	11	0	29	5
70 Costa Rica	33	8	8	9	1	7	8	8	0	28	9
71 Jordan	36	..	6	6	..	5	7	6	..	34	..
72 Syrian Arab Rep.	..	..	..	..	..	..	..	..	..	..	..
73 *Lebanon*	..	..	..	..	..	..	..	..	..	..	..

Upper middle-income

	Food			Gross rents, fuel and power				Transport and communication		Other consumption	
74 Brazil	35	9	10	11	2	6	5	8	1	27	8
75 Malaysia	*30*	..	*5*	*9*	..	*5*	*8*	*16*	..	*27*	..
76 South Africa	..	..	..	..	..	..	..	..	..	..	..
77 Mexico	35d	..	10	8	..	5	5	12	..	25	..
78 Uruguay	31	7	7	12	2	6	4	13	0	27	5
79 Hungary	25	..	9	10	5	5	7	9	2	35	8
80 Poland	29	..	9	7	2	6	7	8	2	34	9
81 Portugal	34	..	10	8	3	6	5	13	3	24	7
82 Yugoslavia	27	..	10	9	4	6	5	11	2	32	9
83 Panama	38	7	3	11	3	8	9	7	0	24	6
84 Argentina	35	4	6	9	2	4	6	13	0	26	6
85 Korea, Rep. of	35	..	6	11	..	4	8	9	..	27	..
86 Algeria	..	..	..	..	..	..	..	..	..	..	..
87 Venezuela	38	..	4	8	..	8	7	10	..	25	..
88 Gabon	..	..	..	..	..	..	..	..	..	..	..
89 Greece	30	..	8	12	3	6	5	13	2	26	5
90 Oman	..	..	..	..	..	..	..	..	..	..	..
91 Trinidad and Tobago	..	..	..	..	..	..	..	..	..	..	..
92 Israel	26	..	4	20	2	6	9	10	..	25	..
93 Hong Kong	19	3	9	12	2	6	5	8	1	39	19
94 Singapore	19	..	8	11	..	7	12	13	..	30	..
95 *Iran, Islamic Rep.*	..	..	..	..	..	..	..	..	..	..	..
96 *Iraq*	..	..	..	..	..	..	..	..	..	..	..
97 *Romania*	..	..	..	..	..	..	..	..	..	..	..

Developing economies
Oil exporters
Exporters of manufactures
Highly indebted countries
Sub-Saharan Africa

High-income oil exporters

	Food			Gross rents, fuel and power				Transport and communication		Other consumption	
98 Saudi Arabia	..	..	..	..	..	..	..	..	..	..	..
99 Kuwait	..	..	..	..	..	..	..	..	..	..	..
100 United Arab Emirates	..	..	..	..	..	..	..	..	..	..	..
101 *Libya*	..	..	..	..	..	..	..	..	..	..	..

Industrial market economies

	Food			Gross rents, fuel and power				Transport and communication		Other consumption	
102 Spain	24	3	7	16	3	7	5	13	3	28	6
103 Ireland	22	4	5	11	5	10	7	11	3	33	5
104 New Zealand	12	..	6	14	2	9	6	19	6	34	9
105 Italy	19	2	8	14	4	10	7	11	3	30	7
106 United Kingdom	12	2	6	17	4	8	6	14	4	36	7
107 Belgium	15	2	6	17	7	10	9	11	3	31	7
108 Austria	16	2	9	17	5	10	8	15	3	26	7
109 Netherlands	13	2	6	18	6	11	8	10	3	33	8
110 France	16	2	6	17	5	13	7	13	3	29	7
111 Australia	13	..	5	21	2	10	8	13	4	31	7
112 Germany, Fed. Rep.	12	2	7	18	5	13	6	13	4	31	9
113 Finland	16	3	4	15	4	9	8	14	4	34	6
114 Denmark	13	2	5	19	5	8	9	13	5	33	7
115 Japan	19	3	6	17	3	10	7	9	1	32	7
116 Sweden	13	2	5	19	4	11	8	11	2	32	7
117 Canada	11	2	6	21	4	5	12	14	5	32	8
118 Norway	15	2	6	14	5	10	8	14	6	32	7
119 United States	13	2	6	18	4	14	8	14	5	27	7
120 Switzerland	17	..	4	17	6	15	..	9	..	38	..

Nonreporting nonmembers

	Food			Gross rents, fuel and power				Transport and communication		Other consumption	
121 *Albania*	..	..	..	..	..	..	..	..	..	..	..
122 *Angola*	..	..	..	..	..	..	..	..	..	..	..
123 *Bulgaria*	..	..	..	..	..	..	..	..	..	..	..
124 *Cuba*	..	..	..	..	..	..	..	..	..	..	..
125 *Czechoslovakia*	..	..	..	..	..	..	..	..	..	..	..
126 *German Dem. Rep.*	..	..	..	..	..	..	..	..	..	..	..
127 *Korea, Dem. Rep.*	..	..	..	..	..	..	..	..	..	..	..
128 *Mongolia*	..	..	..	..	..	..	..	..	..	..	..
129 *USSR*	..	..	..	..	..	..	..	..	..	..	..

Percentage share of total household consumption (range of years, 1980–85)

a. Data relate to government expenditure.   b. Excludes fuel.   c. Includes fuel.   d. Includes beverages and tobacco.

Table 7. Agriculture and food

	Value added in agriculture (millions of current dollars)		Cereal imports (thousands of metric tons)		Food aid in cereals (thousands of metric tons)		Fertilizer consumption (hundreds of grams of plant nutrient per hectare of arable land)		Average index of food production per capita (1979–81=100)
	1970	1986	1974	1986	1974/75	1985/86	1970[a]	1985	1984–86
Low-income economies	74,755 t	202,852 t	21,897 t	18,038 t	5,718 t	6,384 t	168 w	674 w	114 w
China and India	55,045 t	147,927 t	12,724 t	7,457 t	1,582 t	548 t	217 w	939 w	118 w
Other low-income	19,710 t	54,900 t	9,173 t	10,581 t	4,136 t	5,836 t	80 w	234 w	101 w
1 Ethiopia	931	2,403	118	1,047	54	793	4	47	87
2 Bhutan	..	..	3	18	0	3	0	10	107
3 Burkina Faso	126	423	99	82	28	109	3	46	112
4 Nepal	579	..	18	3	0	9	30	187	102
5 Bangladesh[b]	3,636	7,254	1,866	1,214	2,076	1,287	142	592	98
6 Malawi	119	404	17	6	0	5	52	143	90
7 Zaire[b]	585	1,739	343	361	1	101	8	10	100
8 Mali[b]	216	548	281	181	107	83	29	129	101
9 Burma[b]	819	3,899	26	0	9	..	34	198	124
10 Mozambique	..	1,505	62	393	34	252	27	12	85
11 Madagascar[b]	266	1,147	114	208	7	65	56	32	98
12 Uganda	929	2,524	37	17	0	7	13	0	111
13 Burundi	159	636	7	14	6	6	5	18	98
14 Tanzania	473	2,367	431	244	148	66	30	76	92
15 Togo[b]	85	318	6	66	11	9	3	69	91
16 Niger[b]	420	952	155	43	73	97	1	10	85
17 Benin	121	653	8	55	9	11	33	66	114
18 Somalia	167	1,335	42	274	111	126	31	36	98
19 Central African Rep.	60	372	7	40	1	11	11	15	94
20 India	23,227	64,487	5,261	..	1,582	257	114	504	112
21 Rwanda[b]	135	733	3	24	19	25	3	14	87
22 China[b]	31,818	83,440	7,463	7,457	0	290	384	1,692	123
23 Kenya	484	1,770	15	189	2	139	224	460	87
24 Zambia[b]	191	179	93	148	5	82	71	155	96
25 Sierra Leone	108	529	72	130	10	49	13	20	97
26 Sudan	757	2,630	125	636	46	904	31	75	96
27 Haiti	..	..	83	196	25	133	4	35	96
28 Pakistan	3,352	7,357	1,274	1,909	584	384	168	736	104
29 Lesotho	23	49	49	144	14	40	17	117	82
30 Ghana[b]	1,030	2,014	177	154	33	96	9	44	109
31 Sri Lanka	545	1,525	951	927	271	366	496	887	85
32 Mauritania	58	254	115	209	48	137	6	103	88
33 Senegal[b]	208	838	341	544	27	117	20	55	102
34 Afghanistan	..	..	5	126	10	170	24	91	99
35 Chad[b]	142	..	37	83	20	74	7	23	100
36 Guinea[b]	..	791	63	151	49	55	18	2	93
37 Kampuchea, Dem.	..	..	223	100	226	6	13	16	145
38 Lao PDR	..	..	53	34	8	4	4	22	123
39 Viet Nam	..	..	1,854	614	64	17	512	561	114
Middle-income economies	57,710 t	255,490 t	44,011 t	72,109 t	2,263 t	4,149 t	292 w	603 w	103 w
Lower middle-income	28,320 t	122,130 t	15,701 t	27,525 t	1,880 t	4,115 t	150 w	422 w	105 w
40 Liberia	91	368	42	124	3	76	55	100	99
41 Yemen, PDR	..	..	149	561	0	7	0	138	89
42 Indonesia	4,340	19,431	1,919	1,752	301	50	119	947	117
43 Yemen Arab Rep.[b]	118	1,252	158	247	33	57	1	121	109
44 Philippines[b]	1,996	8,029	817	1,094	89	181	214	358	94
45 Morocco[b]	789	3,140	891	1,610	75	142	130	356	109
46 Bolivia[b]	202	1,016	209	529	22	293	13	17	93
47 Zimbabwe	214	562	56	54	0	..	466	622	92
48 Nigeria	3,576	19,964	389	1,596	7	0	3	108	103
49 Dominican Rep.[b]	282	910	252	545	16	125	354	415	100
50 Papua New Guinea[b]	240	858	71	182	..	1	76	225	99
51 Côte d'Ivoire	462	2,645	172	601	4	0	71	118	105
52 Honduras	212	804	52	122	31	135	160	128	86
53 Egypt, Arab Rep.	1,942	8,199	3,877	8,846	610	1,799	1,282	3,473	105
54 Nicaragua[b]	193	649	44	122	3	41	184	494	76
55 Thailand[b]	1,851	6,962	97	191	0	89	76	210	109
56 El Salvador[b]	292	807	75	212	4	278	1,048	1,156	90
57 Botswana[b]	28	45	21	141	5	49	14	4	76
58 Jamaica[b]	93	149	340	364	1	203	886	439	103
59 Cameroon[b]	335	2,509	81	149	4	12	28	81	94
60 Guatemala[b]	..	..	138	242	9	53	224	518	97
61 Congo, People's Rep.[b]	49	173	34	104	2	2	112	69	93
62 Paraguay[b]	191	964	71	25	10	4	58	52	106
63 Peru[b]	1,409	1,824	637	1,767	37	180	297	201	100
64 Turkey	3,383	9,598	1,276	1,065	16	6	166	538	100
65 Tunisia	245	1,220	307	1,312	59	80	82	194	108
66 Ecuador[b]	401	1,704	152	288	13	5	123	285	100
67 Mauritius	30	178	160	168	22	5	2,081	2,615	100
68 Colombia	1,817	5,846	503	909	28	6	310	640	96

Note: For data comparability and coverage, see the technical notes. Figures in italics are for years other than those specified.

	Value added in agriculture (millions of current dollars)		Cereal imports (thousands of metric tons)		Food aid in cereals (thousands of metric tons)		Fertilizer consumption (hundreds of grams of plant nutrient per hectare of arable land)		Average index of food production per capita (1979–81 = 100)
	1970	1986	1974	1986	1974/75	1985/86	1970[a]	1985	1984–86
69 Chile[b]	558	..	1,737	264	323	10	317	391	101
70 Costa Rica[b]	222	883	110	152	1	119	1,086	1,332	92
71 Jordan	44	332	171	728	79	46	20	369	109
72 Syrian Arab Rep.[b]	435	3,500	339	942	47	30	67	407	94
73 Lebanon[b]	136	..	354	518	26	36	1,279	1,190	113
Upper middle-income	**29,390 t**	**143,360 t**	**28,310 t**	**44,584 t**			**402 w**	**739 w**	**102 w**
74 Brazil	4,401	22,940	2,485	5,940	31	6	169	425	106
75 Malaysia[b]	1,198	..	1,017	2,067	1	0	436	1,165	121
76 South Africa	1,362	3,207	127	734			425	657	83
77 Mexico[b]	4,330	11,467	2,881	2,710	..	11	246	693	97
78 Uruguay	268	614	70	131	6	0	392	378	101
79 Hungary[b]	1,010	3,906	408	144	..	..	1,485	2,527	111
80 Poland	..	..	4,185	2,056	..	5	1,715	2,299	107
81 Portugal	..	1,943	1,860	2,052	0	..	411	873	102
82 Yugoslavia	2,212	7,193	992	561			766	1,275	100
83 Panama[b]	149	479	63	113	3	0	391	452	98
84 Argentina[b]	2,438	8,867	0	1			24	43	99
85 Korea, Rep. of[b]	2,311	12,081	2,679	7,408	234	..	2,466	3,764	102
86 Algeria[b]	492	7,401	1,816	4,664	54	4	174	376	101
87 Venezuela[b]	826	4,471	1,270	1,694			165	1,082	93
88 Gabon[b]	60	323	13	74			0	62	98
89 Greece	1,569	5,939	1,341	1,008			858	1,739	104
90 Oman[b]	40	..	52	273			0	1,021	..
91 Trinidad and Tobago	40	262	208	243			640	601	92
92 Israel[c]	295	878	1,176	1,950	53	8	1,394	2,203	105
93 Hong Kong	62	159	657	859			0	0	110
94 Singapore[b]	44	119	682	829			2,667	10,400	97
95 Iran, Islamic Rep.	2,120	..	2,076	4,141			76	609	99
96 Iraq	579	..	870	3,338			35	325	102
97 Romania	..	..	1,381	1,597			559	1,460	112
Developing economies	**132,470 t**	**458,310 t**	**65,908 t**	**90,147 t**	**7,981 t**	**10,526 t**	**232 w**	**644 w**	**110 w**
Oil exporters	**21,070 t**	**112,550 t**	**15,977 t**	**30,813 t**	**1,038 t**	**1,911 t**	**131 w**	**555 w**	**105 w**
Exporters of manufactures	**72,270 t**	**216,070 t**	**29,229 t**	**30,852 t**	**1,900 t**	**567 t**	**341 w**	**950 w**	**116 w**
Highly indebted countries	**27,500 t**	**103,870 t**	**13,655 t**	**20,208 t**	**637 t**	**1,154 t**	**165 w**	**374 w**	**101 w**
Sub-Saharan Africa	**15,500 t**	**60,530 t**	**3,931 t**	**8,730 t**	**910 t**	**3,655 t**	**32 w**	**91 w**	**97 w**
High-income oil exporters	**340 t**	..	**1,327 t**	**7,347 t**			**58 w**	**1,218 w**	..
98 Saudi Arabia[b]	219	3,446	482	4,625			44	2,926	..
99 Kuwait[b]	8	..	101	433			0	2,333	..
100 United Arab Emirates	..	..	132	491			0	2,211	..
101 Libya	93	..	612	1,798			64	265	..
Industrial market economies	**87,730 t**	**304,700 t**	**65,494 t**	**60,855 t**			**986 w**	**1,164 w**	**103 w**
102 Spain[b]	..	14,260	4,675	2,997			595	819	104
103 Ireland	559	3,130	631	553			3,573	7,809	103
104 New Zealand[b]	..	2,960	92	84			8,875	8,748	107
105 Italy[b]	8,195	25,500	8,100	7,360			962	1,723	99
106 United Kingdom	2,976	10,250	7,541	3,861			2,521	3,566	111
107 Belgium[b]	920	2,740	4,585[d]	4,047[d]			5,686[d]	5,223[d]	98
108 Austria[b]	992	3,100	165	86			2,517	2,547	109
109 Netherlands[b]	1,850	7,130	7,199	4,435			7,165	7,812	109
110 France[b]	9,100	27,810	654	1,058			2,424	3,008	107
111 Australia[b]	2,292	8,360	2	26			246	235	101
112 Germany, Fed. Rep.[b]	5,951	17,680	7,164	5,170			4,208	4,273	113
113 Finland	1,205	5,030	222	98			1,931	2,104	110
114 Denmark	882	3,980	462	349			2,254	2,418	123
115 Japan[b]	12,467	61,550	19,557	27,119			3,849	4,273	108
116 Sweden	1,370	3,840	301	140			1,639	1,406	109
117 Canada	3,224	10,850	1,513	822			192	497	108
118 Norway[b]	624	2,580	713	479			2,471	2,776	108
119 United States[b]	27,856	89,490	460	1,246			800	939	99
120 Switzerland[b]	..	..	1,458	926			3,842	4,362	106
Nonreporting nonmembers	..	..	**15,476 t**	**32,847 t**			**561 w**	**1,210 w**	**108 w**
121 Albania	..	..	48	3			745	1,320	97
122 Angola	..	..	149	276	0	53	45	58	90
123 Bulgaria	..	..	649	1,475			1,446	2,090	101
124 Cuba	..	..	1,622	2,162			1,539	1,786	109
125 Czechoslovakia	..	..	1,296	428			2,402	3,365	118
126 German Dem. Rep.	..	..	2,821	2,776			3,202	3,296	110
127 Korea, Dem. Rep.	..	..	1,108	200			1,484	3,575	107
128 Mongolia	..	..	28	55			18	137	97
129 USSR	..	..	7,755	25,473			437	1,093	108

a. Average for 1969–71.   b. *Value added in agriculture* data are at purchaser values.   c. *Value added in agriculture* data refer to net domestic product at factor cost.   d. Includes Luxembourg.

Table 8. Structure of manufacturing

| | Value added in manufacturing (millions of current dollars) | | Distribution of manufacturing value added (percent; current prices) | | | | | | | | | |
| | | | Food and agriculture | | Textiles and clothing | | Machinery and transport equipment | | Chemicals | | Other[a] | |
	1970	1985	1970	1985	1970	1985	1970	1985	1970	1985	1970	1985
Low-income economies	**40,890 t**	**145,750 t**										
China and India	**35,750 t**	**130,700 t**										
Other low-income	**5,140 t**	**15,050 t**										
1 Ethiopia	149	492	46	51	31	23	0	0	2	3	21	22
2 Bhutan[b]	..	..	..	..	..	..	..	..	..	..	..	..
3 Burkina Faso	..	..	69	62	9	18	2	2	1	1	19	17
4 Nepal	32	108	..	..	..	..	..	..	..	..	..	..
5 Bangladesh[b]	387	1,332	30	26	47	36	3	6	11	17	10	15
6 Malawi	..	126	51	49	17	13	3	2	10	11	20	25
7 Zaire[b]	286	59	38	40	16	16	7	8	10	8	29	29
8 Mali[b]	22	82	36	..	40	..	4	..	5	..	14	..
9 Burma[b]	225	680	..	..	..	..	..	..	..	..	..	..
10 Mozambique	..	..	51	..	13	..	5	..	3	..	28	..
11 Madagascar[b]	118	..	36	35	28	47	6	3	7	..	23	15
12 Uganda	158	130	40	..	20	..	2	..	4	..	34	..
13 Burundi	16	87	57	75	19	11	0	0	7	5	17	9
14 Tanzania	116	393	36	28	28	26	5	8	4	7	26	31
15 Togo[b]	25	49	..	..	..	..	..	..	..	..	..	..
16 Niger[b]	30	58	..	..	..	..	..	..	..	..	..	..
17 Benin	19	43	..	58	..	16	..	0	..	5	..	21
18 Somalia	26	138	88	46	6	21	0	0	1	2	6	31
19 Central African Rep.	12	55	..	44	..	19	0	0	..	7	..	30
20 India	6,960	35,597	13	11	21	16	20	26	14	15	32	32
21 Rwanda[b]	8	260	86	77	0	1	3	0	2	12	8	9
22 China[b]	28,794[c]	95,103[c]	..	13	..	13	..	26	..	10	..	38
23 Kenya	174	631	31	35	9	12	18	14	7	9	35	29
24 Zambia[b]	181	513	49	44	9	13	5	9	10	9	27	25
25 Sierra Leone	22	71	..	36	..	4	..	0	..	38	..	22
26 Sudan	140	498	39	22	34	25	3	1	5	21	19	31
27 Haiti[b]	..	..	..	..	..	..	..	..	..	..	..	..
28 Pakistan	1,462	4,949	24	34	38	21	6	8	9	12	23	25
29 Lesotho	3	26	11	12	26	20	0	0	0	0	63	68
30 Ghana[b]	252	526	34	53	16	6	4	2	4	4	41	35
31 Sri Lanka	321	804	26	..	19	..	10	..	11	..	33	..
32 Mauritania	10	..	..	..	..	..	..	..	..	..	..	..
33 Senegal[b]	141	474	51	48	19	15	2	6	6	7	22	24
34 Afghanistan	..	..	..	..	..	..	..	..	..	..	..	..
35 Chad[b]	51	..	..	45	..	40	..	0	..	0	..	15
36 Guinea[b]	..	41	..	..	..	..	..	..	..	..	..	..
37 Kampuchea, Dem.	..	..	..	..	..	..	..	..	..	..	..	..
38 Lao PDR	..	..	..	..	..	..	..	..	..	..	..	..
39 Viet Nam	..	..	..	..	..	..	..	..	..	..	..	..
Middle-income economies	**64,310 t**	**358,300 t**										
Lower middle-income	**15,390 t**	**85,260 t**										
40 Liberia	15	49	..	..	..	..	..	..	..	..	..	..
41 Yemen, PDR	..	..	..	..	..	..	..	..	..	..	..	..
42 Indonesia[b]	994	11,447	..	23	..	11	..	10	..	10	..	47
43 Yemen Arab Rep.[b]	10	259	20	..	50	..	0	..	1	..	28	..
44 Philippines[b]	1,622	8,048	39	34	8	10	8	11	13	11	32	34
45 Morocco[b]	641	2,009	..	26	..	16	..	10	..	11	..	37
46 Bolivia[b]	135	817	33	37	34	16	0	2	3	4	29	41
47 Zimbabwe	293	1,314	24	28	16	16	9	10	11	9	40	36
48 Nigeria	438	7,373	..	29	..	11	..	17	..	9	..	35
49 Dominican Rep.[b]	275	698	74	63	5	7	1	1	6	5	14	24
50 Papua New Guinea[b]	35	203	25	52	1	1	37	10	5	3	33	35
51 Côte d'Ivoire	149	889	27	..	16	..	10	..	5	..	42	..
52 Honduras	91	419	58	56	10	10	1	1	4	4	28	29
53 Egypt, Arab Rep.	..	..	17	20	35	27	9	13	12	10	27	31
54 Nicaragua[b]	159	787	53	54	14	12	2	2	8	10	23	22
55 Thailand[b]	1,048	7,696	43	30	13	17	9	13	6	6	29	34
56 El Salvador[b]	194	598	40	36	30	18	3	4	8	14	18	29
57 Botswana[b]	5	49	..	52	..	12	..	0	..	4	..	32
58 Jamaica[b]	221	409	46	50	7	6	0	0	10	13	36	31
59 Cameroon[b]	119	952	47	50	16	13	5	7	4	6	28	23
60 Guatemala[b]	..	..	42	40	14	10	4	3	12	17	27	29
61 Congo, People's Rep.[b]	..	128	65	47	4	13	1	3	7	9	23	29
62 Paraguay[b]	99	513	56	..	16	..	1	..	5	..	21	..
63 Peru[b]	1,413	3,426	25	25	14	12	7	12	7	11	47	39
64 Turkey	1,930	12,277	26	20	15	14	8	15	7	8	45	43
65 Tunisia	121	981	29	17	18	19	4	7	13	13	36	44
66 Ecuador[b]	305	2,369	43	35	14	13	3	7	8	9	32	37
67 Mauritius	26	185	75	37	6	34	5	4	3	5	12	21
68 Colombia	1,154	5,565	31	33	20	14	8	9	11	13	29	32

Note: For data comparability and coverage, see the technical notes.   Figures in italics are for years other than those specified.

	Value added in manufacturing (millions of current dollars)		Distribution of manufacturing value added (percent; current prices)									
			Food and agriculture		Textiles and clothing		Machinery and transport equipment		Chemicals		Other[a]	
	1970	1985	1970	1985	1970	1985	1970	1985	1970	1985	1970	1985
69 Chile[b]	2,092	..	17	28	12	7	11	4	5	9	55	53
70 Costa Rica[b]	..	..	48	47	12	10	6	6	7	10	28	27
71 Jordan	32	494	21	27	14	6	7	0	6	10	52	57
72 Syrian Arab Rep.[b]	..	..	37	28	40	19	3	10	2	6	19	38
73 Lebanon[b]	..	..	27	..	19	..	1	..	3	..	49	..
Upper middle-income	**48,920 t**	**273,040 t**										
74 Brazil	10,433	58,089	16	15	13	12	22	24	10	9	39	40
75 Malaysia[b]	500	..	26	21	3	6	8	23	9	10	54	40
76 South Africa	3,914	11,096	15	16	13	7	17	16	10	12	45	49
77 Mexico[b]	8,416	43,613	28	24	15	12	13	14	11	12	34	39
78 Uruguay	..	..	34	32	21	20	7	6	6	10	32	32
79 Hungary[b]	..	..	12	8	13	11	28	34	8	12	39	35
80 Poland	..	..	20	17	19	16	24	30	8	6	28	32
81 Portugal	..	..	18	17	19	22	13	16	10	8	39	38
82 Yugoslavia	..	..	10	12	15	17	23	25	7	7	45	40
83 Panama[b]	127	420	41	49	9	8	1	2	5	7	44	35
84 Argentina[b]	5,761	17,954	24	24	14	10	18	16	9	13	35	37
85 Korea, Rep. of[b]	1,880	24,466	26	16	17	17	11	23	11	9	35	36
86 Algeria[b]	682	6,157	32	26	20	20	9	11	4	1	35	41
87 Venezuela[b]	1,849	10,556	30	22	13	8	9	7	8	10	39	54
88 Gabon[b]	..	..	37	..	7	..	6	..	6	..	44	..
89 Greece	1,642	5,448	20	20	20	22	13	14	7	7	40	38
90 Oman[b]	0	267	..	29	..	0	..	0	..	0	..	71
91 Trinidad and Tobago	198	516	..	20	..	4	..	10	..	6	..	60
92 Israel	..	..	15	13	14	9	23	28	8	8	41	42
93 Hong Kong	1,013	6,739	4	5	41	39	16	21	2	2	36	33
94 Singapore[b]	388	4,311	12	6	5	4	28	49	4	8	51	33
95 Iran, Islamic Rep.	1,501	..	30	13	20	22	18	22	6	7	26	36
96 Iraq	325	..	26	..	14	..	7	..	3	..	50	..
97 Romania	..	..	..	..	..	..	..	..	..	..	..	..
Developing economies	**105,200 t**	**504,050 t**										
Oil exporters	**16,010 t**	**114,150 t**										
Exporters of manufactures	**63,780 t**	**289,200 t**										
Highly indebted countries	**38,730 t**	**186,920 t**										
Sub-Saharan Africa	**3,310 t**	**19,130 t**										
High-income oil exporters	**600 t**	**..**										
98 Saudi Arabia[b]	372	7,586	..	..	..	..	..	..	..	..	..	..
99 Kuwait[b]	120	1,654	5	12	4	8	1	4	4	11	86	65
100 United Arab Emirates	..	2,715	..	..	..	..	..	..	..	..	..	..
101 Libya	81	1,215	..	..	..	..	..	..	..	..	..	..
Industrial market economies	**598,270 t**	**2,012,650 t**										
102 Spain[b]	..	44,891	13	17	15	10	16	22	11	9	45	43
103 Ireland	785	696	31	28	19	7	13	20	7	15	30	28
104 New Zealand[b]	1,784	6,040	24	27	13	10	15	17	4	6	43	41
105 Italy[b]	29,205	93,973	10	7	13	13	24	32	13	10	40	38
106 United Kingdom	35,954	101,470	13	15	9	6	31	32	10	11	37	37
107 Belgium[b]	8,226	18,570	17	20	12	8	22	23	9	14	40	36
108 Austria[b]	4,873	18,299	17	18	12	9	19	24	6	6	45	43
109 Netherlands[b]	8,652	23,063	17	19	8	4	27	28	13	11	36	38
110 France[b]	40,502	124,436	14	18	10	7	29	33	8	9	39	34
111 Australia[b]	9,495	30,730	16	17	9	7	24	23	7	7	43	46
112 Germany, Fed. Rep.[b]	70,888	201,640	13	12	8	5	32	38	9	10	38	36
113 Finland	2,588	12,199	13	13	10	7	20	24	6	7	51	50
114 Denmark	2,929	9,729	20	22	8	6	24	24	8	10	40	38
115 Japan[b]	73,339	395,148	8	10	8	6	33	37	11	9	40	38
116 Sweden	8,333	20,878	10	10	6	2	30	35	5	8	49	45
117 Canada	16,710	58,862	16	15	8	7	23	25	7	9	46	44
118 Norway[b]	2,416	7,939	15	20	7	3	23	26	7	7	49	44
119 United States[b]	254,115	803,391	12	12	8	5	31	36	10	10	39	38
120 Switzerland[b]	..	..	10	..	7	..	31	..	9	..	42	..
Nonreporting nonmembers												
121 Albania	..	..	..	..	..	..	..	..	..	..	..	..
122 Angola	..	..	..	..	..	..	..	..	..	..	..	..
123 Bulgaria	..	..	..	..	..	..	..	..	..	..	..	..
124 Cuba	..	..	..	62	..	6	..	11	..	7	..	14
125 Czechoslovakia	..	..	9	9	12	11	34	38	6	8	39	35
126 German Dem. Rep.	..	..	..	..	..	..	..	..	..	..	..	..
127 Korea, Dem. Rep.	..	..	..	..	..	..	..	..	..	..	..	..
128 Mongolia	..	..	..	..	..	..	..	..	..	..	..	..
129 USSR	..	..	..	..	..	..	..	..	..	..	..	..

a. Includes unallocable data; see the technical notes.   b. *Value added in manufacturing* data are at purchaser values.   c. World Bank estimate.

Table 9. Manufacturing earnings and output

| | Earnings per employee | | | | | Total earnings as percentage of value added | | | | Gross output per employee (1980=100) | | | |
| | Growth rates | | Index (1980=100) | | | | | | | | | | |
	1970–80	1980–85	1983	1984	1985	1970	1983	1984	1985	1970	1983	1984	1985
Low-income economies													
China and India													
Other low-income													
1 Ethiopia	−4.7	−3.5	101	94	79	24	20	19	19	61	110	109	113
2 Bhutan	..	..	..	..	..	..	..	..	..	..	..	..	..
3 Burkina Faso	..	1.3	94	105	107	..	18	20	20	..	91	97	106
4 Nepal	..	..	..	..	..	..	..	..	..	..	..	..	..
5 Bangladesh	−2.9	−3.9	84	85	83	26	31	32	32	116	98	98	98
6 Malawi	..	..	105	..	..	36	38	..	..	121	92	..	..
7 Zaire	..	..	..	..	..	..	..	..	..	..	..	..	..
8 Mali	−8.4	..	..	..	..	46	..	..	..	97	..	..	..
9 Burma	..	..	..	..	..	..	..	..	..	..	..	..	..
10 Mozambique	..	..	..	..	..	29	..	..	..	..	..	..	..
11 Madagascar	−0.9	−12.9	60	62	..	36	40	36	..	91	50	57	..
12 Uganda	..	..	..	..	..	..	..	..	..	..	..	..	..
13 Burundi	−6.1	..	133	..	..	..	18	..	..	..	135	..	..
14 Tanzania	..	−14.5	61	53	45	42	35	34	34	122	77	78	74
15 Togo	..	..	..	..	..	..	..	..	..	..	..	..	..
16 Niger	..	..	..	..	..	..	25	25	25	..	..	..	..
17 Benin	..	..	..	..	..	..	25	25	25	..	..	..	..
18 Somalia	−6.4	−7.9	91	71	69	28	30	30	30	..	91	71	69
19 Central African Rep.	..	0.3	101	105	103	..	56	51	51	..	77	74	74
20 India	−0.2	4.6	113	116	122	47	49	48	48	95	125	138	145
21 Rwanda	..	..	..	..	..	22	..	19	..	..	..	..	..
22 China	..	..	..	..	..	..	..	..	..	..	..	..	..
23 Kenya	−3.4	−5.6	80	79	76	53	46	46	46	38	90	90	90
24 Zambia	−3.2	−2.1	96	96	95	33	26	26	26	110	98	97	103
25 Sierra Leone	..	..	..	..	..	..	..	..	..	..	..	..	..
26 Sudan	..	..	..	..	..	31	..	..	..	..	..	..	..
27 Haiti	−3.0	−0.4	108	107	102	..	..	..	..	..	..	..	..
28 Pakistan	3.4	7.0	116	130	134	21	20	20	20	51	129	139	151
29 Lesotho	..	..	112	..	..	..	48	48	48	..	110	137	151
30 Ghana	..	..	48	..	..	23	18	..	..	193	76	..	..
31 Sri Lanka	..	..	..	..	..	..	..	..	..	70	..	..	..
32 Mauritania	..	..	..	..	..	..	..	..	..	..	..	..	..
33 Senegal	−4.8	0.5	105	97	101	..	44	43	44	..	125	96	102
34 *Afghanistan*	..	..	..	..	..	..	..	..	..	..	..	..	..
35 *Chad*	..	..	..	..	..	..	..	..	..	..	..	..	..
36 *Guinea*	..	..	..	..	..	..	..	..	..	..	..	..	..
37 *Kampuchea, Dem.*	..	..	..	..	..	..	..	..	..	..	..	..	..
38 *Lao PDR*	..	..	..	..	..	..	..	..	..	..	..	..	..
39 *Viet Nam*	..	..	..	..	..	..	..	..	..	..	..	..	..
Middle-income economies													
Lower middle-income													
40 Liberia	..	3.1	102	111	107	..	..	..	..	..	..	..	..
41 Yemen, PDR	..	..	..	..	..	..	..	..	..	..	..	..	..
42 Indonesia	4.7	8.1	128	132	153	26	21	18	21	42	129	138	156
43 Yemen Arab Rep.	..	..	..	..	..	..	..	..	..	..	..	..	..
44 Philippines	−3.3	..	..	..	..	21	19	19	20	102	123	114	..
45 Morocco	..	−3.7	88	82	85	..	51	51	51	..	89	83	81
46 Bolivia	2.5	4.4	99	122	..	44	35	35	..	68	66	61	..
47 Zimbabwe	1.6	5.4	106	114	142	43	40	44	44	98	98	104	113
48 Nigeria	0.0	−4.8	86	..	..	18	21	..	..	105	131	..	..
49 Dominican Rep.	−1.0	−3.2	101	101	79	35	23	24	24	63	106	99	91
50 Papua New Guinea	2.9	−0.4	88	89	96	42	37	36	36	..	..	..	..
51 Côte d'Ivoire	−0.9	..	136	..	..	27	..	..	..	52	..	..	..
52 Honduras	−0.4	..	..	..	..	..	38	38	38	..	..	..	..
53 Egypt, Arab Rep.	4.0	2.7	122	117	121	54	57	57	57	91	151	155	172
54 Nicaragua	..	−9.2	76	71	63	16	22	20	22	206	122	107	104
55 Thailand	1.1	10.6	135	151	160	25	24	24	24	70	146	159	163
56 El Salvador	2.4	..	90	..	..	28	28	..	..	71	92	..	..
57 Botswana	*10.4*	−4.2	80	81	85	..	39	40	..	..	70	69	..
58 Jamaica	−0.2	..	..	..	..	43	..	..	..	..	..	..	..
59 Cameroon	..	..	..	..	..	29	37	37	37	..	..	..	..
60 Guatemala	−3.2	1.0	107	110	106	..	23	24	24	..	..	..	..
61 Congo, People's Rep.	..	..	..	..	..	34	..	57	..	..	..	..	..
62 Paraguay	..	..	..	..	..	..	..	..	..	..	..	..	..
63 Peru	..	−1.9	86	87	..	..	19	19	19	83	69	66	79
64 Turkey	3.7	−3.5	96	84	89	26	25	24	24	108	128	131	125
65 Tunisia	4.2	−5.2	83	83	78	44	47	47	47	95	94	91	87
66 Ecuador	2.9	7.1	93	143	140	27	35	44	44	83	115	132	117
67 Mauritius	1.7	1.0	96	92	112	34	50	47	48	139	107	90	104
68 Colombia	−0.2	4.4	109	117	122	25	21	20	21	84	102	111	119

Note: For data comparability and coverage, see the technical notes.   Figures in italics are for years other than those specified.

	Earnings per employee					Total earnings as percentage of value added				Gross output per employee (1980=100)			
	Growth rates		Index (1980=100)										
	1970–80	1980–85	1983	1984	1985	1970	1983	1984	1985	1970	1983	1984	1985
69 Chile	..	0.0	112	105	111	19	17	15	18	60	123	..	..
70 Costa Rica	..	..	..	..	..	41	..	..	..	..	..	..	..
71 Jordan	..	0.6	109	101	..	37	30	30	..	..	157	174	..
72 Syrian Arab Rep.	2.2	−1.4	101	96	..	33	31	31	32	72	136	129	169
73 *Lebanon*	..	..	..	..	..	..	..	..	..	..	..	..	..

Upper middle-income

	1970–80	1980–85	1983	1984	1985	1970	1983	1984	1985	1970	1983	1984	1985
74 Brazil	4.0	−2.1	84	91	93	22	20	20	20	71	71	72	74
75 Malaysia	2.0	8.3	119	125	153	29	30	29	30	96	136	..	..
76 South Africa	2.7	1.3	108	109	106	46	52	50	50	50	93	96	95
77 Mexico	1.2	−5.9	75	73	86	44	24	21	26	77	101	108	107
78 Uruguay	..	−3.7	102	78	96	..	29	21	22	..	114	115	106
79 Hungary	4.0	1.3	101	106	108	28	32	33	34	41	114	116	111
80 Poland	..	..	..	..	..	..	..	..	..	..	..	..	..
81 Portugal	2.5	−1.7	94	87	98	34	44	38	43	..	114	117	120
82 Yugoslavia	1.3	−2.7	92	87	94	39	33	30	30	59	105	109	100
83 Panama	0.2	5.0	117	..	..	32	32	..	..	67	92	92	92
84 Argentina	1.4	4.1	103	126	104	30	20	23	19	79	105	111	103
85 Korea, Rep. of	10.0	4.4	109	119	119	25	26	26	27	40	126	139	139
86 Algeria	0.2	−3.0	88	88	83	45	53	53	53	101	94	93	94
87 Venezuela	3.8	0.5	119	109	110	31	32	26	26	118	116	111	112
88 Gabon	..	..	..	..	..	..	..	..	..	..	..	..	..
89 Greece	5.0	−1.7	91	92	93	32	39	39	39	57	93	93	95
90 Oman	..	..	..	..	..	..	61	61	61	..	..	..	..
91 Trinidad and Tobago	2.7	8.4	136	132	120	..	41	41	41	..	116	111	105
92 Israel	8.8	..	..	..	..	36	68	48	45	..	..	..	..
93 Hong Kong	6.3	3.1	103	106	119	..	47	57	51	..	..	..	..
94 Singapore	3.6	8.9	130	142	152	36	36	36	38	74	106	114	115
95 *Iran, Islamic Rep.*	..	..	..	..	..	25	..	..	..	85	..	..	..
96 *Iraq*	..	..	..	..	..	36	..	..	..	..	..	..	..
97 *Romania*	..	..	..	..	..	..	..	..	..	..	..	..	..

Developing economies
  Oil exporters
  Exporters of manufactures
  Highly indebted countries
  Sub-Saharan Africa

High-income oil exporters

	1970–80	1980–85	1983	1984	1985	1970	1983	1984	1985	1970	1983	1984	1985
98 Saudi Arabia	..	..	..	..	..	..	..	..	..	..	..	..	..
99 Kuwait	..	3.9	113	115	..	12	38	46	..	96	132	..	..
100 United Arab Emirates	..	..	..	..	..	..	..	..	..	..	..	..	..
101 *Libya*	..	..	..	..	..	37	..	..	..	45	..	..	..

Industrial market economies

	1970–80	1980–85	1983	1984	1985	1970	1983	1984	1985	1970	1983	1984	1985
102 Spain	4.5	3.4	101	111	119	52	41	43	43	..	117	122	129
103 Ireland	4.1	7.2	96	120	142	49	36	39	39	..	..	..	..
104 New Zealand	1.2	−2.8	94	92	88	62	62	55	57	..	106	116	..
105 Italy	4.3	0.2	98	104	101	41	45	46	43	57	107	118	114
106 United Kingdom	1.7	3.0	106	109	117	52	44	44	45	..	121	128	130
107 Belgium	4.6	−1.2	97	96	95	46	48	47	46	51	114	117	120
108 Austria	3.4	1.6	104	103	111	47	56	55	56	64	110	115	120
109 Netherlands	2.5	3.0	101	111	114	52	54	57	57	69	107	115	116
110 France	..	..	..	..	..	..	..	..	..	64	105	110	..
111 Australia	2.9	1.3	106	107	106	53	56	51	48	72	101	109	..
112 Germany, Fed. Rep.	3.5	0.5	99	101	102	46	48	48	46	60	108	114	117
113 Finland	2.6	1.9	105	107	110	47	44	43	44	72	109	113	119
114 Denmark	2.5	−0.4	100	98	97	56	53	52	52	64	112	113	109
115 Japan	3.1	2.2	105	107	113	32	36	35	36	45	110	120	130
116 Sweden	0.5	−0.3	96	97	98	52	37	37	37	72	116	121	124
117 Canada	1.8	2.5	101	102	117	53	49	46	49	69	..	..	..
118 Norway	2.6	1.0	98	101	105	50	58	55	57	75	104	109	118
119 United States	0.1	1.3	102	104	106	47	40	39	40	63	107	114	117
120 Switzerland	..	..	..	..	..	..	..	..	..	..	..	..	..

Nonreporting nonmembers

	1970–80	1980–85	1983	1984	1985	1970	1983	1984	1985	1970	1983	1984	1985
121 *Albania*	..	..	..	..	..	..	..	..	..	..	..	..	..
122 *Angola*	..	..	..	..	..	..	..	..	..	..	..	..	..
123 *Bulgaria*	..	..	..	..	..	..	..	..	..	..	..	..	..
124 *Cuba*	..	..	..	..	..	..	..	..	..	..	..	..	..
125 *Czechoslovakia*	..	..	..	..	..	..	..	..	..	..	..	..	..
126 *German Dem. Rep.*	..	..	..	..	..	..	..	..	..	..	..	..	..
127 *Korea, Dem. Rep.*	..	..	..	..	..	..	..	..	..	..	..	..	..
128 *Mongolia*	..	..	..	..	..	..	..	..	..	..	..	..	..
129 *USSR*	..	..	..	..	..	..	..	..	..	..	..	..	..

Table 10. Commercial energy

	Average annual energy growth rate (percent)				Energy consumption per capita (kilograms of oil equivalent)		Energy imports as a percentage of merchandise exports	
	Energy production		Energy consumption					
	1965–80	1980–86	1965–80	1980–86	1965	1986	1965	1986
Low-income economies	**9.1 w**	**6.4 w**	**8.2 w**	**5.6 w**	**131 w**	**314 w**	**5 w**	**9 w**
China and India	**9.1 w**	**6.6 w**	**8.8 w**	**5.8 w**	**146 w**	**394 w**	**4 w**	**6 w**
Other low-income	**9.0 w**	**2.9 w**	**2.9 w**	**3.8 w**	**71 w**	**86 w**	**7 w**	**17 w**
1 Ethiopia	7.5	5.3	4.1	2.1	10	21	8	36
2 Bhutan	..	..			..	..	..	..
3 Burkina Faso			10.5	0.2	7	18	11	7
4 Nepal	18.4	14.6	6.2	11.6	6	23	10	25
5 Bangladesh		17.3	..	8.8	..	46	..	17
6 Malawi	18.2	5.0	8.0	−0.7	25	43	7	8
7 Zaire	9.4	2.7	3.6	0.8	74	73	6	2
8 Mali	38.6	9.4	7.0	2.3	14	23	16	27
9 Burma	8.4	5.3	4.9	5.8	39	76	4	3
10 Mozambique	19.8	−50.1	2.2	1.8	81	86	13	..
11 Madagascar	3.9	11.0	3.5	1.2	34	40	8	12
12 Uganda	−0.5	2.7	−0.5	4.4	36	26	1	6
13 Burundi		15.7	6.0	10.4	5	21	11	6
14 Tanzania	7.3	2.5	3.7	2.0	37	35	10	39
15 Togo	2.9	11.4	10.7	−3.2	27	52	4	13
16 Niger		17.6	12.5	3.3	8	42	9	9
17 Benin			9.9	5.4	21	46	10	45
18 Somalia			16.7	1.8	14	82	8	8
19 Central African Rep.	6.7	1.0	2.2	4.6	22	30	9	1
20 India	5.6	8.9	5.8	6.4	100	208	8	19
21 Rwanda	8.8	8.2	15.2	4.9	8	42	10	25
22 China	10.0	6.0	9.8	5.6	178	532	0	2
23 Kenya	13.1	10.4	4.5	−0.8	110	100	13	21
24 Zambia	25.7	1.0	4.0	−0.4	464	381	6	12
25 Sierra Leone			0.8	−1.8	109	77	11	19
26 Sudan	17.8	0.6	2.0	0.3	67	58	5	..
27 Haiti		5.3	8.4	1.6	24	50	6	4
28 Pakistan	6.5	7.4	3.5	6.9	135	205	7	23
29 Lesotho			..	..	..	..	..	..
30 Ghana	17.7	−10.7	7.8	−4.9	76	131	6	15
31 Sri Lanka	10.4	10.7	2.2	4.1	107	139	6	23
32 Mauritania			9.5	−0.2	48	114	2	8
33 Senegal			7.4	−2.3	79	116	8	25
34 *Afghanistan*	15.7	2.2	5.6	14.3	30	71	8	..
35 *Chad*			..	..	..	..	..	..
36 *Guinea*	16.5	1.8	2.3	0.6	56	59	7	..
37 *Kampuchea, Dem.*		4.6	7.6	2.1	19	60	..	..
38 *Lao PDR*		−0.6	4.2	1.9	22	37	..	..
39 *Viet Nam*	5.3	−0.4	−2.6	1.1	106	87	..	..
Middle-income economies	**4.9 w**	**3.0 w**	**6.6 w**	**2.8 w**	**487 w**	**883 w**	**8 w**	**12 w**
Lower middle-income	**10.6 w**	**2.8 w**	**7.0 w**	**4.1 w**	**179 w**	**346 w**	**8 w**	**12 w**
40 Liberia	14.6	−3.2	7.9	−12.4	182	166	6	10
41 Yemen, PDR			−6.4	2.7	..	714	..	..
42 Indonesia	9.9	0.9	8.4	3.9	91	213	3	14
43 Yemen Arab Rep.			21.0	13.8	7	102	..	..
44 Philippines	9.0	11.6	5.8	−1.9	160	180	12	17
45 Morocco	2.5	−2.5	7.9	2.7	124	246	5	22
46 Bolivia	9.5	−0.6	7.7	−2.0	155	255	1	2
47 Zimbabwe	−0.7	−0.9	5.2	0.4	441	517	7	7
48 Nigeria	17.3	−2.8	12.9	6.5	34	134	7	2
49 Dominican Rep.	10.9	7.3	11.5	2.6	127	337	8	28
50 Papua New Guinea	13.7	6.7	13.0	2.6	56	244	11	..
51 Côte d'Ivoire	11.1	17.0	8.6	2.7	101	175	5	5
52 Honduras	14.0	1.7	7.6	1.5	111	192	5	10
53 Egypt, Arab Rep.	10.7	7.6	6.2	7.3	313	577	11	8
54 Nicaragua	2.6	2.7	6.5	1.7	172	259	6	20
55 Thailand	9.0	47.3	10.1	8.2	81	325	11	13
56 El Salvador	9.0	3.6	7.0	1.5	140	216	5	8
57 Botswana	8.8	2.7	9.5	2.2	191	430	..	..
58 Jamaica	−0.9	4.2	6.1	−4.5	703	844	12	23
59 Cameroon	13.0	20.2	6.3	6.8	67	142	6	4
60 Guatemala	12.5	6.7	6.8	−1.3	150	171	9	10
61 Congo, People's Rep.	41.1	10.1	7.8	5.0	90	225	10	5
62 Paraguay		15.9	9.7	5.1	84	224	17	32
63 Peru	6.6	−0.1	5.0	−0.3	395	478	3	1
64 Turkey	4.3	9.3	8.5	7.3	258	750	12	26
65 Tunisia	20.4	−0.5	8.5	6.5	170	499	12	11
66 Ecuador	35.0	7.7	11.9	2.6	162	575	11	2
67 Mauritius	2.1	6.6	7.2	3.0	160	378	6	6
68 Colombia	1.0	9.4	6.0	2.1	413	728	1	4

Note: For data comparability and coverage, see the technical notes.   Figures in italics are for years other than those specified.

	Average annual energy growth rate (percent)				Energy consumption per capita (kilograms of oil equivalent)		Energy imports as a percentage of merchandise exports	
	Energy production		Energy consumption					
	1965–80	1980–86	1965–80	1980–86	1965	1986	1965	1986
69 Chile	1.8	3.7	3.0	1.2	657	812	5	7
70 Costa Rica	8.2	5.7	8.8	2.3	267	565	8	8
71 Jordan	..	..	9.3	9.2	226	767	33	19
72 Syrian Arab Rep.	56.3	0.3	12.4	4.8	212	914	13	38
73 *Lebanon*	2.0	−7.2	2.0	3.6	713	846	50	..
Upper middle-income	**3.8 w**	**3.0 w**	**6.5 w**	**2.4 w**	**823 w**	**1,527 w**	**9 w**	**12 w**
74 Brazil	8.6	11.7	9.9	4.2	286	830	14	19
75 Malaysia	36.9	19.5	6.7	6.6	312	762	11	4
76 South Africa	5.1	6.5	4.3	3.9	1,744	2,470	5	0
77 Mexico	9.7	2.6	7.9	0.5	604	1,235	4	1
78 Uruguay	4.7	13.7	1.3	−2.8	765	742	13	13
79 Hungary	0.8	2.2	3.8	1.3	1,825	2,985	12	21
80 Poland	4.0	1.7	4.8	0.6	2,027	3,369	..	..
81 Portugal	3.6	7.3	6.5	2.7	506	1,284	13	20
82 Yugoslavia	3.5	3.0	6.0	3.0	898	2,041	7	25
83 Panama	6.9	12.9	5.8	4.9	576	653	..	..
84 Argentina	4.5	2.5	4.3	1.4	975	1,427	8	3
85 Korea, Rep. of	4.1	11.3	12.1	6.2	237	1,408	18	14
86 Algeria	5.3	4.5	11.9	6.8	226	1,034	0	1
87 Venezuela	−3.1	−2.3	4.6	2.4	2,319	2,502	0	0
88 Gabon	13.7	0.2	14.7	3.0	153	1,141	3	1
89 Greece	10.5	10.9	8.5	3.0	615	1,932	29	28
90 Oman	*16.0*	11.9	30.5	10.4	14	2,146	..	1
91 Trinidad and Tobago	3.8	−3.2	6.6	−0.8	2,776	4,778	..	24
92 Israel	−15.2	−19.0	4.4	1.3	1,574	1,944	14	10
93 Hong Kong	..	..	8.4	4.4	424	1,260	4	3
94 Singapore	..	..	10.8	−1.5	670	1,851	17	22
95 *Iran, Islamic Rep.*	3.6	5.2	8.9	2.6	537	958	0	..
96 *Iraq*	6.2	−0.8	7.4	5.2	399	734	0	..
97 Romania	4.3	0.7	6.6	0.7	1,536	3,405	..	..
Developing economies	**5.9 w**	**4.0 w**	**7.2 w**	**3.9 w**	**252 w**	**506 w**	**8 w**	**11 w**
Oil exporters	**5.0 w**	**1.5 w**	**7.8 w**	**2.9 w**	**298 w**	**608 w**	**5 w**	**5 w**
Exporters of manufactures	**7.1 w**	**5.7 w**	**7.8 w**	**4.3 w**	**246 w**	**569 w**	**8 w**	**12 w**
Highly indebted countries	**3.6 w**	**1.9 w**	**6.9 w**	**2.1 w**	**420 w**	**764 w**	**6 w**	**10 w**
Sub-Saharan Africa	**15.3 w**	**−1.0 w**	**6.4 w**	**2.3 w**	**62 w**	**103 w**	**7 w**	**8 w**
High-income oil exporters	**6.4 w**	**−10.7 w**	**7.7 w**	**5.2 w**	**1,345 w**	**3,313 w**	**..**	**..**
98 Saudi Arabia	11.5	−15.0	7.2	5.7	1,759	3,336	0	1
99 Kuwait	−1.6	−1.1	2.1	2.8	..	4,080	0	0
100 United Arab Emirates	14.7	−3.1	36.6	5.7	108	5,086	..	..
101 *Libya*	0.6	−6.8	18.2	4.5	223	2,259	2	1
Industrial market economies	**2.1 w**	**1.9 w**	**3.0 w**	**0.4 w**	**3,745 w**	**4,952 w**	**11 w**	**13 w**
102 Spain	3.6	8.9	6.5	1.2	901	1,928	31	25
103 Ireland	0.1	5.6	3.9	0.8	1,504	2,436	14	8
104 New Zealand	4.7	8.6	3.6	4.2	2,622	4,127	7	9
105 Italy	1.3	1.4	3.7	−0.4	1,568	2,539	16	18
106 United Kingdom	3.6	3.4	0.9	0.8	3,481	3,802	13	9
107 Belgium	−3.9	12.5	2.9	0.2	3,402	4,809	9[a]	9[a]
108 Austria	0.8	−1.0	4.0	1.3	2,060	3,400	10	10
109 Netherlands	15.4	−1.5	5.0	1.1	3,134	5,201	12	11
110 France	−0.9	9.1	3.7	0.6	2,468	3,640	16	14
111 Australia	10.5	6.9	5.0	0.5	3,287	4,710	11	5
112 Germany, Fed. Rep.	−0.1	0.7	3.0	−0.1	3,197	4,464	8	9
113 Finland	3.8	9.5	5.1	3.6	2,233	5,475	11	14
114 Denmark	2.6	55.8	2.4	1.1	2,911	3,821	13	10
115 Japan	−0.4	5.3	6.1	1.5	1,474	3,186	19	18
116 Sweden	4.9	7.7	2.5	2.4	4,162	6,374	12	9
117 Canada	5.7	3.4	4.5	0.9	6,007	8,945	8	4
118 Norway	12.4	5.3	4.1	2.8	4,650	8,803	11	7
119 United States	1.1	0.2	2.3	−0.1	6,535	7,193	8	19
120 Switzerland	3.7	2.0	3.1	2.1	2,501	4,052	8	6
Nonreporting nonmembers	**4.6 w**	**2.9 w**	**4.4 w**	**2.9 w**	**2,509 w**	**4,552 w**	**..**	**..**
121 *Albania*	9.4	−1.3	7.8	0.9	415	1,664	2	..
122 *Angola*	19.9	12.1	5.3	2.7	114	202	..	..
123 *Bulgaria*	1.3	2.7	6.1	1.9	1,788	4,590	..	..
124 *Cuba*	8.1	23.9	5.8	0.8	604	1,086	12	..
125 *Czechoslovakia*	1.0	0.9	3.2	0.8	3,374	4,845	..	..
126 *German Dem. Rep.*	0.8	3.2	2.4	1.5	3,762	5,915	..	..
127 *Korea, Dem. Rep.*	6.4	2.5	6.7	3.4	1,196	2,174	..	..
128 *Mongolia*	10.3	6.7	9.6	3.9	471	1,195	..	..
129 *USSR*	4.9	2.9	4.5	3.2	2,603	4,949	..	..

a. Includes Luxembourg.

Table 11. Growth of merchandise trade

	Merchandise trade (millions of dollars)		Average annual growth rate [a] (percent)				Terms of trade (1980=100)	
	Exports 1986	Imports 1986	Exports 1965-80	Exports 1980-86	Imports 1965-80	Imports 1980-86	1984	1986
Low-income economies	61,228 t	88,754 t	2.7 w	6.5 w	2.7 w	7.2 w	97 m	91 m
China and India	43,161 t	58,845 t	4.8 w	9.5 w	4.5 w	11.9 w	103 m	105 m
Other low-income	17,922 t	29,690 t	0.5 w	0.6 w	1.1 w	−0.1 w	97 m	91 m
1 Ethiopia	453	1,102	−0.5	−2.5	−0.9	10.7	102	127
2 Bhutan	. .	. .	. .	. .	. .	. .	. .	. .
3 Burkina Faso	112	325	4.0	1.6	5.8	−0.9	95	69
4 Nepal	142	459	−2.3	6.7	2.9	6.5	85	97
5 Bangladesh	880	2,701	. .	5.6	. .	3.3	109	109
6 Malawi	243	260	4.3	1.1	3.3	−6.5	97	88
7 Zaire	1,844	1,488	4.6	−4.3	−2.9	−1.2	84	80
8 Mali	383	438	11.0	7.2	6.2	3.4	93	73
9 Burma	299	617	−2.1	−0.2	−5.8	−8.8	76	62
10 Mozambique	159	489	. .	. .	. .	. .	. .	. .
11 Madagascar	331	395	0.7	−3.7	−0.4	−5.0	100	108
12 Uganda	395	344	−3.9	4.4	−5.3	2.2	100	116
13 Burundi	167	207	3.0	11.6	2.0	3.6	101	117
14 Tanzania	343	1,050	−4.0	−9.8	1.6	−1.3	96	104
15 Togo	275	379	4.5	−6.6	8.6	−10.0	92	86
16 Niger	331	436	12.8	−13.4	6.6	−4.4	100	94
17 Benin	181	386	−2.3	−3.5	6.7	−1.2	97	74
18 Somalia	89	440	3.8	−7.9	5.8	−1.7	93	80
19 Central African Rep.	130	219	−0.4	2.0	−4.8	−2.7	95	85
20 India	11,741[b]	16,269[b]	3.7	3.8	1.6	3.6	109	127
21 Rwanda	188	348	5.9	1.3	8.7	6.5	101	133
22 China*	31,148	43,172	5.5	11.7	8.0	16.8	97	83
23 Kenya	1,216	1,649	0.3	−0.9	1.7	−5.2	92	100
24 Zambia	689	714	1.7	−2.1	−5.5	−7.3	70	69
25 Sierra Leone	142	155	−3.9	−3.1	−2.7	−16.5	99	93
26 Sudan	497[b]	1,138[b]	−0.3	6.9	2.4	−4.0	96	70
27 Haiti	373[b]	503[b]	6.8	3.4	8.4	1.5	94	102
28 Pakistan	3,384	5,377	4.3	6.2	0.4	3.8	92	103
29 Lesotho[c]	. .	. .	. .	. .	. .	. .	. .	. .
30 Ghana	863	783	−1.8	−7.1	−1.4	−4.6	98	88
31 Sri Lanka	1,215	1,948	0.5	6.4	−1.2	3.0	118	96
32 Mauritania	419	363	2.7	13.6	6.6	0.0	98	87
33 Senegal	615	1,021	2.4	8.7	4.1	1.8	101	87
34 Afghanistan	552	1,404	. .	. .	. .	. .	. .	. .
35 Chad	120	203	. .	. .	. .	. .	. .	. .
36 Guinea	448	351	. .	. .	. .	. .	. .	. .
37 Kampuchea, Dem.	. .	. .	. .	. .	. .	. .	. .	. .
38 Lao PDR	. .	. .	. .	. .	. .	. .	. .	. .
39 Viet Nam	. .	. .	. .	. .	. .	. .	. .	. .
Middle-income economies	364,355 t	368,656 t	3.2 w	4.6 w	6.1 w	−0.9 w	96 m	94 m
Lower middle-income	84,172 t	98,942 t	6.7 w	2.4 w	6.1 w	−2.4 w	96 m	92 m
40 Liberia	404	235	4.5	−2.0	1.5	−8.8	93	97
41 Yemen, PDR	645	1,543	−13.7	3.2	−7.5	3.1	100	78
42 Indonesia	14,824	13,371	9.6	2.0	14.2	−1.0	96	64
43 Yemen Arab Rep.	20	1,033	−0.3	1.9	25.2	−7.8	95	99
44 Philippines	4,771	5,394	4.7	−1.7	2.9	−6.0	104	101
45 Morocco	2,454	3,803	3.6	3.8	6.6	0.8	88	98
46 Bolivia	563	716	2.8	0.0	5.0	−3.9	90	46
47 Zimbabwe	1,301	1,132	3.5	−2.7	−1.8	−6.7	96	86
48 Nigeria	6,599	4,498	11.4	−6.0	15.1	−17.2	97	44
49 Dominican Rep.	718	1,433	3.7	−3.6	5.5	0.4	88	104
50 Papua New Guinea	1,033	1,130	12.8	3.2	1.2	0.0	103	90
51 Côte d'Ivoire	3,200	2,024	5.6	3.5	8.0	−5.4	99	92
52 Honduras	854	875	3.1	2.6	2.5	0.7	97	103
53 Egypt, Arab Rep.	4,617[b]	9,517[b]	2.8	7.4	6.0	5.2	98	76
54 Nicaragua	247	770	2.4	−3.2	1.3	−0.6	96	97
55 Thailand	8,794	9,178	8.5	9.2	4.1	2.0	82	83
56 El Salvador	757	902	2.4	−6.3	2.7	0.9	99	114
57 Botswana[c]	. .	. .	. .	. .	. .	. .	. .	. .
58 Jamaica	596	964	−0.2	−7.2	−1.9	−1.9	95	109
59 Cameroon	2,059[b]	1,512[b]	5.2	13.8	5.6	−0.5	96	60
60 Guatemala	1,043	898	4.9	−2.5	4.6	−7.1	95	107
61 Congo, People's Rep.	673	629	12.5	5.4	1.0	2.0	97	57
62 Paraguay	234	577	6.6	1.6	4.6	−5.4	94	82
63 Peru	2,509	2,829	2.3	0.1	−0.2	−6.7	84	66
64 Turkey	7,985	11,027	5.5	19.9	7.7	9.9	92	102
65 Tunisia	1,759	2,890	8.5	−0.6	10.4	−2.8	91	81
66 Ecuador	2,181	1,810	15.2	8.4	6.8	−3.3	96	56
67 Mauritius	675	684	3.4	10.4	6.4	2.8	88	99
68 Colombia	5,102	3,862	1.5	4.9	5.3	−3.0	101	98
* Data for Taiwan, China are:	39,758	24,165	19.0	12.7	15.1	4.3	104	107

Note: For data comparability and coverage, see the technical notes.   Figures in italics are for years other than those specified.

	Merchandise trade (millions of dollars)		Average annual growth rate[a] (percent)				Terms of trade (1980=100)	
	Exports 1986	Imports 1986	Exports 1965-80	Exports 1980-86	Imports 1965-80	Imports 1980-86	1984	1986
69 Chile	4,222	3,436	7.9	3.9	2.6	−9.3	80	75
70 Costa Rica	1,125	1,147	7.1	1.2	5.7	−2.9	96	106
71 Jordan	733	2,432	13.6	5.7	9.7	0.1	93	97
72 Syrian Arab Rep.	1,325	2,703	11.4	1.5	8.5	−5.0	97	74
73 *Lebanon*	500	2,203	. .	. .	. .	. .	. .	. .
Upper middle-income	**280,615 t**	**269,715 t**	**1.7 w**	**5.6 w**	**6.0 w**	**−0.1 w**	**94 m**	**96 m**
74 Brazil	22,396	15,555	9.4	4.3	8.2	−5.1	101	125
75 Malaysia	13,874	10,829	4.4	10.2	2.9	5.2	86	64
76 South Africa[c]	18,454	12,989	6.1	−0.4	0.1	−9.5	82	72
77 Mexico	16,237	11,997	7.7	7.7	5.7	−9.2	97	66
78 Uruguay	1,088	820	4.6	0.9	1.2	−11.3	90	99
79 Hungary	9,165	9,599	. .	. .	. .	. .	. .	. .
80 Poland	12,074	11,535	. .	. .	. .	. .	. .	. .
81 Portugal	7,242	9,650	3.4	11.0	3.7	0.8	84	104
82 Yugoslavia	10,353	11,753	5.6	1.5	6.6	−1.6	93	96
83 Panama	2,412	2,955	. .	−2.0	. .	−0.8	97	101
84 Argentina	6,852	4,724	4.7	1.5	1.8	−13.8	99	80
85 Korea, Rep. of	34,715	31,584	27.3	13.1	15.2	9.3	106	111
86 Algeria	7,875	10,162	1.5	0.9	13.1	−3.1	96	44
87 Venezuela	10,029	9,565	−9.5	−1.4	8.7	−7.2	94	47
88 Gabon	1,052	951	8.1	−0.6	10.5	3.1	95	56
89 Greece	5,648	11,350	12.0	4.6	5.2	4.1	93	99
90 Oman	2,527	2,401	. .	6.7	. .	5.1	86	37
91 Trinidad and Tobago	1,376	1,355	−5.5	−8.1	−5.8	−11.9	97	71
92 Israel	7,136	10,737	8.9	6.4	6.3	2.0	91	96
93 Hong Kong	35,440	35,366	9.5	10.7	8.3	7.9	100	108
94 Singapore	22,495	25,511	4.7	6.1	7.0	3.6	102	101
95 *Iran, Islamic Rep.*	*13,435*	*11,635*	. .	. .	. .	. .	. .	. .
96 *Iraq*	. .	10,190	. .	. .	. .	. .	. .	. .
97 *Romania*	12,543	11,437	. .	. .	. .	. .	. .	. .
Developing economies	**425,984 t**	**457,155 t**	**3.1 w**	**4.8 w**	**5.5 w**	**0.5 w**	**96 m**	**93 m**
Oil exporters	**84,587 t**	**90,443 t**	**0.0 w**	**1.8 w**	**8.3 w**	**−5.4 w**	**96 m**	**57 m**
Exporters of manufactures	**217,171 t**	**230,994 t**	**7.7 w**	**8.4 w**	**7.2 w**	**5.4 w**	**101 m**	**108 m**
Highly indebted countries	**98,995 t**	**86,302 t**	**0.4 w**	**1.6 w**	**6.3 w**	**−7.2 w**	**96 m**	**92 m**
Sub-Saharan Africa	**28,285 t**	**29,229 t**	**6.6 w**	**−2.1 w**	**4.9 w**	**−7.5 w**	**97 m**	**87 m**
High-income oil exporters	**43,374 t**	**36,844 t**	**5.6 w**	**−12.5 w**	**19.5 w**	**−7.7 w**	**97 m**	**46 m**
98 Saudi Arabia	20,085	19,112	8.8	−19.2	25.9	−7.7	97	46
99 Kuwait	7,383	5,845	−1.9	−3.8	11.8	−3.1	97	47
100 United Arab Emirates	9,900	7,447	10.9	−1.0	20.5	−4.0	96	53
101 *Libya*	6,006	4,511	3.3	−4.9	15.3	−15.2	91	39
Industrial market economies	**1,443,629 t**	**1,510,671 t**	**7.1 w**	**3.3 w**	**6.7 w**	**4.3 w**	**101 m**	**109 m**
102 Spain	27,187	35,055	14.2	6.4	6.3	2.6	100	120
103 Ireland	12,657	11,619	8.3	9.3	7.1	3.4	101	109
104 New Zealand	5,880	6,033	3.6	4.5	3.1	3.7	97	94
105 Italy	97,811	99,452	8.2	4.3	6.3	2.6	93	108
106 United Kingdom	106,929	126,330	5.5	4.0	4.4	5.6	99	97
107 Belgium[d]	68,892	68,656	7.9	3.8	7.7	6.9	94	102
108 Austria	22,622	26,104	8.4	5.3	8.7	3.8	101	108
109 Netherlands	79,436	75,292	8.4	3.4	6.5	2.8	102	107
110 France	124,948	129,402	8.8	2.1	8.1	2.1	101	114
111 Australia	22,622	26,104	6.0	5.5	4.8	4.3	96	83
112 Germany, Fed. Rep.	243,327	191,084	7.5	4.3	7.1	3.0	96	115
113 Finland	16,356	15,339	5.6	2.8	4.8	1.9	102	114
114 Denmark	21,293	22,878	5.5	4.5	4.6	3.9	99	106
115 Japan	210,757	127,553	11.5	6.4	8.7	3.5	108	156
116 Sweden	37,263	32,693	5.0	5.7	4.5	4.0	100	110
117 Canada	90,193	85,068	6.2	7.2	7.1	5.2	92	89
118 Norway	18,230	20,300	7.5	5.1	6.2	5.8	118	87
119 United States	217,307	387,081	6.9	−2.7	6.2	9.0	112	119
120 Switzerland	37,471	41,039	6.2	3.7	5.6	4.2	113	117
Nonreporting nonmembers	. .	. .	. .	. .	. .	. .	. .	. .
121 *Albania*	. .	. .	. .	. .	. .	. .	. .	. .
122 *Angola*	1,787	1,080	. .	. .	. .	. .	. .	. .
123 *Bulgaria*	*13,348*	*13,656*	. .	. .	. .	. .	. .	. .
124 *Cuba*	. .	. .	. .	. .	. .	. .	. .	. .
125 *Czechoslovakia*	20,456	21,055	. .	. .	. .	. .	. .	. .
126 *German Dem. Rep.*	27,729	27,414	. .	. .	. .	. .	. .	. .
127 *Korea, Dem. Rep.*	. .	. .	. .	. .	. .	. .	. .	. .
128 *Mongolia*	. .	. .	. .	. .	. .	. .	. .	. .
129 *USSR*	97,336	88,871	. .	. .	. .	. .	. .	. .

a. See the technical notes.   b. World Bank estimate.   c. Figures are for the South African Customs Union comprising South Africa, Namibia, Lesotho, Botswana, and Swaziland; trade between the component territories is excluded.   d. Includes Luxembourg.

Table 12. Structure of merchandise exports

	Percentage share of merchandise exports									
	Fuels, minerals, and metals		Other primary commodities		Machinery and transport equipment		Other manufactures		(Textiles and clothing)[a]	
	1965	1986	1965	1986	1965	1986	1965	1986	1965	1986
Low-income economies	17 w	15 w	57 w	29 w	1 w	11 w	28 w	44 w	..	..
China and India	8 w	12 w	45 w	22 w	2 w	14 w	45 w	52 w	..	..
Other low-income	25 w	21 w	69 w	47 w	0 w	2 w	12 w	27 w	5 w	17 w
1 Ethiopia	1	2	98	97	1	0	0	1	0	0
2 Bhutan	..	..	..	..	..	..	4	7	2	..
3 Burkina Faso	1	0	94	87	1	5	22	66	..	43
4 Nepal	0	2	78	31	0	2	..	73	..	57
5 Bangladesh	..	1	..	25	..	0	..	..	..	..
6 Malawi	0	0	99	84	0	5	1	11	0	..
7 Zaire	72	49	20	45	0	1	8	5	0	..
8 Mali	1	0	96	70	1	1	2	29	1	3
9 Burma	5	3	94	84	0	9	0	4	0	0
10 Mozambique	14	..	84	..	0	..	2	..	1	..
11 Madagascar	4	7	90	81	1	2	4	10	1	6
12 Uganda	14	2	86	98	0	0	1	0	0	..
13 Burundi	1	0	94	88	0	0	6	12	1	0
14 Tanzania	4	4	83	79	0	3	13	14	0	..
15 Togo	33	58	62	22	1	1	4	19	0	0
16 Niger	0	81	95	16	1	1	4	2	1	..
17 Benin	1	42	94	36	2	6	3	16	0	..
18 Somalia	6	1	80	98	4	0	10	1	..	..
19 Central African Rep.	1	0	45	67	0	0	54	33	0	..
20 India	10	15	41	23	1	10	48	52	36	18
21 Rwanda	40	5	60	94	0	0	1	1	..	0
22 China*	6	14	48	22	3	16	43	48	..	24
23 Kenya	13	14	81	70	0	2	6	14	0	..
24 Zambia	97	96	3	1	0	1	0	2	0	..
25 Sierra Leone	25	22	14	21	0	0	60	56	0	0
26 Sudan	1	6	98	88	1	3	0	4	0	1
27 Haiti	14	5	61	32	2	10	23	53	..	..
28 Pakistan	2	1	62	31	1	3	35	65	29	51
29 Lesotho[b]	..	..	..	..	..	..	..	..	0	..
30 Ghana	13	30	85	68	1	0	2	2	0	..
31 Sri Lanka	2	7	97	52	0	2	1	39	0	30
32 Mauritania	94	34	5	65	1	0	0	1	0	0
33 Senegal	9	35	88	36	1	7	2	22	1	..
34 Afghanistan	..	47	87	46	..	0	13	7	13	..
35 Chad	5	..	92	..	0	..	3	..	0	..
36 Guinea	..	..	..	..	..	..	..	..	..	..
37 Kampuchea, Dem.	0	..	99	..	0	..	0	..	0	..
38 Lao PDR	62	..	32	..	0	..	6	..	0	..
39 Viet Nam	..	..	..	..	..	..	..	..	..	..
Middle-income economies	31 w	28 w	48 w	20 w	3 w	14 w	15 w	35 w	5 w	11 w
Lower middle-income	29 w	38 w	63 w	34 w	1 w	3 w	7 w	24 w	2 w	..
40 Liberia	72	63	25	36	1	0	3	1	0	..
41 Yemen, PDR	80	92	14	7	2	0	4	0	2	..
42 Indonesia	43	58	53	21	3	3	1	19	0	4
43 Yemen Arab Rep.	9	..	91	..	0	..	0	..	..	..
44 Philippines	11	14	84	26	0	6	6	55	1	7
45 Morocco	40	26	55	27	0	1	5	46	1	18
46 Bolivia	92	90	3	8	0	0	4	2	0	0
47 Zimbabwe	24	23	47	41	6	3	23	34	6	..
48 Nigeria	32	94	65	4	0	0	2	1	0	..
49 Dominican Rep.	10	15	88	56	0	6	2	23	0	..
50 Papua New Guinea	1	54	89	40	0	1	10	5	..	..
51 Côte d'Ivoire	2	6	93	85	1	2	4	7	1	1
52 Honduras	7	7	89	82	0	0	4	10	1	..
53 Egypt, Arab Rep.	8	74	72	14	0	0	20	13	15	9
54 Nicaragua	4	1	90	88	0	0	6	10	0	..
55 Thailand	11	4	84	54	0	9	4	33	0	15
56 El Salvador	2	2	81	75	1	2	16	21	6	7
57 Botswana[b]	..	..	..	..	..	..	..	..	..	..
58 Jamaica	28	15	41	19	0	4	31	63	4	..
59 Cameroon	17	50	77	44	3	1	2	5	0	..
60 Guatemala	0	2	86	66	1	2	13	30	4	5
61 Congo, People's Rep.	5	64	32	17	2	1	61	18	0	..
62 Paraguay	0	0	92	81	0	0	8	19	0	0
63 Peru	45	60	54	18	0	3	1	20	0	..
64 Turkey	9	11	89	33	0	5	2	51	1	29
65 Tunisia	31	27	51	13	0	5	19	55	2	28
66 Ecuador	2	54	96	43	0	1	2	2	1	0
67 Mauritius	0	0	100	58	0	2	0	39	0	..
68 Colombia	18	12	75	70	0	1	6	17	2	3
* Data for Taiwan, China are:	2	2	57	7	4	29	37	62	5	18

Note: For data comparability and coverage, see the technical notes. Figures in italics are for years other than those specified.

	Fuels, minerals, and metals		Other primary commodities		Machinery and transport equipment		Other manufactures		(Textiles and clothing)[a]	
	1965	1986	1965	1986	1965	1986	1965	1986	1965	1986
69 Chile	89	66	7	25	1	3	4	6	0	0
70 Costa Rica	0	1	84	63	1	6	15	30	2	..
71 Jordan	27	21	54	20	11	10	7	49	1	2
72 Syrian Arab Rep.	7	49	83	23	1	3	9	25	7	..
73 *Lebanon*	14	3	52	32	14	10	19	55	2	..
Upper middle-income	**39 w**	**25 w**	**39 w**	**16 w**	**3 w**	**19 w**	**19 w**	**38 w**	**6 w**	**12 w**
74 Brazil	9	19	83	41	2	15	7	26	1	3
75 Malaysia	35	26	59	38	2	26	4	10	0	..
76 South Africa[b]	24	40	44	21	3	3	29	36	1	..
77 Mexico	22	49	62	21	1	18	15	12	3	2
78 Uruguay	0	0	95	58	0	2	5	40	2	14
79 Hungary	5	7	25	23	32	35	37	35	9	6
80 Poland	..	20	..	12	..	35	..	33	..	5
81 Portugal	4	5	34	16	3	16	58	64	24	31
82 Yugoslavia	11	7	33	12	24	34	33	47	8	9
83 Panama	35	10	63	77	0	0	2	13	1	4
84 Argentina	1	4	93	73	1	6	5	16	0	2
85 Korea, Rep. of	15	3	25	6	3	33	56	58	27	25
86 Algeria	58	97	38	1	2	0	2	2	0	0
87 Venezuela	97	90	1	1	0	3	2	6	0	..
88 Gabon	50	65	39	22	1	3	10	10	0	..
89 Greece	8	14	78	35	2	3	11	48	3	29
90 Oman	90	92	10	7	0	0	0	1	..	0
91 Trinidad and Tobago	84	64	9	4	0	9	7	23	0	0
92 Israel	6	2	28	11	2	20	63	67	9	6
93 Hong Kong	2	2	11	6	6	21	81	71	43	35
94 Singapore	21	21	44	12	11	38	24	30	6	5
95 *Iran, Islamic Rep.*	88	..	8	..	0	..	4	..	4	..
96 *Iraq*	95	..	4	..	0	..	1	..	0	..
97 *Romania*	..	..	..	..	..	..	..	..	..	..
Developing economies	**27 w**	**26 w**	**51 w**	**22 w**	**2 w**	**14 w**	**18 w**	**37 w**	**6 w**	**11 w**
Oil exporters	**58 w**	**72 w**	**35 w**	**12 w**	**1 w**	**4 w**	**6 w**	**9 w**	**..**	**..**
Exporters of manufactures	**9 w**	**8 w**	**45 w**	**14 w**	**6 w**	**25 w**	**41 w**	**54 w**	**15 w**	**17 w**
Highly indebted countries	**38 w**	**36 w**	**51 w**	**32 w**	**3 w**	**11 w**	**8 w**	**21 w**	**1 w**	**..**
Sub-Saharan Africa	**33 w**	**48 w**	**59 w**	**40 w**	**1 w**	**1 w**	**7 w**	**10 w**	**0 w**	**..**
High-income oil exporters	**98 w**	**88 w**	**1 w**	**1 w**	**1 w**	**3 w**	**1 w**	**8 w**	**..**	**..**
98 Saudi Arabia	98	90	1	1	1	4	1	5	0	..
99 Kuwait	98	87	1	1	1	4	0	7	0	..
100 United Arab Emirates	99	78	1	4	0	1	0	18	..	..
101 *Libya*	99	99	1	1	1	0	0	0	0	..
Industrial market economies	**9 w**	**8 w**	**22 w**	**12 w**	**32 w**	**42 w**	**37 w**	**37 w**	**6 w**	**4 w**
102 Spain	9	9	51	19	10	31	29	42	6	4
103 Ireland	3	2	63	28	5	31	29	39	7	5
104 New Zealand	1	6	94	68	0	6	5	21	0	3
105 Italy	8	4	14	8	30	34	47	54	15	14
106 United Kingdom	7	15	10	9	41	36	41	40	7	4
107 Belgium[c]	13	9	11	12	20	26	55	54	12	7
108 Austria	8	5	16	8	20	32	55	55	12	9
109 Netherlands	12	18	32	25	21	19	35	38	9	4
110 France	8	5	21	19	26	35	45	41	10	5
111 Australia	13	40	73	39	5	6	10	16	1	1
112 Germany, Fed. Rep.	7	4	5	6	46	48	42	41	5	5
113 Finland	3	5	40	14	12	28	45	53	2	5
114 Denmark	2	4	55	36	22	25	21	35	4	5
115 Japan	2	1	7	1	31	64	60	34	17	3
116 Sweden	9	6	23	10	35	44	33	40	2	2
117 Canada	28	18	35	18	15	42	22	22	1	1
118 Norway	21	53	28	10	17	18	34	20	2	1
119 United States	8	7	27	17	37	48	28	28	3	2
120 Switzerland	3	3	7	4	30	35	60	59	10	6
Nonreporting nonmembers	**..**	**..**	**..**	**..**	**..**	**..**	**..**	**..**	**..**	**..**
121 *Albania*	..	..	..	..	..	..	..	..	..	..
122 *Angola*	6	..	76	..	1	..	17	..	0	..
123 *Bulgaria*	..	..	..	..	..	..	..	..	..	..
124 *Cuba*	4	..	92	..	0	..	4	..	0	..
125 *Czechoslovakia*	..	..	..	..	..	..	..	..	..	..
126 *German Dem. Rep.*	..	..	..	..	..	..	..	..	..	..
127 *Korea, Dem. Rep.*	..	..	..	..	..	..	..	..	..	..
128 *Mongolia*	..	..	..	..	..	..	..	..	..	..
129 *USSR*	..	..	..	..	..	..	..	..	..	..

Percentage share of merchandise exports

a. *Textiles and clothing* is a subgroup of *other manufactures*.   b. Figures are for the South African Customs Union comprising South Africa, Namibia, Lesoth swana, and Swaziland; trade between the component territories is excluded.   c. Includes Luxembourg.

Table 13. Structure of merchandise imports

Percentage share of merchandise imports

	Food 1965	Food 1986	Fuels 1965	Fuels 1986	Other primary commodities 1965	Other primary commodities 1986	Machinery and transport equipment 1965	Machinery and transport equipment 1986	Other manufactures 1965	Other manufactures 1986
Low-income economies	..	**10** *w*	..	**6** *w*	..	**6** *w*	..	**30** *w*	..	**48** *w*
China and India	..	**18** *w*	..	**5** *w*	..	**6** *w*	..	**29** *w*	..	**53** *w*
Other low-income	**19** *w*	**14** *w*	**6** *w*	**10** *w*	**5** *w*	**4** *w*	**29** *w*	**32** *w*	**44** *w*	**38** *w*
1 Ethiopia	6	22	6	15	6	3	37	32	44	28
2 Bhutan	..	..	..	..	..	..	..	..	..	..
3 Burkina Faso	23	20	4	2	14	5	19	33	40	41
4 Nepal	22	10	5	11	14	6	37	22	22	51
5 Bangladesh	..	27	..	6	..	11	..	19	..	37
6 Malawi	15	7	5	7	3	3	21	34	57	50
7 Zaire	18	16	7	3	5	4	33	36	37	41
8 Mali	20	13	6	12	5	2	23	46	47	28
9 Burma	15	6	4	1	5	2	18	43	58	48
10 Mozambique	17	..	8	..	7	..	24	..	45	..
11 Madagascar	19	13	5	15	2	2	25	29	48	41
12 Uganda	7	6	1	7	3	2	38	46	51	38
13 Burundi	16	12	6	5	9	4	15	23	55	56
14 Tanzania	..	4	..	16	..	2	..	30	..	48
15 Togo	15	23	3	8	5	6	31	45	45	17
16 Niger	12	18	6	4	6	11	21	32	55	35
17 Benin	18	16	6	24	7	2	17	17	53	40
18 Somalia	31	15	5	2	8	5	24	47	33	32
19 Central African Rep.	13	16	7	1	2	3	29	38	49	41
20 India	22	10	5	14	14	10	37	22	22	44
21 Rwanda	12	12	7	10	5	8	28	32	49	38
22 China*	..	7	..	1	..	5	..	31	..	56
23 Kenya	10	9	11	15	3	3	34	39	42	34
24 Zambia	9	4	10	12	3	1	33	40	45	42
25 Sierra Leone	17	32	9	10	3	4	30	28	41	26
26 Sudan	23	21	5	9	4	3	21	30	47	37
27 Haiti	25	15	6	3	6	2	14	27	48	53
28 Pakistan	20	18	3	14	5	7	38	32	34	29
29 Lesotho[a]	..	..	..	..	..	..	..	..	..	..
30 Ghana	12	7	4	16	3	3	33	36	48	38
31 Sri Lanka	41	16	8	14	4	2	12	29	34	39
32 Mauritania	9	25	4	7	1	2	56	39	30	27
33 Senegal	36	20	6	16	4	2	15	28	38	34
34 *Afghanistan*	17	10	4	1	1	1	8	24	69	63
35 *Chad*	13	17	20	*1*	3	2	21	*32*	42	*47*
36 *Guinea*	..	12	..	29	..	*3*	..	25	..	*31*
37 *Kampuchea, Dem.*	6	..	7	..	2	..	26	..	58	..
38 *Lao PDR*	32	..	14	..	1	..	19	..	34	..
39 *Viet Nam*	..	..	..	..	..	..	..	..	..	..
Middle-income economies	**15** *w*	**10** *w*	**8** *w*	**11** *w*	**10** *w*	**7** *w*	**28** *w*	**33** *w*	**36** *w*	**43** *w*
Lower middle-income	**16** *w*	**11** *w*	**7** *w*	**11** *w*	**6** *w*	**5** *w*	**30** *w*	**33** *w*	**40** *w*	**40** *w*
40 Liberia	16	21	8	17	3	3	34	30	39	30
41 Yemen, PDR	19	11	40	55	5	2	10	17	26	15
42 Indonesia	6	4	3	14	2	4	39	39	50	38
43 Yemen Arab Rep.	40	26	6	1	6	2	26	32	21	39
44 Philippines	20	8	10	15	7	5	33	22	30	51
45 Morocco	36	17	5	14	10	14	18	26	31	29
46 Bolivia	19	10	1	1	3	2	35	49	42	39
47 Zimbabwe	13	12	8	6	3	2	31	36	46	43
48 Nigeria	9	11	6	3	3	3	34	35	48	49
49 Dominican Rep.	23	15	10	14	4	4	24	27	40	40
50 Papua New Guinea	23	20	5	9	3	1	25	34	45	36
51 Côte d'Ivoire	18	15	6	7	3	3	28	34	46	41
52 Honduras	11	*10*	6	*17*	1	*1*	26	*21*	56	*51*
53 Egypt, Arab Rep.	26	22	7	4	12	6	23	29	31	40
54 Nicaragua	12	14	5	9	2	1	30	21	51	54
55 Thailand	6	5	9	12	6	8	31	34	49	40
56 El Salvador	15	15	5	6	4	4	28	20	48	56
57 Botswana[a]	..	..	..	..	..	..	..	..	..	..
58 Jamaica	20	18	9	14	5	4	23	20	43	44
59 Cameroon	11	11	5	1	4	2	28	37	51	49
60 Guatemala	11	7	7	12	2	3	29	27	50	51
61 Congo, People's Rep.	15	19	6	6	1	3	34	27	44	45
62 Paraguay	14	9	14	18	2	7	37	39	33	27
63 Peru	17	13	3	1	5	3	41	48	34	36
64 Turkey	6	4	10	18	10	8	37	34	37	35
65 Tunisia	16	14	6	7	7	12	31	26	41	42
66 Ecuador	10	5	9	2	4	3	33	52	44	38
67 Mauritius	34	23	5	6	3	4	16	20	43	47
68 Colombia	8	8	1	6	10	6	45	40	35	41
* Data for Taiwan, China are:	13	8	5	12	24	15	29	32	29	33

Note: For data comparability and coverage, see the technical notes. Figures in italics are for years other than those specified.

	Food 1965	Food 1986	Fuels 1965	Fuels 1986	Other primary commodities 1965	Other primary commodities 1986	Machinery and transport equipment 1965	Machinery and transport equipment 1986	Other manufactures 1965	Other manufactures 1986
69 Chile	20	12	6	9	10	3	35	40	30	37
70 Costa Rica	9	7	5	8	2	3	29	29	54	53
71 Jordan	28	22	6	13	6	4	18	25	42	36
72 Syrian Arab Rep.	22	12	10	23	9	4	16	26	43	36
73 *Lebanon*	26	..	8	..	8	..	15	..	43	..
Upper middle-income	**15 w**	**10 w**	**8 w**	**14 w**	**12 w**	**8 w**	**29 w**	**32 w**	**36 w**	**36 w**
74 Brazil	20	15	21	27	9	7	22	25	28	26
75 Malaysia	25	10	12	5	10	4	22	51	32	30
76 South Africa[a]	5	3	5	0	11	4	42	43	37	50
77 Mexico	5	11	2	1	10	8	50	47	33	34
78 Uruguay	7	3	17	21	16	8	24	35	36	32
79 Hungary	12	8	11	20	22	10	27	28	28	34
80 Poland	..	10	..	21	..	9	..	32	..	28
81 Portugal	16	13	8	15	19	9	27	29	30	33
82 Yugoslavia	16	7	6	22	19	12	28	28	32	31
83 Panama	11	10	21	17	2	1	21	26	45	46
84 Argentina	6	7	10	9	21	10	25	31	38	41
85 Korea, Rep. of	15	6	7	16	26	15	13	34	38	30
86 Algeria	26	22	0	1	6	5	15	32	52	41
87 Venezuela	12	14	1	0	5	4	44	45	39	36
88 Gabon	16	21	5	1	2	3	38	37	40	38
89 Greece	15	16	8	17	11	8	35	25	30	34
90 Oman	27	15	19	1	4	3	15	42	34	39
91 Trinidad and Tobago	11	17	50	3	2	5	16	37	22	38
92 Israel	16	9	6	7	12	5	28	34	38	44
93 Hong Kong	25	9	3	3	13	6	13	23	46	59
94 Singapore	23	9	13	20	19	5	14	37	30	30
95 *Iran, Islamic Rep.*	16	..	0	..	6	..	36	..	42	..
96 *Iraq*	24	..	0	..	7	..	25	..	44	..
97 *Romania*	..	..	..	..	..	..	..	..	..	..
Developing economies	**17 w**	**10 w**	**7 w**	**10 w**	**10 w**	**7 w**	**29 w**	**32 w**	**36 w**	**41 w**
Oil exporters	**14 w**	**13 w**	**6 w**	**5 w**	**6 w**	**5 w**	**34 w**	**41 w**	**40 w**	**39 w**
Exporters of manufactures	**22 w**	**9 w**	**7 w**	**11 w**	**17 w**	**9 w**	**23 w**	**30 w**	**31 w**	**42 w**
Highly indebted countries	**14 w**	**11 w**	**7 w**	**11 w**	**10 w**	**7 w**	**34 w**	**35 w**	**35 w**	**35 w**
Sub-Saharan Africa	**15 w**	**12 w**	**6 w**	**7 w**	**4 w**	**3 w**	**30 w**	**34 w**	**45 w**	**42 w**
High-income oil exporters	**20 w**	**15 w**	**2 w**	**2 w**	**5 w**	**2 w**	**32 w**	**35 w**	**40 w**	**45 w**
98 Saudi Arabia	29	17	1	1	5	2	27	34	38	46
99 Kuwait	21	17	1	0	7	3	33	38	39	41
100 United Arab Emirates	15	11	3	7	7	3	34	37	41	42
101 *Libya*	13	15	4	1	3	2	36	33	43	49
Industrial market economies	**19 w**	**10 w**	**11 w**	**12 w**	**19 w**	**7 w**	**19 w**	**33 w**	**31 w**	**37 w**
102 Spain	19	12	10	19	16	11	27	29	28	29
103 Ireland	18	13	8	8	10	5	25	31	39	43
104 New Zealand	7	6	7	9	10	4	33	39	43	43
105 Italy	24	14	16	17	24	11	15	25	21	32
106 United Kingdom	30	12	11	7	25	8	11	33	23	39
107 Belgium[b]	14	11	9	11	21	9	24	28	32	41
108 Austria	14	6	7	9	13	8	31	34	35	43
109 Netherlands	15	14	10	12	13	6	25	28	37	40
110 France	19	11	15	13	18	7	20	29	27	40
111 Australia	5	5	8	5	10	4	37	43	41	44
112 Germany, Fed. Rep.	22	12	8	12	21	9	13	26	35	41
113 Finland	10	6	10	15	12	7	35	36	34	36
114 Denmark	14	11	11	9	11	6	25	31	39	42
115 Japan	22	17	20	31	38	17	9	11	11	24
116 Sweden	12	7	11	11	12	7	30	36	36	39
117 Canada	10	6	7	5	9	5	40	56	34	29
118 Norway	10	6	7	6	12	6	38	40	32	42
119 United States	19	7	10	10	20	5	14	42	36	36
120 Switzerland	16	7	6	6	11	6	24	30	43	51
Nonreporting nonmembers	..	..	..	..	..	..	..	..	..	..
121 *Albania*	..	..	..	..	..	..	..	..	..	..
122 *Angola*	18	..	2	..	2	..	24	..	54	..
123 *Bulgaria*	..	..	..	..	..	..	..	..	..	..
124 *Cuba*	29	..	10	..	3	..	15	..	43	..
125 *Czechoslovakia*	..	..	..	..	..	..	..	..	..	..
126 *German Dem. Rep.*	..	..	..	..	..	..	..	..	..	..
127 *Korea, Dem. Rep.*	..	..	..	..	..	..	..	..	..	..
128 *Mongolia*	..	..	..	..	..	..	..	..	..	..
129 *USSR*	..	..	..	..	..	..	..	..	..	..

a. Figures are for the South African Customs Union comprising South Africa, Namibia, Lesotho, Botswana, and Swaziland; trade between the component territories is excluded.   b. Includes Luxembourg.

Table 14. Origin and destination of manufactured exports

| | Manufactured exports (millions of dollars) | | Destination of manufactured exports (percentage of total) | | | | | | | |
| | | | Industrial market economies | | Nonreporting nonmember economies | | High-income oil exporters | | Developing economies[a] | |
Origin	1965	1986	1965	1986	1965	1986	1965	1986	1965	1986
Low-income economies	**2,420** w	**32,785** w	**56** w	**45** w	**9** w	**3** w	**2** w	**4** w	**33** w	**48** w
China and India	**1,850** w	**27,576** w	**55** w	**39** w	**11** w	**5** w	**2** w	**3** w	**32** w	**53** w
Other low-income	**537** w	**4,939** w	**58** w	**66** w	**4** w	**4** w	**2** w	**8** w	**37** w	**22** w
1 Ethiopia	0	3	67	63	0	21	20	3	13	13
2 Bhutan	. .	. .	. .	. .	. .	. .	. .	. .	. .	. .
3 Burkina Faso	1	18	2	34	0	0	0	0	98	66
4 Nepal	13	95	. .	65	. .	7	. .	0	. .	28
5 Bangladesh	. .	636	. .	67	. .	4	. .	1	. .	28
6 Malawi	0	39	3	39	0	0	0	0	97	61
7 Zaire	28	88	93	22	0	0	0	0	7	78
8 Mali	0	57	14	11	8	0	0	0	78	89
9 Burma	1	38	73	43	1	0	0	7	26	51
10 Mozambique	3	. .	27	2	5	0	0	9	68	89
11 Madagascar	5	41	80	82	0	5	0	0	20	13
12 Uganda	1	1	7	81	0	0	0	1	93	18
13 Burundi	1	19	0	28	0	0	0	0	99	72
14 Tanzania	23	58	93	36	0	2	0	1	7	12
15 Togo	1	52	37	11	0	1	0	0	62	89
16 Niger	1	7	43	. .	0	. .	0	. .	57	. .
17 Benin	1	20	15	82	0	0	0	1	85	18
18 Somalia	4	1	21	65	0	0	2	0	77	33
19 Central African Rep.	14	47	60	9	0	0	0	7	40	93
20 India	828	7,234	55	59	11	10	2	0	32	24
21 Rwanda	0	1	95	93	0	0	0	0	5	7
22 China*	1,021	19,997	. .	32	. .	3	. .	2	. .	62
23 Kenya	13	192	23	8	0	0	2	1	75	91
24 Zambia	1	21	14	67	0	0	0	1	86	32
25 Sierra Leone	53	72	99	99	0	0	0	0	1	1
26 Sudan	2	32	78	. .	0	. .	2	. .	20	. .
27 Haiti	9	236	. .	99	. .	0	. .	0	. .	1
28 Pakistan	190	2,285	40	65	7	4	2	11	52	19
29 Lesotho[b]	. .	. .	. .	. .	. .	. .	. .	. .	. .	. .
30 Ghana	7	22	60	40	10	0	0	1	29	60
31 Sri Lanka	5	505	59	89	5	0	0	1	36	10
32 Mauritania	1	9	61	34	0	0	0	0	39	66
33 Senegal	4	185	48	. .	0	. .	0	. .	52	. .
34 *Afghanistan*	11	40	98	. .	0	. .	0	. .	2	. .
35 Chad	1	. .	6	11	0	0	25	0	69	89
36 *Guinea*	. .	. .	. .	44	. .	0	. .	3	. .	53
37 *Kampuchea, Dem.*	1	. .	28	. .	1	. .	0	. .	71	. .
38 *Lao PDR*	0	. .	13	. .	0	. .	0	. .	87	. .
39 *Viet Nam*	. .	. .	. .	. .	. .	. .	. .	. .	. .	. .
Middle-income economies	**5,475** w	**180,631** w	**45** w	**60** w	**22** w	**7** w	**1** w	**3** w	**33** w	**31** w
Lower middle-income	**714** w	**23,336** w	**38** w	**55** w	**10** w	**2** w	**6** w	**6** w	**36** w	**37** w
40 Liberia	4	6	77	60	0	0	0	1	23	39
41 Yemen, PDR	11	3	32	33	0	4	6	2	62	61
42 Indonesia	27	2,961	25	50	2	0	0	4	73	46
43 Yemen Arab Rep.	0	. .	. .	70	. .	0	. .	23	. .	7
44 Philippines	43	2,808	93	74	0	0	0	1	7	25
45 Morocco	23	1,057	63	53	5	5	0	5	32	36
46 Bolivia	6	11	86	53	0	0	0	0	14	47
47 Zimbabwe	116	365	12	78	2	0	0	0	86	22
48 Nigeria	17	99	85	64	0	0	0	0	15	36
49 Dominican Rep.	3	208	95	87	0	0	0	0	5	13
50 Papua New Guinea	5	61	100	85	0	0	0	0	0	15
51 Côte d'Ivoire	15	289	50	32	0	0	0	0	50	68
52 Honduras	6	91	2	28	0	0	0	0	98	72
53 Egypt, Arab Rep.	126	588	20	46	44	30	4	4	32	21
54 Nicaragua	8	37	4	38	0	0	0	0	96	62
55 Thailand	30	3,944	39	60	0	0	0	8	61	32
56 El Salvador	32	170	1	87	0	0	0	0	99	13
57 Botswana[b]	. .	. .	. .	. .	. .	. .	. .	. .	. .	. .
58 Jamaica	64	394	93	38	0	0	0	0	7	62
59 Cameroon	6	121	46	47	0	0	0	0	54	52
60 Guatemala	26	366	9	7	0	0	0	0	91	93
61 Congo, People's Rep.	24	134	88	39	1	0	0	0	11	61
62 Paraguay	5	44	93	68	0	0	0	0	7	32
63 Peru	5	573	51	72	0	0	0	0	49	27
64 Turkey	11	4,352	83	57	1	2	0	5	15	35
65 Tunisia	23	1,060	19	70	3	3	5	1	73	26
66 Ecuador	3	68	25	30	0	0	0	0	75	70
67 Mauritius	0	277	16	89	0	0	0	0	84	11
68 Colombia	35	902	43	52	0	1	0	0	57	47
* Data for Taiwan, China are:	187	35,943	47	78	0	0	1	3	52	19

Note: For data comparability and coverage, see the technical notes.   Figures in italics are for 1983, 1984 or 1985.

| | Manufactured exports (millions of dollars) | | Destination of manufactured exports (percentage of total) | | | | | | | |
| | | | Industrial market economies | | Nonreporting nonmember economies | | High-income oil exporters | | Developing economies[a] | |
Origin	1965	1986	1965	1986	1965	1986	1965	1986	1965	1986
69 Chile	28	385	38	40	0	..	..	0	62	60
70 Costa Rica	18	404	6	..	0	..	0	..	94	..
71 Jordan	5	298	49	16	0	0	23	22	28	61
72 Syrian Arab Rep.	16	378	5	5	12	66	25	6	59	23
73 *Lebanon*	29	328	19	..	1	..	61	..	19	..
Upper middle-income	**4,878 w**	**161,213 w**	**46 w**	**60 w**	**23 w**	**8 w**	**1 w**	**3 w**	**31 w**	**30 w**
74 Brazil	134	9,068	40	56	1	1	0	1	59	42
75 Malaysia	75	4,974	17	69	0	0	2	2	81	29
76 South Africa[b]	443	7,122	94	..	0	..	0	..	6	..
77 Mexico	165	4,859	71	90	0	1	0	0	29	9
78 Uruguay	10	385	71	51	5	2	0	0	24	47
79 Hungary	1,053	6,450	11	23	65	53	0	2	24	22
80 Poland	..	8,188	..	19	..	42	..	2	..	37
81 Portugal	355	5,707	59	91	18	2	0	0	23	7
82 Yugoslavia	617	8,320	24	30	41	44	1	2	35	24
83 Panama	1	49	7	..	0	..	0	..	93	..
84 Argentina	84	1,804	45	37	1	5	0	0	54	58
85 Korea, Rep. of	104	31,931	68	75	0	0	0	5	32	20
86 Algeria	24	147	50	64	2	3	1	0	48	33
87 Venezuela	51	775	59	..	0	..	0	..	41	..
88 Gabon	10	140	72	..	0	..	0	..	28	..
89 Greece	44	3,048	56	75	6	2	9	5	29	18
90 Oman	0	201	..	30	..	0	..	51	..	19
91 Trinidad and Tobago	28	340	78	78	0	0	0	0	22	22
92 Israel	281	6,052	67	71	1	0	0	0	31	29
93 Hong Kong	995	32,645	71	60	0	0	1	2	28	38
94 Singapore	338	14,672	9	55	0	1	3	4	88	40
95 *Iran, Islamic Rep.*	58	..	61	..	0	..	10	..	28	..
96 *Iraq*	8	..	24	..	1	..	13	..	63	..
97 *Romania*	..	..	..	..	..	..	..	..	..	..
Developing economies	**7,984 w**	**214,337 w**	**47 w**	**56 w**	**19 w**	**7 w**	**2 w**	**3 w**	**32 w**	**32 w**
Oil exporters	**610 w**	**11,240 w**	**52 w**	**..**	**11 w**	**..**	**3 w**	**..**	**34 w**	**..**
Exporters of manufactures	**6,083 w**	**177,532 w**	**42 w**	**54 w**	**24 w**	**8 w**	**1 w**	**..**	**34 w**	**..**
Highly indebted countries	**1,318 w**	**32,115 w**	**43 w**	**..**	**20 w**	**..**	**0 w**	**2 w**	**34 w**	**33 w**
Sub-Saharan Africa	**366 w**	**3,160 w**	**55 w**	**34 w**	**1 w**	**0 w**	**0 w**	**0 w**	**44 w**	**57 w**
High-income oil exporters	**115 w**	**4,498 w**	**30 w**	**..**	**0 w**	**..**	**21 w**	**..**	**49 w**	**..**
98 Saudi Arabia	19	1,818	31	..	0	..	17	..	52	..
99 Kuwait	17	849	18	..	0	..	33	..	49	..
100 United Arab Emirates	0	1,831	..	..	..	..	..	..	..	..
101 *Libya*	7	0	57	..	0	..	0	..	43	..
Industrial market economies	**86,373 w**	**1,151,136 w**	**67 w**	**74**	**2 w**	**2 w**	**1 w**	**2 w**	**30 w**	**22 w**
102 Spain	382	19,742	57	71	9	3	0	2	34	24
103 Ireland	203	8,773	82	94	0	0	0	1	17	5
104 New Zealand	53	1,595	90	73	0	0	0	0	10	26
105 Italy	5,587	85,724	68	75	3	3	2	3	27	19
106 United Kingdom	11,346	80,544	61	72	2	1	1	5	36	22
107 Belgium[c]	4,823	54,342	86	85	1	1	0	1	13	12
108 Austria	1,204	19,622	67	77	12	6	0	1	21	15
109 Netherlands	3,586	46,197	81	85	2	1	1	1	17	12
110 France	7,139	90,495	64	72	2	2	1	2	33	24
111 Australia	432	4,784	57	48	0	0	0	1	43	51
112 Germany, Fed. Rep.	15,764	217,471	76	78	2	3	1	1	22	17
113 Finland	815	13,188	63	66	23	24	0	1	14	10
114 Denmark	967	12,334	79	80	3	2	0	1	17	17
115 Japan	7,704	203,896	47	62	3	2	2	3	49	33
116 Sweden	2,685	31,196	82	85	3	2	0	1	15	12
117 Canada	2,973	53,509	88	94	0	0	0	0	12	6
118 Norway	734	6,825	78	69	2	1	0	1	20	30
119 United States	17,833	162,838	58	63	0	0	1	2	40	35
120 Switzerland	2,646	34,997	75	75	2	2	1	2	22	20
Nonreporting nonmembers	**..**	**..**	**..**	**..**	**..**	**..**	**..**	**..**	**..**	**..**
121 *Albania*	..	..	..	..	..	..	..	..	..	..
122 *Angola*	36	..	3	..	0	..	0	..	97	..
123 *Bulgaria*	..	..	..	..	..	..	..	..	..	..
124 *Cuba*	27	..	27	..	68	..	0	..	5	..
125 *Czechoslovakia*	..	..	..	..	..	..	..	..	..	..
126 *German Dem. Rep.*	..	..	..	..	..	..	..	..	..	..
127 *Korea, Dem. Rep.*	..	..	..	..	..	..	..	..	..	..
128 *Mongolia*	..	..	..	..	..	..	..	..	..	..
129 *USSR*	..	..	..	..	..	..	..	..	..	..

a. Includes unallocable data.   b. Figures are for the South African Customs Union comprising South Africa, Namibia, Lesotho, Botswana, and Swaziland; trade between the component territories is excluded.   c. Includes Luxembourg.

Table 15. Balance of payments and reserves

| | Current account balance (millions of dollars) | | External financing requirement (millions of dollars) | | Receipts of workers' remittances (millions of dollars) | | Net direct private investment (millions of dollars) | | Gross international reserves | | |
| | | | | | | | | | Millions of dollars | | In months of import coverage |
	1970	1986	1970	1986	1970	1986	1970	1986	1970	1986	1986
Low-income economies									3,223 t	33,624 t	4.2 w
China and India									1,023 t	26,898 t	5.5 w
Other low-income									2,200 t	67,27 t	2.2 w
1 Ethiopia	−32	5[a]	−43	−289[a]	..	..	4	..	72	332	3.6
2 Bhutan	..	..	..	..	..	..	..	..	..	..	..
3 Burkina Faso	9	−124[a]	−21	−297[a]	18	150[a]	0	..	36	238	4.4
4 Nepal	8[a]	−112	−16[a]	−182	..	..	..	..	94	146	3.2
5 Bangladesh	−114[a]	−538	−234[a]	−1,084	..	586	..	2	..	430	1.9
6 Malawi	−35	−57[a]	−46	−84[a]	..	..	9	..	29	30	1.0
7 Zaire	−64	−397	−141	−580	2	..	42	5	189	451	2.1
8 Mali	−2	−148	−22	−282	6	45	..	4	1	31	0.7
9 Burma	−63	−210[a]	−81	−310[a]	..	..	..	..	98	131	2.0
10 Mozambique	..	−363	..	−576	..	50	..	..	..	..	..
11 Madagascar	10	−127[a]	−42	−127[a]	..	..	10	..	37	115	2.0
12 Uganda	20	0[a]	19	−25[a]	..	..	4	0[a]	57	29	0.6
13 Burundi	2[a]	−38[a]	−8[a]	−86[a]	..	..	0[a]	6[a]	15	76	3.0
14 Tanzania	−36	−514	−37	−533	..	5	..	..	65	61	0.7
15 Togo	3	−105	−14	−181	..	9	0	13	35	337	7.0
16 Niger	0	−6	−32	−154	..	..	0	..	19	193	4.8
17 Benin	−1	−125[a]	−21	−151[a]	2	35[a]	7	..	16	8	0.3
18 Somalia	−6	−87	−18	−347	..	..	5	0	21	20	0.5
19 Central African Rep.	−12	−86	−24	−188	..	..	1	−1	1	70	2.3
20 India	−386[a]	−3,604[a]	−592[a]	−3,874[a]	113[a]	2,000[a]	..	208[a]	1,023	10,480	6.0
21 Rwanda	7	−69	−12	−186	1	2	0	18	8	162	4.5
22 China	−81[a]	−7,034	−81[a]	−7,158	..	208	..	1,425	..	16,417	5.2
23 Kenya	−49	−42[a]	−86	−42[a]	..	..	14	..	220	445	2.5
24 Zambia	108	−302	107	−323	..	..	−297	..	515	71	0.8
25 Sierra Leone	−16	−36	−20	−68	..	..	8	..	39	14	0.7
26 Sudan	−42	−430[a]	−43	−842[a]	..	109	..	5	22	59	0.4
27 Haiti	2	−70	−5	−173	17	..	3	5	4	23	0.5
28 Pakistan	−667	−788	−705	−1,286	86	2,632	23	159	195	1,465	2.2
29 Lesotho	19[a]	−9	0[a]	−64	29[a]	..	..	4	..	60	1.8
30 Ghana	−68	−43	−76	−166	..	1	68	4	43	624	7.1
31 Sri Lanka	−59	−417	−71	−592	3	324	0	29	43	377	1.8
32 Mauritania	−5	−185	−13	−300	1	2	1	3	3	52	0.9
33 Senegal	−16	−284[a]	−66	−284[a]	3	..	5	−2[a]	22	21	0.2
34 *Afghanistan*	..	−556	..	−748	..	..	..	..	49	636	5.6
35 *Chad*	2	−64	−33	−253	..	1	1	31	2	20	0.6
36 *Guinea*	..	−40	..	−40	..	..	..	..	..	..	..
37 *Kampuchea, Dem.*	..	..	..	..	..	..	..	..	..	..	..
38 *Lao PDR*	..	..	..	..	..	..	..	..	6	..	..
39 *Viet Nam*	..	..	..	..	..	..	..	..	243	..	..
Middle-income economies									15,738 t	126,940 t	3.3 w
Lower middle-income									4,927 t	39,263 t	3.0 w
40 Liberia	−16[a]	51	−27[a]	−11	..	..	28[a]	−6	..	3	0.1
41 Yemen, PDR	−4	−190	−4	−208	60	283	..	..	59	154	3.0
42 Indonesia	−310	−4,004	−376	−4,099	..	71	83	258	160	5,265	3.1
43 Yemen Arab Rep.	−34[a]	−126	−52[a]	−326	45[a]	566	..	5	..	432	5.1
44 Philippines	−48	996	−138	790	..	163	−29	127	255	2,611	3.9
45 Morocco	−124	−210	−161	−370	63	1,395	20	1	142	487	1.1
46 Bolivia	4	−400[a]	2	−482[a]	..	*0*	−76	10[a]	46	492	*5.4*
47 Zimbabwe	−14[a]	−42[a]	−13[a]	−91[a]	..	..	..	..	59	316	2.4
48 Nigeria	−368	370	−412	375	..	..	205	195	224	1,350	2.5
49 Dominican Rep.	−102	−119	−103	−148	25	241	72	50	32	383	2.5
50 Papua New Guinea	−89[a]	−141	−239[a]	−353	..	..	..	91	..	450	3.7
51 Côte d'Ivoire	−38	−110[a]	−73	−110[a]	..	..	31	29	119	37	0.2
52 Honduras	−64	−155	−68	−271	..	..	8	30	20	118	1.1
53 Egypt, Arab Rep.	−148	−6,373[a]	−452	−6,742[a]	29	2,600[a]	..	1,208[a]	165	1,780	1.2
54 Nicaragua	−40	−742[a]	−43	−823[a]	..	..	15	..	49	..	..
55 Thailand	−250	249	−296	88	..	..	43	262	911	3,777	3.8
56 El Salvador	9	39[a]	7	−223[a]	..	*126*	4	*12*	64	353	3.0
57 Botswana	−31	169	−37	68	..	..	6	90	..	1,198	15.0
58 Jamaica	−153	0[a]	−149	0[a]	29	92	161	2[a]	139	98	0.7
59 Cameroon	−30	59[a]	−47	59[a]	..	*10*	16	50[a]	81	71	0.3
60 Guatemala	−8	−11	−8	−36	..	..	29	67	79	566	5.3
61 Congo, People's Rep.	−45[a]	−595	−53[a]	−659	1[a]	..	30[a]	22	9	11	0.1
62 Paraguay	−16	−359	−19	−369	..	*0*	4	32	18	460	4.5
63 Peru	202	−1,055	146	−1,151	..	..	−70	22	339	2,265	6.0
64 Turkey	−44	−1,528	−57	−1,774	273	1,634	58	125	440	2,966	2.5
65 Tunisia	−53	−657[a]	−88	−698[a]	29	320[a]	16	159[a]	60	378	1.2
66 Ecuador	−113	−613	−122	−658	..	..	89	70	76	806	3.0
67 Mauritius	8	99	5	79	..	..	2	7	46	151	2.2
68 Colombia	−293	423	−333	413	6	175	39	673	207	3,481	6.1
* Data for Taiwan, China are:	1	16,217	2	16,210	..	..	61	260	627	48,489	19.6

Note: For data comparability and coverage, see the technical notes. Figures in italics are for years other than those specified.

	Current account balance (millions of dollars)		External financing requirement (millions of dollars)		Receipts of workers' remittances (millions of dollars)		Net direct private investment (millions of dollars)		Gross international reserves		
									Millions of dollars		In months of import coverage
	1970	1986	1970	1986	1970	1986	1970	1986	1970	1986	1986
	−91	−1,091	−95	−1,135	..	..	−79	57	392	2,949	5.5
	−74	−100	−77	−191	..	..	26	62	16	550	4.0
	−20	−42	−130	−671	..	1,182	..	21	258	854	2.9
	−69	−464a	−72	−1,028a	7	293	..	..	57	357	0.9
	..	..	..	..	..	..	..	..	405	4,093	..
ne									10,811 t	87,677 t	3.4 w
	−837	−4,930a	−861	−4,930a	..	2	407	350a	1,190	6,754	2.7
	8	−295	2	−309	..	..	94	528	667	6,942	5.0
	−1,215	3,125	−1,253	3,114	..	..	318	−16	1,057	2,254	1.5
	−1,068	−1,270	−1,098	−1,470	..	..	323	905	756	6,674	3.1
	−45	91	−55	66	..	..	..	−5	186	1,500	11.8
	−25	−1,287	−25	−1,287	..	..	..	..	..	3,979	3.9
...ugal	..	−1,109	..	−1,109	..	..	..	−6	..	882	0.6
Yugoslavia	−158a	1,121	−158a	929	523a	2,529	15a	239	1,565	9,336	9.6
63 Panama	−372	1,097	−378	1,099	441	3,721	..	..	143	2,189	1.4
	−64	441	−79	320	..	..	33	−4	16	170	0.4
84 Argentina	−163	−2,864	−160	−2,864	..	..	11	573	682	4,427	4.5
85 Korea, Rep. of	−623	4,617	−706	4,606	..	..	66	325	610	3,444	1.1
86 Algeria	−125	−2,224	−163	−2,240	211	309	45	290	352	3,843	3.9
87 Venezuela	−104	−2,011	−98	−1,990	..	..	−23	16	1,047	10,917	10.0
88 Gabon	−3	−958	−15	−980	..	0	−1	114	15	131	0.8
89 Greece	−422	−1,676	−424	−3,068	333	942	50	471	318	2,812	2.8
90 Oman	..	−966	..	−966	..	39	..	138	13	1,081	3.6
91 Trinidad and Tobago	−109	−441	−104	−421	3	0	83	−22	43	495	2.8
92 Israel	−562	1,262	−766	−2,939	..	..	40	−39	452	5,057	3.9
93 Hong Kong	225a	1,552a	225a	1,552a	..	..	..	282a	..	..	..
94 Singapore	−572	478	−585	492	..	..	93	582	1,012	12,939	5.4
95 Iran, Islamic Rep.	−507	..	−511	..	..	..	25	..	217	..	..
96 Iraq	105	..	104	..	..	..	24	..	472	..	..
97 Romania	..	1,489	..	1,489	..	..	..	..	..	1,851	1.9
Developing economies									18,961 t	160,565 t	3.5 w
Oil exporters									3,685 t	32,780 t	3.5 w
Exporters of manufactures									5,994 t	73,329 t	3.6 w
Highly indebted countries									5,958 t	47,588 t	3.9 w
Sub-Saharan Africa									2,020 t	6,787 t	2.1 w
High-income oil exporters									2,475 t	37,664 t	7.2 w
98 Saudi Arabia	71	−10,360	152	−7,408	..	..	20	964	670	20,120	6.3
99 Kuwait	853a	6,160	918a	6,342	..	..	..	−288	209	6,494	8.6
100 United Arab Emirates	75a	6,486a	68a	2,616a	..	..	4a	..	..	3,689	5.7
101 Libya	645	1,890	758	1,890	..	..	139	−316	1,596	7,360	11.1
Industrial market economies									72,868 t	610,996 t	3.5 w
102 Spain	79	4,102	79	4,500	469	1,180	179	3,057	1,851	20,548	5.7
103 Ireland	−198	−450	−228	−1,859	..	..	32	161	698	3,377	2.4
104 New Zealand	−232	−1,299	−222	−1,239	40	345	137	101	258	3,780	4.9
105 Italy	902	3,961	1,385	6,948	446	1,205	498	−2,917	5,547	46,049	4.5
106 United Kingdom	1,913	−1,392	2,316	1,825	..	..	−190	−8,378	2,918	25,853	1.5
107 Belgium	717	3,586	904	4,363	154	479	140	−990	2,947	18,900	2.3
108 Austria	−75	133	−73	178	13	267	104	−41	1,806	14,427	4.5
109 Netherlands	−483	4,686	−511	5,665	..	..	−15	−2,198	3,362	28,368	3.6
110 France	−204	2,922	18	5,768	130	320	248	−2,116	5,199	63,450	4.2
111 Australia	−777	−9,652	−682	−9,503	..	..	778	−114	1,709	10,347	3.2
112 Germany, Fed. Rep.	853	37,357	1,899	45,551	..	..	−290	−8,121	13,879	88,941	4.3
113 Finland	−239	−887	−232	−660	..	..	−41	−419	455	2,535	1.5
114 Denmark	−544	−4,313	−510	−4,146	..	..	75	..	488	5,601	2.0
115 Japan	1,980	85,831	2,160	87,301	..	..	−260	−14,250	4,876	51,727	3.6
116 Sweden	−265	3,795	−160	4,651	..	..	−104	−2,300	775	8,923	2.6
117 Canada	1,056	−6,723	739	−6,854	..	..	566	−1,824	4,733	10,961	1.2
118 Norway	−242	−4,440	−200	−3,777	..	12	32	−107	813	12,987	4.8
119 United States	2,330	−141,460	4,680	−127,450	..	..	−6,130	−3,000	15,237	139,884	3.4
120 Switzerland	72	4,525	114	4,427	..	93	..	383	5,317	54,339	9.5
Nonreporting nonmembers									..	..	..
121 Albania	..	..	..	..	..	..	..	..	..	..	..
122 Angola	..	..	..	..	..	..	..	..	..	..	..
123 Bulgaria	..	..	..	..	..	..	..	..	..	..	..
124 Cuba	..	..	..	..	..	..	..	..	..	..	..
125 Czechoslovakia	..	..	..	..	..	..	..	..	..	..	..
126 German Dem. Rep.	..	..	..	..	..	..	..	..	..	..	..
127 Korea, Dem. Rep.	..	..	..	..	..	..	..	..	..	..	..
128 Mongolia	..	..	..	..	..	..	..	..	..	..	..
129 USSR	..	..	..	..	..	..	..	..	..	..	..

a. World Bank estimates.

Table 16. Total external debt

	Long-term debt (millions of dollars)				Use of IMF credit (millions of dollars)		Short-term debt (millions of dollars)		Total external debt (millions of dollars)	
	Public and publicly guaranteed		Private nonguaranteed							
	1970	1986	1970	1986	1970	1986	1970	1986	1970	1986
Low-income economies										
China and India										
Other low-income										
1 Ethiopia	169	1,989	0	0	0	66	..	83	..	2,139
2 Bhutan	..	..	..	..	0	0	..	..	..	..
3 Burkina Faso	21	616	0	0	0	0	..	49	..	665
4 Nepal	3	711	0	0	0	15	..	21	..	747
5 Bangladesh	0	7,282	0	0	0	461	..	125	..	7,868
6 Malawi	122	910	0	0	0	124	..	80	..	1,114
7 Zaire	311	5,430	..	..	0	786	..	318	..	..
8 Mali	238	1,566	0	0	9	85	..	65	..	1,716
9 Burma	106	3,664	0	0	17	47	..	55	..	3,766
10 Mozambique	..	..	..	..	0	0	..	..	..	..
11 Madagascar	90	2,635	0	0	0	184	..	80	..	2,899
12 Uganda	138	929	0	0	0	229	..	35	..	1,193
13 Burundi	7	528	0	0	8	0	..	23	..	551
14 Tanzania	250	3,650	15	0	0	45	..	260	..	3,955
15 Togo	40	882	0	0	0	81	..	87	..	1,050
16 Niger	32	1,026	..	224	0	88	..	121	..	1,460
17 Benin	41	781	0	0	0	0	..	109	..	890
18 Somalia	77	1,415	0	0	0	145	..	20	..	1,580
19 Central African Rep.	24	393	0	0	0	33	..	27	..	453
20 India	8,018	31,913	100	2,598	10	4,274	..	2,303	..	41,088
21 Rwanda	2	412	0	0	3	0	..	27	..	439
22 China	..	17,193	0	0	0	731	..	4,800	..	22,724
23 Kenya	319	3,438	88	263	0	431	..	372	..	4,504
24 Zambia	623	3,575	30	0	0	825	..	900	..	5,300
25 Sierra Leone	60	459	0	0	0	72	..	59	..	590
26 Sudan	307	7,057	0	0	31	740	..	475	..	8,272
27 Haiti	40	585	0	0	2	67	..	46	..	698
28 Pakistan	3,064	11,764	5	30	45	1,036	..	790	..	13,620
29 Lesotho	8	182	0	0	0	0	..	4	..	186
30 Ghana	494	1,413	0	0	46	748	..	224	..	2,385
31 Sri Lanka	317	3,448	..	96	79	286	..	289	..	4,119
32 Mauritania	27	1,637	0	0	0	36	..	88	..	1,761
33 Senegal	100	2,456	31	15	0	247	..	272	..	2,990
34 *Afghanistan*	..	..	..	..	15	0	..	..	..	..
35 *Chad*	32	172	0	0	3	9	..	7	..	187
36 *Guinea*	312	1,421	0	0	3	25	..	69	..	1,516
37 *Kampuchea, Dem.*	..	..	..	..	..	..	..	..	..	..
38 *Lao PDR*	..	..	..	..	..	..	..	..	..	..
39 *Viet Nam*	..	..	..	..	..	..	..	..	..	..
Middle-income economies										
Lower middle-income										
40 Liberia	158	1,002	0	0	4	251	..	50	..	1,303
41 Yemen, PDR	1	1,927	0	0	0	7	..	125	..	2,059
42 Indonesia	2,443	31,901	461	3,828	139	51	..	6,309	..	42,090
43 Yemen Arab Rep.	4	2,052	0	0	0	8	..	249	..	2,308
44 Philippines	625	19,828	919	1,794	69	1,173	..	5,378	..	28,172
45 Morocco	712	14,610	..	..	28	1,026	..	2,189	..	..
46 Bolivia	482	3,523	11	555	6	145	..	397	..	4,619
47 Zimbabwe	233	1,712	..	46	0	234	..	489	..	2,481
48 Nigeria	452	21,496	115	50	0	0	..	330	..	21,876
49 Dominican Rep.	212	2,609	141	146	7	304	..	241	..	3,301
50 Papua New Guinea	36	1,147	173	1,095	0	0	..	62	..	2,304
51 Côte d'Ivoire	255	6,500	11	2,955	0	623	..	787	..	10,865
52 Honduras	90	2,342	19	125	0	98	..	298	..	2,863
53 Egypt, Arab Rep.	1,713	22,788	0	947	49	31	..	4,790	..	28,556
54 Nicaragua	147	5,343	0	0	8	0	..	1,027	..	6,370
55 Thailand	324	11,023	402	3,108	0	988	..	2,840	..	17,959
56 El Salvador	88	1,463	88	83	7	43	..	90	..	1,680
57 Botswana	17	355	0	0	0	0	..	3	..	358
58 Jamaica	160	2,993	822	64	0	678	..	147	..	3,882
59 Cameroon	131	2,267	9	505	0	0	..	761	..	3,533
60 Guatemala	106	2,187	14	119	0	70	..	225	..	2,601
61 Congo, People's Rep.	124	2,861	0	0	0	12	..	662	..	3,534
62 Paraguay	112	1,752	0	86	0	0	..	122	..	1,960
63 Peru	856	11,049	1,799	1,337	10	728	..	2,189	..	15,303
64 Turkey	1,843	23,309	42	503	74	1,085	..	6,911	..	31,808
65 Tunisia	541	5,001	0	250	13	183	..	553	..	5,987
66 Ecuador	193	7,919	49	59	14	486	..	490	..	8,953
67 Mauritius	32	427	0	22	0	158	..	38	..	644
68 Colombia	1,299	11,437	283	1,585	55	0	..	1,597	..	14,619

Note: For data comparability and coverage, see the technical notes.   Figures in italics are for years other than those specified.

| | Long-term debt (millions of dollars) | | | | Use of IMF credit (millions of dollars) | | Short-term debt (millions of dollars) | | Total external debt (millions of dollars) | |
| | Public and publicly guaranteed | | Private nonguaranteed | | | | | | | |
	1970	1986	1970	1986	1970	1986	1970	1986	1970	1986
69 Chile	2,067	15,109	501	2,821	2	1,331	..	1,480	..	20,741
70 Costa Rica	134	3,582	112	306	0	172	..	392	..	4,453
71 Jordan	119	3,079	0	0	0	70	..	985	..	4,134
72 Syrian Arab Rep.	232	3,060	0	0	10	0	..	1,290	..	4,350
73 *Lebanon*	64	211	0	0	0	0	..	240	..	451
Upper middle-income										
74 Brazil	3,421	82,523	1,706	14,641	0	4,501	..	9,010	..	110,675
75 Malaysia	390	16,759	50	2,891	0	0	..	..	..	..
76 South Africa	..	..	..	..	0	0	..	..	..	..
77 Mexico	3,196	74,962	2,770	16,100	0	4,060	..	6,600	..	101,722
78 Uruguay	269	2,759	29	43	18	395	..	573	..	3,770
79 Hungary	..	13,567	0	0	0	1,031	..	2,620	..	17,218
80 Poland	..	35,200	..	0	0	0	..	1,438	..	36,638
81 Portugal	485	13,929	85	641	0	700	..	1,389	..	16,658
82 Yugoslavia	1,199	13,174	854	4,781	0	2,069	..	1,340	..	21,364
83 Panama	194	3,439	0	0	0	353	..	1,010	..	4,802
84 Argentina	1,880	38,453	3,291	4,559	0	2,741	..	3,155	..	48,908
85 Korea, Rep. of	1,840	29,108	175	5,196	0	1,549	..	9,256	..	45,109
86 Algeria	937	14,777	0	0	0	0	..	3,152	..	17,929
87 Venezuela	728	24,485	236	7,934	0	0	..	1,472	..	33,891
88 Gabon	91	1,095	0	0	0	34	..	440	..	1,568
89 Greece	905	15,015	388	1,659	0	0	..	4,188	..	20,862
90 Oman	0	2,501	0	0	0	0	..	496	..	2,997
91 Trinidad and Tobago	101	1,154	0	0	0	0	..	273	..	1,427
92 Israel	2,274	15,938	361	4,470	13	0	..	3,367	..	23,775
93 Hong Kong	..	..	..	..	0	0	..	..	..	..
94 Singapore	152	2,120	248	..	0	0	..	268	..	..
95 *Iran, Islamic Rep.*	..	..	..	..	0	0	..	..	..	..
96 *Iraq*	..	..	..	..	0	0	..	..	..	..
97 *Romania*	..	5,309	0	0	0	714	..	617	..	6,639

Developing economies
Oil exporters
Exporters of manufactures
Highly indebted countries
Sub-Saharan Africa

High-income oil exporters

98 Saudi Arabia
99 Kuwait
100 United Arab Emirates
101 *Libya*

Industrial market economies

102 Spain
103 Ireland
104 New Zealand
105 Italy
106 United Kingdom

107 Belgium
108 Austria
109 Netherlands
110 France
111 Australia

112 Germany, Fed. Rep.
113 Finland
114 Denmark
115 Japan
116 Sweden

117 Canada
118 Norway
119 United States
120 Switzerland

Nonreporting nonmembers

121 *Albania*
122 *Angola*
123 *Bulgaria*
124 *Cuba*
125 *Czechoslovakia*

126 *German Dem. Rep.*
127 *Korea, Dem. Rep.*
128 *Mongolia*
129 *USSR*

Table 17. Flow of public and private external capital

	Disbursements (millions of dollars)				Repayment of principal (millions of dollars)				Net flow[a] (millions of dollars)			
	Public and publicly guaranteed		Private nonguaranteed		Public and publicly guaranteed		Private nonguaranteed		Public and publicly guaranteed		Private nonguaranteed	
	1970	1986	1970	1986	1970	1986	1970	1986	1970	1986	1970	1986
Low-income economies												
China and India												
Other low-income												
1 Ethiopia	28	321	0	0	15	125	0	0	13	195	0	0
2 Bhutan	..	..	..	..	..	..	..	..	..	..	..	..
3 Burkina Faso	2	94	0	0	2	23	0	0	0	71	0	0
4 Nepal	1	142	0	0	2	18	0	0	-2	124	0	0
5 Bangladesh	0	976	0	0	0	162	0	0	0	814	0	0
6 Malawi	40	119	0	0	3	72	0	0	37	47	0	0
7 Zaire	32	233	..	..	28	142	..	..	3	92	..	..
8 Mali	23	173	0	0	0	23	0	0	23	150	0	0
9 Burma	22	379	0	0	13	159	0	0	9	220	0	0
10 Mozambique	..	..	..	..	..	..	..	..	..	..	..	..
11 Madagascar	11	191	0	0	5	51	0	0	5	141	0	0
12 Uganda	27	80	0	0	4	16	0	0	23	63	0	0
13 Burundi	2	103	0	0	0	19	0	0	1	84	0	0
14 Tanzania	51	185	..	..	10	43	..	..	40	142	..	..
15 Togo	4	88	0	0	2	86	0	0	3	2	0	0
16 Niger	12	142	..	66	2	55	..	29	11	87	..	37
17 Benin	2	69	0	0	1	36	0	0	1	33	0	0
18 Somalia	4	125	0	0	1	54	0	0	4	71	0	0
19 Central African Rep.	2	76	0	0	3	9	0	0	-1	67	0	0
20 India	931	3,642	25	849	355	1,582	25	773	576	2,061	0	76
21 Rwanda	0	74	0	0	0	13	0	0	0	61	0	0
22 China	0	6,890	0	0	0	1,367	0	0	0	5,522	0	0
23 Kenya	34	582	..	..	17	256	..	..	17	327	..	..
24 Zambia	351	233	..	..	35	69	..	..	316	164	..	..
25 Sierra Leone	8	25	0	0	10	10	0	0	-3	14	0	0
26 Sudan	52	189	0	0	22	24	0	0	30	165	0	0
27 Haiti	4	43	0	0	4	11	0	0	1	32	0	0
28 Pakistan	489	1,113	3	19	113	708	1	15	377	405	2	4
29 Lesotho	0	22	0	0	0	10	0	0	0	12	0	0
30 Ghana	43	209	0	0	14	60	0	0	29	149	0	0
31 Sri Lanka	66	501	0	8	29	164	0	6	36	337	0	2
32 Mauritania	5	212	0	0	3	46	0	0	1	166	0	0
33 Senegal	19	390	1	5	5	111	3	3	14	279	-2	2
34 *Afghanistan*	..	..	..	..	3	..	0	..	..	..	..	..
35 *Chad*	6	20	0	0	3	2	0	0	3	18	0	0
36 *Guinea*	90	118	0	0	11	84	0	0	80	34	0	0
37 *Kampuchea, Dem.*	..	..	..	..	..	..	..	..	..	..	..	..
38 *Lao PDR*	..	..	..	..	..	..	..	..	..	..	..	..
39 *Viet Nam*	..	..	..	..	..	..	..	..	..	..	..	..
Middle-income economies												
Lower middle-income												
40 Liberia	8	43	0	0	12	13	0	0	-4	30	0	0
41 Yemen, PDR	1	557	0	0	0	77	0	0	1	480	0	0
42 Indonesia	441	4,311	195	550	59	2,385	61	532	383	1,926	134	18
43 Yemen Arab Rep.	4	213	0	0	0	57	0	0	4	156	0	0
44 Philippines	141	1,208	276	110	74	620	186	125	67	588	90	-15
45 Morocco	168	1,353	..	..	37	699	..	..	131	653	..	..
46 Bolivia	55	299	3	0	17	74	2	0	38	225	1	0
47 Zimbabwe	..	287	..	..	5	222	..	..	-5	66	..	..
48 Nigeria	56	1,253	25	0	38	1,233	30	0	18	20	-5	0
49 Dominican Rep.	38	190	22	0	7	122	20	4	31	68	2	-4
50 Papua New Guinea	43	99	111	279	0	83	20	204	43	16	91	75
51 Côte d'Ivoire	78	347	..	..	28	253	..	..	49	93	..	..
52 Honduras	29	207	10	18	3	80	3	29	26	127	7	-11
53 Egypt, Arab Rep.	397	1,550	..	310	309	1,034	..	146	88	516	..	164
54 Nicaragua	44	531	0	0	16	11	0	0	28	520	0	0
55 Thailand	51	1,302	169	587	23	1,192	107	850	28	110	62	-262
56 El Salvador	8	144	24	0	6	115	16	21	2	30	8	-21
57 Botswana	6	31	0	0	0	17	0	0	6	14	0	0
58 Jamaica	15	218	165	7	6	216	164	10	9	2	1	-2
59 Cameroon	29	274	11	207	5	179	2	246	24	95	9	-40
60 Guatemala	37	147	6	15	20	134	2	3	17	14	4	12
61 Congo, People's Rep.	20	519	0	0	6	232	0	0	15	286	0	0
62 Paraguay	15	225	0	0	7	109	0	18	8	115	0	-18
63 Peru	148	476	240	35	100	262	233	105	48	214	7	-70
64 Turkey	329	3,563	1	180	129	1,866	3	79	200	1,697	-2	102
65 Tunisia	89	765	0	50	47	507	0	46	42	258	0	4
66 Ecuador	41	1,071	7	3	16	206	11	34	26	865	-4	-31
67 Mauritius	2	61	0	7	1	36	0	3	1	25	0	4
68 Colombia	254	2,594	0	169	75	924	59	152	179	1,670	-59	17

Note: For data comparability and coverage, see the technical notes. Figures in italics are for years other than those specified.

	Disbursements (millions of dollars)				Repayment of principal (millions of dollars)				Net flow[a] (millions of dollars)			
	Public and publicly guaranteed		Private nonguaranteed		Public and publicly guaranteed		Private nonguaranteed		Public and publicly guaranteed		Private nonguaranteed	
	1970	1986	1970	1986	1970	1986	1970	1986	1970	1986	1970	1986
69 Chile	408	1,000	247	162	165	271	41	163	243	729	206	−1
70 Costa Rica	30	169	30	20	21	182	20	15	9	−13	10	5
71 Jordan	15	608	0	0	3	360	0	0	12	247	0	0
72 Syrian Arab Rep.	60	471	0	0	31	211	0	0	29	261	0	0
73 *Lebanon*	12	38	0	0	2	16	0	0	10	22	0	0
Upper middle-income												
74 Brazil	892	3,170	900	0	256	2,342	200	722	637	828	700	−722
75 Malaysia	45	1,300	12	901	47	1,055	9	803	−2	244	3	97
76 South Africa	..	..	..	..	..	..	..	..	..	..	..	..
77 Mexico	772	3,762	603	1,700	475	2,517	542	1,990	297	1,245	61	−290
78 Uruguay	37	144	13	0	47	85	4	18	−10	59	9	−18
79 Hungary	..	3,895	0	0	..	2,832	0	0	..	1,064	0	0
80 Poland	..	1,118	0	0	..	1,346	0	0	..	−228	0	0
81 Portugal	18	1,885	20	85	63	1,938	22	103	−45	−53	−1	−18
82 Yugoslavia	179	463	465	190	170	934	204	310	9	−471	261	−120
83 Panama	68	213	0	0	24	145	0	0	44	68	0	0
84 Argentina	482	2,303	424	300	344	1,434	428	534	139	869	−4	−234
85 Korea, Rep. of	444	3,235	32	1,666	198	4,664	7	2,699	246	−1,428	25	−1,033
86 Algeria	308	3,430	0	0	34	3,905	0	0	274	−475	0	0
87 Venezuela	226	134	67	0	42	1,332	25	594	184	−1,198	41	−594
88 Gabon	26	252	0	0	9	148	0	0	17	105	0	0
89 Greece	163	2,512	144	217	61	1,090	37	215	102	1,423	107	2
90 Oman	0	790	0	0	0	223	0	0	0	567	0	0
91 Trinidad and Tobago	8	109	0	0	10	136	0	0	−2	−27	0	0
92 Israel	411	658	123	550	26	835	36	574	385	−177	87	−24
93 Hong Kong	..	..	..	..	..	..	..	..	..	..	..	..
94 Singapore	61	447	..	..	6	247	..	..	55	200	..	..
95 *Iran, Islamic Rep.*	..	..	..	..	..	..	..	..	..	..	..	..
96 *Iraq*	..	..	..	..	..	..	..	..	..	..	..	..
97 *Romania*	..	745	0	0	..	1,060	0	0	..	−314	0	0

Developing economies
  Oil exporters
  Exporters of manufactures
  Highly indebted countries
  Sub-Saharan Africa

High-income oil exporters

98 Saudi Arabia
99 Kuwait
100 United Arab Emirates
101 *Libya*

Industrial market economies

102 Spain
103 Ireland
104 New Zealand
105 Italy
106 United Kingdom

107 Belgium
108 Austria
109 Netherlands
110 France
111 Australia

112 Germany, Fed. Rep.
113 Finland
114 Denmark
115 Japan
116 Sweden

117 Canada
118 Norway
119 United States
120 Switzerland

Nonreporting nonmembers

121 *Albania*
122 *Angola*
123 *Bulgaria*
124 *Cuba*
125 *Czechoslovakia*

126 *German Dem. Rep.*
127 *Korea, Dem. Rep.*
128 *Mongolia*
129 *USSR*

a. Disbursements less repayments of principal may not equal net flow, because of rounding.

Table 18. Total external public and private debt and debt service ratios

	Total long-term debt disbursed and outstanding				Total interest payments on long-term debt (millions of dollars)		Total long-term debt service as percentage of:			
	Millions of dollars		As percentage of GNP				GNP		Exports of goods and services	
	1970	1986	1970	1986	1970	1986	1970	1986	1970	1986
Low-income economies										
China and India										
Other low-income										
1 Ethiopia	169	1,989	9.5	35.7	6	52	1.2	3.2	11.3	25.8
2 Bhutan	..	..	..	..	..	..	..	..	..	..
3 Burkina Faso	21	616	6.5	41.8	0	12	0.6	2.3	6.5	14.8
4 Nepal	3	711	0.3	27.7	0	13	0.3	1.2	3.1	9.4
5 Bangladesh	0	7,282	0.0	47.5	0	108	0.0	1.8	0.0	25.1
6 Malawi	122	910	43.2	78.6	4	36	2.3	9.4	7.8	40.1
7 Zaire	..	..	..	..	..	..	..	..	..	..
8 Mali	238	1,566	69.6	95.7	0	13	0.1	2.1	1.0	14.2
9 Burma	106	3,664	4.9	45.3	3	88	0.7	3.0	12.2	55.4
10 Mozambique	..	..	..	..	..	..	..	..	..	..
11 Madagascar	90	2,635	10.4	105.6	2	63	0.8	4.5	3.7	27.7
12 Uganda	138	929	7.3	26.8	5	13	0.5	0.8	2.9	6.5
13 Burundi	7	528	3.1	44.2	0	12	0.3	2.6	2.3	19.0
14 Tanzania	265	3,650	20.7	81.6	..	..	..	..	..	..
15 Togo	40	882	16.0	93.7	1	42	0.9	13.6	3.0	32.5
16 Niger	..	1,251	..	62.0	..	49	..	6.6	..	40.3
17 Benin	41	781	15.1	56.5	0	22	0.6	4.2	2.2	28.8
18 Somalia	77	1,415	24.4	*54.4*	0	18	0.3	2.0	1.8	62.1
19 Central African Rep.	24	393	13.4	41.6	1	9	1.8	1.9	5.3	9.6
20 India	8,118	34,511	15.2	15.1	204	1,359	1.1	1.6	27.3	24.6
21 Rwanda	2	439	0.9	23.9	0	5	0.1	1.0	1.2	7.6
22 China	..	17,193	..	6.3	..	1,014	..	0.9	..	7.8
23 Kenya	406	3,700	26.3	55.5	..	..	..	..	..	..
24 Zambia	653	3,575	37.5	240.5	..	..	..	..	..	..
25 Sierra Leone	60	459	14.3	37.0	3	4	3.1	1.2	10.7	8.2
26 Sudan	307	7,057	15.3	95.9	13	32	1.7	0.8	10.7	7.7
27 Haiti	40	585	10.3	27.4	0	7	1.0	0.9	7.5	6.0
28 Pakistan	3,069	11,794	30.6	36.0	77	358	1.9	3.3	23.7	27.2
29 Lesotho	8	182	7.8	33.4	0	4	0.3	2.5	2.7	4.2
30 Ghana	494	1,413	21.9	*25.6*	12	28	1.2	*1.8*	5.5	10.8
31 Sri Lanka	317	3,544	16.1	55.4	12	121	2.1	4.6	10.9	18.4
32 Mauritania	27	1,637	13.9	210.0	0	31	1.8	9.9	3.3	17.4
33 Senegal	131	2,471	15.5	69.6	2	99	1.1	6.0	4.0	20.2
34 *Afghanistan*	..	..	..	..	..	..	..	..	..	..
35 *Chad*	32	172	9.9	..	0	2	0.9	..	4.0	2.2
36 *Guinea*	312	1,421	47.1	*70.4*	4	19	2.2	3.6	..	..
37 *Kampuchea, Dem.*	..	..	..	..	..	..	..	..	..	..
38 *Lao PDR*	..	..	..	..	..	..	..	..	..	..
39 *Viet Nam*	..	..	..	..	..	..	..	..	..	..
Middle-income economies										
Lower middle-income										
40 Liberia	158	1,002	39.3	99.0	6	15	4.3	2.7	8.1	6.4
41 Yemen, PDR	1	1,927	..	189.7	0	22	..	9.8	0.0	74.6
42 Indonesia	2,904	35,729	29.9	49.7	45	2,363	1.7	7.3	13.9	33.1
43 Yemen Arab Rep.	4	2,052	1.6	41.1	0	42	0.0	2.0	0.0	59.6
44 Philippines	1,544	21,622	21.8	72.2	44	1,092	4.3	6.1	23.0	21.3
45 Morocco	..	..	..	..	..	..	..	..	..	..
46 Bolivia	493	4,078	47.2	90.9	7	132	2.5	4.6	12.6	30.4
47 Zimbabwe	..	1,758	..	33.2	..	..	..	..	..	..
48 Nigeria	567	21,876	5.7	45.0	28	391	1.0	3.3	7.1	23.4
49 Dominican Rep.	353	2,756	26.1	55.5	13	182	2.9	6.2	15.2	21.7
50 Papua New Guinea	209	2,242	33.4	93.1	10	140	4.8	17.7	29.1	35.8
51 Côte d'Ivoire	266	9,455	19.5	106.8	..	..	..	..	..	..
52 Honduras	109	2,467	15.6	72.4	4	117	1.4	6.6	5.0	22.0
53 Egypt, Arab Rep.	1,713	23,735	22.5	58.8	56	766	4.8	4.8	38.0	23.8
54 Nicaragua	147	5,343	19.5	198.2	7	21	3.0	1.2	10.5	12.9
55 Thailand	726	14,130	11.1	35.2	33	1,031	2.5	7.7	13.9	25.4
56 El Salvador	176	1,547	17.3	40.2	9	75	3.1	5.5	12.1	20.8
57 Botswana	17	355	21.2	36.2	0	27	0.6	4.5	0.9	4.3
58 Jamaica	982	3,057	73.1	147.5	63	219	17.4	21.4	43.5	32.7
59 Cameroon	141	2,772	13.0	25.4	5	185	1.0	5.6	4.0	22.8
60 Guatemala	120	2,306	6.5	31.7	7	156	1.6	4.0	8.2	24.3
61 Congo, People's Rep.	124	2,861	46.5	152.1	3	79	3.4	16.5	11.5	39.8
62 Paraguay	112	1,838	19.2	51.5	3	90	1.8	6.1	11.7	25.2
63 Peru	2,655	12,386	38.1	50.5	162	332	7.1	2.8	40.0	20.5
64 Turkey	1,885	23,812	15.0	42.3	44	1,564	1.4	6.2	22.7	32.4
65 Tunisia	541	5,251	38.6	61.5	18	304	4.7	10.0	19.7	30.7
66 Ecuador	242	7,977	14.8	74.4	10	648	2.2	8.3	14.1	33.9
67 Mauritius	32	449	14.3	33.4	2	29	1.4	5.1	3.2	7.7
68 Colombia	1,582	13,022	22.5	41.7	59	970	2.8	6.5	19.0	31.5

Note: For data comparability and coverage, see the technical notes.   Figures in italics are for years other than those specified.

| | Total long-term debt disbursed and outstanding | | | | Total interest payments on long-term debt (millions of dollars) | | Total long-term debt service as percentage of: | | | |
| | Millions of dollars | | As percentage of GNP | | | | GNP | | Exports of goods and services | |
	1970	1986	1970	1986	1970	1986	1970	1986	1970	1986
69 Chile	2,568	17,930	32.1	120.1	104	1,515	3.9	13.1	24.4	37.1
70 Costa Rica	246	3,889	25.3	97.8	14	217	5.7	10.4	19.9	28.9
71 Jordan	119	3,079	22.9	68.9	2	180	0.9	12.1	3.6	28.7
72 Syrian Arab Rep.	232	3,060	10.8	17.7	6	87	1.7	1.7	11.3	15.6
73 *Lebanon*	64	211	4.2	..	1	12	0.2	..	..	..
Upper middle-income										
74 Brazil	5,128	97,164	12.2	37.6	135	7,516	0.9	4.1	12.5	41.8
75 Malaysia	440	19,650	10.8	77.0	25	1,394	2.0	12.7	4.5	20.0
76 South Africa	..	..	..	..	..	..	..	..	..	..
77 Mexico	5,966	91,062	17.0	76.1	283	7,737	3.7	10.2	44.3	51.5
78 Uruguay	298	2,802	12.5	47.1	17	253	2.9	6.0	23.6	22.3
79 Hungary	..	13,567	..	59.6	..	1,112	..	17.3	..	35.9
80 Poland	..	35,200	..	48.5	..	1,264	..	3.6	..	18.5
81 Portugal	570	14,570	9.2	52.2	34	1,241	1.9	11.8	8.8	32.9
82 Yugoslavia	2,053	17,955	15.0	27.8	104	1,492	3.5	4.2	19.7	17.8
83 Panama	194	3,439	19.5	66.5	7	322	3.1	9.0	7.7	7.6
84 Argentina	5,171	43,012	23.2	51.7	338	3,698	5.0	6.8	51.7	64.1
85 Korea, Rep. of	2,015	34,304	22.5	36.1	76	2,896	3.1	10.8	20.4	24.4
86 Algeria	937	14,777	19.3	24.8	10	1,250	0.9	8.7	3.9	54.8
87 Venezuela	964	32,419	8.7	66.9	53	2,257	1.1	8.6	4.2	37.4
88 Gabon	91	1,095	28.7	37.1	3	61	3.7	7.1	5.6	17.5
89 Greece	1,293	16,674	12.7	42.5	63	1,213	1.6	6.4	14.7	31.9
90 Oman	0	2,501	0.0	38.3	0	172	0.0	6.0	..	11.3
91 Trinidad and Tobago	101	1,154	13.3	24.0	6	92	2.1	4.8	4.6	13.2
92 Israel	2,635	20,408	47.9	72.1	34	1,790	1.7	11.3	6.8	27.5
93 Hong Kong	..	..	..	..	..	..	..	..	..	..
94 Singapore	..	..	..	..	..	..	..	..	..	..
95 *Iran, Islamic Rep.*	..	..	..	..	..	..	..	..	..	..
96 *Iraq*	..	..	..	..	..	..	..	..	..	..
97 *Romania*	..	5,309	..	..	..	543	..	..	..	11.9

Developing economies
  Oil exporters
  Exporters of manufactures
  Highly indebted countries
  Sub-Saharan Africa

High-income oil exporters

98 Saudi Arabia
99 Kuwait
100 United Arab Emirates
101 *Libya*

Industrial market economies

102 Spain
103 Ireland
104 New Zealand
105 Italy
106 United Kingdom

107 Belgium
108 Austria
109 Netherlands
110 France
111 Australia

112 Germany, Fed. Rep.
113 Finland
114 Denmark
115 Japan
116 Sweden

117 Canada
118 Norway
119 United States
120 Switzerland

Nonreporting nonmembers

121 *Albania*
122 *Angola*
123 *Bulgaria*
124 *Cuba*
125 *Czechoslovakia*

126 *German Dem. Rep.*
127 *Korea, Dem. Rep.*
128 *Mongolia*
129 *USSR*

Note: Public and private debt includes public, publicly guaranteed, and private nonguaranteed debt; data are shown only when they are available for all categories.

Table 19. External public debt and debt service ratios

	External public debt outstanding and disbursed				Interest payments on external public debt (millions of dollars)		Debt service as percentage of:			
	Millions of dollars		As percentage of GNP				GNP		Exports of goods and services	
	1970	1986	1970	1986	1970	1986	1970	1986	1970	1986
Low-income economies	..	121,205 t	..	19.2 w	..	3,846 t	..	1.5 w	..	14.1 w
China and India	..	49,106 t	..	9.8 w	..	2,129 t	..	1.0 w	..	11.1 w
Other low-income	7,373 t	72,100 t	16.6 w	54.4 w	204 t	1,718 t	1.3 w	3.3 w	7.6 w	20.9 w
1 Ethiopia	169	1,989	9.5	35.7	6	52	1.2	3.2	11.3	25.8
2 Bhutan	..	..	..	..	..	..	..	..	..	..
3 Burkina Faso	21	616	6.5	41.8	0	12	0.6	2.3	6.5	14.8
4 Nepal	3	711	0.3	27.7	0	13	0.3	1.2	3.1	9.4
5 Bangladesh	0	7,282	0.0	47.5	0	108	0.0	1.8	0.0	25.1
6 Malawi	122	910	43.2	78.6	4	36	2.3	9.4	7.8	40.1
7 Zaire	311	5,430	9.1	96.8	9	228	1.1	6.6	4.4	18.2
8 Mali	238	1,566	69.6	95.7	0	13	0.1	2.1	1.0	14.2
9 Burma	106	3,664	4.9	45.3	3	88	0.7	3.0	12.2	55.4
10 Mozambique	..	..	..	..	..	..	..	..	..	..
11 Madagascar	90	2,635	10.4	105.6	2	63	0.8	4.5	3.7	27.7
12 Uganda	138	929	7.3	26.8	5	13	0.5	0.8	2.9	6.5
13 Burundi	7	528	3.1	44.2	0	12	0.3	2.6	2.3	19.0
14 Tanzania	250	3,650	19.5	81.6	7	26	1.3	1.5	5.3	15.3
15 Togo	40	882	16.0	93.7	1	42	0.9	13.6	3.0	32.5
16 Niger	32	1,026	5.0	50.9	1	37	0.4	4.6	4.0	27.9
17 Benin	41	781	15.1	56.5	0	22	0.6	4.2	2.2	28.8
18 Somalia	77	1,415	24.4	54.4	0	18	0.3	2.0	1.8	62.1
19 Central African Rep.	24	393	13.4	41.6	1	9	1.8	1.9	5.3	9.6
20 India	8,018	31,913	15.0	14.0	198	1,115	1.0	1.2	25.8	17.9
21 Rwanda	2	412	0.9	22.4	0	5	0.1	1.0	1.2	7.6
22 China	..	17,193	..	6.3	..	1,014	..	0.9	..	7.8
23 Kenya	319	3,438	20.6	51.6	13	174	1.9	6.5	5.9	22.5
24 Zambia	623	3,575	35.7	240.5	29	55	3.7	8.3	6.4	16.8
25 Sierra Leone	60	459	14.3	37.0	3	4	3.1	1.2	10.7	8.2
26 Sudan	307	7,057	15.3	95.9	13	32	1.7	0.8	10.7	7.7
27 Haiti	40	585	10.3	27.4	0	7	1.0	0.9	7.5	6.0
28 Pakistan	3,064	11,764	30.6	35.9	77	355	1.9	3.2	23.6	26.8
29 Lesotho	8	182	7.8	33.4	0	4	0.3	2.5	2.7	4.2
30 Ghana	494	1,413	21.9	25.6	12	28	1.2	1.8	5.5	10.8
31 Sri Lanka	317	3,448	16.1	53.9	12	113	2.1	4.3	10.9	17.5
32 Mauritania	27	1,637	13.9	210.0	0	31	1.8	9.9	3.3	17.4
33 Senegal	100	2,456	11.9	69.2	2	98	0.8	5.9	2.9	19.9
34 Afghanistan	..	..	..	..	..	..	..	..	..	..
35 Chad	32	172	9.9	21.2	0	2	0.9	0.4	4.0	2.2
36 Guinea	312	1,421	47.1	70.4	4	19	2.2	3.6	..	..
37 Kampuchea, Dem.	..	..	..	..	..	..	..	..	..	..
38 Lao PDR	..	..	..	..	..	..	..	..	..	..
39 Viet Nam	..	..	..	..	..	..	..	..	..	..
Middle-income economies	34,068 w	654,432 w	12.2 w	42.2 w	1,299 w	43,639 w	1.6 w	5.6 w	9.8 w	20.8 w
Lower middle-income	16,006 w	247,863 w	15.2 w	51.9 w	491 w	12,931 w	1.7 w	5.6 w	10.7 w	24.1 w
40 Liberia	158	1,002	39.3	99.0	6	15	4.3	2.7	8.1	6.4
41 Yemen, PDR	1	1,927	..	189.7	0	22	..	9.8	0.0	74.6
42 Indonesia	2,443	31,901	25.2	44.4	24	2,047	0.9	6.2	7.0	27.8
43 Yemen Arab Rep.	4	2,052	1.6	41.1	0	42	0.0	2.0	0.0	59.6
44 Philippines	625	19,828	8.8	66.2	26	962	1.4	5.3	7.5	18.3
45 Morocco	712	14,610	18.2	103.9	24	742	1.6	10.2	8.7	40.4
46 Bolivia	482	3,523	46.1	78.5	7	87	2.2	3.6	11.3	23.7
47 Zimbabwe	233	1,712	15.7	32.4	5	117	0.7	6.4	2.3	22.3
48 Nigeria	452	21,496	4.5	44.2	20	391	0.6	3.3	4.3	23.4
49 Dominican Rep.	212	2,609	15.7	52.5	4	171	0.8	5.9	4.4	20.6
50 Papua New Guinea	36	1,147	5.8	47.6	1	66	0.2	6.2	1.3	12.5
51 Côte d'Ivoire	255	6,500	18.7	73.4	12	532	2.9	8.9	7.1	23.3
52 Honduras	90	2,342	12.9	68.7	3	111	0.8	5.6	2.9	18.5
53 Egypt, Arab Rep.	1,713	22,788	22.5	56.4	56	703	4.8	4.3	38.0	21.3
54 Nicaragua	147	5,343	19.5	198.2	7	21	3.0	1.2	10.5	12.9
55 Thailand	324	11,023	4.9	27.4	16	751	0.6	4.8	3.3	16.1
56 El Salvador	88	1,463	8.6	38.1	4	67	1.0	4.7	3.7	18.0
57 Botswana	17	355	21.2	36.2	0	27	0.6	4.5	0.9	4.3
58 Jamaica	160	2,993	11.9	144.4	9	215	1.1	20.8	2.8	31.7
59 Cameroon	131	2,267	12.1	20.8	4	121	0.8	2.7	3.2	11.2
60 Guatemala	106	2,187	5.7	30.1	6	147	1.4	3.9	7.4	23.4
61 Congo, People's Rep.	124	2,861	46.5	152.1	3	79	3.4	16.5	11.5	39.8
62 Paraguay	112	1,752	19.2	49.1	3	88	1.8	5.5	11.7	22.9
63 Peru	856	11,049	12.3	45.0	44	229	2.1	2.0	11.6	14.4
64 Turkey	1,843	23,309	14.7	41.4	42	1,529	1.4	6.0	22.0	31.3
65 Tunisia	541	5,001	38.6	58.6	18	286	4.7	9.3	19.7	28.5
66 Ecuador	193	7,919	11.8	73.9	7	640	1.4	7.9	8.7	32.3
67 Mauritius	32	427	14.3	31.8	2	28	1.4	4.8	3.2	7.3
68 Colombia	1,299	11,437	18.5	36.6	44	871	1.7	5.7	11.7	27.6

Note: For data comparability and coverage, see the technical notes. Figures in italics are for years other than those specified.

		External public debt outstanding and disbursed				Interest payments on external public debt (millions of dollars)		Debt service as percentage of:			
		Millions of dollars		As percentage of GNP				GNP		Exports of goods and services	
		1970	1986	1970	1986	1970	1986	1970	1986	1970	1986
69	Chile	2,067	15,109	25.8	101.2	78	1,350	3.0	10.9	19.1	30.8
70	Costa Rica	134	3,582	13.8	90.1	7	196	2.9	9.5	10.0	26.3
71	Jordan	119	3,079	22.9	68.9	2	180	0.9	12.1	3.6	28.7
72	Syrian Arab Rep.	232	3,060	10.8	17.7	6	87	1.7	1.7	11.3	15.6
73	*Lebanon*	64	211	4.2	..	1	12	0.2	..	..	..
	Upper middle-income	**18,062 w**	**406,569 w**	**10.4 w**	**37.9 w**	**808 w**	**30,708 w**	**1.5 w**	**5.6 w**	**9.2 w**	**19.7 w**
74	Brazil	3,421	82,523	8.2	31.9	135	6,066	0.9	3.3	12.5	33.2
75	Malaysia	390	16,759	9.5	65.7	22	1,173	1.7	8.7	3.8	13.7
76	South Africa	..	..	..	..	..	..	..	..	..	..
77	Mexico	3,196	74,962	9.1	62.6	216	6,237	2.0	7.3	23.6	36.8
78	Uruguay	269	2,759	11.3	46.4	16	249	2.7	5.6	21.7	20.9
79	Hungary	..	13,567	..	59.6	..	1,112	..	17.3	..	35.9
80	Poland	..	35,200	..	48.5	..	1,264	..	3.6	..	18.5
81	Portugal	485	13,929	7.8	49.9	29	1,205	1.5	11.3	6.8	31.5
82	Yugoslavia	1,199	13,174	8.8	20.4	72	1,052	1.8	3.1	10.0	12.9
83	Panama	194	3,439	19.5	66.5	7	322	3.1	9.0	7.7	7.6
84	Argentina	1,880	38,453	8.4	46.2	121	3,182	2.1	5.5	21.6	52.2
85	Korea, Rep. of	1,840	29,108	20.6	30.6	71	2,332	3.0	7.4	19.5	16.7
86	Algeria	937	14,777	19.3	24.8	10	1,250	0.9	8.7	3.9	54.8
87	Venezuela	728	24,485	6.6	50.5	40	1,764	0.7	6.4	2.9	27.7
88	Gabon	91	1,095	28.7	37.1	3	61	3.7	7.1	5.6	17.5
89	Greece	905	15,015	8.9	38.2	41	1,082	1.0	5.5	9.3	27.5
90	Oman	0	2,501	0.0	38.3	0	172	0.0	6.0	..	11.3
91	Trinidad and Tobago	101	1,154	13.3	24.0	6	92	2.1	4.8	4.6	13.2
92	Israel	2,274	15,938	41.3	56.3	13	1,355	0.7	7.7	2.8	18.9
93	Hong Kong	..	..	..	..	..	..	..	..	..	..
94	Singapore	152	2,120	7.9	11.8	6	174	0.6	2.3	0.6	1.4
95	*Iran, Islamic Rep.*	..	..	..	..	..	..	..	..	..	..
96	*Iraq*	..	..	..	..	..	..	..	..	..	..
97	*Romania*	..	5,309	..	..	..	543	..	..	..	11.9
	Developing economies	**49,458 w**	**775,637 w**	**13.1 w**	**35.5 w**	**1,700 w**	**47,485 w**	**1.5 w**	**4.4 w**	**10.1 w**	**20.0 w**
	Oil exporters	**10,341 w**	**211,266 w**	**12.2 w**	**47.6 w**	**396 w**	**13,642 w**	**1.7 w**	**6.2 w**	**12.0 w**	**30.5 w**
	Exporters of manufactures	..	**260,276 w**	..	**22.7 w**	..	**17,254 w**	..	**3.1 w**	..	**14.0 w**
	Highly indebted countries	**17,926 w**	**354,401 w**	**10.2 w**	**45.8 w**	**877 w**	**24,764 w**	**1.6 w**	**5.0 w**	**12.4 w**	**29.5 w**
	Sub-Saharan Africa	**5,336 w**	**82,360 w**	**13.1 w**	**57.4 w**	**166 w**	**2,404 w**	**1.1 w**	**4.3 w**	**5.3 w**	**19.3 w**

High-income oil exporters

98	Saudi Arabia
99	Kuwait
100	United Arab Emirates
101	*Libya*

Industrial market economies

102	Spain
103	Ireland
104	New Zealand
105	Italy
106	United Kingdom
107	Belgium
108	Austria
109	Netherlands
110	France
111	Australia
112	Germany, Fed. Rep.
113	Finland
114	Denmark
115	Japan
116	Sweden
117	Canada
118	Norway
119	United States
120	Switzerland

Nonreporting nonmembers

121	*Albania*
122	*Angola*
123	*Bulgaria*
124	*Cuba*
125	*Czechoslovakia*
126	*German Dem. Rep.*
127	*Korea, Dem. Rep.*
128	*Mongolia*
129	*USSR*

Table 20. Terms of external public borrowing

	Commitments (millions of dollars)		Average interest rate (percent)		Average maturity (years)		Average grace period (years)		Public loans with variable interest rates, as a percentage of public debt	
	1970	1986	1970	1986	1970	1986	1970	1986	1970	1986
Low-income economies	..	19,695 t	..	5.1 w	..	24 w	..	6 w	..	11.3 w
China and India	..	11,958 t	..	5.9 w	..	18 w	..	5 w	..	18.6 w
Other low-income	2,680 t	7,737 t	3.2 w	3.7 w	28 w	32 w	9 w	8 w	0.2 w	6.2 w
1 Ethiopia	21	257	4.4	2.0	32	35	7	7	0.0	4.1
2 Bhutan	..	..	..	..	..	..	..	..	..	..
3 Burkina Faso	9	59	2.3	2.4	36	31	8	7	0.0	0.4
4 Nepal	17	209	2.8	1.0	27	42	6	9	0.0	1.3
5 Bangladesh	0	783	0.0	1.1	0	41	0	10	0.0	0.1
6 Malawi	14	118	3.8	3.2	29	27	6	8	0.0	4.9
7 Zaire	258	446	6.5	5.2	12	26	4	6	0.0	12.9
8 Mali	34	143	1.1	1.4	25	36	9	9	0.0	0.3
9 Burma	50	193	4.1	2.8	16	33	5	9	0.0	0.3
10 Mozambique	..	..	..	..	..	..	..	..	..	..
11 Madagascar	23	239	2.3	2.3	39	37	9	9	0.0	6.6
12 Uganda	12	0	3.8	0.0	28	0	6	0	0.0	0.3
13 Burundi	1	67	2.9	1.0	5	31	2	8	0.0	1.3
14 Tanzania	284	196	1.2	1.0	39	48	11	10	1.6	4.1
15 Togo	3	38	4.5	2.8	17	27	4	7	0.0	5.1
16 Niger	19	206	1.2	1.1	40	39	8	9	0.0	14.9
17 Benin	7	45	1.8	5.2	32	19	7	5	0.0	5.4
18 Somalia	2	97	0.0	1.2	3	44	3	9	0.0	0.0
19 Central African Rep.	7	88	2.0	2.2	36	37	8	8	0.0	0.0
20 India	954	5,761	2.5	5.1	34	22	8	5	0.0	10.8
21 Rwanda	9	137	0.8	1.3	50	42	10	9	0.0	0.0
22 China	..	6,197	..	6.7	..	14	..	4	..	33.1
23 Kenya	50	327	2.6	6.3	37	20	8	5	0.1	3.6
24 Zambia	557	188	4.2	4.8	27	31	9	7	0.0	16.0
25 Sierra Leone	25	37	2.9	0.5	27	16	6	5	10.6	0.6
26 Sudan	95	271	1.8	1.4	17	34	9	8	0.0	13.4
27 Haiti	5	40	4.8	2.1	10	41	1	10	0.0	1.7
28 Pakistan	951	2,084	2.8	6.6	31	26	12	6	0.0	5.2
29 Lesotho	0	40	5.5	3.0	28	31	2	7	0.0	0.0
30 Ghana	57	141	2.1	3.1	37	44	10	9	0.0	0.0
31 Sri Lanka	81	543	3.0	4.1	26	33	5	9	0.0	8.7
32 Mauritania	7	227	6.0	2.3	11	27	3	7	0.0	3.5
33 Senegal	7	396	3.8	3.2	23	29	7	8	0.0	7.2
34 *Afghanistan*	..	..	..	..	..	..	..	..	..	..
35 *Chad*	10	55	5.7	0.9	8	48	1	11	0.0	0.2
36 *Guinea*	68	67	2.9	0.9	13	46	5	10	0.0	11.9
37 *Kampuchea, Dem.*	..	..	..	..	..	..	..	..	..	..
38 *Lao PDR*	..	..	..	..	..	..	..	..	..	..
39 *Viet Nam*	..	..	..	..	..	..	..	..	..	..
Middle-income economies	9,274 t	51,796 t	6.1 w	7.6 w	17 w	14 w	5 w	5 w	3.6 w	53.3 w
Lower middle-income	3,978 t	23,542 t	4.7 w	7.3 w	21 w	16 w	6 w	5 w	1.7 w	35.1 w
40 Liberia	12	19	6.7	0.0	19	29	5	8	0.0	12.3
41 Yemen, PDR	63	92	0.0	1.4	21	19	11	5	0.0	0.0
42 Indonesia	520	3,930	2.6	7.2	34	16	9	6	0.0	24.5
43 Yemen Arab Rep.	9	196	4.1	4.4	5	21	3	5	0.0	3.4
44 Philippines	171	1,029	0.0	6.0	0	23	0	6	0.8	51.8
45 Morocco	187	1,132	4.6	6.7	20	20	3	6	0.0	34.8
46 Bolivia	24	266	1.9	3.7	47	22	4	6	0.0	23.6
47 Zimbabwe	..	200	..	5.5	..	18	..	4	0.0	28.6
48 Nigeria	65	1,018	6.0	8.6	14	18	4	5	2.7	54.5
49 Dominican Rep.	20	86	2.4	5.5	28	17	5	6	0.0	28.4
50 Papua New Guinea	91	160	6.4	6.9	22	15	8	3	0.0	38.2
51 Côte d'Ivoire	70	591	5.8	7.0	19	17	5	5	9.0	47.2
52 Honduras	23	165	4.1	6.6	30	29	7	8	0.0	17.6
53 Egypt, Arab Rep.	704	1,389	6.0	8.8	19	23	8	10	0.0	2.1
54 Nicaragua	23	160	7.1	4.0	18	17	4	4	0.0	26.6
55 Thailand	106	1,746	6.8	6.2	19	16	4	6	0.0	33.5
56 El Salvador	12	108	4.7	3.1	23	39	6	9	0.0	8.3
57 Botswana	38	43	0.6	6.8	39	20	10	6	0.0	10.4
58 Jamaica	24	183	6.0	6.6	16	16	3	4	0.0	20.4
59 Cameroon	42	247	4.7	7.9	29	15	8	4	0.0	5.0
60 Guatemala	50	120	3.7	5.4	26	22	6	6	10.3	31.2
61 Congo, People's Rep.	32	899	2.8	10.6	17	8	6	2	0.0	31.3
62 Paraguay	14	80	5.7	7.9	25	14	6	4	0.0	15.2
63 Peru	125	290	7.4	7.4	11	12	3	3	0.0	35.7
64 Turkey	484	4,451	3.6	7.4	19	12	5	4	0.9	28.9
65 Tunisia	144	716	3.5	6.9	27	16	6	5	0.0	17.6
66 Ecuador	78	1,090	6.2	7.4	20	13	4	4	0.0	72.1
67 Mauritius	14	128	0.0	7.1	24	17	2	5	6.0	17.6
68 Colombia	363	1,540	6.0	8.5	21	14	5	3	0.0	43.8

Note: For data comparability and coverage, see the technical notes. Figures in italics are for years other than those specified.

	Commitments (millions of dollars)		Average interest rate (percent)		Average maturity (years)		Average grace period (years)		Public loans with variable interest rates, as a percentage of public debt	
	1970	1986	1970	1986	1970	1986	1970	1986	1970	1986
69 Chile	361	754	6.8	8.6	12	19	3	4	0.0	82.6
70 Costa Rica	58	148	5.6	7.8	28	21	6	5	7.5	57.8
71 Jordan	35	272	3.8	7.3	12	13	5	3	0.0	19.8
72 Syrian Arab Rep.	14	264	4.4	5.3	9	15	2	4	0.0	1.1
73 *Lebanon*	7	31	2.9	4.8	22	13	1	3	0.0	11.9
Upper middle-income	5,296 *t*	28,254 *t*	7.1 *w*	7.8 *w*	14 *w*	12 *w*	4 *w*	4 *w*	4.1 *w*	64.4 *w*
74 Brazil	1,436	2,650	6.7	8.7	14	13	3	3	11.8	69.4
75 Malaysia	84	2,550	6.1	6.7	19	14	5	4	0.0	52.2
76 South Africa	..	..	..	..	..	..	..	..	..	..
77 Mexico	858	3,595	7.9	8.4	12	14	3	4	5.7	79.7
78 Uruguay	71	154	7.9	8.5	12	13	3	3	0.7	69.1
79 Hungary[a]	..	3,584	..	7.8	..	9	..	7	..	69.1
80 Poland	..	1,333	..	5.3	..	6	..	3	..	61.7
81 Portugal	59	2,035	4.3	7.9	17	9	4	5	0.0	46.4
82 Yugoslavia	199	13	7.1	9.5	17	9	6	4	3.3	66.7
83 Panama	111	142	6.1	8.5	15	15	4	4	0.0	60.2
84 Argentina	494	1,291	7.3	8.9	12	12	3	3	0.0	83.7
85 Korea, Rep. of	691	3,390	5.8	7.5	19	13	6	4	1.1	45.3
86 Algeria	306	2,149	6.4	7.5	10	9	2	2	2.8	29.3
87 Venezuela	198	638	7.8	8.5	8	20	2	6	2.6	92.7
88 Gabon	33	115	5.1	7.7	11	15	2	5	0.0	7.4
89 Greece	246	2,557	7.2	7.5	9	8	4	5	3.5	63.0
90 Oman	..	612	..	7.8	..	9	..	5	0.0	30.7
91 Trinidad And Tobago	3	91	7.4	7.5	10	10	1	2	0.0	49.8
92 Israel	438	575	10.0	9.5	13	13	4	3	0.0	0.4
93 Hong Kong	..	60	..	..	..	..	..	..	..	..
94 Singapore	69	264	6.9	9.2	18	12	4	6	0.0	18.9
95 *Iran, Islamic Rep.*	..	..	..	..	..	..	..	..	..	..
96 *Iraq*	..	..	..	..	..	..	..	..	..	..
97 Romania	..	456	..	9.3	..	28	..	7	..	36.6
Developing economies	12,908 *t*	71,490 *t*	5.2 *w*	6.9 *w*	20 *w*	16 *w*	6 *w*	5 *w*	2.3 *w*	46.8 *w*
Oil exporters	2,852 *t*	16,036 *t*	6.1 *w*	8.0 *w*	18 *w*	14 *w*	5 *w*	5 *w*	4.0 *w*	54.4 *w*
Exporters of manufactures	..	26,318 *t*	..	7.0 *w*	..	14 *w*	..	5 *w*	..	49.3 *w*
Highly indebted countries	4,781 *t*	16,382 *t*	6.6 *w*	8.0 *w*	14 *w*	16 *w*	3 *w*	4 *w*	5.5 *w*	68.7 *w*
Sub-Saharan Africa	1,880 *t*	7,144 *t*	3.7 *w*	5.4 *w*	26 *w*	25 *w*	8 *w*	6 *w*	1.5 *w*	24.9 *w*

High-income oil exporters

98 Saudi Arabia
99 Kuwait
100 United Arab Emirates
101 *Libya*

Industrial market economies

102 Spain
103 Ireland
104 New Zealand
105 Italy
106 United Kingdom

107 Belgium
108 Austria
109 Netherlands
110 France
111 Australia

112 Germany, Fed. Rep.
113 Finland
114 Denmark
115 Japan
116 Sweden

117 Canada
118 Norway
119 United States
120 Switzerland

Nonreporting nonmembers

121 *Albania*
122 *Angola*
123 *Bulgaria*
124 *Cuba*
125 *Czechoslovakia*

126 *German Dem. Rep.*
127 *Korea, Dem. Rep.*
128 *Mongolia*
129 *USSR*

a. Includes debt in convertible currencies only.

Table 21. Official development assistance from OECD & OPEC members

					Amount					
	1965	1970	1975	1980	1982	1983	1984	1985	1986	1987ᵃ
OECD						Millions of US dollars				
103 Ireland	0	0	9	32	47	32	33	37	58	51
104 New Zealand	0	4	73	75	68	64	56	57	73	..
105 Italy	60	151	202	683	846	841	1,168	1,126	2,424	
106 United Kingdom	472	491	916	1,745	1,720	1,523	1,346	1,456	1,667	1,887
107 Belgium	102	122	394	583	508	460	436	426	516	692
108 Austria	10	21	41	180	239	167	188	258	202	196
109 Netherlands	70	206	686	1,688	1,501	1,205	1,264	1,150	1,747	2,094
110 France	752	937	2,100	4,082	3,856	3,664	3,421	3,807	4,876	..
111 Australia	119	216	578	704	928	821	854	789	817	618
112 Germany, Fed. Rep.	456	603	1,706	3,543	3,124	3,129	2,646	2,827	3,651	4,454
113 Finland	2	9	58	118	155	171	207	239	350	..
114 Denmark	13	72	267	555	515	470	540	526	842	855
115 Japan	244	463	1,205	3,529	3,190	3,955	4,439	3,939	5,761	..
116 Sweden	38	144	662	1,090	1,089	813	800	861	1,167	1,337
117 Canada	96	362	950	1,042	1,240	1,424	1,663	1,634	1,606	1,880
118 Norway	11	50	236	593	675	713	641	671	921	..
119 United States	4,023	3,125	4,139	7,179	8,246	8,359	8,684	9,294	9,395	..
120 Switzerland	12	34	118	263	262	332	293	310	424	532
Total	6,480	7,008	14,339	27,683	28,210	28,143	28,678	29,407	36,497	..
OECD						As percentage of donor GNP				
103 Ireland	0.00	0.00	0.11	0.19	0.25	0.18	0.19	0.22	0.32	0.28
104 New Zealand	0.00	0.06	0.51	0.35	0.25	0.24	0.21	0.23	0.30	..
105 Italy	0.08	0.13	0.09	0.16	0.19	0.20	0.27	0.26	0.50	..
106 United Kingdom	0.48	0.40	0.42	0.39	0.32	0.29	0.28	0.31	0.33	0.28
107 Belgium	0.63	0.47	0.68	0.49	0.49	0.51	0.52	0.52	0.57	0.50
108 Austria	0.11	0.14	0.11	0.24	0.32	0.24	0.27	0.37	0.27	0.17
109 Netherlands	0.36	0.62	0.84	0.99	0.96	0.83	0.91	0.85	1.20	0.98
110 France	0.76	0.62	0.66	0.64	0.60	0.63	0.62	0.71	0.82	..
111 Australia	0.50	0.56	0.60	0.47	0.51	0.43	0.43	0.41	0.43	0.33
112 Germany, Fed. Rep.	0.40	0.35	0.41	0.43	0.41	0.44	0.38	0.42	0.50	0.40
113 Finland	0.02	0.08	0.23	0.24	0.28	0.32	0.39	0.44	0.58	..
114 Denmark	0.13	0.47	0.76	0.82	0.83	0.81	0.95	0.91	1.30	0.87
115 Japan	0.28	0.23	0.24	0.31	0.26	0.32	0.35	0.29	0.37	..
116 Sweden	0.18	0.43	0.98	0.92	0.93	0.78	0.80	0.87	1.06	0.84
117 Canada	0.19	0.44	0.58	0.41	0.42	0.45	0.49	0.46	0.44	0.46
118 Norway	0.16	0.47	0.89	1.12	1.14	1.22	1.09	1.12	1.43	..
119 United States	0.57	0.31	0.26	0.26	0.26	0.24	0.23	0.23	0.22	..
120 Switzerland	0.09	0.15	0.23	0.24	0.24	0.31	0.28	0.29	0.37	0.30
OECD						National currencies				
103 Ireland (millions of pounds)	0	0	4	15	33	26	30	35	43	34
104 New Zealand (millions of dollars)	0	3	53	75	82	88	85	110	143	..
105 Italy (billions of lire)	38	94	132	585	1,144	1,277	2,051	2,150	3,614	..
106 United Kingdom (millions of pounds)	169	205	414	751	985	1,005	1,007	1,134	1,137	1,151
107 Belgium (millions of francs)	5,100	6,090	14,491	17,057	23,197	23,516	25,200	25,313	23,037	25,835
108 Austria (millions of schillings)	260	538	711	2,326	4,079	2,998	3,764	5,336	3,084	2,478
109 Netherlands (millions of guilders)	253	746	1,735	3,356	4,009	3,439	4,056	3,820	4,280	4,242
110 France (millions of francs)	3,713	5,205	9,001	17,250	25,340	27,924	29,903	34,204	33,774	..
111 Australia (millions of dollars)	·106	193	423	632	841	877	942	1,028	1,168	882
112 Germany, Fed. Rep. (millions of deutsche marks)	1,824	2,206	4,198	6,440	7,581	7,989	7,530	8,323	7,928	8,009
113 Finland (millions of markkaa)	6	38	213	438	745	954	1,242	1,483	1,775	..
114 Denmark (millions of kroner)	90	541	1,533	3,126	4,291	4,301	5,589	5,568	6,813	5,848
115 Japan (billions of yen)	88	167	358	800	795	939	1,054	940	971	..
116 Sweden (millions of kronor)	197	743	2,749	4,609	6,844	6,236	6,617	7,411	8,312	8,477
117 Canada (millions of dollars)	104	379	967	1,219	1,529	1,754	2,154	2,231	2,232	2,493
118 Norway (millions of kroner)	79	354	1,232	2,927	4,358	5,201	5,230	5,767	6,807	..
119 United States (millions of dollars)	4,023	3,125	4,139	7,179	8,246	8,359	8,684	9,294	9,395	..
120 Switzerland (millions of francs)	52	147	305	440	533	697	688	761	763	793
OECD						Summary				
ODA (billions of US dollars, nominal prices)	6.48	7.01	14.34	27.68	28.21	28.14	28.68	29.41	36.50	..
ODA as percentage of GNP	0.47	0.34	0.36	0.37	0.35	0.35	0.34	0.34	0.39	..
ODA (billions of US dollars, constant 1980 prices)	21.03	18.68	22.68	27.68	28.63	28.39	28.92	29.17	30.42	..
GNP (trillions of US dollars, nominal prices)	1.37	2.08	3.93	7.42	8.06	8.11	8.44	8.74	9.42	..
GDP deflatorᵇ	0.31	0.38	0.63	1.00	0.99	0.99	0.99	1.01	1.20	..

Errata

The word "export" should be deleted from the
fifth line of the second column in Box 5.1 on page
107. The corrected sentence reads: ". . . in recent
years, several countries — including Argentina,
Brazil, China, India, the Republic of Korea, and
Pakistan — have developed arms industries of
their own."

Errata

Because of methodological problems with rapidly changing exchange rates, Table 21 of the World Development Indicators included in the *World Development Report* overstates most aid ratios for 1986, other than those of the United States. The corrected figures, including minor adjustments to earlier years' data, are given below.

Table 21. Official development assistance from OECD & OPEC members

	1965	1970	1975	1980	1982	1983	1984	1985	1986	1987[a]
OECD					*Millions of US dollars*					
103 Ireland	0	0	8	30	47	33	35	39	62	51
104 New Zealand	..	14	66	72	65	61	55	54	75	..
105 Italy	60	147	182	683	811	834	1,133	1,098	2,404	..
106 United Kingdom	472	500	904	1,854	1,800	1,610	1,429	1,530	1,750	1,887
107 Belgium	102	120	378	595	499	479	446	440	549	692
108 Austria	10	11	79	178	236	158	181	248	198	196
109 Netherlands	70	196	608	1,630	1,472	1,195	1,268	1,136	1,740	2,094
110 France	752	971	2,093	4,162	4,034	3,815	3,788	3,995	5,105	..
111 Australia	119	212	552	667	882	753	777	749	752	618
112 Germany, Fed. Rep.	456	599	1,689	3,567	3,152	3,176	2,782	2,942	3,832	4,454
113 Finland	2	7	48	110	144	153	178	211	313	..
114 Denmark	13	59	205	481	415	395	449	440	695	855
115 Japan	244	458	1,148	3,353	3,023	3,761	4,319	3,797	5,634	..
116 Sweden	38	117	566	962	987	754	741	840	1,090	1,337
117 Canada	96	337	880	1,075	1,197	1,429	1,625	1,631	1,695	1,880
118 Norway	11	37	184	486	559	584	540	574	798	..
119 United States	4,023	3,153	4,161	7,138	8,202	8,081	8,711	9,403	9,564	..
120 Switzerland	12	30	104	253	252	320	285	302	422	532
Total	6,480	6,968	13,847	27,297	27,777	27,592	28,742	29,429	36,678	..
OECD					*As percentage of donor GNP*					
103 Ireland	0.00	0.00	0.09	0.16	0.27	0.20	0.22	0.24	0.28	0.28
104 New Zealand	..	0.23	0.52	0.33	0.28	0.28	0.25	0.25	0.30	..
105 Italy	0.10	0.16	0.11	0.15	0.20	0.20	0.28	0.26	0.40	..
106 United Kingdom	0.47	0.41	0.39	0.35	0.37	0.35	0.33	0.33	0.32	0.28
107 Belgium	0.60	0.46	0.59	0.50	0.58	0.59	0.58	0.55	0.49	0.50
108 Austria	0.11	0.07	0.21	0.23	0.36	0.24	0.28	0.38	0.21	0.17
109 Netherlands	0.36	0.61	0.75	0.97	1.07	0.91	1.02	0.91	1.01	0.98
110 France	0.76	0.66	0.62	0.63	0.74	0.74	0.77	0.78	0.72	..
111 Australia	0.53	0.59	0.65	0.48	0.56	0.49	0.45	0.48	0.47	0.33
112 Germany, Fed. Rep.	0.40	0.32	0.40	0.44	0.48	0.48	0.45	0.47	0.43	0.40
113 Finland	0.02	0.06	0.18	0.22	0.29	0.32	0.35	0.40	0.45	..
114 Denmark	0.13	0.38	0.58	0.74	0.77	0.73	0.85	0.80	0.89	0.87
115 Japan	0.27	0.23	0.23	0.32	0.28	0.32	0.34	0.29	0.29	..
116 Sweden	0.19	0.38	0.82	0.78	1.02	0.84	0.80	0.86	0.85	0.84
117 Canada	0.19	0.41	0.54	0.43	0.41	0.45	0.50	0.49	0.48	0.46
118 Norway	0.16	0.32	0.66	0.87	1.03	1.10	1.03	1.01	1.20	..
119 United States	0.58	0.32	0.27	0.27	0.27	0.24	0.24	0.24	0.23	..
120 Switzerland	0.09	0.15	0.19	0.24	0.25	0.31	0.30	0.31	0.30	0.30
OECD					*National currencies*					
103 Ireland (millions of pounds)	0	0	4	15	33	26	32	37	46	34
104 New Zealand (millions of dollars)	..	13	55	74	87	91	95	109	143	..
105 Italy (billions of lire)	38	92	119	585	1,097	1,267	1,991	2,097	3,578	..
106 United Kingdom (millions of pounds)	169	208	409	798	1,031	1,062	1,070	1,180	1,194	1,151
107 Belgium (millions of francs)	5,100	6,000	13,902	17,399	22,800	24,390	25,527	26,145	24,525	25,835
108 Austria (millions of schillings)	260	286	1,376	2,303	4,026	2,838	3,622	5,132	3,023	2,478
109 Netherlands (millions of guilders)	253	710	1,538	3,241	3,931	3,411	4,069	3,773	4,263	4,242
110 France (millions of francs)	3,713	5,393	8,971	17,589	26,513	29,075	33,107	35,894	35,357	..
111 Australia (millions of dollars)	106	189	402	591	798	802	873	966	1,121	882
112 Germany, Fed. Rep. (millions of deutsche marks)	1,824	2,192	4,155	6,484	7,649	8,109	7,917	8,661	8,323	8,004
113 Finland (millions of markkaa)	6	29	177	414	694	852	1,070	1,308	1,587	..
114 Denmark (millions of kroner)	90	443	1,178	2,711	3,458	3,612	4,650	4,657	5,623	5,848
115 Japan (billions of yen)	88	165	341	760	753	893	1,026	906	944	..
116 Sweden (millions of kronor)	197	605	2,350	4,069	6,201	5,781	6,129	7,226	7,765	8,477
117 Canada (millions of dollars)	104	353	895	1,257	1,477	1,761	2,104	2,227	2,354	2,493
118 Norway (millions of kroner)	79	264	962	2,400	3,608	4,261	4,407	4,946	5,901	..
119 United States (millions of dollars)	4,023	3,153	4,161	7,138	8,202	8,081	8,711	9,403	9,564	..
120 Switzerland (millions of francs)	52	131	268	424	512	672	672	743	759	793
OECD					*Summary*					
ODA (billions of US dollars, nominal prices)	6.48	6.97	13.86	27.30	27.78	27.59	28.74	29.43	36.68	..
ODA as percentage of GNP	0.48	0.34	0.35	0.37	0.38	0.36	0.36	0.35	0.35	..
ODA (billions of US dollars, constant 1980 prices)	20.68	18.41	21.84	27.30	27.99	27.87	29.03	29.14	30.56	..
GNP (trillions of US dollars, nominal prices)	1.35	2.04	3.96	7.39	7.43	7.70	8.03	8.42	10.39	..
GDP deflator[b]	0.31	0.38	0.63	1.00	0.99	0.99	0.99	1.01	1.20	..

	Amount									
	1976	1978	1979	1980	1981	1982	1983	1984	1985	1986
OPEC	*Millions of US dollars*									
48 Nigeria	80	27	29	35	143	58	35	51	45	52
86 Algeria	11	39	281	81	55	129	37	52	52	50
87 Venezuela	109	96	110	135	92	125	142	90	32	85
95 Iran, Islamic Rep.	751	231	−20	−72	−141	−193	10	52	−129	40
96 Iraq	123	123	658	864	207	52	−10	−22	−27	−40
98 Saudi Arabia	2,791	5,250	3,941	5,682	5,514	3,854	3,259	3,194	2,630	3,575
99 Kuwait	706	1,001	971	1,140	1,163	1,161	997	1,020	771	715
100 United Arab Emirates	1,028	889	968	1,118	805	406	351	88	71	72
101 Libya	98	132	145	376	257	44	144	24	149	31
Qatar	180	95	282	277	246	139	20	10	9	3
Total OAPEC	4,937	7,529	7,246	9,538	8,247	5,785	4,798	4,366	3,655	4,406
Total OPEC	5,877	7,883	7,365	9,636	8,341	5,775	4,983	4,559	3,603	4,582
OPEC	*As percentage of donor GNP*									
48 Nigeria	0.19	0.05	0.04	0.04	0.19	0.08	0.05	0.07	0.06	0.10
86 Algeria	0.07	0.15	0.90	0.20	0.13	0.31	0.08	0.10	0.09	0.08
87 Venezuela	0.35	0.24	0.23	0.23	0.14	0.19	0.22	0.19	0.07	0.19
95 Iran, Islamic Rep.	1.16	0.33	−0.02	−0.08	−0.13	−0.15	0.01	−0.01	−0.08	0.03
96 Iraq	0.76	0.55	1.97	2.36	0.94	0.18	−0.09	−0.10	−0.08	−0.13
98 Saudi Arabia	5.95	8.06	5.16	4.87	3.45	2.50	2.86	3.44	2.86	4.52
99 Kuwait	4.82	5.53	3.52	3.52	3.65	4.34	3.73	3.82	3.25	2.99
100 United Arab Emirates	8.95	6.38	5.08	4.06	2.57	1.39	1.30	0.32	0.29	0.34
101 Libya	0.66	0.75	0.60	1.16	0.81	0.15	0.51	0.08	0.58	0.13
Qatar	7.35	3.29	6.07	4.16	3.50	2.13	0.39	0.17	0.18	0.08
Total OAPEC	4.23	4.51	3.31	3.22	2.52	1.81	1.70	1.60	1.39	1.80
Total OPEC	2.32	2.39	1.75	1.79	1.45	0.98	0.86	1.13	0.65	0.95

	Net bilateral flows to low-income economies									
	1965	1970	1975	1980	1981	1982	1983	1984	1985	1986
OECD	*As percentage of donor GNP*									
103 Ireland	..	..	..	..	..	0.02	0.03	0.03	0.05	0.06
104 New Zealand	..	..	0.14	0.01	0.01	0.00	0.00	0.00	0.00	0.00
105 Italy	0.04	0.06	0.01	0.01	0.02	0.04	0.05	0.09	0.12	0.16
106 United Kingdom	0.23	0.15	0.11	0.11	0.13	0.07	0.10	0.09	0.09	0.09
107 Belgium	0.56	0.30	0.31	0.24	0.25	0.21	0.21	0.20	0.23	0.20
108 Austria	0.06	0.05	0.02	0.03	0.03	0.01	0.02	0.01	0.02	0.01
109 Netherlands	0.08	0.24	0.24	0.30	0.37	0.31	0.26	0.29	0.27	0.32
110 France	0.12	0.09	0.10	0.08	0.11	0.10	0.09	0.14	0.14	0.13
111 Australia	0.08	0.09	0.10	0.04	0.06	0.07	0.05	0.06	0.05	0.04
112 Germany, Fed. Rep.	0.14	0.10	0.12	0.08	0.11	0.12	0.13	0.11	0.14	0.12
113 Finland	..	..	0.06	0.08	0.09	0.09	0.12	0.13	0.17	0.18
114 Denmark	0.02	0.10	0.20	0.28	0.21	0.26	0.31	0.28	0.32	0.32
115 Japan	0.13	0.11	0.08	0.08	0.06	0.11	0.09	0.07	0.09	0.10
116 Sweden	0.07	0.12	0.41	0.36	0.32	0.38	0.33	0.30	0.31	0.38
117 Canada	0.10	0.22	0.24	0.11	0.13	0.14	0.13	0.15	0.15	0.12
118 Norway	0.04	0.12	0.25	0.31	0.28	0.37	0.39	0.34	0.40	0.47
119 United States	0.26	0.14	0.08	0.03	0.03	0.02	0.03	0.03	0.04	0.03
120 Switzerland	0.02	0.05	0.10	0.08	0.07	0.09	0.10	0.12	0.12	0.12
Total	0.20	0.13	0.11	0.07	0.08	0.08	0.08	0.07	0.09	0.09

a. Preliminary estimates.   b. See the technical notes.

					Amount					
	1976	1978	1979	1980	1981	1982	1983	1984	1985	1986
OPEC					*Millions of US dollars*					
48 Nigeria	80	27	29	35	143	58	35	51	45	52
86 Algeria	11	39	281	81	55	129	37	52	52	50
87 Venezuela	109	96	110	135	92	125	142	90	32	85
95 Iran, Islamic Rep.	751	231	−20	−72	−141	−193	10	52	−129	40
96 Iraq	123	123	658	864	207	52	−10	−22	−27	−40
98 Saudi Arabia	2,791	5,250	3,941	5,682	5,514	3,854	3,259	3,194	2,630	3,575
99 Kuwait	706	1,001	971	1,140	1,163	1,161	997	1,020	771	715
100 United Arab Emirates	1,028	889	968	1,118	805	406	351	88	71	72
101 Libya	98	132	145	376	257	44	144	24	149	31
Qatar	180	95	282	277	246	139	20	10	9	3
Total OAPEC	4,937	7,529	7,246	9,538	8,247	5,785	4,798	4,366	3,655	4,406
Total OPEC	5,877	7,883	7,365	9,636	8,341	5,775	4,985	4,559	3,603	4,583
OPEC					*As percentage of donor GNP*					
48 Nigeria	0.19	0.05	0.05	0.05	0.18	0.07	0.05	0.07	0.06	0.08
86 Algeria	0.07	0.16	0.94	0.22	0.13	0.27	0.07	0.10	0.09	0.09
87 Venezuela	0.35	0.24	0.24	0.26	0.15	0.19	0.22	0.15	0.06	0.16
95 Iran, Islamic Rep.	1.16	0.32	−0.02	..	..	..	..	..	..	..
96 Iraq	0.76	0.54	1.90	..	..	..	..	..	..	..
98 Saudi Arabia	5.95	7.98	5.09	5.77	3.91	2.41	2.35	2.74	2.64	4.29
99 Kuwait	4.82	5.10	3.99	4.03	3.24	3.71	3.50	3.62	3.03	2.90
100 United Arab Emirates	8.95	6.08	4.91	4.10	2.57	1.34	1.22	0.30	0.26	0.35
101 Libya	0.66	0.68	0.59	1.27	0.87	0.14	0.48	0.09	0.55	..
Qatar	7.35	2.74	6.51	5.02	3.53	2.18	0.40	0.17	0.18	0.07
Total OAPEC	4.23	4.42	3.37	3.33[c]	2.55[c]	1.96[c]	1.88[c]	1.86[c]	1.64[c]	2.06[c]
Total OPEC	2.32	2.38	1.83	2.12[d]	1.74[d]	1.31[d]	1.22[d]	1.21[d]	1.05[d]	1.43[d]

				Net bilateral flows to low-income economies						
	1965	1970	1975	1980	1981	1982	1983	1984	1985	1986
OECD					*As percentage of donor GNP*					
103 Ireland	0.00	0.00	0.00	0.03	0.03	0.04	0.05	0.05	0.06	0.07
104 New Zealand	0.00	0.00	0.07	0.01	0.01	0.00	0.00	0.00	0.00	0.00
105 Italy	0.03	0.03	0.02	0.01	0.02	0.03	0.05	0.08	0.10	0.19
106 United Kingdom	0.23	0.16	0.12	0.16	0.15	0.08	0.09	0.09	0.09	0.10
107 Belgium	0.58	0.29	0.32	0.25	0.21	0.18	0.18	0.19	0.23	0.26
108 Austria	0.06	0.05	0.02	0.03	0.03	0.01	0.02	0.01	0.02	0.02
109 Netherlands	0.08	0.08	0.19	0.34	0.34	0.30	0.25	0.28	0.25	0.38
110 France	0.12	0.09	0.12	0.10	0.12	0.10	0.10	0.13	0.14	0.16
111 Australia	0.08	0.04	0.07	0.04	0.06	0.07	0.04	0.05	0.04	0.03
112 Germany, Fed. Rep.	0.14	0.10	0.13	0.10	0.10	0.12	0.13	0.11	0.14	0.15
113 Finland	0.00	0.00	0.07	0.10	0.10	0.10	0.13	0.15	0.16	0.21
114 Denmark	0.02	0.11	0.20	0.30	0.19	0.25	0.31	0.27	0.31	0.39
115 Japan	0.13	0.05	0.04	0.07	0.06	0.10	0.09	0.08	0.09	0.13
116 Sweden	0.07	0.11	0.44	0.39	0.31	0.33	0.32	0.31	0.31	0.45
117 Canada	0.10	0.23	0.24	0.12	0.13	0.15	0.14	0.15	0.14	0.12
118 Norway	0.04	0.11	0.29	0.36	0.30	0.38	0.38	0.35	0.37	0.50
119 United States	0.25	0.12	0.08	0.03	0.03	0.03	0.03	0.03	0.04	0.03
120 Switzerland	0.02	0.03	0.09	0.08	0.06	0.09	0.11	0.11	0.11	0.14
Total	0.19	0.11	0.10	0.08	0.08	0.08	0.08	0.08	0.08	0.10

a. Preliminary estimates.   b. See the technical notes.   c. Excluding Iraq.   d. Excluding Iraq and Iran.

Table 22. Official development assistance: receipts

	Net disbursements of ODA from all sources								
	Millions of dollars							Per capita (dollars)	As percentage of GNP
	1980	1981	1982	1983	1984	1985	1986	1986	1986
Low-income economies	12,042 *t*	11,590 *t*	11,652 *t*	11,366 *t*	11,573 *t*	13,023 *t*	16,059 *t*	6.4 *w*	2.4 *w*
China and India	2,213 *t*	2,387 *t*	2,069 *t*	2,410 *t*	2,408 *t*	2,467 *t*	3,193 *t*	1.7 *w*	0.6 *w*
Other low-income	9,829 *t*	9,203 *t*	9,583 *t*	8,956 *t*	9,165 *t*	10,556 *t*	12,866 *t*	19.6 *w*	9.0 *w*
1 Ethiopia	212	245	200	339	364	715	642	14.8	11.5
2 Bhutan	8	10	11	13	18	24	40	30.2	19.3
3 Burkina Faso	212	217	213	184	189	198	284	35.0	19.3
4 Nepal	163	181	200	201	198	236	301	17.7	11.7
5 Bangladesh	1,282	1,104	1,346	1,067	1,200	1,151	1,455	14.1	9.5
6 Malawi	143	137	121	117	158	113	203	27.9	17.5
7 Zaire	428	394	348	315	312	325	448	14.1	8.0
8 Mali	267	230	210	215	320	380	372	49.1	22.7
9 Burma	309	283	319	302	275	356	416	10.9	5.1
10 Mozambique	169	144	208	211	259	300	422	29.7	9.8
11 Madagascar	230	234	242	183	153	188	316	30.0	12.7
12 Uganda	114	136	133	137	163	183	198	13.1	5.7
13 Burundi	117	121	127	140	141	142	187	38.7	15.7
14 Tanzania	679	703	684	594	558	487	681	29.5	15.2
15 Togo	91	63	77	112	110	114	174	55.4	18.5
16 Niger	170	194	257	175	161	305	308	46.6	15.2
17 Benin	91	82	81	86	77	96	138	33.1	10.0
18 Somalia	433	374	462	343	350	353	523	94.3	27.8
19 Central African Rep.	111	102	90	93	114	104	139	52.5	14.8
20 India	2,147	1,910	1,545	1,741	1,610	1,527	2,059	2.6	0.9
21 Rwanda	155	153	151	150	165	181	211	33.8	11.5
22 China	66	477	524	669	798	940	1,134	1.1	0.4
23 Kenya	397	449	485	400	411	438	458	21.6	6.9
24 Zambia	318	232	317	217	239	328	464	66.8	31.2
25 Sierra Leone	91	60	82	66	61	66	87	23.2	7.0
26 Sudan	583	632	740	962	622	1,128	940	41.7	12.8
27 Haiti	105	107	128	134	135	153	175	29.0	8.2
28 Pakistan	1,130	764	849	668	683	735	952	9.6	2.9
29 Lesotho	94	104	93	108	101	94	88	55.3	16.1
30 Ghana	192	148	141	110	216	204	371	28.2	6.6
31 Sri Lanka	390	377	416	473	466	484	571	35.4	8.9
32 Mauritania	176	234	187	175	174	201	187	103.1	23.9
33 Senegal	262	397	285	322	368	294	567	83.8	16.0
34 *Afghanistan*	32	23	9	14	7	17	2	0.1	..
35 *Chad*	35	60	65	95	115	182	165	32.0	..
36 *Guinea*	89	106	90	68	123	119	175	27.6	..
37 *Kampuchea, Dem.*	281	130	44	37	17	13	13	1.7	..
38 *Lao PDR*	41	35	38	30	34	37	48	13.1	..
39 *Viet Nam*	228	242	136	106	110	114	147	2.3	..
Middle-income economies	13,589 *t*	13,519 *t*	11,846 *t*	11,712 *t*	11,916 *t*	12,653 *t*	13,395 *t*	11.5 *w*	0.9 *w*
Lower middle-income	11,589 *t*	11,265 *t*	9,956 *t*	9,466 *t*	9,537 *t*	9,536 *t*	10,039 *t*	14.5 *w*	2.0 *w*
40 Liberia	98	108	109	118	133	90	97	43.0	9.6
41 Yemen, PDR	100	87	143	106	102	112	58	26.2	5.7
42 Indonesia	949	975	906	744	673	603	711	4.3	1.0
43 Yemen Arab Rep.	472	411	412	328	325	275	233	28.5	4.7
44 Philippines	300	376	333	429	397	486	956	16.7	3.2
45 Morocco	894	1,033	771	396	352	838	336	15.0	2.4
46 Bolivia	169	169	147	174	172	202	322	49.0	7.2
47 Zimbabwe	164	212	216	208	298	237	225	25.8	4.2
48 Nigeria	36	41	37	48	33	32	60	0.6	0.1
49 Dominican Rep.	125	105	137	103	198	222	106	16.1	2.1
50 Papua New Guinea	326	336	311	333	322	259	263	77.2	10.9
51 Côte d'Ivoire	210	124	137	156	128	125	186	17.5	2.1
52 Honduras	103	109	158	192	290	276	288	63.7	8.5
53 Egypt, Arab Rep.	1,387	1,292	1,416	1,438	1,769	1,766	1,667	33.5	4.1
54 Nicaragua	223	172	121	120	114	102	150	44.3	5.6
55 Thailand	418	406	389	431	474	481	496	9.4	1.2
56 El Salvador	96	167	223	295	263	345	355	72.8	9.2
57 Botswana	106	97	101	104	102	96	102	92.3	10.4
58 Jamaica	136	155	180	181	170	169	177	74.7	8.5
59 Cameroon	265	199	212	129	186	159	225	21.3	2.1
60 Guatemala	73	75	64	76	65	83	135	16.5	1.9
61 Congo, People's Rep.	92	81	93	108	98	71	110	56.4	5.9
62 Paraguay	30	54	85	51	50	50	66	17.4	1.9
63 Peru	203	233	188	297	310	316	272	13.7	1.1
64 Turkey	950	723	642	351	241	175	346	6.7	0.6
65 Tunisia	232	239	210	205	178	163	199	27.3	2.3
66 Ecuador	46	59	53	64	136	136	147	15.2	1.4
67 Mauritius	33	58	48	41	36	28	56	54.6	4.2
68 Colombia	90	102	97	86	88	62	63	2.2	0.2

Note: For data comparability and coverage, see the technical notes.   Figures in italics are for years other than those specified.

	Millions of dollars							Per capita (dollars) 1986	As percentage of GNP 1986
	1980	1981	1982	1983	1984	1985	1986		
69 Chile	−10	−7	−8	0	2	40	−5	−0.4	0.0
70 Costa Rica	65	55	80	252	218	280	196	76.5	4.9
71 Jordan	1,275	1,065	798	787	686	541	537	148.4	12.0
72 Syrian Arab Rep.	1,696	1,500	962	990	853	623	842	77.7	4.9
73 *Lebanon*	237	455	187	127	77	94	62	23.2	..
Upper middle-income	2,000 *t*	2,254 *t*	1,889 *t*	2,246 *t*	2,379 *t*	3,117 *t*	3,357 *t*	7.1 *w*	0.4 *w*
74 Brazil	85	235	208	101	161	123	178	1.3	0.1
75 Malaysia	135	143	135	177	327	229	193	12.0	0.8
76 South Africa	..	..	..	..	..	..	..	..	..
77 Mexico	56	99	140	132	83	144	252	3.1	0.2
78 Uruguay	10	7	4	3	4	5	27	9.0	0.4
79 Hungary	..	..	..	..	..	..	..	..	..
80 Poland	..	..	..	..	..	..	..	..	..
81 Portugal	112	82	49	43	97	101	139	13.7	0.5
82 Yugoslavia	−17	−15	−8	3	3	11	19	0.8	0.0
83 Panama	46	39	41	47	72	69	52	23.3	1.0
84 Argentina	18	44	30	48	49	39	88	2.8	0.1
85 Korea, Rep. of	139	330	34	8	−37	−9	−18	−0.4	0.0
86 Algeria	176	167	136	95	122	173	165	7.4	0.3
87 Venezuela	15	14	13	10	14	11	16	0.9	0.0
88 Gabon	56	44	62	64	76	61	79	77.2	2.7
89 Greece	40	13	12	13	13	11	19	1.9	0.0
90 Oman	168	231	133	71	67	78	84	64.9	1.3
91 Trinidad and Tobago	5	−2	6	5	5	7	19	16.0	0.4
92 Israel	892	773	857	1,345	1,256	1,978	1,937	450.0	6.8
93 Hong Kong	11	9	8	9	14	20	18	3.4	0.0
94 Singapore	14	22	20	15	41	24	30	11.5	0.2
95 *Iran, Islamic Rep.*	31	9	3	48	13	16	27	0.6	..
96 *Iraq*	9	9	6	13	4	26	33	2.0	..
97 *Romania*	..	..	..	..	..	..	..	..	
Developing economies	25,630 *t*	25,109 *t*	23,498 *t*	23,078 *t*	23,489 *t*	25,676 *t*	29,454 *t*	8.1 *w*	1.4 *w*
Oil exporters	4,985 *t*	4,718 *t*	4,177 *t*	3,958 *t*	4,130 *t*	3,907 *t*	4,437 *t*	8.2 *w*	1.0 *w*
Exporters of manufactures	3,449 *t*	3,823 *t*	3,239 *t*	3,933 *t*	3,941 *t*	4,715 *t*	5,497 *t*	2.7 *w*	0.5 *w*
Highly indebted countries	2,307 *t*	2,723 *t*	2,401 *t*	2,376 *t*	2,320 *t*	3,018 *t*	3,287 *t*	5.8 *w*	0.4 *w*
Sub-Saharan Africa	6,971 *t*	6,971 *t*	7,162 *t*	6,964 *t*	7,207 *t*	8,228 *t*	10,018 *t*	23.1 *w*	6.2 *w*
High-income oil exporters	46 *t*	50 *t*	80 *t*	59 *t*	48 *t*	42 *t*	81 *t*	4.2 *w*	0.1 *w*
98 Saudi Arabia	15	30	57	44	36	29	31	2.6	0.0
99 Kuwait	10	10	6	5	4	4	5	2.8	0.0
100 United Arab Emirates	4	1	5	4	3	3	34	24.2	0.2
101 *Libya*	17	11	12	6	5	5	11	2.8	..
Industrial market economies	..	..	..	..	..	..	..	..	..
102 Spain	23	2	22	0	0	0	0	0.0	0.0
103 Ireland									
104 New Zealand									
105 Italy									
106 United Kingdom									
107 Belgium									
108 Austria									
109 Netherlands									
110 France									
111 Australia									
112 Germany, Fed. Rep.									
113 Finland									
114 Denmark									
115 Japan									
116 Sweden									
117 Canada									
118 Norway									
119 United States									
120 Switzerland									
Nonreporting nonmembers	..	..	..	..	..	..	..	..	..
121 *Albania*									
122 *Angola*	53	61	60	75	95	92	131	14.6	..
123 *Bulgaria*									
124 *Cuba*	32	14	16	13	12	18	18	1.8	..
125 *Czechoslovakia*									
126 *German Dem. Rep.*									
127 *Korea, Dem. Rep.*									
128 *Mongolia*									
129 *USSR*									

Table 23. Central government expenditure

	Defense 1972	Defense 1986	Education 1972	Education 1986	Health 1972	Health 1986	Housing, amenities; social security and welfare[a] 1972	1986	Economic services 1972	1986	Other[a] 1972	1986	Total expenditure (percentage of GNP) 1972	1986	Overall surplus/deficit (percentage of GNP) 1972	1986
Low-income economies	..	..	..	..	..	..	..	..	..	..	..	..	..	..	..	..
China and India	..	..	..	..	..	..	..	..	..	..	..	..	..	..	..	..
Other low-income	..	17.7 w	..	9.8 w	..	3.6 w	..	6.2 w	..	23.8 w	..	38.9 w	..	20.8 w	..	−5.1 w
1 Ethiopia	14.3	..	14.4	..	5.7	..	4.4	..	22.9	..	38.3	..	13.7	..	−1.4	..
2 Bhutan	..	..	..	..	..	..	..	..	..	..	..	..	..	..	..	..
3 Burkina Faso	11.5	19.2	20.6	17.7	8.2	6.2	6.6	8.3	15.5	13.9	37.6	34.7	11.1	13.2	0.3	1.6
4 Nepal	7.2	6.2	7.2	12.1	4.7	5.0	0.7	6.8	57.2	48.5	23.0	21.5	8.5	19.7	−1.2	−8.1
5 Bangladesh[b]	5.1	11.2	14.8	9.9	5.0	5.3	9.8	0.6	39.3	41.6	25.9	31.3	9.4	10.9	−1.9	−0.2
6 Malawi[b]	3.1	6.0	15.8	11.0	5.5	6.9	5.8	1.9	33.1	30.5	36.8	43.7	22.1	31.5	−6.2	−8.4
7 Zaire	11.1	..	15.2	..	2.3	..	2.0	..	13.3	..	56.1	..	19.8	..	−3.8	..
8 Mali	..	8.1	..	9.0	..	1.7	..	6.2	..	7.7	..	67.3	..	34.0	..	−9.6
9 Burma	31.6	18.8	15.0	11.7	6.1	7.7	7.5	8.4	20.1	35.1	19.7	18.2	20.0	16.2	−7.3	−0.8
10 Mozambique	..	..	..	..	..	..	..	..	..	..	..	..	..	..	..	..
11 Madagascar	3.6	..	9.1	..	4.2	..	9.9	..	40.5	..	32.7	..	20.8	..	−2.5	..
12 Uganda	23.1	26.3	15.3	15.0	5.3	2.4	7.3	0.8	12.4	14.8	36.6	40.7	21.8	9.4	−8.1	−2.8
13 Burundi	10.3	..	23.4	..	6.0	..	2.7	..	33.9	..	23.8	..	19.9	..	0.0	..
14 Tanzania	11.9	13.8	17.3	7.2	7.2	4.9	2.1	1.4	39.0	24.0	22.6	48.6	19.7	23.9	−5.0	..
15 Togo	..	6.9	..	11.7	..	3.6	..	9.2	..	23.5	..	45.2	..	42.3	..	−5.1
16 Niger	..	..	..	..	..	..	..	..	..	..	..	..	..	..	..	..
17 Benin	..	..	..	..	..	..	..	..	..	..	..	..	..	..	..	..
18 Somalia[b]	23.3	..	5.5	..	7.2	..	1.9	..	21.6	..	40.5	..	13.5	..	0.6	..
19 Central African Rep.	..	..	..	..	..	..	..	..	..	..	..	..	..	..	..	..
20 India	..	18.4	..	2.1	..	2.1	..	5.6	..	23.4	..	48.5	..	16.4	..	−8.1
21 Rwanda	25.6	..	22.2	..	5.7	..	2.6	..	22.0	..	21.9	..	12.5	..	−2.7	..
22 China	..	..	..	..	..	..	..	..	..	..	..	..	..	..	..	..
23 Kenya[b]	6.0	8.7	21.9	19.7	7.9	6.4	3.9	0.5	30.1	27.6	30.2	37.0	21.0	27.8	−3.9	−6.7
24 Zambia[b]	0.0	..	19.0	16.0	7.4	7.2	1.3	2.6	26.7	16.1	45.7	58.1	34.0	38.2	−13.8	−16.3
25 Sierra Leone[b]	..	3.4	..	12.8	..	5.8	..	2.0	..	15.4	..	60.4	..	13.6	..	−8.9
26 Sudan[b]	24.1	..	9.3	..	5.4	..	1.4	..	15.8	..	44.1	..	19.2	..	−0.8	..
27 Haiti	..	..	..	..	..	..	..	..	..	..	..	..	14.5	..	..	..
28 Pakistan	39.9	33.9	1.2	3.2	1.1	1.0	3.2	10.5	21.4	25.8	33.2	25.6	16.9	23.1	−6.9	−9.5
29 Lesotho	0.0	9.6	22.4	15.5	7.3	6.9	6.3	1.5	21.4	25.5	42.7	41.0	14.5	24.2	3.5	−2.6
30 Ghana[b]	7.9	6.5	20.1	23.9	6.3	8.3	4.1	7.3	15.1	15.7	46.6	38.3	19.5	14.0	−5.8	0.1
31 Sri Lanka	3.1	8.0	13.0	8.4	6.4	4.0	19.5	11.1	20.2	10.2	37.7	58.3	25.4	30.5	−5.3	−9.2
32 Mauritania	..	..	..	..	..	..	..	..	..	..	..	..	..	..	..	..
33 Senegal	..	..	..	..	..	..	..	..	..	..	..	..	18.8	..	−2.8	..
34 Afghanistan	..	..	..	..	..	..	..	..	..	..	..	..	..	..	..	..
35 Chad	24.6	..	14.8	..	4.4	..	1.7	..	21.8	..	32.7	..	14.9	..	−2.7	..
36 Guinea	..	..	..	..	..	..	..	..	..	..	..	..	..	..	..	..
37 Kampuchea, Dem.	..	..	..	..	..	..	..	..	..	..	..	..	..	..	..	..
38 Lao PDR	..	..	..	..	..	..	..	..	..	..	..	..	..	..	..	..
39 Viet Nam	..	..	..	..	..	..	..	..	..	..	..	..	..	..	..	..
Middle-income economies	13.8 w	11.7 w	13.2 w	11.2 w	4.9 w	4.8 w	19.1 w	15.2 w	26.6 w	20.0 w	22.4 w	37.1 w	21.7 w	27.5 w	−3.3 w	−5.8 w
Lower middle-income	16.1 w	15.8 w	22.1 w	14.5 w	6.6 w	4.0 w	15.9 w	9.1 w	24.4 w	21.5 w	14.9 w	35.1 w	22.1 w	24.9 w	−5.2 w	−4.5 w
40 Liberia	..	7.7	..	14.2	..	5.7	..	1.8	..	34.5	..	36.2	..	27.1	..	−9.0
41 Yemen, PDR	..	..	..	..	..	..	..	..	..	..	..	..	..	..	..	..
42 Indonesia	18.6	9.3	7.4	8.5	1.4	1.9	0.9	1.4	30.5	19.3	41.3	59.6	15.1	26.9	−2.5	−3.9
43 Yemen Arab Rep.	..	28.8	..	22.5	..	4.7	..	0.0	..	7.8	..	36.1	..	25.5	..	−10.3
44 Philippines[b]	10.9	11.9	16.3	20.1	3.2	6.0	0.7	1.6	17.6	44.9	51.3	15.6	13.4	10.8	−2.0	−1.9
45 Morocco	12.3	16.4	19.2	16.6	4.8	2.8	8.4	6.6	25.6	25.9	29.7	31.7	22.8	35.3	−3.9	−8.4
46 Bolivia	18.8	5.8	31.3	11.6	6.3	1.4	0.0	6.0	12.5	5.8	31.3	69.4	9.6	32.0	−1.8	−28.3
47 Zimbabwe	..	15.2	..	20.9	..	6.2	..	4.7	..	26.0	..	27.0	..	35.2	..	−7.0
48 Nigeria[b]	40.2	..	4.5	..	3.6	..	0.8	..	19.6	..	31.4	..	10.2	..	−0.9	..
49 Dominican Rep.	8.5	8.1	14.2	12.8	11.7	9.0	11.8	13.0	35.4	43.5	18.3	13.6	20.0	15.3	−0.2	−2.0
50 Papua New Guinea[b]	..	4.5	..	17.0	..	9.6	..	2.0	..	18.6	..	48.3	..	34.8	..	−2.6
51 Côte d'Ivoire	..	3.9	..	20.5	..	4.0	..	1.8	..	31.5	..	38.3	..	31.2	..	−3.1
52 Honduras	12.4	..	22.3	..	10.2	..	8.7	..	28.3	..	18.1	..	15.4	..	−2.7	..
53 Egypt, Arab Rep.	..	17.7	..	10.8	..	2.4	..	14.9	..	9.3	..	44.9	..	40.6	..	−10.9
54 Nicaragua	12.3	..	16.6	..	4.0	..	16.4	..	27.2	..	23.4	..	15.5	56.4	−3.9	−15.9
55 Thailand	20.2	20.2	19.9	19.5	3.7	5.7	7.0	4.6	25.6	22.6	23.5	27.4	17.2	21.7	−4.3	−5.6
56 El Salvador	6.6	28.7	21.4	17.5	10.9	7.5	7.6	4.6	14.4	22.6	39.0	19.2	12.8	12.9	−1.0	−0.8
57 Botswana[b]	0.0	6.4	10.1	17.7	6.1	5.0	21.5	7.3	27.9	29.7	34.3	34.0	33.6	49.4	−23.8	31.8
58 Jamaica	..	..	..	..	..	..	..	..	..	..	..	..	..	..	..	..
59 Cameroon	..	8.8	..	14.4	..	5.1	..	11.4	..	33.8	..	26.6	..	22.4	..	0.8
60 Guatemala	11.0	..	19.4	..	9.5	..	4.7	..	23.8	..	31.5	..	9.9	..	−2.2	..
61 Congo, People's Rep.	..	..	..	..	..	..	..	..	..	..	..	..	..	..	..	..
62 Paraguay	13.8	12.1	12.1	12.2	3.5	3.1	18.3	32.3	19.6	10.1	32.7	30.2	13.1	7.9	−1.7	1.5
63 Peru[b]	14.8	..	22.6	..	6.1	..	2.5	..	30.6	..	23.3	..	16.7	14.1	−1.0	..
64 Turkey	15.5	13.5	18.1	11.9	3.2	2.2	0.8	2.8	41.8	24.3	20.6	45.3	22.7	21.8	−2.2	−3.3
65 Tunisia	4.9	7.9	30.5	14.3	7.4	6.5	8.8	12.4	23.3	33.1	25.1	25.7	23.1	36.9	−0.9	−4.6
66 Ecuador[b]	15.7	11.8	27.5	24.5	4.5	7.3	0.8	0.9	28.9	19.8	22.6	35.8	13.4	15.7	0.2	2.1
67 Mauritius	0.8	0.8	13.5	13.4	10.3	7.7	3.1	1.6	13.9	12.4	58.3	64.1	16.3	24.9	−1.2	−3.5
68 Colombia	..	..	..	..	..	..	..	..	..	..	..	..	13.0	..	−2.5	..

Note: For data comparability and coverage, see the technical notes. Figures in italics are for years other than those specified.

| | Percentage of total expenditure | | | | | | | | | | | | Total expenditure (percentage of GNP) | | Overall surplus/deficit (percentage of GNP) | |
| | Defense | | Education | | Health | | Housing, amenities; social security and welfare[a] | | Economic services | | Other[a] | | | | | |
	1972	1986	1972	1986	1972	1986	1972	1986	1972	1986	1972	1986	1972	1986	1972	1986
69 Chile	6.1	10.7	14.3	12.5	8.2	6.0	39.8	42.6	15.3	9.2	16.3	19.0	43.2	33.6	−13.0	−1.1
70 Costa Rica	2.8	2.2	28.3	16.2	3.8	19.3	26.7	26.7	21.8	12.3	16.7	23.3	18.9	29.3	−4.5	−5.0
71 Jordan	..	26.7	..	12.2	..	3.8	..	8.6	..	22.5	..	26.2	..	46.0	..	−10.0
72 Syrian Arab Rep.	37.2	..	11.3	..	1.4	..	3.6	..	39.9	..	6.7	..	28.8	..	−3.5	..
73 *Lebanon*	..	..	..	..	..	..	..	..	..	..	..	..	..	..	..	..
Upper middle-income	**13.1 w**	*10.3 w*	**9.6 w**	*10.2 w*	**4.2 w**	*5.1 w*	**21.4 w**	*17.3 w*	**27.7 w**	*19.6 w*	**24.0 w**	*37.5 w*	**21.6 w**	*28.3 w*	**−2.7 w**	*−6.3 w*
74 Brazil	8.3	*3.1*	8.3	*3.0*	6.7	6.4	35.0	23.7	23.3	*11.2*	18.3	*52.7*	17.4	26.4	−0.3	−11.6
75 Malaysia	18.5	..	23.4	..	6.8	..	4.4	0.0	14.2	..	..	32.7	26.5	36.6	−9.4	−7.2
76 South Africa	..	..	..	..	..	..	..	..	..	..	..	..	21.8	26.8	−4.2	−4.5
77 Mexico	4.2	2.5	16.4	*11.5*	5.1	*1.4*	25.0	*11.4*	34.2	25.7	15.2	*47.5*	12.0	27.3	−3.0	−9.2
78 Uruguay	5.6	10.2	9.5	7.1	1.6	4.8	52.3	49.5	9.8	8.3	21.2	20.1	25.0	24.7	−2.5	−0.7
79 Hungary	..	6.9	..	1.6	..	3.6	..	25.7	..	38.8	..	23.4	..	62.6	..	−3.3
80 Poland	..	..	..	..	..	..	..	..	..	..	..	..	..	42.2	..	−0.3
81 Portugal	..	..	..	..	..	..	..	..	..	..	..	..	..	..	..	..
82 Yugoslavia	20.5	60.0	..	..	..	..	35.6	9.0	12.0	15.4	31.9	15.7	21.1	6.6	−0.4	0.0
83 Panama	0.0	0.0	20.7	16.0	15.1	15.8	10.8	16.7	24.2	9.0	29.1	42.5	27.6	32.5	−6.5	−3.2
84 Argentina	*10.0*	*5.2*	*20.0*	*6.0*	*0.0*	*1.3*	*20.0*	*33.0*	*30.0*	*18.4*	*20.0*	*36.0*	*19.6*	*25.8*	*−4.9*	*−8.0*
85 Korea, Rep. of	25.8	29.2	15.8	18.1	1.2	1.5	5.9	7.2	25.6	16.2	25.7	27.7	18.0	17.8	−3.9	−0.1
86 Algeria	..	..	..	..	..	..	..	..	..	..	..	..	..	..	..	..
87 Venezuela	10.3	*4.9*	18.6	*19.8*	11.7	*8.1*	9.2	*14.0*	25.4	*17.9*	24.8	*35.3*	21.4	*26.6*	−0.3	*2.9*
88 Gabon	..	..	..	..	..	..	..	..	..	..	..	..	40.1	41.0	−12.9	0.1
89 Greece	14.9	..	9.1	..	7.4	..	30.6	..	26.4	..	11.7	..	27.5	50.9	−1.7	−14.4
90 Oman	39.3	41.9	3.7	10.1	5.9	5.0	3.0	1.4	24.4	20.8	23.6	20.8	62.1	63.2	−15.3	−27.9
91 Trinidad and Tobago	..	..	..	..	..	..	..	..	..	..	..	..	..	..	..	..
92 Israel	42.9	*30.1*	7.1	*6.7*	3.6	*3.4*	7.1	*20.4*	7.1	*5.7*	32.2	*33.7*	43.9	*72.1*	−15.7	*−3.5*
93 Hong Kong	..	..	..	..	..	..	..	..	..	..	..	..	..	..	..	..
94 Singapore	20.1	22.5	9.0	21.6	4.5	6.5	2.2	5.7	5.7	17.7	58.6	26.0	29.5	26.5	1.3	2.0
95 *Iran, Islamic Rep.*	24.1	..	10.4	..	3.6	..	6.1	..	30.6	..	25.2	..	30.8	..	−4.6	..
96 *Iraq*	..	..	..	..	..	..	..	..	..	..	..	..	..	..	..	..
97 *Romania*	6.2	*4.7*	3.2	*1.8*	0.5	*0.8*	16.5	*21.9*	..	*55.5*	73.5	*15.4*	..	..	..	..
Developing economies	**14.3 w**	*12.5 w*	**12.5 w**	*10.3 w*	**4.7 w**	*4.5 w*	**16.9 w**	*13.8 w*	**25.6 w**	*20.6 w*	**26.0 w**	*38.3 w*	**18.7 w**	*26.3 w*	**−3.5 w**	*−6.2 w*
Oil exporters	**15.8 w**	*11.2 w*	**15.9 w**	*13.3 w*	**5.4 w**	*4.3 w*	**12.1 w**	*10.8 w*	**32.3 w**	*22.3 w*	**18.5 w**	*38.1 w*	**18.4 w**	*27.0 w*	**−3.2 w**	*−4.7 w*
Exporters of manufactures		*13.6 w*		*5.5 w*		*4.2 w*		*16.2 w*		*20.3 w*		*40.2 w*		*24.7 w*		*−7.0 w*
Highly indebted countries	**10.1 w**	*5.7 w*	**15.8 w**	*10.3 w*	**6.8 w**	*4.9 w*	**29.3 w**	*18.8 w*	**22.5 w**	*18.0 w*	**15.5 w**	*42.3 w*	**17.5 w**	*23.7 w*	**−2.7 w**	*−7.6 w*
Sub-Saharan Africa	..	..	..	..	..	..	..	..	..	..	..	..	..	..	..	..
High-income oil exporters	..	..	..	..	..	..	..	..	..	..	..	..	..	..	..	..
98 Saudi Arabia	..	..	..	..	..	..	..	..	..	..	..	..	..	..	..	..
99 Kuwait	8.4	12.8	15.0	12.6	5.5	7.1	11.9	20.5	16.6	22.4	42.5	24.6	34.4	41.5	17.4	23.6
100 United Arab Emirates[b]	24.4	45.3	16.5	9.7	4.3	6.2	6.1	5.0	18.3	5.1	30.5	28.7	4.3	17.5	0.3	..
101 *Libya*	..	..	..	..	..	..	..	..	..	..	..	..	..	..	..	..
Industrial market economies	**21.7 w**	*16.4 w*	**5.4 w**	*4.5 w*	**11.2 w**	*12.9 w*	**42.3 w**	*39.0 w*	**12.8 w**	*9.5 w*	**12.0 w**	*12.3 w*	**22.2 w**	*28.6 w*	**−1.8 w**	*−5.1 w*
102 Spain	6.5	*4.4*	8.3	*6.2*	0.9	*13.1*	49.8	*48.5*	17.5	*11.7*	17.0	*16.3*	19.8	*29.1*	−0.5	*−7.7*
103 Ireland	..	*3.1*	..	*11.7*	..	*13.2*	..	*30.1*	..	*15.0*	..	*26.9*	33.0	*54.7*	−5.5	*−11.6*
104 New Zealand[b]	5.8	*4.7*	16.9	*10.9*	14.8	*12.5*	25.6	*32.2*	16.5	*12.3*	20.4	*27.4*	29.2	*42.8*	−3.9	*−4.9*
105 Italy	6.3	*3.2*	16.1	*7.2*	13.5	*9.9*	44.8	*30.0*	18.4	*13.2*	0.9	*36.5*	27.6	*50.2*	−8.1	*−14.1*
106 United Kingdom	16.7	*13.3*	2.6	*2.1*	12.2	*12.6*	26.5	*30.2*	11.1	*8.9*	30.8	*33.0*	32.3	*40.6*	−2.7	*−3.4*
107 Belgium	6.7	*5.3*	15.5	*13.0*	1.5	*1.7*	41.0	*41.5*	18.9	*11.9*	16.4	*26.5*	39.9	*56.7*	−4.4	*−10.6*
108 Austria	3.3	*3.1*	10.2	*9.7*	10.1	*12.0*	53.7	*42.6*	11.3	*13.8*	11.4	*18.8*	29.6	*40.5*	−0.2	*−5.9*
109 Netherlands	..	*5.2*	..	*11.1*	..	*10.8*	..	*39.8*	..	*10.7*	..	*22.5*	41.0	*56.6*	0.0	*−1.7*
110 France	..	..	..	..	..	..	..	..	..	..	..	..	32.0	*44.1*	0.7	*−2.8*
111 Australia	14.2	*9.3*	4.2	*7.2*	7.0	*9.5*	20.3	*28.9*	14.4	*7.8*	39.9	*37.3*	18.8	*27.9*	0.3	*−2.3*
112 Germany, Fed. Rep.	12.4	*8.8*	1.5	*0.6*	17.5	*17.9*	46.9	*50.5*	11.3	*6.8*	10.4	*15.4*	24.2	*29.9*	0.7	*−0.7*
113 Finland	6.1	*5.2*	15.3	*13.7*	10.6	*10.6*	28.4	*35.7*	27.9	*21.0*	11.6	*13.7*	24.3	*31.1*	1.2	*−0.5*
114 Denmark	7.3	*5.2*	16.0	*9.2*	10.0	*1.0*	41.6	*40.0*	11.3	*6.8*	13.7	*37.8*	32.6	*39.5*	2.7	*−3.8*
115 Japan	..	..	..	..	..	..	..	..	..	..	..	..	12.7	*17.4*	−1.9	*−4.9*
116 Sweden	12.5	*6.6*	14.8	*8.9*	3.6	*1.1*	44.3	*51.8*	10.6	*6.8*	14.3	*24.8*	27.9	*44.1*	−1.2	*−2.6*
117 Canada	..	*7.6*	..	*3.4*	..	*6.1*	..	*35.0*	..	*14.9*	..	*33.1*	..	*25.4*	..	*−6.2*
118 Norway	9.7	*8.3*	9.9	*8.7*	12.3	*10.5*	39.9	*35.0*	20.2	*19.5*	8.0	*17.9*	35.0	*40.6*	−1.5	*3.9*
119 United States	32.2	*25.8*	3.2	*1.7*	8.6	*11.6*	35.3	*31.0*	10.6	*8.8*	10.1	*21.1*	19.0	*24.5*	−1.5	*−5.0*
120 Switzerland	15.1	*10.3*	4.2	*3.1*	10.0	*13.1*	39.5	*50.6*	18.4	*12.2*	12.8	*10.8*	13.3	*18.6*	0.9	*−0.1*
Nonreporting nonmembers																
121 *Albania*	..	..	..	..	..	..	..	..	..	..	..	..	..	..	..	..
122 *Angola*	..	..	..	..	..	..	..	..	..	..	..	..	..	..	..	..
123 *Bulgaria*	..	..	..	..	..	..	..	..	..	..	..	..	..	..	..	..
124 *Cuba*	..	..	..	..	..	..	..	..	..	..	..	..	..	..	..	..
125 *Czechoslovakia*	..	..	..	..	..	..	..	..	..	..	..	..	..	..	..	..
126 *German Dem. Rep.*	..	..	..	..	..	..	..	..	..	..	..	..	..	..	..	..
127 *Korea, Dem. Rep.*	..	..	..	..	..	..	..	..	..	..	..	..	..	..	..	..
128 *Mongolia*	..	..	..	..	..	..	..	..	..	..	..	..	..	..	..	..
129 *USSR*	..	..	..	..	..	..	..	..	..	..	..	..	..	..	..	..

a. See the technical notes.   b. Refers to budgetary data.

Table 24. Central government current revenue

	Percentage of total current revenue												Total current revenue (percentage of GNP)	
	Tax revenue										Nontax revenue			
	Taxes on income, profit, and capital gain		Social security contributions		Domestic taxes on goods and services		Taxes on international trade and transactions		Other taxes[a]					
	1972	1986	1972	1986	1972	1986	1972	1986	1972	1986	1972	1986	1972	1986
Low-income economies	..	..	..	..	..	..	..	..	..	..	..	..	..	..
China and India	..	..	..	..	..	..	..	..	..	..	..	..	..	..
Other low-income	..	16.8 w	..	..	..	32.2 w	..	28.1 w	..	..	..	19.8 w	..	15.4 w
1 Ethiopia	23.0	..	0.0	..	29.8	..	30.4	..	5.6	..	11.1	..	10.5	..
2 Bhutan	..	..	..	..	..	..	..	..	..	..	..	..	..	..
3 Burkina Faso	16.8	12.4	0.0	7.6	18.0	13.8	51.8	33.9	3.2	6.1	10.2	26.2	11.4	15.1
4 Nepal	4.1	8.0	0.0	0.0	26.5	40.7	36.7	27.7	19.0	6.2	13.7	17.4	5.2	9.2
5 Bangladesh[b]	3.7	9.6	0.0	0.0	22.4	28.1	18.0	22.3	3.8	5.7	52.2	34.3	8.6	9.4
6 Malawi[b]	31.5	34.6	0.0	0.0	24.3	28.5	20.0	21.5	0.4	0.5	23.9	14.9	16.0	22.3
7 Zaire	22.2	26.8	2.2	0.7	12.7	19.2	57.9	37.3	1.4	1.6	3.7	14.4	14.3	19.9
8 Mali	..	9.2	..	3.6	..	31.2	..	21.7	..	19.6	..	14.7	..	16.3
9 Burma	28.7	4.8	0.0	0.0	..	..	13.4	15.9	34.2	40.0	23.8	39.3	12.4	13.7
10 Mozambique	..	..	..	..	..	..	..	..	..	..	..	..	..	..
11 Madagascar	13.1	..	7.2	..	29.9	..	33.6	..	5.5	..	10.8	..	18.3	..
12 Uganda	22.1	5.5	0.0	0.0	32.8	19.1	36.3	75.3	0.3	0.0	8.5	0.0	13.7	5.9
13 Burundi	18.1	..	1.2	..	18.3	..	40.3	..	15.6	..	6.5	..	11.5	..
14 Tanzania	29.9	..	0.0	..	29.1	..	21.7	..	0.5	..	18.8	..	15.8	..
15 Togo	..	30.3	..	6.2	..	7.6	..	32.1	..	1.1	..	22.6	..	32.4
16 Niger	..	..	..	..	..	..	..	..	..	..	..	..	..	..
17 Benin	..	..	..	..	..	..	..	..	..	..	..	..	..	..
18 Somalia[b]	10.7	..	0.0	..	24.7	..	45.3	..	5.2	..	14.0	..	13.7	..
19 Central African Rep.	..	..	..	..	..	..	..	..	..	..	..	..	..	..
20 India	..	14.8	..	0.0	..	38.0	..	26.9	..	0.4	..	19.9	..	13.3
21 Rwanda	17.9	..	4.4	..	14.1	..	41.7	..	13.8	..	8.1	..	9.8	..
22 China	..	..	..	..	..	..	..	..	..	..	..	..	..	..
23 Kenya[b]	35.6	30.2	0.0	0.0	19.9	38.9	24.3	18.0	1.4	0.6	18.8	12.3	18.0	21.5
24 Zambia[b]	49.7	28.4	0.0	0.0	20.2	40.2	14.3	22.6	0.1	1.3	15.6	7.5	23.2	23.9
25 Sierra Leone[b]	..	28.0	..	0.0	..	25.0	..	40.4	..	1.0	..	5.6	..	6.5
26 Sudan[b]	11.8	..	0.0	..	30.4	..	40.5	..	1.5	..	15.7	..	18.0	..
27 Haiti	..	..	..	..	..	..	..	..	..	..	..	..	..	..
28 Pakistan	13.6	11.9	0.0	0.0	35.9	33.0	34.2	31.0	0.5	0.3	15.8	23.8	12.5	16.2
29 Lesotho	10.3	11.1	0.0	0.0	2.5	10.3	74.0	67.8	5.4	0.2	7.8	10.5	15.4	21.9
30 Ghana[b]	18.4	19.4	0.0	0.0	29.4	28.4	40.6	40.8	0.2	0.2	11.5	11.2	15.1	13.9
31 Sri Lanka	19.1	13.0	0.0	0.0	34.7	40.1	35.4	29.7	2.1	1.8	8.7	15.5	20.1	20.6
32 Mauritania	..	..	..	..	..	..	..	..	..	..	..	..	..	..
33 Senegal	20.0	..	..	..	25.9	..	42.7	..	7.5	..	3.8	..	17.0	..
34 Afghanistan	..	..	..	..	..	..	..	..	..	..	..	..	..	..
35 Chad	16.7	21.0	0.0	0.0	12.3	8.5	45.2	46.2	20.5	12.7	5.3	11.6	10.8	..
36 Guinea	..	..	..	..	..	..	..	..	..	..	..	..	..	..
37 Kampuchea, Dem.	..	..	..	..	..	..	..	..	..	..	..	..	..	..
38 Lao PDR	..	..	..	..	..	..	..	..	..	..	..	..	..	..
39 Viet Nam	..	..	..	..	..	..	..	..	..	..	..	..	..	..
Middle-income economies	21.3 w	25.7 w	..	..	23.8 w	25.5 w	14.1 w	8.3 w	..	..	22.5 w	26.3 w	19.1 w	24.0 w
Lower middle-income	19.7 w	31.7 w	..	..	33.9 w	24.3 w	21.1 w	13.7 w	..	..	15.3 w	..	16.7 w	21.4 w
40 Liberia	..	39.7	..	0.0	..	24.9	..	28.6	..	2.5	..	4.3	..	17.8
41 Yemen, PDR	..	..	..	..	..	..	..	..	..	..	..	..	..	..
42 Indonesia	45.5	40.4	0.0	0.0	22.8	23.3	17.6	4.9	3.5	1.8	10.6	29.7	13.4	23.1
43 Yemen Arab Rep.	..	12.2	..	0.0	..	11.6	..	43.1	..	11.7	..	21.4	..	19.5
44 Philippines[b]	13.8	26.6	0.0	0.0	24.3	36.4	23.0	23.7	29.7	2.5	9.3	10.8	12.4	11.5
45 Morocco	16.4	18.7	5.9	5.0	45.7	37.8	13.2	16.1	6.1	7.7	12.6	14.8	18.5	26.8
46 Bolivia	15.4	6.5	..	28.6	30.8	14.3	46.2	28.6	7.7	-6.5	8.0	28.6	7.8	3.2
47 Zimbabwe	..	42.8	..	0.0	..	30.6	..	15.6	..	1.1	..	10.0	..	26.8
48 Nigeria[b]	43.0	..	0.0	..	26.3	..	17.5	..	0.2	..	13.0	..	11.6	..
49 Dominican Rep.	17.9	19.0	3.9	3.5	19.0	33.8	40.3	33.7	1.8	2.2	17.0	7.8	19.4	13.3
50 Papua New Guinea[b]	..	47.9	..	0.0	..	14.3	..	24.1	..	1.9	..	11.8	..	22.4
51 Côte d'Ivoire	..	11.4	..	4.4	..	15.7	..	26.7	..	41.7	..	..	..	28.2
52 Honduras	19.2	..	3.0	..	33.8	..	28.2	..	2.3	..	13.5	..	12.6	..
53 Egypt, Arab Rep.	..	16.4	..	13.3	..	10.8	..	14.1	..	7.2	..	38.2	..	34.3
54 Nicaragua	9.5	14.4	14.0	10.5	37.3	48.5	24.4	7.1	9.0	10.6	5.8	8.9	12.6	39.6
55 Thailand	12.1	20.7	0.0	0.0	46.3	43.9	26.7	22.2	1.8	2.0	11.2	11.1	12.9	16.3
56 El Salvador	15.2	20.0	0.0	0.0	25.6	31.6	36.1	41.4	17.2	-1.8	6.0	8.9	11.6	14.7
57 Botswana[b]	19.9	29.8	0.0	0.0	2.2	0.9	47.2	13.9	0.7	0.1	29.9	55.2	30.7	82.6
58 Jamaica	..	..	..	..	..	..	..	..	..	..	..	..	..	..
59 Cameroon	..	57.2	..	5.4	..	10.9	..	15.2	..	3.3	..	8.0	..	24.3
60 Guatemala	12.7	..	..	..	36.1	..	26.2	..	15.6	..	9.4	..	8.9	..
61 Congo, People's Rep.	19.4	..	0.0	..	40.3	..	26.5	..	6.3	..	7.5	..	18.4	..
62 Paraguay	8.8	12.2	10.4	12.7	26.1	26.1	24.8	11.4	17.0	22.5	12.9	15.1	11.5	9.6
63 Peru[b]	17.2	22.0	..	..	32.2	46.6	15.9	22.6	22.1	1.2	12.6	7.6	15.5	12.9
64 Turkey	..	43.5	..	..	..	31.0	..	6.6	..	4.3	..	14.6	17.6	18.5
65 Tunisia	15.9	12.2	7.1	7.9	31.6	19.8	21.8	28.5	7.8	5.5	15.7	26.2	23.6	34.4
66 Ecuador[b]	19.6	65.0	0.0	0.0	19.1	13.7	52.4	17.3	5.1	2.0	3.8	2.0	13.6	17.7
67 Mauritius	22.7	9.1	0.0	0.0	23.3	19.9	40.2	56.4	5.5	4.4	8.2	10.1	15.6	21.5
68 Colombia	37.2	..	13.9	..	16.0	..	20.3	..	7.2	..	5.5	..	10.6	..

Note: For data comparability and coverage, see the technical notes. Figures in italics are for years other than those specified.

	Percentage of total current revenue												
	Tax revenue												Total current revenue (percentage of GNP)	
	Taxes on income, profit, and capital gain		Social security contributions		Domestic taxes on goods and services		Taxes on international trade and transactions		Other taxes [a]		Nontax revenue			
	1972	1986	1972	1986	1972	1986	1972	1986	1972	1986	1972	1986	1972	1986
69 Chile	14.3	11.7	28.6	7.5	28.6	43.6	14.3	8.8	0.0	7.5	14.3	20.8	30.2	31.7
70 Costa Rica	17.7	10.8	13.4	24.7	38.1	28.2	18.1	21.1	1.6	−0.2	11.0	15.5	15.7	24.5
71 Jordan	..	13.2	..	0.0	..	12.9	..	33.1	..	14.8	..	25.9	..	26.7
72 Syrian Arab Rep.	6.8	..	0.0	..	10.4	..	17.3	..	12.1	..	53.4	..	25.1	..
73 *Lebanon*	..	..	..	..	..	..	..	..	..	..	..	..	..	..
Upper middle-income	**22.5**	**23.8**	..	..	**21.1**	**25.8**	**11.6**	**6.6**	..	..	**24.8**	**28.3**	**20.3**	**25.0**
74 Brazil	20.0	17.7	27.7	20.8	35.4	16.4	7.7	2.4	3.1	3.8	6.2	38.9	18.8	27.2
75 Malaysia	25.2	43.0	0.1	0.7	24.2	17.6	27.9	16.6	1.4	2.2	21.2	19.8	20.3	29.3
76 South Africa	54.8	52.2	1.2	1.2	21.5	32.5	4.6	2.5	5.0	3.1	12.8	8.5	21.2	23.3
77 Mexico	36.4	24.3	19.4	12.9	32.1	67.0	13.2	4.0	−9.8	−17.0	8.6	8.8	10.4	18.1
78 Uruguay	4.7	8.2	30.0	27.3	24.5	43.6	6.1	13.7	22.0	2.5	12.6	4.7	22.7	24.3
79 Hungary	..	15.9	..	24.0	..	29.0	..	6.2	..	11.5	..	13.5	..	59.4
80 Poland	..	25.8	..	24.9	..	29.8	..	7.0	..	6.2	..	6.3	..	42.0
81 Portugal	..	..	..	..	..	..	..	..	..	..	..	..	..	..
82 Yugoslavia	0.0	0.0	52.3	0.0	24.5	63.1	19.5	35.6	0.0	0.0	3.7	1.3	20.7	6.6
83 Panama	23.3	23.1	22.4	20.3	13.2	15.2	16.0	10.6	7.7	3.4	17.3	27.3	21.8	28.3
84 Argentina	0.0	4.9	33.3	27.1	0.0	37.4	33.3	14.7	0.0	6.3	33.3	9.7	14.7	22.8
85 Korea, Rep. of	29.1	25.2	0.7	1.6	41.8	42.7	10.7	14.9	5.2	3.9	12.5	11.7	13.2	18.8
86 Algeria	..	..	..	..	..	..	..	..	..	..	..	..	..	..
87 Venezuela	54.2	58.4	6.0	2.9	6.7	5.4	6.1	15.4	1.1	2.2	25.9	15.6	21.9	31.8
88 Gabon	18.2	44.2	6.0	0.0	9.5	6.5	44.9	16.2	4.2	1.9	17.2	31.2	28.3	42.0
89 Greece	12.2	17.9	24.5	34.9	35.5	36.3	6.7	0.5	12.0	0.2	9.2	10.2	25.4	35.8
90 Oman	71.1	19.8	0.0	0.0	0.0	1.2	3.0	4.4	2.3	0.9	23.6	73.8	47.4	33.5
91 Trinidad and Tobago	..	..	..	..	..	..	..	..	..	..	..	..	..	..
92 Israel	40.0	36.9	0.0	8.8	20.0	29.0	20.0	4.8	10.0	2.8	10.0	17.7	31.3	56.4
93 Hong Kong	..	..	..	..	..	..	..	..	..	..	..	..	..	..
94 Singapore	24.4	27.0	0.0	0.0	17.6	13.8	11.1	3.6	15.5	15.1	31.4	40.6	21.6	27.0
95 *Iran, Islamic Rep.*	7.9	..	2.7	..	6.4	..	14.6	..	4.9	..	63.6	..	26.2	..
96 *Iraq*	..	..	..	..	..	..	..	..	..	..	..	..	..	..
97 Romania	6.3	0.0	7.9	16.5	0.0	0.0	0.0	0.0	0.0	12.3	85.8	71.2	..	..
Developing economies	21.1 w	24.6 w	..	..	25.7 w	26.8 w	16.1 w	10.5 w	..	..	21.4 w	25.5 w	16.2 w	22.7 w
Oil exporters	28.0 w	32.5 w	..	..	19.2 w	23.6 w	14.5 w	8.4 w	..	..	30.6 w	29.0 w	15.9 w	22.6 w
Exporters of manufactures	..	18.0 w	..	..	..	25.1 w	..	8.9 w	..	..	..	31.6 w	..	23.0 w
Highly indebted countries	18.3 w	22.0 w	..	..	28.1 w	32.1 w	13.9 w	8.3 w	..	..	12.4 w	22.9 w	16.4 w	21.3 w
Sub-Saharan Africa	..	..	..	..	..	..	..	..	..	..	..	..	..	..
High-income oil exporters	..	..	..	..	..	..	..	..	..	..	..	..	..	..
98 Saudi Arabia	..	..	..	..	..	..	..	..	..	..	..	..	..	..
99 Kuwait	68.8	0.6	..	..	19.7	0.4	1.5	1.3	0.2	0.0	9.9	97.7	55.2	66.2
100 United Arab Emirates[b]	0.0	..	0.0	..	0.0	..	0.0	..	0.0	..	100.0	..	0.2	..
101 *Libya*	..	..	..	..	..	..	..	..	..	..	..	..	..	..
Industrial market economies	**4.1 w**	**40.0 w**	..	..	**21.2 w**	**17.3 w**	**2.0 w**	**1.2 w**	..	..	**6.2 w**	**9.0 w**	**21.6 w**	**24.1 w**
102 Spain	15.9	22.9	38.9	45.2	23.4	15.8	10.0	4.1	0.7	2.2	11.1	9.8	20.0	23.7
103 Ireland	28.3	33.6	9.0	14.4	32.1	32.1	16.7	7.2	3.2	1.2	10.6	11.5	30.3	45.3
104 New Zealand[b]	61.4	61.8	0.0	0.0	19.9	17.5	4.1	3.5	4.5	1.9	10.0	15.3	28.0	39.5
105 Italy	16.6	38.5	39.2	28.7	31.7	23.5	0.4	0.0	4.3	9.3	7.7	3.1	23.3	36.7
106 United Kingdom	39.4	38.9	15.6	17.5	27.1	30.4	1.7	0.0	5.4	1.9	10.8	11.4	33.1	37.9
107 Belgium	31.3	37.9	32.4	34.0	28.9	21.4	1.0	0.0	3.3	2.1	3.1	4.5	35.6	46.5
108 Austria	20.7	19.4	30.0	36.7	28.3	26.6	5.4	1.4	10.2	7.3	5.5	8.6	29.7	35.0
109 Netherlands	32.5	24.3	36.7	37.9	22.3	20.6	0.5	0.0	3.4	2.3	4.7	14.8	43.4	51.6
110 France	16.9	17.5	37.1	43.8	37.9	29.9	0.3	0.1	2.9	4.0	4.9	4.7	33.0	40.9
111 Australia	58.3	60.0	0.0	0.0	21.9	23.5	5.2	5.2	2.1	0.5	12.5	10.9	20.7	25.8
112 Germany, Fed. Rep.	19.7	17.5	46.6	53.3	28.1	21.8	0.8	0.0	0.8	0.2	4.0	7.3	25.3	29.4
113 Finland	30.0	31.5	7.8	9.6	47.7	45.7	3.1	0.8	5.8	4.4	5.5	7.9	26.5	29.8
114 Denmark	40.0	37.2	5.1	3.7	42.1	41.7	3.1	0.1	2.8	3.8	6.8	13.5	35.5	43.8
115 Japan	64.8	67.4	0.0	0.0	22.6	18.9	3.5	1.7	6.8	7.5	2.4	4.6	11.2	12.6
116 Sweden	27.0	16.0	21.6	29.8	34.0	29.6	1.5	0.5	4.7	8.3	11.3	15.8	32.4	41.1
117 Canada	..	49.3	..	14.5	..	18.5	..	4.7	..	0.0	..	13.0	..	19.7
118 Norway	22.6	20.2	20.6	21.8	48.0	39.7	1.6	0.5	1.0	1.0	6.2	16.7	36.8	48.4
119 United States	59.2	50.1	23.8	33.9	7.1	3.9	1.6	1.7	2.5	0.8	5.7	9.5	17.6	19.5
120 Switzerland	13.9	14.8	37.3	52.7	21.5	20.5	16.7	7.8	2.6	−1.3	8.0	5.5	14.5	18.3
Nonreporting nonmembers	..	..	..	..	..	..	..	..	..	..	..	..	..	..
121 *Albania*	..	..	..	..	..	..	..	..	..	..	..	..	..	..
122 *Angola*	..	..	..	..	..	..	..	..	..	..	..	..	..	..
123 *Bulgaria*	..	..	..	..	..	..	..	..	..	..	..	..	..	..
124 *Cuba*	..	..	..	..	..	..	..	..	..	..	..	..	..	..
125 *Czechoslovakia*	..	..	..	..	..	..	..	..	..	..	..	..	..	..
126 *German Dem. Rep.*	..	..	..	..	..	..	..	..	..	..	..	..	..	..
127 *Korea, Dem. Rep.*	..	..	..	..	..	..	..	..	..	..	..	..	..	..
128 *Mongolia*	..	..	..	..	..	..	..	..	..	..	..	..	..	..
129 *USSR*	..	..	..	..	..	..	..	..	..	..	..	..	..	..

a. See the technical notes.   b. Refers to budgetary data.

Table 25. Money and interest rates

	Monetary holdings, broadly defined					Average annual inflation (GDP deflator)	Nominal interest rates of banks (average annual percentage)			
	Average annual nominal growth rate (percent)		Average outstanding (percentage of GDP)				Deposit rate		Lending rate	
	1965-80	1980-86	1965	1980	1986	1980-86	1980	1986	1980	1986
Low-income economies										
China and India										
Other low-income										
1 Ethiopia	12.7	12.8	12.5	25.2	37.3	3.4	..	..	..	..
2 Bhutan	..	..	..	..	..	..	6.25	5.25	9.38	8.83
3 Burkina Faso	17.1	12.6	9.3	18.5	22.1	6.3	4.00	7.17	14.00	15.67
4 Nepal	17.9	18.6	8.4	21.9	28.7	8.8	8.25	*12.00*	11.33	*12.00*
5 Bangladesh	..	23.8	..	18.6	26.7	11.2	7.92	12.75	16.67	19.00
6 Malawi	15.4	15.9	17.7	20.3	22.0	12.4				
7 Zaire	28.0	56.4	11.7	8.9	10.8	54.1	6.19	6.08	9.38	8.83
8 Mali	14.4	16.0	..	17.4	23.0	7.4	..	..	..	..
9 Burma	11.5	14.3	29.0	23.9	35.8	2.1	..	..	..	..
10 Mozambique	..	..	..	..	..	28.1	..	..	..	..
11 Madagascar	11.9	14.3	19.6	27.6	25.7	17.8	5.63	11.50	9.50	14.50
12 Uganda	*23.2*	77.8	..	12.7	7.8	74.9	6.80	35.00	10.80	33.33
13 Burundi	15.7	11.7	10.1	12.7	17.1	6.4	2.50	8.00	12.00	12.00
14 Tanzania	*20.1*	..	..	37.2	..	21.5	6.25	8.50	11.50	18.50
15 Togo	20.3	12.6	10.9	29.0	45.3	6.7	6.25	5.25	9.38	8.83
16 Niger	18.3	6.6	3.8	13.3	15.9	6.6	6.25	5.25	9.38	8.83
17 Benin	17.3	9.8	10.6	21.1	22.8	8.6	6.25	5.25	9.38	8.83
18 Somalia	20.4	29.4	12.7	25.1	10.7	*45.4*	4.50	*14.00*	7.50	20.58
19 Central African Rep.	12.7	7.5	13.5	18.9	17.4	11.5	5.50	7.25	10.50	12.00
20 India	15.3	17.6	25.7	36.2	43.9	7.8	..	..	16.50	16.50
21 Rwanda	19.0	9.9	15.8	13.6	15.4	5.6	6.25	6.25	13.50	14.00
22 China	..	23.9	..	34.9	56.5	3.8	5.40	..	..	..
23 Kenya	*18.6*	15.2	..	37.7	39.8	9.9	5.75	11.25	10.58	14.00
24 Zambia	12.7	24.4	..	32.6	28.3	23.3	7.00	..	9.50	27.40
25 Sierra Leone	15.9	43.2	11.7	20.6	27.2	33.5	9.17	14.17	11.00	15.00
26 Sudan	21.0	34.5	14.2	28.2	32.3	32.6	..	..	..	..
27 Haiti	20.3	*7.4*	9.9	26.1	..	7.7	10.00	..	..	..
28 Pakistan	14.7	14.8	40.8	38.7	38.4	7.5	..	..	..	..
29 Lesotho	..	20.2	..	..	48.4	13.1	*9.6*	10.04	11.00	13.42
30 Ghana	25.9	42.8	20.3	16.2	11.3	50.8	11.50	17.00	19.00	20.00
31 Sri Lanka	15.1	17.7	31.4	32.9	33.6	13.5	14.50	12.21	19.00	9.80
32 Mauritania	20.7	12.0	5.7	20.5	22.9	9.9	..	*7.33*	..	*10.67*
33 Senegal	15.6	9.8	15.3	27.0	24.5	9.5	6.25	5.25	9.38	8.83
34 *Afghanistan*	14.0	13.8	14.4	26.8	..	..	9.00	9.00	13.00	13.00
35 *Chad*	12.5	19.8	9.3	20.0	25.5	..	5.50	5.50	11.00	11.00
36 *Guinea*	..	..	..	..	..	..	..	..	..	..
37 *Kampuchea, Dem.*	..	..	..	..	..	..	..	..	..	..
38 *Lao PDR*	..	..	..	..	..	..	..	..	..	..
39 *Viet Nam*	..	..	..	..	..	..	..	..	..	..
Middle-income economies										
Lower middle-income										
40 Liberia	..	..	..	..	..	1.1	10.30	7.25	18.40	14.45
41 Yemen, PDR	15.2	13.2	..	114.8	175.0	4.8	..	..	..	..
42 Indonesia	54.4	24.1	..	13.2	26.3	8.9	6.00	*18.00*	9.00	21.49
43 Yemen Arab Rep.	..	23.0	..	74.7	78.3	13.1	..	..	..	..
44 Philippines	17.7	16.7	19.9	19.0	20.9	18.2	12.25	11.25	14.00	17.53
45 Morocco	15.8	14.8	29.4	45.4	53.7	7.7	4.88	8.50	7.00	8.75
46 Bolivia	24.3	642.6	10.9	16.2	13.7	683.7	18.00	..	28.00	..
47 Zimbabwe	..	12.4	..	54.6	45.3	13.0	3.52	10.28	17.54	13.00
48 Nigeria	28.5	9.8	13.9	25.1	34.5	10.5	5.27	*9.12*	8.43	*9.43*
49 Dominican Rep.	18.5	21.1	18.0	23.4	27.7	15.9	..	..	..	..
50 Papua New Guinea	..	9.8	..	32.9	35.5	..	6.90	11.49	11.15	12.33
51 Côte d'Ivoire	20.4	9.4	21.8	26.7	29.4	8.3	6.25	5.25	9.38	8.83
52 Honduras	14.6	10.9	15.4	23.3	29.1	5.2	7.00	10.10	18.50	19.00
53 Egypt, Arab Rep.	17.7	23.2	35.3	49.7	74.0	12.4	7.04	*8.50*	..	..
54 Nicaragua	15.0	..	15.4	21.0	..	56.5	7.50	..	..	..
55 Thailand	17.8	19.0	25.6	35.9	63.0	3.0	12.00	9.75	18.00	*19.00*
56 El Salvador	14.3	18.3	21.6	28.1	32.0	14.9	..	..	..	..
57 Botswana	..	19.7	..	31.1	27.1	7.6	5.00	8.67	8.48	11.00
58 Jamaica	17.2	26.5	24.3	35.6	51.1	19.8	10.29	19.02	13.00	23.00
59 Cameroon	19.1	18.9	12.5	19.7	19.4	11.0	7.50	7.25	13.00	13.00
60 Guatemala	16.3	13.7	15.2	20.5	22.5	11.3	9.00	..	..	..
61 Congo, People's Rep.	14.2	12.3	16.5	14.7	20.1	7.5	6.50	8.00	11.00	11.50
62 Paraguay	21.3	16.8	12.1	19.8	16.7	19.0	..	..	..	..
63 Peru	25.9	100.8	18.7	16.3	15.6	100.1	..	*49.20*	25.67	..
64 Turkey	27.4	51.0	23.0	16.7	25.4	37.3	10.00			
65 Tunisia	17.4	15.3	30.2	42.1	51.5	8.9	2.50	5.25	7.25	9.17
66 Ecuador	22.6	..	15.6	20.2	..	29.5	..	..	..	..
67 Mauritius	21.8	15.6	27.3	41.1	45.0	8.1	*9.25*	9.50	*12.19*	14.33
68 Colombia	26.5	*27.2*	19.8	23.7	..	22.6	*31.30*	*29.10*	19.00	..

Note: For data comparability and coverage, see the technical notes.   Figures in italics are for years other than those specified.

		Monetary holdings, broadly defined					Average annual inflation (GDP deflator)	Nominal interest rates of banks (average annual percentage)			
		Average annual nominal growth rate (percent)		Average outstanding (percentage of GDP)				Deposit rate		Lending rate	
		1965–80	1980–86	1965	1980	1986	1980–86	1980	1986	1980	1986
69	Chile	137.5	..	16.3	17.6	..	20.2	37.46	..	47.14	..
70	Costa Rica	24.6	29.4	19.3	38.8	35.3	32.3	..	16.67	..	21.80
71	Jordan	19.1	12.9	..	88.8	122.6	3.2	..	..	..	..
72	Syrian Arab Rep.	21.9	22.2	24.6	40.5	..	6.2	5.00	..	..	..
73	*Lebanon*	16.2	42.5	83.4	176.1	..	..	..	..	..	..

Upper middle-income

		1965–80	1980–86	1965	1980	1986	1980–86	1980	1986	1980	1986
74	Brazil	43.4	*175.8*	20.6	18.0	..	157.1	..	..	..	..
75	Malaysia	21.5	14.8	26.3	69.8	127.5	1.4	6.23	7.17	7.75	*11.54*
76	South Africa	14.0	14.9	56.6	49.5	52.5	13.6	5.54	10.98	9.50	14.33
77	Mexico	21.9	59.6	27.0	28.7	23.7	63.7	26.15	84.68	28.10	..
78	Uruguay	65.5	51.2	28.0	30.5	39.1	50.4	50.30	61.70	66.62	94.73
79	Hungary	..	7.2	..	46.5	48.0	5.4	3.00	4.00	9.00	11.00
80	Poland	..	23.3	..	58.3	39.0	31.2	3.00	6.00	8.00	12.00
81	Portugal	19.5	..	77.7	97.1	..	22.0	18.20	*26.80*	18.50	*25.59*
82	Yugoslavia	25.7	46.3	43.6	59.1	39.5	51.8	5.88	55.67	11.50	83.00
83	Panama	..	..	..	..	..	3.3	..	..	..	..
84	Argentina	86.5	302.2	..	22.3	17.6	326.2	87.97	61.23	..	..
85	Korea, Rep. of	35.5	18.1	11.1	31.8	41.3	5.4	19.50	10.00	18.00	10.00
86	Algeria	22.1	17.5	32.1	58.5	85.2	6.1	..	..	..	..
87	Venezuela	22.3	15.6	20.5	42.5	67.7	8.7	..	8.93	..	8.49
88	Gabon	25.2	12.1	16.2	15.2	26.3	4.8	7.50	8.00	12.50	11.50
89	Greece	21.4	25.7	35.0	61.6	75.8	20.3	14.50	15.50	21.25	20.50
90	Oman	..	17.4	..	13.8	30.6	*3.6*	..	..	..	..
91	Trinidad and Tobago	22.4	12.4	21.3	30.8	59.4	8.6	*6.57*	5.97	10.00	12.00
92	Israel	52.4	193.8	13.9	56.8	68.9	182.9	..	18.59	176.93	60.27
93	Hong Kong	..	..	..	69.3	..	6.9	..	..	..	..
94	Singapore	17.6	10.7	58.4	74.4	101.6	1.9	9.37	3.91	11.72	6.82
95	*Iran, Islamic Rep.*	28.6	..	21.6	52.1	..	..	..	..	..	..
96	*Iraq*	..	..	19.7	..	..	..	..	..	..	..
97	*Romania*	..	7.5	..	33.2	..	..	..	..	..	..

Developing economies
Oil exporters
Exporters of manufactures
Highly indebted countries
Sub-Saharan Africa

High-income oil exporters

		1965–80	1980–86	1965	1980	1986	1980–86	1980	1986	1980	1986
98	Saudi Arabia	32.1	11.6	16.4	18.6	53.6	−1.3	..	..	..	..
99	Kuwait	17.8	6.4	28.1	34.4	..	..	4.50	*4.50*	6.80	*6.80*
100	United Arab Emirates	..	14.5	..	19.0	..	−1.4	9.47	..	..	..
101	*Libya*	29.2	2.2	14.2	34.7	..	..	5.13	5.50	7.00	7.00

Industrial market economies

		1965–80	1980–86	1965	1980	1986	1980–86	1980	1986	1980	1986
102	Spain	19.7	8.7	60.3	75.2	63.7	11.3	13.05	9.05	16.85	12.19
103	Ireland	16.1	6.5	..	58.1	47.6	..	12.00	6.50	15.96	12.23
104	New Zealand	12.8	16.4	54.8	51.1	55.3	11.0	..	16.32	12.63	..
105	Italy	17.8	12.2	60.0	76.0	66.5	13.2	12.70	8.97	19.03	14.18
106	United Kingdom	13.8	13.3	48.6	46.3	63.5	6.0	14.13	6.89	16.17	10.83
107	Belgium	10.4	6.5	59.2	57.0	56.2	5.7	7.69	5.33	..	10.44
108	Austria	13.3	7.5	49.0	72.6	80.8	4.5	5.00	3.50	..	..
109	Netherlands	14.7	5.8	54.5	79.0	87.7	3.1	5.96	3.93	13.50	8.63
110	France	15.0	10.0	53.5	69.7	68.9	8.8	6.25	5.32	18.73	16.38
111	Australia	13.1	12.7	49.3	44.5	47.7	8.2	8.58	13.96	10.58	19.85
112	Germany, Fed. Rep.	10.1	5.7	46.1	60.4	63.7	3.0	7.95	3.71	12.04	8.75
113	Finland	14.7	14.3	39.1	39.5	48.2	8.1	..	7.33	9.77	9.08
114	Denmark	11.5	16.9	45.8	42.6	57.5	7.3	10.80	6.58	17.20	12.98
115	Japan	17.2	8.6	106.9	134.0	163.5	1.6	5.50	2.32	8.32	5.91
116	Sweden	10.8	..	39.3	40.6	..	8.2	11.25	9.58	15.12	14.18
117	Canada	15.3	6.7	40.5	65.0	62.8	5.6	12.86	8.25	18.25	9.75
118	Norway	12.8	12.9	51.9	52.9	59.9	7.0	5.08	*5.35*	12.63	*13.46*
119	United States	9.2	10.5	63.8	58.7	68.4	4.4	13.07	6.52	15.27	8.35
120	Switzerland	7.1	8.8	101.1	107.4	119.4	4.2	..	3.63	..	5.46

Nonreporting nonmembers

		1965–80	1980–86	1965	1980	1986	1980–86	1980	1986	1980	1986
121	*Albania*	..	..	..	..	..	..	..	..	..	..
122	*Angola*	..	..	..	..	..	..	..	..	..	..
123	*Bulgaria*	..	..	..	..	..	..	..	..	..	..
124	*Cuba*	..	..	..	..	..	..	..	..	..	..
125	*Czechoslovakia*	..	..	..	..	..	..	..	..	..	..
126	*German Dem. Rep.*	..	..	..	..	..	..	..	..	..	..
127	*Korea, Dem. Rep.*	..	..	..	..	..	..	..	..	..	..
128	*Mongolia*	..	..	..	..	..	..	..	..	..	..
129	*USSR*	..	..	..	..	..	..	..	..	..	..

Table 26. Income distribution

| | Year | \multicolumn{6}{c}{Percentage share of household income, by percentile groups of households[a]} |
		Lowest 20 percent	Second quintile	Third quintile	Fourth quintile	Highest 20 percent	Highest 10 percent
Low-income economies							
China and India							
Other low-income							
1 Ethiopia		..	..	..	..	..	..
2 Bhutan		..	..	..	..	..	..
3 Burkina Faso		..	..	..	..	..	..
4 Nepal		..	..	..	..	..	..
5 Bangladesh	1981-82	6.6	10.7	15.3	22.1	45.3	29.5
6 Malawi		..	..	..	..	..	..
7 Zaire		..	..	..	..	..	..
8 Mali		..	..	..	..	..	..
9 Burma		..	..	..	..	..	..
10 Mozambique		..	..	..	..	..	..
11 Madagascar		..	..	..	..	..	..
12 *Uganda*		..	..	..	..	..	..
13 Burundi		..	..	..	..	..	..
14 Tanzania		..	..	..	..	..	..
15 Togo		..	..	..	..	..	..
16 Niger		..	..	..	..	..	..
17 Benin		..	..	..	..	..	..
18 Somalia		..	..	..	..	..	..
19 Central African Rep.		..	..	..	..	..	..
20 India	1975-76	7.0	9.2	13.9	20.5	49.4	33.6
21 Rwanda		..	..	..	..	..	..
22 China		..	..	..	..	..	..
23 Kenya	1976	2.6	6.3	11.5	19.2	60.4	45.8
24 Zambia	1976	3.4	7.4	11.2	16.9	61.1	46.4
25 Sierra Leone		..	..	..	..	..	..
26 Sudan		..	..	..	..	..	..
27 Haiti		..	..	..	..	..	..
28 Pakistan		..	..	..	..	..	..
29 Lesotho		..	..	..	..	..	..
30 Ghana		..	..	..	..	..	..
31 Sri Lanka	1980-81	5.8	10.1	14.1	20.3	49.8	34.7
32 Mauritania		..	..	..	..	..	..
33 Senegal		..	..	..	..	..	..
34 *Afghanistan*		..	..	..	..	..	..
35 *Chad*		..	..	..	..	..	..
36 Guinea		..	..	..	..	..	..
37 *Kampuchea, Dem.*		..	..	..	..	..	..
38 *Lao PDR*		..	..	..	..	..	..
39 *Viet Nam*		..	..	..	..	..	..
Middle-income economies							
Lower middle-income							
40 Liberia		..	..	..	..	..	..
41 Yemen, PDR		..	..	..	..	..	..
42 Indonesia	1976	6.6	7.8	12.6	23.6	49.4	34.0
43 Yemen Arab Rep.		..	..	..	..	..	..
44 Philippines	1985	5.2	8.9	13.2	20.2	52.5	37.0
45 Morocco		..	..	..	..	..	..
46 Bolivia		..	..	..	..	..	..
47 Zimbabwe		..	..	..	..	..	..
48 Nigeria		..	..	..	..	..	..
49 Dominican Rep.		..	..	..	..	..	..
50 Papua New Guinea		..	..	..	..	..	..
51 Côte d'Ivoire	1985-86	2.4	6.2	10.9	19.1	61.4	43.7
52 Honduras		..	..	..	..	..	..
53 Egypt, Arab Rep.	1974	5.8	10.7	14.7	20.8	48.0	33.2
54 Nicaragua		..	..	..	..	..	..
55 Thailand	1975-76	5.6	9.6	13.9	21.1	49.8	34.1
56 El Salvador	1976-77	5.5	10.0	14.8	22.4	47.3	29.5
57 Botswana		..	..	..	..	..	..
58 Jamaica		..	..	..	..	..	..
59 Cameroon		..	..	..	..	..	..
60 Guatemala		..	..	..	..	..	..
61 Congo, People's Rep.		..	..	..	..	..	..
62 Paraguay		..	..	..	..	..	..
63 Peru	1972	1.9	5.1	11.0	21.0	61.0	42.9
64 Turkey	1973	3.5	8.0	12.5	19.5	56.5	40.7
65 Tunisia		..	..	..	..	..	..
66 Ecuador		..	..	..	..	..	..
67 Mauritius	1980-81	4.0	7.5	11.0	17.0	60.5	46.7
68 Colombia		..	..	..	..	..	..

	Year	Percentage share of household income, by percentile groups of households[a]					
		Lowest 20 percent	Second quintile	Third quintile	Fourth quintile	Highest 20 percent	Highest 10 percent
69 Chile		..	..	..	..	..	..
70 Costa Rica	1971	3.3	8.7	13.3	19.8	54.8	39.5
71 Jordan		..	..	..	..	..	..
72 Syrian Arab Rep.		..	..	..	..	..	..
73 *Lebanon*		..	..	..	..	..	..
Upper middle-income							
74 Brazil	1972	2.0	5.0	9.4	17.0	66.6	50.6
75 Malaysia	1973	3.5	7.7	12.4	20.3	56.1	39.8
76 South Africa		..	..	..	..	..	..
77 Mexico	1977	2.9	7.0	12.0	20.4	57.7	40.6
78 Uruguay		..	..	..	..	..	..
79 Hungary	1982	6.9	13.6	19.2	24.5	35.8	20.5
80 Poland		..	..	..	..	..	
81 Portugal	1973-74	5.2	10.0	14.4	21.3	49.1	33.4
82 Yugoslavia	1978	6.6	12.1	18.7	23.9	38.7	22.9
83 Panama	1973	2.0	5.2	11.0	20.0	61.8	44.2
84 Argentina	1970	4.4	9.7	14.1	21.5	50.3	35.2
85 Korea, Rep. of	1976	5.7	11.2	15.4	22.4	45.3	27.5
86 Algeria		..	..	..	..	..	
87 Venezuela	1970	3.0	7.3	12.9	22.8	54.0	35.7
88 Gabon							
89 Greece		..	..	..	..	..	
90 Oman							
91 Trinidad and Tobago	1975-76	4.2	9.1	13.9	22.8	50.0	31.8
92 Israel	1979-80	6.0	12.0	17.7	24.4	39.9	22.6
93 Hong Kong	1980	5.4	10.8	15.2	21.6	47.0	31.3
94 Singapore		..	..	..	..	..	..
95 *Iran, Islamic Rep.*		..	..	..	..	..	..
96 *Iraq*		..	..	..	..	..	..
97 *Romania*		..	..	..	..	..	..
Develong economies							
Oil exporters							
Exporters of manufactures							
High indebted countries							
Sub-Saharan Africa							
High-income oil exporters							
98 Saudi Arabia		..	..	..	..	..	
99 Kuwait		..	..	..	..	..	..
100 Unit Arab Emirates		..	..	..	..	..	
101 *Libya*		..	..	..	..	..	..
Industrial market economies							
102 Spain	1980-81	6.9	12.5	17.3	23.2	40.0	24.
103 Ireland	1973	7.2	13.1	16.6	23.7	39.4	25.1
104 New Zealand	1981-82	5.1	10.8	16.2	23.2	44.7	28.7
105 Italy	1977	6.2	11.3	15.9	22.7	43.9	28.1
106 United Kingdom	1979	7.0	11.5	17.0	24.8	39.7	23.4
107 Belgium	1978-79	7.9	13.7	18.6	23.8	36.0	21.5
108 Austria		..	..	..	..	..	
109 Netherlands	1981	8.3	14.1	18.2	23.2	36.2	21.5
110 France	1975	5.5	11.5	17.1	23.7	42.2	26.4
111 Australia	1975-76	5.4	10.0	15.0	22.5	47.1	30.5
112 Germany, Fed. Rep.	1978	7.9	12.5	17.0	23.1	39.5	24.0
113 Finland	1981	6.3	12.1	18.4	25.5	37.6	21.7
114 Denmark	1981	5.4	12.0	18.4	25.6	38.6	22.3
115 Japan	1979	8.7	13.2	17.5	23.1	37.5	22.4
116 Sweden	1981	7.4	13.1	16.8	21.0	41.7	28.1
117 Canada	1981	5.3	11.8	18.0	24.9	40.0	23.8
118 Norway	1982	6.0	12.9	18.3	24.6	38.2	22.8
119 United States	1980	5.3	11.9	17.9	25.0	39.9	23.3
120 Switzerland	1978	6.6	13.5	18.5	23.4	38.0	23.7
Nonreporting nonmembers							
121 *Albania*		..	..	..	..	..	..
122 *Angola*		..	..	..	..	..	..
123 *Bulgaria*		..	..	..	..	..	..
124 *Cuba*		..	..	..	..	..	..
125 *Czechoslovakia*		..	..	..	..	..	..
126 *German Dem. Rep.*		..	..	..	..	..	..
127 *Korea, Dem. Rep.*		..	..	..	..	..	..
128 *Mongolia*		..	..	..	..	..	..
129 *USSR*		..	..	..	..	..	..

a. These estimates should be treated with caution; see the technical notes.

Table 27. Population growth and projections

	Average annual growth of population (percent)			Population (millions)			Hypothetical size of stationary population (millions)	Assumed year of reaching net reproduction rate of 1	Population momentum 1985
	1965–80	1980–86	1986–2000	1986	1990ᵃ	2000ᵃ			
Low-income economies	**2.3 w**	**1.9 w**	**1.9 w**	**2,493 t**	**2,700 t**	**3,246 t**			
China and India	**2.2 w**	**1.6 w**	**1.6 w**	**1,835 t**	**1,963 t**	**2,281 t**			
Other low-income	**2.7 w**	**2.8 w**	**2.8 w**	**658 t**	**736 t**	**966 t**			
1 Ethiopia	2.7	2.4	2.9	43	49	65	205	2040	1.9
2 Bhutan	1.6	2.0	2.2	1	1	2	4	2035	1.7
3 Burkina Faso	2.0	2.5	2.9	8	9	12	42	2040	1.8
4 Nepal	2.4	2.6	2.5	17	19	24	63	2035	1.8
5 Bangladesh	2.7	2.6	2.5	103	114	145	342	2030	1.9
6 Malawi	2.9	3.2	3.3	7	8	12	42	2040	1.9
7 Zaire	2.8	3.1	3.0	32	36	48	142	2035	1.9
8 Mali	2.1	2.3	2.7	8	8	11	39	2040	1.8
9 Burma	2.3	2.0	2.3	38	42	52	102	2020	1.7
10 Mozambique	2.5	2.7	3.0	14	16	22	74	2040	1.9
11 Madagascar	2.5	3.3	3.2	11	12	16	52	2035	1.9
12 Uganda	2.9	3.1	3.2	15	17	23	82	2040	1.9
13 Burundi	1.9	2.7	3.1	5	5	7	24	2035	1.8
14 Tanzania	3.3	3.5	3.4	23	27	37	123	2035	2.0
15 Togo	3.0	3.4	3.3	3	4	5	16	2035	2.0
16 Niger	2.7	3.0	3.2	7	7	10	36	2040	1.9
17 Benin	2.7	3.2	3.4	4	5	7	22	2035	2.0
18 Somalia	2.7	2.9	3.1	6	6	8	30	2040	1.9
19 Central African Rep.	1.8	2.5	2.9	3	3	4	12	2035	1.8
20 India	2.3	2.2	1.8	781	846	1,002	1,698	2010	1.7
21 Rwanda	3.3	3.3	3.7	6	7	10	40	2040	1.9
22 China	2.2	1.2	1.4	1,054	1,117	1,279	1,695	2000	1.6
23 Kenya	3.6	4.1	3.9	21	25	36	121	2030	2.1
24 Zambia	3.1	3.5	3.4	7	8	11	37	2035	2.0
25 Sierra Leone	2.0	2.4	2.6	4	4	5	18	2045	1.8
26 Sudan	3.0	2.8	2.9	23	25	34	101	2035	1.8
27 Haiti	2.0	1.8	2.0	6	7	8	17	2030	1.7
28 Pakistan	3.1	3.1	3.0	99	113	150	423	2035	1.8
29 Lesotho	2.3	2.7	2.7	2	2	2	6	2030	1.8
30 Ghana	2.2	3.5	3.1	13	15	20	58	2030	1.9
31 Sri Lanka	1.8	1.5	1.5	16	17	20	30	2005	1.7
32 Mauritania	2.3	2.6	2.8	2	2	3	9	2040	1.8
33 Senegal	2.5	2.9	3.0	7	8	10	30	2035	1.9
34 *Afghanistan*	2.4	. .	. .	. .	. .	. .	. .	. .	. .
35 *Chad*	2.0	2.3	2.5	5	6	7	22	2040	1.8
36 *Guinea*	1.9	2.4	2.4	6	7	9	26	2040	1.8
37 *Kampuchea, Dem.*	0.3	. .	. .	. .	. .	. .	. .	. .	. .
38 *Lao PDR*	1.4	2.0	2.8	4	4	5	15	2035	1.8
39 *Viet Nam*	. .	2.6	2.4	63	70	88	168	2015	1.8
Middle-income economies	**2.4 w**	**2.3 w**	**2.1 w**	**1,268 t**	**1,380 t**	**1,680 t**			
Lower middle-income	**2.5 w**	**2.6 w**	**2.3 w**	**691 t**	**758 t**	**941 t**			
40 Liberia	3.0	3.3	3.2	2	3	3	11	2035	1.9
41 Yemen, PDR	2.0	3.1	2.8	2	3	3	9	2035	1.9
42 Indonesia	2.3	2.2	1.8	166	178	207	335	2005	1.8
43 Yemen Arab Rep.	2.8	2.5	3.0	8	9	12	39	2040	1.9
44 Philippines	2.9	2.5	2.3	57	62	76	137	2015	1.8
45 Morocco	2.5	2.5	2.2	22	25	30	59	2020	1.8
46 Bolivia	2.5	2.7	2.6	7	7	9	24	2030	1.8
47 Zimbabwe	3.1	3.7	3.0	9	10	13	33	2025	2.0
48 Nigeria	2.5	3.3	3.3	103	118	164	529	2035	2.0
49 Dominican Rep.	2.7	2.4	2.1	7	7	9	13	2015	1.5
50 Papua New Guinea	2.3	2.1	2.2	3	4	5	10	2025	1.8
51 Côte d'Ivoire	4.2	4.2	3.6	11	12	17	51	2030	2.0
52 Honduras	3.2	3.6	3.0	5	5	7	16	2020	2.0
53 Egypt, Arab Rep.	2.4	2.7	2.2	50	55	67	132	2020	1.8
54 Nicaragua	3.1	3.4	3.0	3	4	5	13	2025	2.0
55 Thailand	2.7	2.0	1.6	53	56	65	99	2000	1.8
56 El Salvador	2.7	1.2	1.9	5	5	6	13	2015	1.8
57 Botswana	3.5	3.5	3.3	1	1	2	5	2025	2.0
58 Jamaica	1.5	1.5	1.4	2	3	3	4	2005	1.7
59 Cameroon	2.7	3.2	3.3	11	12	17	51	2030	1.9
60 Guatemala	2.8	2.9	2.7	8	9	12	29	2025	1.8
61 Congo, People's Rep.	2.7	3.3	3.5	2	2	3	10	2030	1.9
62 Paraguay	2.8	3.2	2.5	4	4	5	10	2015	1.8
63 Peru	2.8	2.3	2.1	20	22	27	48	2015	1.8
64 Turkey	2.4	2.5	1.9	51	56	67	112	2010	1.7
65 Tunisia	2.1	2.3	2.2	7	8	10	18	2015	1.8
66 Ecuador	3.1	2.9	2.4	10	11	13	26	2015	1.9
67 Mauritius	1.6	1.0	1.2	1	1	1	2	2000	1.7
68 Colombia	2.2	1.9	1.8	29	31	37	59	2010	1.7

Note: For data comparability and coverage, see the technical notes. Figures in italics are for years other than those specified.

	Average annual growth of population (percent)			Population (millions)			Hypothetical size of stationary population (millions)	Assumed year of reaching net reproduction rate of 1	Population momentum 1985
	1965-80	1980-86	1986-2000	1986	1990[a]	2000[a]			
69 Chile	1.8	1.7	1.2	12	13	14	20	2000	1.6
70 Costa Rica	2.6	2.4	2.1	3	3	3	5	2005	1.8
71 Jordan	2.6	3.7	3.1	4	4	6	13	2020	1.9
72 Syrian Arab Rep.	3.4	3.5	3.3	11	13	17	42	2020	1.9
73 *Lebanon*	1.6	..	..	..	..	..	..	..	..
Upper middle-income	**2.2 w**	**1.9 w**	**1.8 w**	**577 t**	**622 t**	**739 t**			
74 Brazil	2.4	2.2	1.9	138	150	180	306	2015	1.8
75 Malaysia	2.5	2.7	1.9	16	18	21	33	2005	1.8
76 South Africa	2.4	2.2	2.3	32	36	45	90	2020	1.8
77 Mexico	3.1	2.2	2.1	80	87	107	187	2010	1.9
78 Uruguay	0.4	0.4	0.7	3	3	3	4	2000	1.3
79 Hungary	0.4	−0.1	−0.1	11	11	11	10	2030	1.1
80 Poland	0.8	0.9	0.6	38	39	41	48	2020	1.3
81 Portugal	0.6	0.5	0.3	10	10	11	11	2030	1.3
82 Yugoslavia	0.9	0.7	0.5	23	24	25	27	2030	1.3
83 Panama	2.6	2.2	1.8	2	2	3	4	2005	1.8
84 Argentina	1.6	1.6	1.1	31	33	36	52	2005	1.5
85 Korea, Rep. of	1.9	1.4	1.2	41	44	49	65	1985	1.6
86 Algeria	3.1	3.1	2.9	22	25	33	81	2025	1.9
87 Venezuela	3.5	2.9	2.2	18	20	24	40	2005	1.8
88 Gabon	3.5	4.4	2.8	1	1	1	4	2035	1.7
89 Greece	0.7	0.5	0.3	10	10	10	10	2030	1.2
90 Oman	3.6	4.7	3.2	1	2	2	5	2030	1.9
91 Trinidad and Tobago	1.3	1.5	1.3	1	1	1	2	2010	1.6
92 Israel	2.8	1.7	1.4	4	5	5	7	2005	1.6
93 Hong Kong	2.1	1.2	1.0	5	6	6	7	2030	1.4
94 Singapore	1.6	1.1	0.8	3	3	3	3	2030	1.4
95 *Iran, Islamic Rep.*	3.2	2.8	3.0	46	52	69	169	2025	1.9
96 *Iraq*	3.4	3.6	3.6	16	19	27	75	2025	1.9
97 *Romania*	1.1	0.5	0.5	23	23	24	28	2030	1.3
Developing economies	**2.3 w**	**2.0 w**	**2.0 w**	**3,761 t**	**4,079 t**	**4,926 t**			
Oil exporters	**2.7 w**	**2.7 w**	**2.5 w**	**538 t**	**595 t**	**754 t**			
Exporters of manufactures	**2.2 w**	**1.6 w**	**1.5 w**	**2,132 t**	**2,277 t**	**2,635 t**			
Highly indebted countries	**2.5 w**	**2.4 w**	**2.2 w**	**570 t**	**625 t**	**773 t**			
Sub-Saharan Africa	**2.7 w**	**3.1 w**	**3.2 w**	**424 t**	**482 t**	**659 t**			
High-income oil exporters	**5.3 w**	**4.2 w**	**3.6 w**	**19 t**	**22 t**	**31 t**			
98 Saudi Arabia	4.6	4.1	3.8	12	14	20	54	2025	1.8
99 Kuwait	7.0	4.4	2.9	2	2	3	5	2015	1.8
100 United Arab Emirates	16.1	5.6	2.8	1	2	2	4	2020	1.4
101 *Libya*	4.6	3.9	3.6	4	5	6	17	2025	1.9
Industrial market economies	**0.8 w**	**0.6 w**	**0.4 w**	**742 t**	**756 t**	**782 t**			
102 Spain	1.0	0.6	0.4	39	39	41	41	2030	1.3
103 Ireland	1.2	0.8	1.0	4	4	4	6	2020	1.4
104 New Zealand	1.3	0.9	0.6	3	3	4	4	2030	1.3
105 Italy	0.6	0.3	0.1	57	58	58	46	2030	1.1
106 United Kingdom	0.2	0.1	0.1	57	57	58	56	2030	1.1
107 Belgium	0.3	0.0	−0.1	10	10	10	8	2030	1.1
108 Austria	0.3	0.0	−0.1	8	8	7	6	2030	1.1
109 Netherlands	0.9	0.5	0.3	15	15	15	13	2030	1.2
110 France	0.7	0.5	0.4	55	56	58	58	2030	1.2
111 Australia	1.8	1.4	1.0	16	17	18	20	2030	1.4
112 Germany, Fed. Rep.	0.3	−0.2	−0.3	61	60	59	40	2030	1.0
113 Finland	0.3	0.5	0.2	5	5	5	4	2030	1.1
114 Denmark	0.5	0.0	−0.1	5	5	5	4	2030	1.1
115 Japan	1.2	0.7	0.5	121	124	129	119	2030	1.1
116 Sweden	0.5	0.1	0.0	8	8	8	7	2030	1.0
117 Canada	1.3	1.1	0.7	26	27	28	28	2030	1.3
118 Norway	0.6	0.3	0.2	4	4	4	4	2030	1.2
119 United States	1.0	1.0	0.6	242	249	263	279	2030	1.3
120 Switzerland	0.5	0.3	0.0	7	6	6	5	2030	1.1
Nonreporting nonmembers	**1.0 w**	**1.0 w**	**0.8 w**	**367 t**	**381 t**	**414 t**			
121 *Albania*	2.5	2.1	1.8	3	3	4	6	2005	1.7
122 *Angola*	2.8	2.6	2.8	9	10	13	43	2040	1.9
123 *Bulgaria*	0.5	0.2	0.2	9	9	9	10	2030	1.1
124 *Cuba*	1.5	0.9	0.8	10	11	11	12	2030	1.5
125 *Czechoslovakia*	0.5	0.3	0.3	16	16	16	19	2030	1.2
126 *German Dem. Rep.*	−0.2	−0.1	0.0	17	17	17	15	2030	1.1
127 *Korea, Dem. Rep.*	2.7	2.5	2.1	21	23	28	49	2015	1.8
128 *Mongolia*	3.0	2.8	2.4	2	2	3	6	2020	1.8
129 *USSR*	0.9	1.0	0.7	281	291	312	398	2020	1.3

a. For the assumptions used in the projections, see the technical notes.

Table 28. Demography and fertility

	Crude birth rate per thousand population		Crude death rate per thousand population		Percentage of women of childbearing age		Total fertility rate			Percentage of married women of childbearing age using contraception[a]	
	1965	1986	1965	1986	1965	1985	1965	1986	2000	1970	1985
Low-income economies	**42** *w*	**30** *w*	**16** *w*	**10** *w*	**45** *w*	**50** *w*	**6.4** *w*	**3.9** *w*	**3.5** *w*		
China and India	**41** *w*	**25** *w*	**14** *w*	**9** *w*	**45** *w*	**51** *w*	**6.3** *w*	**3.2** *w*	**2.9** *w*		
Other low-income	**46** *w*	**43** *w*	**21** *w*	**15** *w*	**45** *w*	**46** *w*	**6.6** *w*	**6.0** *w*	**5.1** *w*		
1 Ethiopia	43	47	20	19	46	46	5.8	6.3	5.8	..	2
2 Bhutan	43	40	31	20	47	47	6.0	5.7	5.0	..	..
3 Burkina Faso	48	47	26	19	46	46	6.4	6.5	6.3	..	..
4 Nepal	46	41	24	17	49	46	6.0	5.9	5.2	..	*15*
5 Bangladesh	47	41	21	15	44	46	6.8	5.6	4.4	..	25
6 Malawi	56	53	26	21	45	41	7.8	7.6	6.8	..	..
7 Zaire	47	45	21	15	46	43	6.0	6.1	5.4	..	*1*
8 Mali	50	48	27	19	45	45	6.5	6.5	6.3	..	*2*
9 Burma	40	33	18	10	48	46	5.8	4.4	3.7	..	*5*
10 Mozambique	49	45	27	17	48	44	6.8	6.3	6.1	..	..
11 Madagascar	47	46	22	14	46	44	6.6	6.4	5.7	..	..
12 Uganda	49	50	19	18	45	44	6.9	6.9	6.2	..	*1*
13 Burundi	47	47	24	18	46	46	6.4	6.5	6.2	..	*9*
14 Tanzania	49	50	22	15	46	44	6.6	7.0	6.2	..	..
15 Togo	50	49	22	15	45	45	6.5	6.5	5.7	..	..
16 Niger	48	51	29	21	44	44	6.8	7.0	6.7	..	..
17 Benin	49	49	24	17	45	45	6.8	6.5	6.2	..	*6*
18 Somalia	50	49	26	19	44	47	6.7	6.8	6.5	..	*0*
19 Central African Rep.	34	43	24	16	48	47	4.5	5.7	5.8	..	..
20 India	45	32	20	12	47	48	6.2	4.4	3.2	12	35
21 Rwanda	52	52	17	18	45	44	7.5	8.0	7.1	..	*1*
22 China	38	19	10	7	44	54	6.4	2.3	2.2	1	74
23 Kenya	52	52	20	12	42	41	8.0	7.7	6.6	1	17
24 Zambia	49	49	20	14	45	44	6.6	6.8	5.9	..	..
25 Sierra Leone	48	48	31	24	46	47	6.4	6.5	6.3	..	*4*
26 Sudan	47	45	24	16	46	45	6.7	6.6	5.8	..	..
27 Haiti	43	35	20	13	46	48	6.2	4.8	3.9	..	*7*
28 Pakistan	48	47	21	15	43	47	7.2	6.8	5.4	6	*11*
29 Lesotho	42	41	18	13	46	45	5.8	5.8	5.1	..	..
30 Ghana	47	45	18	13	45	43	6.8	6.3	5.4	..	..
31 Sri Lanka	33	24	8	6	47	52	4.8	2.9	2.4	..	62
32 Mauritania	47	47	26	19	44	45	6.5	6.5	6.3	..	*1*
33 Senegal	47	46	23	18	46	45	6.4	6.5	5.7	..	12
34 *Afghanistan*	54	..	29	..	47	..	8.0	..	..	2	..
35 *Chad*	45	44	28	20	47	48	6.0	5.9	5.7	..	..
36 *Guinea*	46	46	29	23	47	46	5.9	6.0	5.8	..	..
37 *Kampuchea, Dem.*	44	..	20	..	45	..	6.2	..	..	..	..
38 *Lao PDR*	45	39	23	15	48	46	6.2	5.9	5.2	..	..
39 *Viet Nam*	..	34	17	7	..	48	..	4.5	3.3	..	20
Middle-income economies	**39** *w*	**31** *w*	**14** *w*	**9** *w*	**46** *w*	**48** *w*	**5.6** *w*	**4.1** *w*	**3.4** *w*		
Lower middle-income	**44** *w*	**35** *w*	**17** *w*	**10** *w*	**46** *w*	**48** *w*	**6.3** *w*	**4.7** *w*	**3.9** *w*		
40 Liberia	46	46	20	13	45	44	6.4	6.6	5.8	..	7
41 Yemen, PDR	50	49	26	16	45	46	7.0	6.6	5.2	..	..
42 Indonesia	43	28	20	11	49	49	5.5	3.6	2.9	0	40
43 Yemen Arab Rep.	49	49	27	20	46	46	6.8	6.8	6.1	..	*2*
44 Philippines	42	35	12	7	44	49	6.8	4.6	3.4	*16*	44
45 Morocco	49	33	18	10	45	46	7.1	4.5	3.5	1	36
46 Bolivia	46	43	21	14	47	46	6.6	6.1	4.7	..	26
47 Zimbabwe	55	45	17	11	44	41	8.0	6.0	4.4	..	40
48 Nigeria	51	50	23	16	45	44	6.9	6.9	6.1	..	5
49 Dominican Rep.	47	32	13	7	42	50	6.9	3.8	3.0	..	50
50 Papua New Guinea	43	36	20	13	47	47	6.2	5.2	4.2	..	4
51 Côte d'Ivoire	52	49	22	14	47	44	7.4	7.1	6.0	..	3
52 Honduras	51	41	17	8	44	44	7.4	5.7	4.1	..	35
53 Egypt, Arab Rep.	43	34	19	10	47	49	6.8	4.6	3.5	..	32
54 Nicaragua	49	42	16	9	43	45	7.2	5.6	4.2	..	27
55 Thailand	41	25	10	7	44	52	6.3	3.0	2.3	15	65
56 El Salvador	46	37	13	9	44	45	6.7	4.9	3.6	..	47
57 Botswana	53	45	19	11	45	44	6.9	6.6	4.9	..	28
58 Jamaica	38	26	8	6	42	48	5.4	3.0	2.4	..	52
59 Cameroon	40	48	20	13	46	43	5.2	6.9	6.0	..	..
60 Guatemala	46	41	17	9	44	46	6.7	5.8	4.4	..	25
61 Congo, People's Rep.	42	46	18	12	47	43	5.7	6.4	6.2	..	..
62 Paraguay	41	35	8	6	43	49	6.6	4.6	3.4	..	49
63 Peru	45	32	16	10	44	49	6.7	4.1	3.2	..	46
64 Turkey	41	29	15	8	44	49	5.8	3.7	2.9	32	62
65 Tunisia	44	32	16	9	43	48	7.0	4.4	3.3	10	42
66 Ecuador	45	34	13	7	43	47	6.8	4.5	3.3	..	44
67 Mauritius	36	19	8	7	45	53	4.8	2.2	2.1	..	75
68 Colombia	45	27	14	7	44	52	6.5	3.2	2.6	*21*	63

Note: For data comparability and coverage, see the technical notes.   Figures in italics are for years other than those specified.

	Crude birth rate per thousand population		Crude death rate per thousand population		Percentage of women of childbearing age		Total fertility rate			Percentage of married women of childbearing age using contraception[a]	
	1965	1986	1965	1986	1965	1985	1965	1986	2000	1970	1985
69 Chile	32	21	11	6	47	53	4.8	2.5	2.1	..	..
70 Costa Rica	45	29	8	4	42	52	6.3	3.3	2.5	..	68
71 Jordan	..	39	17	7	45	43	..	6.0	4.2	..	27
72 Syrian Arab Rep.	48	45	16	8	41	42	7.7	6.9	4.7	..	..
73 *Lebanon*	40	..	12	..	42	..	6.2	..	..	55	..
Upper middle-income	**34 w**	**27 w**	**11 w**	**8 w**	**46 w**	**49 w**	**4.9 w**	**3.5 w**	**3.0 w**		
74 Brazil	39	29	11	8	46	50	5.6	3.5	2.9	..	65
75 Malaysia	40	29	12	6	43	52	6.3	3.5	2.6	7	51
76 South Africa	40	34	16	10	46	47	6.1	4.5	3.5	..	..
77 Mexico	45	29	11	6	43	47	6.7	3.7	2.8	..	48
78 Uruguay	21	19	10	10	49	46	2.8	2.6	2.2	..	..
79 Hungary	13	12	11	14	48	46	1.8	1.8	1.8	..	73
80 Poland	17	17	7	10	47	48	2.5	2.3	2.1	60	..
81 Portugal	23	13	10	10	48	49	3.1	1.7	1.7	..	70
82 Yugoslavia	21	15	9	9	50	51	2.7	2.0	2.0	59	..
83 Panama	40	27	9	5	44	50	5.7	3.2	2.5	..	61
84 Argentina	22	23	9	9	50	47	3.1	3.2	2.5	..	..
85 Korea, Rep. of	35	20	11	6	46	54	4.8	2.2	2.1	32	70
86 Algeria	50	40	18	9	44	44	7.4	6.1	4.5	..	..
87 Venezuela	42	30	8	5	42	49	6.1	3.8	2.7	..	..
88 Gabon	31	40	22	16	45	49	4.1	5.3	5.8	..	..
89 Greece	18	11	8	9	51	47	2.3	1.8	1.8	..	..
90 Oman	50	45	24	13	46	44	7.2	6.9	5.2	..	..
91 Trinidad and Tobago	33	26	8	7	45	52	4.3	2.9	2.4	44	53
92 Israel	26	22	6	7	46	48	3.8	2.9	2.4	..	..
93 Hong Kong	27	16	6	6	45	54	4.5	1.9	1.9	50	72
94 Singapore	31	16	6	5	45	57	4.7	1.7	1.7	45	74
95 *Iran, Islamic Rep.*	50	41	17	10	42	46	7.8	5.6	4.8	..	..
96 *Iraq*	49	44	18	8	45	44	7.2	6.7	5.6	..	..
97 *Romania*	15	15	9	10	50	47	1.9	2.0	2.1	..	..
Developing economies	**41 w**	**30 w**	**15 w**	**10 w**	**45 w**	**49 w**	**6.1 w**	**4.0 w**	**3.5 w**		
Oil exporters	46 w	37 w	18 w	10 w	46 w	47 w	6.4 w	4.9 w	4.0 w		
Exporters of manufactures	39 w	24 w	13 w	9 w	45 w	51 w	6.0 w	3.1 w	2.8 w		
Highly indebted countries	41 w	33 w	14 w	9 w	45 w	48 w	5.9 w	4.3 w	3.6 w		
Sub-Saharan Africa	48 w	48 w	22 w	16 w	45 w	44 w	6.6 w	6.7 w	6.0 w		
High-income oil exporters	**48 w**	**41 w**	**18 w**	**8 w**	**46 w**	**44 w**	**7.3 w**	**6.8 w**	**5.6 w**		
98 Saudi Arabia	48	42	20	8	46	44	7.3	7.1	5.9	..	..
99 Kuwait	48	32	7	3	46	46	7.4	4.8	3.5	..	..
100 United Arab Emirates	41	28	14	4	..	45	6.8	5.7	4.7	..	..
101 *Libya*	49	44	17	9	45	44	7.4	6.9	5.8	..	..
Industrial market economies	**19 w**	**13 w**	**10 w**	**9 w**	**47 w**	**50 w**	**2.7 w**	**1.7 w**	**1.8 w**		
102 Spain	21	13	8	9	49	47	2.9	1.8	1.8	..	59
103 Ireland	22	18	12	9	42	47	4.0	2.5	2.4	60	..
104 New Zealand	23	16	9	8	45	52	3.6	1.9	1.9	..	..
105 Italy	19	10	10	10	49	48	2.7	1.5	1.5	..	..
106 United Kingdom	18	13	12	12	45	48	2.9	1.8	1.8	75	83
107 Belgium	17	12	12	11	44	48	2.6	1.5	1.5	..	81
108 Austria	18	11	13	11	43	48	2.7	1.5	1.5	..	..
109 Netherlands	20	13	8	9	47	52	3.0	1.5	1.5	..	78
110 France	18	14	11	10	43	48	2.8	1.8	1.8	64	..
111 Australia	20	15	9	7	47	51	3.0	1.9	2.0	67	..
112 Germany, Fed. Rep.	18	10	12	12	45	49	2.5	1.3	1.3	..	78
113 Finland	17	12	10	10	48	47	2.4	1.7	1.7	77	..
114 Denmark	18	11	10	11	47	49	2.6	1.4	1.4	67	..
115 Japan	19	12	7	7	56	51	2.0	1.8	1.8	53	64
116 Sweden	16	12	10	11	47	47	2.4	1.7	1.7	..	78
117 Canada	21	15	8	7	47	53	3.1	1.7	1.7	..	73
118 Norway	18	13	10	11	45	48	2.9	1.6	1.7	..	..
119 United States	19	16	9	9	45	52	2.9	1.9	1.9	65	68
120 Switzerland	19	12	10	9	48	44	2.6	1.5	1.5	..	70
Nonreporting nonmembers	**20 w**	**20 w**	**8 w**	**10 w**	**47 w**	**48 w**	**2.7 w**	**2.5 w**	**2.3 w**		
121 *Albania*	35	26	9	6	44	50	5.3	3.3	2.5	..	..
122 *Angola*	49	48	29	21	46	46	6.4	6.4	6.2	..	..
123 *Bulgaria*	15	13	8	11	51	47	2.1	2.0	2.0	..	..
124 *Cuba*	34	16	8	6	48	55	4.4	1.8	1.8	..	60
125 *Czechoslovakia*	16	14	10	12	46	46	2.4	2.1	2.1	66	..
126 *German Dem. Rep.*	17	13	14	13	40	47	2.5	1.7	1.7	..	..
127 *Korea, Dem. Rep.*	39	29	12	6	45	50	5.6	3.7	2.9	..	..
128 *Mongolia*	42	34	12	8	47	48	5.8	4.7	3.6	..	..
129 *USSR*	18	19	7	10	48	48	2.5	2.4	2.3	..	..

a. Figures include women whose husbands practice contraception; see the technical notes.

Table 29. Health and nutrition

	Population per:				Daily calorie supply per capita		Babies with low birth weights (percent)
	Physician		Nursing person				
	1965	1981	1965	1981	1965	1985	1984
Low-income economies	8,570 w	6,050 w	4,920 w	3,890 w	2,046 w	2,329 w	
China and India	4,230 w	2,550 w	4,450 w	2,920 w	2,061 w	2,411 w	
Other low-income	26,620 w	17,670 w	7,250 w	7,130 w	1,998 w	2,100 w	
1 Ethiopia	70,190	88,150	5,970	5,000	1,832	1,704	10
2 Bhutan	..	19,160		8,310	2,904	2,477	..
3 Burkina Faso	73,960	55,760	4,150	3,070	2,009	2,003	21
4 Nepal	46,180	28,780	..	33,390	1,931	1,997	..
5 Bangladesh	8,400	9,690	..	19,370	1,964	1,804	50
6 Malawi	46,890	52,830	..	2,980	2,132	2,415	20
7 Zaire	35,130	13,430	..	1,740	2,188	2,151	9
8 Mali	51,510	26,030	3,360	2,280	1,860	1,810	13
9 Burma	11,860	4,930	11,370	4,920	1,928	2,508	7
10 Mozambique	18,000	36,970	5,370	5,610	1,982	1,617	16
11 Madagascar	10,620	9,920	3,650	1,730	2,486	2,452	11
12 Uganda	11,110	21,270	3,130	2,000	2,383	2,483	10
13 Burundi	55,910	..	7,320	..	2,391	2,233	14
14 Tanzania	21,700	..	2,100	..	1,970	2,316	12
15 Togo	23,240	21,140	4,990	1,640	2,378	2,221	17
16 Niger	65,540	..	6,210		1,996	2,276	20
17 Benin	32,390	17,010	2,540	1,660	2,008	2,248	10
18 Somalia	36,840	17,460	3,950	2,550	2,145	2,074	..
19 Central African Rep.	34,020	22,530	3,000	2,120	2,130	2,059	23
20 India	4,880	3,700	6,500	4,670	2,100	2,126	30
21 Rwanda	72,480	32,150	7,450	10,260	1,665	1,935	17
22 China	3,790	1,730	3,050	1,670	2,034	2,620	6
23 Kenya	13,280	10,120	1,930	990	2,287	2,214	18
24 Zambia	11,380	7,800	5,820	1,660	2,073	2,126	2
25 Sierra Leone	16,840	19,130	4,470	2,100	1,836	1,784	17
26 Sudan	23,500	9,810	3,360	1,440	1,874	2,168	15
27 Haiti	14,010	9,200	12,900	..	2,007	1,784	17
28 Pakistan	..	2,910	9,910	5,870	1,747	2,180	28
29 Lesotho	20,060	..	4,700	..	2,065	2,299	11
30 Ghana	13,740	6,680	3,730	630	1,949	1,785	15
31 Sri Lanka	5,800	7,460	3,210	1,260	2,155	2,485	25
32 Mauritania	36,470	..	..	..	2,070	2,071	10
33 Senegal	21,130	13,070	2,640	1,990	2,474	2,418	10
34 Afghanistan	15,770	..	24,430	..	2,203	2,179	20
35 Chad	72,480	..	13,610	..	2,393	1,733	11
36 Guinea	54,430	56,170	4,750	6,250	1,899	1,731	18
37 Kampuchea, Dem.	22,410	..	3,670	..	2,276	2,171	..
38 Lao PDR	26,510	..	5,320	..	1,958	2,317	35
39 Viet Nam	..	4,110	..	1,260	2,031	2,281	25
Middle-income economies	9,830 w	4,940 w	3,290 w	1,400 w	2,358 w	2,719 w	
Lower middle-income	17,340 w	7,880 w	4,780 w	1,760 w	2,117 w	2,511 w	
40 Liberia	12,360	9,340	2,290	2,920	2,155	2,373	..
41 Yemen, PDR	12,870	7,110	1,850	820	1,999	2,255	12
42 Indonesia	31,740	12,330	9,500	2,300	1,792	2,476	14
43 Yemen Arab Rep.	58,240	7,120	..	3,450	2,002	2,266	..
44 Philippines	..	6,850	1,130	2,640	1,936	2,260	15
45 Morocco	12,120	18,570	2,290	900	2,182	2,729	9
46 Bolivia	3,300	2,000	3,990	..	1,868	2,171	10
47 Zimbabwe	8,010	7,100	990	1,000	2,089	2,144	15
48 Nigeria	29,530	9,400	6,160	2,690	2,185	2,139	25
49 Dominican Rep.	1,700	1,400	1,640	1,240	1,870	2,530	15
50 Papua New Guinea	12,640	15,610	620	930	1,908	2,145	25
51 Côte d'Ivoire	20,640	..	2,000	..	2,357	2,308	14
52 Honduras	5,370	3,100	1,530	690	1,963	2,224	9
53 Egypt, Arab Rep.	2,300	760	2,030	790	2,435	3,275	0
54 Nicaragua	2,560	2,230	1,390	590	2,398	2,464	15
55 Thailand	7,230	6,870	5,020	2,140	2,200	2,399	12
56 El Salvador	..	2,550	1,300	..	1,859	2,155	9
57 Botswana	27,460	7,400	17,720	700	2,015	2,159	12
58 Jamaica	1,990	2,830	340	550	2,232	2,578	10
59 Cameroon	26,720	13,990	5,830	1,950	2,043	2,080	13
60 Guatemala	3,690	..	8,250	1,360	2,028	2,345	10
61 Congo, People's Rep.	14,210	..	950	..	2,255	2,511	15
62 Paraguay	1,850	1,750	1,550	650	2,627	2,873	7
63 Peru	1,650	1,440	900	1,010	2,324	2,120	9
64 Turkey	2,900	1,530	2,290	1,240	2,636	3,218	8
65 Tunisia	8,000	3,620	1,150	950	2,296	2,796	7
66 Ecuador	3,000	..	2,320	..	1,942	2,005	..
67 Mauritius	3,930	1,820	2,030	580	2,272	2,717	9
68 Colombia	2,500	..	890	..	2,174	2,588	10

Note: For data comparability and coverage, see the technical notes. Figures in italics are for years other than those specified.

		Population per:			Daily calorie supply per capita		Babies with low birth weights (percent)
	Physician		Nursing person				
	1965	1981	1965	1981	1965	1985	1984
69 Chile	2,100	*1,930*	600	*450*	2,591	2,544	7
70 Costa Rica	2,010	*1,440*	630	. .	2,366	2,807	10
71 Jordan	4,710	1,190	1,810	1,160	2,282	2,968	10
72 Syrian Arab Rep.	5,400	2,190	. .	1,390	2,144	3,235	9
73 *Lebanon*	1,010	510	2,030	. .	2,428	3,046	10
Upper middle-income	**2,310** *w*	**1,380** *w*	**1,690** *w*	**900** *w*	**2,621** *w*	**2,967** *w*	
74 Brazil	2,500	1,300	1,550	1,140	2,405	2,657	9
75 Malaysia	6,220	3,910	1,320	1,390	2,249	2,601	10
76 South Africa	2,050	. .	490	. .	2,643	2,926	12
77 Mexico	2,080	1,210	980	. .	2,643	3,126	15
78 Uruguay	880	500	590	*190*	2,811	2,791	8
79 Hungary	630	390	240	160	3,186	3,544	10
80 Poland	800	550	410	230	3,238	3,224	8
81 Portugal	1,240	500	1,160	. .	2,531	3,122	8
82 Yugoslavia	1,200	700	850	300	3,287	3,499	7
83 Panama	2,130	1,010	680	. .	2,255	2,423	8
84 Argentina	600	. .	610	. .	3,209	3,216	6
85 Korea, Rep. of	2,700	1,390	2,990	350	2,255	2,806	9
86 Algeria	8,590	*2,630*	11,770	*1,010*	1,682	2,799	12
87 Venezuela	1,210	1,000	560	. .	2,321	2,485	9
88 Gabon	. .	2,550	*770*	. .	1,881	2,448	16
89 Greece	710	390	600	370	3,086	3,637	6
90 Oman	23,790	1,410	6,420	. .	. .	. .	14
91 Trinidad and Tobago	3,810	1,500	560	390	2,497	2,915	. .
92 Israel	400	400	300	130	2,795	3,019	7
93 Hong Kong	2,460	1,290	1,220	790	2,502	2,692	8
94 Singapore	1,900	1,100	600	340	2,214	2,696	8
95 *Iran, Islamic Rep.*	3,800	2,900	4,170	1,160	2,140	3,115	4
96 *Iraq*	5,000	1,810	2,910	2,250	2,138	2,891	15
97 *Romania*	760	700	400	280	2,994	3,413	6
Developing economies	**8,990** *w*	**5,690** *w*	**4,360** *w*	**3,230** *w*	**2,149** *w*	**2,460** *w*	
Oil exporters	**18,400** *w*	**7,020** *w*	**5,850** *w*	. .	**2,115** *w*	**2,664** *w*	
Exporters of manufactures	**3,870** *w*	**2,340** *w*	**3,980** *w*	**2,660** *w*	**2,155** *w*	**2,483** *w*	
Highly indebted countries	**7,930** *w*	**4,580** *w*	**2,070** *w*	. .	**2,425** *w*	**2,607** *w*	
Sub-Saharan Africa	**33,830** *w*	**25,310** *w*	**4,820** *w*	**2,800** *w*	**2,098** *w*	**2,097** *w*	
High-income oil exporters	**7,500** *w*	**1,380** *w*	**4,440** *w*	**580** *w*	**1,969** *w*	**3,213** *w*	
98 Saudi Arabia	9,400	1,800	6,060	730	1,866	3,057	6
99 Kuwait	800	700	270	180	2,963	3,102	7
100 United Arab Emirates	. .	720	. .	390	2,672	3,652	7
101 *Libya*	3,850	620	850	360	1,923	3,585	5
Industrial market economies	**870** *w*	**550** *w*	**420** *w*	**180** *w*	**3,137** *w*	**3,357** *w*	
102 Spain	800	360	1,220	280	2,844	3,303	1
103 Ireland	950	770	170	140	3,530	3,736	4
104 New Zealand	820	610	570	150	3,311	3,393	5
105 Italy	1,850	750	790	250	3,113	3,493	7
106 United Kingdom	870	680	200	120	3,346	3,148	7
107 Belgium	700	370	590	130	. .	3,679	5
108 Austria	720	440	350	170	3,303	3,440	6
109 Netherlands	860	480	270	170	3,149	3,348	4
110 France	830	460	*380*	110	3,303	3,358	5
111 Australia	720	520	150	140	3,174	3,302	6
112 Germany, Fed. Rep.	640	420	500	170	3,143	3,519	6
113 Finland	1,300	460	180	100	3,119	2,961	4
114 Denmark	740	420	190	140	3,417	3,489	6
115 Japan	970	740	410	210	2,669	2,695	5
116 Sweden	910	410	310	100	2,922	3,007	4
117 Canada	770	550	190	120	3,289	3,443	6
118 Norway	790	460	340	70	3,047	3,171	4
119 United States	670	500	310	180	3,292	3,682	7
120 Switzerland	710	390	270	130	3,413	3,406	5
Nonreporting nonmembers	**770** *w*	**300** *w*	**370** *w*	. .	**3,155** *w*	**3,304** *w*	
121 *Albania*	2,100	. .	550	. .	2,398	2,716	7
122 *Angola*	13,150	. .	3,820	. .	1,912	1,926	19
123 *Bulgaria*	600	400	410	190	3,434	3,593	6
124 *Cuba*	1,150	720	820	*370*	2,371	3,088	8
125 *Czechoslovakia*	540	350	200	130	3,406	3,473	6
126 *German Dem. Rep.*	870	490	. .	. .	3,222	3,769	6
127 *Korea, Dem. Rep.*	. .	. .	. .	. .	2,330	3,113	0
128 *Mongolia*	710	400	310	240	2,594	2,814	10
129 *USSR*	480	270	280	. .	3,231	3,332	6

Table 30. Education

Percentage of age group enrolled in education

	Primary Total 1965	Primary Total 1985	Primary Male 1965	Primary Male 1985	Primary Female 1965	Primary Female 1985	Secondary Total 1965	Secondary Total 1985	Secondary Male 1965	Secondary Male 1985	Secondary Female 1965	Secondary Female 1985	Tertiary Total 1965	Tertiary Total 1985
Low-income economies	74 w	99 w	..	110 w	..	88 w	22 w	34 w	..	41 w	..	26 w	2 w	..
China and India	83 w	110 w	..	121 w	..	98 w	25 w	37 w	..	45 w	..	29 w	2 w	..
Other low-income	44 w	67 w	58 w	75 w	31 w	56 w	9 w	22 w	13 w	28 w	4 w	16 w	1 w	5 w
1 Ethiopia	11	36	16	44	6	28	2	12	3	14	1	9	0	1
2 Bhutan	7	25	13	32	1	18	0	4	0	6	..	1	..	0
3 Burkina Faso	12	32	16	41	8	24	1	5	2	7	1	3	0	1
4 Nepal	20	79	36	104	4	47	5	25	9	35	2	11	1	5
5 Bangladesh	49	60	67	70	31	50	13	18	23	26	3	10	1	5
6 Malawi	44	62	55	71	32	53	2	4	3	6	1	2	0	1
7 Zaire	70	98	95	112	45	84	5	57	8	81	2	33	0	2
8 Mali	24	23	32	29	16	17	4	7	5	10	2	4	0	1
9 Burma	71	102	76	..	65	..	15	24	20	..	11	..	1	..
10 Mozambique	37	84	48	94	26	74	3	7	3	9	2	4	0	0
11 Madagascar	65	121	70	125	59	118	8	36	10	43	5	30	1	5
12 Uganda	67	..	83	..	50	..	4	..	6	..	2	..	0	1
13 Burundi	26	53	36	61	15	44	1	4	2	5	1	3	0	1
14 Tanzania	32	72	40	90	25	85	2	3	3	4	1	2	0	0
15 Togo	55	95	78	118	32	73	5	21	8	33	2	10	0	2
16 Niger	11	28	15	36	7	20	1	6	1	9	0	3	..	1
17 Benin	34	65	48	87	21	43	3	20	5	29	2	12	0	2
18 Somalia	10	25	16	32	4	18	2	17	4	23	1	12	0	..
19 Central African Rep.	56	73	84	107	28	..	2	13	4	..	1	..	..	1
20 India	74	92	89	107	57	76	27	35	41	45	13	24	5	..
21 Rwanda	53	64	64	66	43	63	2	2	3	3	1	2	0	0
22 China	89	124	..	132	..	114	24	39	..	45	..	32	0	2
23 Kenya	54	94	69	97	40	91	4	20	6	25	2	16	0	1
24 Zambia	53	103	59	106	46	96	7	19	11	24	3	14	..	2
25 Sierra Leone	29	..	37	..	21	..	5	..	8	..	3	..	0	..
26 Sudan	29	49	37	58	21	41	4	19	6	22	2	17	1	2
27 Haiti	50	78	56	83	44	72	5	18	6	19	3	17	0	1
28 Pakistan	40	47	59	61	20	32	12	17	18	24	5	9	2	5
29 Lesotho	94	115	74	102	114	127	4	22	4	18	4	26	0	2
30 Ghana	69	66	82	75	57	59	13	39	19	45	7	27	1	2
31 Sri Lanka	93	103	98	105	86	102	35	63	34	60	35	67	2	5
32 Mauritania	13	..	19	..	6	..	1	..	2	..	0	..	..	..
33 Senegal	40	55	52	66	29	45	7	13	10	18	3	9	1	2
34 *Afghanistan*	16	..	26	..	5	..	2	..	4	..	1	..	0	..
35 *Chad*	34	38	56	55	13	21	1	6	3	11	0	2	..	0
36 *Guinea*	31	30	44	42	19	19	5	12	9	18	2	6	0	2
37 *Kampuchea, Dem.*	77	..	98	..	56	..	9	..	14	..	4	..	1	..
38 *Lao PDR*	40	91	50	101	30	79	2	19	2	23	1	15	0	1
39 *Viet Nam*	..	100	..	107	..	94	..	43	..	44	..	41	..	..
Middle-income economies	85 w	104 w	92 w	109 w	79 w	101 w	22 w	49 w	26 w	57 w	19 w	51 w	5 w	14 w
Lower middle-income	75 w	104 w	84 w	111 w	66 w	100 w	16 w	42 w	21 w	50 w	12 w	41 w	4 w	13 w
40 Liberia	41	..	59	..	23	..	5	..	8	..	3	..	1	..
41 Yemen, PDR	23	66	35	96	10	35	11	19	17	26	5	11	..	..
42 Indonesia	72	118	79	121	65	116	12	39	18	45	7	34	1	7
43 Yemen Arab Rep.	9	67	16	112	1	22	0	10	..	17	..	3	..	..
44 Philippines	113	106	115	105	111	106	41	65	42	63	40	66	19	38
45 Morocco	57	81	78	98	35	63	11	31	16	38	5	25	1	9
46 Bolivia	73	91	86	96	60	85	18	37	21	40	15	34	5	20
47 Zimbabwe	110	131	128	135	92	128	6	43	8	51	5	35	0	3
48 Nigeria	32	92	39	103	24	81	5	29	7	..	3	..	0	3
49 Dominican Rep.	87	124	87	121	87	126	12	50	11	44	12	57	2	..
50 Papua New Guinea	44	64	53	..	35	..	4	14	6	..	2	..	..	2
51 Côte d'Ivoire	60	78	80	92	41	65	6	20	10	27	2	12	0	3
52 Honduras	80	102	81	103	79	102	10	36	11	31	9	36	1	10
53 Egypt, Arab Rep.	75	85	90	94	60	76	26	62	37	73	15	52	7	23
54 Nicaragua	69	101	68	96	69	107	14	39	15	23	13	55	2	10
55 Thailand	78	97	82	..	74	..	14	30	16	..	11	..	2	20
56 El Salvador	82	70	85	69	79	70	17	24	18	23	17	26	2	14
57 Botswana	65	104	59	98	71	109	3	29	5	27	3	31	..	1
58 Jamaica	109	106	112	106	106	107	51	58	53	56	50	60	3	..
59 Cameroon	94	107	114	116	75	97	5	23	8	29	2	18	0	2
60 Guatemala	50	76	55	80	45	69	8	17	10	17	7	16	2	8
61 Congo, People's Rep.	114	..	134	..	94	..	10	..	15	..	5	..	1	..
62 Paraguay	102	101	109	104	96	98	13	31	13	31	13	30	4	10
63 Peru	99	122	108	125	90	120	25	65	29	68	21	61	8	24
64 Turkey	101	116	118	119	83	112	16	42	22	47	9	28	4	9
65 Tunisia	91	118	116	127	65	108	16	39	23	46	9	33	2	6
66 Ecuador	91	114	94	117	88	117	17	55	19	51	16	53	3	33
67 Mauritius	101	106	105	105	97	106	26	51	34	53	18	49	3	1
68 Colombia	84	117	83	116	86	119	17	50	18	50	16	51	3	13

Note: For data comparability and coverage, see the technical notes.   Figures in italics are for years other than those specified.

		Percentage of age group enrolled in education												
		Primary						Secondary						Tertiary	
		Total		Male		Female		Total		Male		Female		Total	
		1965	1985	1965	1985	1965	1985	1965	1985	1965	1985	1965	1985	1965	1985
69	Chile	124	109	125	*108*	122	106	34	69	31	*63*	36	69	6	16
70	Costa Rica	106	101	107	101	105	100	24	41	23	39	25	43	6	23
71	Jordan	95	*99*	105	*98*	83	*99*	38	*79*	52	*80*	23	78	2	*37*
72	Syrian Arab Rep.	78	108	103	116	52	101	28	61	43	72	13	49	8	*17*
73	*Lebanon*	106	. .	118	. .	93	. .	26	. .	33	. .	20	. .	14	. .
	Upper middle-income	97 *w*	105 *w*	100 *w*	108 *w*	93 *w*	102 *w*	29 *w*	57 *w*	31 *w*	66 *w*	26 *w*	63 *w*	7 *w*	16 *w*
74	Brazil	108	104	109	*108*	108	99	16	35	16	. .	16	. .	2	*11*
75	Malaysia	90	99	96	100	84	99	28	53	34	52	22	53	2	6
76	South Africa	90	. .	91	. .	88	. .	15	. .	16	. .	14	. .	4	
77	Mexico	92	115	94	116	90	114	17	55	21	56	13	54	4	16
78	Uruguay	106	110	106	111	106	109	44	70	42	. .	46	. .	8	32
79	Hungary	101	98	102	98	100	99	. .	72	. .	71	. .	72	13	15
80	Poland	104	101	106	102	102	100	58	78	52	75	64	81	18	17
81	Portugal	84	112	84	*120*	83	*119*	42	*47*	49	*43*	34	*51*	5	*13*
82	Yugoslavia	106	96	108	96	103	96	65	82	70	84	59	80	13	20
83	Panama	102	105	104	107	99	102	34	59	32	56	36	63	7	26
84	Argentina	101	108	101	107	102	108	28	70	26	66	31	75	14	36
85	Korea, Rep. of	101	96	103	96	99	96	35	94	44	97	25	91	6	32
86	Algeria	68	94	81	104	53	83	7	51	10	59	5	43	1	6
87	Venezuela	94	108	93	109	94	108	27	45	27	41	28	50	7	26
88	Gabon	134	*123*	146	*124*	122	*121*	11	25	16	*30*	5	20	. .	4
89	Greece	110	*106*	111	*106*	109	*106*	49	86	57	87	41	84	10	*21*
90	Oman	. .	89	. .	97	. .	80	. .	32	. .	43	. .	21	. .	1
91	Trinidad and Tobago	93	95	97	93	90	96	36	76	39	74	34	79	2	4
92	Israel	95	99	95	98	95	101	48	76	46	73	51	80	20	34
93	Hong Kong	103	*105*	106	*106*	99	*104*	29	69	32	66	25	72	5	13
94	Singapore	105	*115*	110	*118*	100	*113*	45	*71*	49	70	41	*73*	10	*12*
95	*Iran, Islamic Rep.*	63	112	85	122	40	101	18	46	24	54	11	37	2	5
96	*Iraq*	74	100	102	108	45	92	28	55	42	69	14	39	4	*10*
97	*Romania*	101	98	102	98	100	97	39	75	44	74	32	76	10	11
	Developing economies	78 *w*	101 *w*	84 *w*	110 *w*	62 *w*	92 *w*	22 *w*	39 *w*	28 *w*	45 *w*	14 *w*	33 *w*	3 *w*	8 *w*
	Oil exporters	69 *w*	107 *w*	78 *w*	113 *w*	59 *w*	101 *w*	14 *w*	44 *w*	20 *w*	53 *w*	9 *w*	42 *w*	2 *w*	10 *w*
	Exporters of manufactures	86 *w*	109 *w*	. .	119 *w*	. .	98 *w*	27 *w*	40 *w*	. .	48 *w*	. .	33 *w*	3 *w*	. .
	Highly indebted countries	88 *w*	104 *w*	91 *w*	108 *w*	84 *w*	99 *w*	21 *w*	47 *w*	23 *w*	57 *w*	20 *w*	57 *w*	5 *w*	16 *w*
	Sub-Saharan Africa	41 *w*	75 *w*	52 *w*	85 *w*	31 *w*	67 *w*	4 *w*	23 *w*	6 *w*	26 *w*	2 *w*	14 *w*	0 *w*	2 *w*
	High-income oil exporters	43 *w*	86 *w*	60 *w*	82 *w*	25 *w*	69 *w*	10 *w*	56 *w*	15 *w*	55 *w*	5 *w*	41 *w*	1 *w*	11 *w*
98	Saudi Arabia	24	69	36	77	11	61	4	42	7	51	1	33	1	*11*
99	Kuwait	116	101	129	102	103	99	52	83	59	85	43	80	1	16
100	United Arab Emirates	. .	99	. .	99	. .	99	. .	58	. .	53	. .	65	0	8
101	*Libya*	78	127	111	. .	44	. .	14	87	24	. .	4	. .	1	11
	Industrial market economies	107 *w*	102 *w*	107 *w*	101 *w*	106 *w*	101 *w*	63 *w*	93 *w*	65 *w*	91 *w*	61 *w*	92 *w*	21 *w*	39 *w*
102	Spain	115	104	117	*108*	114	*107*	38	91	46	*88*	29	*91*	6	*27*
103	Ireland	108	*100*	107	*100*	108	*100*	51	96	53	*91*	50	*101*	12	22
104	New Zealand	106	106	107	*107*	104	106	75	85	76	*84*	74	86	15	35
105	Italy	112	98	113	*99*	110	*99*	47	75	53	*74*	41	*73*	11	26
106	United Kingdom	92	101	92	*103*	92	*103*	66	89	67	*83*	66	*87*	12	22
107	Belgium	109	95	110	94	108	96	75	96	77	94	72	97	15	31
108	Austria	106	99	106	100	105	98	52	79	52	77	52	81	9	27
109	Netherlands	104	*95*	104	*94*	104	*96*	61	*102*	64	*103*	57	*100*	17	*31*
110	France	134	114	135	*108*	133	*106*	56	96	53	88	59	95	18	30
111	Australia	99	106	99	106	99	105	62	95	63	94	61	97	16	28
112	Germany, Fed. Rep.	. .	96	. .	96	. .	96	. .	74	. .	73	. .	75	9	30
113	Finland	92	104	95	104	89	103	76	102	72	95	80	110	11	33
114	Denmark	98	98	97	*98*	99	*99*	83	*103*	98	*104*	67	*103*	14	29
115	Japan	100	102	100	101	100	102	82	96	82	95	81	97	13	*30*
116	Sweden	95	98	94	97	96	99	62	83	63	79	60	88	13	38
117	Canada	105	105	106	106	104	104	56	103	57	103	55	103	26	55
118	Norway	97	97	97	*97*	98	*97*	64	97	66	95	62	*100*	11	31
119	United States	. .	101	. .	101	. .	101	. .	99	. .	99	. .	98	40	57
120	Switzerland	87	. .	87	. .	87	. .	37	. .	38	. .	35	. .	8	22
	Nonreporting nonmembers	102 *w*	105 *w*	103 *w*	. .	102 *w*	. .	66 *w*	92 *w*	60 *w*	. .	72 *w*	. .	27 *w*	21 *w*
121	Albania	92	97	97	99	87	95	33	69	40	74	26	64	8	7
122	*Angola*	39	*93*	53	. .	26	. .	5	*13*	6	. .	4	. .	0	*1*
123	*Bulgaria*	103	102	104	102	102	101	54	100	54	99	55	100	17	18
124	*Cuba*	121	105	123	108	119	101	23	85	23	82	24	88	3	21
125	*Czechoslovakia*	99	97	100	97	97	98	29	39	23	28	35	50	14	16
126	*German Dem. Rep.*	109	101	107	102	111	100	60	79	62	80	57	77	19	31
127	*Korea, Dem. Rep.*	. .	. .	. .	. .	. .	. .	. .	. .	. .	. .	. .	. .	. .	. .
128	*Mongolia*	98	*105*	98	*104*	97	*106*	66	*88*	65	*84*	66	*92*	8	*26*
129	*USSR*	103	106	103	. .	103	. .	72	99	65	. .	79	. .	. .	21

Table 31. Labor force

	Percentage of population of working age (15-64 years)		Percentage of labor force in						Average annual growth of labor force (percent)		
			Agriculture		Industry		Services				
	1965	1985	1965	1980	1965	1980	1965	1980	1965-80	1980-85	1985-2000
Low-income economies	**54** w	**59** w	**77** w	**72** w	**9** w	**13** w	**14** w	**15** w	**2.1** w	**2.3** w	**1.9** w
China and India	**55** w	**61** w	**77** w	**72** w	**9** w	**14** w	**14** w	**14** w	**2.1** w	**2.3** w	**1.6** w
Other low-income	**52** w	**52** w	**79** w	**71** w	**8** w	**10** w	**13** w	**19** w	**2.2** w	**2.5** w	**2.6** w
1 Ethiopia	52	51	86	80	5	8	9	12	2.1	1.7	2.2
2 Bhutan	55	55	95	92	2	3	4	5	1.8	1.9	1.9
3 Burkina Faso	48	44	89	87	3	4	7	9	1.6	1.9	2.2
4 Nepal	56	54	94	93	2	1	4	7	1.6	2.3	2.3
5 Bangladesh	51	53	84	75	5	6	11	19	1.9	2.8	3.0
6 Malawi	51	47	92	83	3	7	5	9	2.2	2.6	2.6
7 Zaire	52	51	82	72	9	13	9	16	1.7	2.3	2.5
8 Mali	53	50	90	86	1	2	8	13	1.7	2.5	2.7
9 Burma	57	54	64	53	14	19	23	28	2.2	1.9	1.8
10 Mozambique	55	51	87	85	6	7	7	8	3.2	..	..
11 Madagascar	54	51	85	81	4	6	11	13	2.1	1.9	2.3
12 Uganda	52	52	91	86	3	4	6	10	3.0	2.7	3.0
13 Burundi	53	52	94	93	2	2	4	5	1.2	2.0	2.4
14 Tanzania	53	50	92	86	3	5	6	10	2.8	2.8	3.0
15 Togo	52	50	78	73	9	10	13	17	2.7	2.3	2.5
16 Niger	51	51	95	91	1	2	4	7	1.8	2.3	2.6
17 Benin	52	49	83	70	5	7	12	23	1.9	2.0	2.5
18 Somalia	49	53	81	76	6	8	13	16	3.1	2.0	1.7
19 Central African Rep.	57	55	88	72	3	6	9	21	1.2	1.3	1.8
20 India	54	56	73	70	12	13	15	17	1.7	2.0	1.8
21 Rwanda	51	49	94	93	2	3	3	4	2.9	2.8	2.9
22 China	55	65	81	74	8	14	11	12	2.4	2.5	1.4
23 Kenya	48	45	86	81	5	7	9	12	3.6	3.5	3.7
24 Zambia	51	48	79	73	8	10	13	17	2.7	3.2	3.5
25 Sierra Leone	54	55	78	70	11	14	11	16	0.9	1.1	1.4
26 Sudan	53	52	82	71	5	8	14	21	2.4	2.8	3.1
27 Haiti	52	51	77	70	7	8	16	22	1.0	2.0	2.2
28 Pakistan	50	53	60	55	18	16	22	30	2.6	3.2	2.8
29 Lesotho	56	52	92	86	3	4	6	10	1.8	2.0	2.1
30 Ghana	52	48	61	56	15	18	24	26	1.9	2.7	2.9
31 Sri Lanka	54	62	56	53	14	14	30	33	2.2	1.6	1.6
32 Mauritania	52	53	89	69	3	9	8	22	1.8	2.7	3.1
33 Senegal	53	52	83	81	6	6	11	13	3.1	1.9	2.1
34 *Afghanistan*	55	..	69	..	11	..	20	..	1.7	..	..
35 *Chad*	55	55	92	83	3	5	5	12	1.6	1.8	2.1
36 *Guinea*	55	52	87	81	6	9	7	10	1.7	1.6	1.8
37 *Kampuchea, Dem.*	52	..	80	..	4	..	16	..	1.2	..	..
38 *Lao PDR*	56	53	81	76	5	7	15	17	1.6	1.8	2.2
39 *Viet Nam*	..	55	79	68	6	12	15	21	1.8	..	..
Middle-income economies	**54** w	**57** w	**56** w	**43** w	**17** w	**23** w	**27** w	**34** w	**2.5** w	**2.5** w	**2.4** w
Lower middle-income	**52** w	**55** w	**65** w	**55** w	**12** w	**16** w	**23** w	**29** w	**2.4** w	**2.6** w	**2.5** w
40 Liberia	51	52	79	74	10	9	11	16	2.6	2.2	2.7
41 Yemen PDR	52	51	54	41	12	18	33	41	1.6	2.8	3.1
42 Indonesia	53	56	71	57	9	13	21	30	2.1	2.4	2.2
43 Yemen Arab Rep.	54	51	79	69	7	9	14	22	0.7	2.6	3.4
44 Philippines	52	56	58	52	16	16	26	33	2.5	2.5	2.4
45 Morocco	50	52	61	46	15	25	24	29	2.9	3.3	3.1
46 Bolivia	53	53	54	46	20	20	26	34	2.0	2.7	2.7
47 Zimbabwe	51	45	79	73	8	11	13	17	3.0	2.7	3.0
48 Nigeria	51	49	72	68	10	12	18	20	3.0	2.6	2.9
49 Dominican Rep.	47	53	59	46	14	15	27	39	2.8	3.5	2.9
50 Papua New Guinea	55	54	87	76	6	10	7	14	1.9	2.2	2.0
51 Côte d'Ivoire	54	54	81	65	5	8	15	27	2.7	2.7	2.6
52 Honduras	50	50	68	61	12	16	20	23	2.8	3.9	3.9
53 Egypt, Arab Rep.	54	55	55	46	15	20	30	34	2.2	2.6	2.7
54 Nicaragua	48	50	57	47	16	16	28	38	2.9	3.8	3.9
55 Thailand	51	59	82	71	5	10	13	19	2.8	2.5	1.7
56 El Salvador	50	60	59	43	16	19	26	37	3.3	2.9	3.3
57 Botswana	50	48	89	70	4	13	8	17	2.4	3.5	3.4
58 Jamaica	51	56	37	31	20	16	43	52	2.0	2.9	2.4
59 Cameroon	55	50	86	70	4	8	9	22	1.7	1.8	2.2
60 Guatemala	50	53	64	57	15	17	21	26	2.3	2.8	3.3
61 Congo, People's Rep.	55	51	66	62	11	12	23	26	2.0	1.8	2.2
62 Paraguay	49	51	55	49	20	21	26	31	3.2	3.1	2.8
63 Peru	51	56	50	40	19	18	32	42	2.9	2.9	2.8
64 Turkey	53	57	75	58	11	17	14	25	1.7	2.3	2.0
65 Tunisia	50	56	49	35	21	36	29	29	2.8	3.1	2.8
66 Ecuador	50	53	55	39	19	20	26	42	2.7	3.1	2.9
67 Mauritius	52	63	37	28	25	24	38	48	2.6	3.3	2.1
68 Colombia	49	59	45	34	21	24	34	42	2.6	2.8	2.3

Note: For data comparability and coverage, see the technical notes.   Figures in italics are for years other than those specified.

	Percentage of population of working age (15-64 years)		Agriculture		Industry		Services		Average annual growth of labor force (percent)		
	1965	1985	1965	1980	1965	1980	1965	1980	1965-80	1980-85	1985-2000
69 Chile	56	63	27	17	29	25	44	58	2.2	2.6	1.7
70 Costa Rica	49	59	47	31	19	23	34	46	3.8	3.1	2.4
71 Jordan	27	49	37	10	26	26	37	64	1.7	4.4	4.2
72 Syrian Arab Rep.	46	48	52	32	20	32	28	36	3.3	3.5	4.0
73 *Lebanon*	51	..	29	..	24	..	47	..	1.7	..	..
Upper middle-income	**56** *w*	**59** *w*	**45** *w*	**29** *w*	**23** *w*	**31** *w*	**32** *w*	**40** *w*	**2.6** *w*	**2.3** *w*	**2.3** *w*
74 Brazil	53	59	49	31	20	27	31	42	3.3	2.3	2.1
75 Malaysia	50	59	59	42	13	19	29	39	3.4	2.9	2.6
76 South Africa	54	55	32	17	30	35	39	49	1.8	2.8	2.8
77 Mexico	49	54	50	37	22	29	29	35	3.9	3.2	3.0
78 Uruguay	63	63	20	16	29	29	51	55	0.4	0.6	0.9
79 Hungary	66	66	32	18	40	44	29	38	0.1	0.0	0.3
80 Poland	62	66	44	29	32	39	25	33	1.1	0.7	0.7
81 Yugoslavia	63	68	57	32	26	33	17	34	0.9	1.0	0.7
81 Portugal	62	64	38	26	30	37	32	38	1.2	1.0	0.8
83 Panama	51	58	46	32	16	18	38	50	2.7	3.0	2.6
84 Argentina	63	60	18	13	34	34	48	53	1.1	1.1	1.5
85 Korea, Rep. of	53	64	55	36	15	27	30	37	2.8	2.7	1.9
86 Algeria	50	49	57	31	17	27	26	42	2.2	3.6	3.7
87 Venezuela	49	56	30	16	24	28	47	56	4.2	3.5	3.0
88 Gabon	61	58	83	75	8	11	9	14	1.7	2.3	2.5
89 Greece	65	65	47	31	24	29	29	40	0.5	0.6	0.3
90 Oman	53	50	62	50	15	22	23	28	3.8	5.2	2.7
91 Trinidad and Tobago	53	61	20	10	35	39	45	51	1.9	2.5	2.1
92 Israel	59	60	12	6	35	32	53	62	3.0	2.2	2.1
93 Hong Kong	56	68	6	2	53	51	41	47	3.9	2.5	1.4
94 Singapore	53	67	6	2	27	38	68	61	4.2	1.9	0.8
95 *Iran, Islamic Rep.*	50	53	49	36	26	33	25	31	3.2	3.3	3.2
96 *Iraq*	51	50	50	30	20	22	30	48	3.6	3.7	4.0
97 *Romania*	65	66	57	31	26	44	18	26	0.2	0.7	0.7
Developing economies	**54** *w*	**58** *w*	**70** *w*	**62** *w*	**12** *w*	**16** *w*	**18** *w*	**22** *w*	**2.3** *w*	**2.4** *w*	**2.1** *w*
Oil exporters	**52** *w*	**53** *w*	**61** *w*	**49** *w*	**15** *w*	**19** *w*	**24** *w*	**31** *w*	**2.8** *w*	**2.8** *w*	**2.8** *w*
Exporters of manufactures	**55** *w*	**61** *w*	**71** *w*	**66** *w*	**11** *w*	**16** *w*	**16** *w*	**17** *w*	**2.2** *w*	**2.2** *w*	**1.6** *w*
Highly indebted countries	**53** *w*	**56** *w*	**51** *w*	**40** *w*	**18** *w*	**23** *w*	**31** *w*	**37** *w*	**2.9** *w*	**2.5** *w*	**2.5** *w*
Sub-Saharan Africa	**52** *w*	**50** *w*	**79** *w*	**75** *w*	**8** *w*	**9** *w*	**13** *w*	**16** *w*	**2.5** *w*	**2.4**	**2.7** *w*
High-income oil exporters	**53** *w*	**54** *w*	**58** *w*	**35** *w*	**15** *w*	**21** *w*	**28** *w*	**44** *w*	**5.6** *w*	**4.4** *w*	**3.4** *w*
98 Saudi Arabia	53	54	68	48	11	14	21	37	4.9	4.4	3.5
99 Kuwait	60	58	2	2	34	32	64	67	6.9	6.2	3.5
100 United Arab Emirates	..	67	21	5	32	38	47	57	..	5.2	2.1
101 *Libya*	53	50	41	18	21	29	38	53	3.6	3.7	3.5
Industrial market economies	**63** *w*	**67** *w*	**14** *w*	**7** *w*	**38** *w*	**35** *w*	**48** *w*	**58** *w*	**1.3** *w*	**1.0** *w*	**0.5** *w*
102 Spain	64	65	34	17	35	37	32	46	0.6	1.3	0.8
103 Ireland	57	60	31	19	28	34	41	48	0.8	1.6	1.6
104 New Zealand	59	65	13	11	36	33	51	56	1.9	1.8	1.2
105 Italy	66	67	25	12	42	41	34	48	0.3	0.7	0.2
106 United Kingdom	65	65	3	3	47	38	50	59	0.3	0.5	0.2
107 Belgium	63	68	6	3	46	36	48	61	0.7	0.7	0.1
108 Austria	63	67	19	9	45	41	36	50	0.2	0.8	0.1
109 Netherlands	62	69	9	6	41	32	51	63	1.4	1.4	0.5
110 France	62	66	18	9	39	35	43	56	0.8	0.9	0.5
111 Australia	62	66	10	7	38	32	52	61	2.4	1.8	1.3
112 Germany, Fed. Rep.	65	70	11	6	48	44	41	50	0.3	0.7	−0.5
113 Finland	65	67	24	12	35	35	41	53	0.7	0.9	0.3
114 Denmark	65	66	14	7	37	32	49	61	1.2	0.6	0.2
115 Japan	67	68	26	11	32	34	42	55	1.0	0.9	0.5
116 Sweden	66	65	11	6	43	33	46	62	1.1	0.3	0.3
117 Canada	59	68	10	5	33	29	57	65	3.2	1.4	0.9
118 Norway	63	64	16	8	37	29	48	62	1.8	0.8	0.7
119 United States	60	66	5	4	35	31	60	66	2.2	1.2	0.8
120 Switzerland	65	67	9	6	49	39	41	55	0.8	0.7	−0.1
Nonreporting nonmembers	**61** *w*	**65** *w*	**34** *w*	**22** *w*	**34** *w*	**39** *w*	**32** *w*	**39** *w*	**1.3** *w*	**1.1** *w*	**0.8** *w*
121 *Albania*	52	59	69	56	19	26	12	18	2.8	2.9	2.4
122 *Angola*	54	52	79	74	8	10	13	17	2.2	1.7	2.1
123 *Bulgaria*	67	67	46	18	31	45	23	37	0.2	0.0	0.2
124 *Cuba*	59	66	33	24	25	29	41	48	2.3	2.3	1.7
125 *Czechoslovakia*	65	64	21	13	47	49	31	37	0.9	0.4	0.7
126 *German Dem. Rep.*	61	67	15	11	49	50	36	39	0.5	0.9	0.2
127 *Korea, Dem. Rep.*	52	58	57	43	23	30	20	27	2.7	3.0	2.8
128 *Mongolia*	54	56	54	40	20	21	26	39	2.7	3.0	2.8
129 *USSR*	62	66	34	20	33	39	33	41	1.2	0.9	0.5

283

Table 32. Urbanization

	Urban population				Percentage of urban population				Number of cities of over 500,000 persons	
	As percentage of total population		Average annual growth rate (percent)		In largest city		In cities of over 500,000 persons			
	1965	1985	1965–80	1980–85	1960	1980	1960	1980	1960	1980
Low-income economies	17 w	22 w	3.6 w	4.0 w	10 w	16 w	31 w	55 w	54 t	148 t
China and India	18 w	23 w	3.0 w	3.6 w	7 w	6 w	33 w	59 w	49 t	114 t
Other low-income	13 w	20 w	4.9 w	5.4 w	26 w	30 w	19 w	40 w	5 t	34 t
1 Ethiopia	8	15	6.6	3.7	30	37	0	37	0	1
2 Bhutan	3	4	3.7	5.2	..	..	0	0	0	0
3 Burkina Faso	6	8	3.4	5.3	..	41	0	0	0	0
4 Nepal	4	7	5.1	5.6	41	27	0	0	0	0
5 Bangladesh	6	18	8.0	7.9	20	30	20	51	1	3
6 Malawi	5	..	7.8	..	..	19	0	0	0	0
7 Zaire	19	39	7.2	8.4	14	28	14	38	1	2
8 Mali	13	20	4.9	4.5	32	24	0	0	0	0
9 Burma	21	24	2.8	2.8	23	23	23	23	1	2
10 Mozambique	5	19	11.8	5.3	75	83	0	83	0	1
11 Madagascar	12	21	5.7	5.3	44	36	0	36	0	1
12 Uganda	6	7	4.1	3.0	38	52	0	52	0	1
13 Burundi	2	2	1.8	2.7	..	..	0	0	0	0
14 Tanzania	6	14	8.7	8.3	34	50	0	50	0	1
15 Togo	11	23	7.2	6.4	..	60	0	0	0	0
16 Niger	7	15	6.9	7.0	..	31	0	0	0	0
17 Benin	11	35	10.2	4.4	..	63	0	63	0	1
18 Somalia	20	34	6.1	5.4	..	34	0	0	0	0
19 Central African Rep.	27	45	4.8	3.9	40	36	0	0	0	0
20 India	19	25	3.6	3.9	7	6	26	39	11	36
21 Rwanda	3	5	6.3	6.7	..	..	0	0	0	0
22 China	18	22	2.6	3.3	6	6	42	45	38	78
23 Kenya	9	20	9.0	6.3	40	57	0	57	0	1
24 Zambia	24	48	7.1	5.5	..	35	0	35	0	1
25 Sierra Leone	15	25	4.3	5.1	37	47	0	0	0	0
26 Sudan	13	21	5.1	4.8	30	31	0	31	0	1
27 Haiti	18	27	4.0	4.1	42	56	0	56	0	1
28 Pakistan	24	29	4.3	4.8	20	21	33	51	2	7
29 Lesotho	2	17	14.6	5.3	..	..	0	0	0	0
30 Ghana	26	32	3.4	3.9	25	35	0	48	0	2
31 Sri Lanka	20	21	2.3	8.4	28	16	0	16	0	1
32 Mauritania	7	31	12.4	3.4	..	39	0	0	0	0
33 Senegal	27	36	4.1	4.0	53	65	0	65	0	1
34 *Afghanistan*	9	..	6.0	..	33	17	0	17	0	1
35 *Chad*	9	27	9.2	3.9	..	39	0	0	0	0
36 *Guinea*	12	22	6.6	4.3	37	80	0	80	0	1
37 *Kampuchea, Dem.*	11	..	1.9	..	..	..	..	..	..	..
38 *Lao PDR*	8	15	4.8	5.6	69	48	0	0	0	0
39 *Viet Nam*	..	20	..	3.4	..	21	..	50	..	4
Middle-income economies	37 w	48 w	4.4 w	3.5 w	28 w	27 w	37 w	49 w	59 t	131 t
Lower middle-income	27 w	36 w	4.5 w	3.7 w	29 w	31 w	31 w	46 w	22 t	55 t
40 Liberia	23	37	6.2	4.3	..	..	0	0	0	0
41 Yemen, PDR	30	37	3.2	4.9	61	49	0	0	0	0
42 Indonesia	16	25	4.7	2.3	20	23	34	50	3	9
43 Yemen Arab Rep.	5	19	10.7	7.3	..	25	0	0	0	0
44 Philippines	32	39	4.0	3.2	27	30	27	34	1	2
45 Morocco	32	44	4.2	4.2	16	26	16	50	1	4
46 Bolivia	40	44	2.9	5.6	47	44	0	44	0	1
47 Zimbabwe	14	27	7.5	5.0	40	50	0	50	0	1
48 Nigeria	15	30	4.8	5.2	13	17	22	58	2	9
49 Dominican Rep.	35	56	5.3	4.2	50	54	0	54	0	1
50 Papua New Guinea	5	14	8.4	4.9	..	25	0	0	0	0
51 Côte d'Ivoire	23	45	8.7	6.9	27	34	0	34	0	1
52 Honduras	26	39	5.5	5.2	31	33	0	0	0	0
53 Egypt, Arab Rep.	41	46	2.9	3.4	38	39	53	53	2	2
54 Nicaragua	43	56	4.6	4.5	41	47	0	47	0	1
55 Thailand	13	18	4.6	3.2	65	69	65	69	1	1
56 El Salvador	39	43	3.5	4.0	26	22	0	0	0	0
57 Botswana	4	20	15.4	4.5	..	..	..	..	..	..
58 Jamaica	38	53	3.4	3.2	77	66	0	66	0	1
59 Cameroon	16	42	8.1	7.0	26	21	0	21	0	1
60 Guatemala	34	41	3.6	4.2	41	36	41	36	1	1
61 Congo, People's Rep.	35	40	3.5	3.6	77	56	0	0	0	0
62 Paraguay	36	41	3.2	3.7	44	44	0	44	0	1
63 Peru	52	68	4.1	3.8	38	39	38	44	1	2
64 Turkey	32	46	4.3	4.4	18	24	32	42	3	4
65 Tunisia	40	56	4.2	3.7	40	30	40	30	1	1
66 Ecuador	37	52	5.1	3.7	31	29	0	51	0	2
67 Mauritius	37	54	4.0	2.1	..	..	..	..	..	..
68 Colombia	54	67	3.5	2.8	17	26	28	51	3	4

Note: For data comparability and coverage, see the technical notes. Figures in italics are for years other than those specified

	Urban population				Percentage of urban population				Number of cities of over 500,000 persons	
	As percentage of total population		Average annual growth rate (percent)		In largest city		In cities of over 500,000 persons			
	1965	1985	1965-80	1980-85	1960	1980	1960	1980	1960	1980
69 Chile	72	83	2.6	2.1	38	44	38	44	1	1
70 Costa Rica	38	45	3.7	3.8	67	64	0	64	0	1
71 Jordan	47	69	5.3	4.0	31	37	0	37	0	1
72 Syrian Arab Rep.	40	49	4.5	5.5	35	33	35	55	1	2
73 *Lebanon*	49	..	4.6	..	64	79	64	79	1	1
Upper middle-income	**49** *w*	**65** *w*	**3.8** *w*	**3.2** *w*	**27** *w*	**26** *w*	**39** *w*	**50** *w*	**37** *t*	**76** *t*
74 Brazil	50	73	4.5	4.0	14	15	35	52	6	14
75 Malaysia	26	38	4.5	4.0	19	27	0	27	0	1
76 South Africa	47	56	2.6	3.3	16	13	44	53	4	7
77 Mexico	55	69	4.5	3.6	28	32	36	48	3	7
78 Uruguay	81	85	0.7	0.9	56	52	56	52	1	1
79 Hungary	43	55	1.8	1.3	45	37	45	37	1	1
80 Poland	50	60	1.8	1.6	17	15	41	47	5	8
81 Portugal	24	31	2.0	3.3	47	44	47	44	1	1
82 Yugoslavia	31	45	3.0	2.5	11	10	11	23	1	3
83 Panama	44	50	3.4	2.6	61	66	0	66	0	1
84 Argentina	76	84	2.2	1.9	46	45	54	60	3	5
85 Korea, Rep. of	32	64	5.7	2.5	35	41	61	77	3	7
86 Algeria	38	43	3.8	3.7	27	12	27	12	1	1
87 Venezuela	72	85	4.5	3.5	26	26	26	44	1	4
88 Gabon	8	12	4.2	4.6	..	..	..	..	..	..
89 Greece	48	65	2.5	1.9	51	57	51	70	1	2
90 Oman	4	9	8.1	7.3	..	..	..	..	..	..
91 Trinidad and Tobago	30	64	5.0	3.3	..	..	0	0	0	0
92 Israel	81	90	3.5	2.4	46	35	46	35	1	1
93 Hong Kong	89	93	2.3	1.3	100	100	100	100	1	1
94 Singapore	100	100	1.6	1.2	100	100	100	100	1	1
95 *Iran, Islamic Rep.*	37	54	5.5	4.6	26	28	26	47	1	6
96 *Iraq*	51	70	5.3	6.3	35	55	35	70	1	3
97 *Romania*	34	51	3.4	1.0	22	17	22	17	1	1
Developing economies	**24** *w*	**31** *w*	**3.9** *w*	**3.8** *w*	**19** *w*	**21** *w*	**34** *w*	**46** *w*	**113** *t*	**279** *t*
Oil exporters	29 *w*	41 *w*	4.3 *w*	3.5 *w*	24 *w*	24 *w*	34 *w*	48 *w*	17 *t*	47 *t*
Exporters of manufactures	23 *w*	29 *w*	3.2 *w*	3.5 *w*	12 *w*	12 *w*	37 *w*	46 *w*	70 *t*	154 *t*
Highly indebted countries	44 *w*	57 *w*	3.5 *w*	3.5 *w*	23 *w*	23 *w*	35 *w*	50 *w*	29 *t*	67 *t*
Sub-Saharan Africa	13 *w*	25 *w*	6.2 *w*	5.7 *w*	22 *w*	32 *w*	8 *w*	42 *w*	2 *t*	14 *t*
High-income oil exporters	**40** *w*	**73** *w*	**9.5** *w*	**6.0** *w*	**29** *w*	**28** *w*	**0** *w*	**34** *w*	**0** *t*	**3** *t*
98 Saudi Arabia	39	72	8.5	6.1	15	18	0	33	0	2
99 Kuwait	78	92	8.2	5.1	75	30	0	0	0	0
100 United Arab Emirates	56	79	18.9	5.5	..	..	..	..	..	..
101 *Libya*	29	60	9.7	6.7	57	64	0	64	0	1
Industrial market economies	**70** *w*	**75** *w*	**1.4** *w*	**1.5** *w*	**18** *w*	**18** *w*	**48** *w*	**55** *w*	**104** *t*	**152** *t*
102 Spain	61	77	2.4	1.6	13	17	37	44	5	6
103 Ireland	49	57	2.2	2.7	51	48	51	48	1	1
104 New Zealand	79	83	1.5	0.9	25	30	0	30	0	1
105 Italy	62	67	1.0	0.9	13	17	46	52	7	9
106 United Kingdom	87	92	0.5	0.3	24	20	61	55	15	17
107 Belgium	93	96	0.5	0.4	17	14	28	24	2	2
108 Austria	51	56	0.1	0.7	51	39	51	39	1	1
109 Netherlands	86	88	1.5	0.9	9	9	27	24	3	3
110 France	67	73	2.7	1.0	25	23	34	34	4	6
111 Australia	83	86	0.2	1.4	26	24	62	68	4	5
112 Germany, Fed. Rep.	79	86	0.8	0.1	20	18	48	45	11	11
113 Finland	44	60	2.5	2.9	28	27	0	27	0	1
114 Denmark	77	86	1.1	0.3	40	32	40	32	1	1
115 Japan	67	76	2.1	1.8	18	22	35	42	5	9
116 Sweden	77	86	1.0	1.2	15	15	15	35	1	3
117 Canada	73	77	1.5	1.7	50	32	50	32	1	1
118 Norway	37	73	5.0	0.9	14	18	31	62	2	9
119 United States	72	74	1.2	2.3	13	12	61	77	40	65
120 Switzerland	53	60	1.2	0.9	19	22	19	22	1	1
Nonreporting nonmembers	**52** *w*	**65** *w*	**2.4** *w*	**1.8** *w*	**9** *w*	**8** *w*	**23** *w*	**32** *w*	**31** *t*	**59** *t*
121 *Albania*	32	34	3.4	3.3	27	25	0	0	0	0
122 *Angola*	13	25	6.4	5.8	44	64	0	64	0	1
123 *Bulgaria*	46	68	2.8	1.7	23	18	23	18	1	1
124 *Cuba*	58	71	2.7	0.8	32	38	32	38	1	1
125 *Czechoslovakia*	51	66	1.9	1.4	17	12	17	12	1	1
126 *German Dem. Rep.*	73	76	0.1	0.6	9	9	14	17	2	3
127 *Korea, Dem. Rep.*	45	63	4.6	3.8	15	12	15	19	1	2
128 *Mongolia*	42	55	4.5	3.3	53	52	0	0	0	0
129 *USSR*	52	66	2.2	1.6	6	4	21	33	25	50

Table 33. Women in Development

| | Population ratios — Females per 100 males | | | | Health and welfare — Life expectancy at birth (years) | | | | Births attended by health staff (percent) | Maternal mortality (per 100,000 live births) | Infant mortality (per 1,000 live births) | | Education — Females per 100 males | | | |
| | Total | | Age 0–4 | | Female | | Male | | | | | | Primary | | Secondary[a] | |
	1965	1985	1965	1985	1965	1986	1965	1986	1984	1980	1965	1986	1965	1985	1970	1985
Low-income economies	96 w	95 w	97 w	95 w	50 w	61 w	47 w	60 w	. .	329 w	122 w	69 w	53 w	74 w	39 w	60 w
China and India	95 w	94 w	97 w	95 w	51 w	64 w	48 w	63 w	. .	237 w	115 w	56 w	. .	75 w	. .	61 w
Other low-income	99 w	99 w	98 w	97 w	44 w	54 w	43 w	52 w	52 w	607 w	150 w	106 w	47 w	68 w	37 w	53 w
1 Ethiopia	104	99	101	99	43	48	42	45	58	2,000[b]	165	155	38	64	32	64
2 Bhutan	98	94	95	94	32	45	30	46	3	. .	184	139	. .	52	. .	32
3 Burkina Faso	101	104	100	99	40	49	37	45	. .	. .	193	140	48	58	33	47
4 Nepal	99	98	98	94	40	47	41	48	10	850	184	130	. .	41	16	30
5 Bangladesh	93	95	95	96	44	50	45	51	. .	600	153	121	44	67	. .	38
6 Malawi	104	103	100	100	40	47	39	44	59	250	200	153	. .	77	39	48
7 Zaire	107	103	97	99	45	54	42	50	. .	800[b]	141	100	48	75	26	40
8 Mali	104	108	102	100	39	48	37	45	. .	. .	207	144	49	59	29	42
9 Burma	103	100	98	97	49	61	46	58	97	135	122	64	. .	. .	65	. .
10 Mozambique	104	105	100	99	39	49	36	46	28	479[b]	168	120	. .	78	. .	49
11 Madagascar	105	101	100	99	45	55	42	52	62	300	201	130	83	. .	70	74
12 Uganda	103	102	100	100	47	49	44	46	. .	300	121	105	. .	. .	31	. .
13 Burundi	105	105	101	99	45	50	42	47	12	. .	142	114	42	72	17	43
14 Tanzania	103	103	100	99	45	55	41	51	74	370[b]	138	108	60	99	38	58
15 Togo	104	108	100	99	44	54	40	51	. .	476[b]	153	96	42	63	26	32
16 Niger	101	102	101	100	39	46	35	43	47	581[b]	180	135	46	56	35	39
17 Benin	104	108	100	99	43	52	41	48	34	1,680[b]	166	117	44	50	44	39
18 Somalia	102	99	100	99	40	48	37	45	2	1,100	165	134	27	52	27	58
19 Central African Rep.	107	107	103	99	41	51	40	48	. .	600	167	134	34	64	20	36
20 India	94	94	98	94	44	56	46	57	33	500	151	86	57	67	40	52
21 Rwanda	104	104	100	100	51	50	47	47	. .	210	139	116	69	96	44	26
22 China	95	94	97	95	56	70	50	68	. .	44	90	34	. .	81	. .	67
23 Kenya	103	101	100	99	50	59	46	56	. .	510[b]	112	74	57	93	42	62
24 Zambia	101	103	100	99	46	54	43	51	. .	140	121	82	78	89	49	58
25 Sierra Leone	105	103	100	99	34	42	31	40	25	450	209	154	55	. .	40	. .
26 Sudan	98	98	96	99	41	51	39	47	20	607[b]	160	108	55	68	40	74
27 Haiti	105	105	98	97	47	56	44	53	20	367	178	119	. .	86	. .	91
28 Pakistan	93	91	95	93	44	51	46	52	24	600	149	111	31	47	25	34
29 Lesotho	102	102	99	99	50	57	47	53	28	. .	142	102	157	125	111	150
30 Ghana	103	101	100	99	49	56	46	52	73	1,400[c]	119	89	71	78	36	62
31 Sri Lanka	93	97	97	96	65	72	63	68	87	90	63	29	86	93	101	108
32 Mauritania	102	102	101	100	39	49	36	45	23	119	178	127	31	67	13	40
33 Senegal	102	101	100	99	42	49	40	46	. .	530[c]	171	130	57	68	39	50
34 *Afghanistan*	96	. .	93	. .	35	. .	35	. .	. .	640	. .	. .	17	. .	16	. .
35 *Chad*	104	103	100	99	38	46	35	44	. .	. .	183	134	. .	39	9	18
36 *Guinea*	101	105	101	99	36	43	34	41	. .	. .	196	148	. .	46	30	35
37 *Kampuchea*	100	. .	97	. .	46	. .	43	. .	. .	. .	134	. .	56	. .	. .	. .
38 *Lao PDR*	97	102	98	98	. .	51	. .	48	. .	. .	. .	146	59	81	34	73
39 *Viet Nam*	. .	105	. .	97	. .	68	. .	63	100	110	. .	47	. .	91	. .	90
Middle-income economies	101 w	100 w	97 w	97 w	56 w	65 w	53 w	61 w	53 w	381 w	109 w	65 w	77 w	88 w	82 w	92 w
Lower middle-income	101 w	100 w	97 w	97 w	50 w	61 w	47 w	57 w	38 w	586 w	133 w	77 w	73 w	86 w	59 w	79 w
40 Liberia	102	100	99	99	46	56	43	52	89	173	138	87	. .	. .	30	. .
41 Yemen, PDR	98	103	97	97	39	51	38	49	10	100	. .	142	. .	36	25	48
42 Indonesia	103	101	97	97	45	58	43	55	31	800	136	87	. .	92	64	73
43 Yemen Arab Rep.	97	110	97	97	38	47	37	44	12	. .	200	152	5	24	3	11
44 Philippines	98	98	97	96	57	65	54	62	. .	80	72	46	94	96	. .	100
45 Morocco	100	100	97	97	51	62	48	58	. .	327[b]	145	85	42	62	40	74
46 Bolivia	102	103	98	98	47	55	42	52	. .	480	160	113	68	88	64	86
47 Zimbabwe	102	100	99	99	50	60	46	56	69	145[b]	103	74	. .	94	63	68
48 Nigeria	103	102	100	99	43	52	40	49	. .	1,500	177	104	63	79	51	. .
49 Dominican Rep.	97	99	97	97	57	68	54	64	98	56	110	67	. .	96	. .	122
50 Papua New Guinea	92	94	95	95	44	54	44	51	34	1,000	140	64	61	. .	. .	. .
51 Côte d'Ivoire	98	91	100	99	44	54	40	51	. .	. .	149	96	51	70	27	41
52 Honduras	99	99	97	96	52	66	48	62	50	82	128	72	. .	99	. .	. .
53 Egypt, Arab Rep.	99	99	96	96	50	63	48	59	24	500	172	88	64	76	45	. .
54 Nicaragua	101	100	98	97	52	63	49	60	. .	65	121	65	99	108	. .	183
55 Thailand	99	99	96	97	58	66	54.	62	33	270	88	41	89	. .	69	. .
56 El Salvador	99	99	97	97	56	66	53	57	35	74	120	61	91	99	77	94
57 Botswana	111	111	100	99	49	62	46	56	. .	250	112	69	129	110	. .	115
58 Jamaica	109	103	100	97	67	76	64	71	89	102	49	19	. .	97	111	106
59 Cameroon	105	103	100	99	47	58	44	54	. .	303	143	96	66	84	36	59
60 Guatemala	97	98	97	97	50	63	48	58	. .	105	112	61	80	83	82	. .
61 Congo, Peoples Rep.	104	105	101	99	51	60	48	56	. .	. .	118	75	71	94	43	71
62 Paraguay	102	100	97	96	67	69	63	65	22	469	73	43	88	91	91	98
63 Peru	100	101	98	96	52	62	49	59	44	314	130	90	82	93	74	88
64 Turkey	96	97	97	97	55	67	52	62	. .	207	152	79	66	89	37	59
65 Tunisia	96	98	96	97	52	65	51	61	60	1,000[c]	145	74	52	80	44	69
66 Ecuador	100	100	98	97	57	68	55	64	27	220	112	64	91	97	76	100
67 Mauritius	100	101	97	96	63	70	59	63	84	52	67	35	90	98	66	90

Note: For data comparability and coverage, see the technical notes.   Figures in italics are for years other than those specified.

	Population ratios Females per 100 males				Life expectancy at birth (years)				Births attended by health staff (percent)	Maternal mortality (per 100,000 live births)	Infant mortality (per 1,000 live births)		Education Females per 100 males			
	Total		Age 0–4		Female		Male						Primary		Secondary[a]	
	1965	1985	1965	1985	1965	1986	1965	1986	1984	1980	1965	1986	1965	1985	1970	1985
68 Colombia	102	100	97	96	59	68	54	63	51	126	96	47	102	100	95	100
69 Chile	101	101	97	96	63	75	57	68	95	55	107	20	96	95	130	109
70 Costa Rica	98	98	97	96	66	76	63	71	93	26	72	18	..	94	111	107
71 Jordan	94	94	96	97	52	67	49	63	75	..	115	46	72	91	53	94
72 Syrian Arab Rep.	95	96	94	95	54	66	51	62	37	280	114	50	47	85	36	69
73 *Lebanon*	99	..	96	..	64	..	60	..	..	..	56	..	..	..	77	..
Upper middle income	**101 w**	**100 w**	**96 w**	**96 w**	**62 w**	**70 w**	**58 w**	**64 w**	**76 w**	**121 w**	**83 w**	**50 w**	**82 w**	**90 w**	**111 w**	**109 w**
74 Brazil	98	100	96	97	59	68	55	62	73	154	104	65	..	..	99	..
75 Malaysia	97	99	96	96	60	71	56	67	82	59	55	27	..	94	..	98
76 South Africa	103	99	99	98	54	63	49	59	..	550c	124	74	..	..	..	..
77 Mexico	100	100	97	96	61	72	58	65	..	92	82	48	..	95	..	86
78 Uruguay	100	103	96	96	72	74	65	68	..	56	48	28	..	95	129	..
79 Hungary	107	106	94	96	72	75	67	67	99	28	39	19	94	95	202	186
80 Poland	106	104	95	96	72	76	67	68	..	12	42	18	..	94	251	268
81 Portugal	108	110	94	97	69	76	63	70	..	15	65	18	95	91	97	116
82 Yugoslavia	104	103	95	95	68	74	64	68	..	27	72	27	91	94	86	92
83 Panama	96	96	96	96	65	74	62	70	83	90	56	24	93	92	102	108
84 Argentina	98	101	96	97	69	74	63	67	..	85	58	33	97	..	156	..
85 Korea, Rep. of	100	98	95	97	58	73	55	66	65	34	63	25	91	94	65	88
86 Algeria	104	101	102	97	51	63	49	60	..	129	154	77	62	77	40	72
87 Venezuela	97	99	97	97	65	73	61	66	82	65	65	37	98	96	102	119
88 Gabon	104	105	100	99	44	54	41	50	..	124b	153	105	84	98	43	77
89 Greece	106	103	94	95	72	79	69	74	..	12	34	12	92	94	91	101
90 Oman	98	91	97	97	44	56	42	53	60	..	174	103	..	79	38	51
91 Trinidad and Tobago	101	101	98	98	67	72	63	67	..	..	42	21	97	99	101	101
92 Israel	98	99	95	96	74	77	71	73	99	5	27	12	..	98	133	126
93 Hong Kong	97	90	95	96	71	79	64	73	..	6	28	8	..	91	74	105
94 Singapore	94	96	95	95	68	75	64	70	100	11	26	9	85	89	103	102
95 *Iran, Islamic Rep.*	98	96	98	94	52	59	53	59	..	..	157	109	46	77	49	68
96 *Iraq*	97	97	96	96	53	65	51	62	60	..	119	71	42	81	41	56
97 *Romania*	104	102	95	96	70	73	66	68	99	175	44	26	94	..	..	..
Developing economies	**97 w**	**97 w**	**97 w**	**96 w**	**52 w**	**63 w**	**49 w**	**60 w**	**44 w**	**346 w**	**118 w**	**67 w**	**62 w**	**78 w**	**59 w**	**67 w**
Oil exporters	**101 w**	**100 w**	**98 w**	**97 w**	**49 w**	**61 w**	**47 w**	**57 w**	**35 w**	**704 w**	**139 w**	**83 w**	**62 w**	**86 w**	**56 w**	**77 w**
Exporters of manufactures	**96 w**	**95 w**	**97 w**	**95 w**	**53 w**	**65 w**	**50 w**	**64 w**	**..**	**217 w**	**109 w**	**54 w**	**62 w**	**76 w**	**63 w**	**67 w**
Highly indebted countries	**100 w**	**100 w**	**97 w**	**97 w**	**57 w**	**66 w**	**53 w**	**60 w**	**68 w**	**384 w**	**107 w**	**64 w**	**81 w**	**89 w**	**87 w**	**92 w**
Sub-Saharan Africa	**103 w**	**102 w**	**100 w**	**99 w**	**44 w**	**52 w**	**41 w**	**49 w**	**48 w**	**973 w**	**161 w**	**113 w**	**57 w**	**76 w**	**40 w**	**55 w**
High-income oil exporters	**92 w**	**80 w**	**96 w**	**97 w**	**51 w**	**66 w**	**48 w**	**62 w**	**86 w**	**47 w**	**138 w**	**62 w**	**34 w**	**81 w**	**22 w**	**74 w**
98 Saudi Arabia	96	84	96	97	50	65	47	61	..	52	148	64	29	77	16	70
99 Kuwait	64	74	97	96	65	75	61	71	99	13	43	19	76	95	73	89
100 United Arab Emirates	71	47	..	96	59	71	56	67	96	..	100	33	..	93	52	95
101 *Libya*	93	85	97	97	51	63	48	61	76	..	138	85	39	..	21	..
Industrial market economies	**104 w**	**104 w**	**96 w**	**96 w**	**74 w**	**79 w**	**68 w**	**73 w**	**99 w**	**11 w**	**24 w**	**9 w**	**95 w**	**95 w**	**95 w**	**98 w**
102 Spain	106	104	96	96	74	79	68	73	96	11	38	11	93	93	..	102
103 Ireland	99	99	96	95	73	76	69	71	..	7	25	9	..	..	..	..
104 New Zealand	99	100	95	96	74	77	68	71	99	14	20	11	94	95	..	98
105 Italy	104	105	96	96	73	79	68	74	..	13	36	10	93	95	86	94
106 United Kingdom	106	104	95	96	74	78	68	72	98	..	20	9	..	..	..	..
107 Belgium	104	104	95	96	74	78	68	72	100	10	24	10	94	95	..	97
108 Austria	114	110	96	96	73	77	66	70	..	11	28	10	95	95	95	93
109 Netherlands	100	101	95	96	76	80	71	74	..	5	14	8	95	98	91	112
110 France	105	103	96	96	75	80	68	74	..	13	22	8	95	93	..	110
111 Australia	98	99	95	96	74	80	68	75	99	11	19	10	95	95	..	98
112 Germany, Fed. Rep.	111	108	95	96	73	78	67	72	..	11	24	9	94	96	92	98
113 Finland	107	107	96	98	73	79	66	72	..	5	17	6	..	95	..	114
114 Denmark	102	102	95	96	75	78	71	73	..	4	19	8	96	96	102	105
115 Japan	104	103	96	96	73	81	68	75	100	15	18	6	96	95	101	99
116 Sweden	100	101	95	95	76	80	72	74	100	4	13	6	96	95	..	107
117 Canada	99	101	95	96	75	80	69	73	99	2	24	8	94	93	95	95
118 Norway	101	101	95	96	76	80	71	74	100	4	17	9	..	96	97	104
119 United States	103	105	96	96	74	79	67	71	100	9	25	10	..	96	..	95
120 Switzerland	105	103	96	95	75	80	69	74	..	5	18	7	..	96	..	99
Nonreporting nonmembers	**116 w**	**110 w**	**95 w**	**98 w**	**72 w**	**73 w**	**65 w**	**65 w**	**98 w**	**..**	**33 w**	**30 w**	**..**	**..**	**..**	**..**
121 *Albania*	98	97	96	95	67	75	65	68	..	..	87	41	..	91	..	..
122 *Angola*	104	103	101	99	37	45	34	43	15	..	192	139	..	..	..	..
123 *Bulgaria*	100	101	95	95	73	75	66	69	100	22	31	15	93	94	..	..
124 *Cuba*	95	97	96	95	69	77	65	73	99	31	38	14	95	90	118	107
125 *Czechoslovakia*	105	105	95	97	73	75	64	66	100	8	26	14	93	97	..	..
126 *German, Dem. Rep.*	119	110	95	96	74	75	67	68	..	17	25	9	..	93	101	98
127 *Korea, Dem. Rep.*	105	102	103	96	58	71	55	65	100	41	63	25	..	..	..	..
128 *Mongolia*	100	100	98	97	58	66	55	62	100	140	88	47	..	..	..	..
129 *USSR*	119	112	95	99	74	73d	66	64d	100	..	28	30d	..	..	..	..

a. See the technical notes.   b. Data refer to maternal mortality in hospitals and other medical institutions only.   c. Includes only community data from rural areas.
d. New estimates.

287

Technical notes

This eleventh edition of the World Development Indicators provides economic and social indicators for selected periods or years in a form suitable for comparing economies and groups of economies. It contains two new tables: one presenting a picture of women's demographic status and their access to some health and education services, and the other providing information on the structure of household consumption. To balance this addition, two tables have been dropped this year, one on the origin and destination of merchandise exports and one on life expectancy and related indicators; most of the latter are now included in the table on women. This makes a total of 33 main tables in which the statistics and measures have been chosen to give a broad perspective on development.

Considerable effort has been made to standardize the data; nevertheless, statistical methods, coverage, practices, and definitions differ widely. In addition, the statistical systems in many developing economies are still weak, and this affects the availability and reliability of the data. Moreover, intercountry and intertemporal comparisons always involve complex technical problems, which are not able to be fully and unequivocally resolved. The data are drawn from sources thought to be most authoritative, but many of them are subject to considerable margins of error. Readers are urged to take these limitations into account in interpreting the indicators, particularly when making comparisons across economies.

To facilitate international comparisons, national accounts constant price data series based on years other than 1980 are, for the first time, partially re-based to a 1980 base. This is accomplished by *rescaling*, which moves the year in which current and constant price versions of the same time series have the same value, without altering the trend of either. A *rescaling deviation* occurs between constant price gross domestic product (GDP) by industrial origin and GDP by expenditure when components of GDP are individually rescaled, and summed up to measure GDP. Such rescaling deviations are absorbed in *private consumption, etc.* on the assumption that GDP by industrial origin is a more reliable estimate than GDP by expenditure.

This approach takes into account the effects of changes in intersectoral relative prices between the original and the new base period. Because private consumption is calculated as a residual, the national accounting identities are maintained. It does, however, involve incorporating in private consumption whatever statistical discrepancies arise for *expenditure* in the rebasing process. The value added in services sector also includes a statistical discrepancy as reported by the original sources. In previous editions, GDP in each country's own original base year was simply rescaled, for presentational purposes, to equal its nominal value in 1980. This meant that the usual national accounting identities failed to hold true.

All growth rates shown are in constant prices and, unless otherwise noted, have been computed by using the least-squares method. The least-squares growth rate, r, is estimated by fitting a least-squares linear trend line to the logarithmic annual values of the variable in the relevant period. More specifically, the regression equation takes the form of $\log X_t = a + bt + e_t$, where this is equivalent to the logarithmic transformation of the compound growth rate equation, $X_t = X_o (1 + r)^t$. In these equations, X is the variable, t is time, and $a = \log X_o$ and $b = \log (1 + r)$ are the parameters to be estimated; e is the error term. If b^* is the least-squares estimate of b, then the annual average growth rate, r, is obtained as [antilog (b^*)] -1.

Table 1. Basic indicators

Population estimates for mid-1986 are based on data from the U.N. Population Division or from World Bank sources. These are normally projections, usually based on data from the most recent population censuses or surveys, which, in some cases, are neither very recent nor very accurate. *Note* that refu-

Box A Basic indicators for U.N. and World Bank member countries with populations of less than 1 million

	Population (thousands) mid-1986	Area (thousands of square kilometers)	GNP per capita[a] Dollars 1986	GNP per capita[a] Average annual growth rate (percent) 1965-86	Average annual rate of inflation[a] (percent) 1965-80	Average annual rate of inflation[a] (percent) 1980-86	Life expectancy at birth (years) 1986
Guinea-Bissau	905	36	170	−2.0	. .	32.9	39
Gambia, The	773	11	230	0.7	8.3	10.9	43
Maldives	189	0[b]	310	1.8	. .	. .	54
Comoros	409	2	320	0.6	. .	. .	56
São Tomé and Principe	111	1	340	0.7	. .	5.3	65
Cape Verde	335	4	460	. .	. .	16.0	65
Guyana	799	215	500	−2.0	8.1	10.2	66
Solomon Islands	283	28	530	. .	. .	6.9	58
Western Samoa	165	3	680	. .	. .	12.8	65
Swaziland	689	17	690	2.8	9.1	9.6	55
Tonga	98	1	740	. .	. .	. .	64
St. Vincent and the Grenadines	119	0[b]	960	1.1	11.1	5.1	69
Belize	170	23	1,170	2.2	7.4	1.6	66
Dominica	85	1	1,210	−0.4	12.9	4.7	75
Grenada	98	0	1,240	. .	11.2	5.0	68
St. Lucia	140	1	1,320	2.3	9.4	3.9	72
St. Kitts and Nevis	43	0[b]	1,700	3.6	9.3	5.2	70
Fiji	707	18	1,810	2.7	10.4	4.9	68
Antigua and Barbuda	81	0[b]	2,380	0.4	9.1	6.1	73
Suriname	402	163	2,510	3.7	. .	0.5	66
Malta	360	0[b]	3,450	7.7	3.5	1.8	75
Cyprus	672	9	4,360	. .	. .	7.4	74
Barbados	254	0[b]	5,150	2.4	11.2	7.0	74
Bahamas, The	236	14	7,190	−0.3	6.4	5.2	70
Bahrain	431	1	8,510	. .	. .	−1.8	70
Qatar	317	11	13,200	. .	. .	. .	69
Iceland	243	103	13,410	3.1	26.9	46.7	77
Brunei	232	6	15,400	. .	. .	−4.4	74
Luxembourg	366	3	15,770	4.1	6.5	6.5	74
Djibouti	361	22	. .	. .	. .	. .	49
Equatorial Guinea	381	28	. .	. .	. .	. .	45
Kiribati	65	1	. .	. .	. .	5.6	52
Seychelles	66	0[b]	. .	. .	12.1	3.8	70
Vanuatu	135	15	. .	. .	. .	4.6	63

Note: Countries with italicized names are those for which no GNP per capita can be calculated. Figures in italics are for years other than those specified.
a. See the technical note to Table 1. b. Less than 500 square kilometers.

gees not permanently settled in the country of asylum are generally considered to be part of the population of their country of origin.

The data on *area* are from the FAO *Production Yearbook, 1986*. For basic indicators for U.N. and World Bank member countries with populations of less than 1 million, see the table in *Box A*.

Gross national product (GNP) measures the total domestic and foreign output claimed by residents and is calculated without making deductions for depreciation. It comprises GDP (defined in the note for Table 2) plus net factor income from abroad, which is the income residents receive from abroad for factor services (labor and capital) less similar payments made to nonresidents who contributed to the domestic economy.

GNP per capita figures are calculated according to the *World Bank Atlas* method. The Bank recognizes that perfect cross-country comparability of GNP per capita estimates cannot be achieved. Beyond the classic, strictly intractable, index number problem, two obstacles stand in the way of adequate comparability. One concerns GNP and population estimates themselves. There are differences in national accounting and demographic reporting systems and in the coverage and reliability of underlying statistical information, between various countries. The other relates to the conversion of GNP data, expressed in different national currencies, to a common numéraire—conventionally the U.S. dollar—to compare them across countries.

Recognizing that these shortcomings affect the comparability of the GNP per capita estimates, the World Bank has introduced several improvements in the estimation procedures. Through its regular review of member countries' national accounts, the Bank also systematically evaluates the GNP estimates, focusing on the coverage and concepts employed and, where appropriate, making adjustments to improve comparability. As part of the review, Bank staff estimates of GNP (and sometimes of population) may be developed for the most recent period. The Bank also systematically assesses the appropriateness of official exchange rates as conversion factors. An alternative conversion factor is used (and reported in the *World Tables*) when the official exchange rate is judged to diverge by an exceptionally large margin from the rate effectively applied to foreign transactions. This applies to only a small number of countries.

The *Atlas* conversion factor for any year is the average of the exchange rate for that year, and the exchange rates for the two preceding years, which have been adjusted for differences in relative inflation between the country and the United States. This three-year average smooths fluctuations in prices and exchange rates for each country. The resulting GNP in U.S. dollars is divided by the midyear population for the latest year to derive per capita GNP.

The 1986 GNP per capita figures are based on conversion factors averaged over 1984 and 1985, when the dollar was at its highest level in recent history, as well as 1986. Hence, the relative GNP value of the United States and of those countries with currencies linked to the dollar has been raised, while the relative GNP value of countries not directly linked to the dollar—notably in Europe and Japan—has been lowered.

The following formulas describe the procedures for computing the conversion factor for year *t*:

$$(e^*_{t-2,t}) = \frac{1}{3} \left[e_{t-2} \left(\frac{P_t}{P_{t-2}} \Big/ \frac{P^\$_t}{P^\$_{t-2}} \right) + e_{t-1} \left(\frac{P_t}{P_{t-1}} \Big/ \frac{P^\$_t}{P^\$_{t-1}} \right) + e_t \right]$$

and for calculating per capita GNP in U.S. dollars for year *t*:

$$(Y^\$_t) = Y_t / N_t \div e^*_{t-2,t}$$

where

Y_t = current GNP (local currency) for year *t*

P_t = GNP deflator for year *t*

e_t = annual average exchange rate (local currency/U.S. dollar) for year *t*

N_t = mid-year population for year *t*

$P^\$_t$ = U.S. GNP deflator for year *t*.

Because of problems associated with the availability of comparable data and the determination of conversion factors, information on GNP per capita is not shown for nonreporting nonmarket economies.

The use of official exchange rates to convert national currency figures to the U.S. dollar does not attempt to measure the relative domestic purchasing powers of currencies. The United Nations International Comparison Program (ICP) has developed measures of real GDP on an internationally comparable scale by using purchasing power parities (PPPs) instead of exchange rates, as conversion factors. Information on the ICP has been published in five studies and in a number of other reports.

The ICP project has covered more than 70 countries in five phases, at five-year intervals. Phase IV results for 1980, covering 60 countries, were included in last year's report. Phase V results for 1985 are now available for 25 (mainly industrial) countries, and those for many of the remaining countries (especially African) should be available by the end of the year. The Bank is currently reviewing the data and methodology underlying the latest estimates and will include an updated comparison of ICP and *Atlas* numbers in a future edition of the *Atlas* or another statistical publication. The United Nations and its regional economic commissions, as well as other international agencies, such as the European Communities, the Organisation for Economic Co-operation and Development, and the World Bank are working to improve the methodology and extend annual purchasing power comparisons to all countries. However, exchange rates remain the only generally available means of converting GNP from national currencies to U.S. dollars.

The *average annual rate of inflation* is that measured by the growth rate of the GDP implicit deflator for each of the periods shown. The GDP deflator is first calculated by dividing, for each year of the period, the value of GDP at current values by the value of GDP at constant values, both in national currency. The least-squares method is then used to calculate the growth rate of the GDP deflator for the period. This measure of inflation, like any other, has limitations. For some purposes, however, it is used as an indicator of inflation because it is the most broadly based deflator, showing annual price movements for all goods and services produced in an economy.

Life expectancy at birth indicates the number of years a newborn infant would live if patterns of mortality prevailing for all people at the time of its birth were to stay the same throughout its life. Data are from the U.N. Population Division, supplemented by World Bank estimates.

The *summary measures* for GNP per capita and life expectancy in this table are weighted by population. Those for average annual rates of inflation are weighted by the share of country GDP valued in current U.S. dollars.

Tables 2 and 3. Growth and structure of production

Most of the definitions used are those of the U.N. *System of National Accounts* (SNA), series F, no. 2, revision 3. Estimates are obtained from national sources, sometimes reaching the World Bank through other international agencies but more often collected by World Bank staff during missions.

GDP measures the total final output of goods and services produced by an economy—that is, by residents and nonresidents—regardless of the allocation to domestic and foreign claims. It is calculated without making deductions for depreciation. While SNA envisages estimates of GDP by industrial origin to be at producer prices, many countries still report such details at factor cost, which differs from producer prices because of the treatment of certain commodity taxes. Overall, GDP at producer prices is equal to GDP at purchaser values, less import duties. For individual sectors, say agriculture, values at producer prices differ from purchaser values because of indirect taxes minus subsidies and, at least in theory, because purchaser prices include retail and wholesale service and transport costs. International comparability of the estimates is affected by the fact that countries are, in practice, about evenly divided in terms of the valuation system they use in reporting value added by production sectors. As a partial solution, GDP estimates are shown at purchaser values if the components are on this basis, and such instances are footnoted. However, for a few countries in Tables 2 and 3, GDP at purchaser values have been replaced by GDP at factor cost. *Note* that in editions before 1986, *GDP at producer prices* and *GDP at purchaser values* were referred to as *GDP at factor cost* and *GDP at market prices*, respectively.

The figures for GDP are dollar values converted from domestic currencies by using single-year official exchange rates. For a few countries where the official exchange rate does not reflect the rate effectively applied to actual foreign exchange transactions, an alternative conversion factor is used (and reported in the *World Tables*). *Note* that this table does not use the three-year averaging computation used for calculating GNP per capita in Table 1.

Agriculture covers forestry, hunting, and fishing as well as agriculture. In developing countries with high levels of subsistence farming, much of agricultural production is either not exchanged or not exchanged for money. This increases the difficulty of measuring the contribution of agriculture to GDP and reduces the reliability and comparability of such numbers. *Industry* comprises value added in mining, *manufacturing* (also reported as a subgroup), construction, and electricity, water, and gas. Value added in all other branches of economic activity, including imputed bank service charges, import duties, and any statistical discrepancies noted by national compilers, are categorized as *services, etc.*.

Partially rebased 1980 series in domestic currencies, as explained above, are used to compute the growth rates in Table 2. The sectoral shares of GDP in Table 3 are based on current price series.

In calculating the *summary measures* for each indicator in Table 2, partially rebased constant 1980 U.S. dollar values for each economy are calculated for each of the years of the periods covered; the values are often aggregated across countries for each year; and the least-squares procedure is used to compute the growth rates. The average sectoral percentage shares in Table 3 are computed from group aggregates of sectoral GDP in current U.S. dollars.

Tables 4 and 5. Growth of consumption and investment; structure of demand

GDP is defined in the note for Table 2, but for these two tables it is in purchaser values.

General government consumption includes all current expenditure for purchases of goods and services by all levels of government. All expenditure, including capital expenditure, on national defense and security is regarded as consumption expenditure.

Private consumption, etc. is the market value of all goods and services purchased or received as income in kind by households and nonprofit institutions. It excludes purchases of dwellings, but includes imputed rent for owner-occupied dwellings (see Table 6 for details). In practice, it includes any statistical discrepancy in the use of resources. At constant prices, this means that it also includes the rescaling deviation from partial rebasing.

Gross domestic investment consists of the outlays for additions to the fixed assets of the economy, plus net changes in the level of inventories.

Gross domestic savings are calculated by deducting total consumption from gross domestic product.

Exports of goods and nonfactor services represent the value of all goods and nonfactor services provided to the rest of the world; they include merchandise, freight, insurance, travel, and other nonfactor services. The value of factor services, such as investment income, interest, and labor income, is excluded.

The *resource balance* is the difference between exports of goods and nonfactor services and imports of goods and nonfactor services.

Partially rebased 1980 series in constant domestic currency units (see above) are used to compute the indicators in Table 4. Table 5 uses national accounts series in current domestic currency units. Similarly, the growth rates in Table 4 are calculated from the constant 1980 price series; the shares of GDP in Table 5, from current price series.

The *summary measures* are calculated by the method explained in the note for Tables 2 and 3.

Table 6. Structure of consumption

Percentage shares of selected items in total household consumption expenditure are computed from SNA-defined details of GDP (expenditure at national market prices) mainly as collected for the International Comparison Program (ICP) phases IV and V. For countries not covered by the ICP, less detailed national accounts estimates are included, as available. The data covers 79 countries and refer to estimates generally for a year between 1980 and 1985, inclusive. In some instances, they refer to earlier years and are therefore italicized. *Consumption* here refers to private (nongovernment) consumption as defined in the SNA and in the notes to Tables 2, 4, and 5, except that education and medical care comprise government as well as private outlays. This ICP concept of consumption enhances international comparability because it is less sensitive to differing national practices regarding the financing of health and education services.

A major sub-item of *food* is presented: *cereals and tubers*. The sub-item comprises rice, flour, bread, all other cereals and cereal preparations, potatoes, yams, and other tubers. For industrialized market economies, this sub-item does not include tubers. *Gross rents, fuel and power* consist of actual, and imputed rents, and repair and maintenance charges, as well as the sub-item *fuel and power* (for heating, lighting, cooking, air conditioning, and so forth). Note that this item excludes energy used for transport (rarely more than 1 percent of the total, in developing countries). As mentioned above, *medical care* and *education* include government as well as private consumption expenditure. *Transport and communication* also include the purchase of *motor cars*, which are reported as a sub-item. *Other consumption*, the residual group, includes beverages and tobacco, nondurable household goods and household services, recreational services, and services supplied by hotels and restaurants. It also includes the separately reported sub-item, *other consumer durables*, comprising household appliances, furniture, floor coverings, recreational equipment, and watches and jewellery.

Estimating the structure of consumption is one of the weakest aspects of national accounting in developing countries. The structure is estimated through household expenditure surveys and similar sampling techniques, and shares any bias of the technique. For example, some countries limit surveys to urban areas or, even more narrowly, to capital cities. This tends to produce exceptionally low shares for *food* and high shares for *transport and communications, gross rents*, and *other consumption*, which includes meals purchased outside the home. Controlled food prices and incomplete national accounting for subsistence activities also contribute to low food shares.

Table 7. Agriculture and food

The basic data for *value added in agriculture* are from the World Bank's national accounts series at current prices in national currencies. This is in contrast to last year's edition, which showed constant price data for this indicator. The value added in current prices in national currencies is converted to U.S. dollars by applying the single-year conversion procedure, as described in the technical note for Tables 2 and 3.

The figures for the remainder of this table are from the Food and Agriculture Organization (FAO).

Cereal imports are measured in grain equivalents and defined as comprising all cereals under the *Standard International Trade Classification* (SITC), Revision 2, Groups 041–046. *Food aid in cereals* covers wheat and flour, bulgur, rice, coarse grains, and blended foods. The figures are not directly comparable since cereal imports are based on calendar-year and recipient-country data, whereas food aid in cereals is based on data for crop years reported by donor countries and international organizations. Furthermore, food aid information by donors may not correspond to actual receipts by beneficiaries during a given period and is sometimes not reported to FAO or other relevant international organizations. The earliest available food aid data are for 1974.

Fertilizer consumption is measured in relation to arable land. This includes land under temporary crops (double-cropped areas are counted once), temporary meadows for mowing or pastures, land under market or kitchen gardens, land temporarily fallow or lying idle, as well as land under permanent crops.

The *index of food production per capita* shows the average annual quantity of food produced per capita in 1984–86 in relation to that produced in 1979–81. The estimates are derived by dividing the quantity of food production by the total population. For this index *food* is defined as comprising nuts, pulses, fruits, cereals, vegetables, sugar cane, sugar beet, starchy roots, edible oils, livestock, and livestock products. Quantities of food production are measured net of animal feed, seeds

for use in agriculture, and food lost in processing and distribution.

The *summary measures* for fertilizer consumption are weighted by total arable land area; the *summary measures* for food production are weighted by population.

Table 8. Structure of manufacturing

The basic data for *value added in manufacturing* are from the World Bank's national accounts series at *current* prices in national currencies—unlike last year's edition, which provided *constant* price values. The figures shown are dollar values converted from national currencies by using single-year official exchange rates. For a few countries where the official exchange rate does not reflect the rate effectively applied to actual foreign exchange transactions, an alternative conversion factor is used.

The basic data for *distribution of value added* among manufacturing industries are provided by United Nations Industrial Development Organization (UNIDO), and are in national currencies at current prices.

The classification of manufacturing industries is in accord with the U.N. *International Standard Industrial Classification of All Economic Activities* (ISIC). *Food and agriculture* comprise *ISIC* Division 31; *textiles and clothing,* Division 32; *machinery and transport equipment,* Major Groups 382–84; and *chemicals,* Major Groups 351 and 352. *Other* comprises wood and related products (Division 33), paper and related products (Division 34), petroleum and related products (Major Groups 353–56), basic metals and mineral products (Divisions 36 and 37), fabricated metal products and professional goods (Major Groups 381 and 385), and other industries (Major Group 390). When data for textiles, machinery or chemicals are shown as not available, they are also included in *other.*

Table 9. Manufacturing earnings and output

Four indicators are shown—two relate to real earnings per employee, one to labor's share in total value added generated, and one to labor productivity in the manufacturing sector. The indicators are based on data from UNIDO, although the deflators are from other sources, as explained below.

Earnings per employee are in constant prices and are derived by deflating nominal earnings per employee, as computed by UNIDO, by the country's consumer price index (CPI). The CPI is from the IMF's *International Financial Statistics* (IFS). *Total earnings as percentage of value added* are derived by dividing total earnings of employees by value added in current prices, to show labor's share in income generated in the manufacturing sector. *Gross output per employee* is in constant prices and is presented as a measure of labor productivity. To derive this indicator, UNIDO data on *gross output per employee* in current prices are adjusted using the implicit deflators for value added in manufacturing or in industry, taken from the World Bank's national accounts data files.

To improve cross-country comparability, UNIDO has, where possible, standardized the coverage of establishments to those with 5 or more employees.

The concepts and definitions are in accordance with the *International Recommendations for Industrial Statistics* published by the United Nations. *Earnings* (wages and salaries) cover all remuneration to employees paid by the employer during the year. The payments include (a) all regular and overtime cash payments and bonuses and cost of living allowances; (b) wages and salaries paid during vacation and sick leave; (c) taxes and social insurance contributions and the like, payable by the employees and deducted by the employer; and (d) payments in kind.

The value of *gross output* is estimated on the basis of either production or shipments. On the production basis it consists of (a) the value of all products of the establishment, (b) the value of industrial services rendered to others, (c) the value of goods shipped in the same condition as received, (d) the value of electricity sold, and (e) the net change of the value of work-in-progress between the beginning and the end of the reference period. In the case of estimates compiled on a shipment basis, the net change between the beginning and the end of the reference period in the value of stocks of finished goods is also included. *Value added* is defined as the current value of gross output less the current cost of (a) materials, fuels and other supplies consumed, (b) contract and commission work done by others, (c) repair and maintenance work done by others, and (d) goods shipped in the same condition as received.

The term *employees* in this table combines two categories defined by the U.N.: *regular employees* and *persons engaged*. Together these groups comprise regular employees, working proprietors, active business partners, and unpaid family workers; they exclude homeworkers. The data refer to the average number of employees working during the year.

Table 10. Commercial energy

The data on energy are from U.N. sources. They refer to commercial forms of primary energy—petroleum and natural gas liquids, natural gas, solid fuels (coal, lignite, and so on), and primary electricity (nuclear, geothermal, and hydroelectric power)—all converted into oil equivalents. Figures on liquid fuel consumption include petroleum derivatives that have been consumed in nonenergy uses. For converting primary electricity into oil equivalents, a notional thermal efficiency of 34 percent has been assumed. The use of firewood, dried animal excrement, and other traditional fuels, although substantial in some developing countries, is not taken into account because reliable and comprehensive data are not available.

Energy imports refer to the dollar value of energy imports—Section 3 in the *SITC*, Revision 1—and are expressed as a percentage of earnings from merchandise exports.

Because data on energy imports do not permit a distinction between petroleum imports for fuel and for use in the petrochemicals industry, these percentages may overestimate the dependence on imported energy.

The *summary measures* of *energy production* and *consumption* are computed by aggregating the respective volumes for each of the years covered by the periods and then applying the least-squares growth rate procedure. For *energy consumption per capita*, population weights are used to compute summary measures for the specified years.

The summary measures of *energy imports as a percentage of merchandise exports* are computed from group aggregates for energy imports and merchandise exports in current dollars.

Table 11. Growth of merchandise trade

The statistics on merchandise trade, Tables 11 through 14, are primarily from the U.N. trade data system, which accords with the U.N. *Yearbook of International Trade Statistics*—that is, the data are based on countries' customs returns. However, more recent statistics are often from secondary sources, notably the IMF; in footnoted cases, World Bank estimates are reported. Secondary sources and World Bank estimates are based on aggregated reports that become available before the detailed reports submitted to the U.N. become available. In some cases, they also permit coverage adjustments for significant components of a country's foreign trade that are not subject to regular customs reports. Such cases are identified in the country notes to the *World Tables*. Values in these tables are in current U.S. dollars.

Merchandise exports and imports, with some exceptions, cover international movements of goods across customs borders. Exports are valued f.o.b. (free on board) and imports, c.i.f. (cost, insurance, and freight), unless otherwise specified in the foregoing sources. These values are in current dollars; *note* that they do not include trade in services.

The *growth rates of merchandise exports and imports* are in constant terms and are calculated from quantum indexes of exports and imports. Quantum indexes for developing countries and high-income oil exporters are obtained from the export or import value index as deflated by the corresponding price index. To calculate these quantum indexes, the World Bank uses its own price indexes, which are based on international prices for primary commodities and unit value indexes for manufactures. These price indexes are both country-specific and disaggregated by broad commodity groups, which ensure consistency between data for a group of countries and those for individual countries.

Such data consistency will increase as the World Bank continues to improve its trade price indexes for an increasing number of countries. For industrial economies the indexes are as reported by the IMF, in accordance with national methodologies.

The *terms of trade*, or the net barter terms of trade, measure the relative movement of export prices against that of import prices. Calculated as the ratio of a country's index of average export prices to its average import price index, this indicator shows changes over a base year in the level of export prices as a percentage of import prices. The terms-of-trade index numbers are shown for 1984 and 1986, where 1980 = 100. The price indexes are from the sources cited above for the growth rates of exports and imports.

The *summary measures* for the growth rates are calculated by aggregating the 1980 constant U.S. dollar price series for each year and then applying the least-squares growth rate procedure for the periods shown. *Note* again that these values do not include trade in services.

Tables 12 and 13. Structure of merchandise trade

The shares in these tables are derived from trade values in current dollars reported in the U.N. trade data system and the U.N. *Yearbook of International Trade Statistics*, supplemented by other secondary sources and World Bank estimates as explained in the note to Table 11.

Merchandise exports and imports are defined in the note to Table 11.

The categorization of exports and imports follows the *SITC*, series M, no. 34, Revision 1. Estimates from secondary sources also usually follow this definition.

In Table 12, *fuels, minerals, and metals* are the commodities in *SITC* Section 3 (mineral fuels, and lubricants and related materials), Divisions 27 and 28 (minerals and crude fertilizers, and metalliferous ores) and Division 68 (nonferrous metals). *Other primary commodities* comprise *SITC* Sections 0, 1, 2, and 4 (food and live animals, beverages and tobacco, inedible crude materials, oils, fats, and waxes) less Divisions 27 and 28. *Machinery and transport equipment* are the commodities in *SITC* Section 7. *Other manufactures* represent *SITC* Sections 5 through 9 less Section 7 and Division 68. *Textiles and clothing*, representing *SITC* Divisions 65 and 84 (textiles, yarns, fabrics, and clothing), are shown as a subgroup of *other manufactures*. *Note* that because of a lack of detailed information for many countries, this definition is somewhat broader than that used for exporters of manufactures defined on page xi.

In Table 13, *food* commodities are those in *SITC* Sections 0, 1, and 4 and Division 22 (food and live animals, beverages, oils and fats, and oilseeds and nuts), less Division 12 (tobacco). *Fuels* are the commodities in *SITC* Section 3 (mineral fuels, lubricants and related materials). *Other primary commodities* comprise *SITC* Section 2 (crude materials, excluding fuels), less Division 22 (oilseeds and nuts) plus Divisions 12 (tobacco) and 68 (nonferrous metals). *Machinery and transport equipment* are the commodities in *SITC* Section 7. *Other manufactures*, calculated as the residual from the total value of manufactured imports, represent *SITC* Sections 5 through 9 less Section 7 and Division 68.

The *summary measures* in Table 12 are weighted by total merchandise exports of individual countries in current dollars; those in Table 13, by total merchandise imports of individual countries in current dollars. (See the note to Table 11.)

Table 14. Origin and destination of manufactured exports

The value of *manufactured exports*, reported by country of origin, conforms to Table 12, where separate shares in total merchandise exports are given for machinery and transport equipment and for other manufactures. The *destination of manufactured exports* is based on the highly detailed Commodity Trade file maintained at the U.N.'s International Computing Center. While the two are conceptually the same, differences may arise because aggregate estimates by country of origin (included in Table 12) tend to be more current and comprehensive. When data on values of manufactured exports are not available from U.N., supplementary sources including IMF and World Bank data files are used.

Manufactured goods are the commodities in *SITC*, Revision 1, Sections 5 through 9 (chemicals and related products, basic manufactures, manufactured articles, machinery and transport equipment, and other manufactured articles and goods not elsewhere classified) excluding Division 68 (nonferrous metals). This definition is somewhat broader than the one used to define exporters of manufactures (see page xi) because the highly detailed information used for country classification is not generally available on a current basis.

In the *destination* columns, *industrial market economies* also include Gibraltar, Iceland, and Luxembourg; *high-income oil exporters* also include Bahrain, Brunei, and Qatar. The *summary measures* are weighted by manufactured exports of individual countries in current dollars.

Table 15. Balance of payments and reserves

The statistics for this table are normally as reported by the IMF but do include recent estimates by World Bank staff and, in rare instances, the Bank's own coverage or classification adjustments to enhance international comparability. Values in this table are in current U.S. dollars.

The *current account balance* is the difference between exports of goods and services (factor and nonfactor) as well as inflows of unrequited transfers (private and official), and imports of goods and services as well as unrequited transfers to the rest of the world. The *external financing requirement* equals the current account balance except that it excludes net official unrequited transfers, treating them as akin to official capital movements. The difference between the two measures is essentially foreign aid in the form of grants, technical assistance, and food aid, which, for most developing countries, tends to make current account deficits smaller than the financing requirement.

Workers' remittances cover remittances of income by migrants who are employed or expect to be em-

ployed for more than a year in their new economy, where they are considered residents. These remittances are classified as private unrequited transfers, while those derived from shorter term stays are included in services, as labor income. The distinction accords with internationally agreed guidelines, but many developing countries classify workers' remittances as a factor income receipt (and hence a component of GNP). The World Bank adheres to international guidelines in defining GNP and, therefore, may differ from national practices.

Net direct private investment is the net amount invested or reinvested by nonresidents in enterprises in which they or other nonresidents exercise significant managerial control, including equity capital, reinvested earnings, and other capital. The net figures subtract the value of direct investment abroad by residents of the reporting country.

Gross international reserves comprise holdings of monetary gold, special drawing rights (SDRs), the reserve position of IMF members in the Fund, and holdings of foreign exchange under the control of monetary authorities. The data on holdings of international reserves are from IMF data files. The gold component of these reserves is valued throughout at year-end London prices: that is, $37.37 an ounce in 1970 and $390.90 an ounce in 1986. The reserve levels for 1970 and 1986 refer to the end of the year indicated and are in current dollars at prevailing exchange rates. Because of differences in the definition of international reserves, in the valuation of gold, and in reserve management practices, the levels of reserve holdings published in national sources do not have strictly comparable significance. Reserve holdings at the end of 1986 are also expressed in terms of the number of months of imports of goods and services they could pay for, with imports at the average level for 1986.

The *summary measures* are computed from group aggregates for gross international reserves and total imports of goods and services, in current dollars.

Table 16. Total external debt

The data on debt in this and successive tables are from the World Bank Debtor Reporting System, supplemented by World Bank estimates. That system is concerned solely with developing economies and does not collect data on external debt for other groups of borrowers, nor from economies that are not members of the World Bank. The dollar figures on debt shown in Tables 16 through 20 are in U.S. dollars converted at official exchange rates.

The data on debt include private nonguaranteed debt reported by twenty-two developing countries and complete or partial estimates (depending on the reliability of information) for an additional twenty-six countries.

Public loans are external obligations of public debtors, including the national government, its agencies, and autonomous public bodies. *Publicly guaranteed loans* are external obligations of private debtors that are guaranteed for repayment by a public entity. These two categories are aggregated in the tables. *Private nonguaranteed loans* are external obligations of private debtors that are not guaranteed for repayment by a public entity.

Use of IMF credit denotes repurchase obligations to the IMF for all uses of IMF resources, excluding those resulting from drawings in the reserve tranche and on the IMF Trust Fund and the structural adjustment facility. It is shown for the end of the year specified. It comprises purchases outstanding under the credit tranches, including enlarged access resources, and all of the special facilities (the buffer stock, compensatory financing, and extended Fund facility). Trust Fund and structural adustment facility loans are included individually in the Debtor Reporting System and are thus shown within the total of public long-term debt. Use of IMF credit outstanding at year-end (a stock) is converted to U.S. dollars at the dollar-SDR exchange rate in effect at year-end.

Short-term external debt is debt with an original maturity of one year or less. Available data permit no distinctions between public and private nonguaranteed short-term debt.

Total external debt is defined for the purpose of this report as the sum of public, publicly guaranteed, and private nonguaranteed long-term debt, use of IMF credit, and short-term debt.

Table 17. Flow of public and private external capital

Data on *disbursements* and *repayment of principal* (amortization) are for public, publicly guaranteed, and private nonguaranteed long-term loans. The *net flow* estimates are disbursements less the repayment of principal.

Table 18. Total external public and private debt and debt service ratios

Total long-term debt data in this table cover public and publicly guaranteed debt and private non-

guaranteed debt. The ratio of debt service to exports of goods and services is one of several conventional measures used to assess the ability to service debt. The average ratios of debt service to GNP for the economy groups are weighted by GNP in current dollars. The average ratios of debt service to exports of goods and services are weighted by exports of goods and services in current dollars.

Table 19. External public debt and debt service ratios

External public debt outstanding and disbursed represents public and publicly guaranteed loans drawn at year-end, net of repayments of principal and write-offs. For estimating external public debt as a percentage of GNP, the debt figures are converted into U.S. dollars from currencies of repayment at end-of-year official exchange rates. GNP is converted from national currencies to U.S. dollars by applying the conversion procedure described in the technical note to Tables 2 and 3.

Interest payments are actual payments made on the outstanding and disbursed public and publicly guaranteed debt in foreign currencies, goods, or services; they include commitment charges on undisbursed debt if information on those charges is available.

Debt service is the sum of actual repayments of principal (amortization) and actual payments of interest made in foreign currencies, goods, or services on external public and publicly guaranteed debt. Procedures for estimating total long-term debt as a percentage of GNP, average ratios of debt service to GNP, and average ratios of debt service to exports of goods and services are the same as those described in the note to Table 18.

The *summary measures* are computed from group aggregates of debt service and GNP in current dollars.

Table 20. Terms of external public borrowing

Commitments refer to the public and publicly guaranteed loans for which contracts were signed in the year specified. They are reported in currencies of repayment and converted into U.S. dollars at average annual official exchange rates.

Figures for *interest rates*, *maturities*, and *grace periods* are averages weighted by the amounts of the loans. Interest is the major charge levied on a loan and is usually computed on the amount of principal drawn and outstanding. The maturity of a loan is the interval between the agreement date, when a loan agreement is signed or bonds are issued, and the date of final repayment of principal. The grace period is the interval between the agreement date and the date of the first repayment of principal.

Public loans with variable interest rates, as a percentage of public debt, refer to interest rates that float with movements in a key market rate; for example, the *London interbank offered rate* (LIBOR) or the U.S. *prime rate*. This column shows the borrower's exposure to changes in international interest rates.

The *summary measures* in this table are weighted by the amounts of the loans.

Table 21. Official development assistance from OECD and OPEC members

Official development assistance (ODA) consists of net disbursements of loans and grants made on concessional financial terms by official agencies of the members of the Development Assistance Committee (DAC) of the Organisation for Economic Cooperation and Development (OECD) and members of the Organization of Petroleum Exporting Countries (OPEC), to promote economic development and welfare. While this definition aims at excluding purely military assistance, the borderline is sometimes blurred; the definition used by the country of origin usually prevails. ODA also includes the value of technical cooperation and assistance. All data shown are supplied by the OECD, and all U.S. dollar values are converted at official exchange rates.

Amounts shown are net disbursements to developing countries and multilateral institutions. The disbursements to multilateral institutions are now reported for all DAC members on the basis of the date of issue of notes; some DAC members previously reported on the basis of the date of encashment. *Net bilateral flows to low-income economies* exclude unallocated bilateral flows and all disbursements to multilateral institutions.

The nominal values shown in the summary for ODA from OECD countries were converted at 1980 prices using the dollar GDP deflator. This deflator is based on price increases in OECD countries (excluding Greece, Portugal, and Turkey) measured in dollars. It takes into account the parity changes between the dollar and national currencies. For example, when the dollar depreciates, price changes measured in national currencies have to be adjusted upward by the amount of the depreciation to obtain price changes in dollars.

The table, in addition to showing totals for OPEC, shows totals for the Organization of Arab Petroleum Exporting Countries (OAPEC). The donor members of OAPEC are Algeria, Iraq, Kuwait, Libya, Qatar, Saudi Arabia, and United Arab Emirates. ODA data for OPEC and OAPEC are also obtained from the OECD.

Table 22. Official development assistance: receipts

Net disbursements of ODA from all sources consist of loans and grants made on concessional financial terms by all bilateral official agencies and multilateral sources to promote economic development and welfare. They include the value of technical cooperation and assistance. The disbursements shown in this table are not strictly comparable with those shown in Table 21 since the receipts are from all sources; disbursements in Table 21 refer to those made by members of the OECD and OPEC only. Net disbursements equal gross disbursements less payments to the originators of aid for amortization of past aid receipts. Net disbursements of ODA are shown per capita and as a percentage of GNP.

The *summary measures* of per capita ODA are computed from group aggregates for population and for ODA. *Summary measures* for ODA as a percentage of GNP are computed from group totals for ODA and for GNP in current U.S. dollars.

Table 23. Central government expenditure

The data on central government finance in Tables 23 and 24 are from the IMF *Government Finance Statistics Yearbook, 1987* and IMF data files. The accounts of each country are reported using the system of common definitions and classifications found in the IMF *Manual on Government Finance Statistics* (1987). The shares of total expenditure and revenue by category are calculated from series in national currencies. Because of differences in coverage of available data, the individual components of central government expenditure and current revenue shown in these tables may not be strictly comparable across all economies.

Moreover, inadequate statistical coverage of state, provincial, and local governments, dictated by the use of central government data, may seriously understate or distort the statistical portrayal of the allocation of resources for various purposes, especially in countries where lower levels of government have considerable autonomy and are responsible for many economic and social services. In addition, *central government* can mean either of two accounting concepts: *consolidated* or *budgetary*. For most countries, central government finance data have been consolidated into one overall account, but for others only the budgetary central government accounts are available. Since all central government units are not included in the budgetary accounts, the overall picture of central government activities is incomplete. Countries reporting budgetary data are footnoted.

It must be emphasized that the data presented, especially those for education and health, are not comparable across countries for the above and other reasons. In many economies private health and education services are substantial; in others public services represent the major component of total expenditure but may be financed by lower levels of government. Great caution should therefore be exercised in using the data for cross-country comparisons.

Central government expenditure comprises the expenditure by all government offices, departments, establishments, and other bodies that are agencies or instruments of the central authority of a country. It includes both current and capital (development) expenditure.

Defense comprises all expenditure, whether by defense or other departments, on the maintenance of military forces, including the purchase of military supplies and equipment, construction, recruiting, and training. Also in this category is expenditure on strengthening public services to meet wartime emergencies, on training civil defense personnel, on supporting research and development, and on funding administration of military aid programs.

Education comprises expenditure on the provision, management, inspection, and support of pre-primary, primary, and secondary schools; of universities and colleges; and of vocational, technical, and other training institutions by central governments. Also included is expenditure on the general administration and regulation of the education system; on research into its objectives, organization, administration, and methods; and on such subsidiary services as transport, school meals, and school medical and dental services. *Note* that Table 6 provides an alternative measure of expenditure on education, private as well as public, relative to household consumption.

Health covers public expenditure on hospitals, medical and dental centers, and clinics with a major medical component; on national health and medical insurance schemes; and on family planning and preventive care. Also included is expen-

diture on the general administration and regulation of relevant government departments, hospitals and clinics, health and sanitation, and national health and medical insurance schemes; and on research and development. *Note* that Table 6 provides a more comprehensive measure of expenditure on medical care, private as well as public, relative to household consumption.

Housing and community amenities and social security and welfare cover public expenditure on housing, such as income-related schemes; on provision and support of housing and slum clearance activities; on community development; and on sanitary services. They also cover public expenditure on compensation to the sick and temporarily disabled for loss of income; on payments to the elderly, the permanently disabled, and the unemployed; and on family, maternity, and child allowances. They also include the cost of welfare services, such as care of the aged, the disabled, and children; as well as the cost of general administration, regulation, and research associated with social security and welfare services.

Economic services comprise public expenditure associated with the regulation, support, and more efficient operation of business; economic development; redress of regional imbalances; and creation of employment opportunities. Research, trade promotion, geological surveys, and inspection and regulation of particular industry groups are among the activities included. The five major categories of economic services are industry, agriculture, fuel and energy, transport and communication, and other economic affairs and services.

Other covers expenditure on the general administration of government not included elsewhere; for a few economies it also includes amounts that could not be allocated to other components.

Overall surplus/deficit is defined as current and capital revenue and grants received, less total expenditure and lending minus repayments.

Summary measures for the components of central government expenditure are computed from group totals for expenditure components and central government expenditure in current dollars. Those for total expenditure as a percentage of GNP and for overall surplus/deficit as a percentage of GNP are computed from group totals for the above total expenditures and overall surplus/deficit in current dollars, and GNP in current dollars, respectively. Since 1986 data are not available for more than half the countries, by weighting, 1985 data are used for the summary measures in Tables 23 and 24.

Table 24. Central government current revenue

Information on data sources and comparability is given in the note to Table 23. Current revenue by source is expressed as a percentage of total current revenue, which is the sum of tax revenue and nontax revenue and is calculated from national currencies.

Tax revenue is defined as all government revenue from compulsory, unrequited, nonrepayable receipts for public purposes, including interest collected on tax arrears and penalties collected on nonpayment or late payment of taxes. Tax revenue is shown net of refunds and other corrective transactions. *Taxes on income, profit, and capital gain* are taxes levied on the actual or presumptive net income of individuals, on the profits of enterprises, and on capital gains, whether realized on land sales, securities, or other assets. *Social security contributions* include employers' and employees' social security contributions as well as those of self-employed and unemployed persons. *Domestic taxes on goods and services* include general sales, turnover or value added taxes, selective excises on goods, selective taxes on services, taxes on the use of goods or property, and profits of fiscal monopolies. *Taxes on international trade and transactions* include import duties, export duties, profits of export or import monopolies, exchange profits, and exchange taxes. *Other taxes* include employers' payroll or labor taxes, taxes on property, and taxes not allocable to other categories. They may include negative values that are adjustments; for instance, taxes collected on behalf of state and local governments and not allocable to individual tax categories.

Nontax revenue comprises all government revenue that is not a compulsory nonrepayable payment for public purposes. Receipts from public enterprises and property income are included in this category. Proceeds of grants and borrowing, funds arising from the repayment of previous lending by governments, incurrence of liabilities, and proceeds from the sale of capital assets are not included.

Summary measures for the components of current revenue are computed from group totals for revenue components and total current revenue in current dollars; those for current revenue as a percentage of GNP are computed from group totals for total current revenue and GNP in current dollars. Since 1986 data are not available for more than half the countries, by weighting, 1985 data are used for the summary measures for Tables 23 and 24.

Table 25. Money and interest rates

The data on monetary holdings are based on the IMF's *International Financial Statistics* (*IFS*). *Monetary holdings, broadly defined*, comprise the monetary and quasi-monetary liabilities of a country's financial institutions to residents other than the central government. For most countries, monetary holdings are the sum of *money* (*IFS* line 34) and *quasi-money* (*IFS* line 35). *Money* comprises the economy's means of payment: currency outside banks and demand deposits. *Quasi-money* comprises time and savings deposits and similar bank accounts that the issuer will readily exchange for money. Where nonmonetary financial institutions are important issuers of quasi-monetary liabilities, these are also included in the measure of monetary holdings.

The growth rates for monetary holdings are calculated from year-end figures, while the average of the year-end figures for the specified year and the previous year is used for the ratio of monetary holdings to GDP.

The *nominal interest rates of banks*, also from *IFS*, represent the rates paid by commercial or similar banks to holders of their quasi-monetary liabilities (deposit rates) and charged by the banks on loans to prime customers (lending rate). They are, however, of limited international comparability partly because coverage and definitions vary, and partly because countries differ in the scope available to banks for adjusting interest rates to reflect market conditions.

Since interest rates (and growth rates for monetary holdings) are expressed in nominal terms, much of the variation between countries stems from differences in inflation. For easy reference, the Table 1 indicator of recent inflation is repeated in this table.

Table 26. Income distribution

The data in this table refer to the distribution of total disposable household income accruing to percentile groups of households ranked by total household income. The distributions cover rural and urban areas and refer to different years between 1970 and 1986.

The data for income distribution are drawn from a variety of sources including the Economic Commission for Latin America and the Caribbean (ECLAC), Economic and Social Commission for Asia and the Pacific (ESCAP), International Labour Organisation (ILO), the Organisation for Economic Co-operation and Development (OECD), the U.N.

National Account Statistics: Compendium of Income Distribution Statistics, 1985, the World Bank, and national sources.

Collection of income distribution data is not systematically organized or integrated with the official statistical system in many countries, and the data are derived from surveys designed for other purposes, most often consumer expenditure surveys, that also collect some information on income. These surveys use a variety of income concepts and sample designs, and in many cases their geographic coverage is too limited to provide reliable nationwide estimates of income distribution. Therefore, while the estimates shown are considered the best available, they do not avoid all these problems and should be interpreted with extreme caution.

The scope of the indicator is similarly limited. Because households vary in size, a distribution in which households are ranked according to per capita household income, rather than according to total household income, is superior for many purposes. The distinction is important because households with low per capita incomes frequently are large households, whose total income may be high, and conversely many households with low household incomes may be small households with high per capita incomes. Information on the distribution of per capita household income exists for only a few countries and is infrequently updated; for this reason this table is unchanged from last year's version. The World Bank's Living Standards Measurement Study and the Social Dimensions of Adjustment project, covering Sub-Saharan African countries are assisting a few selected countries to improve their collection and analysis of data on income distribution.

Table 27. Population growth and projections

The *growth rates of population* are period averages calculated from midyear populations.

The estimates of *population* for mid-1986 are based on data from the U.N. Population Division and from World Bank sources. In many cases the data take into account the results of recent population censuses. *Note* again that refugees not permanently settled in the country of asylum are generally considered to be part of the population of their country of origin.

The *projections of population* for 1990 and 2000, and to the year in which the population will eventually become stationary (see definition below) are made for each economy separately. Information on total population by age and sex, fertility rates, mortality rates, and international migration in the base year 1985 is projected on the basis of generalized assumptions until the population becomes stationary. The base-year estimates are from updated computer printouts of the U.N. *World Population Prospects as Assessed in 1986,* from the most recent issues of the U.N. *Population and Vital Statistics Report,* from World Bank country data, and from national censuses.

The *net reproduction rate* (NRR) indicates the number of daughters a newborn girl will bear during her lifetime, assuming fixed age-specific fertility and mortality rates. The NRR thus measures the extent to which a cohort of newborn girls will reproduce themselves under given schedules of fertility and mortality. An NRR of 1 indicates that fertility is at replacement level: at this rate childbearing women, on average, bear only enough daughters to replace themselves in the population.

A *stationary population* is one in which age- and sex-specific mortality rates have not changed over a long period, while age-specific fertility rates have simultaneously remained at replacement level (NRR=1). In such a population, the birth rate is constant and equal to the death rate, the age structure is constant, and the growth rate is zero.

Population momentum is the tendency for population growth to continue beyond the time that replacement-level fertility has been achieved; that is, even after the NRR has reached 1. The momentum of a population in any given year is measured as a ratio of the ultimate stationary population to the population of that year, given the assumption that fertility remains at replacement level. For example, the 1985 population of India was estimated at 765 million. If NRR was 1 in 1985, the projected stationary population would be 1,698 million–reached in the middle of the 22nd century—and the population momentum would be 1.7.

A population tends to grow even after fertility has declined to replacement level because past high growth rates will have produced an age distribution with a relatively high proportion of women in, or still to enter, the reproductive ages. Consequently, the birth rate will remain higher than the death rate, and the growth rate will remain positive for several decades. It takes at least 50 to 75 years, depending on the initial conditions, for a population's age distribution to adjust fully to changed fertility rates.

To make the projections, assumptions about future mortality rates are made in terms of female life expectancy at birth (that is, the number of years a newborn girl would live if she remained subject to the mortality risks prevailing for the cross-section of population at the time of her birth). Economies are divided according to whether their primary school enrollment ratio for females is above or below 70 percent. In each group a set of annual increments in female life expectancy is assumed, depending on the female life expectancy in 1980–85. For a given life expectancy at birth, the annual increments during the projection period are larger in economies with a higher primary school enrollment ratio and a life expectancy of up to 62.5 years. At higher life expectancies, the increments are the same.

To project fertility rates the year in which fertility will reach replacement level is estimated. These estimates are speculative and are based on information on trends in crude birth rates (defined in the note to Table 28), total fertility rates (also defined in the note to Table 28), female life expectancy at birth, and the performance of family planning programs. For most economies it is assumed that the total fertility rate will decline between 1986 and the year of reaching a net reproduction rate of 1, after which fertility will remain at replacement level. For most countries in Sub-Saharan Africa and for a few countries in Asia and the Middle East, total fertility rates are assumed to remain constant for some time and then to decline until replacement level is reached; for a few countries they are assumed to increase and then to decline.

In some countries, fertility is already below replacement level or will decline to below replacement level during the next 5 to 10 years. It is assumed, in order to make estimates of the stationary population for them, that fertility rates in these economies will regain replacement levels. The total fertility rates in industrial economies are assumed to remain constant until 1995–2000 and then to increase to replacement level by 2030.

International migration rates are based on past and present trends in migration flow. The estimates of future net migration are speculative. For most economies the net migration rates are assumed to be zero by 2000, but for a few they are assumed to be zero by 2025.

The estimates of the hypothetical size of the stationary population and the assumed year of reaching replacement-level fertility are speculative. *They should not be regarded as predictions.* They are included to show the long-run implications of recent fertility and mortality trends on the basis of highly stylized assumptions. A fuller description of the methods and assumptions used to calculate the estimates is available from the World Bank's *World Population Projections*, 1987–88 edition.

Table 28. Demography and fertility

The *crude birth and death rates* indicate the number of live births and deaths occurring per thousand population in a year. They come from the sources mentioned in the note to Table 27.

The *percentage of women of childbearing age* has been added to provide a more complete picture of fertility patterns. Comparison of 1965 and 1985 data adds an interesting aspect to the pattern of reproduction during the past two decades. *Childbearing age* is generally defined as 15 to 49, although for some countries contraceptive usage is measured for other age groups: 15 to 44, 18 to 44, and 19 to 49.

The *total fertility rate* represents the number of children that would be born to a woman, if she were to live to the end of her childbearing years and bear children at each age in accordance with prevailing age-specific fertility rates. The rates given are from the sources mentioned in the note to Table 27.

The *percentage of married women of childbearing age using contraception* refers to women who are practicing, or whose husbands are practicing, any form of contraception (see definitions of childbearing age earlier in this note).

Data are mainly derived from the World Fertility Surveys, the Contraceptive Prevalence Surveys, Demographic and Health Surveys, World Bank country data, and the U.N. *Recent Levels and Trends of Contraceptive Use as Assessed in 1983*. For a few countries for which no survey data are available, program statistics are used; these include Bangladesh, India, Indonesia, and several African countries. Program statistics may understate contraceptive prevalence because they do not measure use of methods such as rhythm, withdrawal, or abstinence, or contraceptives not obtained through the official family planning program. The data refer to a variety of years, generally not more than three years distant from those specified.

All *summary measures* are country data weighted by each country's share in the aggregate population.

Table 29. Health and nutrition

The estimates of *population per physician and nursing person* are derived from World Health Organization (WHO) data and have been slightly revised to take account of more recent estimates of population. For a few countries the information shown relates to a year later than 1981. The figure for *physicians* normally refers to the total number of registered practitioners in the country. *Nursing persons* include graduate, practical, assistant, and auxiliary nurses; the inclusion of auxiliary nurses provides more realistic estimates of available nursing care. Because definitions of doctors and nursing personnel vary—and because the data shown are for a variety of years, generally not more than three years distant from those specified—the data for these two indicators are not strictly comparable across countries.

The *daily calorie supply per capita* is calculated by dividing the calorie equivalent of the food supplies in an economy by the population. Food supplies comprise domestic production, imports less exports, and changes in stocks; they exclude animal feed, seeds for use in agriculture, and food lost in processing and distribution. These estimates are from FAO.

A new column on the percentage of *babies with low birth weights* relates to children born weighing less than 2,500 grams. Low birth weight is frequently associated with maternal malnutrition, and tends to raise the risk of infant mortality and to lead to poor growth in infancy and childhood, thus increasing the incidence of other forms of retarded development. The figures are derived from both WHO and UNICEF sources and are based on national data. The data are not strictly comparable across countries as they are compiled from a combination of surveys and administrative records, and other such sources.

The *summary measures* in this table are country figures weighted by each country's share in the aggregate population.

Table 30. Education

The data in this table refer to a variety of years, generally not more than two years distant from those specified, and are mostly from Unesco. However, disaggregated figures for males and females sometimes refer to a year earlier than that for overall totals.

The data on *primary* school enrollments are estimates of children of *all* ages enrolled in primary school. Figures are expressed as the ratio of pupils to the population of school-age children. While many countries consider primary school age to be 6 to 11 years, others do not. The differences in country practices in the ages and duration of schooling are reflected in the ratios given. For some countries with universal primary education, the gross enrollment ratios may exceed 100 percent, because some pupils are younger or older than the country's standard primary school age. The data on *secondary* school enrollments are calculated in the same manner, but again the definition of secondary school age differs among countries. It is most commonly considered to be 12 to 17 years. Late entry of more mature students as well as repetition and the phenomenon of *bunching* in final grades can influence these ratios.

The *tertiary* enrollment ratio is calculated by dividing the number of pupils enrolled in all post-secondary schools and universities by the population, age 20 to 24. Pupils attending vocational schools, adult education programs, two-year community colleges, and distance education centers (primarily correspondence courses) are included. The distribution of pupils across these different types of institutions varies among countries. The *youth* population, that is 20 to 24 years, is used as the denominator since it represents an average tertiary level cohort. While in higher income countries, youths aged 18 to 19 may be enrolled in a tertiary institution (and are included in the numerator), in developing and in many industrialized countries, many people older than 25 years are also enrolled in such an institution. These data and definitions come from Unesco.

The *summary measures* in this table are country enrollment rates weighted by each country's share in the aggregate population.

Table 31. Labor force

The *population of working age* refers to the population aged 15 to 64. The estimates are from the International Labour Organisation (ILO) based on U.N. population estimates.

The *summary measures* are weighted by population.

The *labor force* comprises economically active persons aged 10 years and over, including the armed forces and the unemployed, but excluding so-called *economically inactive* groups. The concept of *economically active* is restrictive and does not, for example, include activities of homemakers and other care-givers. *Agriculture, industry,* and *services* are defined as in Table 2. The estimates of the sectoral distribution of the labor force are from the ILO, *Labour Force Estimates and Projections, 1950–2000* (1986) and, in a few instances, from the World Bank. Labor force numbers in several developing countries appear to reflect a significant underestimate of female participation rates and are therefore themselves underestimates.

The *summary measures* are weighted by the labor force.

The *labor force growth rates* are from ILO data and are based on age-specific activity rates reported in the source cited above.

The application of ILO activity rates to the Bank's latest population estimates may be inappropriate for some economies in which there have been significant changes in unemployment and underemployment, as well as in international and internal migration. The labor force projections for 1985–2000 should thus be treated with caution.

The *summary measures* are country growth rates weighted by each country's share in the aggregate labor force in 1980.

Table 32. Urbanization

The data on *urban population as a percentage of total population* are from the U.N. publication *The Prospects of World Urbanization, Revised as of 1984–85,* 1987, supplemented by data from various issues of the U.N. *Demographic Yearbook,* and from the World Bank.

The growth rates of urban population are calculated from the World Bank's population estimates; the estimates of urban population shares are calculated from the sources cited above. Data on urban agglomeration in large cities are from the U.N. *Patterns of Urban and Rural Population Growth, 1980.*

Because the estimates in this table are based on different national definitions of what is *urban,* cross-country comparisons should be interpreted with caution. Data on urban population are from population censuses, which are conducted at only five or even ten-year intervals. Since for this reason new data are infrequently available, this table remains unchanged from last year.

The *summary measures* for urban population as a percentage of total population are calculated from country percentages weighted by each country's share in the aggregate population; the other *summary measures* in this table are weighted in the same fashion, using urban population.

Table 33. Women in development

This new table draws together some basic indicators of the condition of women in society. It reflects their demographic status and their access to some health and education services. The table mostly presents series previously published in the World Development Indicators, but which have now been disaggregated to show both the differences between the sexes and the changes in these differences over time. Statistical anomalies become more visible when social indicators are analyzed by gender, at least in some instances because basic reporting systems are weak in areas of special importance for monitoring the role of women in development. Indicators drawn from censuses and surveys, such as those on population, tend to be about as reliable for women as for men; indicators based largely on administrative records, such as maternal and infant mortality, are less reliable. Considerable work remains to be done to develop a statistical framework for this area, and the reliability of the data, even in the series shown in this table, varies significantly.

The first four columns show the ratios of females to males for the total population and for the under-five age-group. In general, throughout the world, more males are born than females. Under good nutritional and health conditions and in times of peace, male children have a higher death rate than females, and females tend to live longer. In the industrial market economies, these factors have resulted in ratios of about 103 to 105 females per 100 males in the general population. The figures in these columns reveal that there are cases where the number of females is much smaller than what would be a normal demographic pattern. In some countries, the apparent imbalance may be the result of migration, for example Kuwait and United Arab Emirates, where males enter the country to work on contracts. In others, male out-migration or the disproportionate effect of war creates a reverse imbalance of fewer than expected males and may partly hide, or compensate for, the excessive female mortality.

Typically, however, in the absence of such factors, a female-to-male ratio significantly below 100 in the general population of a country reflects the effects of discrimination against women. Such discrimination affects mostly three age groups. Very young girls, who may get a smaller share of scarce food or receive less prompt costly medical attention; childbearing women; and to a lesser extent the resourceless elderly. This pattern of discrimination is not uniformly associated with development. There are low- and middle-income countries (and within countries, regions) where the composition of the population is quite "normal." In many others, however, the numbers starkly demonstrate why better associating women with development is, literally, vital.

The health and welfare indicators in the next five columns draw attention, in particular, to the conditions associated with childbearing. This activity still carries the highest risk of death for women of reproductive age in developing countries. The indicators may reflect, but do not measure, both the availability of health services for women and the general welfare and nutritional status of mothers.

Life expectancy at birth is defined in the note to Table 1.

Births attended by health staff show the percentage of births recorded where a recognized health service worker was in attendance. The data are from the World Health Organization (WHO). *Maternal mortality* usually refers to the number of female deaths that occur during childbirth, per 100,000 live births. Since for some countries "childbirth" is defined more widely than for others—to include complications of pregnancy or of abortion—and since many pregnant women die because of lack of suitable health care, maternal mortality is difficult to measure consistently and reliably across countries. The data in these two series are drawn from diverse national sources and collected by WHO, although many national administrative systems are weak and do not record vital events in a systematic way. The data are derived mostly from official community reports and hospital records, and some reflect only deaths in hospitals and other medical institutions. Sometimes smaller private and rural hospitals are excluded, and sometimes even relatively primitive local facilities are included. The coverage is therefore not always comprehensive, and the figures should be treated with extreme caution.

Clearly, many maternal deaths go unrecorded, particularly in countries with remote rural populations; this accounts for some of the very low numbers shown in the table, especially for several African countries. Moreover, it is not clear whether an increase in the number of mothers in hospital re-flects more extensive medical care for women or more complications in pregnancy and childbirth because of poor nutrition, for instance. (See Table 29 for low birth weight data.)

These time series attempt to bring together readily available information not always presented in international publications. WHO warns that there are "inevitably gaps," in the series, and it has invited countries to provide more comprehensive figures. They are reproduced here, from the 1986 WHO publication *Maternal Mortality Rates*, mainly as part of the international effort to highlight data in this field. The reference year of 1980 represents any year from 1977 to 1984.

The *infant mortality* rate is the number of infants who die before reaching one year of age, per thousand live births, in a given year. The data are from a variety of U.N. sources—"Infant Mortality: World Estimates and Projects, 1950–2025" in the *Population Bulletin* (1983), recent issues of *Demographic Yearbook*, and *Population and Vital Statistics Report*—as well as from the World Bank.

The *education* indicators, based on Unesco sources, show the extent to which females are enrolled at school at both primary and secondary levels, compared with males. All things being equal, and opportunities being the same, the ratios for females should be close to 100. However, inequalities may cause the ratios to move in different directions. For example, the number of females per 100 males will rise at secondary school level if male attendance declines more rapidly in the final grades because of males' greater job opportunities, conscription into the army, or migration in search of work. In addition, since the numbers in these columns refer mainly to general secondary education, they do not capture those (mostly males) enrolled in technical and vocational schools or in full time apprenticeships, as in Eastern Europe.

Bibliography

National accounts and economic indicators	International Monetary Fund. 1987. *Government Finance Statistics Yearbook*. Vol. XI Washington, D.C.. U.N. Department of International Economic and Social Affairs. Various years. *Statistical Yearbook*. New York. FAO, IMF, UNIDO, and World Bank data; and national sources.
Energy	U.N. Department of International Economic and Social Affairs. Various years. *World Energy Supplies*. Statistical Papers, series J. New York. World Bank data.
Trade	International Monetary Fund. Various years. *International Financial Statistics*. Washington, D.C.. U.N. Conference on Trade and Development. Various years. *Handbook of International Trade and Development Statistics*. Geneva. U.N. Department of International Economic and Social Affairs. Various years. *Monthly Bulletin of Statistics*. New York. ———. Various years. *Yearbook of International Trade Statistics*. New York. FAO, IMF, U.N., and World Bank data.
Balance of payments, capital flows, debt and aid	The Organisation for Economic Co-operation and Development. Various years. *Development Co-operation*. Paris. ———. 1986. *Geographical Distribution of Financial Flows to Developing Countries*. Paris. IMF, OECD, and World Bank data; and the World Bank Debtor Reporting System.
Labor force	International Labour Office. 1986. *Labour Force Estimates and Projections, 1950–2000*. 3rd ed. Geneva. International Labour Organisation tapes.
Population	U.N. Department of International Economic and Social Affairs. Various years. *Demographic Yearbook*. New York. ———. Various years. *Population and Vital Statistics Report*. New York. ———. 1980. *Patterns of Urban and Rural Population Growth*. New York. ———. 1982. ''Infant Mortality: World Estimates and Projections, 1950–2025.'' *Population Bulletin of the United Nations*, no. 14. New York. ———. Updated printouts. *World Population Prospects as Assessed in 1982*. New York. ———. 1983. *World Population Trends and Policies: 1983 Monitoring Report*. New York. ———. 1984. *Recent Levels and Trends of Contraceptive Use as Assessed in 1983*. New York. ———. 1987. *The Prospects of World Urbanization, Revised as of 1984–85*. New York. World Bank data.

Social indicators

Food and Agriculture Organization. 1981. *Fertilizer Yearbook 1982.* Rome

———. 1983. *Food Aid in Figures* (December). Rome.

Institute for Resource Development/Westinghouse. 1987. *Child Survival: Risks and the Road to Health.* Columbia, Md.

Sivard, Ruth. 1985. *Women–A World Survey.* Washington, D.C.: World Priorities.

U.N. Department of International Economic and Social Affairs. Various years. *Demographic Yearbook.* New York.

———. Various years. *Statistical Yearbook.* New York.

U.N. Educational Scientific and Cultural Organization. Various years. *Statistical Yearbook.* Paris.

UNICEF. 1986. *The State of the World's Children 1986.* Oxford: Oxford University Press.

World Health Organization. Various years. *World Health Statistics Annual.* Geneva.

———. 1986. *Maternal Mortality Rates;* A Tabulation of Available Information, 2nd Edition. Geneva.

———. Various years. *World Health Statistics Report.* Geneva.

FAO and World Bank data.